TALMUD ESER SEFIROT
(The Study of the Ten Sefirot)

Volume Two

Rav Yehuda Leib Ashlag (Baal HaSulam)

LAITMAN
KABBALAH
PUBLISHERS

TALMUD ESER SEFIROT
The Study of the Ten Sefirot
Volume Two
Preliminary Edition

Laitman Kabbalah Publishers, 2022
Copyright [c] 2022 by Laitman Kabbalah Publishers
1057 Steeles Avenue West, Suite 532
Toronto, ON M2R 3X1, Canada

All rights reserved.

Contact Information
E-mail: info@kabbalah.info
Website: www.kabbalah.info

Toll free in USA and Canada: 1-866-LAITMAN
1057 Steeles Avenue West, Suite 532, Toronto,
ON, M2R 3X1, Canada

No part of this book may be used or reproduced
in any manner without written permission of the publisher,
except in the case of brief quotations embodied
in critical articles or reviews.

ISBN: 9798362069599

Translation: Chaim Ratz
Content Editing: Shaul Dar
Editing and Proofreading: Mary Miesem
Cover Design: Inna Smirnova
Printing and Post Production: Uri Laitman

FIRST EDITION: November 2022
First printing

Contents

VOLUME 2

PART FIVE 7
   Additional Explanation about the Matter of the Inversion of the *Panim*
   and the Making Order of the *Kelim* 115
   Table of Questions for Topics 118
   Table of Questions for the Meaning of the Words 163

PART SIX 173
   Histaklut Pnimit 250
   Cause and Consequence 271
   Table of Questions and Answers for the Meaning of the Words 289
   Table of Questions for Topics 298

PART SEVEN 335
   Histaklut Pnimit 423
   Table of Questions for the Meaning of the Words 434
   Table of Questions for Topics 454

PART EIGHT 489

PART SIXTEEN 565

PART FIVE

Eser Sefirot de Akudim in the second *Hitpashtut* called *Matei ve Lo Matei*

1.	*3	22.	24	43.	54
2.	3	23.	24	44.	57
3.	4	24.	25	45.	58
4.	4	25.	26	46.	59
5.	6	26.	27	47.	63
6.	*6	27.	*28	48.	68
7.	9	28.	29	49.	69
8.	9	29.	29	50.	*72
9.	10	30.	30	51.	74
10.	13	31.	31	52.	75
11.	15	32.	32	53.	76
12.	16	33.	33	54.	76
13.	17	34.	33	55.	*77
14.	18	35.	*33	56.	79
15.	*19	36.	39	57.	79
16.	21	37.	39	58.	80
17.	21	38.	40	59.	80
18.	22	39.	41	60.	80
19.	22	40.	43	61.	82
20.	22	41.	49	62.	83
21.	23	42.	52		

1. *Know, that since these *Eser Sefirot* are called *Olam ha Akudim*, they are *Orot* and *Anafim* that came out of *Peh de AK*. It is known that the *Behinat Yod Sefirot* in her will be inside her, in that *Peh* itself.

   Also, there are ten *Shorashim* there of these ten *Sefirot* that came out, in the tenth *Sefira* in her, called the *Malchut* in her. These are called *Olam Akudim*.

   They are also called *Eser Sefirot* from *Keter* to *Malchut*. They are *Shorashim* to these ten *Sefirot de Akudim* that came out for so it is in all the *Olamot*.

Ohr Pnimi

1. There are ten *Shorashim* there...in the tenth *Sefira*...called the *Malchut* in her.

   We have already learned the matter of the *Hitpashtut* of each *Partzuf*. The *Ohr Elyon* expands for *Zivug de Hakaa* on the *Masach* in *Kli Malchut* first. This *Ohr Hozer* rises from the *Masach* upward and clothes the *Eser Sefirot* in the *Ohr Elyon*, and this *Halbasha* is called *Eser Sefirot* of *Rosh*.

   Afterwards, *Malchut* expands through the *Ohr Hozer* that she raised to *Eser Sefirot* from her and within her from above downward. This *Halbasha* is called *Guf*, and in the *Partzufim* of AK they are called *Akudim*.

   You find that the *Malchut* with the *Eser Sefirot* of her *Ohr Hozer* extend and emanate the *Eser Sefirot* of the *Guf*. That is why her *Eser Sefirot* are called *Shorashim* to the *Sefirot* of the *Guf*.

2. It writes above that when the *Orot* left to the *Maatzil Ohr Keter* remained in permanent *Dvekut* with the *Maatzil* and did not come. The thing is that it stood there below *Sefirat Malchut* in the *Eser Sefirot*, called *Shorashim* of the *Akudim*.

   All these *Eser* are in *Sefirat Malchut* from the general *Eser Sefirot* of the *Peh* of *Adam Kadmon* Himself. Thus, the *Behinat Malchut* in the *Eser* above-mentioned *Shorashim* emanated these *Eser Sefirot* called *Akudim* and is considered their *Maatzil*.

Ohr Pnimi

2. Stood there below *Sefirat Malchut*.

   It has already been explained that *Hitpashtut Aleph de Akudim* was in *Komat Keter* since the *Zivug de Hakaa* was there in the *Masach* in *Aviut Dalet*. It is known that this *Komat Keter* did not come down again in *Hitpashtut Bet* after it departed from *Hitpashtut Aleph de Akudim*. Rather, it remained in its source, in the *Maatzil*, meaning *Malchut* of *Rosh*, which is considered his *Maatzil*, as the Rav writes here.

It is written, that he stood there below *Sefirat Malchut*, called *Shorashim de Akudim* in the *Eser Sefirot*. In other words, this *Komat Keter* that returned to the *Maatzil*, meaning to *Malchut de Rosh* is an *Anaf* of *Malchut*. Hence, when he retuned to her he stands beneath her.

We must know the difference between *Malchut de Rosh* that owns the *Masach*, where there is the *Zivug de Hakaa* and the *Ohr Hozer*, and the *Ohr Keter* that rose. This is considered the same *Ohr* that had already been clothed in the *Kli*, but then departed from there and is now considered *Ohr* without a *Kli*, and remember that for all the rest.

3. Hence, all the aforementioned *Shorashim* face down to shine in *Olam Akudim* through that *Keter* of *Akudim* that remained there under the *Malchut* of the *Shorashim*, as mentioned above. Also, the *Keter Elyon* of the *Shorashim* also yearns to bestow in the *Keter* of *Akudim* that rose there.

This is so because the *Shorashim* always yearn to shine in the *Anafim*, as they are their sons. They shine in them enough to satisfy them so that the *Anafim*, which are their sons, will also mate and produce posterity.

Ohr Pnimi

3. **All the aforementioned *Shorashim* face down to shine in *Olam Akudim* through that *Keter*.**

It means that even after the *Histalkut* of the *Akudim*, the *Kelim de Akudim* must receive *Ohr* from the *Eser Sefirot* of the *Rosh* in order to revive them. This is a miniature luminescence that suffices only to sustain them.

They need to receive this luminescence through the *Ohr Keter* that stands under *Malchut de Rosh*. This is because the rule is that every thing that comes and pours to the *Partzuf* is poured by the *Sefirat Keter* of that *Partzuf*, as it is the *Shoresh Elyon* of those *Eser Sefirot*.

Hence, here too, even though the *Ohr Keter* has already left the *Partzuf* the *Kelim* still cannot receive the *He'arah* for sustenance except through the *Ohr Keter* that stands under the *Malchut* of *Rosh*.

The *Keter Elyon* of the *Shorashim* also yearns to bestow... ...and produce posterity.

It means that besides the vitality that the branches receive from their *Ohr Keter* that stands under *Malchut* of the *Rosh*, they have a yearning to give to the *Shorashim Elyonim* in the *Rosh* plentiful *He'arah* that suffices for them to mate and produce progeny.

This lush *He'arah* is only given to them through the *Keter Elyon* of the *Shorashim*, meaning through the *Zivug* in the *Masach de Malchut* of *Rosh* that bestows upon the *Ohr Keter* that stands under that *Malchut*. From there it is poured to the *Anafim*, as we shall see ahead.

4. **The *Anaf* also wishes to receive *He'arah* and suck from the *Shorashim*. Hence, both the *Zachar* and the *Nekeva* in the *Kli* of *Keter* of the Upper *Anafim* rise upward under the *Keter*, which rose under *Malchut* of the *Shorashim* and there receive their *He'arah* from Him.**

Once they receive all that they need the *Keter* of the *Anafim*, which always stands there, now turns His face from them upward to the *Shorashim*, and His *Achoraim* facing the above *Zachar* and *Nekeva*.

Ohr Pnimi

4. **The *Zachar* and the *Nekeva* in the *Kli* of *Keter* of the Upper *Anafim*.**

They are the *Reshimo de Keter* with the *Reshimo de Behina Gimel* contained in the *Masach* that rose and departed from *Hitpashtut Aleph* to the *Malchut* of *Rosh* (explained in Part 4, Chap 4, Ohr Pnimi item 50).

Behina Dalet did not leave a *Reshimo*. Where then did the *Reshimo de Komat Keter* come here from? Indeed, every *Behina* consists of two kinds of *Reshimot*. There is *Reshimo de Hamshacha*, which belongs to the bottom *Behina* of the degree, and there is *Behinat Reshimo* of *Hitlabshut Ohr*, which belongs to the Upper *Behina* in the *Koma* of the degree. (In that regard see Part 4, Histaklut Pnimit item 41).

These two *Reshimot* are as *Zachar* and *Nukva*. The *Reshimo de Hitlabshut* is the *Behinat Zachar* in the *Reshimo*, and the *Reshimo de Hamshacha* is the *Behinat Nekeva* in the *Reshimo*.

Know, that only the *Behinat Nekeva* in the *Reshimo de Behina Dalet*, which belongs to *Malchut* disappeared. However, the *Behinat Zachar* of the *Reshimo* that belongs to *Keter* remained and is contained in the *Masach* that rose to the *Malchut of Rosh*.

Rise upward... ...and there receive their *He'arah* from Him.

The ascent is performed through the *Hizdakchut* of the *Masach* in *Tabur de Hitpashtut Aleph* until it becomes as pure as the *Maatzil*, meaning *Malchut de Rosh*, since the *Hishtavut Tzura* unites the spirituals into one. Since the *Masach de Guf* becomes as *Zach* as the *Masach* of the *Rosh*, it is considered to have risen and united into one with it, in its place.

It is known that *Histalkut* is not conducted in the *Rosh* at all. Rather, the *Masach* there is always in a *Zivug de Lo Pasik* with the *Ohr Elyon*. Hence, the *Masach* that rose there was also incorporated in its *Zivug* and receives from the *Ohr Elyon* together with it.

It is written, "both the **Zachar** and the **Nekev**... ...rise upward etc. under **Malchut** of the **Shorashim** and there receive their **He'arah** from Him." In other words, by incorporating in the *Zivug Elyon* there.

Once they receive all that they need.

It means until they became suitable to expand to their place to the *Guf* with this *He'arah* that they received.

Now turns His face from them upward.

It means that the *Zivug* that belongs to the *Ohr Keter* stops. At that time it stops its *He'arah* from expanding to the ZON below it. This is called that its *Achoraim* is opposite the ZON because the prevention of *He'arah* is called *Achor*.

The reason for the cessation of his *He'arah* will be explained below. It is because the *Zivug* reached the *Nukva* contained in the *Reshimo*, which is *Aviut de Behina Gimel* that extends only from *Komat Hochma* of the *Shorashim Elyonim*, not from the *Keter de Shorashim*.

Therefore the *Ohr Keter* below *Malchut* does not receive any more *Ohr* for the ZON beneath it. After the above *Zivug de Behina Gimel* is performed, the *Zachar* and *Nekeva* immediately expand to the *Guf*, to the *Kli de Keter* found there and the second *Hitpashtut de Akudim* occurs.

5. The reason that they have to rise up is that these ***Kelim*** of ***Akudim*** are the first ***Kelim*** that were emanated. No ***Kelim*** were emanated above them since the ***Ohr*** there is enormous and the ***Kelim*** cannot exist there.

    Hence, if the *Ohr Elyon* had extended down to their place when they are in their *Kelim*, the *Kelim* would have been annulled. Thus it was necessary that only the *Orot* of the ZON in the *Kli* would rise up.

Ohr Pnimi

5. **These *Kelim* of *Akudim* are the first *Kelim*.**

    This means the *Kelim* of the first *Hitpashtut* when the *Zachar* and *Nekeva* of *Keter* rose from there (see above Part 4, Chap 1 item 5).

    If the *Ohr Elyon* had extended down... ...the *Kelim* would have been annulled.

It means that if *Komat Keter* had expanded back to the *Kelim* as it first was, before the its *Histalkut*, the *Kelim* made during the *Histalkut* would have been annulled again for the reason the Rav mentioned above (Part 4, Chap 6 item 3).

It was necessary that only the *Orot* of the ZON in the *Kli* would rise up.

These *ZON de Keter* that rose above the *Masach* that purified have only *Aviut de Behina Gimel*. Hence, they extend only *Komat Hochma* and *Ohr Hochma* clothes *Kli de Keter*, *Ohr Bina* in *Kli de Hochma* etc.

It turns out that each *Kli* lacks much of the measure of *Ohr* meant for it. *Kli de Keter* now has only *Ohr Hochma*, which is much lower than it. Also, *Kli Hochma* has only *Ohr Bina* etc. Because of that the *Aviut* became apparent in the *Kelim* in a way that they could not be annulled.

6. *Now we shall explain the existence of this ascent. It is said that when **Lo Matei** in the **Keter**, since ZON of the **Keter** rise up to the place of this *Keter* at the end of the *Shorashim Elyonim*, they cannot be together there because He is greater than them.

Hence, they remain in His place and He rises to the place of *Shoresh* of *Malchut*. Then the *Shoresh* of *Malchut* also rises to the *Shoresh* of *Yesod* where they both remain as *Yesod*, which is ZON. Then, *Shoresh Keter Elyon* gives below after there is already a preparation for the *Tachtonim* to receive. At that time the *Nukva* of *Keter* is incorporated in the *Zachar*.

Ohr Pnimi

6. **Lo Matei in the Keter, since ZON of the Keter rise up.**

The matter of *Histalkut Komat Keter de Hitpashtut Aleph* is called *Lo Matei* in *Keter*. This is the matter of *Histalkut ZON* of the *Keter* upward, meaning they rise there to be incorporated in the *Zivug Elyon* in the *Malchut* of the *Rosh*.

This has already been explained elaborately in Part 4, chapter 4, *Ohr Pnimi* item 50 and study it there. I shall only bring an extract of it here sufficiently to explain the Rav's words here.

It explains there that the whole reason for the *Histalkut Orot* from *Hitpashtut Aleph de Akudim* was only because of the ascent of *Malchut*, meaning the *Hizdakchut* of the *Masach* in *Kli Malchut*. When *Malchut* rose to ZA, which is *Behina Gimel*, *Komat Keter* disappeared.

Afterwards, when it too rose from the *Kli* of *Keter* to the *Maatzil*, meaning to *Malchut* of *Rosh*, the entire *Ohr* of that *Hitpashtut* disappeared. Thus, all these *Orot* that departed from there left *Reshimot* after them in their *Kelim*, except *Malchut*, meaning *Behina Dalet* who did not leave any *Reshimo* after her departure.

It is also explained there that *Malchut*, meaning the *Masach* in her, is incorporated in the *Reshimot* that the *Orot* left behind in those *Behinot*, when it purifies and ascends from *Behina* to *Behina*. It is so because when the *Masach* purified from *Behina Dalet* to *Behina Gimel*, which is the *Kli de ZA*, it mingles with the *Reshimo* that remains there from the *Ohr ZA* after its *Histalkut*.

Also, when it rose to *Hochma*, it mingled with the *Reshimo de Hochma*, and when it rose to *Keter* it mingled in the *Reshimo de Keter*. Afterwards, when it rose from the *Keter* to the *Maatzil* the *Masach* is found to be containing all the *Reshimot* that exist in the *Eser Sefirot de Hitpashtut Aleph* except the *Reshimo de Behina Dalet*. This is because it disappeared even from the *Malchut de Hitpashtut Aleph* itself.

Know, that the essence of those *Reshimot* contained in the *Masach* are the very *Aviut* of *Behina Gimel* that remained from *Komat Hochma*. It is also *Aviut* from *Behina Dalet* from the perspective of the *Hitlabshut*, remaining from *Komat Keter*. This is because the *Reshimot* from the *Komot* that are lower than them are incorporated in the Upper *Reshimot*.

You should know that these two above *Reshimot* can still be a single degree although *Komat Keter* is far more valuable than *Komat Hochma*, but with a differentiation of *Zachar* and *Nekeva*. This is because the *Reshimo* of *Komat Keter* is only half a *Reshimo*. Moreover, it lacks that most important half.

It is already presented above that each *Reshimo* is discerned by two: *Reshimo de Hamshacha* and *Reshimo de Hitlabshut*. This means that the measure of the *Koma* is measured by the measure of the *Aviut* in the *Masach*, where the more *Av* draws a higher *Koma*.

However, since the higher *Koma* needs a purer *Kli*, we come to find two opposite ends in each *Koma*, set one atop the other. On the one hand, the greater *Koma* must have the most *Av Masach* and *Kli*, which are the *Kelim* for *Hamshacha* for the great *Koma*. On the other hand, it must have the finest vessels of reception to fit the clothing of the greatest *Ohr*.

Hence, each of these *Reshimot* that remained from *Hitpashtut Aleph* is evaluated by the two above halves, the *Reshimo de Hamshacha* and the *Reshimo de Hitlabshut*. Know, that the *Reshimo de Hamshacha* is the most important, as this is what the *Zivug Elyon* is made on. Also, the *Ohr Hozer* that connects and clothes the *Ohr Elyon* in the *Partzuf* rises from it.

From the explanation you can thoroughly understand why the *Reshimo de Komat Keter* with the *Reshimo de Komat Hochma* are considered *Zachar* and *Nukva*. It seems very puzzling since it is known that *Zachar* and *Nekeva* should be equal to each other. Otherwise how will they have contact with each other, how will they affect and receive from one another?

Here, the *Zachar* will be from *Komat Keter* and the *Nekeva* from *Komat Hochma* and the value of *Keter* is known to be far greater than *Keter*. We learned that the *Reshimo de Komat Keter* is only half a *Reshimo*, and the weaker half too since it is unfit to draw the *Ohr* on its own.

Yet, the *Reshimo de Behina Gimel* is a complete *Reshimo*, both from the perspective of the *Hamshacha*, and from the perspective of the *Hitlabshut*. Hence, you find that the complete *Reshimo de Behina Gimel* equalizes with the half *Reshimo de Komat Keter*. Understand that and remember it through the rest here.

We will explain below how these *Zachar* and *Nekeva* connect with the *Masach* in *Malchut* of *Rosh* in one *Zivug* because of their ascent there. For that reason they return and extend *Hitpashtut Ohr Elyon* to the *Partzuf* once more. This is named *Hitpashtut Bet*.

It is written, "when *Lo Matei* in the *Keter*, since ZON of the *Keter* rise up etc. Then, *Shoresh Keter Elyon* gives below." It is as we've written above that when *Lo Matei* in *Keter*, meaning in *Hitpashtut Aleph*, generally called *Keter*, *Behinat Zachar* and *Nekeva* rise from that *Komat Keter*.

The *Zachar* is discerned as the *Reshimo de Keter* of *Komat Keter* and the *Nekeva* is discerned as the *Reshimo de Hochma* of that *Komat Keter*. They rise under *Malchut de Rosh* and are renewed there in a new *Zivug* as he will explain henceforth.

They remain in His place... ...the Shoresh of Malchut also rises to the Shoresh of Yesod.

Here you must know this rule, that the ascent of the *Anafim* means the *Hizdakchut* of the *Aviut* in them, which causes the ascent of their *Shorashim*. Even though *Hizdakchut* does not apply in the *Shorashim*, which are the *Eser Sefirot de Rosh*, still the ascent of the *Shorashim* extends from the *Hizdakchut* in the *Anafim* themselves.

This is because the *Anafim* relate to the *Shorashim* as the "actual to the potential". In fact, they are one entity and the actual has only what is in the potential. Hence, if there is any manifestation of the *Anafim*, which are *Sefirot de Guf*, that manifestation must first appear in the *Eser Sefirot* of the *Shorashim*.

Thus, it is true that this matter of *Hizdakchut* and *Histalkut Orot* from their *Hitlabshut* in the *Kelim* cannot occur in the *Eser Sefirot de Rosh*. This is because the *Hitlabshut Orot* in the *Kelim* is essentially only in potential there. However, the matter of the ascent of the place of the *Zivug* is certainly there though it occurred because of the ascent of the *Anafim* there.

This concept is among the most important in this wisdom. He elaborates on this matter below in all its details, but here he speaks in general. He says that the ascent of ZON of *Komat Keter de Guf* below *Malchut* of the *Rosh* causes the *Hitkalelut Ohr Keter* in the *Behinat Kli Malchut* of the *Rosh*.

These two mixtures are: *Hitkalelut ZON de Keter* of the *Guf* under *Malchut de Rosh* in the place of *Ohr Keter de Guf*, and the *Hitkalelut Ohr Keter* of the *Guf* in *Kli Malchut* itself. They cause the *Shoresh de Malchut*, meaning the *Masach* contained in *Kli Malchut* of the *Rosh*, to rise to the place of the *Shoresh* of *Yesod*, meaning the *Aviut de Behina Gimel*.

Shoresh Keter Elyon gives below.

This is refers to abundant bestowal by way of *Zivug* to produce progeny which are the *Eser Sefirot de Hitpashtut Bet* called *Partzuf AB de AK*, considered a progeny and the son of the first *Partzuf de AK*.

Preparation for the *Tachtonim* to receive.

This means the *Tikun* of the *Masach* to be suitable and fitting to mate with the *Ohr Elyon*.

The *Nukva* of *Keter* is incorporated in the *Zachar*.

It means that this *Zivug* is not done on the *Reshimo de Behina Gimel*, which is the *Behinat Nekeva*. Rather, it is done on the *Behinat Reshimo de Behina Dalet*, which is the *Behinat Zachar de Keter*. However, the *Nekeva* is incorporated in the *He'arat Zivug* with it, as we will explain below.

7. Interpretation: There are several rules: One, when two *Orot* are in two *Kelim*, each on its own. Afterwards, when the two *Orot* enter one *Kli*, it will be called *Klalut* (from the word *Kolel* – containing). This is because they are contained in one another in one *Kli*.

There is yet another reality. Since these two *Behinot Orot Zachar* and *Nekeva* are in two *Kelim*, what happens to them is what is written in *Parashat Truma*, as then there is AHaVaH in them. This means that the *He'arah* of the *Zachar* is incorporated in the *Nekeva* and both are in one *Kli*.

Also, the *He'arat Nukva* returns to be contained in the *Kli* of the *Zachar*. Thus they are four *Orot*, two in each *Kli*, intermingled. This is the meaning of the four *Otiot* of AHaVaH.

Ohr Pnimi

7. **One, when two *Orot* are in two *Kelim* etc. contained in one another in one *Kli*.**

   Interpretation: Any spiritual separation is through *Shinui Tzura* and any spiritual unification is through *Hishtavut Tzura*. Hence, if for example one *Ohr* is clothed in *Behina Dalet* and the other in *Behina Gimel* they are considered two. This is because the *Shinui Tzura* separates between them. They are considered two separate *Orot* in two *Kelim* in themselves.

   However, when the *Kli de Behina Dalet* is purified and remains in *Behina Gimel* too, the two *Kelim* mingle and become one *Kli*, since both are in even *Tzura*. The two *Orot* are also mingled in their *He'arah*. Even though they both originate from the *Eser Sefirot de Ohr Yashar*, they are two kinds, such as one being *Ruach* and the other is *Nefesh*.

   Two *Orot* are in two *Kelim* etc. Then there is *AhaVaH*.

   This refers to the *Zivug de Neshikin* and will be explained in its place.

8. **There is yet another kind of *Klalut*. This is the reality we are in, which are two *Orot* without *Kelim*, which are ZON of the *Keter* that rose up and are not in the *Kli*. It is because then their *Klalut* would be in the form of receiving *He'arah* from one another, and this is their *Klalut*.**

Ohr Pnimi

8. **The reality we are in, which are two *Orot* without *Kelim*.**

   Here the *Zachar* and the *Nekeva* are considered in ascent because of the *Hizdakchut* of the *Masach* from all the *Aviut* that was in it, as it completely equalized its form with the *Maatzil*.

   These *Zachar* and *Nekeva de Keter* are nothing but silent *Reshimot* that have no *Aviut* at all. Yet, they were first in *Behinat Hitlabshut* in the *Guf*, one in *Komat Keter de Guf* and the other in *Komat Hochma* in the *Guf*. Hence, we call them *Zachar* and *Nekeva*.

   This is the precision that the Rav makes for us here, "which are two *Orot* without *Kelim*, which are ZON of the *Keter* that rose up." This means that these ZON have nothing of the *Behinat Kelim* since they are considered to be in ascent.

9. **Now the *Nukva* is contained in the *Dechura* since the *Nukva* is *Ohr Hochma* and the *Zachar* is *Ohr* of *Keter* that remained in the *Kli*. Hence, it is the *Zachar* that now receives from its *Shoresh*, the *Shoresh* of *Keter*.**

This extends to it by purifying that *Keter* that remained above at the end of the *Shorashim*; it is greatly purified by the Upper *He'arah* of the *Shoresh* of *Keter*. Then, a great *Ohr* shines in that *Zachar* of the *Keter* and the *Nekeva* is incorporated in the *Zachar* and receives *He'arah* from it until these three *Behinot* are even in their *He'arah*.

They are the *Zachar* and *Nekeva* of the *Kli Keter* and that *Keter* that is on them. Once they are even, they will receive their *Ohr* from the *Shoresh* of the *Keter Elyon*.

Ohr Pnimi

9. **The *Nukva* is *Ohr Hochma*.**

Meaning, it is the *Behinat Reshimo* that left *Ohr Komat Hochma* after its *Histalkut*.

The *Zachar* is *Ohr* of *Keter* that remained in the *Kli*.

This refers to the *Behinat Reshimo* that the *Ohr* of *Komat Keter* left after its *Histalkut* when it remained in *Kli de Komat Keter*. Now it rose to the *Maatzil* through the *Masach* that was purified.

This extends to it by purifying that *Keter* that remained above at the end of the *Shorashim*.

Here the Rav gives us a complete order of *Zivug* and birth of a lower *Partzuf* by the Upper One. Hence, we must know these things for a very accurate understanding.

He wrote that these *Reshimot* that rose from the *Histalkut de Hitpashtut Aleph* are the *Reshimo* from the *Ohr* that remains in *Kli de Hochma*. They rose under *Malchut* of the *Rosh* to the place where the general *Ohr* of *Komat Keter* of *Hitpashtut Aleph* was after its *Histalkut* from there.

It turns out that here in *Malchut* of the *Rosh*, we have three kinds of *Orot* of the *Guf de Partzuf Aleph* of AK that emerged after the *Histalkut* and came to the *Rosh* of that *Partzuf*. These are the general *Komat Keter* of the *Guf* and the *Reshimo* that that *Komat Keter* left in the *Kli de Keter* of the *Guf* after its *Histalkut*.

Afterwards it too rose to the *Rosh* by its *Hitkalelut* in the *Masach de Malchut de Guf* that ascended. That *Reshimo* is called *Zachar de Kli de Keter*.

We must understand that this *Reshimo* is an *Anaf* of the general *Komat Keter* mentioned above. Indeed, it is more of a branch since it is an actual part of *Atzmuto*. The only difference between them is that the general *Ohr de Komat Keter* was removed from the *Guf* entirely immediately after the *Masach* purified from the *Aviut de Behina Dalet*. The *Reshimo* is that part that it left there in its *Kli*, and thus you find that they are one *Atzmut*.

There is yet another (second) *Reshimo* here, namely the *Ohr* that the *Ohr* of *Komat Hochma* of the *Guf de AK* left inside its *Kli* after its *Histalkut* from that *Guf*. It is called the *Nekeva* of the *Keter* since it too rose from her *Kli de Guf* to the *Rosh* by her *Hitkalelut* in the *Masach* that was purified.

We have already elaborated on that in Part 4, Chap 4 *Ohr Pnimi* item 50. We must scrutinize thoroughly well there for all the things from there should have been copied here had I not spared the length. Hence, I am being very brief here.

Remember these three names of the three *Orot* well. They are: *Zachar de Keter, Nekeva de Keter*, and *Ohr Keter*, according to their above explanation because it is impossible to explain them every time. Also, remember that all these three *Orot* are *Anafim* of *Malchut de Rosh* since she brought them out to the *Guf* by the force of the *Shinui Tzura* and the *Aviut Guf* that she gave them, called *Aviut* from above downward.

Now that they have purified from this *Aviut* once more they have returned to her once more and were incorporated in her as in the beginning. This is considered that the three *Orot* rose to the place of *Malchut de Rosh*.

However, their order of positioning there is considered that every *Anaf* stands under its proximate *Shoresh*. This is because the *Ohr Keter*, which is the general *Ohr* that rose and departed from the *Guf* is the closest to *Malchut*.

The *Zachar de Keter* stands behind it since it is a branch of the *Ohr Keter*, which is the *Reshimo* that the *Ohr Keter* left in its *Kli*. The *Nekeva de Keter* stands behind, as she is from *Behinat Aviut de Behina Gimel*, being a branch of the *Zachar de Keter*, which is from *Behina Dalet*.

Know, that the ascents of *Zachar* and *Nekeva de Keter* to the *Rosh* caused two *Zivugim* by this ascent. The *Masach* and the *Malchut* of the *Rosh* immediately rose to the *Yesod de Rosh*. It means that *Malchut* left the *Behina Dalet* in her and acquired the *Aviut de Behina Gimel* of the *Rosh*.

The reason for her ascent is that the *Histalkut Orot de Hitpashtut Aleph* of the *Guf* caused a cessation of the bestowal of *Malchut de Rosh* since she no longer had anyone to give to. The whole matter of *Malchut de Rosh* stands only for bestowal, as she is not fitting for reception from the *Tzimtzum* onward.

Instead, she raises *Ohr Hozer* through the *Zivug de Hakaa* that occurs in her. Through that *Ohr Hozer* she raises she gives and extends the *Ohr Elyon* into the *Guf*. Thus, during the *Histalkut* of the *Orot de Guf* she cannot give to the

Guf but only a restricted bestowal, sufficient only to sustain the *Kelim de Guf* so that they are not completely annulled.

Hence, when the *Masach* and the *Reshimot de ZON de Keter* in it returned to the place of *Malchut* where the *Zivug* did not stop, they immediately condense in the *Behinat Aviut de Rosh* in the entire measure contained in the *Reshimot*.

Since *Behina Dalet* did not leave a *Reshimo* they could not because more *Av* than the measure of *Aviut de Behina Gimel*. It is considered that she rose to the place of *Yesod* to make a new *Zivug de Hakaa* there on *Masach de Behina Gimel*.

Thus, the *Nekeva de Keter* can receive her bestowal. This is one *Zivug* that the ZON induced by their ascent to the *Rosh*.

However, there is *Reshimo de Behina Dalet* here too though it is from *Behinat Hitlabshut*, meaning *Behinat Zachar de Keter*. In itself, that *Reshimo* is fitting for extension of the *Ohr* through it, meaning to make a *Zivug de Hakaa* with the *Ohr Elyon*, to raise *Ohr Hozer* and the *Ohr Hozer* will draw the *Ohr* to it. Despite that, it is fitting to connect with the *Nekeva*, meaning *Aviut de Hamshacha*, and examine that thoroughly.

Thus, *Malchut de Rosh* made a *Behinat Zivug de Hakaa* here on the common *Aviut* from *Behina Dalet de Hitlabshut* and from *Behina Gimel de Hamshacha*. By that she raised *Ohr Hozer* up to *Komat Keter* of the *Rosh* since she was aided by the *Aviut de Behina Dalet* of *Hitlabshut*.

Thus we have thoroughly explained the two *Zivugim* that the ascents of ZON de Keter induced in the *Malchut de Rosh* by their ascent and *Hitkalelut* in her: The first is the *Zivug* on the common *Aviut* from *Behina Dalet de Hitlabshut* and *Behina Gimel* of *Hamshacha*. In this *Zivug* she extended *Komat Keter de Rosh*. The second is the *Zivug* on the *Aviut de Behina Gimel* only. In this *Zivug* she extends merely *Komat Hochma* of *Rosh*.

From the explained thus far you will thoroughly understand the Rav's words here in item six. He says, **"ZON of the Keter rise up to the place of this Keter at the end of the Shorashim Elyonim."**

This means that so is their presence in the *Rosh* measured, each *Anaf* under its *Shoresh*; the *Nekeva* under the *Zachar* and the *Zachar* under the *Ohr Keter* (see *Ohr Pnimi* this imem, par. "Remember"). It is written, **"He rises to the place of Shoresh of Malchut,"** and then the *Shoresh of Malchut* also rises in the *Shoresh* of the *Yesod* where they both remain as *Yesod*, which is ZON.

This means that in order to bestow to the ZON *de Keter* that rose she leaves her *Behina Dalet*, namely the place of *Malchut of Rosh* and receives the *Aviut de Behina Gimel* which is the place of *Yesod* of the *Rosh*.

However, note that the Rav is precise in saying "**they both remain as *Yesod*, which is ZON.**" This indicates the difference here. In several places where the *Malchut* rises to *Yesod* the *Yesod* rises to the *Sefira* above it. This is because *Malchut* acquired *Aviut de Behina Gimel* and the *Zivug* that emerges on *Aviut de Behina Gimel* extends merely *Komat Hochma*.

At that time the *Ohr Hochma* comes in *Kli de Keter*, the *Bina* in *Kli de Hochma*, ZA in *Kli de Bina* and *Malchut* in *Kli de ZA*. Here, however, the ZA did not rise to *Kli de Bina*, but they both remained as *Yesod*, as the Rav says.

The reason for it is thoroughly explained with the above words "However, there is *Reshimo*". Here there was a common *Zivug* from *Aviut de Hitlabshut* of *Behina Dalet* with the *Aviut de Hamshacha de Behina Gimel* that the *Malchut de Rosh* was mixed with by the *Zachar* and the *Nekeva de Keter* that rose in her.

Because of this association with *Behina Dalet de Hitlabshut* a *Zivug de Hakaa* was made in her extending *Komat Keter* of the *Rosh*. Hence, the *Ohr Keter* comes in its *Kli* and the *Sefirot* did not change their places.

Naturally, the *Yesod* also remained in its *Kli* along with the *Malchut* that rose to it. Thus, now there are two *Orot* together in the *Kli* of *Yesod*. They are also the connection *Zachar* and *Nekeva*, meaning its own *Ohr*, which is *Zachar* and the *Ohr Malchut*, which is *Nekeva*. That is why it is written, "**which is ZON.**"

It is written, "**Then, *Shoresh Keter Elyon* gives below after there is already a preparation for the *Tachtonim* to receive.**" It means that the *Koma* that emerges by that common *Zivug* is *Komat Keter* of the *Rosh*.

Hence, *Shoresh Keter Elyon*, meaning *Keter de Rosh* gives below to the *Ohr Keter*, which is contained in *Kli Malchut*. From the *Ohr Keter* that *Ohr* comes to his *Reshimo*, called *Zachar de Kli de Keter*. From the *Zachar* the *Ohr* reaches the *Nukva de Kli de Keter* since the three of them are mingled together.

It is written, "**At that time the *Nukva* of *Keter* is incorporated in the *Zachar*.**" It means that the unique *Zivug* for her was not done in *Malchut de Rosh*, namely the above second *Zivug* on *Aviut de Behina Gimel* alone. Rather, it is mingled together with the *Reshimo de Hitlabshut* of the *Zachar*; and examine that thoroughly.

It is written here in item nine, "**This extends to it by purifying that *Keter* that remained above at the end of the *Shorashim*.**" There is a very important concept here.

The *Zivug* that is made here now is *Zivug Elyon de Rosh*. Thus, how will the *Ohr Keter* be mingled in this *Zivug*, which is an *Ohr* that has already clothed the *Aviut* of the *Guf*, which is very far from the *Behinat Rosh*? This is what the Rav tells us here, "**This extends to it by purifying that *Keter*.**"

This means that the *Masach de Guf* rose and was purified from any *Aviut* in the *Guf* until it rose to the *Rosh*. Hence, the entire *Behinat Guf* contained in the *Ohr Keter* had been completely sucked out. It became just as *Zach* as *Behinat Rosh* and therefore mingled in the *Malchut* in the *Zivug de Rosh* and received the *Ohr* of *Keter* of the *Rosh* and poured upon the ZON *de Kli de Keter*.

The *Nekeva* is incorporated in the *Zachar*.

As it is written in the previous item, her *Behina Gimel* mingled and participated with the *Behina Dalet de Hitlabshut* of the *Zachar*. After that she departed from this participation since *Malchut de Rosh* made a special *Zivug* on the *Behina Gimel* of the *Nekeva*, as he explains below.

These three *Behinot* are even in their *He'arah*. They will receive their *Ohr* from the *Shoresh* of the *Keter Elyon*.

The three of them were incorporated in this *Zivug* of *Malchut de Rosh* in the common *Masach* from the *Aviut* of *Hitlabshut* of *Behina Dalet* with the *Aviut* of *Hamshacha de Behina Gimel*. The *Ohr Hozer* that rose from here clothed through *Komat Keter Elyon*, namely *Keter de Rosh*.

In addition, the matter of the *Hitkalelut* of these three *Orot* has already been explained above. Each *Anaf* is incorporated in its proximate *Shoresh*, meaning the *Nukva de Keter* in the *Zachar de Keter*, the *Zachar de Keter* in the *Ohr Keter*, and the *Ohr Keter* in *Malchut*.

10. The *Nukva* of the *Keter* must also receive from her *Shoresh Elyon*, which is the Upper *Hochma*. Hence, the *Shoresh* of the Upper *Hochma* descends in *Bina*, *Bina* in *Hesed* etc. until *Yesod* descends in *Malchut*.

Afterwards, that *Keter*, which rose to the place of *Shoresh* of *Malchut*, descends in His place. He cannot be there since He has no similarity with the *Shoresh* of *Malchut*. In addition, He is a branch and *Malchut* is a *Shoresh*. Hence, although He receives from *Keter*, He is worse than her.

However, He comes down to His place and can there be together with ZON that were in His place. This is so because then they are all equal, having received equally from the *Shoresh* of the *Keter Elyon*.

Ohr Pnimi

10. **The *Nukva* of the *Keter* must also receive from her *Shoresh Elyon*.**

Interpretation: This great *Zivug* that was made on the common *Masach* of the *Zachar* and the *Nukva* together that extended the great *Ohr de Keter Elyon* remained entirely in the *Rosh*. It cannot expand to the *Guf* because the *Behinat Aviut* of *Hamshacha de Behina Dalet* is absent there.

This matter of the association that was made with the *Behinat Hamshacha de Behina Dalet* and the matter of the association that was made with the *Hamshacha de Behina Gimel* was enough for the *Eser Sefirot* of the *Rosh*. This is so because there is no actual *Behinat Hitlabshut* in them. However, it is not enough for actual *Hitlabshut* inside the *Guf*.

Hence, the *Behinat Aviut de Hitlabshut* awakened in the *Zachar de Kli de Keter* to expand with this great *Ohr* into actual *Behinat Hitlabshut*, meaning to clothe in the *Eser Sefirot de Guf*. Because of that the *Behinat Guf* contained in the *Ohr Keter* that stands at the place of *Malchut de Rosh* immediately became apparent.

Along with it His *Tzura* became different from the *Malchut de Rosh*. In that it is considered to have instantly become separated from the *Malchut* and left there to His place, as the *Shinui Tzura* separates and departs the spirituals from one another.

Since He left the place of *Malchut*, you find that he immediately separated from the *Ohr* of the *Keter Elyon* and only the previous restricted *He'arah* remained in Him. It is called that the *Ohr Keter* returned His face upward and His posterior downward.

He writes, "**The *Nukva* of the *Keter* must also receive from her *Shoresh Elyon*.**" It means that the *Zivug* is not completed by the great *Zivug de Komat Keter Elyon* for its *He'arah* does not expand to the *Guf*. Thus, there is a need for the *Zivug* made on the *Behinat Nekeva de Keter*, meaning the complete *Aviut de Behina Gimel* both from the *Behinat Hamshacha* and from the *Behinat Hitlabshut*.

From her *Shoresh Elyon*, which is the Upper *Hochma*.

It is written above that the *Reshimo* that remained from *Komat Hochma de Hitpashtut Aleph* after its *Histalkut* is *Behinat Aviut de Behina Gimel*. It is made here into *Behinat Nukva de Keter* and it is the source of this second *Hitpashtut*.

Hence, the *Shoresh* of the Upper *Hochma* descends in *Bina*, *Bina* in *Hesed* etc.

The *Behinat Zivug* made on the *Behinat Nekeva de Keter*, which is *Behina Gimel*, causes the descent of the degrees from *Rosh* to *Sof*. *Keter* descends to the degree of *Hochma*, *Hochma* descends to the degree of *Bina*, *Bina* descends to the degree of *Hesed* etc. Finally, *Yesod* descends to the degree of *Malchut*.

The reason for it is that this *Zivug* occurs on *Aviut de Behina Gimel*. It does not raise *Ohr Hozer* and extends only *Komat Hochma*. Hence, with regard to this *Zivug*, you find that the *Ohr Hochma* descends and clothes *Kli de Keter*.

It is considered that the *Keter* descended from its degree and came to the degree of *Hochma*. Similarly, *Ohr Bina* clothes *Kli de Hochma* and *Sefirat Hochma* descends to the degree of *Bina* etc. until *Ohr Malchut* clothes *Kli de Yesod* and the *Yesod* descends to the degree of *Malchut*.

That *Keter* etc. since He has no similarity with the *Shoresh* of *Malchut*.

During the ascent of the *Masach* and the *Sefirot* up to the *Maatzil*, meaning they purified from the *Behinat Aviut de Guf* entirely, meaning from above downward. By that they have come to *Hishtavut Tzura* with *Malchut de Rosh*.

Thus, it is considered that the *Ohr de Komat Keter* that rose from the *Guf* came to the place of *Malchut* since it is then as *Zach* as *Malchut* and there is no disparity of form between them, as the Rav says (item 9). He wrote, "**This extends to it by purifying that *Keter* that remained above at the end of the *Shorashim*"** (see *Ohr Pnimi* item 9).

However, afterwards this first above *Zivug* that extended the *Komat Keter Elyon* has been completed in the form of from below upward as it is in the *Rosh*. Then came His time to turn around and expand from above downward too for *Hitlabshut* in the *Guf* as it is in all the *Zivugim*.

At that time the *Ohr Keter* in the place of *Malchut de Rosh* awakened to expand to the *Guf* once more as it was there to begin with. However, the *Behinat Nukva* of the *Rosh* was not in her place in *Behina Dalet* since the *Behina Dalet de Behinat Hamshacha* was missing there (*Ohr Pnimi* item 10). Thus, she could not expand from above downward to *Eser Sefirot* from her and within her through the *Tabur de Guf*, and all this great *Ohr* of this *Zivug* remained in the *Rosh*.

Still, because the *Ohr Keter* had awakened to return and expand in the *Guf* as in the beginning, even though it did not return, it still caused this awakening to disclose the *Aviut de Guf* from the time it was there in the beginning. Since the *Aviut de Guf* appeared in it, its *Tzura* has changed form that of *Malchut* of *Rosh*. He no longer has any semblance to her since He has grown as far from her as the *Guf* is far from the *Rosh*.

He writes, "**Afterwards, that *Keter*, which rose to the place of *Shoresh* of *Malchut*, descends in His place. He cannot be there since He has no similarity with the *Shoresh* of *Malchut*. In addition, He is a branch and *Malchut* is a *Shoresh*.**" It means that after the *Zivug* is completed the *Aviut de Guf* awakened in Him and His *Tzura* was changed from *Malchut* until He had no likeness with her.

Hence, He was completed to descend from there and return to His place. It is written, "for this is a root and that is a branch." This is because the *Behinat Guf* is a branch and the *Behinat Rosh* is a *Shoresh*.

He comes down to His place.

It is below *Kli Malchut* of the *Rosh*, meaning intermediate between *Rosh* and *Guf*. This is because it cannot descend and expand to the *Guf* since the *Nukva* of the *Rosh* does not expand in her *Eser Sefirot de Ohr Hozer* to become *Kelim* to clothe Him, as written in the previous item. He also cannot be in the *Rosh* because of the above *Shinui Tzura*. Hence, He is regarded as intermediate between them.

They are all equal, having received equally from the *Shoresh* of the *Keter Elyon*.

Before the second *Zivug* was made on the *Masach de Aviut* from *Behina Gimel* only on the *Behinat Nekeva de Keter*, the *Nekeva* was still mingled with the *Behina Dalet* of the *Zachar* and the *Zachar de Keter* was contained in the *Ohr Keter*. Hence, now the three of them are equal in their reception from the *Keter Elyon*, meaning what they still receive from *Komat Keter* of *Rosh*.

11. **At that time the *He'arat Shoresh Hochma* extends below and the *Zachar* is incorporated in the *Nukva*. The *Nukva* receives first since she equalizes in virtue with the *Zachar* and they both receive from the *Shoresh* of the *Keter Elyon* equally.**

Since they now receive from *Shoresh Hochma*, the *Nukva* first receives from all three here. They receive from her and incorporate in her, as it is written, "A virtuous woman is a crown to her husband."

Ohr Pnimi

11. **At that time the *He'arat Shoresh Hochma* extends below.**

It means that the *Zivug* is made on the *Masach* of *Behina Gimel* of the *Malchut de Rosh* without the participation of the *Aviut de Hamshacha de Behina Dalet*. At that time the *Ohr Hozer* that ascends from below upward attains no more than *Komat Keter Elyon*, but only up to *Komat* Upper *Hochma* of the *Rosh*. It is written about that, "**At that time the *He'arat Shoresh Hochma* extends below**," meaning the *Hochma* of the *Rosh*.

The *Zachar* is incorporated in the *Nukva* etc. receive from the *Shoresh* of the *Keter Elyon* equally.

Interpretation: now that the *Zivug* is made on *Masach de Behina Gimel* that extends only *Komat Hochma* of the *Rosh*, you find that the *Ohr Hochma* of the *Rosh* clothed the *Behinat Kli de Keter* of the *Rosh*. *Keter* and *Hochma* were incorporated in one another in the *Rosh* too. It follows that the *Zachar*, which is *Reshimo de Komat Keter*, and the *Nekeva*, being *Reshimo de Komat Hochma*, were also intermingled, and the *Zachar* receives the *Ohr Zivug* of the *Nekeva*.

It is written, "**The *Nukva* receives first since she equalizes in virtue with the *Zachar* and they both receive from the *Shoresh* of the *Keter Elyon* equally.**" Also, now that the *Ohr Hochma* came to *Kli de Keter* of the *Rosh* they receive from the *Kli de Keter* too, both of them equally.

The *Nukva* first receives from all three here. They receive from her etc.

This means that in the beginning, in the first *Zivug*, extending *Komat Keter* of the *Rosh*, the *Ohr Zivug* belonged to the *Ohr Keter* that rose from the *Guf* to *Malchut de Rosh*. However, *Nukva* did not have any connection to this *Ohr de Keter Elyon* since she is the *Reshimo de Komat Hochma*.

It follows, that *Nukva* receives from all of these three *Orot* because of her *Hitkalelut* in them. Now, however, when the *Zivug* is made on her *Behina*, namely *Behina Gimel*, the *Nukva* is found to be the primer receiver of the three *Orot*. This is so because the other two do not belong to *Komat Hochma* but receive from it.

12. Yet, the reasons for the descent of the *Shoresh Hochma* below in the place of the *Shoresh Bina* etc. are several. The first is that when she is near the *Shoresh Keter* she cannot shine below and her *Ohr* is annulled in the *Ohr* that extends from *Keter*.

Moreover, she must draw nearer down so that *Nukva* in the *Keter* may receive from Him first. This causes the closeness of the *Shoresh* to her on degree more than the closeness of the *Zachar* in *Keter* to His *Shoresh*.

In addition, we have explained that the *Shorashim* never cease giving below since the *Tachtonim* want to receive. Hence, the *Shoresh* of *Keter* does not stop pouring down the whole time ZON are outside their *Kli*.

It follows, that reason *Hochma* cannot bestow. Thus, when *Hochma* departs and descends below to the place of *Bina*, her place will remain vacant. While the *Shefa* pours from the *Shoresh* of *Keter* fills that vacant *Halal*, *Hochma* pours below. It follows, that then even if *Keter* bestows, He does not revoke the *He'arat Hochma*.

Ohr Pnimi

12. She is near the *Shoresh Keter* she cannot shine below and her *Ohr* is annulled in the *Ohr* that extends from *Keter*.

It means that if the degrees had not descended but the *Ohr Keter* would be in *Kli de Keter* and the *Ohr Hochma* in *Kli Hochma* etc. then the *Ohr Hochma* would not have been able to pour to the *Guf*. This is so because it is then annulled in the *Ohr Keter*, as all the lower *Sefirot* are annulled and become indistinguishable compared to the highest *Sefira* in the degree.

For that reason, though each degree contains *Eser Sefirot*, it is named only after the highest among them. Hence, it is impossible for the *Zivug* to be made only on *Behina Gimel* for then the degrees come down and the *Ohr Hochma* comes to *Kli de Keter*. In that state the *Ohr Hochma* will be the highest *Sefira* and its *He'arah* will be distinguishable.

ZON are outside their Kli. It follows, that reason Hochma cannot bestow.

This means that as long as they are the *Rosh*, they are there without a *Kli*. Hence, as long as the degrees are in their place and the *Ohr Keter Elyon* is in its own *Kli*, its *He'arah* always reaches the ZON and they cannot receive from another *Ohr* that is smaller than that. Thus, the descent of the degrees is required, that *Ohr Keter* will not shine in its *Kli*, but *Ohr Hochma*.

Thus, when Hochma departs and descends below to the place of Bina, her place will remain vacant.

Interpretation: When the degree of *Hochma* descends to the degree of *Bina*, the degree of *Hochma* is found to be vacant and there is no other place for *Ohr Hochma* to clothe if not *Kli de Keter*, as its own *Kli* serves the *Ohr Bina*.

While the Shefa pours from the Shoresh of Keter fills that vacant Halal, Hochma pours below.

It follows, that while an *Ohr* that extends from the *Kli* fulfills it from the missing degree of *Hochma*, meaning that *Ohr Hochma* itself clothes there, the degree of *Hochma* gives below and is not annulled in the *Ohr Keter*. This is because now it is the highest *Sefira* in the *Rosh* and no degree is higher.

13. However, the descent of *Hochma* below will not diminish her *He'arah* when the *Maatzil* grows one degree farther. This is because the *Ohr Keter Elyon* fulfills that place of *Halal*.

    Otherwise, had a vacant *Halal* been left there, the *Ohr* would cease from the *Maatzil* to *Hochma* and she would even lose the *Hochma*. It would have been better to leave her in her place. Now, however, when *Ohr Keter* fulfills the place of that *Halal*, there is a passageway to the *Ohr* of the *Maatzil* to pour in the *Shoresh Hochma*, and she is not lost at all.

Ohr Pnimi

13. **Will not diminish her *He'arah* when the *Maatzil* grows one degree farther.**

    Thus, after the *Kli de Hochma* descends to the degree of *Bina* because *Ohr Bina* clothed it, it did not create any cessation between the *Sefirot* because of the missing degree of *Hochma* there. This is so for the above reason that no vacant *Halal* remained there inside the degrees, as *Kli de Keter* where *Ohr Hochma* clothed fills the place of that want.

    It is written, "**Now, however, when *Ohr Keter* fulfills the place of that *Halal*, there is a passageway to the *Ohr* of the *Maatzil* to pour in the *Shoresh Hochma*.**" This means that the *Ohr Hochma* poured from the *Maatzil* is poured in *Kli de Keter* and the *Keter* fills the place of *Hochma*.

14. **After ZON have received from the *Shoresh* of *Hochma* too, they do not need to suck any longer. Then ZON descend in their *Kli*, the *Shoresh Hochma* rises to her place, and the *Shoresh Keter* gathers a part of the *Ohr* to it.**

    That *Keter* at the end of the *Shorashim* receives only the vitality it needs. Now He is called *Behinat Matei* in the *Keter* to the *Kli* since the *Ohr* returned to its *Kli*.

    However, the *Shoresh Keter Elyon* is called *Lo Matei* below in *Akudim*. Thus, we have deduced that the *Ohr* in the first *Kli* is called *Keter*, containing only *Ohr Hochma* since the *Ohr Keter* remained above at the end of the *Shorashim*. This is the meaning of, "In wisdom hast Thou made them all."

Ohr Pnimi

14. **After ZON have received from the *Shoresh* of *Hochma* too, they do not need to suck any longer.**

    The *Zivug* was made on the complete *Aviut de Behina Gimel*, both from the perspective of the *Hamshacha* and the perspective of the *Hitlabshut*. Afterwards the *Nukva* of the *Keter* can expand from above downward in *Eser Sefirot* to the *Guf* with the *Ohr* that she receives from the *Rosh*. The *Zachar de Kli de Keter* expands along with her and descends to the *Guf*. This is why it is written that then ZON descend in their *Kli*, meaning the *Guf*.

    Then ZON descend in their *Kli*, the *Shoresh Hochma* rises to her place, and the *Shoresh Keter* gathers a part of the *Ohr* to it.

    The matter of the decline of the above degrees that was made in the *Rosh*, was only for the time of the *Zivug*. However, after the *Zivug* and after ZON came down into their *Kli*, the degrees returned to their place as in the beginning, the *Ohr Keter Elyon* returned to *Kli de Keter*, *Ohr Hochma* to *Kli de Hochma* etc.

Yet, the *Keter Elyon* did not shine to the *Ohr Keter* below *Malchut* until it could expand to the *Guf* as in the beginning, but, "**the Shoresh Keter gathers a part of the Ohr to it. That Keter at the end of the Shorashim receives only the vitality it needs,**" and not in a way that it can expand to the *Guf* as in the beginning, for the above reason.

Matei in the Keter to the Kli.

This is because that *Ohr* of the *Zivug* that is made in *Behinat Nekeva de Keter de Behina Gimel* of the *Rosh*, which is in *Komat Hochma*, clothing *Kli de Keter*. It comes down with the above *Zachar* and *Nukva* into the *Guf* and clothes *Kli de Keter de Guf* too.

It is written, "**since the Ohr returned to its Kli.**" This refers to *Kli de Keter* that belongs to *Ohr Hochma*, since it extends so from the *Behinat Zivug*, hence its name, *Matei* in *Keter de Guf*.

The Shoresh Keter Elyon is called Lo Matei below in Akudim.

It means that when it is written *Matei* in *Keter de Guf* it does not mean that *Ohr Keter* of the *Rosh* shines in the *Guf*, as this *Ohr Keter* is always *Lo Matei* in the *Guf*. Rather, it means *Ohr Hochma* of the *Rosh*, but clothing in *Kli de Keter*.

Thus, we have deduced etc. containing only Ohr Hochma.

He lets us know that in this entire *Hitpashtut Bet*, when it writes *Ohr Keter* it means only *Ohr Hochma*, as we have learned here that there is no *Ohr Keter* in the *Guf* at all, but only *Ohr Hochma*. However, because it clothes in the *Kli de Keter*, we called it *Ohr Keter*.

15. *Now we will explain this reality of the *Histalkut Ohr Elyon*. When evaluating this reality of the *Kli* that contains all the *Ohr*, it is necessary that when the *Ohr* leaves it, there will be parts in it that are suitable for looking to that *Ohr*.

When it draws far from them, the *Panim* to *Panim* looking draws as far from them as it has drawn far. The lesson in that is that when the *Ohr* departs from the tenth part of that *Kli*, which will be later called *Malchut*, that tenth part of that *Kli*, from which that *Ohr* departed, thus becomes a *Kli*.

At that time the *Kli* turns its *Panim* down because it has now been discerned as a *Kli*. When separated from its *Ohr*; it is unable to look at it *Panim be Panim*. In that state it turns its *Panim* after it has become a *Kli* and then it looks at the *Ohr Elyon* that has drawn far from it only through the *Achor*.

Ohr Pnimi

15. Parts in it that are suitable for looking to that *Ohr*.

    The place of bestowal or the place of reception in the *Kli*, is called *Panim*. The bestowal or the reception themselves are called *Histaklut* or *Habata* (gazing).

    It is written, "**When evaluating this reality of the *Kli* that contains all the *Ohr*, it is necessary that when the *Ohr* leaves it, there will be parts in it that are suitable for looking to that *Ohr*.**" This is so because each *Histalkut* is done by *Hizdakchut* of the *Aviut* in the corrected *Masach* in the *Kli*.

    It is known that there are four *Behinot* in the *Masach*. For example, if *Behina Dalet* of the *Kli* is purified and the *Ohr* departs from the *Kli* because of that, three *Behinot* of *Aviut* still remain in the *Kli* from which the *Ohr* has not departed and they are still suitable for *Habata* on the *Ohr*.

    The *Panim* to *Panim* looking draws as far from them as it has drawn far.

    If the *Aviut* has been purified from *Behina Dalet*, the *Ohr* is distanced from the *Kli* in the measure of *Behina Dalet*, not from the three other *Behinot*. If it is also distanced from *Behina Gimel*, the *Ohr* will be distanced from the *Kli* in the measure of *Aviut* of *Behina Gimel* too, and not from the rest of the *Kli* which is from *Behina Bet* upward.

    At that time the *Kli* turns its *Panim* down.

    Here we must remember everything the Rav wrote regarding *Hitpashtut Aleph de Akudim* in Part 4 regarding the descending *Ohr Hozer* from the *Komot* that emerge during the *Hizdakchut* that shines to the empty *Kelim* located under the place of the *Zivug*. Also, the issue of *Hakaa* that these *He'arot* made with the *Reshimot* that remain in those *Kelim* (see Part 4, Chap 9 and *Ohr Pnimi* items 50, 90).

    From there you will understand that after the *Aviut* has been purified from *Behina Gimel* to *Behina Bet* (for example), the *Zivug* is made in *Behina Bet* and *Behina Gimel* remains empty without its *Ohr*. At that time the *Ohr Hozer* descends from the *He'arat Zivug de Behina Bet* into the *Kli* of the empty *Behina Gimel*.

    Then there is *Hakaa* and *Bitush* between the descending *Ohr Hozer* and the *Reshimo* in the empty *Kli* since the *Reshimo* is from the *Histalkut* of the *Zivug*. For that reason the *Reshimo* must exit there and ascend above the *Kli* as *Tagin*, making room for the *Ohr Hozer* to come down into its *Kli*. Know, that this

Ohr Hozer that descended into the empty *Kli* operates in the *Kli* that will turn its *Panim* downward and its *Achor* upward, as the Rav says here.

You already know that from the *Behina* of *Hamshacha* of *Ohr* in the *Kli*, the wall of the *Kli* is divided into two halves called *Panim* and *Achor* or *Pnimiut* and *Hitzoniut* (see Part 4, Chap 5 item 3). Accordingly, you find that that empty *Kli* of the above *Behina Gimel* is divided into *Panim* and *Achor*.

Its more *Av* half of the wall is called *Panim* since it extends the *Ohr Elyon* to it through a *Zivug*, and the half of the wall that is not so *Av* is called *Achor*. This is because it is silent in the *Kli*, and the *Ohr* has no contact with it.

All this refers only to a time when the *Ohr* is present in the degree. However, during the *Histalkut* of the *Ohr* from the degree *de Behina Gimel* to *Behina Bet*, made in the *Zivug de Behina Bet* when the *He'arah* of this *Zivug* descends to the empty *Kli* of the empty *Behina Gimel*, the two halves of the wall are turned. The half of *Panim* becomes *Achor*, and the half of *Achor* becomes *Panim*.

This is because the descending *Ohr Hozer* from *Behina Bet* into the empty *Kli* becomes distant from the *Aviut de Behina Gimel* there since it is *Ohr* from *Behina Bet*. It draws nearer to the half of the wall of the *Kli* that is closest to *Behina Bet* and shines there.

Thus, the most *Av* of that *Kli* does not receive any *He'arah* from that *Ohr Hozer* and now becomes *Behinat Achor* of the *Kli*. The most *Zach* of that *Kli* now becomes the *Panim* of the *Kli* since the *Ohr* shines only in its *Zach* part.

This is the meaning of, **"At that time the *Kli* turns its *Panim* down,"** since it cannot receive anything from the *He'arat Zivug* made in the Upper *Behina*. The *Panim* becomes *Achor* and turns its *Achoraim* upward since it is now all that receives from the *He'arat Ohr Hozer* that descended to it, and the *Achor* becomes *Panim*. This is called inversion.

It has now been discerned as a *Kli*.

However, afterwards, when the *Behina* above it also becomes a *Behinat Kli*, meaning the *Zivug* departs from there too, the *He'arat Ohr Hozer* stops coming down to it. Then the *Kli* returns its *Panim* upward as in the beginning since its *Achor* has now lost all its merit, as the *Reshimo* now begins to shine to the *Kli* and the *He'arat Reshimo* only the *Behinat Panim* of the *Kli*. It is like the *Ohr* prior to its departure, not reaching its *Behinat Achor*. You find that the *Kli* has been restored as in the beginning.

It looks at the *Ohr Elyon* etc. through the *Achor*.

This means that then you find that the *He'arat Zivug* that descends to it from the highest *Behina* is received only through the *Achor* of the *Kli*, which is the more *Zach* part of it. This is considered that the *Kli* turned its *Achoraim* upward.

16. Now the *Ohr Elyon* too will be called *Achor* during its *Histalkut* and that *Kli* will be *Achor be Achor* with that *Ohr*. After that *Ohr* also leaves, one more portion, which will later be called *Behinat Yesod*, departed from all of it. Then, that part will also turn its *Panim* from the *Ohr Elyon* for it will not be able to receive it.

    In that state, the first *Behinat Kli*, called *Malchut*, will be able to turns its *Panim* upward since the *Ohr* drew far from it. At that time *Malchut* and *Yesod* will be *Panim be Panim* but *Yesod* will be *Achor be Achor* with the *Ohr Elyon*.

    Ohr Pnimi

16. **Now the *Ohr Elyon* too will be called *Achor*.**

    The matter of the appellations *Panim* and *Achor* applies only to the *Kelim*. This is because in the *Ohr* they are called *Hitpashtut* and *Histalkut*. The Rav calling the *Histalkut Ohr* here by the name *Achor* is only in allegory, since he wants to compare the matter of the *Histalkut Ohr* with the matter of the *Achor* in the *Kelim* and call them *Achor be Achor*. The Rav has already explained the reason that the empty *Kelim* are called *Achor* and *Histalkut* in Part 4, Chap 3 item 4.

    Will be able to turns its *Panim* upward since the *Ohr* drew far from it.

    This is so because after the *Zivug* stops at the highest *Behina* too and the *He'arat Zivug* stops descending to the *Kli*, the *Reshimo* shines in the *Kli* once more. Then the *Kli* returns its *Panim* upward as in the beginning since it does not receive any *He'arah* now.

17. Also, when *Behinat Ohr* of *Hod* departs, *Hod* will be *Achor be Achor* with the *Ohr Elyon*. Then *Yesod* will turn its *Panim* to *Hod*, *Hod* and *Yesod* will be *Panim be Panim* and *Malchut* will be *Panim be Achor*, the *Panim* of *Malchut* in the *Achoraim* of *Yesod*.

    This is so because the desire and the yearning of the *Sefira* to return its *Panim* to the *Ohr*. However, the near *Sefira* to the *Ohr* cannot return its *Panim* to it yet, before it draws the measure of one *Sefira* far from the *Ohr*.

    Ohr Pnimi

17. **Before it draws the measure of one *Sefira* far from the *Ohr*.**

    As long as there is *Zivug* in the highest *Sefira*, the *He'arat Zivug* comes from there to the empty *Sefira* below it. At that time this *He'arah* reaches only the

Behinat Achor in the *Kli* and not at all the *Panim*. Thus, the *Panim* of the *Kli* are turned downward.

However, after the *Ohr* departs from the highest *Sefira* as well, the *He'arat Zivug* reaches only from the *Elyon* to the *Tachton*, meaning from the cause to the consequence but not from above its cause. This is so even though there is still *Zivug* in the *Sefira* above the Upper One.

Thus, the *He'arat Reshimo* returns and returns its *Panim* upward. This is his precision, "Before it draws the measure of one *Sefira* far from the *Ohr*," and examine carefully.

18. Also, when the *Ohr* leaves the *Behinat Netzah*, *Netzah* will be *Achor be Achor* with the *Ohr Elyon* and *Panim be Panim* with the *Hod*. *Yesod* will be *Panim be Achor* with the *Hod* and *Malchut* too *Panim be Achor* with the *Yesod* etc. similarly until the *Ohr* departs from all ten parts of the *Kli*.

    In that state all the *Sefirot* will be *Panim be Achor*, the *Panim* of the inferior in the *Achor* of the superior. However, the *Keter* will be *Panim be Panim* with the *Hochma* since the *Keter* is *Achor be Achor* with the *Ohr Elyon* for the above reason. Therefore, *Keter* and *Hochma* must be *Panim be Panim*.

Ohr Pnimi

18. **The *Keter* is *Achor be Achor* with the *Ohr Elyon*.**

    This is because *Behina Dalet* did not leave a *Reshimo*. It is known that *Behina Dalet* extends the *Ohr Keter*. Although *Ohr Keter* itself left a *Reshimo* in its *Kli*, it is still only *Behinat Reshimo de Hamshacha* (see *Ohr Pnimi* item 6). This is considered the *Behinat Achor* with regard to the *Behinat Hamshacha*. For that reason it is also considered its *Achoraim* being turned upward, and *Panim* downward.

    Keter and Hochma must be Panim be Panim.

    Hochma has a complete *Reshimo* from the *Behinat Hamshacha*. This *Reshimo* brings its *Panim* upward once again. *Keter* lacks the *Reshimo de Hamshacha*, hence its *Achoraim* are turned upward. Hence, they are found to be equalized with one another, which is called *Panim be Panim*. This will be clarified below.

19. Thus we have explained the *Histalkut* and how the *Kelim* were made by that. Yet, we have explained how there are *Kli Malchut* and *Yesod* etc. in this *Kli*. Yet, this is not why it is called *Kelim*, since it is still not apparent that they are ten *Sefirot*, and also that the *Ohr* departed together.

The thing is that it is like one long *Kli* whose parts are not equal according to the distancing of those parts from one end to the other. Thus we have explained the existence of the *Ohr*, its *Hitpashtut* and its *Histalkut*, and they are two *Behinot*.

20. Now there is another *Hitpashtut* and *Histalkut*, as will be explained, and then the four *Behinot* will be completed. The thing is that when this *Behinat Kli* was completed and became a *Kli* by the *Histalkut* of the *Ohr*, when the *Ohr* expands in this *Kli* once more, there will remain a discernment of *Orot* and *Kelim*.

    However, when the *Ohr* expands in this *Kli* for the second time, it does not expand in the first order, but appears and disappears. This is the meaning of what is written in the Zohar, "*Matei ve Lo Matei*." These two *Behinot* are called *Hitpashtut* and *Histalkut*, by which the four *Behinot* will be completed.

Ohr Pnimi

20. "*Matei ve Lo Matei*." These two *Behinot* are called *Hitpashtut* and *Histalkut*, by which the four *Behinot*.

    This refers to the four *Otiot* of the Name *HaVaYaH*. This is because these two *Behinot* of *Hitpashtut* and *Histalkut de Hitpashtut Aleph de Akudim* that he introduced above (item 19) are the two *Otiot Yod, Hey* of *HaVaYaH*. These two *Behinot* of *Hitpashtut* and *Histalkut* in *Hitpashtut Bet de Akudim*, called *Matei ve Lo Matei*, are the two *Otiot Vav, Hey* of *HaVaYaH*.

    The beginning of the *Matei* of *Ohr* inside the *Kli de Keter*.

    Will be explained below.

21. The thing is that first the *Ohr* enters the *Kli* of *Keter* and then leaves it. After that the *Ohr* enters *Kli* of *Hochma* and leaves once more. It does the same in all ten *Kelim*, and this is called *Matei ve Lo Matei* that is always mentioned in the Zohar.

    It is always in the nature of that *Ohr* to come and shine and then leave, as it is the nature of a candle's flame to sway. Also, the *Ohr* always remains *Matei ve Lo Matei* in these *Kelim* called *Akudim*. Because they are in one *Kli*, that *Kli* has no power to tolerate the *Ohr* if it is not *Matei ve Lo Matei*.

    Thus we have explained the four *Behinot* that are the first *Hitpashtut* and its *Histalkut*, and the second *Hitpashtut* and its *Histalkut*. We have also explained that the second *Hitpashtut* and *Histalkut* are called *Matei ve Lo*

Matei. For that reason this *Kli* is called *Akudim*, since it is one *Kli* that connects and ties ten *Orot* within it.

Ohr Pnimi

21. Because they are in one *Kli*, that *Kli* has no power to tolerate the *Ohr*.

    Until *Olam ha Nekudim* there is no more than one *Kli* in the entire *Eser Sefirot*. Even though we refer to the other *Sefirot* as *Kelim*, it is only in metaphor, to simplify matters, as the Rav has written above (Part 4, Chap 1).

    This is the reason for the *Hizdakchut* and the *Histalkut Orot de Hitpashtut Aleph de Akudim* as well as the *Matei ve Lo Matei de Hitpashtut Bet de Akudim*, as the Rav wrote above (Part 4, Chap 1 item 3). Since the ten inner *Orot* and the ten surrounding *Orot* are connected and tied to a single *Kli* etc. they beat on each other and strike one another.

    Hence the *Aviut* in the *Masach* is purified and the *Orot* depart. It is the same manner in all these ten exits and ten entrances that were here in *Hitpashtut Bet*. They are also for the reason that that the *Ohr Makif* and *Ohr Pnimi* that are connected together in their *Shoresh* in *Malchut* of the *Rosh* strike each other as they depart from there to the *Guf*.

    This is because the *Masach* prevents the *Ohr Makif* from expanding to its place in the *Guf*, meaning from *Tabur* down. For that reason it purifies the *Masach* and the *Masach* cannot tolerate and limit the *Ohr Pnimi* inside the *Kelim* and the *Orot* leave and return as we have written before (see Part 4, Chap 1, item7 *Ohr Pnimi*).

22. This also explains how come the *Kli* is considered one *Kli*, alone, and the *Orot* are considered ten. This is because when the *Ohr* leaves, everything is considered one *Kli* and not ten *Kelim*.

    However, regarding the *Orot* in them, when they return to expand in a real *Hitpashtut*, which is the second *Hitpashtut*, it does not expand in one time inside the *Kli* as it departed. Rather, it enters and exits ten exits and ten entrances.

    It enters and exits ten times, once in *Keter*, once in *Hochma* and so forth in all of them, hence they are called ten *Orot*. The *Kli*, however, is made at once by *Histalkut Aleph* when it left at one time. For that reason it is called one *Kli*.

Ohr Pnimi

22. Hence they are called ten *Orot*. The *Kli*, however, is made at once.

Compared to the *Kli*, all these departures are considered one *Histalkut*. This is because here there is still only one *Kli*, only *Kli Malchut*. There is no recognition of a *Kli* in the first nine *Sefirot* and all these exits and entrances made in it are considered as one long *Kli* whose parts are not equal as the Rav says above (item 19). Know, that all these are preparations for the *Tikun* of the *Eser Kelim* in the *Eser Sefirot*.

Things are done gradually: in *Hitpashtut de AK* there is still no recognition through the *Histalkut*. Even the discernment in the *Orot* does not show that they are ten *Orot*. In *Hitpashtut Bet* there is a discernment in the *Eser Sefirot* that they are ten *Orot*, and in the *Hitpashtut* of the *Eser Sefirot* in *Olam Nekudim* there is a recognition of the *Eser Kelim* in the GAR and not in the seven lower *Sefirot*. It is completed in *Olam Atzilut* and ten complete *Kelim* are made in all ten *Sefirot*.

23. These four *Behinot* are the actual four *Otiot HaVaYaH*. The *Yod-Vav* are two *Behinot Hitpashtut,* and the *Heys* (pl. for *Hey*) are two *Behinot Histalkut*.

    You already know that the name *HaVaYaH* begins only from *Hochma* downward. The reason is that these four *Behinot* belong only to *Hochma* and under, but *Keter* contains only two *Behinot*. For this reason it is called *Yod-Hey, Yod-Hey-Vav-Hey*.

    This is the meaning of, "for the Lord is God, an everlasting Rock." This is because He first began to picture and create the world in them. This is the meaning of *Akudim*, which are the *Yod-Hey HaVaYaH*. This because *Yod-Hey* in *Keter*, *HaVaYaH* in all the other *Partzufim*.

Ohr Pnimi

23. The *Yod-Vav* are two *Behinot Hitpashtut,* and the *Heys* are two *Behinot Histalkut*.

    The first *Hitpashtut* is the *Yod*; the second *Hitpashtut* is the *Vav*. The first *Histalkut* is the First *Hey* and the second *Histalkut* is the last *Hey*.

    HaVaYaH begins only from Hochma downward.

    It is known that the *Yod* means *Hochma*, *Vav* means ZA, the First *Hey* means *Bina* and the last *Hey* means *Malchut*. *Keter*, however, is not implied in the four *Otiot*, except in the tip of the *Yod*. This is so for the reason that the Rav explains below.

24. The reason is that below, the nine *Sefirot* have the four deficits of the *Ohr*. This in itself will cause the giving of the Name of the *Ohr Elyon,* making these four deficits capable of being called *HaVaYaH*.

They are those: The first is the *Hitpashtut* of the *Ohr* for the first time. At that time the *Ohr* begins to expand in *Keter*, the first among them. At that time all nine below it lack that *Ohr*.

Thus, when the *Ohr* appeared in the reality of *Keter*, all the rest were still absent. This is the first deficit in the first *Hitpashtut* of the nine *Kelim*. This deficit is absent in *Keter*.

Ohr Pnimi

24. The four deficits of the *Ohr*. This in itself will cause the giving of the Name of the *Ohr Elyon*, making these four deficits capable of being called *HaVaYaH*.

    Interpretation: the meaning of the *Otiot* is *Kelim* that were emanated and made by the *Nitzotzin* that fell from the *Ohr Hozer* of the four *Komot* that came out during the *Histalkut* of the *Ohr* of *Hitpashtut Aleph*. They came into the empty *Kelim* after the *Histalkut* of the *Ohr* from them.

    As has been explained in the Rav's words above (Part 4, chap3 item 12 (see *Ohr Pnimi* there item 100), any "Name" implies attainment, since "anything that we do not attain, we do not call by a name." It is known that there is no attainment in the *Ohr* without a *Kli*, and it has also been explained (Part 4, Chap 1 item 9) that the *Hitpashtut* of the *Ohr* and its *Histalkut* are the reason for the making of the *Kli*.

    Thus, the lack of *Ohr* makes for the extistence of the *Kelim* and the Holy Names. It is written, "**the nine *Sefirot* have the four deficits of the *Ohr*. This in itself will cause the giving of the Name of the *Ohr Elyon*, making these four deficits capable of being called *HaVaYaH*.**" In other words, it is so that there will be a possibility to attain Him in that Name.

    The *Hitpashtut* of the *Ohr* for the first time etc. This is the first deficit in the first *Hitpashtut* of the nine *Kelim*.

    This means that when the *Ohr* begins to expand in the *Keter* the *Ohr* is in *Behinat Ohr Yashar, Rachamim*. At that time all nine below it lack that complete *Ohr*.

    Although they are considered *Ohr Hozer* and *Din* and are therefore called *Nekudot*, hence there is a blemish here in the lower nine of *Hitpashtut Aleph*. However, here there is no blemish in the *Keter* whatsoever, hence the *Keter* is not implied in the *Otiot* of the Name *HaVaYaH*, as they imply the lack of the *Ohr*.

Rather, the *Hitpashtut* of the nine *Sefirot* below *Keter*, being the four *Komot HB ZON* that came out as *Ohr Hozer* and *Din*, imply the *Yod* of *HaVaYaH*. also, the *Histalkut* of the entire *Hitpashtut Aleph* in general is the meaning of the *Hey de HaVaYaH*. They are called the *Yod-Hey de Keter*, as the whole of *Hitpashtut Aleph* is called *Keter*.

25. In the second *Hitpashtut*, this deficit will also be in the nine *Sefirot* once more, not in the *Keter*. Hence, there are two deficits in the nine *Sefirot* and not in *Keter*. This is so because when no *Ohr* is emanated, it is not called a deficit.

    However, once this *Ohr* begins to expand, it first expands in *Keter*. At that time the nine *Sefirot* will be considered lacking that *Ohr*, as the *Ohr Keter* preceded them. However, the other two deficits are found in both *Keter* and the nine *Sefirot*, and it is the two *Behinot Histalkut*, since this is called a true deficit whether to the nine *Sefirot* or to the *Keter* Himself.

Ohr Pnimi

25. **In the second *Hitpashtut*, this deficit will also be in the nine *Sefirot* once more, not in the *Keter*.**

    This is so because in *Hitpashtut Bet* too only *Keter* came out in *Behinat Taamim*. However, the other nine *Sefirot* came out during the *Hizdakchut* as *Nekudot* and that lack appeared in them a second time.

    Hence, the *Keter de Hitpashtut Bet* is not implied in the four *Otiot HaVaYaH*, even in *Hitpashtut Bet*, as that lack is not in it but only from *Hochma* down. These are the four *Komot HB ZON* that emerge because of the *Hizdakchut* of the *Masach* (as he writes below) called *Nekudot*. They are implied in the *Vav* of *HaVaYaH* and the general *Histalkut* of this *Hitpashtut Bet* is the last *Hey* of *HaVaYaH*.

    The Rav says above (item 23) about this *Hitpashtut Bet*, *HaVaYaH* in the all the other *Partzufim*. This is because the two lacks of *Hitpashtut Aleph* are present in this *Hitpashtut Bet* too, as we shall see below.

    The nine *Sefirot* will be considered lacking that *Ohr*, as the *Ohr Keter* preceded them.

    It means that the matter of the lack in them is only compared to the *Ohr Keter* that preceded them in its merit. Compared to Him, they are considered *Ohr Hozer* and *Din* though in themselves they are *Rachamim* since they too extend from the *Maatzil* from above downward, as the Rav wrote above (Part 4, Chap 2 item 1).

It is known that all that extends from above downward is *Rachamim*. Yet, compared to the *Ohr Keter* they are considered *Din* since they only exit by the power of the *Histalkut* of His *Ohr* (see Part 4, Chap 6 and *Ohr Pnimi* item 9). However, the two *Behinot* of the general *Histalkut* of *Hitpashtut Aleph* and *Hitpashtut Bet* implied in the two *Otiot Hey* of the Name *HaVaYaH* are a true lack and *Behinat Din* in themselves too, as the Rav says above.

We understand from all the above that the *Yod* in the *HaVaYaH* is the *Ohr* of *Nekudot* of *Hitpashtut Aleph*, meaning the nine *Sefirot* from *Hochma* downward that came out there during the *Histalkut Ohr Taamim*.

The First *Hey* in the Name *HaVaYaH* is the general *Histalkut* of this *Hitpashtut Aleph*, the *Vav* in the Name *HaVaYaH* implies the *Ohr Nekudot* of *Hitpashtut Bet*. The last *Hey* in the Name *HaVaYaH* implies the general *Histalkut* of this *Hitpashtut Bet*. Thus, the two expansions of *Ohr Nekudot* imply the *Yod-Vav* in the Name *HaVaYaH* and the two departures imply the *Hey-Hey* in the Name *HaVaYaH*.

He writes (item 23), "**Yod-Hey in Keter, HaVaYaH in all the other Partzufim.**" It means that that the *Hitpashtut* of the nine *Sefirot* from *Hochma* downward that came out during the *Histalkut Ohr Keter de Hitpashtut Aleph* and the *Histalkut Ohr de Hitpashtut Aleph* in general, is the meaning of the "**Yod-Hey in Keter.**"

This is so because as a whole, *Hitpashtut Aleph* is called *Keter*, as it is known that it is *Partzuf Keter de AK*. These two lacks of the *Ohr*, meaning the *Histalkut* compared to *Keter*, and not compared to themselves.

The *Behina* of its real *Histalkut*, in themselves too, is necessarily received inside *Hitpashtut Bet*. This is because all the forces that appear in the *Elyon* must necessarily be in its *Tachton*.

Hence, these *Yod-Hey de Hitpashtut Aleph* are in *Hitpashtut Bet* too. Added to them are these two lacks of the *Ohr* in their own *Behina*, which are *Behinat Histalkut* compared to the *Keter* of *Hitpashtut Bet*, and compared to the value of the lower nine themselves. It is also the real collective *Behinat Histalkut* of *Hitpashtut Bet*, implied in the *Vav-Hey*.

Thus, we have all four *Otiot* of the Name *HaVaYaH* here in *Hitpashtut Bet*. It is written, "**HaVaYaH in all the other Partzufim,**" meaning the *Partzufim* of *Hitpashtut Bet*.

26. We shall explain this matter that writes that these **Behinot** are called, "for the Lord is God, an everlasting Rock." This is the meaning of the verse, "extol Him that rideth upon the skies, whose name is the Lord (ה״יב)."

We must be meticulous with this verse. He should have said, "ה"י" (Lord) is His name, but what is "ה"יב"? The thing is that the entire name is contained in the "ה"יב" and this is the meaning of, "whose name is the Lord (ה»יב)."

The "ה"י" in its fullest is *Yod* (comprised of the letters *Yod, Vav, Dalet*), *He* (comprised of the letters *Hey, Aleph*), twenty-six in *Gimatria*, which is *HaVaYaH*. Thus, "ה"יב" is the actual name and the name "ה"י" in *Keter*. It implies how the name *HaVaYaH* emerged from it containing all the four *Otiot HaVaYaH*.

Ohr Pnimi

26. Thus, "ה"יב" is the actual name etc. It implies how the name *HaVaYaH* emerged from it containing all the four *Otiot HaVaYaH*.

    This is the meaning of the verse, "extol Him that rideth upon the skies (Heb: *Aravot*)": *Aravot* implies *Eruv* (lit. mixture) of *Midat ha Rachamim* with *Din*. It begins in the *Partzufim* of *Hitpashtut Bet* and says, "whose name is the Lord (ה»יב)."

    (ה»יב) implies *Keter* where there is still no mixture. Hence, the *HaVaYaH* of *Hitpashtut Bet* extends from it and in all the other *Partzufim* until *Olam ha Atzilut*, where the mixture ends, and ten *Kelim* emerge.

    This is the entire reason for giving a good reward to the righteous, as it is written above (Part 4, Chap 1 item 4 in *Ohr Pnimi*). This is the meaning of the verse, "extol Him that rideth upon the skies," who mixed and associated *Midat ha Rachamim* with *Din*. It came out of the meaning of "ה"י" His Name in *Keter*.

    This is the meaning of *Hitpashtut* and *Histalkut* and in that "exult ye before Him," for in that was all the good reward prepared and concealed for the righteous.

27. *Know, that all these *Kelim* did not gain *Aviut* and become *Kelim* only after the *Histalkut* of *Ohr Malchut*. At that time He turned His *Panim* from the *Kli*. It is so because the *Ohr Elyon* of the *Kli* of *Keter* departed and rose to the *Maatzil*. Despite that, because *Ohr Hochma* rose in its place the *Kli* of *Keter* does not gain *Aviut* and materialize. It is the same way in all the other *Orot*.

    You find that it's been explained in the previous study that *Ohr Keter* of *Akudim* leaves first of all and *Ohr Malchut* leaves last of all. It follows, that the existence of *Behinat Kli* begins only from below upward.

Also, the *Kli* of *Malchut* is made before all the others. This is because since *Ohr Malchut* leaves last, when it leaves its own *Kli* the *Kli* does not become more *Av* until its *Histalkut* from its entire *Kli* is completed.

At that time the nine Upper *Kelim* still have *Ohr* though none of them as any a part of the *Ohr* that reaches its actual part. For that reason they do not become *Av* and materialize.

Kli Malchut, however, has been entirely emptied of her *Ohr*. Also, there is no other *Ohr* below her to rise inside her. Hence, she gains *Aviut* and becomes a *Kli*.

Despite that, she does not become completely *Av* until the *Ohr* departs from her entirely, three degrees etc. The reason for it will be understood with the above mentioned, that any less than three is considered alone. Thus, after the *Ohr* departed by three complete degrees the *Kli* becomes completely dark and its making is complete.

Ohr Pnimi

27. Until the *Ohr* departs from her entirely, three degrees etc.

The *Kli* is made only by the complete *Histalkut* of the *Ohr* from it, both *Ohr Pnimi* and *Ohr Makif*. It is known that up to two degrees, the *Kli* still receives *Ohr Makif*. For that reason it does not become a *Kli* until the *Ohr* draws far from it by three degrees.

Take *Kli de ZA* for example. When *Ohr ZA* leaves the *Kli* and rises to *Bina*, it is no longer considered as distancing of the degree since it still receives *Yechida de Ohr Pnimi*. Only when it departs and rises to *Hochma* does it depart one degree from the *Kli* and receives the first *Ohr Makif*.

Afterwards, when it departs two degrees and ascends to *Keter*, it still receives the second *Ohr Pnimi*. Thus, the *Kli* is not yet entirely dark, until it leaves from the *Keter* to the *Maatzil* as well. At that time the *Kli* does not attain any *Ohr*, and it is completed.

The same applies to *Kli Malchut*. When the *Ohr* departs one degree from her, meaning when *Ohr Malchut* ascends to ZA, she still receives the first *Ohr Makif*. When it departs two degrees, meaning when it ascends to *Bina*, it still receives the second *Ohr Makif*. Only when *Ohr Malchut* ascends to *Hochma*, which is the third degree, no *He'arah* is received, the *Kli Malchut* becomes completely dark, and it is completed.

Hence, the *Kelim* were not completed from *Bina* upward. This is because even when *Ohr Bina* ascends to *Keter*, *Bina* still receives *Yechida de Ohr Pnimi*. This is not considered a distancing in the degree at all, much less with *Keter* and *Hochma*. Study all that in the Rav's words above (Part 4, Chap 6 item 15).

Besides the above, there is yet another condition for the completion of the *Kli*, namely the completeness of the outer half of the wall of the *Kli*, mentioned in the Rav's words above (Part 4, Chap 4 item 3). As long as there is not the outer half of the wall of the *Kli* that belongs to the *Makifim*, the *Kli* is not completed.

Thus, the *Kelim de GAR* did not attain any *Orot Makifim* during their ascent to the *Maatzil*, as the Rav says there. Consequently, the *Kelim de GAR* are found to be lacking the outer half of the wall of their outer *Kli*. For that reason they were only completed later, in *Hitpashtut Bet*, as the Rav says here.

28. You find that after the *Histalkut* of *Ohr Malchut* it rose to its *Shoresh* inside *Peh de AK*. At that time the work of the seven lower *Kelim* from *Hesed* to *Malchut* ends. Thus, the end of their work was through the *Histalkut Orot*, and when they departed, their *Kelim* were made.

However, the work of the three Upper *Kelim* of *Keter Hochma Bina* was not over since they have not yet distanced three complete degrees from the *Ohr Malchut* that rose to the *Maatzil*. Yet, the end of their work was afterwards when the *Orot* returned to come down a second descent into the above *Kelim*.

Ohr Pnimi

28. Yet, the end of their work was afterwards when the *Orot* returned to come down a second descent.

It is so because then the *Hitzoniut* of their *Kelim* is completed and the *Orot* are also permanently diminished there. This is because only *Ohr Hochma* comes to *Kli de Keter* and *Ohr Bina* to *Kli de Hochma* etc. That completes their *Behinat Kelim*.

29. We shall add another explanation about making those *Kelim*. It has been explained in the previous study that the three kinds of *Orot* that came out of *AHP de AK* are considered *NRN* and clothe each other.

However, the *Ohr* that comes out of the *Eynaim de AK* is called *Neshama* to *Neshama*, which is called *Haya*. Its place is up there in the *Ayin* but it expands below, as we shall explain.

This is so because it stands in its place as *Ohr Makif* to them. From them downward expands a very minute *Ohr* called *Reiah*. It is not a complete *Hevel* like the *Havalim* that extend from the *AHP*. Those are complete tangible and sensed *Havalim*. In addition, since it is a very frail and thin *Ohr*, the *Behinat Kelim* of *Akudim* that exit from the *Peh* were made of it and the *Orot* are not made since it is a frail *Ohr*.

However, the *Ohr AHP* was not an actual tangible and sensed *Hevel*. Even the *Behinat Kelim* couldn't have been made since they are lower *Orot* than the *Ohr Eynaim*. For that reason they come out actual, sensed *Hevel* and thus the *Behinot Orot* that are called *NRN* were made.

Ohr Pnimi

29. **Orot that came out of AHP de AK are considered NRN.**

This has already been explained in the Rav's words above (Part 4, Chap 6 item 6) and in *Ohr Pnimi*.

The Ohr that comes out of the Eynaim etc. Its place is up there in the Ayin etc. as Ohr Makif.

This refers to *Behinat Ohr Makif de Yechida* to ZA. However, as the Rav says (Part 4, Chap 6 item 17), it does not reach the *Nukva* even as *Behinat Ohr Makif*.

A very minute Ohr called Reiah. It is not a complete Hevel like the Havalim that extend from the AHP. Those are complete tangible and sensed Havalim.

The *Ohr Hozer* that expands from above downward with the *Ohr Yashar* inside it into *Eser Sefirot* called *Guf* is called *Hevel*. This is because it comes out of the *Zivug de Hakaa* in the *Aviut* in the *Masach*.

If there is a lot of *Aviut* the *Ohr Hozer* is greater and the *Koma* is greater. Hence, until *Behina Bet*, the *Aviut* in the *Masach* is considered sufficient to raise *Ohr Hozer* to extend the *Ohr* from below upward in a sufficient measure to afterwards expand from above downward into *Behinat Guf* as well. For that reason the *Ohr Hozer* is called "Complete *Hevel*".

However, the *Aviut* from *Behina Aleph*, called *Eynaim*, note that the *Aviut* of that *Behina* is very thin and frail. It is a not a complete *Hevel* that can also expand from above downward and for that reason no *Ohr* comes from it into the *Guf*.

It is written, "**since it is a very frail and thin Ohr, the Behinat Kelim of Akudim etc. were made of it.**" It means that we discern only the *Behinat Ohr Yashar* in the *Ohr Eynaim*.

This is the *Behinat Atzmut Ohr* that makes a *Zivug de Hakaa* in the *Orot de AHP* and generates the *Kelim* for them as he explains before us. However, in itself, the *Zivug* is insufficient to generate *Komat Ohr* to the *Guf* as the AHP, only as a frail *Ohr*.

30. Let us return to the matter of the *Reiah* of the *Eynaim*. It is said that the making of the *Kelim* was through its *Histaklut, Reiah* and *Habata* in the *Ohr Akudim*, called the above mentioned *Nefesh*.

    This is the meaning of the verse, "And God saw the light, that it was good; and God divided" etc. The *Ruach* and the *Neshama*, which are the *Orot Awzen* and *Hotem*, are called complete *Ohr*. The *Nefesh*, which is *Akudim* that exit from the *Peh,* are implied in the excess word "the", in what the text says "the light."

    He said that since God is the emanator, He sees and looks at the *Nefesh,* called "the" and then divides. This is considered making the *Kelim* that separate, limit and place a ration and measurement in the *Orot* and their parts are separated from one another.

Ohr Pnimi

30. Its *Histaklut, Reiah* and *Habata* in the *Ohr Akudim,* called the above mentioned *Nefesh*.

    The *Peh de Rosh* is called *Nefesh*. The *Hitpashtut Ohr* is called *Histaklut* and *Habata*. Hence, the *Hitpashtut Ohr Elyon* to the *Masach* in *Kli Malchut* for *Zivug de Hakaa* is called *Histaklut* and *Habata* in the *Nefesh*, meaning the *Masach* in *Malchut*.

    The emanator, He sees and looks at the *Nefesh,* called "the".

    As has been written in the previous item, the *Masach* in *Kli Malchut* is called *Nefesh* and is called "the", as the Rav has written, and examine carefully (Part 3, Chap 3 item 3).

31. There is *Ohr Yashar* and *Ohr Hozer* in this *Reiah*. In the *Histaklut* of this *Reiah* as *Ohr Yashar* in the *Ohr Nefesh* there was sufficient ability to make the *Kelim* of the First Three. Yet, the seven lower *Kelim* were not finished until the *Histaklut Ohr Yashar* extended down to the tenth *Kli* of *Malchut*.

    Afterwards the two *Orot* returned, being the *Ohr* of the *Reiah* of *Ayin* and the *Ohr Nefesh* that extended from the *Peh*. Both returned to depart upward from below upward and the seven lower *Kelim* were made during their *Histalkut* from below upward as *Ohr Hozer*. Yet, the first three *Kelim* were made in the *Ohr Yashar* from above downward through the *Histaklut Ohr Yashar de Eynaim* in the *Ohr Nefesh*.

Ohr Pnimi

31. There is *Ohr Yashar* and *Ohr Hozer* in this *Reiah*.

This is because the *Hitpashtut Ohr Elyon* in the *Partzuf* is called *Reiah* and that part of the *Ohr* that is received in the *Partzuf* is called *Ohr Yashar*, meaning up to *Kli Malchut*. That part of the *Ohr* that is not received in the *Partzuf* because of the *Masach* that pushes it back, which was suitable for clothing in *Malchut*, is called *Ohr Hozer*. This is why it is said that there is *Ohr Yashar* and *Ohr Hozer* in this *Reiah*.

In the *Histaklut* of this *Reiah* as *Ohr Yashar* in the *Ohr Nefesh*.

This refers to *Malchut*, called *Nefesh*. The *Ohr Nefesh* refers to the *Ohr Hozer* that she raises up from her upward clothing the *Ohr Elyon* as *Eser Sefirot* of the *Rosh*.

It is written, "there was sufficient ability to make the *Kelim* of the First Three." It means that the *Kelim* of the *Eser Sefirot de Rosh*, which are from below upward, are considered the *Shorashim* of the *Kelim*.

The seven lower *Kelim* were not finished until the *Histaklut Ohr Yashar* extended down to the tenth *Kli* of *Malchut*.

She is called *Malchut de Malchut*, or *Nefesh de Malchut*. This is because this above-mentioned *Malchut* of the *Rosh*, called *Nefesh* or "the" expanded in itself into *Eser Sefirot* from her and within her through her own *Malchut*, meaning *Malchut de Malchut*.

These *Eser Sefirot* are called *Guf* or the seven lower *Sefirot*. They are called AK in *Akudim*, expanding form *Peh de AK* through its *Tabur* because *Malchut* of the *Rosh* is called *Peh* and *Malchut de Malchut* is called *Tabur*.

The *Ohr* of the *Reiah* of *Ayin* and the *Ohr Nefesh* that extended from the *Peh*.

Meaning the *Ohr Yashar* and *Ohr Hozer* because the *Ohr Reiah* is *Ohr Yashar* and the *Ohr Nefesh* is the *Ohr Hozer* that ascends from the *Malchut*.

Both returned to depart upward from below upward etc. the seven lower *Kelim* were made during their *Histalkut* from below upward as *Ohr Hozer*.

Meaning through the *Masach*, as it is written at length above (Part 4). In the *Hizdakchut* of the *Masach* from *Behina Dalet* to *Behina Gimel* the *Zivug* from *Behina Dalet* stops. The *Ohr Hozer* with the *Ohr Yashar de Komat Keter* within it leaves, rises up and the *Zivug* is made in *Behina Gimel*, which is *Behinat ZA de Ohr Yashar*. Then the *Ohr Hozer* of that *Zivug* connects and clothes only *Komat Hochma*.

Ohr Hochma comes in *Kli de Keter*, *Ohr Bina* in *Kli de Hochma* and *Ohr ZA* in *Kli de Bina*, *Ohr Malchut* in *Kli ZA* and *Kli Malchut* remains without *Ohr*. Then *Kli Malchut* darkens and thickens and becomes a *Kli*, as the Rav has written (item 27).

Afterwards, when the *Masach de Behina Gimel* purified into *Behina Bet*, which is *Bina de Ohr Yashar*, and the *Ohr Hozer* and *Ohr Yashar de Komat Hochma* departed, *Komat Bina* was extended. At that time the *Ohr Bina* clothes *Kli de Keter*, *Ohr ZA* in *Kli de Hochma* and *Ohr Malchut* in *Kli de Bina*. Hence, *Kli de ZA* too remains without *Ohr*. In that state *Kli de ZA* also darkens and thickens, thus becoming a *Kli*.

When it purifies from *Behina Bet* to *Behina Aleph*, which is *Hochma de Ohr Yashar*, *Komat Bina* departs and *Komat ZA* extends. Then *Ohr ZA* comes in *Kli de Keter* and the *Kli Bina* too remains without *Ohr*. Thus *Kli de Bina* too darkens and thickens etc. similarly.

Thus, the *Kelim de Guf* are made only through the *Histalkut Ohr Yashar* and the *Ohr Hozer* upward, as then they darken, thicken, and become *Kelim*.

However, only the two *Kelim* of ZA and *Malchut* were entirely completed through this *Histalkut* in both their inner half for *Ohr Pnimi* and their outer half for *Ohr Makif* (*Ohr Pnimi* item 27).

However, the three *Kelim Keter Hochma Bina* were not yet completed here in this *Histalkut* since they still lack the outer half of their walls. This is so because they did not have any ascents to attain *Kelim* and *Orot Makifim*, hence they were only completed afterwards, in *Hitpashtut Bet*.

Yet, the first three Kelim were made in the Ohr Yashar from above downward through the Histaklut Ohr Yashar de Eynaim in the Ohr Nefesh.

It means that their *Kelim de GAR*, the *Eser Sefirot de Rosh*, were made through the *Hitpashtut Ohr Yashar* from above downward into *Zivug de Hakaa* in the *Malchut*. *Malchut* raised *Ohr Hozer* from below upward and clothed the *Ohr Yashar de Eynaim*, as the Rav has written at length in the beginning of Part 3.

32. Now we shall explain how that second return of *Orot* was. Know, that their second return is not like their first descent. This is because then all ten *Orot* came down to their place.

However, in this second descent, had they all descended back to their place, the **Kelim** that have already been made by their **Histalkut** would have nullified as in the beginning. They would not have been able to tolerate their *Orot*, as it happened to them before.

Therefore, it became necessary that the *Ohr Elyon* in all of them, being *Keter*, which is great and equal to all the nine *Orot* put together, would always remain above, attached to the *Shoresh* that emanates it, which is the *Toch* of the *Peh* of AK.

33. Only the lower nine *Orot* came out of it again. They expanded in the following manner: *Ohr Hochma* entered the *Kli* of *Keter*; *Ohr Bina* entered the *Kli* of *Hochma* etc. until you find that *Ohr Malchut* entered the *Kli* of *Yesod*.

    Now there are two changes from the way it was at first. The greatest of all *Orot* put together, namely *Keter*, remained above in its *Shoresh*.

    Moreover, even though the *Kli* of *Keter* does not have the power to tolerate its own great *Ohr*, it can tolerate the *Ohr Hochma*, which is much smaller than *Keter*. It is similar in all the other *Sefirot*, and for the above two reasons there is now an ability in these *Kelim* to tolerate their *Ohr* and they are not cancelled as in the beginning.

34. We will explain below that all nine *Orot Tachtonim* enter the *Kli* of *Keter* together. Afterwards only *Ohr Hochma* remains inside it while the other eight *Orot* descend and enter the *Kli* of *Bina* and so on similarly with all of them.

    However, that does not add or subtract. We have a great rule in our hands: the *Elyon* is greater than everything below it. Hence, even when the nine *Orot* enter the *Kli* of *Keter* together, all the eight *Tachtonim* are of no consequence compared to the *Ohr Hochma* that is higher than them and emanated them.

    It has already been explained that the *Ohr Hochma* can tolerate the *Kli* of *Keter* since it is a higher *Behina*. Thus, of course it will tolerate the rest of the eight *Orot* below it, and likewise in the rest of the *Kelim*.

    The *Ohr* that is designated to the *Kli* does not enter it, only a small *Ohr* in its place. For that reason they can tolerate the *Orot* and are not cancelled as in the beginning.

35. *We must thoroughly explain the meaning of *Matei ve Lo Matei*. It is said that in the beginning the *Ohr* comes in *Keter* and nine *Orot* are contained in Him.

    Afterwards it returns to being *Behinat Lo Matei*, when the *Ohr* that reaches the *Keter* exits there once more. However, the nine other *Orot* remained in *Keter* since *Keter* has the power to tolerate them.

In that state, when the *Ohr* is *Lo Matei* in the *Keter*, *Keter* extends the nine *Orot* to *Hochma Panim be Panim* and places them in *Hochma*. At that time *Hochma* turns her *Panim*, after receiving the nine *Orot*, and shines to *Bina Panim be Panim*. It is only *He'arah,* but she still does not give her the seven *Orot*.

Ohr Pnimi

35. **In the beginning the *Ohr* comes in *Keter* and nine *Orot* are contained in Him.**

    In order to understand the Rav's words here we must thoroughly remember and clearly understand all his words in the beginning of the Part from item 1 to item 15 and what we explained there, as it is because it is impossible to repeat all that length from there. Here we shall briefly review the item headlines.

    First examine the order of the ascents of the *Sefirot* to the *Maatzil* after their *Histalkut* from the first *Hitpashtut* explained in Part 4, Chap 4 item 6. The gist of all the above is that the *Zivug de Hakaa* made in the first *Partzuf de AK* was on the corrected *Masach* in *Kli Malchut* that was in the *Gadlut* of the *Aviut*, meaning *Aviut de Behina Dalet*.

    Hence, that *Malchut* raised the greatest *Ohr Hozer*, up to *Komat Keter*. This *Ohr Hozer* rose and clothed the *Ohr Elyon* from below upward, and these *Eser Sefirot* are called *Eser Sefirot* of *Rosh*.

    It is the conduct of the *Malchut* and the *Ohr Hozer* that as it clothes from below upward, to the same extent it inverts and expands the *Kli Malchut* from above downward from her and within her up to that *Malchut de Malchut*. There it descends and clothes the entire *Komat Ohr Yashar* that is clothed in the *Rosh*.

    This *Hitlabshut* is called *Hitpashtut Aleph de AK*. It is also called *Eser Sefirot de Guf*, the *Malchut* of the *Rosh* is called *Peh*, and *Malchut de Malchut*, which is *Malchut de Guf*, is called *Tabur*.

    Since there is still no apparent limitation in *Malchut* of the *Rosh*, the *Ohr Makif* and the *Ohr Pnimi* shine there equally. However, when the *Ohr* expands from there into the *Eser Sefirot de Guf* through the *Tabur*, being *Malchut de Guf*, the *Masach de Tabur* stopped the *Ohr Yashar* and did not let it expand below *Tabur*. That means that that *Ohr Yashar* ascribed to the first nine *Sefirot* called *Ohr Pnimi* clothed the nine *Sefirot de Guf* through the *Tabur*. Also, that *Ohr Yashar* ascribed to *Malchut* could not enter and clothe its place below

Tabur since of the *Masach* there and remained outside the *Partzuf* as *Ohr Makif*.

Hence, there was a *Hakaa* and *Bitush* between the *Ohr Makif* and the *Ohr Pnimi* on that *Gevul*, called *Masach de Tabur*. This is because the *Ohr Makif* also wanted to come down and clothe in its place as did the *Ohr Pnimi* since both of them illuminated equally in the *Rosh*. For that reason the *Ohr Makif* overpowered and purified the *Masach* from its *Aviut* so that its force of detainment would disappear from it and the *Ohr Makif* would be able to clothe too.

Understand that thoroughly for this is the explanation of the whole issue of the *Hizdakchut* of the *Masach* in each and every *Partzuf*. There is no apparent limitation on the *Ohr Makif* in any *Rosh*. Hence, it too wishes to clothe in the *Guf*.

Thus, it purifies the *Aviut* in the *Masach*, meaning the *Behinat* detainment in it. This is because the measure of the *Aviut* in the *Masach* is the measure of its detainment; they are one matter in it.

Indeed, the *Ohr Makif* purified the entire *Aviut* present in the *Masach* all at once and brought it to the *Maatzil*, meaning to *Peh de Rosh*, where it is not limited at all. It means that the *Masach* purified from the entire *Aviut de Guf* and all that remained in it is the *Behinat Shoresh* in it, which is the *Behinat Masach de Malchut* of the *Rosh*. This is called the ascent to the *Peh*, as *Hishtavut Tzura* makes the spirituals into one.

However, since there are four degrees in the *Aviut*, it is necessary that that the *Masach* that had *Behinat Aviut de Behina Dalet* and has completely purified necessarily went through the same four degrees one by one. Also, the *Ohr Elyon* never stops shining even for a moment, except it is not discerned in the *Olamot* unless there is a proper receiver to receive its *Ohr*.

For that reason we discern that the *Ohr Elyon* mates with the *Masach* as it passes through the four degrees found from *Behina Dalet* to the complete purification. It generates four *Komot* of *Ohr* on its way according to the measure of the *Aviut* that the *Masach* stands in since as long as there is some measure of *Aviut* that merits a *Zivug*, *Ohr Elyon* still connects and clothes it.

Also, when the *Koma* departs, though it certainly leaves at once, we still discern four stops along its way. For example: when it purifies from *Behina Dalet* to *Behina Gimel*, when *Komat Keter* disappears from the *Partzuf*, since there are five degrees, KHB, ZA and *Malchut* in *Komat Keter*, we discern four stops on its way as in the order of its *Histalkut*.

Keter in the *Koma* disappears first and only the lower nine *Sefirot* remain there. You then find that *Hochma* rose to the place of *Keter* and *Bina* to the place of *Hochma* etc. until *Malchut* in the place of ZA. Afterwards the *Hochma* disappears from the *Koma* and then *Bina* ascends to the place of *Keter* and ZA to the place of *Hochma*. After that ZA too disappears from the *Koma* and *Malchut* rises to the place of *Keter*.

Finally, *Malchut* too disappears from the *Koma* and you find that the entire *Komat Keter* has departed from the *Partzuf*. Thus, even in *Komat* we discern that it makes four stops during its *Histalkut*.

Before the *Masach* comes to the *Aviut de Behina Gimel* only one *Behina* of *Hizdakchut* is discernible there. That *Hizdakchut* rejects and expels the *Ohr Hozer* as it is then unfit for *Zivug*, as it is occupied in its purification from that attribute.

It is also known that the *Masach de Tabur* of the above *Hitpashtut Aleph* that purified and reached the *Peh* was incorporated in all the *Reshimot* of the *Eser Sefirot de Guf* except *Behina Dalet*, which did not leave its *Reshimot* of bestowal. All that was left of her was the *Reshimo de Hitlabshut*, see *Ohr Pnimi* item 9 throughout as all of it is needed here.

It explains there that we regard primarily the highest *Behina* in them, which is *Behina Gimel* that extends *Komat Hochma*. However, there is *Behinat Reshimo de Behina Dalet de Hitlabshut* too there, called *Behinat Zachar de Kli de Keter*.

On the one hand it is much higher than *Behina Gimel*, since it is from *Behinat Komat Keter*. However, since it does not have the *Behinat Aviut* of *Hamshacha* it must connect with a *Behinat Nekeva*, meaning with *Behinat Aviut* of *Hamshacha*, which is the *Reshimo* of *Behina Gimel* that has *Behinat Hamshacha* too.

Now we shall come to the heart of the examination of the Rav's words. He says, **"in the beginning the *Ohr* comes in *Keter* and nine *Orot* are contained in Him."**

There are two things to discern here: A – Why has the order been reversed here from what it was in *Hitpashtut Aleph*? There the *Ohr* came into *Malchut* first, and here it began to expand in *Keter* first. B – Why did all the *Orot* come each into its designated *Kli*, and here they all came together into one *Kli* of the *Keter*?

Indeed, if we understand where these *Kelim* came here from, these two above questions will be clarified simply. We must know that the Rav speaks briefly and says that the *Orot* expanded back to the empty *Kelim* after the *Orot* have departed from within them. This means that it does not only speak of the first *Partzuf* where the *Histalkut* occurred.

However, this is a matter of a special *Partzuf*, completely separated from the first *Partzuf*. This is because the first *Partzuf* is called *Partzuf Galgalta de AK* and this *Hitpashtut Bet* is called *Partzuf AB de AK*. It is considered a child and a progeny of the first *Partzuf* since this *Hitpashtut Bet* was born and came out of this *Zivug*.

The Rav has already thoroughly explained to us the order of that *Zivug* (items 9-15). We should not repeat the words, but we must understand the rule that the whole matter of the *Histalkut* of the *Orot* and the empty *Kelim* that remained, spoken of in the first *Partzuf*, all that already belongs to the second *Partzuf*.

This is so because there is no absence in the spiritual and any matter of *Shinui Tzura* discerned in the spirituals means additional *Tzura*, not an absence or replacement. Hence, all these empty *Kelim* spoken of in the first *Partzuf* are the *Kelim* of this *Hitpashtut Bet*, where the *Orot* return and expand a second time.

Thus, the *Zivugim* were made on the *Masach* contained of the two *Reshimot* mentioned in the Rav's words above, which are the *Reshimo de Behina Dalet*, called *Zachar*, and the *Reshimo de Behina Gimel*, called *Nekeva*. Afterwards these two *Komot* expanded into the *Kli de Keter* that remained empty from the time of *Hitpashtut Aleph*, and this *Hitpashtut Bet* was contained in those two *Komot*.

All the *Komot* were contained in *Komat Keter* in *Hitpashtut Aleph*, and all four *Komot HB ZON* came out through the *Hizdakchut Masach* of the *Aviut de Behina Dalet*, which is *Komat Keter*. Similarly here, all nine *Sefirot* are contained in the first *Koma* of *Zachar* and *Nekeva* that came out inside the *Kli de Keter*.

This is so because afterwards that *Masach de Behina Dalet* and *Behina Gimel* purified and the *Zachar* and *Nekeva* came out to the *Kli* of *Hochma* etc. similarly, just as it was in the order of *Hitpashtut Aleph*.

Now you can simply understand that it was not possible for the *Koma de Behina Gimel* and *Behina Dalet*, which are close to the degree of *Keter* (see item 9) to clothe *Kli de Hochma*, which is much smaller than them. Also, they have no interest in clothing the *Komot HB ZON* since every single *Sefira* from those *Eser Sefirot de Zachar* and *Nekeva* are of the same *Koma*. In other words, each of them is close to *Komat Keter*, and how can any of them clothe the other low *Komot HB ZA* and *Malchut*.

Lo Matei, when the Ohr that reaches the Keter exits there once more.

It is because the *Masach* of *Behina Dalet de Zachar* purified to *Behina Gimel* and the *Masach de Behina Gimel* of the *Nekeva* to *Behina Bet*. Hence, the two *Komot de Zachar* and *Nekeva de Keter* departed and this is the meaning of his words, "**the Ohr that reaches the Keter exits there once more.**" This matter of *Hizdakchut* that happened in the *Zachar* and *Nekeva de Keter* is also because of the *Bitush* and *Hakaa de Ohr Makif* and *Ohr Pnimi* as in *Hitpashtut Aleph*.

The nine other Orot remained in Keter.

It means that the above *Aviut* of *Behina Bet* remains in it, where the *Zivug* that comes out on this *Aviut* elicits *Komat Bina* and *Bina* contains within it *Komat ZA* and *Malchut*, which are eight *Orot*. There is also *Behina Gimel* of the *Zachar de Keter*. Thus there are nine *Orot* in *Kli de Keter* that remains after the *Hizdakchut* of her own *Behina*.

Lo Matei in the Keter, Keter extends the nine Orot to Hochma Panim be Panim.

You already know that these *Kelim de Hitpashtut Bet* are the same empty *Kelim* that remained after *Hitpashtut Aleph*. Also, the order of the making of these *Kelim* has been explained in the Rav's words above (item 26).

First, *Malchut* was made since she was the first to be emptied of her *Ohr*. Afterwards, when *Kli de ZA* was emptied from its *Ohr* the *Kli de ZA* was made. Then, when *Kli de Bina* was emptied, the *Kli de Bina* was made etc.

The reason for it is that it did not rise and depart with the *Ohr Yashar*, as the Rav explained above (Part 4, Chap 2, item 7). Hence, each and every *Kli* was made with the *Histalkut Ohr* from inside it since then the *Ohr Av* remained below and became a *Kli*.

You find that the *Kelim* were arranged from the time they were made one above the other: *Malchut* first, *ZA* atop her, *Bina* atop him, up to *Kli Keter* above all. Hence, know that here too in *Hitpashtut Bet*, even before the *Orot* expanded, the *Kelim* are already arranged and stand from above downward, *Keter* at their head and finally *Malchut*, meaning as they came out in *Hitpashtut Aleph*.

Thus, when the *Orot* expanded and came out of the *Zivug de Komat Keter* and *Hochma*, where all these *Eser Sefirot* were on an equal *Koma*, close to *Keter*, they've found the *Kli de Keter* suited for them standing ready for them.

While *Lo Matei* in the *Keter* means that the *Behina Dalet de Zachar de Keter* purified and *Behina Gimel de Nukva de Keter*, the *Komat Keter de Zachar* and *Komat Hochma de Nukva* departed. It follows that all these *Eser Sefirot de*

Zachar and Nekeva lost, the Komat Keter in them and the Eser Sefirot de Zachar were diminished into Komat Hochma, and the Eser Sefirot de Nekeva diminished into Komat Bina.

Thus, this Koma is no longer ascribed to the Keter at all, but to Kli de Hochma. Therefore the Keter pours them to the Kli de Hochma, as the Rav says.

Yet, we must understand how the Orot extend from the Kli de Keter to the Kli de Hochma. After all, there is a great distance between these Kelim. Kli de Keter is in Aviut de Behina Gimel, and it is known that Shinui Tzura separates and distances the spirituals.

Thus, how do they touch one another so as to be able to bestow upon each other? We must not be mistaken to say that the Kli de Keter purified to Behina Gimel and thus became equal with the Kli de Hochma since it is known that no Hizdakchut is applied in the Kelim whatsoever. The whole issue of the above Hizdakchut relates only to the Masach in the Kelim, not to the Kelim themselves.

However, we must remember what the Rav explained above (item 15 and in Ohr Pnimi), and then the Kli turns its Panim. It has been explained there that when the Ohr leaves the Kli, the Kli turns its Panim downward and its Achoraim upward, the Panim of the Kli becomes the Achor and the Achor becomes the Panim, and examine it there.

Here, however, the Ohr that belongs to Kli de Keter departed because the Behina Dalet de Zachar and Behina Gimel de Nekeva have departed and a Zivug was made on the Behina Gimel de Zachar and Behina Bet de Nekeva. After that the Kli de Keter turned its Panim downward, which is the great Aviut that was in it. Its entire Panim and importance has now become very bad, and Achor, meaning the pure side of it has become the most important.

Now you can see that after the Kli de Keter turned its Achoraim upward, it equalized with the Kli de Hochma. This is because the whole Shinui Tzura that was in Kli de Keter is the great Aviut of Behina Dalet and Behina Gimel in it, for this is its entire merit over the Kli de Hochma. Now all that Aviut has been annulled from it because of the turning of its Panim downward, and thus it is now considered equalized in form with Hochma.

It is written, **"Keter extends the nine Orot to Hochma Panim be Panim."** It implies that because of the Histalkut Ohr Keter, Kli de Keter has turned its Panim downward. Therefore, it is standing Panim be Panim with Kli de Hochma.

This is so because now too the Panim de Keter is the Behina Bet and Behina Gimel, meaning that pure side that prior to that was the Behinat Achor of

Keter. In fact, it is equal to the *Panim de Hochma*; hence it can pour the *Ohr* to *Hochma*, as they are in *Hishtavut Tzura* with one another. This is the reason that the Rav wrote above that any giving of *Orot* is always in *Behinat Panim be Panim*.

The matter of these nine *Orot* that *Hochma* received from *Keter* has already been explained above. They are the remains of the *Aviut* that was left of the *Zachar de Keter* after its *Hizdakchut*.

This is *Behinat Reshimo de Hochma* of the first *Hitpashtut* that was contained in the *Zachar de Keter* (see *Ohr Pnimi* item 6), and this is one *Ohr*. Also, she received the rest of the *Aviut de Nekeva de Keter*, which is *Behina Bet* and *Komat Bina* where the two *Komot* are incorporated, *de ZA* and *de Malchut*. They are eight *Orot* together and with the *Behina Gimel de Zachar*, they are nine *Orot*.

Hochma turns her Panim, after receiving the nine Orot, and shines to Bina.

This refers to the turning of the *Panim* only of the *Zachar de Hochma*, not the *Behinat Nekeva de Hochma*. This is so because the turning of the *Panim* means *Hizdakchut* of the *Aviut* and the *Histalkut Ohr* from there since then the *Kli* turns its *Panim* downward, as the Rav says (item 15).

In that state the *Masach de Aviut de Behina Gimel* of the *Zachar* purifies into *Behinat Aviut* of *Behina Bet* and you find that the *Kli de Zachar* turns its *Panim* downward and its *Achoraim* upward. It means that the importance of *Behinat Gadlut* of the *Aviut* in it is cancelled (see *Ohr Pnimi* item 15).

At that time that residue *de Zachar de Hochma* is poured to the *Kli de Bina*. This is the meaning of *Hochma* turning her *Panim* after having received the nine *Orot* and shining to *Bina*, meaning the *Behinat Zachar* of the *Kli de Bina*.

However, the Rav did not explain any *Hizdakchut* in the *Zachar de Kli de Keter*. Rather, he wrote it along with the *Nekeva de Keter* in a single *Hizdakchut*.

This is so because the *Zachar de Keter* does not have any *Behinat Aviut* of *Hamshacha*, but only from *Behinat Hitlabshut*, and there is no *Hizdakchut* in its own *Behinat Hitlabshut* since there is no *Behinat Aviut* in it. Instead, it is incorporated and connects with the *Aviut* of the *Nekeva* (*Ohr Pnimi* item 9, par. "However"). Thus, the matter of its *Hizdakchut* comes along with the *Hizdakchut* of the *Masach* of the *Nekeva*, therefore the Rav write them as a single *Hizdakchut*.

However, the *Zachar de Kli de Hochma*, which is the *Behinat Reshimo de Ohr Hochma* that remains in *Hitpashtut Aleph* as in the previous item, also has *Behinat Aviut de Hamshacha*. For that reason it is necessary that it will purify before the *Nekeva* purifies since its measure of *Aviut* is greater, as it is *Behina Gimel* and the *Nekeva* is *Behina Bet*.

It is only *He'arah*, but she still does not give her the seven *Orot*.

It means that it gives only one *Ohr* of the *Zachar de Kli de Bina* since its time has now come to purify, and it gives its remains to *Bina*. However, the time of the *Nekeva* to purify has not come yet; thus it does not give the seven *Orot* related to the *Nekeva de Bina*, as has been explained in the previous item.

36. Afterwards the *Ohr Keter* retuned to being *Matei* in *Keter* and *Ohr Hochma* was once more concealed in *Keter* because of its desire to unite with the *Keter*. At that time *Kli Hochma* turned its *Panim* to *Keter* and gave it its *Ohr*. Yet, *Ohr Bina* that was in *Hochma* does not rise to *Keter* with it because of the craving of the sons, of which she is the mother.

We have already explained that there is return of *Panim* and *Achor* only in *Behinat Kelim*. However, in the *Orot* themselves there is no *Panim* and *Achor*, only *Hitpashtut* and *Histalkut*.

Ohr Pnimi

36. ***Matei* in *Keter* and *Ohr Hochma* was once more concealed in *Keter*.**

Interpretation: when *Hochma* purified and her *Ohr de Zachar* and *Nekeva* departed and rose to the *Keter*, *Nukva de Keter* returned to thicken in her *Aviut de Behina Gimel* and *Ohr Hochma* was elicited to *Kli de Keter*. Thus, the *Ohr* was once more *Matei* in the *Keter*.

The reason for it is because the *Zachar* of the *Hochma* that rose to the *Kli de Keter* is *Behinat Reshimo* that remained from the *Hitpashtut Aleph* from the *Aviut de Behina Gimel* that was there. Thus, it rose and was incorporated in the *Nekeva de Keter* that was also *Behinat Aviut de Behina Gimel* before it purified. Hence, because of the present ascent of the *Zachar de Hochma*, its previous *Aviut* has now returned and the *Zivug Elyon* on it returned.

***Hochma* turned its *Panim* to *Keter* and gave it its *Ohr*.**

This means that the *Hochma* returned her *Panim* up against the *Keter*. Afterwards she returned and purified once more from her *Behina Bet* too and the *Komat Bina* disappeared from her and came to the *Keter*. It is so because prior to that he says that *Hochma* turned her *Panim* down toward *Bina* because of the *Hizdakchut Zachar de Hochma*.

He tells us that after *Bina* received the remains *de Zachar de Hochma*, *Kli de Hochma* returned her *Panim* toward *Keter* once more. This is because there was still *Komat Ohr Bina* in the *Aviut de Behina Bet* in her from which she has not purified.

Rather, after she returned her *Panim* to *Keter*, her time to purify from *Behina Bet* arrived. Then *Komat Ohr Bina* disappeared as well, which she gave to the *Keter*.

Ohr Bina that was in Hochma does not rise to Keter with it.

This refers to *Ohr ZA* ascribed to *Kli de Bina*. However, *Ohr Bina* does not belong to *Bina* in *Hitpashtut Bet*, but to *Hochma*. It is written that the *Kli de Hochma* gave her *Ohr* to *Keter*, meaning her *Ohr Bina*.

This is so because she purified from *Behina Bet* and all that was left in her is the *Aviut de Behina Aleph*, which is *Ohr* of *Komat ZA*, which belongs to *Kli de Bina*. He says about that *Ohr* that it remained in *Kli de Hochma* and did not rise to *Keter*. The Rav calls it *Ohr Bina* because it is related to *Kli de Bina*.

37. **Yet, after Kli Hochma turned his Panim opposite Keter and his Ohr rose there, he then turned his Panim down opposite Bina and gave her the seven Orot. You should also know that any giving of Orot is always regarded as Panim be Panim.**

Ohr Pnimi

37. **His Panim down opposite Bina and gave her the seven Orot.**

The matter of the *Histalkut Ohr* from *Kli de Hochma* causes the turning of his *Panim* down. This is considered *Hishtavut* with the *Panim de Bina* since he cancelled his prior *Panim*, meaning his *Behina Bet* and turned his *Achor*, namely *Behina Aleph*, into *Behinat Panim*.

It follows that now it is *Panim be Panim* with *Bina* and can therefore give her the *Koma* of *Behina Aleph* which is *Komat ZA*. Now she is named after the highest *Sefira*, being *Ohr Hesed*, containing all seven lower *Sefirot HGT NHYM*.

It is written, "**turned his Panim down opposite Bina and gave her the seven Orot.**" Now there are eight *Orot* in *Bina*. Those are the remains of the *Ohr Zachar* that she received from the *Hochma*, which is *Behina Bet*. This is in addition to the seven lower ones contained in *Behina Aleph* that have now received from the *Nekeva de Hochma*, thus eight *Orot*.

Any giving of Orot is always regarded as Panim be Panim.

It has been explained above that the giver and the receiver should equalize their *Tzura* with one another. Hence, as long as his *Panim* are upward he is much higher than the receiver and they do not touch each other. For that reason he does not give except if he cancels his *Panim* and places his *Achor* forward.

In that state the *Panim* of the giver and the receiver are equal. This is called *Panim be Panim*. Examine the interpretation of the matter carefully in *Ohr Pnimi* item 15.

38. However, *Bina* did not turn her *Panim* to shine in *Hesed* below since there was no power in *Hesed* and *VAK* to receive such a great *Ohr Panim be Panim*, only *Achor be Achor*. This is so because there is *Ohr* of *VAK* here and the *Ohr* of *Bina* which is greater than all of them together.

Yet, in the beginning when there were still no *Orot* in *Bina* except what she gave to *Hochma*, she turned her *Panim* and illuminated to *Bina* only *He'arah Panim be Panim*. This is not so in *Hesed* since *Bina* has the strength to receive their *Orot*, as the seven *Orot Tachtonim* were annulled with respect to her *Ohr*, and she can certainly receive her own *Ohr*.

The *Ohr* of *Hochma*, though his *Ohr* is greater than her *Ohr*, you already know that *Abba ve Ima* "stay as one and come out as one" and she can receive the *Ohr Hochma*. It is not so in *Hesed* since there is a big difference between that and the *Ohr Bina*, and he cannot receive it *Panim be Panim*.

Ohr Pnimi

38. **Bina did not turn her *Panim* to shine in *Hesed* below since there was no power.**

You should know that here in *Bina* there are three *Orot*: The first is the *Ohr Zachar* that she received from the *Hizdakchut Zachar de Hochma*, which is *Behina Bet*.

The second is the *Behinat Reshimo de Kli Bina* herself as there is in each and every *Kli* from the time of *Hitpashtut Aleph*. This is considered the *Behinat Nekeva* of *Bina*.

The third is the *Ohr Hesed*, meaning the *Komat ZA* that she now received from the remains of the *Hizdakchut* of *Behina Bet de Kli de Hochma*. This is considered *Behinat* progeny of *Bina* and not at all from the *Behinat Ohr Bina*. This third *Ohr* is called *VAK* whose property is that lacks *He'arat GAR*, meaning the *Ohr Hochma*, and it has only *Behinat Hassadim*.

It is written, "**Bina did not turn her *Panim* to shine in *Hesed* below since there was no power in *Hesed* and *VAK* to receive such a great *Ohr Panim be Panim*.**" It means that now the *Ohr Hesed* is in *Katnut*, meaning only *Ohr*

Hassadim without any *He'arat GAR*. This is so because it comes out of the *Zivug* on *Masach de Behina Aleph* that does not have *He'arat Hochma*.

For that reason it does not have the power to receive anything from the *Bina*, comes down and clothes the *Kelim de VAK*. Consequently, it still remains in *Kli Bina* and did not expand to *Kli de Hesed*.

The seven *Orot Tachtonim* were annulled with respect to her *Ohr*.

It means that although *Bina* received the *Ohr Hesed* within her, which is the *Ohr* of the seven lower *Sefirot* that lack GAR, she still did not lose the *Ohr* of her own GAR because of that. This is because the *Ohr ZAT* is cancelled in her compared to her own great *Ohr*, which are her own *Zachar* and *Nukva* from *Behina Bet*.

The *Ohr* of *Hochma*, though his *Ohr* is greater than her *Ohr*.

This revolves around the *Zachar de Kli de Hochma* (see item 35) and it is called *Ohr Hochma*. This is because the above matter of the *Hizdakchut* regarding the *Zachar de Hochma* is *Behinat Zivug* between the *Zachar* and the *Nukva* of *Hochma* where by mating them together the *Ohr Zachar de Bina* was born.

The *Nukva de Kli de Hochma* has *Koma de Behina Bet* and the *Zachar de Hochma* has *Koma de Behina Gimel*. Thus, when the *Zachar* purified from *Behina Gimel* to *Behina Bet*, you find that it equalized its *Koma* to its *Nukva*.

At that time they were both mingled together in a common *Masach de Behina Bet* and the *Zivug de Hakaa* was made on it. Thus, a new *Koma de Behina Bet* was elicited, made of the *Zachar* and *Nekeva* together.

This new *Koma* is that which descended and became the *Zachar de Kli de Bina*. Its *Koma* is equal with the *Nekeva de Kli de Hochma*, hence it is called *Ohr Hochma*. This is the meaning of, **"and she can receive the *Ohr Hochma*,"** meaning the *Behinat Zachar*, whose *Koma* is equal to the *Ohr Bina* in *Kli de Hochma*.

***Abba ve Ima* "stay as one and come out as one".**

This is because even *Bina de Ohr Yashar* is considered *Etzem Hochma de Ohr Yashar*, much less here, when *Hochma* too has only *Komat Bina*.

39. Let us return to the matter that when it returns to being *Lo Matei* in *Keter*, it is then *Matei* in *Hochma* and *Ohr* of *Hochma* descends in it. Then the seven sons in *Bina* are grown and do not need their mother. At that time *Bina* ascends to *Hochma* due to her desire to cleave to her.

This is called *Lo Matei* in the *Ohr Bina*. After that *Bina* turns her *Panim* downward, the seven *Orot* in her descend and all are given to *Hesed Panim be Panim*.

39. Lo Matei in Keter, it is then Matei in Hochma and Ohr of Hochma descends in it.

This is because the *Aviut de Behina Gimel* of the *Nukva de Keter* returned and purified. At that time the *Kli de Keter* turns its *Panim* downward and once more gives its remains, meaning *Behina Bet*, to the *Hochma* as before. It follows, that the *Ohr of Hochma* descends once more as in the beginning.

The seven sons in Bina are grown and do not need their mother. At that time Bina ascends to Hochma.

After the *Ohr Hochma* descended to *Kli de Hochma* this *He'arah* reaches *Kli de Bina* too for the above reason that *Abba ve Ima* come out as one. In other words, they emerge on a single *Behinat Aviut*, hence "stay as one," meaning their *Koma* is the same.

Since the *He'arah* reached *Bina*, it receives *Ohr Hesed* for this *He'arat Hochma* as well. At this time it attains his *Behinat Gadlut*, meaning *Behinat GAR de VAK*.

He writes, "**Then the seven sons in Bina are grown and do not need their mother.**" This is because once they have attained *He'arat Hochma* they have become grown since they have acquired *Behinat Rosh*. This is why they do not need their mother.

Prior to that the *VAK* were *Behinat Ohr de Hassadim* without any *He'arat Hochma*. Thus, they needed to receive their sustenance from the *Kli de Bina*, which is *Behinat GAR* and *Behinat Atzmut*.

They could not separate the *Kli de Bina* from the *Kelim de VAK* because of the lack of sustenance, as there is no sustenance and *Atzmut* except in *Behinat Hochma*. However, now that they have attained *Hochma* they have become grown and have stance and power to expand in the *Kelim*.

At that time Bina ascends to Hochma.

This is because it is impossible for the *Elyon* to bestow upon the *Tachton* except by turning the *Panim*, meaning to equalize with the *Tachton*. At that time it is considered close to it and gives it its remains.

Thus, *Bina* ascends to *Hochma*, meaning the *Zachar* and the *Nukva* of *Bina* purify from their *Behina Bet* to *Behina Aleph*. Now *Behina Aleph* has become the *Panim* and thus *Kli de Bina* is found *Panim be Panim* with the *Kli de Hesed* as they are now both from *Aviut de Behina Aleph*, which is called *Panim be Panim*.

At that time the *Zachar* and the *Nekeva* of *Kli de Bina* depart and rise to the *Kli de Hochma*. *Hochma* and *Bina* are then found in one *Kli* of *Behinat Hochma*, and thus there is the dominion of the *Kli* of *Hochma* in the *Partzuf*.

There is yet another profundity here: In fact, the *Behinat Bina* is discerned as the *Achoraim* to the *Hochma* from the *Shoresh* of the *Ohr Yashar*. It is the meaning of the *Yod* י and *Nun* נ of the *Tzadik* צ being opposite to one another as it is written in the Zohar (Bereshit). It is also as the Rav implies here in the meaning of "because He delighteth in mercy."

This means that *Bina* craves *Hassadim* more than *Hochma* and therefore had to ascend to the *Kli de Hochma* so as not to stop at the *Ohr Hesed* with her *Behinat Achoraim*. At that time *Ohr Hesed* can receive a greater *He'arah* than the *Hochma*.

40. Afterwards the **Ohr** returns to being **Matei** in **Keter** and then both **HB** ascend there because of the desire they have. In that state you find that there is a big distance between the sons and the **Ohr GAR** for there are two distances between them, **Bina** and **Hochma,** which have no **Ohr** in them.

    Hence, at that time **Ohr Hesed** ascends to **Bina** and is called **Lo Matei** in **Hesed**. In that state the **Kli Hesed** turns its **Panim** and gives the six **Orot** below in **Gevura**.

Ohr Pnimi

40. **The Ohr returns to being Matei in Keter and the both HB ascend there.**

    This is because *Hochma* purified once more from the *Aviut de Behina Dalet* in the *Masach* in her and the *Orot* departed from there and rose to the *Keter*. This caused the awakening of the *Aviut* in *Nukva de Keter* by the force of the *Reshimo de Zachar de Hochma* that rose inside her being *Behina Gimel*.

    For that reason she received the *Aviut de Behina Gimel* in her once more, the *Komat Hochma* expanded to her once more and the *Ohr Hochma Matei* in *Kli de Keter*. Know, that the Rav names the *Hizdakchut* of the *Aviut* by the name "craving to rise to the *Elyon*" because *Hizdakchut* and ascent are one and the same.

    Two distances between them, Bina and Hochma, which have no Ohr.

    In order explain the matter of these two distances that were made because of the ascent of *HB* to *Keter* and in order to make it possible to continue to explain the Rav's words I must elaborate here. It is in order to comprehensively clarify in a thorough understanding the attribute of these ten *Kelim* that remained from *Hitpashtut Aleph de AK* after the *Histalkut* of their *Orot* within them and their setting here in the *Partzuf de Hitpashtut Bet de AK*.

Most importantly, we must thoroughly understand the matter of *Panim* and *Achor* of those *Kelim* for until now we explained only from the *Behinat Aviut* in the *Masach* that mates with the *Ohr Elyon*. The greatest *Aviut* in the degree is its *Panim*, and its least measure of *Aviut* is in the *Achor* of the degree.

Now we shall explain the *Panim* and *Achor* in the property of the *Kelim* in themselves, according to how they were affected by the *Hitpashtut* and *Histalkut de Hitpashtut Aleph*.

The primary disclosure of the forces in the ways of the *Orot* comes mostly through the property of the *Kelim* themselves, hence the *Kelim* are called tubes. They are like the nature of the water that adopt their form through the *Tzinorot* (pl. for *Tzinor*) by which they come, whether abundantly or scantly, whether to the east or to the west. Also, the *Orot* are activated in the properties of the *Kelim* they are clothed in, hence, we must understand them thoroughly.

You find that the *Ohr Keter* in *Hitpashtut Aleph* did not come back down to *Hitpashtut Bet*, but remained standing in the *Rosh* under the *Malchut* of the *Rosh*. When ZON *de Kli de Keter* of *Hitpashtut Bet* should rise and receive their *Shefa*, he turns his *Panim* to them, meaning he gives them all that they need.

However, it is only while they are with him in the *Malchut* of the *Rosh*. After they are filled with their *Shefa* and descend to the *Guf*, he immediately turns his *Achoraim* to them, meaning he denies them of the *Shefa* that they need.

We must understand that thing. If he prevents the *Shefa* from them once more, how has the ascent to the *Rosh* helped? The thing is that indeed they received their fill during the ascent, meaning according to the *Masachim* in them, which are *Behina Dalet de Zachar* and *Behina Gimel de Nekeva*. That *Komat Zivug* is close to *Komat Keter* and they descended to *Keter de Guf* with all this great *Shefa*.

However, we must therefore understand what was the benefit in that root *Keter* turning its *Achoraim* to ZON *de Keter* that descended to the *Guf*. Indeed, much is done because of that: because of it the *Kli de Keter de Guf* must be in *Behinat Achoraim* toward *Hochma* as well because this *Kli* is indeed the *Kli* of that root *Keter* from the time of *Hitpashtut Aleph*. After all, it is from her that he departed and rose to the *Rosh*.

By so doing he operates on her when he is in the *Rosh* too, as she equalizes with him as he stands at the *Rosh*. For that reason the *Kli* too must be in *Behinat Achoraim* to all the lower nine *Sefirot* from her.

This means that she does not give them from that *Shefa* that she received in the *Rosh*, except through the *Achoraim*, meaning by preventing the *He'arat Hochma* from them. This is because *Hochma* is always called *Ohr Panim*, or *Ohr GAR*, and remember that in all the places. Thus, the nine lower *Sefirot* cannot receive from the *Keter* but only *Behinat VAK*, meaning lacking *He'arat Hochma*, and examine thoroughly.

The meaning of *Panim* and *Achor de Kelim* is simple: the place of bestowal in it is called *Panim*, and that *Behina* through which it does not bestow is called *Achor*. It is like a person who negotiates with his friend; he stands opposite him, at his fore side, not behind him.

Yet, you will understand that even though the *Keter* bestows through its *Achoraim*, you can once call it *Panim* even though it has no *He'arat Hochma*, meaning the side that is the place of bestowal. Hence, we must understand it only according to the relevant matter.

The *Masach de Keter* purified from the *Aviut de Behina Dalet* and *Behina Gimel* in it to *Behina Gimel* and *Behina Bet*, fitting for the *Ohr Hochma*. At that time the *Kli de Keter* must turn its *Panim* downward and its *Achoraim* upward. This is because its *Achoraim* detain the *He'arat Hochma* completely because of the root *Keter* of the *Rosh* that stands under *Malchut de Rosh*.

However, the cause of the above turning of the *Panim* is the matter of the *Hizdakchut* of the *Masach de Zachar de Keter*, which is the *Reshimo* that the root *Keter* left in this *Kli de Keter* after its *Histalkut* from it. Since that *Reshimo* departed from there because it purified and came to *Aviut de Behina Gimel*, the dominion of the root *Keter* on its *Kli* stopped.

At that time the *Kli* turns its *Panim* downward and everything that is ascribed to the *He'ara* of the root *Keter* ascends once more to it, to the *Rosh*. The remains, meaning the *Reshimo de Behina Gimel de Hitpashtut Aleph*, which is the *Zachar de Hochma*, and the *He'arat* new *Zivug* that came out on the *Aviut de Behina Gimel* that the *Nukva de Keter* left after her *Hizdakchut*, became the *Nekeva de Kli de Hochma*.

Now we shall explain the *Panim* and *Achor* of the *Kli de Hochma*. *Hochma*'s conduct is to bestow only *Hochma*. Hence, the place of the bestowal of *Hochma* is her *Panim* and the place of bestowal of *Ohr Hassadim* is her *Behinat Achoraim*.

In other words, it is the complete opposite from *Keter*. The *Panim* of *Keter* is to bestow *VAK* and *He'arat GAR* is in her *Achor*. At the same time the *Panim de Hochma* is *He'arat GAR* from the *Behinat Ohr Hochma* and her *Achor* is *He'arat VAK*.

The *Panim* and *Achor* de *Keter* of *Bina* is also opposite from *Kli de Hochma* though not completely opposite since the *Shoresh* of *Bina* is *Etzem Hochma*. However, her nature is to always yearn for *Ohr Hassadim*, as the Rav has written regarding "because He delighteth in mercy."

Bina is called "He" and she craves and wants *Hassadim*. Hence, when she has *Hassadim* in the *Partzuf*, she becomes *Etzem Hochma* once more, as the Rav wrote above regarding **"Abba ve Ima stay as one and come out as one."**

However, *Kli de Bina* is primarily distinguished by her craving for *Hassadim*, hence her *Panim* is *He'arat Hassadim* and her *Achor* is *He'arat Hochma*, the opposite of *Kli de Hochma*.

Now we shall briefly explain the *Kelim* of the seven lower *Sefirot* HGT NHYM. You must remember the Rav's words above (Part 4, Chap 6 item 8) that ZA has only five *Ktzavot*, being five *Hassadim* from *Hesed* to *Hod* though *Yesod* does not take its own private *Hesed*, but all five *Ktzavot* are incorporated in it.

In essence, there are two general *Orot* in all the degrees, which are *Ohr Hochma* and *Ohr Hassadim*. There are also five *Behinot Aviut* in the *Masach* according to the five *Behinot de Ohr Yashar* called KHB *Tifferet* and *Malchut*.

These five *Behinot* are called KHB TM only when the GAR are *Behinat Ohr Hochma*. However, in a place where all those five *Behinot* contain only *Ohr de Hassadim*, they are called HGT NH. The names of the first three *Behinot* KHB have been changed to HGT and the names of the last two *Behinot Tifferet* and *Malchut* have been changed to *Netzah* and *Hod*.

He writes, **"they are five Hassadim from Hesed to Hod."** This means that even the First three *Behinot* are also only *Ohr Hassadim* and not *Ohr Hochma* at all, and understand and remember that. The *Yesod* and the *Malchut* are only two containers of the above five *Ktzavot*.

One container is from the perspective of their being five sweetened *Hassadim* in *Midat ha Rachamim*, and one container is from the perspective of their being in *Midat ha Din*. At that time they are called five *Gevurot* or that the five *Hassadim* and five *Gevurot* are contained together.

However, in order to understand the attributes of these five *Ktzavot* we need the Rav's words here regarding *Matei ve Lo Matei* for they were not explained anywhere else in all of the Rav's writings. Hence, these words of his need close attention.

Let us clarify once more the birth of the first *Hesed* of these five *Hassadim*, brought in the Rav's words (item 37). ZON de *Hochma* departed to *Keter* since the *Aviut de Behina Bet* purified to *Behina Aleph* and its *Zivug* raises only *Ohr* de VAK that are now contained in the first *Hesed*. At that time the *Kli de Hochma* turned its *Panim* downward since it cancelled its *Behinat Panim* and turned its *Achoraim* upward.

This means that its previous *Achor*, meaning *He'arat Hassadim*, has now become a place of bestowal. By that it equalized itself with the *Panim of Bina*, as it is written, "because He delighteth in mercy." In that state he gave her the seven *Orot* that are now contained in the first *Ohr Hesed*. Thus, *Ohr Hesed* is found in *Kli de Bina*.

You must remember that besides this *Ohr Hesed* there are two other *Orot* that precede it in that *Kli de Bina*. They are the *Zachar*, born of the *Zivug ZON de Kli de Hochma*, which is truly *Behina Bet*, *Komat Bina* like the *Nekeva de Hochma* herself.

However, since he is born through the turning of the *Panim de Kli de Hochma* (see the Rav's words item 35 and in *Ohr Pnimi* there) it is thus considered *Behinat VAK of Hochma*. You should also know that he is the *Shoresh de Israel Saba* in all the *Partzufim*.

There is yet another, second *Ohr* there, being the *Reshimo de Kli de Bina*, which is there from the time of *Hitpashtut Aleph*. [Besides the *Masach* being incorporated of all the *Reshimot* in those *Kelim* as it travels to the *Maatzil*, it is certain that the majority of the *Reshimot* remained in their place in their own *Kelim* and did not ascend with the *Masach* to the *Maatzil*.]

That *Reshimo* is the *Behinat Nekeva* that exists in *Kli de Bina*, and you should know that she is the *Shoresh* to all the *Behinot* of *Tvuna* in all the *Partzufim*. However, this *Ohr Hesed* that *Hochma* now gave to *Bina* is considered the son of *Bina* and not actually her.

Keep in mind the relationship between the ZON in *Kli de Hochma* with the ZON in *Kli de Bina*, as in fact they are *Ohr* of the same *Koma of Bina*. However, ZON *de Bina* relate to ZON *de Hochma* as *Israel Saba ve Tvuna* relate to Upper *AVI*. The YESHSUT are only the *VAK of AVI* themselves though they are both discerned as one *Koma of Aviut de Behina Bet*.

From this you can see that the primary division of AVI and YESHSUT to two *Partzufim* GAR and VAK is only to procreate the *Katnut* of the seven lower *Sefirot*. This is because it is impossible for *Kli de Hochma* to dispense the *Ohr Hesed*, which is *Behinat VAK* without GAR if not through the *Achoraim* of *Hochma*.

Hence, it turns the *Panim* backwards, and this inversion divides the *Kli de Hochma* into two *Partzufim*: *Partzuf* GAR, where the *Panim* remain in their place, and *Partzuf* VAK *de Hochma*, which turned its *Panim* backward, giving *Ohr* VAK that lacks GAR. YESHSUT is also named VAK after the inversion of the *Panim de Kli de Hochma*.

However, in order to procreate the *Gadlut* of ZA, meaning the GAR that belong to those five *Hassadim*, *Kli de Hochma* must return its *Panim* upward once more as in the beginning. Then it is considered that ZON *de Bina* and the ZON of *Hochma* that were divided into GAR and VAK due to the inversion of the *Panim de Hochma*, now the *Hochma* returned and revoked that inversion of the *Panim*. Now there is no longer dispensing of GAR and dispensing of VAK in the *Kli de Hochma*.

You find that ZON *de Bina* return and rise to ZON *de Hochma* and become one *Partzuf* once more. Know, that this matter is implemented in the *Partzufim* of *Atzilut* as well.

When AVI want to dispense *Mochin de* GAR to the ZA, AVI and YESHSUT become one *Partzuf* once more. This too is for the above reason that the *He'arat* VAK was cancelled from the *Hochma* and the *Panim* returned to its place as in the beginning.

From the explained you can thoroughly understand the order of the birth of the first *Ohr Hesed* in its *Behinat Gadlut* brought in the Rav's words (item 39). To summarize his words, it returned to being *Lo Matei* in *Keter* and then *Matei* in *Hochma* when *Ohr* of *Hochma* that was in *Keter* descended to *Hochma*. At that time the sons in *Bina* are grown and then *Bina* ascends to *Hochma* because of the craving in her to cleave to her, the seven *Orot* descend and are given to the *Hesed Panim be Panim*.

Interpretation: The ZON *de Keter* purified once more and departed to the root *Keter* that stands under *Malchut de Rosh*. At that time the *Kli de Keter* turned its *Panim* below and gave its remains, being ZON *de Hochma*, to the *Kli de Hochma*.

The *Behinat Panim* of ZON *de Hochma* returned to its place as in the beginning and then "**Bina ascends to Hochma**." It means that *Bina* and *Hochma* have become one *Partzuf*, similar to AVI and YESHSUT that became one *Partzuf*.

Consequently, that *Hesed* in *Kli de Bina* receives the *He'arat Ohr Hochma* since the *Kli* is united with the *Ohr Hochma*. You find that *Hesed* returned to *Behinat* GAR, which is called that it has become grown.

He writes, "**Then the seven sons in Bina are grown and do not need their mother.**" That means that they have acquired *Behinat He'arat Hochma* and GAR, and in that the ZAT are discerned as grown.

It has already been explained above that before the *Ohr Hesed* acquires the *Gadlut* it cannot spread below. This is because it cannot separate from the *Kli de Bina* which is its entire sustenance and *Atzmut* in the *Behinat GAR*. Hence, it is considered to need its *Ima*, though now that it has already attained the *Ohr Hochma* itself it no longer needs the sucking of the *Kli de Bina*, hence, it is written, **"and do not need their mother."**

At that time the *Kli* of *Bina* turned her *Panim* downward and the seven *Orot* in her descend and all of them are given to *Hesed Panim be Panim*. You must remember that the *Behinat Panim de Kli de Bina* is for *He'arat Hassadim* and her *Achor* is for *He'arat Hochma*.

When she is in that state she cannot administer *He'arat Ohr Hesed* with *He'arat Hochma*. However, it has been explained that the returning of the *Panim de Kli of Hochma* instigated the unification of the two *Kelim Bina* and *Hochma* into one because the *Kli de Hochma* has already cancelled her *He'arat VAK*.

Hence, you find that the *Kli de Bina* has inverted her *Panim* backwards by the force of this unification. The previous *Achor* has now become *Behinat Panim*. It means that that *Achor* that prevented the distribution of *He'arat Hochma* has now become the dispenser of *He'arat Hochma*.

This is because her *Kli* received that property of *Panim* and *Achor* found in *Hochma*. For that reason the *Bina* has now dispensed the ZAT to *Kli de Hesed* in *He'arat Hochma*.

Now you can thoroughly see the attribute of *Sefirat Hesed de ZA* to its fullest. The *Behinat Etzem* of the *Kli de Hesed* is *Behinat Keter de VAK* as it has already been explained that *HGT de ZA* are the change of the name of *KHB*. Yet, *KHB de Ohr Hassadim*, meaning *KHB* of the *Koma de Behina Aleph* are called *HGT*.

Thus, *Kli de Hesed* is *Behinat Kli de Keter de ZA* though it is still not considered *Keter*, only *Hochma de ZA*. This is because of the *Ohr* in it, as it has no *Ohr Keter* at all, but only *He'arat Hochma* that it received when it was in *Kli de Bina* and united into one with the *Kli de Hochma*. This is why it is called *Hochma*. There are other reasons too, but there is nothing to add here.

Now we shall explain the order of the emanation of the *Kli* of *Gevura* brought in the Rav's words here in item 40. He writes, **"Afterwards the Ohr returns to being Matei in Keter and then both HB ascend there. In that state you find that there is a big distance between the sons and the Ohr GAR for there are two distances between them, Bina and Hochma, which have no Ohr in them. Hence, at that time Ohr Hesed ascends to Bina and is called**

Lo Matei in *Hesed*. In that state the *Kli Hesed* turns its *Panim* and gives the six *Orot* below in *Gevura*." Thus far his words.

You must remember the two issues there are in the matter of the inversion of the *Panim* downwards. We have learned above that they are, one – from the perspective of the *Kli*, meaning her place of dispensing, whether *Behinat Hochma* or *Behinat Hassadim* and not *Hochma*.

The second matter is from the perspective of the *Zivug*. Concerning the measure of the *Aviut* of the *Masach*, the most *Av Behina* in the degree is considered the *Panim* and the *Behinat* least *Aviut* is the *Behinat Achor* in that degree.

Accordingly, you always find that the *Elyon* wants to bestow upon the *Tachton* and must turn its *Panim* downward. This means that he is purified from the measure of the *Aviut* in him, which is his *Panim*, and remains in a lesser *Aviut*, equal to the degree of the *Aviut* of the lower degree. This is so because then it is considered close to him and can administer in him.

Now you can see that in every place that the matter of the distribution of *Bina* to *Kli de Hesed* is brought here, *Bina* purified from *Behina Bet* to *Behina Aleph*. This is because then she is *Panim be Panim* with the *Kli de Hesed* from the *Masach* side in her. It turns out that when *Bina* dispenses the *Ohr Hesed* to the *Kli de Hesed*, the *Bina* purifies to *Behina Aleph*.

There was a whole order of gradual *Hizdakchut* here: First, the *Keter* purified from *Behina Gimel* to *Behina Bet* at which time the *Ohr Keter* disappeared to the *Shoresh* and gave *Behina Bet* to *Kli de Hochma*. Afterwards *Kli de Bina* unites with it into one and then *Behina Bet* too purifies to *Behina Aleph*. At that time the *Orot de Kelim* of *Hochma* and *Bina* disappear to *Keter* and *Behina Aleph* is dispensed to *Kli de Hesed* in *He'arat Hochma*.

It has already been explained above that when the four *Orot Zachar* and *Nekeva de Hochma* and the *Zachar* and *Nekeva de Bina* rise to the *Keter*, they awaken *Behinat Aviut de Behina Gimel* in the *Keter* once more. The *Eser Sefirot* in *Komat Hochma* elicits there by the power of the *Zivug Elyon* as in the beginning and the *Ohr Hochma* returns to *Kli de Keter*. This is called *Matei* in the *Keter*.

You find that at the coming of *Hesed* to its *Kli* it causes the existence of *Matei* in the *Keter*. This is because then the *Behina Bet* in *HB* purifies to *Behina Aleph* and their four *Orot* rise to *Kli de Keter*, inducing a new *Zivug* there on *Komat Behina Gimel*. The *Ohr Hochma* is once more *Matei* in the *Kli* of *Keter* as in the beginning.

It is written, "**Afterwards the Ohr returns to being Matei in Keter and then both HB ascend there.**" It means that because of the ascent of the four *Orot de HB* the *Ohr* is *Matei* in *Kli de Keter*.

"**In that state you find that there is a big distance between the sons and the Ohr GAR for there are two distances between them.**" Interpretation: It has been explained that the *Panim de Keter* is for *He'arat VAK* without GAR as it is written, "because He delighteth in mercy," (*Ohr Pnimi* item 40, par "And the *Panim*").

These are the two distances that now rest on the *Ohr Hesed* and deprive the *He'arat GAR* from it, which it previously received from the *Hochma*. It is written, "**In that state you find that there is a big distance between the sons and the Ohr GAR.**"

It means that these two *Achoraim de Bina* and *Keter* draw the GAR very far from the sons, which are ZAT that are contained in the *Ohr Hesed*. It is written,"**for there are two distances between them, Bina and Hochma, which have no Ohr.**"

In other words, had the *Ohr* been in *Hochma*, it would have been possible for the *Ohr Hesed* to receive from *Hochma* and *Achor de Bina* would not have prevented it since it did not prevent it in the beginning. However, now that there is no *Ohr* even in *Hochma* due to the *Achoraim de Keter*, hence that *He'arah* that *Hesed* previously received is also prevented from *Hochma*.

He writes, "**Hence, at that time Ohr Hesed ascends to Bina.**" After the GAR disappears from the *Ohr Hesed* and returns to its *Katnut*, it needs its *Ima Bina* once more to suck *He'arat GAR* of the *Kli* from there as in the beginning.

He writes, "**In that state the Kli Hesed turns its Panim and gives the six Orot below in Gevura.**" This is because the *Panim de Kli de Hesed* is for *He'arat Hochma* after it received *He'arat Hochma*, and its *Achor* is for *He'arat Hassadim*.

This is so because in several places where there is *Hochma* and *Hassadim* in the degree, the *Hochma* is considered *Panim* and the *Hassadim* as *Achoraim*. For that reason the *Achor de Hesed* is considered *He'arat Hassadim*.

However, now that the *He'arat Hochma* has disappeared from it and its *Ohr* disappeared to *Kli de Bina*, it turns out that he turned his *Panim* downward and gave the remains of the *Ohr* in it to *Kli de Gevura*, and then *Matei* in *Gevura*.

Now you can thoroughly understand the property of *Sefirat Gevura de ZA* to the fullest. Essentially, the *Kli de Gevura* is the *Behinat Hochma* of the VAK, as has been explained above that the HGT are *Behinat KHB de VAK*.

Thus, the *Kli de Gevura* is indeed considered *Behinat Bina*. This is so because its *Ohr* is *Behinat VAK de He'arat Hochma* in *Hesed*, such as ZON of the Upper *Bina*, which are *Behinat Vav Ktzavot* of the Upper *Hochma*. Thus, the *Ohr* of *Gevura* is *Behinat Bina de VAK*.

Accordingly, the two *Sefirot de* ZA, *Hesed* and *Gevura* have been explained. They are *Behinat Hochma* and *Bina* of the ZA though their *Kelim* have the value of *Keter* and *Hochma*.

41. Afterwards it returned to being **Lo Matei** in **Keter**, and then it is **Matei** in **Hochma**. At that time **Bina** is suitable to remain there in **Hochma** as in the beginning, but because of the **Ohr Hesed** in her place she comes down with him.

It is so "because He delighteth in mercy" and you already know that *Bina* is called "He". When *Bina* descends in her place, *Hesed* does not need her and he descends to his place, and is called *Matei* in *Hesed*.

Then the *Ohr Gevura* ascends in *Hesed* and this is called *Lo Matei* in *Gevura*. At that time *Kli* of *Gevura* turns her *Panim* downward and gives the five *Orot* below in *Tifferet*. This is called *Matei* in *Tifferet*.

Ohr Pnimi

41. **Lo Matei in Keter.**

This is so because the *Aviut de Behina Gimel de Nekeva* and *Behina Dalet de Zachar* in *Kli de Keter* purified once more. At that time the ZON *de Keter* departed to its *Shoresh* and then turned its *Panim* downward.

In other words, it cancelled its *Panim* and the *Achoraim* became *Panim*. After that it gave the remains of it, being the *Aviut de Behina Gimel de Zachar* and *Behina Bet de Nekeva* to *Kli de Hochma*, and then it is *Matei* in *Hochma*.

At that time Bina is suitable to remain there in Hochma as in the beginning.

After the *Panim* returned to its place in the *Hochma*, the HB immediately return to one degree. At that time *Bina* is in *Kli de Hochma*.

However, it does not remain so here since *Hochma* turned her *Panim* down and her *Achoraim* up. She returned the ZON *de Bina* to *Kli de Bina* and they were divided into two *Partzufim* once more, and examine it carefully.

First, when *Kli de Hochma* received her *Orot* ZON and the *Panim* of *Hochma* returned to its place as in the beginning, it is certain that *Bina* and *Hochma* joined and became one *Kli*. It is so for the same reason mentioned above regarding the birth of *Gadlut Hesed*.

Here too when the *Hesed* is in *Kli de Bina*, joined with *Kli de Hochma*, he receives *He'arat Hochma* as in the beginning. Thus you find once more that *Hesed* has grown and does not need its *Ima*.

Yet, it is still impossible for it to descend from itself to its *Kli*, except through the influence of *Bina*. Hence, *Hochma* had to return ZON *de Bina* to *Kli de Bina*, as then *Bina* returns her *Panim* downward too and returns the *Ohr Hesed* to its place, to its *Kli*.

But because of the Ohr Hesed in her place she comes down with him.

In other words, had *Bina* remained connected to *Kli de Hochma*, *Hesed* would have remained in her place and would not have descended to his *Kli de Hesed*.

"Because He delighteth in mercy."

This is the whole property of *Bina*; she craves *Hassadim* more than the *Ohr Hochma*. This is the cause of the *Hizdakchut* of *Aviut de Behina Gimel de Zachar de Hochma* to *Behina Bet* and afterwards the *Behina Bet de Bina* to *Behina Aleph*, whose *Ohr* is *Ohr Hassadim*.

At that time she is *Panim be Panim* with the *Kli de Hesed* and then gives the *Ohr Hesed* back to *Kli de Hesed*. It is written, **"When Bina descends in her place, Hesed does not need her and he descends to his place."** This is so because after he had already received *He'arat Hochma* from the time the *Kli de Bina* and *Kli de Hochma* were connected, he no longer needs the sucking of the *Kli de Bina*, hence he descends to his place.

Lo Matei in Gevura. At that time Kli of Gevura turns her Panim downward.

The entire division of *Gevura* from *Hesed* was because of the two distances, meaning because of the return of ZON *de Keter* to their place when their *Achoraim* detained the *Ohr Hochma* from the *Kli de Hochma*. At that time the *He'arat Hochma* stopped from *Hesed*, hence he turned his *Panim* downward and gave *Behinat VAK* to the *Gevura*.

Thus, now that *Hesed* attained his GAR once more, it is natural that *Behinat Ohr Gevura* that departed from the GAR returned to *Kli de Hesed* once more as in the beginning before they separated.

See and understand that it is completely similar to the comportment of the *Kelim de Hochma* and *Bina*. The division of the *Orot de ZON de Hochma* and *ZON de Bina* was made because of the inversion of the *Achoraim de Kli de Hochma*. This means that *Hochma* abandoned the dispensing of her GAR and gave only VAK, which are *Behinat ZON de Kli de Bina*.

Similarly, the *Orot de Hesed* and *Gevura* were divided by the inversion of the *Panim de Kli de Hesed*. After the *He'arat GAR* was deprived of him because of the two distances, he turned his *Panim* and dispensed VAK without GAR, which is the *Ohr* of *Gevura*.

After it is *Lo Matei* in *Keter* and his force of *Achor* was cancelled and he returned the *Ohr Hochma* to *Kli de Hochma*, the *Panim* of *Hochma* returned to its place as in the beginning. Thus, the *Orot de ZON de Hochma* and *ZON de Bina* reunited into a single *Partzuf*.

Similarly here, after the *Hesed* acquired *He'arat Hochma* when he was in *Kli de Bina* at the time she was joined with *Hochma*, he returned with the *Gadlut* to his place. At that time his *Panim* returned as in the beginning, and thus the *Orot* of *Hesed* and *Gevura* unite into one *Ohr*.

All this is because the *Ohr* is only divided into GAR and VAK because some element compels it to. Consequently, as soon as that element is cancelled they return to a single *Ohr* as in the beginning.

He writes, "**Lo Matei in Gevura. At that time Kli of Gevura turns her Panim downward and gives the five Orot below in Tifferet. This is called Matei in Tifferet.**" This is because when the *Ohr Gevura* joins the *Ohr Hesed* into one, that connection operates on their *Kelim* as well.

Since the *Kli de Gevura* joined with the *Kli de Hesed*, by that she returned her *Panim* below, since she cancelled her *Panim* that detained the dispensing of GAR and returned her *Panim* upwards. In other words, she turned to dispense *He'arat GAR* like the *Kli de Hesed*.

At that time she dispensed her remains, ascribed to *Tifferet*, to the *Kli de Tifferet* and *Tifferet* receives *He'arat GAR* as well. This is the meaning of *Tifferet* being called *Vav* ו with a *Rosh*. It is the same *He'arat GAR* that it receives through the dispensing of the *Ohr Gevura* when *Gevura* is connected into one with the *Ohr Hesed*.

Now you can understand what is brought in several places that *Tifferet* is merged of *Hesed* and *Gevura* together. It means that it receives the remains of the *Ohr Gevura* from the time it is connected into one with the *Ohr Hesed*.

Now we understand *Sefirat Tifferet de ZA* from its origin. Its *Kli* is *Behinat Bina de VAK* because the HGT are the KHB of the VAK. However, it is regarded as merely *Behinat Sefirat Daat de VAK*.

This is so because of its *Ohr*, which is *Behinat Daat*. However, first we must know what is the *Ohr Daat*. After all we only have ten *Sefirot* KHB HGT

NHYM. It is known that it is written in Sefer Yetzira (Book of Creation), "Ten and not eleven." Thus, what is that *Ohr Daat*?

Know, that the source of that *Ohr* is the interchanging of the *Orot* here in *Hitpashtut Bet*. Here *Ohr Hochma* comes to *Kli de Keter*, *Ohr Bina* to *Kli de Hochma*, *Ohr Hesed* to *Kli de Bina* and *Malchut* to *Kli de ZA*, as we learn from the Rav's words.

Note, that this *Ohr Hesed* that comes to *Kli de Bina* is the origin of the *Ohr Daat*, hence the Rav calls it "*Bina's* son". Its *Behinat AVI* are the *Zachar* and *Nekeva* in *Kli de Bina*. The *Zachar* is *Behinat Hochma de Kli de Bina* and the *Nekeva* is *Behinat Bina de Kli de Bina*. *Ohr Hesed* is the *Behinat Daat* between this *HB*, which is always called "the son of *HB*".

More precisely, the *ZON de Kli de Hochma* are both considered *Behinat Hochma* and *Behinat Abba*, and the *ZON* in *Kli de Bina* are both considered *Behinat Bina* and *Behinat Ima*. The *Ohr Hesed* in *Kli de Bina* is considered *Behinat Daat* and *Behinat* son of these *AVI*.

This clarifies that the *Ohr Hesed* was originally emanated from the remains of the *Ohr* of *ZON de Hochma* after they purified into *Behina Aleph*. It came to *Kli de Bina*, which is discerned as its *Ima*, and lingered there in the intestine of the *Kli de Bina* until it acquired *He'arat Hochma*, meaning until it grew. At that time it came out to the place of the *Kelim de VAK*, called "*Avir ha Olam*", and there is nothing more to add here.

Now we have explained the *Ohr Daat* from its *Shoresh*, that it is a son and a progeny that was renewed because of the interchanging of the *Orot* in *Hitpashtut Bet*. For that reason it comes and clothes *Kli de Bina* though it is only *Ohr ZA* and *Behinat VAK*, having no equivalence with *Behinat GAR*.

This is so because the difference between *GAR* and *VAK* is so far, as between an *Ohr* and its *Kli*. Yet, because of the interchanging of the *Orot* this *Ohr de VAK* came and clothed the *Kli de GAR*. This is a very wonderful matter. Examine this for there is no need to elaborate here in what is not necessary for our issue.

From all that has been explained thus far you can see that these three *Sefirot HGT de ZA* are not considered that essence of *ZA*, but *Behinat GAR KHB* or *HBD de ZA*. It has been written above that the five *Ktzavot HGT NH* are the very five *Behinot KHB*, *ZA* and *Malchut*. Yet, when they are *Behinat Ohr Hassadim* and *Ohr VAK*, their names change to *HGT NH*.

Thus, the actual *Behinat ZA* begins at the fourth end of the five *Hassadim Netzah* since it is opposite the fourth *Behina*, called *ZA*. The *Tifferet*, however, is opposite the third *Behina*, called *Bina*, and remember that.

Therefore, *Orot de HGT* are also *Behinat GAR*, but begin from *Hochma* for the above reason. The *Ohr Hesed* is considered *Ohr Hochma* of the *VAK*, *Ohr Tifferet* is considered that same *Ohr Hesed* from the point of its clothing in *Kli de Bina*, meaning *Behinat Ohr Daat* and the son of *HB*.

This is the actual *Behinat Ohr VAK*. The *Orot de Hesed* and *Gevura*, however, are considered *Behinat He'arot Hochma* and *Bina* that reached that *Ohr Hesed* though they are not the *Atzmut Ohr Hesed* in its own essence.

The reason for it is the attitude of the *Kelim*. *Hesed* and *Gevura* are originally in *Behinat Kelim de Keter* and *Hochma*. Since this *Ohr Hesed* never clothed in these *Kelim*, it also does not clothe the *Kelim de Hesed* and *Gevura*.

However, since it clothed the *Kli de Bina*, it takes its place in the *Kelim de VAK* in the *Kli Tifferet* in the place of *Bina*. Hence, the *Tifferet* is considered the gist of the *Partzuf de ZA*, the *Guf de Ilana*. The above *Atzmut Ohr Hesed* inside it is considered the *Shokaim de Ilana* (shins of the tree), and all the other *Sefirot* of the *ZAT* are considered the *Anafim* that hang in the *Tifferet*.

42. After that it is *Matei* in *Keter* once more and then *Lo Matei* in *Hochma* and *Bina* since the two rise to *Keter* together. In that state it is *Lo Matei* in *Hesed*, as he rises to the place of *Bina*, as in the beginning because of the two distances between them.

At that time it is *Matei* in *Gevura* and then it is *Lo Matei* in *Tifferet*, as the *Ohr Tifferet* ascends in *Gevura* because of the yearning. At that time the *Kli Tifferet* turns his *Panim* and gives the four *Orot* in *Netzah*, and this is called *Matei* in *Netzah*.

Ohr Pnimi

42. It is *Matei* in *Keter* once more and then *Lo Matei* in *Hochma* and *Bina* etc.

You already know that the coming of *Hesed* to its *Kli* makes it *Matei* in *Keter* (see *Ohr Pnimi* item 40, par. "You find"). This is so because there is no giving of *Orot* except *Panim be Panim*, as the Rav says above.

Hence, *Bina* must purify from *Behina Bet* to *Behina Aleph* and then the *Orot de HB* depart to the *Keter* and induce a *Zivug Elyon* there on *Aviut de Behina Gimel*. At that time the *Ohr Matei* in *Komat Hochma* as in the beginning.

Then *Lo Matei* in *HB* because the *Achoraim de Kli de Keter* stop and detain the *He'arat GAR*. Because of that *Lo Matei* in *Hesed* too since there are two vacant distances without *Ohr*, which are *HB*.

Since the *Ohr* is *Lo Matei* in *Hochma* you find that even the *He'arat Hochma* in *Hesed* stops from it and *Hesed* returns to its *Katnut*. In that state it needs its *Ima Bina* once more to suck *He'arat GAR* from her.

Thus, *Hesed* ascends to the *Bina* and his *Kli* turns its *Panim* downward and the *Ohr de Gevura* descends to the *Kli de Gevura* and is *Matei* in *Gevura*. At that time it is *Lo Matei* in *Tifferet* since the *Achoraim de Gevura* stop and detain the *He'arat GAR* of the *Ohr Tifferet*.

For that reason the *Ohr Tifferet* rises to *Kli de Gevura*, as it did not descend from the *Gevura* except by the force of the *He'arat GAR* of the dominion of *Hesed* over *Gevura*. Now that the dominion of *Gevura* has come once more, the *Gevura* raises his *Ohr* to her once more, as in the beginning.

At that time *Kli de Tifferet* turns its *Panim* downward for it must revoke the influence of its *GAR*, which was its previous *Panim*, and make its *Achor* the *Panim* of bestowal. After that it lowers the remains of the *Ohr* in it to *Netzah* and this is called *Matei* in *Netzah*.

Now we shall understand *Sefirat Netzah de ZA* thoroughly. The *Kli de Netzah* is the *Behinat ZA* itself since the *Hesed* of the five *Hassadim* corresponds to *Behina Gimel* of the *Keter* and the *Dalet Behinot de Ohr Yashar*. It is so because the *HGT* are considered *KHB de Hassadim* and *Netzah* and *Hod* are *Behinot ZA* and *Malchut de Hassadim*.

You find that from the perspective of the *Ohr Sefirat Tifferet* is the gist of the *Ohr ZA*. The *Etzem Ohr Daat* clothes the *Kli de Tifferet* and this is because of the interchanging of the *Orot*. Since *Ohr Hochma* clothed in *Keter* and *Ohr Bina* in *Kli de Hochma*, you find that *Ohr ZA* clothes in *Kli de Tifferet*, which is *Behinat Bina* of the five *Hassadim*.

However, from the perspective of the *Kelim*, the *Netzah* is considered the *Atzmut* of *ZA* and the *Ohr* of *Netzah* is the *Behinat VAK* that remains in *Kli de Tifferet* after its *Histalkut* from there to *Gevura*. The difference between it and *Sefirat Gevura* is that the *Ohr* of the *Gevura* is evaluated as *VAK de Hochma* although it is also discerned as *VAK*.

This is so because it is the remains of *Hesed* from the *Behinat He'arat Hochma* in it, and is evaluated like the *Ohr ZON de Kli de Bina*. However, the *Ohr Netzah* is *Behinat VAK de Ohr ZA* since we learned there that the *Ohr* of *Tifferet* is actually *Behinat Ohr ZA*.

We must predominantly discern here that how the *Orot* and the *Kelim de HGT* here relate to the *Orot* and *Kelim de NHYM* is the same as how the *GAR* relates to *VAK*. This is because the *HGT* correlate to *GAR de Hey Behinot* and *NHYM* correlate to *ZA* and *Malchut de Hey Behinot*.

43. After that it returns to being **Lo Matei in Keter** and then it is **Matei in Hochma**. It is also **Matei in Bina** because of the **Hesed** there "because He delighteth in mercy."

At that time it is also **Matei in Hesed** for then **Hesed** descends to his place, and it is then **Lo Matei in Gevura** because **Gevura** ascends with the **Hesed**. At that time it is **Matei in Tifferet** and **Ohr** descends in **Tifferet**.

Then it is **Lo Matei in Netzah** since the **Ohr Netzah** ascends with the **Tifferet**. At that time it is **Matei in Hod** since then the *Kli* of *Netzah* turns his *Panim* and gives the three *Orot* to *Hod*, at which time the *Hod* turns his *Panim* to *Yesod* and shines in him.

Ohr Pnimi

43. **Lo Matei in Keter and then it is Matei in Hochma.**

This is because the *Zachar* and *Nekeva de Ohr Keter* purified to *Behina Bet*. Then their *Achoraim* was cancelled and they dispensed the *Ohr Bina* to the *Kli* of *Hochma*, they are *Matei* in *Hochma* and the *Panim de Hochma* returned to its place as in the beginning.

It is also Matei in Bina because of the Hesed there.

This means that *Hochma* turned her *Panim* downward, gave the *Zachar* and *Nekeva* of *Bina* to *Kli de Bina* and is *Matei* in *Bina* too. He explains the reason: "because of the *Hesed* there" so that he may correct the *Hesed* and lower it to his *Kli* (see *Ohr Pnimi* item 41).

Matei in Hesed for then Hesed descends to his place.

Through the *Hizdakchut Behina Bet* in *Bina* to *Behina Aleph*. This is *Behinat Ohr* of the five *Hassadim* that belong to the *VAK*. At that time the *Ohr Hesed* descends to its *Kli*, is *Matei* in the *Hesed* and its *Panim* return to its place.

Lo Matei in Gevura because Gevura ascends with the Hesed.

The whole *Ohr Gevura* is discerned as the *Achoraim* and the *VAK* of the *Ohr Hesed*. Since the *Panim* of *Hesed* returned to its place the *Achoraim* that was in *Gevura* was cancelled and incorporated once more in the *Panim de Ohr Hesed*. In that state the *Kli de Gevura* returns and turns its *Panim* downward, giving the *Ohr Tifferet* in *He'arat GAR* to the *Tifferet* (see *Ohr Pnimi* item 41).

Lo Matei in Netzah since the Ohr Netzah ascends with the Tifferet.

This too is for the above reason that *Ohr Netzah* is only *Behinat Achoraim* and *VAK* of the *Ohr Tifferet*. Thus, when the *Panim* of *Tifferet* returned to its place it pulls its *VAK* to it as *Hesed* pulled the *Ohr Gevura* and as *Hochma* that pulled *ZON de Bina* to herself.

Matei in Hod since then the Kli of Netzah turns his Panim.

After the *Ohr de Netzah* rose to the *Panim* of the *Kli de Tifferet* it thus turns the *Panim* of its *Kli* to its *Achoraim*. This is because the previous dispensing of *GAR* is detained in it in *Behinat Achor*. Now it has become the place of bestowal as the *Panim de Kli* of the *Hesed* that now controls it. At that time it gives its remains to the *Hod* in dispensing of *GAR*.

Now we have found the way to understand the *Sefira* of *Hod* of the *ZA* from its origin. Know, that this *Sefira* is the axis that all the corrections depend on and revolve around.

Its *Kli* is the last fifth *Behina* of the five *Behinot KHB ZA* and *Malchut*, meaning the original *Kli Malchut*. This is because the four previous *Hassadim* correspond to *KHB ZA*, and *Hesed* is fifth, meaning the *Hod* which is opposite *Malchut*.

You already know that all those *Kelim de Hitpashtut Bet* are the *Kelim* of *Hitpashtut Aleph* that have been emptied of their *Orot*. It turns out that the *Kli de Hod* is the *Behina Dalet de Hitpashtut Aleph* that has been emptied of her *Ohr* and did not leave any *Reshimo* after her (see the Rav's words Part 4, Chap 2 item 6).

However, the *Ohr* of the *Hod* is not the *Ohr Malchut*, but the *Ohr ZA*, meaning what reached her from the remains of *Netzah* when he was connected with the *Ohr de He'arat GAR* of the *Tifferet*. Moreover, it is the most important *Ohr* among the *Sefirot* of *NHYM*. From the perspective of the *Orot* it is *Behinat GAR* of *ZA*, not *ZA* himself.

Thus, he is more important than *Netzah*, as *Netzah* is from the *Behinat Achoraim* and *VAK* of the *Ohr Tifferet*, but the *Hod* is called the "fifth *Hesed*" since he is *Behinat He'arat GAR* that is in *NHYM*. Though it is *Behina Dalet* from the perspective of the *Kli*, being the greater *Din* in the *Eser Sefirot*, its gist is of course the *Ohr* in it. This *Ohr* is now very sweetened, meaning from *He'arat GAR* in *Tifferet*, and examine carefully.

Hod turns his Panim to Yesod and shines in him.

You already know that all this *Ohr* that extends in *Matei ve Lo Matei* from *Bina* to *Hod* is *Ohr de Hassadim*. In other words, it is the *Behinat Koma* that emerged on the *Aviut de Behina Aleph* that remained after the *Hizdakchut* of *Bina*.

The matter of the difference of *Matei ve Lo Matei* is primarily through the changes of *He'arat GAR* in *Hassadim* or *Hassadim* without *He'arat GAR*. However, there was no difference between them in the stature of the *Koma* since they are all at the level of *Behina Aleph*.

Here *Sefirat Hod* turned its *Panim* backward though it had not completed the *Hizdakchut de Behina Aleph*, only cancelled the *Behinat He'arat GAR* in it, which is the *Panim* and turned the *Achor* into *Behinat Panim*. However, here we must know what the Rav has written that the ZON in *Kli de Bina* mated and procreated one *Hey*. The *Vav* ו inside the *Hey* ה was given to *Kli de Yesod* and the *Dalet* ד on the *Vav* was given to the *Kli de Malchut*.

Interpretation: *Bina* turned her *Panim* for the first time and purified from her *Aviut de Behina Bet* into *Behina Aleph* that equalized her *Panim* to the *Panim de Kli de Hesed*. At that time she also lowered one *Ohr* that was born by the *Zivug* of the *Zachar* and *Nekeva* in herself.

This *Ohr* is *Behinat Nukva* and is therefore called *Hey*. Thus, *Behinat Zachar* and *Nekeva* descended to the *Kelim de VAK* too, as they descended to the *GAR de Hitpashtut Bet*.

The *Zachar* is the above *Ohr Daat* and the *Nekeva* is that *Ohr* born by the *Zivug* of ZON *de Bina*, called *Hey*. All these *Orot* that come and are born through a *Zivug*, the Rav names *He'arot* (see item 35).

He says there that *Hochma* turned her *Panim* and shines for *Bina*. He also says that the *Hod* turned his *Panim* to the *Yesod* and shines in him. Also, he says below that so it was in all the *VAK*, which turn their *Panim* and shine below. All these are *Hamshachot* (pl. for *Hamshacha*) of the *Orot* that come by the *Zivug*, for which he names them *He'arot*.

It is written, "**Hod turns his Panim to Yesod and shines in him.**" It means that there was not a complete *Hizdakchut*, only what is sufficient to illuminate the *Hey* of *Bina* to the *Yesod*. Afterwards, when there was a complete *Hizdakchut*, the *Ohr* that belongs to *Yesod* descended to *Yesod*.

Yet, this *Hey* that was born from ZON *de Bina* is the beginning of the association of *Midat ha Rachamim* in *Din*, hence it is worthwhile to expand the understanding of it. We have already discussed this *Hidush* that was made in *Hitpashtut Bet* when the *Ohr ZA* was emanated and elicited through the *Hochma* and not through *Bina* as it would be in the *Eser Sefirot de Ohr Yashar* and as it was in *Hitpashtut Aleph*.

This *Hidush* came here by the inversion of the *Orot*. Besides that there is yet another great *Hidush* here: *Ohr Malchut* was emanated by the *Bina* and not by the ZA, as in *Eser Sefirot de Ohr Yashar* and as it was in *Hitpashtut Aleph*.

The *Ohr Daat* was emanated from the *Hizdakchut* of the *Zachar* and *Nekeva* of *Kli de Hochma*, which is the *Ohr Zeir Anpin*. Similarly, *Ohr Malchut* emerged by the *Hizdakchut* of the *Zachar* and *Nekeva de Kli de Bina*, namely the *Hey*, which belongs to *Malchut*, as she is *Ohr Nekeva*.

Now you will thoroughly understand the difference between *Ohr Daat*, which is *Ohr ZA*, and the *Ohr* of the above *Hey*, which is the *Ohr Malchut*, meaning according to their emanation. In fact, when they were emanated, both came out in *Behinat Koma* of *Behina Aleph*.

This is so because *Behina Bet de ZON* of the *Kli de Hochma* purified to *Behina Aleph*, which is *Ohr Hesed*, (see item 37), called *Ohr Daat* or *Ohr ZA*. Similarly, the *Behina Bet* of the *Zachar* and *Nekeva de Bina* purified into *Behina Bet*, which is the above *Ohr Hey*, being the *Ohr Malchut*.

Therefore, you find that the *Ohr Hesed*, which is the *Ohr ZA*, and the *Ohr* of the *Hey*, which is the *Ohr Malchut*, are of equal *Koma*. This is so because both are *Behina Aleph*, as both came from the *Hizdakchut* of *Behina Bet*.

Yet, the difference between them is as great as the measure of the difference between *ZON de Hochma* and *ZON de Bina*. It has been clarified above that *ZON de Bina* are considered the *Achoraim* and *Behinat VAK* of the *ZON de Hochma*.

It is therefore obvious that the consequences that stem from them are also as far as *GAR* is far from *VAK*. The *Ohr Hesed* that was emanated by the *ZON de Hochma* is considered the *Behinat Panim* and *GAR* compared to the *Ohr Hey*, which is considered the *Achoraim* and *VAK* compared to the *Ohr Hesed*, being the *Ohr ZA*. It is analogous to the ratio in the progenitors, and examine well.

Now we can thoroughly understand what the Rav stresses above (item 38), **"However, Bina did not turn her Panim to shine in Hesed below since there was no power in Hesed and VAK to receive such a great Ohr Panim be Panim, only Achor be Achor."**

In that he refers to the above *Ohr Hey*, which he names *He'arah* since it came out through a *Zivug* and in the regular order of *Hizdakchut* and emanation of the *Orot* from one another.

He stresses in that regard that the *Ohr* of this *Hey* did not come to the *VAK* before the seven *Orot* that come in the regular order of the *Hizdakchut*. It is similar to the *Zachar* of *Bina*, born out of the *Zivug ZON de Hochma*, which comes to *Kli de Bina* before the *Ohr Hesed* comes through the ordinary *Hizdakchut*, as the Rav has written before (item 35).

The reason is that if the *Ohr* of the *Hey* had come before the *Hizdakchut* to *Behina Aleph*, meaning before the time of the descent of *Hesed*, like the *Zachar* of *Bina*, it would have been the *Koma* of the *Hey* that was in *Behina Bet*. This is so because the *Aviut de Bina* had not yet purified to *Behina Aleph*, but only when *Hesed* was given to the *Kli de Hesed*.

This is what the Rav stresses, "**since there was no power in Hesed and VAK to receive such a great Ohr.**" How is it possible that the *Ohr Koma* of *Behina Bet* would come and clothe the *Kelim de VAK*, which are *Behina Aleph*?

Thus, first *Bina* was compelled to purify from *Behina Bet* to *Behina Aleph*, at which time the *Ohr Hey* purified to the measure of *Behina Aleph*. Then both of them came out, meaning the *Ohr Hesed* and the *Ohr Hey*, and came to *Kli de Hesed*. This *Hey* then moved from *Kli* to *Kli* until it came to the *Kli* of *Yesod* which is its place.

Now you can also see what the Rav answers there and says that the *Hochma* could have illuminated to the *Bina* before it purified to *Behina Aleph*, before *Abba ve Ima* remain as one and come out as one. He wishes to say that *Hochma* emanated and gave the *Zachar de Bina* to the *Kli* of *Bina* before she was purified to *Behina Aleph*.

This is because the *Kli* of *Bina* is indeed a *Kli de Behina Bet* like the *Koma* of the *Ohr Hochma*, hence it does not need to purify and lessen its *Koma* to *Behina Aleph*. This is not so with *Bina* to the *Kelim de Hesed* and the rest of the *VAK*, which are *Kelim* of *Behina Aleph*, as how can they receive the *Ohr* of the *Hey* while it has *Koma de Behina Bet*?

It is written, "**at which time the Hod turns his Panim to Yesod and shines in him.**" It has been explained that this *Hey* is considered the *Ohr Achoraim* and *VAK*.

Thus, since the *Panim* of the *Hod* is from *Behinat He'arat GAR*, it therefore cannot dispense the *Ohr* of the *Hey*, which is *Behinat Ohr Achoraim*, unless through turning the *Panim* downward and the *Achoraim* upward. In other words, her *Achor*, which dispenses *VAK* and prevents *GAR* will not become the giver, and will then give the above *Ohr Hey* to *Yesod*.

44. **It is the same matter in all the VAK since when the Orot are given in them they turn their Panim and shine below. This is because it is precisely Bina who did not turn her Panim to Hesed since there is no power in Hesed to receive the Ohr Bina. The VAK, however, have the ability in themselves to receive Ohr from one another since all the VAK are equal.**

Ohr Pnimi

44. **It is the same matter in all the VAK since when the *Orot* are given in them they turn their *Panim* and shine below.**

As it has been written above, this *Hey* emerged by the *Zivug* from the *Zachar* and *Nekeva de Kli de Bina*, when *Bina* purified from *Behina Bet* to *Behina Aleph*, to give the *Ohr Hesed* in *Kli de Hesed*. At that time the *Ohr* of this *Hey* emerged with it too, *Hesed* gave to *Gevura* etc. until she reached *Kli de Hod* and *Hod* gave to *Yesod*.

It is written, "**It is the same matter in all the VAK since when the *Orot* are given in them they turn their *Panim* and shine below.**" In other words, that same *Ohr* of the *Hey* that came out by a *Zivug*, whose dispensing is always referred to by the Rav as *He'arah*.

45. **After that it returned to being *Matei* in *Keter* and then *Lo Matei* in *Hochma* and *Bina* since they both rise there. It is also *Lo Matei* in *Hesed* because it rose to *Bina* and it is *Matei* in *Gevura*.**

At that time it is *Lo Matei* in *Tifferet* and then it is *Matei* in *Netzah* and *Lo Matei* in *Hod*. In that state the *Hod* turns its *Panim* and gives the two *Orot* to *Yesod*, then it is *Matei* in *Yesod*. Then the *Yesod* turns its *Panim* and shines to *Malchut*, etc. in all the VAK.

Ohr Pnimi

45. **Returned to being *Matei* in *Keter* etc. and *Lo Matei* in *Hod*.**

It has already been repeatedly explained above that the dispensing of *Bina* to the *Kli de VAK* causes *Matei* in *Keter*. In that state the *Achor* of *Kli de Keter* dominate, preventing any *He'arat GAR* in the *Partzuf*, even in the *Kli de Hochma*, much less in the *Kelim* below that receive from the *Kli* of *Hochma*. Hence, the *He'arat GAR* departs from the *Kli de Hod* and the *Kli* turns its *Panim* down, giving the rest to *Yesod*.

However, regarding their turning of the *Panim* of the *Kli de Hod*, there is also a matter of the *Hizdakchut* of the *Aviut de Behina Aleph* to *Behinat Keter*. The *Ohr* that comes out has but *Komat Malchut*, as the Rav has written above that *Komat Malchut* clothed the *Kli de Yesod*.

In this manner, there were two *Behinot* regarding the turning of the *Panim de Hod*, both the matter of the administering of the *Achoraim* instead of the *Panim* as before, and the matter of the *Hizdakchut* of the *Aviut de Behina Aleph*. The latter dominated all five *Ktzavot*, *Hesed* through *Hod*, and now *Hod* has purified from its *Behina Aleph* and gave only *Komat Malchut* to the *Kli de*

Yesod. The reason for it is that there is no more than five *Ktzavot* in the *Koma de Behina Aleph*.

Now *Sefirat Yesod de ZA* has been clarified for us. Its *Kli* is from *Behinat Malchut* since the *Kli de Hod* of the *ZA* is also a *Kli* of *Malchut*, and all the more so the *Kli* that follows it.

Thus, all of these three *Kelim Hod*, *Yesod* and *Malchut* are a mere *Hitpashtut* of *Kli Malchut*. They expand primarily because of that above-mentioned *Hey* that descended from the *Zivug ZON de Bina*, but also because of the *Ohr Achoraim* that remained from the *Kli de Hod* after it turned her *Panim* because of the dominion of the *Achor de Keter*. It is so because these two *Orot* are specific to the *Kli de Yesod*.

Thus, the *Kli de Yesod* is discerned as *Kli Malchut* and the *Ohr* in it is combined of *Din* and *Rachamim*. This is because the *Ohr* of the *Achoraim* that remains of *Sefirat Hod* after she had turned her *Panim* is discerned as the hardest *Din* in all five *Ktzavot de ZA*.

This is so because it is the *Kli de Behina Dalet* from the time of *Hitpashtut Aleph*. However, when *He'arat GAR* of *Tifferet* it was to the contrary, considered *Hesed* reached it.

This is so because the *He'arat GAR* turns everything to *Hesed*. Yet, when the *He'arat GAR* is absent, only the *Midat Din* remains in it, and that *Midat Din* came down to the *Kli* of *Yesod*.

You must know that that was a *Hidush* in the *Partzuf*. Until now none of *Midat ha Din* appeared in the *Partzuf* in all five *Ktzavot*. On the contrary, the *Ohr de Hassadim* of the *Koma de Behina Aleph* dominated the entire *Partzuf* though once in *He'arat GAR* and once without *He'arat GAR*.

Now, however, *Komat Ohr Hassadim* has already purified from *Sefirat Hod* and there is only *Komat Malchut* there. Since the *He'arat GAR* disappeared from the *Partzuf*, there appeared the entire *Din* force in *Kli de Hod* and that residue descended to *Kli de Yesod*. Thus you find that this *Din* force is a *Hidush* that has now appeared in the *Kli de Yesod*.

Thus, now all five *Ktzavot* are considered *Behinat Hey Gevurot* because of the *Hidush Tzura* that they have acquired in the *Kli de Yesod*. Hence, now there are two *Behinot*: *Hey Hassadim* in the *Hey Ktzavot* from *Hesed* to *Hod*, and the second is since they are five *Gevurot*, meaning in the *Kli de Yesod*.

However, there is yet another *Ohr* of the *Hey* in the *Kli de Yesod*, meaning what reached it from the *Zivug ZON de Bina*. It is a very big *Ohr* since from the *Shoresh* of its emanation, it is *Behina Bet*, since it comes from the *Zivug de ZON* of *Behina Bet*.

Afterwards, when it descended along with the *Ohr Hesed* to the *Kelim de VAK*, it was lessened to *Komat Malchut* once more. However, since it is from *Zivug de Behina Bet*, it is considered *Ohr Hesed*, but on a low *Koma*.

Thus, from her perspective the *Hey Ktzavot* are regarded as *Hey Hassadim* once more, sweetening the above *Hey Gevurot* that descended to the *Kli de Yesod* from the residue of the *Ohr Hod*. Thus we have thoroughly learned that the *Ohr Yesod* is a combined *Ohr* of *Hesed* and *Din*, called *Hey Hassadim* and *Hey Gevurot*.

The *Hey Gevurot* are from the remains of the *Ohr VAK*, and the *Hey Hassadim* are from the residue of the *Zachar* and the *Nekeva de Kli de Bina*. They mix and join together in the *Kli* of *Yesod*. Bear in mind that all this is done here during, and because of the dominion of the *Achor de Kli de Keter*.

46. **Afterwards it returned to being Lo Matei in Keter and then it is Matei in HB and Hesed and then it is Lo Matei in Gevura, Matei in Tifferet and Lo Matei in Netzah, Matei in Hod and Lo Matei in Yesod, as it ascended in Hod.**

    At that time it turns its Panim and gives Ohr to Malchut below in her place, and then it is Matei in Malchut. Now the first Behinot are complete, which is the reality of the Hitpashtut. Thus, all ten Orot reached the Malchut.

Ohr Pnimi

46. *Lo Matei in Keter* etc. *Matei in Hod and Lo Matei in Yesod,* as it ascended in *Hod*. At that time it turns its *Panim* and gives *Ohr* to *Malchut* below in her place, and then it is *Matei in Malchut*.

    The matter of *Lo Matei in Keter* has already been explained, being because of the regular *Hizdakchut* through the *Bitush de Ohr Makif* and *Ohr Pnimi*, at which time the *Behina Gimel* in the *Kli* purified into *Behina Bet*. The *Ohr* that elicits in that *Zivug* is *Komat Bina* and that remains gave the *Keter* to the *Kli de Hochma*.

    Since the *He'arat GAR* returned to the *Partzuf*, all the *Behinot Panim* and *Hochma, Bina,* and *Hesed, Tifferet* and *Hod*, returned to their original place. Then the *Ohr Yesod* rises and joins the *He'arat Panim de GAR* of the *Hod* for the above reason.

    At that time the *Kli de Yesod* turns its *Panim* downward, meaning it administers *Behinat He'arat GAR*, relating to the dominion of the *Kli de Hod* on it. However, it is not from *Behina Aleph* but only from *Komat Ohr Malchut*, as the *Ohr* that remains in the *Kli de Yesod* is only *Komat Malchut*, and then it is *Matei in Malchut*.

However, here we must know what is the *Ohr* of *Yesod* that rose to *Hod* and what is its residue, which it gave to the *Kli de Malchut*. We thoroughly know the origin of the above *Hey* that descended to *Kli de Yesod*.

You already know that this *Hey* is a result of the *Zivug ZON* in *Kli de Bina*. We must also discern a shape of *Dalet* ד over *Vav* ו in this *Hey* ה.

This *Vav* in the *Pnimiut* of the *Partzuf* has no *Rosh* and there is a significant indication here since this *Hey* consists of the *Zachar* and *Nekeva* in *Bina*. Hence, the *Behinat Nekeva* in the *Hey* is the *Dalet* and the *Behinat Zachar* in the *Hey* is the *Vav* without the *Rosh* inside it.

The meaning of the words is that the matter of the cessation of the left leg in the *Hey* implies the cessation of the *GAR* from the *VAK* that had been prepared and made inside the *Kli de Bina*. There is a great *Hidush* to discern: the *Nekeva* is more important than her *Zachar* since the *Zachar* is resultant from the *Zivug Zachar* and *Nekeva de Kli de Hochma* when the *Zachar* is in *Behinat Harkanat Rosh* (see the Rav's words item 35).

The *Hochma* turned her *Panim* and shines to *Bina Panim be Panim*, only *He'arah*. It means that the *Zachar* in *Kli de Hochma*, which is *Behina Gimel*, turned its *Panim* and purified into *Behina Bet* like the *Nukva* of *Kli de Hochma*.

You find that the *Zachar* lowered its *Rosh* since the *GAR de Hochma* is called *Rosh*. Now, after it departed from the *Aviut de Behina Gimel*, the entire *Ohr Hochma* disappeared from it, and it equalizes with *Komat Bina* of its *Nekeva*. At that time they mated and procreated the above *Zachar* of *Kli de Bina*.

It is known that any offspring and resultant is considered *VAK* of its *Maatzil*, meaning the *Zachar* and *Nekeva de Hochma* that gave birth to it. When they procreated it they both had only *Komat Bina*, hence their offspring is merely *VAK* of that *Koma*.

However, the *Nekeva* of the *Kli de Bina* is discerned as the *Reshimo* of *Bina* that remained in that *Kli* from the time of *Hitpashtut Aleph* that the *Ohr Bina* of *Hitpashtut Aleph* left there when departing from there. That *Ohr Bina* had *Komat Keter* there since all *Eser Sefirot de Hitpashtut Aleph* had *Komat Keter*.

Thus, you see the great importance of this *Reshimo* that remained in *Kli de Bina*. However, it became a *Nukva* to the *Zachar de Keter de Kli de Bina*, which lacks even the *GAR de Bina*.

That was so because this *Reshimo* has a very small *Ohr*, as all her *Ohr* has already departed. She is but a *Reshimo*, meaning a very small *Ohr* that must remain after every *Ohr* when it leaves its place. Hence, since the *Reshimo* has no *Ohr*, she became a *Behinat Nekeva* to the above *Ohr Zachar*, which is much lower than her, so as to receive *Ohr* from it, and examine that.

Now you will thoroughly understand the meaning of this above *Hey* that was emanated from those *Zachar* and *Nekeva*. The truncated *Vav* without the *Rosh* that stands inside that *Hey* is the *Behinat Zachar* in that resultant. This is because it is *Behinat VAK de Komat Bina* without the *Behinat Rosh de Komat Bina*.

The *Dalet* that surrounds that truncated *Vav* in the *Hey* is the *Behinat Nekeva* in this resultant. It is regarded as the *Rosh* over the truncated *Vav* since it is completely *Behinat GAR*.

Yet, it lacks the *Ohr*, which the truncated *Vav* has, whose entire *Ohr* is only what she receives from that truncated *Vav*. Hence, it is called *Dalet*, indicating that she is poor and devoid of *Shefa* from her own *Behina* and must receive from her *Zachar*.

That cessation that was made in the left leg of the *Hey* indicates that she divided into two separate degrees from one another. This is what has now been made by the ascent of the *Ohr Yesod* to *Sefirat Hod*.

You know the two kinds of *Orot* in the *Kli de Yesod*. The first is the *Behinat Dinim* that remained in the *Hod* after the *He'arat GAR* disappeared there, and the second is the *Ohr* of the *Hey* that was drawn to it from the *ZON* in *Bina*.

After the *Ohr Matei* in *Hod*, being *Behinat He'arat GAR* that departed from the *Ohr* of *Yesod* when that *Ohr* is in *Hod*, it causes its residue to descend to *Yesod*. Now you find that when the *Ohr* descended to the *Hod* once more, the residue that descended to *Yesod* has certainly returned to its *Shoresh*, to *Hod* since now it has *He'arat GAR* there once more.

That *Ohr* that rose there took the *Behinat* truncated *Vav* inside the *Hey* in the *Yesod* along with it and raised it to the *Hod*. Thus, two *Orot* rose from the *Yesod*. The first is the *Ohr* above *Malchut*, meaning the residue that it took from *Hod* first. The second is the truncated *Vav* inside the *Hey*.

The reason for it is that although that *Vav* is not at all from *Behinat Hod*, it still rose there. This is so because it was first connected to the *Ohr* of *Malchut* in order to sweeten it.

The *Ohr Malchut* is discerned as the *Hey Gevurot* and the *Hey* is the *Behinat Hey Hassadim*, and they were sweetened in one another. That sweetening comes only from the *Vav* inside the *Hey* since it is the entire *Ohr* inside the *Hey* though it certainly took the *He'arat GAR* in her from the *Dalet*, meaning only during the *Lo Matei* in *Hod*, and it was in the *Yesod* without *He'arat GAR*.

Now, however, that it is *Matei He'arat GAR* in *Hod* once more, it no longer needs the *He'arat GAR* in the *Behina* of the *Dalet*. Therefore, it only took the *Behinat Vav* when it rose up there, not the *Behinat Dalet* that surrounds it. You should also know that that *Behina* of *Dalet* ד that surrounds it came down and clothed the *Kli Malchut*.

Now we can thoroughly understand *Sefirat Malchut*. This is because the *Kli* in her is *Kli Malchut*, extending from *Kli de Hod* and the *Ohr* in her is the *Behinat Dalet* ד that surrounds the *Vav* from the *Behinat Hey* that extends from ZON *de Bina*.

However, the *Ohr* of *Malchut* herself is what clothed here in the *Kli* of *Yesod*. For that reason *Malchut* is called *Aspaklaria* that does not shine, as the Rav says above (Part 4).

You find that there are four males and four females in this *Hitpashtut Bet*. The first two couples are ZON *de Keter* and ZON *de Hochma*. The males in them are more important than the females since the *Zachar de Keter* is from *Behina Dalet de Hitlabshut* but the *Nekeva de Keter* is only from *Behina Gimel*.

The *Zachar de Kli de Hochma* is from *Behina Gimel*, but the *Nekeva de Kli de Hochma* is from *Behina Bet*. Thus, the males are greater than the females.

However, in both, the males and females are found in one *Kli*. They are close since the males are from the *Reshimot* that remained after the *Histalkut* of *Hitpashtut Aleph*, hence they are devoid of *Ohr*. The females, however, are from the new, second *Hitpashtut* and are filled with *Ohr*.

However, in the *Zachar* and *Nekeva de Kli de Bina*, the *Nekeva* is greater than the *Zachar*. This is because the *Zachar* is *Behinat VAK de Bina*, hence they are both in one *Kli*, as the *Nekeva* is from the *Reshimo* and lacks *Ohr* and the *Zachar* comes from the *Zivug* of ZON *de Hochma*, hence it is filled with *Ohr*.

Also, though the *Zachar* in *Kli de Keter* is a *Reshimo*, considered devoid of *Ohr*, that absence concerns only its GAR. From the perspective of VAK, however, it is filled with *Ohr*.

Yet, there are many discernments in the *Zachar* and *Nekeva* of the VAK. The *Zachar*, being the *Ohr* ZA, is emanated by the *Hochma*, which is the *Ohr Hesed* in the *Kli de Bina* and then expands to the *Kli de ZA*. The *Nekeva*, however, is a upshot of *Bina*, meaning the *Hey* that was emanated by the ZON of *Bina*.

We must still discern another *Behinat Zachar* and *Nekeva* there, namely the *Zachar* and *Nekeva* in *Yesod* and *Malchut*. There the *Zachar* is smaller than the *Nekeva* since the *Zachar* is the *Behinat Vav* without the *Rosh* inside the *Hey* that extends from the *Zachar* of *Bina*, which is *Behinat VAK*. Nevertheless, they are not in one *Kli* but the *Zachar* is in the upper *Kli*, which is the *Yesod*, and the *Nekeva* is in the lower *Kli*, being *Malchut*.

These two above *Behinot* ZON inside the seven lower *Sefirot* are sometimes considered one, and sometimes two. This is because in *Gadlut*, the *Nekeva* has all the above *Hey* and all the *VAK* are then considered the *Zachar* of that *Hey*.

However, in *Katnut* only the *Yesod* is considered *Behinat Zachar* and then *Malchut* has only the *Dalet* ד in the *Hey* ה, as the truncated *Vav* takes the *Yesod*. There are many changes in that too and this is not the place to elaborate.

We must also note here that there are three divisions in the lower seven, which are *Behinat Rosh, Toch, Sof*. The first are *Hesed* and *Gevura*, which are *Behinat Rosh* of the *VAK*. The second are *Tifferet* and *Netzah*, which are the *Behinat Toch* of the *VAK*. The third are *Hod, Yesod, Malchut*. These are the *Behinat Sof* of the *VAK*.

The matter of *Matei ve Lo Matei* depends only on *Keter* and *Hochma*. This is so because the *Achor de Keter* denies *He'arat GAR* from the entire *Partzuf*, except when *Keter's* dominion is cancelled, meaning by the *Hizdakchut* of the *Aviut* in the *Masach* in it, which belongs to its *Koma*. At that time the *Ohr* departs from *Keter* and its residue is *Matei* in *Hochma* from which appears *He'arat GAR* in the *Partzuf*.

Hence, if *Matei* in *Keter*, *He'arat GAR* is denied even from the *Hochma*. Therefore, at that time the *Behinat VAK* of the seven lower *Sefirot* control, namely the *VAK de Rosh* in them, which is *Sefirat Gevura*.

If *Lo Matei* in *Keter*, at which time *Matei* in *Hochma*, then comes the dominion of the *He'arat GAR* in the *RTS* of the seven lower *Sefirot*, meaning their *Behinat He'arat GAR de Rosh*, which is *Hesed*. Also, their *Behinat He'arat GAR* of their interior, which is the *Tifferet*, their *Behinat He'arat GAR de Sof*, which is *Hod*, from which comes the *Behinat GAR* without the *VAK* to the *Malchut*, called *Dalet* ד over the *Vav* ו in the form of the *Ot Hey* ה.

This *Dalet* ד means cessation of *Ohr* from the *Partzuf*. Because all the *Aviut* in the *Masach* purified and the *Zivug* stopped, there is no *Ohr Hozer* to clothe the *Ohr Yashar* there any longer, and the *Ohr Yashar* stops too. All the *Sefirot* return to the *Maatzil* through *Hitkalelut* of all the *Reshimot* in them within the *Masach*, as the *Masach* ascends to the *Maatzil*.

Now the first Behinot are complete, which is the reality of the Hitpashtut.

This refers to *Hitpashtut Bet*, called *Partzuf AB de AK*.

Thus, all ten Orot reached the Malchut.

It means that the *Hizdakchut* reached *Komat Malchut*. At that time the *Masach* is clean from any *Aviut* from the *Behinat Guf* until its *Tzura* is equal to the *Behinat Masach* of *Malchut* of the *Rosh*. It is considered to have risen there and become incorporated in the *Zivug de Lo Pasik* in the *Malchut* of *Rosh*.

In that state the *Reshimot* of the *Sefirot Guf* contained in it in the full measure of their *Aviut* reawaken, and it thickens once more in the *Aviut* from the *Behinat Guf*. Thus its *Tzura* has been differentiated from the *Malchut* in the *Rosh* once more and it is therefore considered to have departed there and become separated. At that time a *Zivug Elyon* comes out on it, extending a new *Koma* of *Eser Sefirot* to the *Guf*.

It has been explained there that the last *Behina* does not leave a *Reshimo*. Since here the last *Behina* was *Behina Gimel*, you find that *Behina Gimel* did not leave a *Reshimo*, hence it is not contained in the *Masach*.

The greatest *Reshimo* in it is *Behina Bet*. Hence, when the *Masach* regained the *Aviut* through its *Hitkalelut* in the *Zivug* of *Rosh* it could not thicken more than *Behina Bet*. You find that the *Koma* that came out there reached no more than *Komat Bina*. This is the second *Behina* of the *Hitpashtut* of the *Ohr* after its second *Histalkut*.

47. The second *Behina* is simple since now it returned to being *Matei* in *Keter*. At that time it is *Lo Matei* in *Hochma*, *Bina* and *Hesed*, and *Matei* in Gevura. *Lo Matei* in *Tifferet* and *Matei* in *Netzah*, *Lo Matei* in *Hod* and *Matei* in *Yesod*, and *Lo Matei* in *Malchut*, etc. etc.

Ohr Pnimi

47. The second *Behina* is simple since now it returned to being *Matei* in *Keter*.

As has been explained in the previous item, after the second *Histalkut* that was made, the *Masach* with the *Reshimot* contained in it returned to the *Masach* in the *Malchut* of the *Rosh* where a new *Zivug* emerged on that *Masach*. Since all it had is *Aviut* of *Behina Bet*, it extended only *Komat Bina*. This *Komat Bina* expanded once more into the *Guf* to the *Kli de Keter*, and this is *Matei* in *Keter*, meaning the *Ohr Bina* in *Kli de Keter*.

Here too the *Kelim* preceded the *Orot* since all those *Kelim* that remained empty after the second *Histalkut* of *Partzuf AB* passed to this new *Partzuf*. It is written above regarding AB that all the empty *Kelim* that remained after the first *Histalkut* passed to *Hitpashtut Bet*, called AB, and so it is here. Also, all four *Behinot* of *Zachar* and *Nekeva* that were in *Partzuf AB* apply here too, but with a different *Koma* since there is only a small *Koma* here in the *Partzuf* in general.

Let us explain the four couples of *Zachar* and *Nekeva* in this *Partzuf*. That *Koma* of the *Ohr Bina* that descended to the *Keter* is the *Behinat Nekeva* of the *Kli de Keter*.

The *Reshimo* of *Behina Dalet de Hitlabshut* was made into the *Behinat Zachar de Kli de Keter de AB* in *Partzuf AB* (see *Ohr Pnimi* item 6, and all the Rav's words there apply here too). Similarly here, the *Reshimo* of *Behina Gimel* from the *Behinat Hitlabshut* that remained in *Kli de Keter* of *Partzuf AB* was made here into the *Zachar de Keter* of the *Partzuf de Komat Bina*.

It receives from the *Ohr Hochma* that rose under the *Malchut* of *Rosh de AB* during the second *Histalkut* and does not return to the *Guf* of *Partzuf Bina*. In other words, it is exactly like the *Zachar de Keter* of the *Partzuf AB*.

Hence, *Keter* of *Partzuf Bina* too denies the *He'arat GAR* from the *Partzuf* since the *Achoraim* of the *Ohr Hochma* under the *Malchut de Rosh* is below, meaning it does not expand to the *Guf*.

It controls the *Kli de Keter*, which also turns its *Achoraim* below, meaning without expanding to the *Guf*. It controls the *Kli de Keter*, which also turns its *Achoraim* below and illuminates only *He'arat VAK* and denies *He'arat GAR* from the *Partzuf*.

It is written, "**Matei in Keter. At that time it is Lo Matei in Hochma, Bina and Hesed.**" This is because the *Achoraim* of *Kli Keter* deny any *He'arat GAR* from the *Partzuf*, even from the *Kli de Hochma*, much less for *He'arat GAR* of the *Rosh, Toch, Sof* of the seven lower *Sefirot*.

It is written, "**Matei in Gevura. Lo Matei in Tifferet and Matei in Netzah, Lo Matei in Hod and Matei in Yesod, and Lo Matei in Malchut.**" It means that then the *Ohr* comes to the *Kelim de VAK* of the *Rosh, Toch, Sof* of the seven lower *Sefirot*, which are *Sefirat Gevura*, *Sefirat Netzah* and *Sefirat Yesod*.

The *Ohr Lo Matei* in the *Kelim de GAR* of the seven lower *Sefirot*, being *Hesed*, *Tifferet*, and *Hod*. This is so because the *Achoraim de Keter* denies them of *He'arat GAR*, as we have explained.

Etc. etc. When *Lo Matei* in *Keter* since the *Behina Gimel* and *Behina Bet* in it purified and the *Ohr Keter* returned to its place, *Keter*'s power of dominion has ceased. At that time it residue descends to *Hochma* and the *Kelim de He'arat GAR* in the *RTS* of the seven lower *Sefirot*, which are *Hesed*, *Tifferet*, and *Hod*, attain their dominion, and the *Malchut* receives her *Behina* of *Dalet* ד.

Now we shall explain the *Zachar* and *Nekeva de Kli de Hochma*. The *Zachar* and *Nekeva* in the *Kli de Keter* mate and procreate *Zachar* and *Nekeva* in their image. The *Zachar* extends from the *Tzura* of the *Zachar*, meaning *Behinat*

VAK without GAR, since the *Achoraim* of the *Ohr Hochma* that stand under *Malchut de Rosh* is turned down toward the *Ne'etzalim* in the *Guf*.

Hence, the *Zachar de Keter* has only VAK without GAR and for that reason the *Zachar* that is born from him has only VAK without GAR. The *Nekeva de Keter* also administers her *Tzura* to the *Nekeva* that was born from her, which is the *Behinat Ohr Bina*.

After that the *Kli de Keter* purifies and turns its *Panim* downward, meaning it purifies to *Behina Aleph* and gives these three *Orot* to the *Kli de Hochma*. These are the *Zachar*, which is *Behinat VAK de Hochma*, and *Nekeva*, which is *Behinat Ohr Bina* and *Koma* of *Behina Aleph* which is the *Ohr Hesed* that also contains the seven lower *Sefirot*. In other words, it is just as we have explained in the emanation of ZON *de Kli de Bina* in the above *Partzuf AB*.

The only difference is that here the degrees are lower and all the *Behinot Ohr* in the *Kli de Bina de AB* are here in the *Kli de Hochma*, and the *Kli de Bina* is incorporated here with the *Kli de Hochma*. However, *Reshimot* ZON from the time it was in *Partzuf AB* from before the second *Histalkut* did remain in the *Bina*, though not distinguished by a name since they are equal with the ZON in the *Kli de Hochma*.

Also, there was a *Zivug* in ZON *de Kli de Bina* in *Partzuf AB* that procreated one *Hey* that came down with the *Ohr* of the seven lower *Sefirot* until it reached *Yesod* and *Malchut*. The *Vav* in her took the *Yesod* and the *Dalet* in her took the *Malchut*.

In just that manner the ZON in *Kli de Hochma* mated here in *Partzuf Bina* and procreated one *Hey* too, which in turn descended with the ZAT, *Kli* by *Kli* until it reached the *Kelim de Yesod* and *Malchut*. The *Yesod* took the *Vav* in her and *Malchut* took the *Dalet* in her.

Thus we have explained the four males and four females in the *Kelim de Eser Sefirot* of the new *Partzuf* here from *Komat Bina*. This is because the *Zachar* of *Kli de Keter* is *Behinat VAK de Hochma* and the *Nekeva de Keter* is the *Komat Bina*.

The *Zachar* and *Nekeva* in the *Kli de Hochma* are also VAK *de Hochma* to the *Zachar*, and *Komat Bina* to the *Nekeva*. In every place, the upshots are considered *Behinat VAK* compared to their progenitors. Here, however, the *Zachar de Keter* has a great, immense *Ohr*, called VAK *de Hochma* because of the *Achoraim de Ohr Hochma* in the *Rosh* that control it so as to give only VAK.

Hence, its progeny is considered VAK too, like him, since he comes in *Kli de Hochma* that has no *Achoraim*. Also, the *Nekeva* is considered *Komat Bina* as the *Nukva de Keter* that procreated her since she also has a *Reshimo de Komat*

Bina in the *Kli de Hochma* that remained there since the time of the *Hitpashtut AB*. It connects with this *Nukva* and thus she too attains *Komat Bina*. Thus we learn that the *Behinot ZON de Kli* of *Hochma* is *VAK de Hochma* to the *Zachar* and *Komat Bina* to the *Nekeva*, like *ZON de Keter*.

We have already learned that the *ZON de Kli* of *Bina* are the *Behinot* of the *Reshimot* that remained from the time of the previous *Hitpashtut de AB*. They are mixed with the *Zachar* and *Nekeva de Kli de Hochma* since they are close to one another.

The *Zachar* in *ZON de ZAT* is the *Ohr Hesed* that was emanated by the *ZON de Kli de Keter* after their *Hizdakchut* to *Behina Aleph*. The *Nekeva* in the *ZAT* is the above *Hey* that was emanated by the *ZON* in *Kli de Hochma*. This *Hey* was also divided into *ZON*, meaning to *Vav* and *Dalet*. The *Vav* clothed in the *Kli de Yesod* and the *Dalet* in the *Kli Malchut*, and these are the *Behinot* Small *ZON* in the *ZAT*.

You find that all the conducts of emanation present in *Hitpashtut Bet*, called *AB de AK*, were also present in *Partzuf Bina de AK*, only one degree lower. The *Behinat ZON de Hochma de AB* rose in *Partzuf Bina* to *ZON de Keter*. The *Behinat ZON de Bina de AB* rose here to *ZON de Hochma*.

Also, the *Ohr ZA* emanated in *Partzuf AB* from the *Kli Hochma* is emanated from the *Kli Keter* here. In addition, the *Hey* that was emanated from the *Kli Bina* in *Partzuf AB*, is emanated here from the *Kli de Hochma*, etc. similarly.

All this stems from the general decline that was here when *Hochma* remained in the *Rosh* and only *Ohr Bina* came to clothe in the *Guf*. You find that *Ohr Bina* clothed *Kli de Keter* and *Ohr ZA* came to *Kli de Hochma*, meaning after the *ZON de Keter* purified to *Behina Aleph*. *Ohr Malchut* is in *Kli de Bina* since that *Hey* that was emanated from the *Hochma* came to the *Kli de Bina* and from there expanded to the *ZAT*.

Now we shall explain the order of *Matei ve Lo Matei*, practiced in *Partzuf Bina de AK*, also called *Partzuf SAG de AK* and the matter of *Matei ve Lo Matei* that is permanent in this *Partzuf*. We have already explained the order of the first *Hitpashtut* of this *Partzuf* (*Ohr Pnimi* item 47).

We learned there that when *Komat Bina* expanded to the *Partzuf* and *Ohr Bina Matei* in *Kli de Keter*, the *Ohr* reaches all the *Kelim* of the dominion of *VAK* in the *Partzuf* according to their impressions during *Hitpashtut Bet* before its *Histalkut*.

This is so because these are the very *Kelim* that had come into that *Partzuf Bina*. Hence, the *Ohr* reached the three *Kelim de Behinat Achoraim* in the *Rosh*, *Toch*, *Sof* in *ZAT*, which are *Gevura*, *Netzah*, *Yesod*.

Their *He'arah* continues until the *ZON de Kli de Keter* purified to *Behina Aleph* and these *ZON* rose to their *Shoresh*. At that time *Matei* in *HB* to the *Zachar*, meaning in the *ZON* in *Hochma* and *Bina*, which are *Behinat VAK de Hochma*, and *Behinat Komat Bina* to the *Nekeva*.

Then *He'arat GAR* reaches the *Partzuf* and *Matei* in all the *Kelim de Panim* present in the *RTS* in the *ZAT*. These are *Hesed, Tifferet, Hod*, and the fourth *Ohr* to *Malchut*.

We could say that *Lo Matei* in *Hochma* before the *Kli de Keter* purified to *Behina Aleph*, at which time it turned its *Panim* and gave the *Ohr Hesed* to the *Kli de Hochma*. Thus, *ZON de Hochma* too should have lessened to *Behina Aleph*.

The thing is that the *Kli de Keter* dispensed the *ZON* to *Kli de Hochma* from *Behinat He'arah* before it purified to *Behina Aleph* [as the Rav wrote regarding the *Zachar de Kli de Bina* that was emanated from the *Kli de Hochma* during *Hitpashtut Bet* (item 38 and *Ohr Pnimi* there)].

Only after the *ZON* descended to the *Kli* of *Hochma* did the *Kli de Keter* purify and lowered *Behina Aleph*, meaning the *Ohr Hesed*, to the *Kli* of *Hochma*. Now there are three *Orot* in this *Kli*, which are *Zachar*, in *VAK de Hochma*, *Nukva* in *Komat Bina*, and *Ohr Hesed*, which is the *Ohr ZA*.

You also know that *ZON de Hochma* mated and procreated *Hey* ה, which is the *Behinat Nekeva* to the *Ohr Hesed* that came to *Kli de Bina*. At that time the *ZON de HB* purified from *Behina Bet* to *Behina Aleph* and turned their *Panim* downward, as with *Hitpashtut Bet*, giving the *Ohr Hesed* with the above *Hey* to the *Kli de Hesed*.

After that *Gevura* rose to the *Kli de Hesed* and the *Kli de Gevura* turned its *Panim* downward, giving her residue in *He'arat GAR* to the *Tifferet*. Then *Lo Matei* in *Netzah* since it rose to the *Tifferet* and turned its *Panim* down, giving its residue to *Hod* in *He'arat GAR*. After that *Lo Matei* in *Yesod* since it rose to *Hod*, at which time *Yesod* turned its *Panim* and gave its residue to *Malchut*, which is the *Dalet* ד of the above *Hey* ה.

You should also remember what the Rav wrote above that the *Kelim* illuminated for each other before they turned their *Panim* to give the *Orot*. This is because they are all on an even *Koma*.

This means that they gave the *Hey* ה that was born from the above *Zivug ZON* to each other before they turned their *Panim*. Only *Bina* could not give the above *Hey* to *Hesed* before she turned her *Panim*. This is so because there is a difference of *Koma* between the *Bina* and the *Kli de Hesed*; one is *GAR* and the other is *VAK*.

This is not so between the *Kelim de ZAT* themselves, whose *Koma* is even (see item 38). Therefore, after the above ה reached the *Kli de Hesed*, the *Kli de Hesed* gave it to the *Kli de Gevura* before she turned her *Panim* downward.

Hence, afterwards, when she turned her *Panim* downward, she gave the above ה along with her residue to the *Kli de Tifferet*. *Kli de Tifferet* gave the above ה to *Kli de Netzah* before it turned its *Panim* downward.

Afterwards, when the *Kli de Netzah* turned its *Panim* downward, it gave the above ה to *Kli de Hod*, along with its residue. Similarly, *Kli de Hod* gave the ה to the *Kli de Yesod* before turning its *Panim* down. Afterwards, when it turned its *Panim* downward, it gave the *Dalet* ד of that ה to the *Kli de Malchut*.

You already know the two matters regarding the turning of the *Panim* downward (see *Ohr Pnimi* item 40, paragraph, "You must remember"). The first is from the *Behinat Kli*. It turns the place of her administration from *He'arat VAK* to *He'arat GAR*, or vise versa. The second is from the *Behinat Masach*, where its greater *Aviut* is the *Behinat Panim*, and the lesser *Aviut* is the inverting of the *Panim*.

In all the *Kelim de ZA*, whose *Koma* is even from *Behina Aleph*, the turning of the *Panim* in them is only from the *Behinat Kelim*. Still, the *Masach* did not purify during the turning of the *Panim*, except in the turning of the *Panim* in Yesod.

In that state the *Masach de Behina Aleph* had already purified to *Komat Malchut*. Thus, after the *Ohr* of the *Dalet* ד reached *Malchut* as well, *Malchut* too purified and the entire *Aviut* ceased in the *Masach*.

In that state the *Zivug* had been cancelled and all the *Ohr* departed from the *Partzuf*. Then all the *Orot* rise in *Behinat MAN* to the *Kli de Keter*, to the ZON de *Keter* there, and then their *Masach* thickens to *Behina Bet* once more.

It mates with the *Ohr Elyon* once more and once again extends *Komat Bina*, as in the beginning. *Ohr Bina* is then *Matei* in *Kli de Keter*, and is *Matei* in *Gevura*, *Netzah* and *Yesod* as well. It is not *Matei* in *Hochma*, *Bina*, and *Hesed*, *Tifferet*, *Hod*, and *Malchut*.

After that the *Masach de Behinat ZON de Keter* purifies once more and then *Matei* in HB, *Hesed*, and *Tifferet*, in *Hod* and in *Malchut*. It is *Lo Matei* in *Keter*, *Gevura*, *Netzah*, and *Yesod*.

Since it is *Matei* to *Malchut*, the *Zivug* stops, and the *Orot* depart and rise to *Kli de Keter* as MAN to the ZON there. *Komat Bina* extends to the *Keter* once more and it is once more *Matei* in *Keter*, *Gevura*, *Netzah*, *Yesod*, and *Lo Matei* in *Hochma*, *Bina*, *Hesed*, *Tifferet*, *Hod*, and *Malchut*, and so on and so forth.

This is so because thus the *Orot* always turn in this *Partzuf*, once in *Keter, Gevura, Netzah, Yesod*, and once in *Hochma, Bina, Hesed, Tifferet, Hod*, and *Malchut*. They are like candlelight, swaying here and there.

The reason for it is that the *Masach de Behina Bet* is a frail *Masach*, as it is *Behinat Achoraim de Bina* to the *Hochma*. It sucks its power from there, as you already know that the *Behinat Achoraim de Bina* on the *Hochma* is rooted back in *Bina* of the *Ohr Yashar*. It turns backwards to *Hochma* and extends *Hassadim* from *Keter* in the form of *Yod* י and *Nun* נ of the *Tzadik* צ, which are opposite to one another.

For this reason the craving for *Hassadim* was imprinted in *Bina*, to prefer the *Ohr Hassadim* to the *Ohr Hochma*, as it is written, "because He delighteth in mercy," as the Rav says above (item 43). Hence, after the *Zivug* is made on the *Masach* of *Behina Bet* and the *Ohr* expands to the *Partzuf*, *Bina* already has *Ohr Hassadim* abundantly.

At that time the *Masach* weakens and purifies because the *Achoraim de Ima* on the *Hochma* cancel too. Though she prefers *Ohr Hassadim* to *Ohr Hochma*, it is only when there is a need for *Ohr de Hassadim*. However, after there is *Ohr Hassadim* abundantly, she turns herself back to the *Ohr Hochma* and cancels her *Achoraim*.

Naturally, the *Masach* that is supported by these *Achoraim* gradually purifies as well, until it purifies into *Behinat Keter*. At that time the *Zivug* stops, and when the *Orot* depart from the *Partzuf* and their *Reshimot* ascend to *Kli de Keter*, contained in the purified *Masach*, *Bina* feels the lack of *Hassadim* once more and her *Achoraim* return to *Hochma*, to its place.

In that state the *Masach* of *Behina Bets* there thickens once more by the force of the *Achoraim de Bina*, and the *Zivug* returns once more, extending the *Koma de Behina Bet*. The abundant *Ohr de Hassadim* returns to the *Partzuf* and *Bina* annuls her *Achoraim* over *Hochma* once more.

After that the *Masach* purifies once more, until it purifies entirely. *Ohr Hassadim* ceases once more and the craving *Reshimot* again rise to *Behinat MAN* to the *Kli de Keter*. She feels the lack of *Hassadim* once more and returns her *Achoraim* to *Hochma*, at which time the *Masach* thickens to *Behina Bet* once more and mates with the *Ohr Elyon* and so on and so forth like a swaying candlelight.

It has now been explained how the *Matei ve Lo Matei* in this *Partzuf* is fixed and always existing. The *Koma de Behina Bet Matei* to the *Kli de Keter, Netzah* and *Yesod* also *Matei* in *Gevura*. These are *Behinat Ohr Hassadim* without

He'arat GAR, but it is in great abundance since they extend from the *Kli de Keter*.

For that reason *Bina* cancels her *Achoraim* and the *Masach* purifies. At that time *Matei* in *Hochma*, *Bina* and *He'arat GAR* reaches the *Partzuf*, and *Matei* in the *Kelim de Panim* as well, which are *Hesed*, *Tifferet*, and *Hod*, until *Matei* in *Malchut*.

At that time the *Aviut* of the *Masach* ceases and the *Zivug* stops. The *Masach* with the *Reshimot* of the *Orot* rises to *Kli de Keter* because of the *Hishtavut Tzura*.

In that state *Bina* feels the lack of *Hassadim*, returns her *Achoraim* to *Hochma* as in the beginning and the *Masach* thickens to *Behina Bet* once more and mates with the *Ohr Elyon*. *Ohr Bina* is *Matei* to the *Kli de Keter* once more; it is again *Matei* in *Keter*, *Gevura*, *Netzah*, and *Yesod*, and *Lo Matei* in *Hochma*, *Bina*, and *Hesed*, *Tifferet*, *Hod*, and *Malchut*, and so on and so forth.

48. Now there are several *Behinot*: The first is the unending craving of the *Ohr* of the *Tachton* to cleave to the *Elyon*. When there is *Matei* in *Yesod* there is *Lo Matei* in *Malchut* since then the *Ohr Malchut* ascends there in *Yesod* because of the craving.

    It is similar in all the other *Sefirot* except the *Hesed* with the *Bina*. This is because when there is *Lo Matei* in *Bina*, there is *Lo Matei* in *Hesed*, due to the two distances. When it is *Matei* in *Bina*, it is also *Matei* in *Hesed*, as *Ohr Hesed* is not equal to the entire *Ohr Bina*.

    However, that one moment when *Bina* descends to her place, she finds *Hesed* in her place and *Hesed* descends to his place instantly. This is the meaning of the VAK being a degree in and of themselves and cannot cleave to *Bina*, which is from GAR.

    The matter of *Matei ve Lo Matei* in GAR is also a different matter. This is because when it is *Matei* in *Keter*, both *Hochma* and *Bina* rise up in *Keter*. For that reason the GAR are regarded as one.

    When *Lo Matei* in *Keter*, then *Matei* in *Hochma*. *Bina* should remain there and be *Lo Matei* in *Bina*. However, "because He delighteth in mercy," it is *Matei* in *Bina* too.

49. You should also know that the measure of time of *Lo Matei* in the *Sefira* is only one moment. This is the meaning of, "For His anger is but for a moment."

    It is so because the *Histalkut* of the *Ohr* when it is *Lo Matei* was because of the wrath and also because the *Tachtonim* do not have the strength.

However, the continuation of *Behinat Matei,* which is the return of the *Ohr* below to revive the *Olamot,* has no measure since it will be according to the act of the *Tachtonim.*

This is the meaning of, "life in His will," according to the desire that will then be, meaning according to the act of humans, so will the stretch of these lives be. Indeed, we have explained above that the first *Histalkut* of the *Orot* was in order to make a *Kli.*

Now that the *Orot* returned a second time in *Hitpashtut Bet,* the *Kelim* were annulled as in the beginning. Hence, the first *Ohr,* being *Ohr Keter,* had to have remained above in all of them and not permeate these *Kelim.*

Thus, only nine *Orot* came in this order, *Ohr Hochma* in the *Kli* of *Keter,* and *Ohr Bina* in the *Kli* of *Hochma,* etc. similarly. Finally, *Ohr Malchut* permeates *Kli Yesod.*

Now the first *Ohr* did not return to the *Kli* that concerns it, which first departed from it. Instead, a different, smaller *Ohr* came in its place. Hence, the *Kelim* remained as *Kelim;* they did not return to being *Orot,* as before.

When the *Orot* began to enter the *Kelim,* the nine *Orot* entered *Keter,* which is the *Ohr Hochma.* This is called *Matei* in *Keter.* After that the *Ohr* that reaches *Keter* departed, namely *Ohr Hochma,* and this is called *Lo Matei.* We should not elaborate in that since we have already elaborated sufficiently in *Behinat Matei ve Lo Matei.*

Yet, the reason that all nine *Orot* entered the *Kli* of *Keter* together in *Hitpashtut Aleph* is that one entered the other. *Ohr Malchut* entered the *Kli* of *Keter.* Afterwards this *Ohr* was pushed down to the place of *Hochma.* Then *Ohr Yesod* entered *Keter* etc. similarly.

Finally, all ten *Orot* entered in the amount of the ten *Kelim.* The reason is understood with the above. In the beginning, when *Ohr Keter* was with them and they all illuminated from its side, none of those *Kelim* had the strength to receive inside, but only one *Ohr.*

Now, however, when *Ohr Keter* did not enter the *Kli,* but remained above and turned its Achoraim downward, because of that there is now strength to instill all the *Orot* together into one *Kli.* This is so because all nine *Orot* that now enter *Keter,* are smaller than the first *Ohr Keter* and there is ability to receive them.

Also, when all eight *Orot* entered *Kli de Hochma,* it has the power to receive them, as they are all smaller than *Ohr Hochma,* etc. similarly in all of them.

Ohr Pnimi

49. The measure of time of *Lo Matei* in the *Sefira* is only one moment.

This means that the length of time of the departure of the *Ohr* from the entire *Partzuf* is a moment, meaning the time for the ascents of the *Orot* to MAN to the *Kli de Keter*, to the ZON there. It is so because at that time there is no *Zivug* in the *Partzuf* since the *Masach* purified from its entire *Aviut*. For that reason it is considered a time of wrath.

He thus tells us that the matter of *Matei ve Lo Matei* in the *Partzuf* sways here and there incessantly since at the moment of *Lo Matei* in *Malchut*, the *Orot* rise to ZON *de Keter* and the *Achoraim de Bina* return to their place at once. Then the aviut *de Behina Bet* returns and the *Ohr* of *Komat Bina Matei* to the *Keter* at once.

Thus, this whole thing is like candlelight, swaying here and there. This is because the darkness that is made in the *Partzuf* during the ascent of the *Orot* to MAN and before the *Zivug* is made, is very short.

Because of the wrath and also because the *Tachtonim* do not have the strength… in order to make a *Kli*.

All of these three reasons are one thing. This is the meaning of what our sages wrote, "In the beginning, it came up in the thought to create the world in *Midat ha Din*; He saw that the world does not exist, He brought *Midat ha Rachamim* and associated it with *Midat ha Din* (Part 4, Chap 1, Ohr Pnimi item 4).

It means that the *Shoresh* of *Midat ha Din* is *Behina Dalet*. This is what emerged first, in *Hitpashtut Aleph*, when there was only one *Kli* of *Malchut* there from the *Behina* of *Aviut de Behina Dalet*. This is the meaning of, "came up in the thought to create the world in *Midat ha Din*.

However, he saw that the world does not exist, that there is no force in the *Tachtonim* to receive the *Ohr* from this hard *Mida* (the noun of *Midat*). Hence, he associated *Midat ha Rachamim* with it, which is the *Behinat Bina*, called *Midat ha Rachamim* in all the places.

This is implied in the Zohar (Ruth) relating to the verse, "So they two went," which are the two *Heyin* of the Name *HaVaYaH* that were contained as one. It explains that the first *Hey* is the Name *HaVaYaH* is *Behinat Bina*, and the last *Hey* of the Name *HaVaYaH* is the *Behinat Malchut*. They were associated together for the purpose of correcting the world, meaning *Midat ha Rachamim* with *Midat ha Din*.

This association did not occur at once, but bit-by-bit, in the order of the concatenation of the *Partzufim* and the degrees. This work was done entirely by the *Histalkut* of the *Orot*.

It is so because during the first *Histalkut* the *Masach* of *Behina Dalet* had already began to mingle in the first nine *Sefirot* through its ascent from degree to degree until it reached the *Maatzil*. Also, most of the force of the *Din* disappeared from the *Masach* there since *Behina Dalet* did not leave a *Reshimo* for the *Hamshacha* of the *Orot*.

That became the *Shoresh* of the division of the degree to *Zachar* and *Nekeva*, since only half a *Reshimo* of *Behina Dalet* returned for *Hitpashtut Bet*, meaning the *Reshimo de Hitlabshut*. This became the *Behinat Zachar de Kli de Keter* of *Hitpashtut Bet*, and it is indeed considered half a thing since it lacks the *Behinat Hamshacha* of *Orot*.

For this reason it has become obligated to complete the degree of *Behina Gimel* in *Behinat Hamshacha*. Note, that the rule that a *Zachar* without a *Nekeva* is half a *Guf* extends from here.

Afterwards, in the second *Histalkut*, the *Reshimo* of *Hamshacha de Behina Gimel* disappeared as well, and only *Behina Bet* remained, though the *Zachar* of *Behina Gimel* from *Behinat Hitlabshut* participated with her in *Kli de Keter*. This association extends here too in all the couples of *Zachar* and *Nekeva* in this *Partzuf Bina*.

However, it still could not be finished before the elicitation of *Bina* outside GAR and the coming to *Behinat VAK*. This matter was prepared by the *Matei ve Lo Matei* that sways in this *Partzuf Bina*, as it is written in its place.

At that time *Olam Nekudim* came out, where the *Bina* emerged from *Behinat GAR* to *Behinat VAK*. Yet, there was the breaking of the vessels and the matter was ended in *Olam ha Tikun*, in *Olam ha Atzilut*, where the complete association of *Midat ha Rachamim* with *Midat ha Din* emerged.

Thus you see how the *Matei ve Lo Matei* in this *Partzuf* is the origin of the association of *Midat ha Rachamim* with *Din*. He says that the matter of the *Histalkut* of the *Ohr* that always sways because of the *Matei ve Lo Matei* is "because of the wrath," meaning due to the force of the *Din* in *Behina Dalet*, and the world does not exist in it.

This is so because the *Tachtonim* do not have the strength, which is also the same, meaning that the world cannot exist in it. It is "in order to make a *Kli*," meaning so that the *Atzmut* can clothe in it in a way that there will not be *Hizdakchut* and *Histalkut Orot* any more.

This was made only at the completion of the association of *Midat ha Rachamim* and *Midat ha Din* together, and not before. This is so because until then the *Orot* were departing in each *Partzuf* and the *Kelim* were not fit for their task. He writes, "in order to make a *Kli*." Thus, all these three reasons that the Rav mentions are one thing.

The act of humans, so will the stretch of these lives be.

Note that this does not refer to the order of the emanation of the *Partzufim* from above downward since there are still no people here who can corrupt or correct. Instead, this refers to the time after the four *Olamot* are proper. At that time the actions of the *Tachtonim* can prolong the Upper Life in this *Partzuf*, or shorten it.

The good deeds draw increased *Shefa*. Also, it is known that any *Hidush* of administration must extend from *Ein Sof*. Thus, if one causes a renewal of administration in one's actions, it extends from *Ein Sof*, travels through *Olam ha Tzimtzum* and from there to the first *Partzuf de AK*. From there on to the second *Partzuf de AK* and from there to this third *Partzuf*, where the matter of *Matei ve Lo Matei* is set. From here on to the rest of the degrees in the four *Olamot ABYA*, reaching this world to be received by Man.

Hence, if the act is complete, you find that the *Shefa* travels through this *Partzuf Bina* and sways there in a way of *Matei ve Lo Matei*. When the time of *Matei ve Lo Matei* reaches that degree to which the *Shefa* is ascribed, it does not move from there quickly, but stretches the time.

By that the *Shefa* extends the time of reception when it reaches a person in this world too. This is called that one's life is prolonged. If, however, the act is flawed, the *Shefa* sways through there very quickly because when the *Shefa Matei* in the designated degree, it does not extend time. Instead, it immediately comes to a state of *Lo Matei*.

Thus, when the *Shefa* reaches a person in this world, he unable to keep it, but only to a very short time. This is the meaning of the wicked being "of few days, and full of trouble." However, here we must remember the meaning of time in spirituality as it has been explained in the end *Histaklut Pnimit* Part 1.

50. ***When the *Orot* reenter, *Ohr Hochma* enters in *Keter*. At that time the *Ohr Keter* inside it, which remained during the *Histalkut* since the *Kli* is not completed before the *Ohr* drifts three degrees away from it, and this does not apply to GAR, then the *Ohr Keter* that remained there inside the *Ohr Hochma* now enters and clothes inside it.**

It becomes a *Neshama* to it since it is the *Ohr Keter* and becomes *Dechura* while the *Hochma* around it becomes *Nukva*. At that time the selected *Ohr* clothes inside *Hochma* and what slightly darkened due to the distance of the *Orot* from there will remain as *Kli*.

It is so for two reasons: A – because of the distancing of the *Ohr* from there, which induces darkness to it. Moreover, even the best of it leaves and clothes inside the *Ohr Hochma* that enters there.

At that time the first *Ohr* that remains from *Keter* is deducted and becomes a *Kli* for *Keter* since the *Ohr Hochma* severs them. Thus, on the contrary, the coming of the *Orot* in their current *Hitpashtut* is the cause of the making of the *Kli* in these *GAR*. The *Kelim* were not made during their *Histalkut*.

There is yet another reason: The *Ohr* of *Behinat Keter* remained above since it never again entered these *Kelim*, but only remained at the end of these *Yod Shorashim* or *Orot* above. It turned its *Achoraim* downward, hence the *Orot* are now fewer than in the beginning, even during the *Histalkut*.

It is similar in the second *Kli* of *Hochma* that *Ohr Bina* entered inside it. At that time the *Ohr Hochma* clothes inside it and the *Ohr* that remains darkens and becomes a *Kli* because of its distancing, though it is not complete remoteness.

Now there are *Zachar* and *Nekeva* in the *Keter* together and *Zachar* and *Nekeva* in *Hochma*. You find that *Keter* and *Hochma* are never cancelled from existence and make females from males since their *Orot* themselves remain in their place, though they are not as complete as in the beginning. Moreover, the rest of the *Orot* that have now come, are added to them and become females to them.

Ohr Pnimi

50. **Three degrees away from it, and this does not apply to GAR.**

    It has already been explained above in *Ohr Pnimi* regarding the Rav's words (item 27) that there are two necessary conditions to complete the *Kli*. The first is completing the outer half of the wall. This is discerned as the place to receive the *Ohr Makif*.

    Since there is no *Ohr* that does not have *Pnimi* and *Makif*, there is also no *Kli* that does not have a *Kli Pnimi* and *Kli Hitzon*, qualified to receive the two *Behinot* in the *Ohr*. Hence, the Rav calls them two halves of the wall (see

Part 4, Chap 5, item 5), since it is a necessary condition in the wall of the *Kli*, meaning as a qualification of the *Kli* to receive any *Ohr* within. This is the first condition.

The second condition is that at one time it will be empty of any *Ohr*, even *Behinat Ohr Makif*, as it is the *Histalkut* of the *Ohr* that makes it a *Kli*.

For this reason the *Kelim* that were made in *Hitpashtut Aleph* were only for the ZAT, which are ZON since *Malchut* attained the inner NRNHY in completeness during the *Hitpashtut*. Hence, when she rose to ZA, she acquired the first *Ohr Makif* and when she rose to *Bina* she attained the second *Ohr Makif*. When she rose to *Hochma* she no longer received any *Ohr*, as the Rav says (Part 4, Chap 6, item 15).

Hence, when she drifted three degrees away from her *Kli*, namely *Hochma*, *Bina*, and ZA, and came to *Hochma*, the two above conditions were completed, as she had already attained the outer half of the wall to receive the two *Makifim*. After that she does not receive any *Ohr*, hence her *Kli* is completed.

However, the ZA is not finished before it comes to the *Maatzil* because when ZA ascends to *Keter*, it receives the second *Ohr Makif* there. For that reason there is no longer complete *Histalkut* of the *Ohr* from its *Kli*. Afterwards, when it departs from *Keter* too and comes to the *Maatzil*, its *Kli* darkens and ends.

However, the GAR, which are KHB, did not receive any *Makifim* there in *Hitpashtut Aleph*. Also, the *Ohr* did not stop entirely from them since even when the *Bina* comes to *Keter* she still receives her *Behinat* inner *Yechida*. For this reason they lack the two conditions and that is why they were not made into *Kelim* to the GAR in that *Hitpashtut Aleph*.

The selected Ohr clothes inside Hochma and what slightly darkened due to the distance of the Orot from there will remain as Kli.

This means that the *Reshimo* consists of *Ohr* and *Kli* like the collective *Ohr* from which it remained. You already know from the Rav's words above (Part 4, Chap 6 item 2) that before it departed in *Hitpashtut Aleph*, the two *Orot* were mixed with the *Kelim*, and there is no discrimination of a *Kli* there.

Hence, the other *Reshimot* that remain of these *Orot* too, were also mixed of *Ohr* and *Kli* together (see Part 4, *Histaklut Pnimit* item 48). It is all the more so in the *Kelim de GAR* as even the *Kelim* themselves are still not considered *Kelim*.

Hence, now the *Orot* returned in *Hitpashtut Bet* and came *Zachar* and *Nekeva* in *Kli de Keter*. The *Zachar* is from the *Behinat Reshimo de Ohr Keter de Hitpashtut Aleph*. The *Reshimo* is divided into two *Behinot Ohr* and *Kli* in it.

The best in it, the *Behinat Ohr*, becomes the *Behinat Ohr* of the *Zachar de Kli de Keter*, and the worst in it, the *Behinat Kli* that was mixed in it, departs from it because of the *Ohr Hochma* that clothed that *Kli de Keter* too. Since the *Ohr Hochma* clothed in the *Kli* of the *Reshimo* the *Hochma* separates between the *Ohr* of the *Reshimo* and its *Kli*. At that time the *Kli* darkens and the *Behinat Kli* ends in it, as the Rav says.

Their current *Hitpashtut* is the cause of the making of the *Kli* in these GAR.

This is so because the *Ohr* of *Hochma* that clothed the *Kli de Keter* separated between the *Ohr* and the *Kli* of the *Reshimo*, which weakens the *Reshimo* of *Hitpashtut Aleph* too. As long as the *Reshimo* is complete, the *Kli* is strengthened by the *Reshimo* in it even after the *Ohr* drifts three degrees away from it.

However, now the *Behinat Reshimo* too has weakened after the *Behinat Kli* has been deducted from it. By that it also attains the *Behinat* outer half of the wall, since the *Kli* consists of the *Behina Gimel* too because of her clothing of *Ohr Hochma*, which is *Behina Gimel*, being *Behinat Hitzoniut* to *Behina Dalet*.

Similarly, the *Kli de Hochma* of *Hitpashtut Aleph* that *Ohr Bina* clothes, attains half of its outer wall since *Ohr ZA* is *Behina Aleph*, being *Hitzoniut* to *Behina Bet*. Thus, the *Kelim de GAR* were made by the current *Hitpashtut* and the *Etzem* of the *Hitpashtut* causes them to be made into *Kelim*.

The Rav gives three reasons here regarding the completion of the *Kelim de GAR*:

1. Due to the exit and distancing of the best *Ohr* of the *Reshimo* from the worst, most *Av Ohr* in it. Hence, the *Ohr Av* of the *Reshimo* became a complete *Kli*.

2. The coming of a new *Ohr* of *Hochma*, clothing that *Ohr Av* of the *Reshimo* which comes between and separates the best *Ohr* of the *Reshimo* from the most *Av Ohr* of the *Reshimo*. This makes the *Av Ohr* a complete *Kli*.

3. Because of the *Achoraim* of the *Ohr Keter* that remains standing in the *Rosh* and did not expand to the *Guf* once more in this *Hitpashtut Bet*. These *Achoraim* lessen the *Ohr GAR* even more than it was during the departure itself. Thus, it darkens the *Kelim* more than a distance of three degrees and therefore they have not become *Kelim* during the making of the *Achoraim* of the *Kelim* under the *Malchut* of the *Rosh*.

Zachar and Nekeva in the Keter together and Zachar and Nekeva in Hochma.

The *Reshimo de Keter de Hitpashtut Aleph* has become the *Zachar de Keter*, and the *Reshimo de Hochma* of *Hitpashtut Aleph* has become the *Zachar de Hochma*.

Also, *Ohr Hochma de Hitpashtut Bet* that comes anew has become the *Behinat Nekeva de Kli de Hochma*.

51. It is the same matter in *Bina* too, except there is a difference in her, which is that some *Ohr Bina* remains in her during the *Histalkut*, and now *Ohr Hesed* enters her.

    It is known that *Hesed* is the son of *Bina* and it cannot be the *Zachar* while the *Ohr Bina* itself a *Nekeva* to it. If we say that the *Ohr Bina* will be a *Zachar* and the *Ohr Hesed* will be a *Nekeva*, that too is impossible.

    This is why that turning *Panim be Panim* that we described above is needed. When the eight *Orot* are given to her, *Hochma* turns her *Panim* downward and the *Zachar* and *Nekeva* of *Hochma* mate there in their place.

    They educe one *Ohr* through their *Zivug*, called *Yod*, which is then dispensed below by turning their *Panim* to *Bina*. At that time that *Yod* clothes inside the *Ohr Bina* as the others did, the *Yod* becomes a *Zachar*, and the *Bina Nukva*.

    Afterwards, when the seven *Orot* are placed in the *Kli* of *Bina*, the *Ohr Hesed* is placed in her and the *Ohr Hesed* remains in her in *Behinat MAN* permanently.

Ohr Pnimi

51. That the *Ohr Bina* will be a *Zachar* and the *Ohr Hesed* will be a *Nekeva*, that too is impossible.

    This is so because the *Eser Sefirot* are discerned as two males, being *Hochma* and *ZA*, and two *Nekevot* (pl. for *Nekeva*), which are *Bina* and *Malchut*. *Zachar* means *Hitpashtut* of *Ohr* and *Nekeva* means reception of *Ohr*.

    Your sign is that the *Zachar* faces downwards to dispense to the *Tachtonim*, and the *Nekeva* faces upward, to receive. This relationship is rooted back in the *Eser Sefirot* of *Ohr Yashar* since *Keter de Ohr Yashar* is the *Shoresh* and the first *Hitpashtut* from the *Shoresh* is *Ohr Hochma*. The second *Hitpashtut* is *Ohr de Hassadim*, meaning the *ZA*, and they are both discerned as *Zecharim* (pl. for *Zachar*).

    Bina is the *Nekeva* of *Hochma*, and *Malchut* is the *Nekeva* of the *ZA*. He writes that it cannot be said that *Ohr Bina* will be a *Zachar* and *Ohr Hesed* will be a *Nekeva*. This is so because the nature of the *Orot* is opposite at their *Shoresh*: *Ohr Hesed* is *Zachar*, meaning *Ohr ZA*, and *Ohr Bina* is *Nekeva*, as we have explained.

Hochma* turns** her *Panim* downward etc. This has already been explained above (*Ohr Pnimi* item 35, sub header "Hochma***") and study it there.

Mate etc. one *Ohr* through their *Zivug*, called *Yod*.

Regarding this *Zivug* see *Ohr Pnimi* item 35. Although this *Zachar* comes from the *Zivug de HB*, it is considered their *Behinat VAK* where each upshot is regarded as *VAK* of its progenitors. However, since it is *VAK de Hochma*, which is *Yod* י, its own value is also considered *Yod*. However, a true *Behinat VAK* is always named in *Vav* ו.

That *Yod* clothes inside the *Ohr Bina*.

This means the reshimot that remain in the *Kli de Bina* from the time of *Hitpashtut Aleph*, after the *Ohr Bina* departed from there. It is so because all the *Orot* left *Reshimot* there in their *Kelim* during their *Histalkut* from them, as the Rav says above (Part 4, Chap 2 item 2), and that *Reshimo* in *Kli de Bina* became the *Behinat Nekeva* to the י.

52. This *Ohr* of *Bina* is among the first *Orot* that remained there, and this *Yod* that it came into from the *Zivug de ZON* inside *Hochma* is renewed. Hence, how will *Bina*, which is the *Shoresh*, become a *Nekeva* to this renewed *Ohr*, which is from *Hochma*?

The answer is that we have already explained that this *Ohr* of *Bina* is not a great *Ohr*, since there are three distances between it and the *Ohr*, though they are not three complete distances. It is not so in the *Hochma* above.

In addition, this *Ohr Bina* remained here during the *Histalkut*, when his intention was not to shine, but the Upper *Nukva* in *Hochma* intended to shine at the time of the *Hitpashtut*. Hence, the son, begotten by both can be more interior than this *Bina*, much less form the *Hesed* that now came, though it too is from the *Behina* of *Hitpashtut*. However, it is still three degrees below *Hochma*.

Ohr Pnimi

52. **This *Ohr* of *Bina* is among the first *Orot* that remained there.**

It means that this is what remains of the *Orot* of the first *Hitpashtut de AK*, as mentioned in the previous item.

53. Generally speaking, there is *YH* in *Keter*, which is *ZON*, *Keter* and *Hochma*. In *Hochma* there is *ZON*, and this is another *YH*, and it is *HB*. In *Bina* there is another *YH*, which is *ZON*. It is the renewed *Hochma* from the *Zivug Elyon* in *ZON* in *Hochma*, which is *Yod*. The *Bina* is

Nekeva to him and it is the *Ot Hey*. Thus there are YH here as well. There is also *Ohr Hesed* in her, which is *Behinat* son.

In addition, every one of these GAR is called *Ot Yod* in the filling. The *Keter* contains *Yod YH*, and the *Kli* itself is the *Dalet* of the *Yod*. *Hochma* too contains *Yod*, which is YH, ZON, and the *Dalet* is the *Kli*.

However, *Bina* is called *Yod* in the *Behinat* three *Orot* in her, ordered as YDV, and they are *Hochma, Bina*, and *Hesed*. Yet, the *Kli* is not mentioned here.

There is yet another reason why the drop of *Yod* from the *Zivug Hochma* is the husband of this lower *Bina*: Since when ZON in *Hochma* mate, they do not educe that drop from her *Atzmut*, but from above, meaning from the *Keter*. This is why his force is greater than the *Ohr* of the lower *Bina*.

Ohr Pnimi

53. *Bina* is called *Yod* in the *Behinat* three *Orot* in her, ordered as YDV.

    The *Zachar* is named *Yod* after the *Hochma*, being her upshot. The *Nekeva*, which is *Bina*, with the *Ohr Hesed* in her, is the *Hey* ה. The *Ohr Hesed* is considered the *Vav* ו in the *Hey* and the *Bina* is considered the *Dalet* ד that surrounds the *Vav*. This is so because it is the *Behinat* GAR of that *Vav*.

54. However, there was no existence of ZON in the rest of the *Sefirot*, as they are all males, and they are also complete *Kelim*. Only that *Ohr* that has reentered is present.

    Thus, the *Ohr* of *Gevura* entered in *Hesed* and etc. similarly until you find that the *Ohr* of *Malchut* is in *Kli* of *Yesod*. Here there is also a first question: How will a *Zachar* be turned into a *Nekeva*?

    Know, that this is why ZON in *Bina* had to mate and educe one *Hey* in its mold. It was divided into two, which are DV, and the *Ot Vav* entered the *Kli Yesod*, as a *Zachar* of *Malchut* there, since this *Ot Vav* is several degrees higher than the *Ohr Malchut* in *Yesod*.

    This is why they are ZON. Afterwards, the *Ot Dalet* descended in *Malchut* and completed there in her place. Thus, there are ZON in the *Dalet Behinot*, which are KHB *Yesod*. This is the reason for the above question in these four, unlike in the others.

Ohr Pnimi

54. *Ohr* of *Malchut* is in *Kli* of *Yesod*.

    After the *Behina Aleph* of the *Ohr Hod* had purified into *Behinat Keter*, meaning extending only *Komat Ohr Malchut*, the *Ohr* was given to the *Kli* of *Yesod*.

This is why he writes, "**Ohr of Malchut is in Kli of Yesod**" (see above *Ohr Pnimi* item 45).

Vav entered the Kli Yesod, as a Zachar of Malchut there, since this Ot Vav is several degrees higher.

This *Vav* ו is from *Komat Behina Aleph*. After *Bina* purified into *Koma de Behina Aleph*, the above *Hey* ה to the *Kelim de VAK* along with the *Ohr Hesed*.

Hod too gave the above *Hey* ה to the *Yesod* as mere *He'arah* and not through the *Hizdakchut* of *Behina Aleph* (see the Rav's words item 43). After the *Hod* illuminated the *Hey* in it, it purified into *Komat Malchut* and gave this residue to the *Yesod*.

Thus, the ו from the ה that took the *Yesod* has *Koma* of *Behina Aleph*, like the ZA. Hence, it is the *Zachar* of the *Kli de Yesod* to the *Ohr* of *Komat Malchut* in it, which is the *Nekeva* in it.

He writes, "This *Ot Vav* is several degrees higher than the *Ohr Malchut* in *Yesod*." The first is that it is *Komat Behina Aleph*, and the second is that it comes from the *Zivug* of *ZON de Bina*.

55. *We have already explained that there are five **Orot** in two **Kelim**. This is because there is **ZON** in the **Kelim** of **Hochma** and there is **ZON** in the **Kli** of **Bina**, and a son, which is the above **Hesed**.

These ascents depend on the actions of the ***Tachtonim***. Sometimes all five *Orot* ascend, and sometimes only four ascend and the *Ohr Hesed*, which is a son, remains below in the *Kli* of *Bina*.

We have explained above that there is ZON in each of these GAR. They are called **YH**, *Yod* in the *Zachar*, and *Hey* in the *Nukva*.

Know, that when all these five *Orot* rise in *Keter*, they are sometimes incorporated in the ***Nukva***, and sometimes in the ***Dechura***. Sometimes some of them are in *Nukva* and some of them in the *Dechura*. Know, that when only four *Orot* ascend, they always incorporate only in the *Nukva*.

Ohr Pnimi

55. **There is ZON in the Kli of Bina, and a son, which is the above Hesed.**

The *Zachar* is the *Yod* that was born by the *ZON de Kli de Hochma*, and the *Nekeva* is the *Reshimo* that remained in the *Kli de Bina* from the time of *Hitpashtut Aleph*. The son there is the *Ohr Hesed* that dispensed *Hochma* to the *Kli de Bina* after *ZON de Hochma* had purified to *Behina Aleph* (see item 51).

These ascents depend on the actions of the *Tachtonim*.

When *Lo Matei* in *Hochma* and *Bina* because they purified to *Behina Aleph* and *Komat HB* disappeared from the *Partzuf*, HB rise to the *Keter*. Through their ascent to ZON *de Keter*, they induce the return of the *Aviut* of *Behina Gimel* to the *Masach de ZON de Keter*.

At that time they mate with the *Ohr Elyon* once more and once more extend *Komat Hochma* as in the beginning (see *Ohr Pnimi* item 36). It is similar in the second *Behina* of the *Hitpashtut*, meaning *Partzuf Bina de AK*.

When *Lo Matei* in *Hochma*, *Bina*, and *Hesed, Tifferet, Hod,* and *Malchut* (see *Ohr Pnimi* item 47, par. "You already know the two matters"), all the *Orot* rise to the *Keter*, to the ZON there. This causes the return of the *Aviut de Behina Bet* to the *Masach* there.

Then *Komat Bina* emerges once again as in the beginning on these two kinds of ascents, namely the ascents of *Hitpashtut Bet*, called *Partzuf Hochma de AK*, and the ascents of the second *Behina* of the perpetual *Hitpashtut* in *Matei ve Lo Matei*, called *Partzuf Bina de AK* (see the Rav's words item 47). Al the words of the Rav before us revolve around that. Regarding his statement that they are dependent on the actions of the *Tachtonim*, that has been explained above (*Ohr Pnimi* item 49, subsection **"The act of humans"**).

Sometimes all five *Orot* ascend, and sometimes only four ascend and the *Ohr Hesed*, which is a son, remains below in the *Kli* of *Bina*.

It is so because only four *Orot* rise in *Partzuf Hochma*, which are ZON *de Kli de Hochma*, and ZON *de Kli de Bina*. But, the *Ohr Hesed* that contains the entire ZAT does not ascend throughout the rest of *Hitpashtut Bet* of the first *Behina* until the completion of that *Hitpashtut* (see item 46 and *Ohr Pnimi* item 47).

In this manner, only the four *Orot* in HB rose to *Keter* throughout all exits and entrances. It is so because only *Behina Bet* purified and her *Koma* disappeared in the *Shoresh* in *Keter*.

Yet, *Behina Aleph* did not purify but only at the end of the *Hitpashtut*, which is only at the coming of the *Orot* to *Yesod* and *Malchut*. At that time the perpetual *Hitpashtut* of *Matei ve Lo Matei* begins, called *Partzuf Bina*.

Five *Orot* ascend in this *Partzuf* since here too the *Ohr Hesed* that contains the whole ZAT rises to *Keter*. This is so because here the *Matei ve Lo Matei* applies perpetually, because every time it *Matei* to *Malchut*, it is after the *Hizdakchut de Behina Aleph*.

When *Malchut* too purifies, all the *Orot* rise to *Keter*. Thus, every time it is *Lo Matei* in the *Malchut*, the five *Orot*, which are ZON *de HB*, and the *Hesed* that contains ZAT, rise to the *Keter*. He writes that sometimes four *Orot* rise, meaning in *Partzuf Hochma*, and sometimes five *Orot* ascend, meaning in *Partzuf Bina*.

Only four *Orot* ascend, they always incorporate only in the *Nukva*.

You know that there are *Zachar* and *Nekeva* in the *Kli de Keter*. There are two *Kelim* in *Partzuf Hochma de AK*, which is *Hitpashtut Bet*, one for the *Zachar* and the other for the *Nekeva*. Hence, when the *Orot* rise to the *Keter*, they all come, meaning the four *Orot*, to the *Kli* of the *Nekeva* since she receives them for MAN within her, but not the *Zachar* since all the ascents for MAN are only to the *Nekeva*.

However, when five *Orot* rise, it is depicted only in a *Partzuf* where there is perpetual *Matei ve Lo Matei*. Every *Lo Matei* in *Malchut*, all the *Orot* rise to MAN to the *Keter*, meaning the *Hesed* too.

Since there is not more than one *Kli de Zachar* in *Partzuf Bina*, the *Nukva* too clothes the *Kli de Zachar*. Hence, the *Orot* must ascend to the *Kli de Zachar*, since the *Nukva* is there too.

56. We shall now explain this division, and say, that before these *Orot* rise above to be incorporated in the *Keter*, the name **YH** in the *Keter* is *Pashut* without filling. Yet, there will be filling in them when these *Orot* ascend upwards.

There are three fillings, in *Yodin*, in *Heyin*, or in *Alephin*. When only four *Orot* ascend, they are all incorporated in the *Nukva*, which is the *Hey* of the name **YH** in the *Keter*. At that time the filling of that *Hey* is in *Yod*, like this: **HY**.

Ohr Pnimi

56. **The name YH in the Keter is *Pashut* without filling.**

It is so because the *ZON de Keter* purified from the *Behina Gimel* in them, the *Zivug* stopped, the *Komot* of the *ZON* departed to their *Shoresh*, and only the *Reshimot* of ZON remained in *Kli de Keter*. At that time they are considered a simple name **YH**, without the filling in them, meaning the measure of *Aviut* that extends the measure of their *Koma* and fills them with their *Ohr*.

In *Yodin*, in *Heyin*, or in *Alephin*.

The *Aviut de Behina Gimel* that extends *Komat Hochma* is called "filling of *Yodin*". *Aviut de Behina Bet* that extends *Komat Bina* is also called "filling of *Yodin*", except the *Aleph* in the *Vav* in it, such as this *Yod* יוד, *Hey* ה', *Vav* ואו, *Hey* ה'. The *Behinat ZA* is *HaVaYaH* in filling of *Alephin*, and the *Behinat Malchut* is *HaVaYaH* in filling of *Heyin*.

When only four *Orot* ascend, they are all incorporated in the **Nukva**, which is the *Hey* of the name **YH**.

It means that the *Kli de Nukva* is the *Hey* ה *de YH*, because only the *Kelim* are called *Otiot* and not the *Orot* themselves, and remember that (see the Rav's words in Part 4, Chap 3, item 12). The fulfillment of that *Hey* is in the *Yod*, like this: הי. It is so because the *Aviut de Behina Gimel* is called *Yod*.

It has been explained above (*Ohr Pnimi* item 40) that because of the ascent of the *Zachar de Hochma* from *Aviut de Behina Gimel*, the *Nukva de Keter* returns and receives this *Aviut de Behina Gimel* in her *Masach*. It follows that the *Hey*, which is *Nukva de Keter*, is filled with *Yod*.

57. The thing is that when four *Orot* ascend in the *Nukva* the lower three are cancelled in the first, since *Ohr Hochma* always cancels the others, and then all three are annulled in the *Ot Yod* י, which is the *Hochma*. This is why the filling of this *Hey* ה is with *Yod* י.

Ohr Pnimi

57. *Hochma* always cancels the others, and then all three are annulled in the *Ot Yod* י.

It means that *Komat Hochma* contains within it all the other lower *Komot*, as the Rav says above (item 37): "We have a great rule in our hands: the *Elyon* is greater than everything below it." Thus, each *Koma* is named only after its highest *Sefira*.

58. However, know that **ZON** in the *Keter* rise above in their *Shorashim*, which is the meaning of *Lo Matei*. At that time the nine *Sefirot* in each of them rise, and two *Malchuyot* (pl. for *Malchut*) remain below, the *Zachar Malchut* and the *Nekeva Malchut*. They are called **YH** since they are *Pshutim* (pl. for *Pashut*), without filling.

Ohr Pnimi

58. Two *Malchuyot* (pl. for *Malchut*) remain below, the *Zachar Malchut* and the *Nekeva Malchut*. They are called **YH** since they are *Pshutim* (pl. for *Pashut*), without filling.

This means that the *Reshimot* that remain from the *Orot* ZON after their departure are the *Behinot Malchut* of the ZON. This is because a *Reshimo* is considered *Behinat Malchut* of the *Ohr* that departed and they are simple, without filling, meaning the measure of *Aviut* in the *Masach* that extends the measure of the *Koma*. Since their measure of *Aviut* has purified, the *Orot* departed, and this is why they are simple.

59. Yet, you should know that then the two *Melachim* are equal. Although the *Zachar* is greater than the *Nukva*, still, now they are equal since the *Behinat Ohr Zachar* is in the form of *Histalkut*, as mentioned above. When these *Orot* wanted to depart in order to make a *Kli*, these *Orot* remained in *Keter Hochma Bina*, as we have said above, I wish to say the *Reshimot*.

It turns out, that the *Ohr Zachar* of the *Keter* is in the form of *Histalkut*, the *Ohr Nukva* in the *Keter* is in the form of *Panim*, and hence the *Ohr Zachar* and the *Ohr Nekeva* are equal this time. Moreover, since the *Zachar* left itself outside, under the *Shorashim*, the *Zachar* has a great craving to ascend once more, which is not so in the *Nukva*.

Hence, almost all the *Ohr Zachar* rises upwards and only very little *Ohr* remains. Yet, because the *Nukva* does not have a *Shoresh* above like the *Zachar* in the *Keter*, she does not have such a craving and desire to rise, and most of the *Ohr* remains in her *Kli*.

For that reason they cannot be equal, the two *Malchuyot* together, *Zachar* and *Nekeva*. Yet when they return, the *Zachar* comes with all its *Ohr* and also takes a great *Ohr* from the *Shoresh* of *Keter* above it. Thus, when they return, the *Nukva* cannot receive the entire *Ohr* of the *Zachar*, only the VAK.

60. In order to understand that, there is one thing you must know first, and this is it: There is a difference between the first time in *Atzilut* and the time that follows. The first time in all of them is when the *Ohr Zachar* of *Keter* remains during the first *Histalkut*.

Afterwards, in *Hitpashtut Bet*, when the *Hochma* enters the *Kli* of *Keter*, it does not enter the *Kli* of the *Zachar*, but only enters in the *Kli* of the *Nekeva* itself, which is the *Hey* of the YH. Thus ZON are in two *Kelim*.

However, in *Histalkut Bet*, when both ZON rose up and equalized together, they all received *He'arah* from the *Keter Elyon* together. Hence, when they come and return in their *Kelim*, both enter the *Kli* of the *Zachar* and the *Malchut* of the *Nukva* remains in her *Kli* of Hey ה.

Ohr Pnimi

60. There is a difference between the first time in *Atzilut* and the time that follows.

It has been explained above that first the *Ohr* expanded in *Matei ve Lo Matei* in ten exits and ten entrances of all ten *Orot* until it came to the *Malchut*. After that it became *Matei ve Lo Matei* a second time, perpetual. This means that every time the *Hitpashtut* reaches *Malchut* it returns.

It has been explained that the first *Behina*, meaning the *Matei ve Lo Matei* that reached the *Malchut* once, is called *Partzuf Hochma de AK*, or *AB de AK*. The perpetual *Matei ve Lo Matei* that goes back and forth is another *Behina*, called *Partzuf Bina de AK*, or *SAG de AK*.

He writes, "There is a difference between the first time in *Atzilut*," meaning the *Matei ve Lo Matei* once until it reaches *Malchut*. "The time that follows" means the *Matei ve Lo Matei* after it reached the *Malchut* in the first time, which is the perpetual *Matei ve Lo Matei*.

The first time in all of them etc. are in two Kelim etc.

It is so because these two *Kelim* of *Zachar* and *Nekeva* emerged right at the time of the coming of the *Ohr* back to the *Partzuf* by the double *Haka'ot* (pl. for *Hakaa*) of the *Reshimo* that remains in *Keter* to the *Ohr* that comes to the *Partzuf* anew.

The Rav explains (Part 4, Chap 4, item 6) that a small *Ohr* does not strike a bigger *Ohr*. Still, because there is merit in the *Ohr Hochma* that comes anew from above unlike the *Reshimo*, whose *Zivug* and her *Ohr* have already departed, the *Hochma* can strike the *Reshimo* and educe *Nitzotzin* from her.

Yet, this reason is sufficient only for the *Ohr Hochma*. Because of its coming anew from the *Zivug* above, it thus equalizes with the *Reshimo* whose *Zivug* has already departed.

However, this is not enough for *Partzuf Bina de AK* since although *Ohr Bina* came anew, its power is still not enough to strike the *Reshimo* and educe *Nitzotzin* for the *Kli*. For that reason a *Kli* for the *Nekeva* was not made here, but it is clothed in the *Kli de Zachar* that remains of the previous *Hitpashtut Bet*.

Furthermore, the Rav has already written (Part 4, Chap 3, item 10) that the whole reason for the beating of the *Orot* on each other is only between two opposite and contradicting *Orot* in their nature. The *Reshimo de Keter* prevents *He'arat GAR* because of the *Achoraim de Ohr Keter* that stands at the *Rosh* (see *Ohr Pnimi* item 40, paragraph "The *Masach de Keter* purified"). Also, the whole *He'arah* of *Ohr Hochma* is only *Behinat GAR*, as it is written there.

Since they are divided in their nature, they beat on each other. However, in *Partzuf Bina*, whose *Reshimo* remains from the *Ohr Hochma de Hitpashtut Bet* and the *Ohr* that comes anew is the *Ohr Bina*, it is known that *Hochma* and *Bina* are not in disparity of nature. On the contrary, *AVI* stay as one (as the Rav says in item 39).

Hence, there is no *Hakaa* between the *Reshimo* and the *Ohr Bina*, there are no *Nitzotzin* for new *Kelim* from the *Nekeva*, and for this reason, the *Nekeva* clothes in *Kli de Zachar*. This does not contradict what the Rav wrote above (item 3), that the *Ohr Hochma* clothed in the bad *Ohr de Reshimo de Keter* and the *Ohr* of the *Reshimo de Keter* inside *Hochma*. Thus, the *Ohr Hochma* and the *Reshimo* have only one *Kli*, while here he says that they have two *Kelim*.

The thing is that they clothe each other like the particular degrees in the *Partzufim* of *Atzilut*. This means that the *Kli de Hochma* clothes in *Kli de Keter*, and the *Ohr Av* of the *Reshimo* clothes inside *Kli de Hochma*. *Ohr Hochma* clothes inside the *Ohr Av* of the *Reshimo* and the selected *Ohr* of the *Reshimo* clothes inside the *Ohr Hochma*.

In *Histalkut Bet*, when both ZON rose up etc. both enter the *Kli* of the *Zachar*.

The *Histalkut* of the *Matei ve Lo Matei* of the first time is called *Histalkut Bet*. This is because *Partzuf Keter de AK* is *Hitpashtut Aleph*, and the *Histalkut* of *Partzuf Keter* is called *Histalkut Aleph*. *Partzuf Hochma de AK* is *Hitpashtut Bet* and the *Histalkut* of *Partzuf Hochma* is called *Histalkut Bet*.

As in the first *Histalkut*, the Rav explained above (item 6) that prior to *Hitpashtut Bet*, the *ZON de Keter* rose up, being the *Reshimo de Behina Dalet de Hitlabshut* and the *Reshimo de Behina Gimel*. There, both received *He'arah* from the *Keter Elyon*.

Similarly, in the second *Histalkut*, prior to the *Hitpashtut* of *Partzuf Bina*, the two *Reshimot* rose. These are the *Reshimo de Behina Gimel* of *Hitlabshut* and the *Reshimo de Behina Bet*, which are *Behinat ZON de Keter de Partzuf Bina*.

Both of them rose to the *Malchut de Rosh* and there received *He'arah* from the *Keter Elyon* together. Through this *He'arah*, the *Nekeva* acquired *Hishtavut* with the *Zachar*, and for that reason the *Nekeva* could clothe the *Kli* of the *Zachar*.

61. **This is always so after the first time since the ZON always remain in the *Kli Zachar* and mate there together. It turns out that the *Yod*, which is the *Kli* of the *Zachar*, were both ZON.**

When they mate, the *Nukva* does not tolerate the *Ohr Zachar*, except from its VAK. Two sons stem from the *Zivug* of these ZON that were incorporated in the simple *Ot Yod*, following their example. They are the VD (Vav Dalet) filling of *Yod*.

Ohr Pnimi

61. **The *Nukva* does not tolerate the *Ohr Zachar*, except from its VAK.**

This is because the *Ohr Hochma* remains in the *Rosh* under the *Malchut* because its *Achoraim* is below and prevents *He'arat GAR* from the *Keter de Guf* (*Ohr Pnimi* item 40, par. "We must understand that thing.").

There it explains it regarding *Partzuf Hochma*, and the same applies in *Partzuf Bina* as well. This is because there is one reason for both: Since the *Ohr* that remains in the *Rosh* cannot expand to the *Guf* by itself. Although its *Reshimo* shines in the *Guf*, such a *He'arah* is still considered to be through the *Achoraim*, preventing *He'arat GAR*. This is why he says, "the *Nukva* does not tolerate the *Ohr Zachar*, except from its *VAK*."

Two sons stem from the *Zivug* of these *ZON* that were incorporated in the simple *Ot Yod*, following their example. They are the *VD* (*Vav Dalet*) filling of *Yod*.

It means that as the ZON *de Keter* in the *Partzuf Hochma de AK* emanated the ZON to *Kli de Hochma* of that *Partzuf*, so here the ZON *de Keter* in *Partzuf Bina* educed the ZON to the *Kli Hochma* here, through their *Zivug* together. The difference is in the measure of the *Koma*, since in *Partzuf Hochma* the ZON *de Kli de Hochma* are regarded as YH (see the Rav's words item 53).

Here, however, there is only *Behinat Ohr Bina* even in ZON *de Keter*. Hence there is no longer *Behinat GAR* in the ZON *de Hochma* that were emanated by their *Zivug*, but *Behinat VAK de GAR*. This is because it is similar to the ZON *de Kli de Bina*, emanated from the ZON *de Hochma* in *Partzuf Hochma de AK*.

It is so because the *Komat ZON de Keter* of *Partzuf Bina* is equal to the *Komat ZON de Hochma* in *Partzuf Hochma de AK* (see *Ohr Pnimi* item 47, par. "Now we shall explain"). For that reason the *Zachar* in *Kli de Hochma* here is not called *Yod*, but *Vav*, since the *VAK* is always called *Vav*. He writes that they are VD in filling of *Yod*, like the ZON in *Bina de Partzuf Hochma*.

62. The thing is that since the *Zachar* does not mate in the *Nukva*, only in the form of its *VAK*, its son is in the shape of *Vav* as well. Yet, the *Nukva* is the shape of *Dalet*, since she has all the *Yod Kelim*, except her *Ohr VAK* is annulled in her first four, hence the name *Dalet*. Thus, the filling of *Yod*, which is *VD*, and all this, is called *Yod*, which are ZON.

Afterwards she is the *Ot Hey* of the YH, which is the *Kli* of the *Nukva*, and *Malchut* of the *Nukva* remains there. When the four lower *Orot* rise in this *Ot Hey*, it is filled with the *Ot Yod*, and becomes *Hey* ה, though the shape of this *Hey* is such as this VD, hence it is ten.

Ohr Pnimi

62. The *Zachar* does not mate in the *Nukva*, only in the form of its *VAK* etc. is in the shape of *Vav* etc. the *Nukva* is the shape of *Dalet*.

This is so because the *Zachar* extends from a *Zachar* which is *Behinat Ohr Hochma*. However, since it does not mate for these ZON, but from the *Behinat VAK* in it, the *Zachar* has only *VAK de Hochma*. For this reason it is called *Vav* ו.

The *Nekeva* extends from the *Nukva de Kli de Keter*, which is the *Komat Bina*. It is called *Dalet* ד because although it has GAR, its VAK are contained in the GAR.

Thus, the filling of *Yod*, which is VD.

This explains the matter of the ascents of the *Orot* of *Partzuf Bina*. It states that if five *Orot* ascend, they all ascend to the *Zachar*. It has been explained that the reason is that the ZON in this *Partzuf* have only one *Kli*, which is a *Kli de Zachar*, called *Yod* י.

It has also been explained that all those five *Orot* that rose to *Kli de Keter* are incorporated in the *Orot Elyonim*, which are ZON de *Hochma*, called *Vav* ו *Dalet* ד. We have also learned that this is the meaning of the VD in filling of *your*, since when they rise to the *Kli de Zachar*, called *Yod*, and the ascending *Orot* are called VD, the *Zivug* returns to the *Partzuf*.

This is the deduction that he wanted to teach to us in this study. Below he will also bring the ascents of *Partzuf Hochma* to the *Kli de Nukva* of the *Keter*.

When the four lower *Orot* rise in this *Ot Hey*, it is filled with the *Ot Yod*.

This refers to the conclusion from the second division, when four *Orot* ascend, meaning in *Partzuf Hochma*, when they rise to the *Nukva de Kli de Keter*.

It has been explained that the *Kli* of the *Nukva de Keter* is called *Hey* ה and the *Orot* that ascend to it are its filling, since they return the *Zivug Elyon* to her.

This explains why these four *Orot* are called *Yod*, named after the highest *Sefira* in these *Orot*, which is the *Behinat Zachar* of the *Kli de Hochma* (being *Behina Gimel* and *Ohr Hochma*, extending to ZON de *Hochma* through a *He'arah* from ZON de *Keter*). It is called *Yod*, and all the *Orot* incorporate in it. Hence, this ה is filled with the *Ot Yod* י and becomes HY.

The Rav speaks above (item 55) of three divisions regarding the ascents of the *Orot* and their incorporation in ZON de *Keter*: The first, when they rise and incorporate in the *Nukva de Keter*, the second, when they incorporate in the *Dechura de Keter*, and the third is when some incorporate in the *Nukva*, and some in the *Dechura*. Only the first two divisions have been explained here, and he did not explain to us the third division at all.

However, he has already explained that third division to us (item 7), as that is where he began to talk of these three kinds of *Hitkalelut*. He mentions three general kinds there:

1. When the ZON incorporate in one another in one *Kli*.
2. When their *He'arot* mingle in one another when they are in two *Kelim*.
3. When they incorporate in one another when they are two *Orot* without *Kelim*.

The meaning of the words is as written above.

The first incorporation is that the ZON are incorporated in one *Kli*, meaning in *Partzuf Bina de AK*, where there is no *Hakaa* of *Reshimo* and the *Ohr Bina* on each other. For this reason the *Kli* for the *Nekeva de Keter* did not emerge. Thus, the *Nekeva* clothes in the *Kli de Zachar*.

The second incorporation is that the ZON have two *Kelim*. It is in *Partzuf Hochma de AK* where there is *Hakaa* of the *Reshimo* and the *Ohr Hochma* on each other. Two *Kelim* emerge, one for the *Zachar* and one for the *Nekeva*.

The third incorporation is when *Lo Matei* in *Keter*, and the ZON themselves rise to the *Malchut* of the *Rosh*. At that time they expand and exit their *Kelim de Guf*. They are two *Orot* without *Kelim*.

The Rav did not explain the first two incorporations at all because he relied himself on what has been elaborately explained here, because these are the first two incorporations that have been thoroughly explained before us. The third division is what he did not explain here, being the third incorporation there, which the Rav explained extensively above.

He explains there that the ZON that rose to the *Rosh* have two *Zivugim* there: the first *Zivug* is when the *Nekeva* is incorporated in the *Zachar*. That *Zivug* comes out on *Aviut* of *Behina Dalet*, at the measure of the *Zachar*. At that time they extend the *Ohr* in *Komat Keter Elyon*.

The second *Zivug* is when the *Zachar* is incorporated in the *Nekeva* and the *Zivug* comes out on the measure of *Aviut* of the *Nekeva*, meaning *Behina Gimel*. Then the *Ohr* is extended only at the level of *Komat Hochma* (see there and in *Ohr Pnimi* item 9).

It has been explained there (*Ohr Pnimi* item 6) that in this ascent of the ZON to the *Rosh*, all the *Sefirot* below *Keter* are also included. However, they are all annulled in the ZON de *Keter*, hence they do not merit a name.

Here, all five *Orot* in the *Partzuf* rose, and the *Ohr Hesed*, which contains the ZAT, was included in these ZON. At that time all five *Orot* are somewhat incorporated in the *Kli de Nekeva*, and somewhat incorporated in the *Kli de Zachar*.

In other words, when the *Nekeva* incorporates in the *Zachar* and the *Zivug* is made in the *Behinat Zachar*, the five *Orot* are incorporated in the *Zachar*. In the second *Zivug*, when the *Zachar* is incorporated in the *Nekeva* and the *Zivug* is made in *Behinat Nekeva*, the five *Orot* are also contained in the *Nekeva*. Thus, the five *Orot* are somewhat incorporated in the *Zachar*, by the first *Zivug*, and somewhat in the *Nekeva*, by the second *Zivug*.

The shape of this Hey is such as this VD, hence it is ten.

This is because there is a *Hey* ה whose shape is *Vav* ו *Dalet* ד, and there is a *Hey* ה whose shape is *Yod* י *Dalet* ד. He says that the *Hey* that implies the *Nekeva de Keter* has a shape of ו ד, which is ten in *Gimatria*, indicating that this *Hey* has ten *Kelim*. It means that all *Eser Sefirot* of the *Koma* are contained in the *Hey*, as he has written above that the entire new *Koma* that came out in *Hitpashtut Bet*, which is the *Komat Hochma*, is the *Behinat Ohr Nekeva de Keter*.

Additional Explanation about the Matter of the Inversion of the Panim and the Making Order of the Kelim

Brought here from item 15 to item 20 in the Rav's words

Although matters are clear enough in their place in *Ohr Pnimi*, I still find that the readers become confused. It is hard for them to arrange the matters and understand the Rav's words there.

It is so because here we must remember the matters of the *Histalkut* of the *Ohr*, and the matter of the *Hizdakchut* of the *Masach* separately, as well as the separate matter of the inversion of the *Panim de Kelim*. On top of that, we must remember the picture of the *Kelim*, each of them in itself.

The making of the *Kelim* is done only after the *Histalkut* of the last *Ohr* from the *Kli*, as the Rav says in item 27. He says: "Know, that all these *Kelim* did not gain *Aviut* and become *Kelim* only after the *Histalkut* of *Ohr Malchut*. At that time He turned His *Panim* from the *Kli*." Thus, the matter of the inversion of the *Panim de Kelim* begins in each and every *Kli* from the time of the *Histalkut Ohr Malchut* from it.

You already know the attribute of the *Kelim*, that each and everyone must have a *Behinat Aviut* that is adequate to its *Komat Ohr* as the *Kli* is only named after the highest *Sefira* in its *Koma*. If the highest *Sefira* is *Hochma*, it is called merely a *Kli* of *Hochma*, though all the *Sefirot* below *Hochma* are necessarily there. Similarly, if the highest *Sefira* is *Keter*, it is only called *Kli de Keter*, etc. similarly.

You also know the measure of the *Aviut* in each *Kli* necessary for the measure of its *Koma*. The *Kli de Keter*, in which there is *Komat Yechida*, must be in a *Kli* of *Aviut de Behina Dalet*. If the *Masach* on the *Aviut de Behina Dalet* in the *Kli* purifies, the entire *Ohr Keter* immediately disappears from there, as it is only *Ohr Yechida*. However, it contains all the *Orot* below this *Ohr*.

Moreover, had the *Kli* itself been lacking this *Aviut de Behina Dalet*, it would not have been qualified to receive the *Masach de Behina Dalet* at all. Thus, it is certain that it is not at all *Kli de Keter* that is arranged only according to the *Aviut* in it.

It is likewise in all the *Kelim*, and this is simple since there is the *Behinat Aviut* in the *Kli* itself, at which time we are talking about the *Masach*. However, if the *Kli* itself is missing, the *Masach* will not be able to complete it, since *Masach* means a detainment on a certain measure of *Aviut* in the *Kli*.

You also know that the matter of the *Aviut* in the *Kli* and the matter of the *Hitlabshut* of the *Ohr*, are two opposites. For example, *Kli de Malchut* has *Aviut de Behina Dalet*. Yet, it is unfit to clothe the *Komat Yechida* for that, since she lacks the *Behinat Hitlabshut* of that *Koma*, which is *Kli Keter*.

It follows, that the distinction between the *Kli de Keter* and the *Kli de Malchut* is in that the *Kli de Keter* has *Behina Dalet de Hamshacha*, as well as *Behinat Keter de Hitlabshut*. Conversely, the *Kli Malchut* has only *Behina Dalet de Hamshacha*, but is devoid of *Behina Dalet de Hitlabshut*, meaning *Behinat Kli Keter*.

Similarly, the difference between *Kli de Hochma* and *Kli de ZA* is that *Kli de Hochma* has *Behina Gimel de Hamshacha*, and also *Kli de Hochma*, being *Behina Gimel de Hitlabshut*. However, *Kli ZA* has only *Behina Gimel de Hamshacha*, and only *Kli de ZA* from *Behinat Hitlabshut*. It is fit to clothe only *Komat Ruach*, which is the *Koma de Behina Aleph*, lacking the *Behina Gimel de Hitlabshut*.

Now you understand that when the *Ohr* departs from *Malchut* because the *Masach de Behina Dalet* purified, and *Malchut* rises to ZA, in fact, only the *Ohr Yechida* departed from the *Partzuf*, from the *Kli* of *Keter*. This is because now it lacks the *Behinat Hamshacha*.

However, the *Ohr Malchut* did not leave at all, since it rose to *Kli de ZA*. Nonetheless, by that only *Kli de Malchut* was made, not the *Kli de Keter*.

This is so because *Kli Malchut* remained entirely without *Ohr*. However, *Kli de Keter* still has *Ohr*. Although it is *Ohr Hochma*, which is much lower than its *Behina*, it is not considered sufficient *Histalkut* to turn its *Panim* downward.

It will make a *Kli* only after *Ohr Malchut* departs from the *Kli de Keter* too, as the Rav says above. Hence *Malchut* alone becomes a *Kli* since she is completely without *Ohr*.

Also, when, for example, *Ohr Malchut* departed from ZA and rose to *Bina*, the *Kli de ZA* turned its *Panim* downward even though the *Ohr ZA* has not yet departed, since it rose to *Bina*, but the *Ohr Hochma* has now departed from the *Kli Hochma*. Nevertheless, *Hochma* did not become a *Kli*, only ZA was made into a *Kli* since only ZA has now been left without *Ohr*, while in *Kli Hochma* there is still *Ohr Bina* there etc. similarly.

It therefore follows, that after all the *Orot* have departed from the *Partzuf*, all the *Kelim* remained *Panim de Tachton* in *Achor de Elyon*, except the *Kelim* de *Keter* and *Hochma*, which remained *Panim be Panim*. It is so because then all the *Kelim* returned their *Panim* as in the beginning and the *Panim de Kli Malchut*, which is *Behina Dalet*, are found opposite the *Achor de Kli ZA*, which is *Behina Bet*.

Also, the *Panim de Kli ZA*, which is *Behina Gimel* is opposite the *Achor de Kli de Bina*, which is *Behina Aleph*. The *Panim de Bina*, which is *Behina Bet* is opposite the *Achor de Hochma*, which is *Behina Bet* too, but the *Keter* keeps its *Panim* below since it cannot return its *Panim* as in the beginning since the *Reshimo de Behina Dalet* disappeared.

For this reason it remained in *Behina Gimel* below, opposite *Hochma*, whose *Panim* is also *Behina Gimel*. Thus, *Keter* and *Hochma* are found to be *Panim be Panim*.

We must also understand that the matter of the measurements of *Koma* that extend according to the *Aviut* in the *Masach*, are arranged according to the measure of the *Hitlabshut* of the *Sefirot de Ohr Yashar*.

For example, when it states *Komat ZA*, it refers to the measure of *Ohr* that *Behina Gimel de Ohr Yashar*, named ZA, can receive inside it, which are two *Orot*, *Ruach Nefesh*. Also, when it talks about *Komat Behina Bet*, meaning the measure of *Hitlabshut* in *Behina Bet de Ohr Yashar*. Also, *Komat Hochma* is as the measure of the *Hitlabshut* of *Hochma de Ohr Yashar* etc. similarly.

Table of Questions for Topics

43. What is *YH* in *Keter*, *HaVaYaH* in the rest of the *Partzufim*?
44. Why do the four *Otiot HaVaYaH* imply discernments of lacks?
45. What do the *YV de HaVaYaH* imply?
46. What do the *Hey Hey de HaVaYaH* imply?
47. Why are the *Shorashim* of the *Sefirot* in *Malchut* of the *Rosh*?
48. Where does the *Ohr Keter* that did not expand to the *Guf* stand?
49. What is the function of the *Ohr Keter* that did not return to the *Guf*?
50. Why must the *Kelim de Guf* receive the *Orot* through the *Ohr Keter*?
51. What is the meaning of the location of the *Ohr Keter* under *Malchut de Rosh*?
52. What is the inversion of the *Panim de Ohr Keter* to the *Shorashim* and its *Achoraim* to the *Anafim*?
53. What is the sufficient *Yenika* of the *Orot*?
54. What is sufficient *He'arah* to generate offspring?
55. What causes the *Ohr Keter* to return its *Panim* to the *Anafim*?
56. What causes the *Ohr Keter* to return its *Achoraim* to the *Anafim*?
57. How will the *Sefirot de Guf* generate changes in the *Rosh*?
58. What are *ZON de Keter de Hitpashtut Bet*?
59. What causes *ZON* to rise to *Malchut* of the *Rosh*?
60. What is a sufficient reception for *ZON* from the *He'arat Rosh*?
61. What is the result of the ascent of *ZON* to the *Malchut* of the *Rosh*?
62. Why are all the *Eser Sefirot* of *Histalkut Aleph* that rose to the *Rosh* called *ZON de Keter*?
63. How do the *Reshimo de Keter* connect with the *Reshimo de Hochma* into *Behinat ZON* of a single degree?
64. What is the place of *ZON de Keter* when they ascend in the *Rosh*?
65. Who causes the ascent of the *Malchut* of the *Rosh* to *Yesod de Rosh*?
66. What does preparation of the *Tachtonim* to receive mean?
67. What are the three kinds of Generality?
68. Why are the *Reshimo de Keter* and *Reshimo de Nekeva* called *Zachar* and *Nekeva*?

69. What are the *Behinot* of the Orot de ZON de Keter of Hitpashtut Bet?
70. How do the three *Orot, Ohr Keter* and *Zachar* and *Nekeva de Keter* stand at the *Malchut* of the *Rosh*?
71. How many *Zivugim* are there to the ZON *de Keter* in the *Rosh*?
72. How is the *He'arat Keter Elyon* extended by the ZON that rose to the *Rosh*?
73. How is it possible that *Malchut de Rosh* would rise to *Behina Gimel* and the *Orot* would not change their places?
74. When are the ZON together in the *Yesod de Rosh*?
75. What is the *Hitkalelut* of the *Nekeva* in the *Zachar*?
76. What causes the descent of the degrees?
77. Why does the *He'arat Keter Elyon de Zivug Aleph* of the *Rosh* not extend to the *Guf*?
78. What makes *Ohr Keter* exit *Malchut* of the *Rosh*?
79. What caused the *Zachar de Keter* mingle with the *Nekeva* in *Zivug Bet*?
80. What does the *Hitkalelut* of ZON de Keter do in the two *Zivugim* of the *Rosh*?
81. How were ZON *de Kli de Keter* emanated?
82. How were ZON *de Kli de Hochma* emanated?
83. How were ZON *de Kli de Bina* emanated?
84. How many *Zivugim* are there in ZON *de Keter*, in ZON *de Hochma* and in ZON *de Bina* when they rise in *Malchut* of the *Rosh*?
85. What is the difference between ZON *de Keter de AB de AK* and ZON *de Keter de SAG de AK*?
86. What is the difference between ZON de Hochma de AB de AK and ZON de Hochma de SAG de AK?
87. What is the difference between ZON *de Bina de AB de AK* and ZON *de Bina de SAG de AK*?
88. What is the difference between the Five *Ktzavot de AB* and the *Five Ktzavot de SAG*?
89. What are the five *Orot* in the two *Kelim*?
90. When is the name YH in *Keter Pashut* and when is it with a filling?
91. When do four *Orot* ascend and when do five *Orot* ascend to the *Keter*?
92. What is the filling in the *YH de Keter* when four Orot rise to *Keter*?
93. What is the meaning of the *Otiot* of the filling?

94. What are the fillings of *Yodin*, *Heyin*, and *Alephin*?
95. What is the meaning of *YH* without a filling?
96. When do *ZON de Keter* equalize with each other and when is the *Zachar* greater than the *Nekeva*?
97. When are *ZON de Keter* in two *Kelim* and when are they in one *Kli*?
98. Why are *ZON de SAG de AK* in one *Kli*?
99. How does the *Nekeva de Keter* receive from *Keter Elyon*?
100. Why does the *Nekeva de Partzuf SAG de AK* receive only *VAK* of the *Zachar*?
101. Why is *ZON de Hochma* of *SAG de AK* called *VH* and not *YH*?
102. When do the *Orot* ascend and incorporate in the *Zachar de Keter* and when do the *Orot* ascend and incorporate in the *Nekeva de Keter*?
103. When do the *Orot* ascend, some in the *Nekeva* and some in the *Zachar* of *Keter*?
104. Why was the ascent of *MAN* not caused in *Hitpashtut Aleph*, when *HB* rose to *Keter*, as in the ascent of *HB* to *Keter* in *Hitpashtut Bet*?
105. What is raising *MAN*?
106. Why did all the *Orot* ascend to *MAN* to *Keter* in all the exits and the *Lo Matei* of *Hitpashtut Bet*, and not to *Rosh*, as in *Hitpashtut Aleph*?
107. What are the first *Kelim de Akudim*?
108. What causes annulment of the *Kelim*?
109. Where did the *Kelim* for the *Partzuf* of *Hitpashtut Bet* come from?
110. Where did the *Kelim* for *Partzuf SAG de AK* come from?
111. Why do *ZON de AB* have two *Kelim* and *ZON de SAG* only one *Kli*?
112. Why did all the *Orot* come to *Kli de Keter* together in *Hitpashtut Bet*?
113. What are *Panim* and *Achor de Kelim*?
114. Why are the *Kelim de Hitpashtut Bet* arrnged one below the other?
115. What are the *Panim* and *Achor de KHB*?
116. Why are there no *Kelim* in the *Partzuf* due to the *Hitpashtut Bet* of itself?
117. What is the difference between *Hitpashtut Aleph* and *Hitpashtut Bet*?
118. How are the *Kelim de GAR* made?
119. What are the causes of the completion of the *Kelim de GAR*?
120. What are the parts in the Kli that are worthy of looking into the *Ohr* even during the *Histalkut*?

121. What causes the *Kli* to turn its *Panim* downward and its *Achoraim* upward?
122. What causes the *Kli* to turn its *Panim* to its place as in the beginning?
123. What is *Histaklut* in the *Ohr Elyon* through the *Achor*?
124. How will the *Orot* be extended from *Keter* to *Hochma* when they are so far from each other?
125. What two kinds of inversions of the *Panim* are implemented in the degrees?
126. What causes the division of the *Sefirot Hochma* and *Bina*?
127. Why do all the *Sefirot* remain in *Panim* and *Achor* after *Histalkut Aleph*?
128. Why did *Keter* and *Hochma* remain *Panim be Panim* after *Histalkut Aleph*?
129. Why is *Keter Achor be Achor* with the *Ohr Elyon*?
130. What is the meaning of a Moment in spirituality?
131. When is the *Kli Malchut* completed in *Histalkut Aleph*?
132. When is *Kli ZA* completed in *Histalkut Aleph*?
133. Why is any less than three is considered filled?
134. Why is the ascent of ZA to *Bina* not considered remoteness of degree?
135. When was there *Lo Matei* in *Keter* for the first time?
136. Why is *Histalkut Aleph* called *Lo Matei* in *Keter*?
137. Who causes the *Lo Matei* in *Hitpashtut Bet* every time?
138. Why were the *Matei ve Lo Matei* made into ten *Orot* and were not made into ten Kelim?
139. Why is the permanent *Matei ve Lo Matei* compared to a flame swaying here and there?
140. What is the ratio between ZON de *Hochma* and ZON de *Bina*?
141. How is *Hesed* emanated?
142. What is *Behinat Kli de Hesed*?
143. What is *Behinat Ohr de Hesed*?
144. What is the order of the emanation of the *Ohr* of *Gevura*?
145. What is the property of *Sefirat Gevura*?
146. What is the difference between ZON de *Bina* and *Sefirat Gevura*?
147. What is the order of the emanation of the *Ohr Tifferet*?
148. What is the property of the *Kli de Tifferet*?
149. How is the *Ohr Hesed* different when it is in *Bina* from when it is in *Tifferet*?

150. What is *Ohr Daat* at its *Shoresh*?
151. What is the essence of *Behinat ZA* in the *Hey Ktzavot*?
152. What are the *Behinot RTS* in ZAT?
153. What is the difference between *Hesed* and *Gevura*, and *Tifferet*?
154. Why is the essence of *Ohr Hesed* not clothed in the *Sefirot* of *Hochma* and *Gevura*?
155. How is *Sefirat Netzah* emanated?
156. What is the attribute of *Sefirat Netzah*?
157. What is the difference between HGT and NHY?
158. What is the attribute of the *Kli de Hod*?
159. What is *Sefirat Yesod*?
160. In which *Sefira* did *Ohr Malchut* clothe?
161. What is the *Ohr* that clothed in *Kli Malchut*?
162. What is the ratio between ZON de Hochma and ZON de Bina?
163. How many *Behinot ZON* are there in *Hitpashtut Bet*?
164. What is the attribute of the four ZON couples of *Hitpashtut Bet*?
165. In which *Behina* did the *Zivug* stop and the *Ohr* of *Hitpashtut Bet* depart entirely?
166. What is the second *Behina* of *Hitpashtut Bet*?
167. How was *Partzuf SAG de AK* emanated?
168. What are the ZON of *Kelim de KHB*?
169. What are the names of ZON de KHB?
170. What are the *Otiot* that designate ZON and the *Kelim* of KHB?
171. How many *Behinot* are there in *Hitpashtut Bet*?
172. What is the meaning of Only *He'arah*, without giving *Orot*?
173. Why did *Hochma* illuminate the *Vav* to *Bina* before the giving of the *Orot*?
174. Why did *Keter* not give the *Yod* to *Hochma* from *Behinat He'arah*?
175. When does *Hesed* need its mother and when does it not?
176. Why does *Bina* rise to *Hochma* before it gives the *Ohr Hesed* to *Kli de Hesed*?
177. How did the *Hey de Zivug* ZON of *Bina* reach the *Kli Malchut*?
178. What is the difference between the *Ohr Hesed* and the *Hey* from *Zivug* ZON de Bina?

179. How is the *Hey* separated into two separated degrees?
180. Why can't the *Ohr Hesed* be a *Zachar* to *Bina*?
181. Why can't the *Ohr Hesed* be a *Nekeva* to *Bina*?
182. Which *Ohr* descended to complement the *Malchut*?
183. What are the ZON in *Yesod*?
184. How did the *Reshimo de Kli de Bina*, which is GAR, become a *Nekeva* to the *Yod* that was born from the *Zivug ZON de Hochma*, which is VAK?
185. What are the five *Hassadim* and five *Gevurot* in the five *Ktzavot*?
186. What are the five *Hassadim* and five *Gevurot* in *Yesod*?
187. What is *Matei* in *Keter de Hitpashtut Bet*?
188. Why is it that when *Matei* in *Keter*, *Lo Matei* in *Hochma* and *Bina*?
189. Why is it that when *Matei* in *Hochma*, *Lo Matei* in *Bina*?
190. Why is it that when *Matei* in *Bina*, *Lo Matei* in *Hesed*?
191. What is *Matei* in *Hesed* and in *Tifferet*?
192. What is *Matei* in *Keter Partzuf SAG de AK*?
193. What is *Matei* in *Hochma de SAG de AK*?
194. What is *Matei* in *Bina de SAG de AK*?
195. What is *Matei* in *Hesed de SAG de AK*?
196. What is *Matei* in *Hod* and not *Matei* in *Yesod de SAG de AK*?
197. Why is it that when *Matei* in *Keter, Gevura, Netzah,* and *Yesod, Lo Matei Hochma, Bina* and *Hesed, Tifferet, Hod,* and *Malchut de SAG de AK*?
198. Why is it that when *Matei* in *Hochma, Bina,* and *Hesed, Tifferet, Hod,* and *Malchut, Lo Matei* in *Keter, Gevura, Netzah,* and *Yesod de SAG de AK*?
199. Why is it that when *Matei* in *Malchut de SAG de AK*, it returns to being *Matei* in *Keter,* and so on and so forth?
200. Why does the *Masach de Behina Bet* rely on the *Achoraim de Bina*?
201. Why are the *Eser Sefirot de Rosh* always called GAR, and the *Eser Sefirot de Guf* named "The Seven Lower *Sefirot*"?
202. Why is every *Partzuf Tachton* considered *Behinat VAK* with respect to its *Elyon*?

43. What is YH in *Keter*, *HaVaYaH* in the rest of the *Partzufim*?

The *Hitpashtut* and *Histalkut* that were in *Partzuf Keter de AK* is called YH. *Hitpashtut Bet* and *Histalkut Bet* that were in *Partzuf AB de AK* is called VH.

The YH in *Hitpashtut Aleph* are also contained in *Hitpashtut Bet* since all the forces in the *Elyon* are necessarily present in the *Tachton* as well. You find, that YH is in the *Keter*, meaning in *Partzuf Keter de AK*, and *HaVaYaH* in the rest of the *Partzufim*.

(Item 23, and *Ohr Pnimi* par. "He writes")

44. Why do the four *Otiot HaVaYaH* imply discernments of lacks?

The *Otiot* are *Kelim*. It is known that the *Histalkut* of the *Ohr* and its absence cause the making of the *Kli*. Hence it is necessary that in each *Ot* of the four *Otiot HaVaYaH* there is some *Behina* of lack of *Ohr*. This is the cause for the making of that *Ot*, meaning that *Kli*, and for this reason the *Otiot* are *Behinot* lackes.

(*Ohr Pnimi* Item 24)

45. What do the YV de *HaVaYaH* imply?

The *Yod* implies the *Hitpashtut Ohr* of the *Nekudot de Partzuf Keter*, which are the *Komot* that came out there from *Hochma* down. *Vav* implies the *Hitpashtut Ohr* of the *Nekudot* of *Partzuf AB de AK*, meaning from *Hochma* down of this *Partzuf* too.

However, there is no sign for the *Hitpashtut* of *Komat Keter* in the four *Otiot HaVaYaH*, neither for *Keter de Partzuf Keter*, nor for *Keter de Partzuf AB*. It is so because there is no discernment of a lack there, for which the *Otiot* would be written (see answer 44).

(Item 24)

46. What do the *Hey Hey de HaVaYaH* imply?

The First *Hey* implies the general *Histalkut de Hitpashtut Aleph*, and the last *Hey* implies the general *Histalkut de Hitpashtut Bet*.

(There, and *Ohr Pnimi*)

47. Why are the *Shorashim* of the *Sefirot* in *Malchut* of the *Rosh*?

Because the whole matter of the vessels of reception, called *Guf*, are because of the *Ohr Hozer* that *Malchut* raises in her *Hakaa* on the *Ohr Elyon* from her and above in the *Eser Sefirot de Rosh*. Through this *Ohr Hozer*, *Malchut* acquires strength to expand from her and within her from above downward to *Eser Sefirot de Hitlabshut*, called *Guf*.

It means that the entire amount that the *Ohr Hozer* clothed in the *Eser Sefirot de Rosh* from below upward themselves invert and clothe the *Eser Sefirot* of the *Guf*. Thus, *Eser Sefirot de Guf* are *Anafim* (lit. Branches) of the *Malchut de Rosh*.

(Item 1)

48. **Where does the *Ohr Keter* that did not expand to the *Guf* stand?**

    It stands under *Malchut* of the *Rosh*, meaning under its *Shoresh*.

    (There)

49. **What is the function of the *Ohr Keter* that did not return to the *Guf*?**

    It gives to its *Anaf* (lit. Branch) that stands at the *Kli de Keter de Guf*, which is the *Behinat Zachar* of *Keter*. It also detains the *He'arat GAR* from expanding to the *Partzuf*.

    (*Ohr Pnimi* item 40 par. "We must understand")

50. **Why must the *Kelim de Guf* receive the *Orot* through the *Ohr Keter*?**

    Because although the *Orot* departed from the *Guf*, they still receive enough *Ohr* to sustain them. They receive this *He'arah* through the *Keter* that departed from them and rose under *Malchut de Rosh*, since it is the *Shoresh* for every *Eser Sefirot de Guf*, as the *Ohr Keter* always contains all the *Eser Sefirot* that expand through it.

    (Item 3, and *Ohr Pnimi* there)

51. **What is the meaning of the location of the *Ohr Keter* under *Malchut de Rosh*?**

    It indicates that it is an *Ohr* without a *Kli*, hence it cannot expand from above downward to the *Guf*. Its being under the *Malchut de Rosh* and above the *Kelim de Guf* indicates that it is a middle, an intermediate between *Behinat Rosh* and *Behinat Guf*, shining from its place to the *Guf* through its *Reshimo* that stands at *Keter de Guf*.

    (There)

52. **What is the inversion of the *Panim de Ohr Keter* to the *Shorashim* and its *Achoraim* to the *Anafim*?**

    It causes its *Anafim* in the *Guf*, which are ZON in *Kli de Keter* that receive its *He'arah*, to not be able to bestow that great *Ohr* that they receive from it to the *Tachtonim* from *Keter de Guf*. This is so because *Achoraim de Ohr Keter* are *Behinat* detainment and cessation on its *He'arah* so as not to expand from *Kli de Keter de Guf* downward.

    (Items 4 and 5)

53. **What is the sufficient *Yenika* of the *Orot*?**

    It is a sufficient *He'arah* to descend below to *Hitlabshut* in the *Guf* to mate and generate offspring.

    (Item 3)

54. **What is sufficient *He'arah* to generate offspring?**

    Through two *Zivugim* that are induced in *Malchut*, ZON acquire the force to descend downward to *Hitlabshut* in the *Guf* and generate offspring.

    (Ohr Pnimi item 3, Sub Header "The *Keter*")

55. **What causes the *Ohr Keter* to return its *Panim* to the *Anafim*?**

    Through the ascents of the *Zachar de Keter*, namely *Behina Dalet de Hitlabshut*, with the *Nekeva de Keter*, namely *Behina Gimel* in complete *Aviut* both from *Hamshacha* and from *Hitlabshut*, these ZON incorporate in one another in a common *Aviut*.

    At that time the *Zachar* attains both from *Behinat Hamshacha* and these common MAN themselves cause a *Behinat Zivug Elyon* in *Malchut* of the *Rosh* and the *Koma* that comes out of this *Zivug* attains up to *Keter de Rosh*. Also, the *Ohr Keter* in *Malchut* receives this great *Ohr* and administers it to its *Anafim*, which are ZON. This is considered that it returned its *Panim* to its *Anafim*.

    (Ohr Pnimi item 9, par. "Thus, *Malchut de Rosh*")

56. **What causes the *Ohr Keter* to return its *Achoraim* to the *Anafim*?**

    The ascents of ZON to the *Rosh* mean that the *Aviut* in them purified and their *Tzura* equalized with *Behinat Malchut de Rosh*. This causes the *Zivug* in *Malchut de Rosh*, extending the *Ohr* from *Keter Elyon* (see answer 55).

    At that time the *Ohr Keter* returns its *Panim* to the *Anafim* and dispenses them the *Ohr de Keter Elyon*. However, after the second *Zivug*, when ZON have already sucked enough to descend to the *Guf* for *Hitlabshut* in the *Kelim*, the *Orot de* ZON are found to be returning and thickening in the *Aviut de Guf*.

    At that time they cause that *Behinat* intermediate *Aviut* (mentioned in answer 51) that exists in the *Ohr Keter*. This is its *Behinat Achoraim*, preventing its *He'arah* from the *Guf* since it lacks the *Behina Dalet de Hamshacha*. For this reason no vessel of reception extends from the first *Zivug*, and this lack of vessels of reception is in itself its *Behinat Achoraim* to the *Anafim*.

    (Ohr Pnimi item 10)

57. **How will the *Sefirot de Guf* generate changes in the *Rosh*?**

    These changes and operations that the *Behinot Guf* cause to be renewed in the *Eser Sefirot* of the *Rosh*, do not refer to the very essence of the *Eser Sefirot de Rosh*, but only to the *Malchut* and the *Masach* in it. This is according to the *Ohr Hozer* that she raises up from below upward.

For this reason *Malchut* is considered the *Shoresh* of all the *Kelim* and the *Orot* in them and all the incidents in the *Eser Sefirot de Guf*. Hence, when her *Anafim* acquire equivalence of form with her, they instantly return to her, as a branch that returns to its root.

Through this return, the branches are renewed and they cause *Behinat* renewed *Aviut* in the *Masach* in *Malchut*. The *Ohr Elyon*, which does not stop for a moment mates on the new form of *Aviut* that the *Masach* attained by the *Hitkalelut* of the *Anafim* in it. At that time a *Koma* of new *Eser Sefirot* comes out "in potential", appearing "de facto" from there to the *Guf*.

(*Ohr Pnimi* item 6, Sub Header **"They"**)

58. **What are ZON *de Keter de Hitpashtut Bet*?**

    The *Zachar de Keter de Keter* is the *Behinat Reshimo de Kli de Keter de Hitpashtut Aleph* that was renewed in the *Zivug Elyon* of the *Rosh*. The *Nekeva* is the actual *Ohr* of *Komat Hochma* that came out through a *Zivug de Ohr Elyon* on *Aviut de Behina Gimel* from *Malchut de Rosh* upward, which turned over and descended to the *Guf* from *Malchut* down.

    (Item 9, and *Ohr Pnimi*, Sub Header **"This extends"**)

59. **What causes ZON to rise to *Malchut* of the *Rosh*?**

    The *Hizdakchut Masach* in *Tabur de Hitpashtut Aleph* until it became *Zach* in equal form to the *Masach de Malchut de Rosh* is considered that the *Masach* of *Tabur* rose to the *Rosh*. As it ascends, in the order of degrees of the *Eser Sefirot de Guf*, the *Masach* is incorporated with all the *Reshimot* in the *Guf*.

    The two *Reshimot de Zachar* and *Nekeva de Keter* are the Upper ones among them, containing all of them, hence when this *Masach* rose to the *Rosh*, it brought these *Reshimot* along with it, meaning ZON *de Keter*. Thus, the *Hizdakchut* of the *Masach de Hitpashtut Aleph* caused ZON *de Keter* to ascend upward to the *Rosh*.

    (*Ohr Pnimi* item 4, Sub Header **"Rise"**)

60. **What is a sufficient reception for ZON from the *He'arat Rosh*?**

    After the two *Zivugim* of ZON in the first *Zivug* ended, which was the *Hitkalelut* of the *Nekeva* in the *Zachar*, they extended the *Ohr* from the *Keter Elyon*. However, they still did not have the strength to turn over and expand downward to the *Guf*.

    This is so because the *Aviut de Behina Dalet* of the *Zachar* was lacking the *Behinat Hamshacha* of *Behina Dalet* since *Malchut* did not leave a *Reshimo*. That

Aviut de Behina Dalet de Hitlabshut was sufficient to make a *Zivug de Rosh* by joining with the *Reshimo de Behina Gimel*. However, she was still not enough to make a *Behinat* vessel of reception for *Hitlabshut* in the *Guf* through this *Ohr Hozer*.

Hence, the ZON could not descend to the *Guf* until a second *Zivug* was made, where there was a *Hitkalelut* of the *Zachar* in the *Nekeva*, and the *Zivug* came out on *Behina Gimel*, which has *Behinat Hamshacha* as well. At that time *Malchut de Rosh* could expand from her and within her to *Eser Sefirot de Guf* through the *Chazeh* and the ZON could come down.

(*Ohr Pnimi* item 4, Sub Header **"Once"**)

61. **What is the result of the ascent of ZON to the *Malchut* of the *Rosh*?**

ZON's ascent upwards was caused by the making of a *Zivug* on *Behina Gimel*. That, in turn, lowered only *Komat Hochma* to the *Guf* and *Ohr Keter* remained in the *Rosh*.

Thus, the degrees descended because the *Ohr Hochma* clothed in *Kli de Keter* and the *Ohr Bina* in *Kli de Hochma* etc. It therefore follows that each and every *Kli* remained lacking much of that measure of *Ohr* that it had in *Hitpashtut Aleph*.

For this reason the *Aviut* in the *Kelim* had been recognized and they were completed in a way that they will not be cancelled by the *Ohr* clothing in them. It follows that the ascents of ZON caused the completion of the *Kelim*.

(*Ohr Pnimi* item 5, Sub Header **"It was"**)

62. **Why are all the *Eser Sefirot* of *Histalkut Aleph* that rose to the *Rosh* called ZON de Keter?**

This is because the Upper *Sefira* contains all the *Sefirot* below it. Hence, the *Reshimo de Behina Dalet* contains all the *Reshimot* below her, but because she lacks *Behinat Hamshacha*, she must therefore join with the *Behina Gimel*. Hence, *Behina Gimel* too merits a name, and they are all named after the two *Reshimot*, which are ZON de Kli de Keter.

(*Ohr Pnimi* item 6, par. "Know, that the essence")

63. **How do the *Reshimo de Keter* connect with the *Reshimo de Hochma* into *Behinat* ZON of a single degree?**

The *Reshimo de Behina Dalet*, which is the *Zachar de Keter*, is only half a *Reshimo*, its weaker half, which is only *Behinat Hitlabshut*. However, the *Reshimo de Behina Gimel* is complete with two *Behinot Aviut*: *Hitlabshut* and *Hamshacha*. The *Zachar* becomes needy of the *Nekeva*, to the extent that there is *Hishtavut* between them, and they become ZON of a single degree.

(*Ohr Pnimi* item 6, par. "You should know")

64. **What is the place of ZON de Keter when they ascend in the Rosh?**

    Under the root *Ohr Keter* that stands under *Malchut* of the *Rosh*, since the ZON are the *Anafim* of that *Ohr Keter*.

    (Item 9, and *Ohr Pnimi* par. "Remember these three names")

65. **Who causes the ascent of the Malchut of the Rosh to Yesod de Rosh?**

    The coming of *Behina Gimel*, which is the *Nekeva de Kli de Keter* to the place of *Malchut de Rosh*. It causes a corresponding ascent of *Malchut de Rosh* to *Yesod de Rosh*, being *Behina Gimel de Rosh*.

    (*Ohr Pnimi* item 6, Sub Header **"They remain"**)

66. **What does preparation of the Tachtonim to receive mean?**

    See answer to question No. 13.

67. **What are the three kinds of Generality?**

    - The first is the *Hitkalelut* of the *Orot* ZON when whey are without *Kelim*, meaning when they ascend to the *Rosh*. At that time they have both purified and acquired the form of *Malchut de Rosh*, which is not considered an actual *Kli*, where ZON are incorporated in one another in two *Zivugim*.
    - The second is when they are in two *Kelim* and their *He'arah* is incorporated in one another, which is in ZON *de Kli de Keter* of *Partzuf AB*.
    - The third is in *Partzuf SAG de AK*, when the *Nekeva* is clothed there in the *Kli Zachar de Keter*.

    (*Ohr Pnimi* Item 62 par. "However, he has already")

68. **Why are the Reshimo de Keter and Reshimo de Nekeva called Zachar and Nekeva?**

    The *Reshimo de Behina Dalet* is half a *Reshimo* from the *Behinat Aviut de Hitlabshut*, devoid of *Behinat Aviut de Hamshacha*. Hence, she is not suitable to extend any *Ohr*, unless in joining with the *Reshimo de Nekeva*, namely *Aviut de Behina Gimel*, which is complete with *Behinat Hamshacha* too. For this reason these two *Reshimot* are considered as two parts of a body; one gives the *Hitlabshut*, and one gives the *Hamshacha*. For this reason they are called ZON.

69. **What are the Behinot of the Orot de ZON de Keter of Hitpashtut Bet?**

    The *Zachar* is the *Behinat Ohr Keter*, and the *Nekeva* is *Behinat Ohr Hochma*.

    (Item 4, and *Ohr Pnimi* there)

70. **How do the three Orot, Ohr Keter and Zachar and Nekeva de Keter stand at the Malchut of the Rosh?**

Each *Anaf* stands under its proximate *Shoresh*. The *Ohr Keter* under the *Malchut* of the *Rosh*, the *Ohr Zachar*, which is the *Reshimo* of that *Ohr Keter* stands below it, and the *Ohr Nekeva*, which is the *Reshimo de Aviut de Behina Gimel*, considered an *Anaf de Behina Dalet*, stands under the *Zachar*.

(Item 9, and *Ohr Pnimi* par. "Remember these three names")

71. **How many *Zivugim* are there to the *ZON de Keter* in the *Rosh*?**

    They make two *Zivugim*: The first is on the common *Aviut* from *Behina Dalet de Hitlabshut* with *Behina Gimel de Hamshacha*. This *Zivug* extends nearly *Komat Keter*. The second is a *Zivug* made only on *Aviut de Behina Gimel*. This *Zivug* extends only *Komat Hochma*.

    (Item 9, and *Ohr Pnimi* Sub Header **"The *Nekeva*"**)

72. **How is the *He'arat Keter Elyon* extended by the *ZON* that rose to the *Rosh*?**

    ZON de Kli de Keter that participate in their kinds of *Aviut* together cause the ascent of *Malchut* to the *Yesod de Rosh*, which is *Behina Gimel de Rosh*. Also, they are incorporated there together like ZON *de Keter de Guf*.

    This is so because *Malchut* is *Behina Dalet* and the *Yesod* is *Behina Gimel*. Thus, the *Ohr Yesod* did not rise upward and *Malchut* did not purify from her *Behina Dalet* when she rose to the *Yesod*, but only to the extent of the lack of *Hamshacha* that the *Zachar de Kli de Keter* lacked.

    Hence, the *Zivug* that emerged on the common *Aviut* of *Yesod* and *Malchut de Rosh* extended nearly *Komat Keter*. The *Orot de Rosh* did not change their places and the *Ohr Keter* remained in its place and did not descend to the degree of *Hochma*. For this reason the *He'arat Keter Elyon* was elicited by that *Zivug*.

    (Item 9, and *Ohr Pnimi* par. "However, note")

73. **How is it possible that *Malchut de Rosh* would rise to *Behina Gimel* and the *Orot* would not change their places?**

    When *Malchut de Rosh* is not completely purified to *Behina Gimel*, but receives *Behina Dalet de Hitlabshut* of the *Zachar de Kli de Keter* inside her, she then participates with *Behina Gimel de Rosh*. In this manner she extends the *Ohr de Keter Elyon* and the *Orot* do not change their places, see answer 72.

    (Item 9, and *Ohr Pnimi* par. "The reason for it")

74. **When are the ZON together in the *Yesod de Rosh*?**

    During the ascent of *Malchut de Rosh* to *Yesod de Rosh* only in the form of association, not in the form of *Hizdakchut*, see answer 73.

    (Item 6)

75. **What is the *Hitkalelut* of the *Nekeva* in the *Zachar*?**

    Behina Gimel, which is the *Nekeva* that has *Behinat Hamshacha* as well, participates with the *Behina Dalet de Zachar* and incorporates with him in one *Masach*. At that time it draws upon it nearly *Komat Keter*.

    (Item 9, and *Ohr Pnimi* Sub Header **"The *Nekeva*"**)

76. **What causes the descent of the degrees?**

    Malchut de Rosh ascends to *Yesod* from *Behinat Hizdakchut* to *Behina Gimel* and a *Zivug Elyon* in *Komat Hochma* emerges on the *Masach* in her. At that time the degrees descend there since the *Ohr Hochma* clothes in *Kli de Keter*, the *Ohr Bina* in *Kli de Hochma*, etc.

    It follows that *Keter* descended to the degree of *Hochma* and *Hochma* descended to the degree of *Bina* etc. This is so because the *Kli* is drawn primarily after the *Ohr* in it. When *Ohr Hochma* clothes *Kli de Keter*, the *Keter* descends to the degree of *Hochma* etc.

    (Item 10, and *Ohr Pnimi* Sub Header **"Hence, the *Shoresh*"**)

77. **Why does the *He'arat Keter Elyon de Zivug Aleph* of the *Rosh* not extend to the *Guf*?**

    Because a *Behinat Hamshacha* from the *Aviut de Behina Dalet* is missing there. Because of that lack, *Malchut* cannot expand from her and within her to *Eser Sefirot de Guf* to *Malchut de Malchut*, called *Tabur*.

    (Item 10, and *Ohr Pnimi* par. "He writes")

78. **What makes *Ohr Keter* exit *Malchut* of the *Rosh*?**

    When *Keter's* time to go back down to the *Guf* from above downward comes, though it has not returned, still the *Behinat Guf* contained in it since it was in *Hitpashtut Aleph* has awakened. This is in disparity of form from *Behinat Malchut* of the *Rosh*, and it is known that *Shinui Tzura* separates and parts the spirituals. For this reason it is considered to have left *Malchut* of the *Rosh*.

    (Item 10, and *Ohr Pnimi* par. "Still")

79. **What caused the *Zachar de Keter* mingle with the *Nekeva* in *Zivug Bet*?**

    The previous *Hitkalelut* of the *Nekeva* in the *Zachar* that was in the first *Zivug* that equalized them together, caused the *Zachar* later mingle with the *Nekeva* in a second *Zivug*.

    (Item 11)

80. **What does the *Hitkalelut* of ZON de Keter do in the two *Zivugim* of the *Rosh*?**

It is through these *Zivugim* that ZON are incorporated. The *Zachar* is incorporated in the new *Koma* of *Ohr Hochma* that expands and descends to the *Guf* entirely, and the *Nekeva* acquired *He'arah* from *Keter Elyon*. In that they unite and mingle in *Kli de Keter* of the *Guf* as well, and both receive from the *Achoraim* of the *Ohr Keter* as well.

(*Ohr Pnimi* item 40, par. "We must understand")

81. **How were ZON de Kli de Keter emanated?**

Through the ascent of the *Masach de Tabur* of *Histalkut Aleph* to the *Rosh*. It raised these two *Reshimot de Behina Dalet* and *Behina Gimel* with it. These, in turn, are ZON *de Kli de Keter*, where they mingled in *Malchut* of the *Rosh* in the two *Zivugim*, received their completion, and descended to the *Guf* to the *Kli Keter*.

(*Ohr Pnimi* item 40, par. "The *Masach*")

82. **How were ZON de Kli de Hochma emanated?**

The *Nukva* left the *Achoraim de Kli de Keter* because of the *Bitush de Ohr Makif* and *Ohr Pnimi*, and also purified from *Behina Gimel* to *Behina Bet*. At that time *Komat Bina* emerged on *Behina Bet* and gave to *Kli de Hochma*.

Also, the *Zachar de Keter*, which is *Behina Dalet*, purified into *Behina Gimel* and gave this residue to the *Kli* of *Hochma*. He became the *Zachar de Kli de Hochma*, and *Komat Bina* that was emanated from the *Nekeva* became *Behinat Nekeva de Kli de Hochma*.

(*Ohr Pnimi* item 35, par. "However, we must remember")

83. **How were ZON de Kli de Bina emanated?**

The *Zachar* was emanated by the inversion of the *Panim de Kli de Hochma* to illuminate without giving *Orot*, meaning only the inversion of the *Panim* from *Behinat GAR* to *Behinat VAK*. It still did not purify to *Behina Aleph*.

At that time ZON *de Kli de Hochma* mated and procreated the *Zachar de Bina*, which is *Yod*, from the *Behinat VAK* in them. They gave it to the *Kli de Bina*, where he became *Behinat Zachar de Bina*.

Afterwards the *Kli de Hochma* purified into *Behina Aleph*, over which extended a *Koma* of *Ohr Hesed* and gave it to the *Kli de Bina*. This is considered a son of *Bina*, and the *Reshimo* found in the *Kli de Bina* from the time of *Hitpashtut Aleph* became the *Behinat Nekeva* of *Bina*.

(*Ohr Pnimi* item 35, Sub Header **"Hochma turns"**)

84. **How many *Zivugim* are there in ZON de Keter, in ZON de Hochma and in ZON de Bina when they rise in Malchut of the Rosh?**

    Two *Zivugim*: 1 - The *Hitkalelut* of the *Nekeva* in the *Zachar* and the *Koma* that extends in the measure of the *Zachar*; 2 - The *Hitkalelut* of the *Zachar* in the *Nekeva* and the *Koma* extended in the measure of the *Nekeva*.

    (Ohr Pnimi item 9, par. "Hence, when the *Masach*")

85. **What is the difference between ZON de Keter de AB de AK and ZON de Keter de SAG de AK?**

    In ZON de Keter de AB de AK, the first *Zivug* is nearly in *Komat Keter*, and the second *Zivug* is in *Komat Hochma*. However, ZON de Keter de SAG, the first *Zivug* is nearly in *Komat Hochma* and the second *Zivug* is in *Komat Bina*.

86. **What is the difference between ZON de Hochma de AB de AK and ZON de Hochma de SAG de AK?**

    In Hochma de AB the *Zachar* is in *Komat Hochma* and the *Nekeva* is in *Komat Bina*. In ZON de Hochma de SAG de AB the *Zachar* is in *Komat Bina*, extended from *Zivug* ZON de Keter, and the *Nekeva* is the *Behinat Reshimo de Bina* found in *Kli de Hochma* since *Hitpashtut Aleph*.

    (Ohr Pnimi item 47, par. "Now we shall explain")

87. **What is the difference between ZON de Bina de AB de AK and ZON de Bina de SAG de AK?**

    In ZON de Bina de AB the *Zachar* is *Behinat VAK de GAR*, meaning *VAK de Hochma*, and the *Nekeva* is *Behinat Reshimo de Hitpashtut Aleph*. In ZON de Bina de SAG they are *Behinot Reshimot* that remained from *Hitpashtut Bet*, from *Orot de ZON de Bina de AB* after their *Histalkut*.

    (Ohr Pnimi item 47, par. "We have already learned")

88. **What is the difference between the Five *Ktzavot* de AB and the Five *Ktzavot* de SAG?**

    Hey *Ktzavot* de AB contain *He'arat Hochma*, but the Hey *Ktzavot* de SAG contain only *He'arat Bina*.

    (There)

89. **What are the five *Orot* in the two *Kelim*?**

    Two *Orot* in *Kli de Hochma*, which are ZON, and three *Orot* in *Kli de Bina*, which are *Zachar* and *Nekeva de Bina* and the *Ohr Hesed* in *Bina*, containing the whole ZAT.

    (Ohr Pnimi item 55, Sub Header **"These ascents"**)

90. **When is the name YH in *Keter Pashut* and when is it with a filling?**

    When the *Masach* purifies and there is no *Zivug* in *Keter*, the name YH is *Pashut*, without filling. When there is a *Zivug* in *Keter*, the name YH is in filling.

    (Item 56)

91. **When do four *Orot* ascend and when do five *Orot* ascend to the *Keter*?**

    Four *Orot* rise in *AB de AK* and five *Orot* rise in *SAG de AK*.

    (*Ohr Pnimi* item 55, Sub Header "Sometimes")

92. **What is the filling in the *YH de Keter* when four *Orot* rise to *Keter*?**

    The *Hey de YH* is filled with *Yod* like this: *Hey Yod*. This is because the lower three of the four *Orot* are cancelled in the *Elyon* in them, which is the *Ohr Hochma* implied in the *Yod*.

    (Item 56)

93. **What is the meaning of the *Otiot* of the filling?**

    The *Otiot* themselves are the *Kelim*, and their filling is the measurements of the *Aviut* found in the *Masach* in them. They are the measurement of the height of the *Koma*.

94. **What are the fillings of *Yodin*, *Heyin*, and *Alephin*?**

    The measure of *Aviut de Behina Gimel* and *Behina Bet* are *Yodin*, the measurements of *Aviut de Behina Aleph* is *Alephin*, and the *Behinot Ohr Malchut* are the *Heyin*.

    (*Ohr Pnimi* item 56, Sub Header "In *Yodin*")

95. **What is the meaning of YH without a filling?**

    When the *Otiot* are without filling, it indicates that there is no *Aviut* in the *Masach* in them and there is no *Zivug de Hakaa* that extends *Ohr*.

    (Item 58)

96. **When do ZON *de Keter* equalize with each other and when is the *Zachar* greater than the *Nekeva*?**

    The *Zachar* and the *Nekeva* are equal to each other when they are without *Ohr*, but only as *Reshimot*. Although the *Zachar* is a *Reshimo* of the *Keter* and the *Nekeva* is a *Reshimo* of *Hochma*, which is much lower than *Keter*, still, because it is devoid of *Behina Dalet de Hamshacha*, it is not destined to return to the *Partzuf*. For this reason his *Reshimo* is very small.

    However, the *Reshimo* of the *Nekeva* is complete in *Behinat Hamshacha* too, and her *Ohr*, which is the *Ohr Hochma*, is destined to return to the *Partzuf* entirely. Thus, a great *Ohr* still remains in her *Reshimo* until she equalizes with the *Reshimo de Zachar*, though she is from *Behinat Keter*.

Nevertheless, after they ascended to the *Rosh* they were mingled there in two *Zivugim*. In the first *Zivug*, the *Reshimo de Zachar* received the *He'arat Keter Elyon*, at which time the *Zachar* is much greater than the *Nukva*.

Even though the *Nekeva* is incorporated in him, she can still receive only *VAK* from him, not the *He'arat GAR*. Thus, the *Nekeva* is considered *Behinat VAK* with respect to the *Zachar*.

(Item 59)

97. When are ZON de Keter in two Kelim and when are they in one Kli?

ZON are found in two *Kelim* in the first *Behina de Hitpashtut Bet*, called *AB de AK*. In the second *Behina de Hitpashtut Bet*, called *SAG de AK*, ZON are found in one *Kli*.

(Item 60)

98. Why are ZON de SAG de AK in one Kli?

Because of the *Hitkalelut* of the *Nekeva* in the *Zachar* in the two *Zivugim* of the *Rosh*, her measure of *Ohr* grew extensively and she needs a new *Kli* that will fit her measure of *Ohr*. She acquires that *Kli* in *Partzuf AB* by the *Hakaa* of the *Reshimo* and the *Ohr Hochma* on each other.

Because there was no *Hakaa* in SAG, *Nitzotzin* were not educed for the purpose of the *Kli de Nekeva*. For this reason she must clothe in the *Kli Zachar*.

(*Ohr Pnimi* item 60)

99. How does the Nekeva de Keter receive from Keter Elyon?

In *Histalkut Bet*, when ZON rose to *Malchut* of the *Rosh*, two *Zivugim* were incorporated there, similar to the ascents of ZON after *Histalkut Aleph*. Here too the *Nekeva* received *He'arat Keter Elyon* in the first *Zivug*, but the difference is that here the degrees descended and there was *Ohr Hochma* in *Kli de Keter Elyon*.

100. Why does the Nekeva de Partzuf SAG de AK receive only VAK of the Zachar?

The *Ohr Keter* that remained in the *Rosh* and did not return to *Guf de AB*, it turned to its *Anafim* and prevented *He'arat GAR* from them. Similarly, the *Ohr Hochma* that did not return to the *Guf de Partzuf SAG de AK* turned its *Achoraim* too to the *Anafim* and prevented *He'arat GAR* from them. Thus, the *Nekeva* could not receive from the *Ohr Zachar*, but only *He'arat VAK*.

(*Ohr Pnimi* item 61)

101. **Why is ZON de Hochma of SAG de AK called VH and not YH?**

Because here in *Partzuf SAG*, the degrees and ZON *de Keter* descended similarly to ZON *de Hochma de AB*. Also, ZON *de Hochma* here are similar to ZON *de Bina* in *Partzuf AB*.

Hence, ZON *de Hochma* here contain only *Behinat VAK de Hochma*, like the *Zachar de Bina de AB*, called *Dalet*. The *Zachar*, which is VAK, is called *Vav*, since every VAK is *Vav* and not *Yod*. Still, in themselves they are sometimes called YH too, like ZON *de Bina de AB*.

(*Ohr Pnimi* item 61, Sub Header "Two sons")

102. **When do the *Orot* ascend and incorporate in the *Zachar de Keter* and when do the *Orot* ascend and incorporate in the *Nekeva de Keter*?**

It is a rule that there is only ascent of MAN to the *Nekeva*. Hence, when four *Orot* rise to *Keter*, which are ZON *de Hochma*, ZON *de Bina* and the *Ohr Hesed* remain in the *Partzuf*.

This is in *Partzuf AB de AK*, where the *Ohr Hesed* remained before it completed all of its ten inlets. At that time the *Orot* rise in the *Kli de Nekeva* of the *Keter*, since there are two kinds of *Kelim* to ZON.

However, when five *Orot* rise to *Keter*, which is only in *Partzuf SAG*, as there is a perpetual *Matei ve Lo Matei* there, every time *de Matei* to *Malchut*, all the *Orot* ascend to *Keter* and it returns to being *Matei* in *Keter*. Thus, five *Orot* ascend here. These are ZON *de Hochma*, ZON *de Bina*, and the *Ohr Hesed*, containing the entire ZAT.

Here the *Orot* rise to the *Kli* of the *Zachar de Keter*, called *Yod*, because there is only one *Kli* to the ZON here. Thus, although they too rise to the *Nekeva*, here the *Nekeva* itself is here in a *Kli de Zachar*, hence the *Orot* rise after it to the *Kli Zachar* too.

All this refers only to the ascent of the *Orot* to *Keter*, but at the end of the departure, when they rise to the *Rosh*, all the *Orot* incorporate in the ZON *de Keter* and annul in them. This is because the *Orot Elyonim* are somewhat incorporated in the *Zachar* and some in the *Nekeva*, like the two *Zivugim* that ZON make there.

In the first *Zivug*, the *Nekeva de Keter* too is incorporated in the *Zachar*, and in the second *Zivug*, made in the attribute of the *Nekeva*, all the *Orot* are contained there in the *Nekeva*. For this reason some of the *Orot* are contained in the *Zachar* and some in the *Nekeva*.

(*Ohr Pnimi* item 62, par. "However, he has already")

103. **When do the *Orot* ascend, some in the *Nekeva* and some in the *Zachar* of *Keter*?**

See above answer 102.

104. **Why was the ascent of MAN not caused in *Hitpashtut Aleph*, when HB rose to *Keter*, as in the ascent of HB to *Keter* in *Hitpashtut Bet*?**

The *Histalkut* of *Hitpashtut Aleph* is considered as one *Histalkut*, instantaneous. This is so because only one *Kli* was made there and all five *Komot* that came out there are considered one *Ohr* because of the *Hizdakchut* of the *Masach*.

Here, however, in *Hitpashtut Bet*, the *Kelim* precede the *Orot*. This is because all the *Kelim* with the *Nitzotzin* and the *Reshimot* in *Hitpashtut Aleph* moved to *Behinot Kelim de Hitpashtut Bet* and were placed one under the other even before the *Ohr* of *Hitpashtut Bet* returned to the *Partzuf*.

Hence, each and every *Kli* here is considered a separate matter in itself. When the *Zivugim de ZON* are made in *Malchut* of the *Rosh* and the *Komat Hochma* descends to the *Partzuf*, she becomes completely clothed in *Kli de Keter* and the *Ohr Lo Matei* in any other *Kli*.

Hence, the *Kli Keter* is considered a special *Partzuf*, having its own *Hitpashtut* and its own *Histalkut*, and similarly in the rest of the *Kelim*. Hence, the *Kli de Keter* became qualified to return to its *Aviut* and to its *Zivug* through the ascent of the *Orot de HB* in a way that will be explained below (answer 105).

However, the *Kli de Keter de Hitpashtut Aleph* is connected with the nine lower *Sefirot* into one degree and one *Behina*. There is no difference between the *Kelim de HB* and the *Kli de Keter* since all of them together are only one *Ohr* clothed in one *Kli*.

105. **What is raising MAN?**

Each *Anaf* that is emanated and leaves its *Shoresh* is in its greatest wholeness during the process of its emanation, before it is separated and comes to its own authority and degree. This is so because then it is in the place of its *Shoresh* and is considered a part of it, in the form of eating what its mother eats.

However, afterwards, when it comes down to its place, it diminishes and lessens according to its property. This creates a permanent nexus between each *Anaf* and its *Shoresh*, where the *Shoresh* tends to enhance its *Anaf* to the same measure it was in, before it descended to its place.

This first beginning was rooted in the *Shoresh* and it wishes to keep it always. Yet, because of the *Katnut* of the *Kelim* of the *Anaf*, they cannot receive the administration of the *Shoresh*; they receive only according to their ability.

Hence, when the *Anaf* rises to its *Shoresh* once more, it awakens the *Shoresh* to extend the same *Orot* it had when it emanated it, and adapts itself to the *Anaf* until it can give it the entire *Gadlut* it gave it since the beginning of it creation. This is the meaning of ascents of MAN. It means that it awakens new *Orot* in its *Shoresh* because of its ascent to it.

You already know that there are two kinds of inversions of *Panim* downward during the emanation of a lower degree: the first is the inversion of the *Panim* of the *Kli* that the *Keter* cancelled its *Behinat Panim*. This was only to dispense GAR, and it made it into *Panim* in order to emanate the *Zachar de Kli de Hochma*.

The second is the inversion of the *Panim de Behinat Masach*, meaning *Hizdakchut* from the great *Aviut* to the lesser *Aviut*, meaning the *Hizdakchut* of *Behina Gimel* of the *Nekeva de Keter* to *Behina Bet*, which is *Komat Bina*, who did that for the *Nekeva de Hochma*.

Thus, when ZON *de Hochma* too were purified from *Behina Bet* to *Behina Aleph* and the *Zivug* stopped from them for their *Koma*, the same two kinds of inversion of *Panim* occurred in them to emanate ZON of *Bina*. You find that *Kli de Hochma* too acquired a *Behinat Panim* of VAK, like the *Kli de Keter*.

This *Hishtavut Tzura* returned the *Orot de HB* to the *Kli de Keter*, and then *Kli de Keter* too returned its *Panim* of *He'arat VAK* to their place as in the beginning. In order to illuminate its *Anafim* to ZON *de Hochma*, with whom they now united as in the beginning of their *Atzilut* before they came down to their place, ZON *de Keter* returned and corrected their *Masach* in *Aviut* of *Behina Gimel* and *Behina Dalet* as in the beginning.

They extended the same two *Zivugim* of theirs and dispensed their *Orot* to the designated *Anafim* that they are connected with. This is called "ascents of MAN".

106. Why did all the Orot ascend to MAN to Keter in all the exits and the Lo Matei of Hitpashtut Bet, and not to Rosh, as in Hitpashtut Aleph?

The matter of the ascent to *Malchut* of *Rosh* means *Hishtavut* with *Malchut de Rosh*. This is only after the *Masach* had been entirely purified from all its *Aviut*. Hence, in all these exits and entrances that were in *Hitpashtut Bet*, before the *Ohr de Matei* to *Malchut*, the *Masach* still did not purify entirely.

This is because until *de Matei* to *Hod*, its still had *Aviut de Behina Aleph*, and when *de Matei* to *Yesod* it still had *Aviut de Shoresh*, which extends *Komat Malchut*. Therefore, it is still in *Shinui Tzura* from *Malchut* of the *Rosh*.

However, after *de Matei* to the *Kli Malchut*, it purified completely like the *Behinat Malchut* of the *Rosh*. At that time it rose to the *Malchut* of the *Rosh* and the *Zivugim* for its lower *Partzuf*, called *SAG*, were made there. This is because the ascents of all the *Orot* to *Rosh* always elicit another *Partzuf*, a son of the previous *Partzuf*.

107. **What are the first *Kelim de Akudim*?**

    These are the *Kelim* of *Hitpashtut Aleph de AK*. Before him there was no *Hitlabshut* in the *Olamot*.

    (*Ohr Pnimi* item 5)

108. **What causes annulment of the *Kelim*?**

    The *Hizdakchut* of the *Masach* from the *Behinat Aviut* in the *Kli* causes the annulment of the *Kli*, as it is unfit to receive any *Ohr* when it lacks a *Masach*. Also, the return of the *Ohr Keter* as it was in *Hitpashtut* causes the annulment of the *Kelim*, because the *Kelim* mix with the *Orot*.

    (*Ohr Pnimi* item 5, Sub Header **"If the *Ohr*"**)

109. **Where did the *Kelim* for the *Partzuf* of *Hitpashtut Bet* come from?**

    They were gathered from many *Behinot*:

    1. From the *Kelim* that were emptied in *Histalkut Aleph* and were arranged here one below the other, *Keter* first, *Hochma* next, and so on, and *Malchut* last. These are primarily *Kelim de Zecharim*, though the *Nekevot* too were mingled there with the *Zecharim*.
    2. The *Nitzotzin* from the *Hakaa* of the *Reshimot* with the descending *Ohr Hozer* that fell into these *Kelim*, as written in Part 4.
    3. The *Kelim de Ohr Hochma* itself. After *Malchut* of the *Rosh* extended *Komat Hochma* of *Rosh*, she expanded once more from above downward into *Eser Sefirot* from her and within her to her *Malchut*, called *Chazeh*.
    4. These are the *Kelim* that were made by the *Hakaa* of *Ohr Reshimo* and *Ohr Hochma* on each other. The *Kelim* for GAR were made from their *Nitzotzin*.
    5. These are the *Kelim* that were made anew in *Hitpashtut Bet* itself by *Histalkut Bet* here in ten exits *de Lo Matei*, though they belong to *Partzuf SAG*.

110. **Where did the *Kelim* for *Partzuf SAG de AK* come from?**

    All the *Kelim* that were emptied from the *Orot* of *Partzuf AB*, moved to *Partzuf SAG* by the very same ways explained above in answer 109 regarding the transference of the *Kelim de Hitpashtut Aleph* to *Hitpashtut Bet*.

111. **Why do ZON de AB have two *Kelim* and ZON de SAG only one *Kli*?**

    Since there were no *Haka'ot* here to generate *Nitzotzin* for the *Nekeva*.

112. **Why did all the *Orot* come to *Kli de Keter* together in *Hitpashtut Bet*?**

Because that *Zivug* which is made on the *Behinot Reshimot* called ZON de *Kli de Keter* was at nearly *Komat Keter*. Hence, they could only come down and clothe in their designated *Kli*, being *Kli de Keter*. However, after they were purified and their *Koma* lessened to the *Koma* of the other *Sefirot*, they descended and clothed in them to that extent.

(*Ohr Pnimi* item 35, par. "Now you can")

113. **What are *Panim* and *Achor de Kelim*?**

A place of bestowal is called *Panim*, and the place through which it does not bestow is called *Achor*. It makes no difference if that place is administration of GAR or administration of VAK.

(*Ohr Pnimi* item 40, par. "The meaning of *Panim* and *Achor*")

114. **Why are the *Kelim de Hitpashtut Bet* arranged one below the other?**

Because thus was their beginning when they were made in *Histalkut Aleph*, where *Keter* is above all and *Malchut* is at the end.

115. **What are the *Panim* and *Achor de KHB*?**

- The *Panim de Kli Keter* is *He'arat VAK* that prevents GAR, and the *Achor* is *He'arat GAR*.
- The *Panim de Kli de Hochma* is *He'arat GAR* and the *Achor* is *He'arat VAK*.
- The *Panim de Kli de Bina* is *He'arat VAK*, which is *Hassadim*, but it depends on a reason in the form of "because He delighteth in mercy." If there is *He'arat Hassadim* in the *Partzuf*, the reason is cancelled, and then it cancels her *Achoraim*.
- The *Panim de Kli de Hesed* is *He'arat GAR* and its *Achor* is *He'arat VAK* since it extends from the *He'arat Hochma* and resembles her.
- The *Panim de Gevura* is *He'arat VAK* and her *Achor* GAR. This is because she extends from the *He'arat Kli de Bina* and resembles her.
- The *Panim de Tifferet* is a mixture of *He'arat HG* together, meaning from the *Behinat Gevura* when she is incorporated in the *Panim de Hesed*, and his *Achor* is *He'arat VAK*.
- The *Panim de Netzah* is *He'arat VAK* and his *Achor* is *He'arat GAR*.
- The *Panim de Hod* is *He'arat GAR* and his *Achor* is *He'arat VAK*.
- The *Panim de Yesod* is *He'arat VAK*, and his *Achor* is *He'arat GAR*.
- The *Panim de Malchut* is *He'arat GAR*.

(*Ohr Pnimi* item 40, par. "The meaning of *Panim* and *Achor*")

116. **Why are there no *Kelim* in the *Partzuf* due to the *Hitpashtut Bet* of itself?**

    This is because a *Kli* is not completed before the *Ohr* drifts three distances from it. Because of that only the *Kelim de* ZON were completed, and they move to the next *Partzuf*, where the *Ohr* returns in the same empty *Kli*. Thus, the *Kelim* that were made in *Histaklut Bet* of the *Partzuf* are only for the needs of the second *Partzuf*.

117. **What is the difference between *Hitpashtut Aleph* and *Hitpashtut Bet*?**

    In *Hitpashtut Aleph* there was only one *Hitpashtut* and one *Histalkut*, though it departed gradually. However, in *Hitpashtut Bet* it expanded by and order of *Matei ve Lo Matei*, creating ten exits and ten entrances until *de Matei* to *Malchut*.

    (Item 20)

118. **How are the *Kelim de* GAR made?**

    The *Kelim de* GAR, being KHB, were made by *Hitpashtut Bet* itself, since the *Ohr Hochma* dressed there in *Kli de Keter* and the *Zachar de Keter* clothes inside the *Ohr Hochma*. By that the bad *Ohr* falls from within the *Reshimo* and becomes a *Behinat Kli* below the *Ohr Hochma*, as the *Ohr Hochma* clothes in it.

    It follows, that *Hochma* separates between the *Ohr Reshimo*, which is the *Zachar de Keter*, and the bad *Ohr* that was separated from him, the *Kli de Keter* becomes very dark, and in that state its *Behinat Kli* is finished. The *Kelim de Hochma* and *Bina* are made similarly.

    (Item 50)

119. **What are the causes of the completion of the *Kelim de* GAR?**

    There are three causes here:

    1. Because of the division and the departure of the good *Ohr* of the *Reshimo* from the bad *Ohr* in it.
    2. Because of the coming of the *Ohr Hochma* in the middle, separating between the good *Ohr* of the *Reshimo* and the bad *Ohr* that was separated from it.
    3. Because of the *Achoraim* of the root *Ohr Keter* that did not return for *Hitpashtut Bet*. It remained standing under *Malchut* of the *Rosh* with its *Achoraim* to the *Anafim*, meaning to the *Sefirot de Guf*. These *Achoraim* of the *Ohr Keter* diminish the *Ohr* extensively and darken the *Sefirot* KHB even more than they had during *Histalkut Aleph* itself. For this reason they darken the *Kelim* as if the *Ohr* is far three degrees.

    (*Ohr Pnimi* item 50. par. "The Rav gives")

120. **What are the parts in the *Kli* that are worthy of looking into the *Ohr* even during the *Histalkut*?**

These are the *Behinot* that exist in the *Hitzoniut* of the *Kli*. They are not as *Av* as the inner half of the wall. For example: if the *Pnimiut* of the *Kli* is *Behina Dalet* and *Komat Keter* leaves it, the *Hitzoniut* of the *Kli*, which is *Behina Gimel*, is fit to receive more *Ohr* from the *He'arat Zivug* of its Upper *Behina*, being *Komat Behina Gimel*. Also, her *Behina Bet* is fit to receive more of the *He'arat Zivug* in the degree above the Upper.

(Item 15)

121. **What causes the *Kli* to turn its *Panim* downward and its *Achoraim* upward?**

When the *Ohr* departs from the degree and the *Zivug* is made in the degree above it, such as in *Behina Bet*, the *Ohr Hozer* descends from the *He'arat Zivug de Behina Bet* to the lower *Behina Gimel*. At that time there is a *Bitush* between the *Reshimo de Behina Gimel* and the descending *Ohr Hozer*.

This is so because the *He'arah de Behina Bet* is in oppositeness to the *Reshimo de Behina Gimel*. At that time the *Reshimo* leaves its place and rises above the *Kli*, giving room for the *Ohr Hozer* to clothe in the *Kli de Behina Gimel*.

Thus, this *Ohr Hozer* clothes the outer half of the wall of that *Kli*, which fits its measure of *Koma*, being in *Behina Bet* and *Behina Gimel*, which is *Achor de Behina Gimel*. You find that the *Panim de Behina Gimel* remains empty of *Ohr*, and the *Achor de Behina Gimel*, which is the *Behina Bet*, is filled with *Ohr*.

This is called turning its *Achoraim* upwards and its *Panim* downwards. It follows, that the *Ohr Hozer* that descends from the *He'arat Zivug* of the Upper degree causes the *Kli* of the lower degree to turn its *Panim* downward.

(*Ohr Pnimi* item 15, par. "All this refers")

122. **What causes the *Kli* to turn its *Panim* to its place as in the beginning?**

After the *Zivug* stops from the adjacent Upper degree as well and the *Ohr Hozer* that descends into her *Kli* stops, the *Reshimo* returns into her *Kli*. Thus, you find that the *Kli* returns its *Panim* upwards and its *Achoraim* downward as in the beginning.

This is because now the *Achor* of the *Kli* cannot receive the *He'arat Reshimo*, which is *Behina Gimel*, it returns to being *Hitzoniut* of the *Kli* as in the beginning, and the entire *He'arat Reshimo* comes to the *Kli*, which is *Behina Gimel*.

(*Ohr Pnimi* item 16, Sub Header **"Will be able"**)

123. **What is *Histaklut* in the *Ohr Elyon* through the *Achor*?**

    The *Ohr* departs from the *Kli* and the *Zivug* is made in the degree above it, such as when it departs from *Behina Gimel* and the *Zivug* is made in *Behina Bet*. At that time the *Achor* of this *Kli*, which is *Behina Bet*, looks at the *Ohr Elyon*, meaning it receives from the *He'arat Zivug* there.

    (*Ohr Pnimi* item 15, Sub Header **"It looks"**)

124. **How will the *Orot* be extended from *Keter* to *Hochma* when they are so far from each other?**

    Their *Komot* equalize with one another and they are *Panim be Panim* by the *Hizdakchut* of the *Aviut* and the turning of the *Panim* downward.

    (*Ohr Pnimi* item 35, par. "However, we must remember")

125. **What two kinds of inversions of the *Panim* are implemented in the degrees?**

    An Upper degree cannot dispense to the lower one except though *Hishtavut* with it, at which time they are close to one another. Hence, there is a measure of inversion of the *Panim de Elyon* to the measure of the *Panim* of the *Tachton*, and this is called *Panim be Panim*.

    There are two *Behinot* of inversion of the *Panim*:

    1. Every *Kli* is defined by its *Behinat* bestowal, by its nature, whether *He'arat VAK* or *He'arat GAR*. This is because *Kli de Keter* naturally administers VAK, not GAR.

        Thus, when it dispenses to *Hochma*, whose *Panim* is GAR, the *Keter* must invert its *Panim* downward and its *Achoraim* upward to *Behinat Panim*, in order to equalize its *Panim* with the *Panim de Hochma*. It is similar in all the other *Sefirot*.

    2. The second is the *Hishtavut Koma*, also named "inversion of the *Panim* downward". For example, *Komat Keter* cannot administer to the degree of *Hochma* except through the *Hizdakchut* of the *Aviut de Behina Dalet* to *Behina Gimel* that extends *Komat Hochma*. In that state, *Komat Keter* is equal to the degree of *Hochma*, and the *Keter* dispenses its *He'arah* to the *Hochma*.

    (*Ohr Pnimi* item 40, par. "The *Masach*")

126. **What causes the division of the *Sefirot Hochma* and *Bina*?**

    The inversion of the *Panim de Kli de Hochma* downward and the making of the *Achor*, which is *He'arat VAK*, into her *Panim*, like the *Panim de Kli* of *Bina*. By so doing, *Hochma* is divided into two *Behinot*, meaning administration of GAR and administration of VAK.

The *Kli Hochma* itself is considered administration of GAR, and the *Kli de Bina*, which received *VAK de Hochma*, is considered administration of *VAK*.

(*Ohr Pnimi* item 40, par. "Keep in mind")

127. **Why do all the *Sefirot* remain in *Panim* and *Achor* after *Histalkut Aleph*?**

    This is because once the *Zivug* stops form the highest *Behina*, from the *Kli* whose *Ohr* has emptied, the *Reshimo* returns to her place and the *Kli* returns its *Panim* to its place as in the beginning (see answer 122). Hence, all the *Kelim* remain in *Behinat Panim* and *Achor* after the completion of the *Histalkut*, meaning the *Panim* of the *Tachton* in the *Achor* of the *Elyon*.

    (Item 18)

128. **Why did *Keter* and *Hochma* remain *Panim be Panim* after *Histalkut Aleph*?**

    Because *Behina Dalet* did not leave a *Reshimo*. It is known that *Behina Dalet* serves as *Panim* to the *Kli de Keter*, which is the most *Av* in the *Masach*, called *Panim*. That which is not so *Av* is considered the *Achor de Keter*.

    It is considered that its *Panim* is downward and equalizes with the *Panim de Hochma* since it has grown close to *Behina Gimel* of the *Hochma*. Even though *Reshimo de Behina Dalet de Hitlabshut* remains there, it is not enough to return the *Panim de Kli de Keter* as in the beginning. Also, this causes the *Ohr Keter* to remain in the *Peh* and not return in *Hitpashtut Bet*.

    (*Ohr Pnimi* item 18)

129. **Why is *Keter Achor be Achor* with the *Ohr Elyon*?**

    Because the *Kli* lacks its primary *Reshimo*, which is a *Reshimo de Hamshacha*, and the *Reshimo de Hitlabshut* that remains in it is considered the *Achor de Kli de Keter*. Also, her *Ohr* up in the *Rosh* stands with its *Achoraim* to the *Anafim* in the *Guf*.

    (There)

130. **What is the meaning of a Moment in spirituality?**

    See at the end of Histaklut Pnimit Part 1. It explains there that Spiritual Time is considered motion, and Spiritual Motion is considered a *Hidush Tzura* that is attained there. From that we understand that the slightest *Shinui Tzura*, the slightest there is, is called "A Moment".

131. **When is the *Kli Malchut* completed in *Histalkut Aleph*?**

    When the *Ohr Malchut* rose to *Kli de Hochma*, a distance of three degrees has been made between the *Ohr* and the *Kli*, and then the *Kli* darkened and was completed.

    (Item 17 and *Ohr Pnimi* there)

132. **When is *Kli ZA* completed in *Histalkut Aleph*?**

    When *Ohr ZA* rose to its *Shoresh* to the *Rosh*. This is because then a distance of three degrees without *Ohr* has been made between the *Ohr* and the *Kli*, hence the *Kli* was darkened and completed (see below answer 134).

    (There)

133. **Why is any less than three is considered filled?**

    This is so because up to three degrees, the *Kli* still receives from *Orot Makifim*. This is so because when *Ohr Malchut* ascends to ZA, *Malchut* receives one *Makif*. When it rises to *Bina*, she receives a second *Makif*, but when *Ohr Malchut* rises to *Kli de Hochma*, it no longer receives any *He'arah*, hence the *Kli* darkens and is completed.

    (There)

134. **Why is the ascent of ZA to *Bina* not considered remoteness of degree?**

    As long as there is some *Ohr* in a *Kli*, even though it is not its own *Behina*, it is not considered remoteness of degree. Hence, when *Ohr ZA* rises to *Kli de Bina*, at which time *Ohr Malchut* rises to *Kli de ZA*, it is still considered having *Ohr Pnimi* in its *Kli*.

    However, afterwards, when *Ohr ZA* rose to *Kli de Hochma*, it is considered remoteness of one degree. When it rises to *Kli de Keter*, it is considered remoteness of two degrees, when the *Kli* still receives from *Orot Makifim*; it is still not completely darkened. Only when it rises to the *Maatzil* is it completely darkened and its *Kli* is completed.

    (Items 50 and 27)

135. **When was there *Lo Matei* in *Keter* for the first time?**

    In the *Histalkut Orot de Hitpashtut Aleph*, called *Partzuf Keter*. For this reason it is called *Histalkut* of the *Ohr Keter*.

    (*Ohr Pnimi* item 6)

136. **Why is *Histalkut Aleph* called *Lo Matei* in *Keter*?**

    See above answer 135.

137. **Who causes the *Lo Matei* in *Hitpashtut Bet* every time?**

    The *Bitush* and *Hakaa* of *Ohr Makif* in *Ohr Pnimi*.

    (*Ohr Pnimi* item 6)

138. **Why were the *Matei ve Lo Matei* made into ten *Orot* and were not made into ten *Kelim*?**

    Because with respect to the *Kli* itself, there is only one *Hizdakchut* and one *Histalkut* here. This is so because in the end, there is only one *Kli Malchut* here, and no *Kelim* were added to the *Kli Malchut* by all these *Histalkuiot* (pl. for *Histalkut*). The *Eser Sefirot* that we discern are like one long *Kli* containing ten parts, not equal to each other.

(Item 22, and *Ohr Pnimi* there)

139. **Why is the permanent Matei ve Lo Matei compared to a flame swaying here and there?**

Because at the moment *de Matei* to *Malchut* and the *Ohr* departed from the *Partzuf* entirely, it immediately returned to being *Matei* in *Keter*, until the disappearance of the *Ohr* was like a flame swaying here and there.

(*Ohr Pnimi* item 49)

140. **What is the ratio between ZON de Hochma and ZON de Bina?**

Although they are discerned as one *Koma*, namely *Koma de Behina Bet*, they are still related as *VAK* relates to *GAR*. This is because *ZON de Hochma* are considered *GAR* and *ZON de Bina* are considered *VAK de GAR*.

It is like *YESHSUT de Atzilut* compared to *AVI de Atzilut*. The *Zachar de Kli de Bina* was born from *Zivug ZON de Hochma* when they turned their *Panim* downwards, meaning when they cancelled the *He'arat GAR* in them and received the *Panim de VAK*.

Hence, the *Zachar* was born in *Behinat Achoraim de Hochma* and in *Behinat VAK*. The *Nekeva de Bina* is *Behinat GAR*, which is a *Reshimo* without *Ohr*, and she receives all the *Ohr* in her through the *Zachar*, which is *VAK*, and for this reason the force of the *Zachar* is on her.

Also, the *Kli Bina* is also *Behinat VAK de GAR* in its *Atzmut*, in the form of "because He delighteth in mercy." Thus, *ZON de Bina* are considered *Behinat VAK de GAR*.

(*Ohr Pnimi* item 40, par. "Keep in mind")

141. **How is Hesed emanated?**

First it was *Lo Matei* in *Keter*. Due to the *Bitush de Ohr Makif* and *Ohr Pnimi* on each other, the *ZON de Keter* were purified, which are *Behina Dalet* and *Behina Gimel* to *Behina Gimel* and *Behina Bet*.

They gave them to the *Hochma* in *Behinot ZON de Hochma*, and then the *Panim de Hochma* returned to their place as in the beginning. Hence, *ZON de Bina* returned and rose to *Hochma* since *VAK* always join their *GAR* when they are disclosed.

Thus, now *Hochma* joined *Bina* into one degree. Consequently, the *Ohr Hesed* which is in *Kli de Bina* now receives *He'arat Hochma*, because of the unification of *Hochma* and *Bina*.

Hesed became great because it acquired *He'arat Hochma*. This means that it no longer needs to suck from the *Kli de Bina* to *Behina Aleph* in order to equalize with the *Kli de Hesed*, and the *Ohr Hesed* was lowered to the *Kli de Hesed*.

(*Ohr Pnimi* item 40, par. "Interpretation")

142. **What is *Behinat Kli de Hesed*?**

    It is *Behinat Keter* of the *Hey Behinot de Ohr Hassadim*, since KHB of the *Ohr Hassadim* is called HGT.

    (*Ohr Pnimi* item 40, par. "Now you can thoroughly see")

143. **What is *Behinat Ohr de Hesed*?**

    It is evaluated as *Behinat Ohr Hochma* in *Kli de Keter*. This is because *Hesed* has only that *He'arat Hochma* that the general *Ohr Hesed* received while being in *Kli de Bina*.

    Also, everything that if found in the general *Ohr Hesed* below the *Ohr Hochma* that it received, no longer belongs to the *Sefirat Hesed*, but to the six lower *Sefirot* below *Hesed*. Hence, the *Hesed* is considered *Behinat Hochma* in *Kli de Keter*, since its *Kli* is *Behinat Keter*, as written in answer 142.

    (There)

144. **What is the order of the emanation of the *Ohr* of *Gevura*?**

    This is the rule: the coming of the *Ohr Hesed* to its *Kli* causes being *Matei* in *Keter*. This is because then the ZON *de Bina* purified to *Behina Aleph* in order to be *Panimbe Panim* with the *Kli* of the *Hesed*.

    For this reason the entire *Komat Ohr Bina* disappeared and four *Orot de HB* rose to the *Keter*. At that time they induced a new *Zivug* and *Matei* in *Keter*. You find that the *Achoraim de Keter* returned to its place as in the beginning, and *He'arat GAR* was prevented from the entire *Partzuf*.

    Since the *He'arat GAR* stopped from the *Ohr Hesed*, it immediately becomes needy of its mother *Bina* in order to suck *He'arat GAR* from *Kli de Bina*. Hence, it rises to *Bina* and the *Kli de Hesed* turns its *Panim* downward, giving its remains, meaning everything below its own *Behina*, to *Kli de Gevura*.

    (There)

145. **What is the property of *Sefirat Gevura*?**

    Her *Kli* has the ratio of *Hochma* to *Ohr de Hassadim*. This is so because KHB *de Hassadim* are called HGT and her *Ohr* is *Behinat VAK de He'arat Hochma* in *Hesed*, which is as VAK *de GAR* compared to the *Ohr Hesed*.

It is like the *Zachar de Kli de Bina*, which is the *Behinat VAK de GAR* compared to *Hochma* (see answer 140). Thus, the property of *Ohr Gevura* compared to the *Ohr Hesed* is as the value of ZON *de Bina* compared to ZON *de Hochma*.

This is the meaning of "I am Understanding (*Bina*), Power (*Gevura*) is mine," since their value is the same and there is no difference between them, but only in the measure of the *Koma*; one is *Komat Behina Bet*, and the other is *Komat Behina Aleph*.

(*Ohr Pnimi* item 40, par. "Now we shall explain")

146. **What is the difference between ZON *de Bina* and *Sefirat Gevura*?**

See above answer 145.

147. **What is the order of the emanation of the *Ohr Tifferet*?**

After it returned to being *Lo Matei* in *Keter*, its *Achoraim* were cancelled on the GAR and ZON *de Hochma* returned to their place. *Kli de Hochma* turned its *Panim* without *Hizdakchut* and placed ZON *de Bina* to their place. After that ZON *de Bina* returned to *Behina Aleph*, and lowered the *Ohr Hesed* to its place.

This is because after the *He'arat GAR* returned to the *Partzuf* and *Hesed* acquired *He'arat Hochma*, it no longer needs its *Ima Bina*. At that time the *Ohr Gevura* rises to *Hesed* since when GAR reappears, its VAK immediately joins with it. In that state *Kli de Gevura* turns its *Panim* downward and places its residue, meaning every thing that is below *Behinat Ohr Gevura*, to the *Kli Tifferet*.

(*Ohr Pnimi* item 40, par. "Now we shall explain the order")

148. **What is the property of the *Kli de Tifferet*?**

Its *Kli* is *Behinat Bina* of *Ohr de Hassadim*. Its *Ohr* is the *Atzmut Ohr Hesed* that was in *Kli de Bina*. This is because the *Orot de Hesed* and *Gevura* are only *He'arot* GAR and VAK *de Hochma* that the *Ohr Hesed* received, but the *Tifferet* is the *Etzem* of this *Ohr* of *Hassadim*. The value of the *Sefira* is as the value of the *Daat* that mates between *Hochma* and *Bina*, since it is *Behinat Ohr Hesed* in *Kli de Bina*, which is the *Ohr Daat*.

(There)

149. **How is the *Ohr Hesed* different when it is in *Bina* from when it is in *Tifferet*?**

The difference is in the value. It is like the difference between the Lower *Daat* and the Upper *Daat*. When *Ohr Hesed* is in *Bina*, it unites the HB into a single *Partzuf*, in the sense that it receives the *He'arat Hochma* from the same time *Hochma* and *Bina* returned to the first *Partzuf*.

When it is in *Tifferet* it is in the form of the Lower *Daat*, uniting all the *Orot Hesed* and *Gevura* into one in the sense that it receives *He'arat Hesed* from the same time *Gevura* rose to *Hesed* and united with it into a single *Ohr*. Because of that beginning, the uniting of *Hochma* and *Gevura* into one has been imprinted in it forever, since it cannot receive its *Shefa* from them in another way. It is like Upper *Daat*, which cannot receive *He'arat Hochma* except through *Hochma* and *Bina* to one *Partzuf*.

(*Ohr Pnimi* item 41, par. "Now we understand *Sefirat Tifferet*")

150. **What is *Ohr Daat* at its *Shoresh*?**

It is a new upshot that emerged during the concealment of the *Ohr Keter* from the *Partzuf de AB* and the replacement of the *Orot*. Because the *Ohr Hochma* clothed in the *Kli Keter*, *Ohr ZA* ascended to clothe in *Kli Bina* to be emanated by the *Hochma*.

In so doing, two *Behinot Ohr ZA* emanated: The first relates to *Partzuf Keter*, when the *Orot* are in their actual place, at which time ZA was emanated by *Bina*, clothing in *Kelim de VAK*. The second relates to *Partzuf Hochma*, when the *Orot* changed their places. At that time the *Ohr ZA* was emanated by *Hochma*, clothing *Kelim de GAR*, meaning in *Kli de Bina*.

Hence, from here on all the *Partzufim* contain two *Behinot* ZA in every *Partzuf*. The Upper ZA, which acquired a place of GAR, is called *Sefirat Daat*, and the Lower ZA, standing in its actual place in *VAK* is called ZA.

(*Ohr Pnimi* item 41, par. "Now we have explained the *Ohr Daat*")

151. **What is the essence of *Behinat ZA* in the *Hey Ktzavot*?**

From the perspective of the *Ohr*, which is the primary, *Sefirat Tifferet* is the essence of ZA. This is because the *Ohr Tifferet* is the *Atzmut* of the *Ohr Hesed* in *Kli de Bina*. For this reason it is called *Vav* ו with a *Rosh*, as *Behinot GAR* of *Bina* rest on it since it was in *Kli de Bina*.

However, from the perspective of the *Kli*, it is *Sefirat Netzah*, being the fourth tip in the five *Ktzavot*, opposite the fourth *Behina* in the *Hey Behinot KHB* ZA and *Malchut*. Thus you find that the ZA in the five *Behinot* is opposite the *Netzah* in the *Hey Hassadim*.

(There par. "From all")

152. **What are the *Behinot RTS* in ZAT?**

Hesed and *Gevura*, which are opposite HB, are *Behinat Rosh* of the ZAT. *Tifferet* and *Netzah* are *Behinat Toch* of the ZAT. One is from the perspective of the *Ohr*, and the other is from the perspective of the *Kli* (see answer 151).

Hod, Yesod, Malchut, are the *Behinat Sof* of the ZAT since *Hod* is the fifth tip of the *Hey Ktzavot*, corresponding to *Malchut* in the *Hey Behinot*, and *Yesod* and *Malchut* extended from it.

(There)

153. **What is the difference between *Hesed* and Gevura, and *Tifferet*?**

    Hesed and *Gevura* are not the *Etzem Ohr Hesed*, but *He'arot Hochma* and *Bina* that reached *Hesed* when it clothed in the *Kli* of *Bina*, but *Tifferet* is indeed the essence and the *Atzmut* of the *Ohr Hesed*.

    (*Ohr Pnimi* item 41, par. "Therefore, *Orot de HGT*")

154. **Why is the essence of *Ohr Hesed* not clothed in the *Sefirot* of *Hochma* and *Gevura*?**

    It is because of the property of their *Kelim*. *Kelim de Hesed* and *Gevura* are *Behinat Keter* and *Hochma*, in which the *Ohr Hesed* has no *Shoresh*. This is so because it only clothed the *Kli de Bina de GAR*.

    For this reason, the *Atzmut Ohr Hesed* cannot clothe in *Behinat Hey Hassadim* too, but in *Kli de Tifferet*, which is the *Bina de Hey Hassadim*, not in *Hesed* and *Gevura*, which are *Keter* and *Hochma de Hey Hassadim*.

    Ohr Hesed never clothed *Keter* and *Hochma*, and therefore the *Kelim de Hesed* and *Gevura* only have *He'arot Hochma* and *Bina* that reached the reception of the *Ohr Hesed* when it was in *Kli de Bina*. Also, the *Atzmut Ohr Hesed* clothed in *Kli de Tifferet*.

    (There)

155. **How is *Sefirat Netzah* emanated?**

    When it returns to being *Matei* in *Keter*, when the dominion of the *Achoraim de Keter* returns as in the beginning and *He'arat GAR* is prevented from the entire *Partzuf*, *Ohr Hesed* departs to *Bina* once more. Its VAK is *Matei* in *Gevura* and the *Ohr Tifferet* too departs and returns to its *Shoresh* in the *Kli Gevura*, its VAK is given to the *Kli de Netzah* and *Matei* in *Netzah*.

    (*Ohr Pnimi* item 42)

156. **What is the attribute of *Sefirat Netzah*?**

    The *Kli* is the *Atzmut* of ZA since it is the fourth tip, opposite ZA of the *Hey Behinot*. Its *Ohr* is *Behinat VAK* from the *Atzmut* of the *Ohr ZA*, which is the *Ohr Tifferet* since after *Ohr Tifferet* concealed in its *Shoresh* in *Gevura*, *Tifferet* gave its VAK to *Netzah* (see answer 155).

    (*Ohr Pnimi* item 42, par. "Now we shall understand *Sefirat Netzah*")

157. What is the difference between *HGT* and *NHY*?

Even though every *Behinat* seven lower *Sefirot* is *Behinat VAK*, they still have *He'arat GAR* in them. Hence, as we discern two *Behinot* in GAR, GAR *de VAK* and *VAK de VAK*, so we have two *Behinot* in VAK, GAR *de VAK* and VAK *de VAK*.

This is so because *HGT* are considered GAR *de VAK*, and *NHY* are VAK *de VAK*. For this reason *NHY* are considered outside the *Guf*, as they are *Behinat Ohr de Hassadim*, lacking *He'arat Hochma*.

The entire sustenance of the *Guf* is only *Ohr Hochma* since it is the *Atzmut* of the *Ohr Elyon*. However, it is impossible that *NHY* will be completely emptied of *He'arat Hochma* since they would be completely cancelled.

Instead, there is a *Behinat Reshimo de HGT* in them, which means a minute *He'arah*, and for this reason the *NHY* are called *Gimel Go Gimel*. It means that the *Reshimot* of the *Sefirot HGT* are concealed in the three *Sefirot NHY* in a way that suffices for their sustenance.

158. What is the attribute of the *Kli de Hod*?

The *Kli* is *Behinat Hesed*, the fifth of the *Hey Hassadim* in the *Hey Behinot*, meaning *Behina Dalet*, which is *Midatha Din*. However, this is from the aspect of her being incorporated in ZA, and her *Ohr* is the remains of *Netzah*.

However, from the aspect of the *Hitkalelut Netzah* in *Tifferet*, the *Ohr Netzah* is then incorporated in *He'arat GAR* too from the *Behinat Ohr Daat* that shines in *Tifferet*. Hence, the *Ohr Hod* is considered merely *Behinat He'arat GAR de Ohr Daat*, and nothing of *He'arat GAR de Hochma* and *Bina*.

This is so because its entire *He'arah* extends from the connection of GAR and VAK *de Ohr Tifferet*, meaning the connection of *Netzah* with *Tifferet* after the *He'arat GAR* is extended to the *Partzuf*. You already know that the *Ohr Tifferet* is merely the *Behinat Ohr Daat*, and not from *Hochma* and *Bina*, whose place is in the *Kelim de Hesed* and *Gevura*.

(There)

159. What is *Sefirat Yesod*?

Its *Kli* is from *Behinat Malchut* since it extends from *Hod*, which is the *Shoresh* of *Malchut* of the *Hey Hassadim*, and the *Ohr* in it is mingled of *Din* and *Rachamim*. This is so because it has two *Orot*: The first is the remains of the *Ohr* that *Hod* gave it, which is *Komat Malchut*, which is *Behinat Din*. The second *Ohr* is the *Hey* that reached from the *Zivug de ZON de Bina* that the *Hod* illuminated for before it purified to *Komat Malchut*.

(*Ohr Pnimi* item 45, par. "Thus, the *Kli de Yesod*")

160. **In which *Sefira* did *Ohr Malchut* clothe?**

Ohr Malchut clothed in the *Kli Yesod*. This is because after the *Hod* purified from *Behina Aleph* to *Behinat Keter*, the *Koma* educed on that *Masach* has only *Komat Malchut*, and then he gives it to the *Kli de Yesod*.

(*Ohr Pnimi* item 46, par. "That cessation")

161. **What is the *Ohr* that clothed in *Kli Malchut*?**

The *Ohr* of the *Dalet* ד, surrounding the Truncated *Vav* ו inside the *Hey* ה that reached *Yesod* from *Zivug ZON de Bina*, is *Behinat GAR* without *VAK*, meaning without *Ohr Hassadim*. She descended from *Yesod* and clothed in *Malchut*.

(*Ohr Pnimi* item 47, par. "Now we shall explain the *Zachar*")

162. **What is the ratio between *ZON de Hochma* and *ZON de Bina*?**

See above answer 140.

163. **How many *Behinot ZON* are there in *Hitpashtut Bet*?**

They are four *Behinot ZON*: *ZON de Kli Keter*, *ZON de Kli Hochma*, *ZON de Kli Bina*, and *ZON de Kli de Yesod* and *Malchut*.

164. **What is the attribute of the four *ZON* couples of *Hitpashtut Bet*?**

In the first two couples, which are *ZON de Keter* and *ZON de Hochma*, the *Zecharim* are more important than the *Nekevot*. This is because the *Zachar de Keter* is from *Behina Dalet de Hitlabshut*, but the *Nekeva* is only from *Behina Gimel*. The *Zachar de Kli de Hochma* is only from *Behina Gimel*, but the *Nekeva de Kli de Hochma* is from *Behina Bet*. Thus, the *Zecharim* are more important than the *Nekevot*.

However, in *ZON de Kli de Bina*, the *Nekeva* is greater than the *Zachar*. This is because the *Zachar* is *Behinat VAK* of *Hochma* and the *Nekeva* is *Behinat GAR*, as she is the *Reshimo de Ohr Bina* from the time of *Hitpashtut Aleph*.

ZON, however, that is in the *Kli* of *Yesod*, the *Zachar* is found to be greater than the *Nekeva* since the *Zachar* is the Truncated *Vav* inside the *Hey*, extending from *Zivug Bina*. It is given to *Yesod* from *Sefirat Hod* without *Hizdakchut*, but as mere *He'arah*, hence it is *Behinat Hassadim de Behina Aleph*, and also extends from a higher place than *Zivug ZON de Bina*.

Nevertheless, the *Nekeva* in *Yesod* is the residue of the *Ohr Hod* after its *GAR* disappeared and after it purified from *Behina Aleph* to *Komat Malchut*. Thus, it is found to be much lower than her *Zachar*.

(*Ohr Pnimi* item 40, par. "You find that there are four males")

165. **In which *Behina* did the *Zivug* stop and the *Ohr* of *Hitpashtut Bet* depart entirely?**

When the *Ohr Dalet* in the *Matei* in *Zivug ZON de Bina* to *Malchut*. This is because the *Masach* has been entirely purified from all its *Aviut* until it equalized to *Behinat Malchut* of *Rosh*, considered that it rose to the *Rosh*, to the *Maatzil*, at which time all the *Orot* departed from the *Partzuf*.

(*Ohr Pnimi* item 46, par. "This *Dalet*")

166. **What is the second *Behina* of *Hitpashtut Bet*?**

It is the *Behinat* perpetual *Matei ve Lo Matei*. Every time the *Ohr Matei* to *Malchut*, it immediately returns to be *Matei* in *Keter*, *Gevura*, *Netzah*, and *Yesod*, and *Lo Matei* in *Hochma*, *Bina*, and *Hesed*, *Tifferet*, *Hod*, and *Malchut*.

Afterwards, *Keter* returns to being in *Lo Matei*, and *Matei* in *Hochma*, *Bina*, and *Hesed*, *Tifferet*, *Hod*, and *Malchut*, and *Lo Matei* in *Keter*, *Gevura*, *Netzah*, and *Yesod*, and so on and so forth continually. This *Behinat Hitpashtut* of the perpetual *Matei ve Lo Matei* is called *Partzuf SAG de AK*, or *Bina de AK*.

(*Ohr Pnimi* item 47)

167. **How was *Partzuf SAG de AK* emanated?**

When it is *Matei* in *Malchut de AB de AK*, which is the *Behina Aleph de Hitpashtut Bet*, the *Masach* purifies entirely, and equalizes with *Malchut* of the *Rosh*, since the *Hishtavut Tzura* unites the spirituals into one. This *Masach* that rose to the *Rosh* consists of all the *Reshimot* of the *Sefirot de Hitpashtut Bet*.

These are five *Orot*: *ZON de Hochma*, *Bina*, and the *Ohr Hesed* that contains *ZAT*, which are all included in *ZON de Keter*. However, the *Reshimo de Behina Gimel*, which is *Behinat Aviut* of *Hamshacha* that was in *Hitpashtut Bet*, and is the last *Behina* here, disappeared like the last *Behina* of *Partzuf Keter*. This is the *Behina Dalet* that disappeared in *Histalkut Aleph* there.

The rule is that the last *Behina* does not leave a *Reshimo*, and this applies to every single *Histalkut*. Hence, only the *Reshimo de Behina Bet* remained here after the second *Histalkut*.

However, the *Behinat Reshimo de Hitlabshut* of *Behina Gimel* remained as well, as the *Behina Dalet de Hitlabshut* remained after *Histalkut Aleph*. This is so because only the *Behinat Hamshacha* is lost from each last *Behina*, but not the *Behinat Hitlabshut*.

Hence, these two *Reshimot*, *Behina Gimel de Hitlabshut* and *Behina Bet*, containing *Behinat Hamshacha*, caused two Upper *Zivugim* in the *Rosh*. It is similar to the two *Zivugim de ZON de Keter* after *Histalkut Aleph*, because they were incorporated in one another.

In the first *Zivug*, the *Nekeva* was incorporated in the *Zachar* in *Behina Gimel*. At that time *Komat Eser Sefirot* came out nearly in the *Koma* of the Upper

Hochma. However, they still could not expand and descend below to the *Guf* since *Behina Gimel* is devoid of *Hamshacha*.

Afterwards, a second *Zivug* was made, where the *Zachar* was incorporated in the *Nekeva* in *Behina Bet*, at which time *Eser Sefirot* in *Komat Bina* extended. Now that she contains *Behinat Hamshacha* too, *Malchut* of this *Komat Bina* can expand from her and within her into *Eser Sefirot* and descend to the *Guf*.

At that time the above ZON descend to the *Kli de Keter* of the *Guf*, filled with *Ohr* from the above two *Behinot Zivugim*, and the perpetual *Matei ve Lo Matei* is made in them. Now, every time it is *Matei* to the *Malchut*, they return to the *Keter*, and this is called *Partzuf SAG de AK*.

(*Ohr Pnimi* item 47)

168. **What are the ZON of Kelim de KHB?**

    The ZON *de Kelim de KHB* of AB *de AK* are all *Behinat YH*. The *Zachar de Kli de Keter* is *Behinat Reshimo de Behina Dalet de Hitlabshut*. Its *Ohr* extends from the first *Zivug* in the *Rosh*, but consists of the second *Zivug* of *Rosh* in the *Ohr Hochma* as well.

    The *Nekeva* of the *Kli de Keter* is the *Etzem Komat Hochma* that expanded in *Partzuf AB*. Her *Ohr* is from the second *Zivug* of the *Rosh*, but she was contained in the first *Zivug de Rosh* too, in the Upper *Ohr Keter*.

    In ZON *de Kli de Hochma* the *Zachar* is from the *Zachar de Keter* after it has purified to *Behina Gimel*. The *Nekeva* is from the *Nekeva de Kli de Keter* after she has purified to *Behina Bet*, and the entire GAR in the *Partzuf* extends only through these ZON *de Hochma*.

    In ZON *de Kli de Bina*, the *Zachar* is born from the *Zivug* ZON *de Hochma* after they inverted the *Panim* from GAR to *He'arat VAK*. The *Nekeva* is the *Behinat Reshimo* that remained in *Kli de Bina* from the time of the first *Histalkut*.

    (Items 50 and 51)

169. **What are the names of ZON de KHB?**

    They are all called *YH*.

170. **What are the Otiot that designate ZON and the Kelim of KHB?**

    Each of them is called *Ot Yod*, filled. The *Zachar de Kli de Keter* is called *Yod*, the *Nekeva*, *Vav*, and the *Kli de Keter*, *Dalet*. Also, the *Zachar de Hochma* is called *Yod*, the *Nekeva*, *Vav*, and the *Kli de Hochma*, *Dalet*.

    In *Bina*, however, there is a difference: the *Zachar* is called *Yod*, the *Nekeva* is called *Dalet*, and the *Kli* does not merit a name, but the *Ohr Hesed* in it is called *Vav*.

    (Item 53)

171. **How many *Behinot* are there in *Hitpashtut Bet*?**

    Four *Behinot* ZON, three in *KHB* one ZON in *Yesod*.

    (Item 54)

172. **What is the meaning of Only *He'arah*, without giving *Orot*?**

    It is *Ohr* that is born by *Zivug* ZON for the purpose of a lower degree. However, giving *Orot* refers to an *Ohr* that hangs down and descends from *Sefira* to *Sefira* through the *Hizdakchut* of the *Masach*.

    (Item 35)

173. **Why did *Hochma* illuminate the *Vav* to *Bina* before the giving of the *Orot*?**

    It is because giving the seven *Orot* to the *Bina* was through *Hizdakchut* to *Behina Aleph*, but the *Zachar de Bina* that was emanated by *Hochma* was in *Komat Behina Bet*, but in the form of *Achoraim*. Hence, it administered it to the *Kli Bina* only in inverting of *Panim* to VAK, before it purified to *Behina Aleph*.

174. **Why did *Keter* not give the *Yod* to *Hochma* from *Behinat He'arah*?**

    This is because the *Achoraim* of the *Ohr Keter* that stands under *Malchut de Rosh* and detains the influence of the *Ohr Keter* to *Kli de* GAR. However, after ZON *de Keter* purified and the *Behinat Ohr Keter* departed to its *Shoresh*, its *Achoraim* were cancelled, and their residue was given to *Kli de Hochma*, being ZON *de Kli* of *Hochma*.

175. **When does *Hesed* need its mother and when does it not?**

    During the control of the *Achoraim de Keter*, which prevents *He'arat* GAR from the *Partzuf* and the two *Sefirot Hochma* and *Bina* are without *Ohr*, there is no *He'arat* GAR in *Hesed*. For this reason it needs its *Ima Bina* and rises to her to suck GAR from the place of *Bina*.

    However, when *Matei* in the two *Sefirot Hochma* and *Bina*, there is *He'arat* GAR in the *Partzuf*, and *Hesed* has *He'arat Hochma*. At that time it does not need its mother and can come down to its own degree.

    (*Ohr Pnimi* item 39, Sub Header **"The seven sons"**)

176. **Why does *Bina* rise to *Hochma* before it gives the *Ohr Hesed* to *Kli de Hesed*?**

    Because of the manifestation of *He'arat* GAR in *Kli de Hochma*. As the *Gadlut* illuminated to the *Hesed*, so it extended the ZON *de Bina* to it and united with them into one *Partzuf*. Then *Bina* purified from *Behina Bet* to *Behina Aleph* in order to be *Panim be Panim* with the *Kli Hesed*, and placed the *Ohr Hesed* there.

177. **How did the *Hey de Zivug ZON* of *Bina* reach the *Kli Malchut*?**

Bina purified from *Behina Bet* to *Behina Aleph* to give the *Ohr Hesed* to the *Kli de Hesed*. At that time it placed the *Hey* that was born of her *Zivug* along with the *Ohr Hesed* there. *Hesed* gave to *Gevura* in Only *He'arah* before it departed to *Kli de Bina*, *Gevura* to *Tifferet* etc. until it reached her place to *Yesod*. He took the *Vav* in her and gave the *Dalet* to *Malchut*.

(Item 44, and *Ohr Pnimi* there)

178. **What is the difference between the *Ohr Hesed* and the *Hey* from *Zivug ZON de Bina*?**

Ohr Hesed is *Behinat Ohr Panim*. Its *He'arah* is from the *Behinat Panim* of *Hochma*, and the beginning of its emanation was also through ZON de *Hochma*. However, the *Hey* is from *Behinat Achoraim* since she was emanated by ZON de *Kli* of *Bina*, which are *Behinat VAK de Hochma*.

Yet, she contains *Behinat GAR* from *Reshimo de Bina*, though these GAR are dark since they are from *Behinat Histalkut*, hence, they are subordinate to the VAK of the *Zachar*.

(*Ohr Pnimi* item 43, par. "Now we can thoroughly understand")

179. **How is the *Hey* separated into two separated degrees?**

When *He'arat GAR* returns to the *Partzuf* and *Matei* in *Hod*, the *Ohr Yesod* departed and rose to its *Shoresh* to *He'arat GAR* in *Hod*. Then the Truncated *Vav* rose along with it when they are united in one another, and the *Ohr* of the *Dalet* descended to the *Malchut*.

(*Ohr Pnimi* item 46, par. "The meaning of the words")

180. **Why can't the *Ohr Hesed* be a *Zachar* to *Bina*?**

Since the difference between VAK and GAR is great, it is utterly impossible that the *Ohr Hesed*, which is complete VAK, will be a *Zachar* to *Behinat Bina*, which is GAR.

(*Ohr Pnimi* item 51)

181. **Why can't the *Ohr Hesed* be a *Nekeva* to *Bina*?**

Because the *Ohr Hesed*, which is ZA, is a *Zachar* at its origin *de Ohr Yashar*, and a *Zachar* does not become a *Nekeva*. In addition, their VAK and GAR cannot be in one degree.

(There)

182. Which *Ohr* descended to complement the *Malchut*?

Ot Dalet of the *Hey de Zivug ZON de Bina* complemented the *Malchut de AB*, which does not have an *Ohr*.

(Item 54)

183. What are the ZON in *Yesod*?

The *Vav* of the *Hey de Zivug Bina* that descended to the *Yesod* is the *Zachar* of *Yesod*, and the *Ohr Malchut* that received from the remains of *Hod*, which is the *Nekeva*.

(Item 54)

184. How did the *Reshimo de Kli de Bina*, which is GAR, become a *Nekeva* to the *Yod* that was born from the *Zivug ZON de Hochma*, which is VAK?

When she is only *Behinat Reshimo* that remained from the time of *Histalkut Aleph*, and she is without *Ohr*, she therefore equalizes with the *Zachar* that extends from the *Zivug ZON de Hochma*, which is filled with *Ohr*.

(*Ohr Pnimi* item 46, par. "However, here we must know")

185. What are the five *Hassadim* and five *Gevurot* in the five *Ktzavot*?

Two *Orot* contain all the degrees. These are *Ohr Hochma* and *Ohr Hassadim*. Hence, the *Hey Behinot*, called KHB, ZA, and *Malchut*, are called by these names only when they are *Ohr Hochma*. However, when they are *Ohr de Hassadim* they are called *Hey Ktzavot*. This is so when they have *Komat Ohr de Behina Aleph*, but, when they have only *Ohr Malchut*, they are called *Hey Gevurot*.

(*Ohr Pnimi* item 60)

186. What are the five *Hassadim* and five *Gevurot* in *Yesod*?

There are two *Orot* in *Yesod*: One is the *Behinat* Truncated *Vav*, extending from *Zivug ZON de Bina*, and the other is the *Behinat Ohr Malchut*. It comes to it from the residue of the *Hod* after it purified from the *Behina Aleph* in it to *Komat Malchut*.

The five *Hassadim* were divided into two *Behinot* from this *Hizdakchut*, *Komat Behina Aleph*, and *Komat Malchut*. They are called *Hey Hassadim* when they are in *Komat Behina Aleph*, and they are called *Hey Gevurot* when they are in *Komat Malchut*.

Since *Yesod* received the *Komat Malchut*, it follows that *Yesod* received all *Hey Gevurot* together. It turns out that all *Hey Ktzavot* are incorporated in it in the *Behinat Hey Gevurot* that came to it from the remains of the *Hod* after it diminished to *Komat Malchut*.

For this reason the *Yesod* is called the general *Hey Ktzavot*, as they are all in it in the form of *Gevurot*. However, these five *Gevurot* in *Yesod* are sweetened in the *Ohr Hassadim* of the Truncated *Vav* that it received from ZON de *Bina*.

It received this *Vav* from *Hod* before it purified into *Komat Malchut*, hence it is still in a measure of *Koma* of *Behina Aleph*. Thus, the five *Gevurot* in *Yesod* are sweetened in the *Ohr Hassadim* in this *Vav*. It follows that only in *Yesod* are there five *Hassadim* and five *Gevurot* sweetened together.

(*Ohr Pnimi* item 46, par. "The meaning of the words")

187. What is *Matei* in *Keter de Hitpashtut Bet*?

Two *Komot*: nearly *Komat Keter* and *Komat Hochma*, called ZON. They were extended by two *Zivugim de Malchut* of the *Rosh*, expanded and descended to *Kli de Keter de Partzuf AB*, called *Hitpashtut Bet*. They contain all the *Sefirot* below them in this *Partzuf*.

(*Ohr Pnimi* item 35, par. "Thus, the *Zivugim*")

188. Why is it that when *Matei* in *Keter*, *Lo Matei* in *Hochma* and *Bina*?

Because the *Ohr Achoraim* of the *Ohr Keter* that remained in the *Rosh* and did not return to the *Guf* prevent *He'arat GAR* from the *Partzuf*. Hence, as long as its *Reshimo* shines by the force of its *He'arah* in *Kli de Keter*, you find that it is *Lo Matei* in *Hochma* and *Bina*, as they are from *Behinat He'arat GAR*.

(*Ohr Pnimi* item 40, par. "We must understand that")

189. Why is it that when *Matei* in *Hochma*, *Lo Matei* in *Bina*?

Since the *Orot de Bina* are only VAK that were emanated by the *Achoraim de Hochma* when it turned its *Panim* downward. Thus, when *de Matei* in *Hochma* and the *Panim de Kli de Hochma* returned to its place as in the beginning, ZON de *Bina* instantly returned to their *Behinat GAR*, to the *Kli de Hochma*.

It is because the VAK and the GAR that come from one degree are difference from each other, but by a reason that compels them to. Hence, when the reason is cancelled they immediately return to their place.

(*Ohr Pnimi* item 40, par. "However, in order to procreate")

190. Why is it that when *Matei* in *Bina*, *Lo Matei* in *Hesed*?

This is because *Bina* cannot dispense the *Ohr Hesed* before she is purified to *Behina Aleph* and before she turns her *Panim* downward. For this inversion of the *Panim*, the *Ohr Bina* must leave the *Kli de Bina* and *Lo Matei* in *Bina*. Hence, as much as it is *Matei* in *Bina*, it is *Lo Matei* in *Hesed*.

(*Ohr Pnimi* item 39, Sub Header **"At that time"**)

191. **What is *Matei* in *Hesed* and in *Tifferet*?**

Ohr de Hassadim in *He'arat Hochma Matei* to *Kli de Hesed* and *Ohr He'arat Hochma* alone is ascribed to the *Hesed*. It gives to *Gevura* anything below this *He'arat Hochma*, and the *Ohr Hassadim* in its *Atzmut* with *He'arat GAR* through the return of *Gevura* to *Hesed* is *Matei* to *Kli de Tifferet*.

(*Ohr Pnimi* item 40, par. "Now you can thoroughly see", and *Ohr Pnimi* item 42, par. "Now we shall understand *Sefirat Netzah*")

192. **What is *Matei* in *Keter Partzuf SAG de AK*?**

Two *Komot*. These are nearly *Komat Hochma*, and *Komat Bina*. They are called ZON for they were extended by two *Zivugim* in *Malchut* of the *Rosh* that expanded and descended from there to the *Kli de Keter de Partzuf SAG*.

(*Ohr Pnimi* item 47, par. "Let us explain the four couples")

193. **What is *Matei* in *Hochma de SAG de AK*?**

ZON *de Kli de Hochma de SAG* were emanated by the inversion of the *Panim de Kli de Keter*. They are considered *Behinat VAK de ZON de Keter*. However, any *He'arat GAR* in *Partzuf Bina* comes from these ZON, which is because of the *Reshimo de Ohr Bina* that remained in the *Kli Hochma* from the time of *Hitpashtut Bet*. The value of these ZON *de Hochma* is similar to the value of ZON *de Bina* of *Partzuf AB*.

(*Ohr Pnimi* item 47, par. "Now we shall explain the *Zachar*")

194. **What is *Matei* in *Bina de SAG de AK*?**

They contain the *Reshimot de Kli Bina* of *Partzuf AB* and receive their *He'arah* from ZON *de Kli de Hochma*.

(*Ohr Pnimi* item 47, par. "Now we shall explain the *Zachar*")

195. **What is *Matei* in *Hesed de SAG de AK*?**

The *Ohr Hassadim* in *He'arat Bina* and the *Hey* from *Zivug* ZON *de Kli de Hochma*.

(*Ohr Pnimi* item 47, par. "We could say")

196. **What is *Matei* in *Hod* and not *Matei* in *Yesod de SAG de AK*?**

When *de Matei He'arat GAR* to the *Kli de Hod*, *Ohr Yesod* returns to it, which is *Behinat VAK* of that *Ohr*.

(There)

197. **Why is it that when *Matei* in *Keter, Gevura, Netzah*, and *Yesod*, *Lo Matei Hochma, Bina* and *Hesed, Tifferet, Hod*, and *Malchut de SAG de AK*?**

Because the *Ohr Hochma* that remained in the *Rosh* and did not return to this *Hitpashtut de SAG* turns its *Achoraim* to its *Anafim* in *Kli de Keter*. Because of these *Achoraim de Hochma*, *ZON de Keter* cannot dispense *Behinat GAR* to the *Partzuf*.

Hence, when the *Ohr Matei* in *Keter*, *He'arat GAR* is prevented from the entire *Partzuf* and only the *Kelim de Behinat VAK* shine, which are *Gevura*, *Netzah*, and *Yesod*. It is *Lo Matei* in *Hochma*, *Bina*, and *Hesed*, *Tifferet*, *Hod*, and *Malchut*, since their *Panim* are *Behinat GAR*.

(*Ohr Pnimi* item 47, par. "Now we shall explain the order")

198. **Why is it that when Matei in Hochma, Bina, and Hesed, Tifferet, Hod, and Malchut, Lo Matei in Keter, Gevura, Netzah, and Yesod de SAG de AK?**

This is because each *Sefira* where *He'arat GAR* is *Matei*, its *VAK*, being in the *Sefira* below it, instantaneously return to it. When *Matei* in *Hochma* and *Bina*, *He'arat GAR* returns to the *Partzuf* and *Matei* in *Hesed*. Thus, its *VAK* in *Gevura* return to it. At that time *Matei* in *Tifferet* and *VAK de Netzah* return to it and *Matei* in *Hod* and *VAK* in *Yesod* return to *Hod*, and *Matei* in *Malchut*.

(*Ohr Pnimi* item 47, par. "We could say")

199. **Why is it that when Matei in Malchut de SAG de AK, it returns to being Matei in Keter, and so on and so forth?**

This is because the reason for the *Hizdakchut* of the *Masach de Behina Bet* is because this *Masach* relies on the *Achoraim de Bina*, which stop the *Hochma*, as the *Yod*, *Nun de Tzadik*, which are opposite to one another. These *Achoraim de Bina* depend on a reason. They are not from *Bina* herself since *Bina* is *Atzmut Hochma* and these *Achoraim* of hers is because *Bina de Ohr Yashar* craves *Hassadim*, as it is written, "because He delighteth in mercy."

Hence, in order to be able to extend *Hassadim*, she turned her *Achoraim* to the *Ohr Hochma*. Thus you find that the lack of *Hassadim* is the reason for the *Achoraim de Bina*.

It follows, that when the *Zivug* was made on the *Masach de Behina Bet* and the *Ohr* is poured to the *Partzuf*, *Bina* already has an abundance of *Ohr Hassadim*. At that time the *Achoraim de Ima* are cancelled since she did not prefer the *Ohr Hassadim* to the *Ohr Hochma*, but when she was devoid of *Hassadim*.

However, once she has *Hassadim* abundantly, she turns herself back to the *Ohr Hochma*, canceling her *Achoraim*. At that time the *Masach* that relies on her *Achoraim* is purified too, as its force of detainment weakens, though it does not purify instantaneously, but gradually.

First it is *Lo Matei* in *Keter*, *Matei* in *Hochma* and *Bina*, and *He'arat GAR* returns to the *Partzuf*. This *He'arah* was by inversion of the *Panim* and not by *Hizdakchut*.

Afterwards, ZON de Keter purified from *Behina Gimel* and *Behina Bet* to *Behina Bet* and *Behina Aleph*. The *Ohr Hesed* was given to the *Kli* of *Hochma*, and from there to the *Kelim de VAK*, and the *Kelim de Panim* illuminated. These are *Hesed*, *Tifferet*, *Hod*, and *Malchut*.

In other words, it is in the form of *Matei ve Lo Matei* as it was in *Partzuf AB*, until the *Ohr* reached *Malchut*. At that time the *Masach* purified and all the *Ohr* stopped from the *Partzuf*. The *Masach* that consists of all the *Reshimot* rises to the *Kli* of *Keter* and *Bina* feels a lack of *Hassadim* once more.

For this reason she returns her *Achoraim* to *Hochma* and the *Masach de Behina Bet* recovers as in the beginning. Once again it draws the *Koma* of *Behina Bet* to the *Keter* and the *Ohr Hassadim* returns to fill the *Partzuf* abundantly. At that time *Bina* cancels her *Achoraim* and the *Masach* weakens once more, and so on and so forth continuously.

(*Ohr Pnimi* item 47, par. "The reason for it")

200. **Why does the *Masach de Behina Bet* rely on the *Achoraim de Bina*?**

    Because indeed, there is only *Kli Malchut* here. The *Tzimtzum* and the *Masach* do not apply to any *Behina* of the Upper nine at all. The whole issue of the *Masach* that rose to the first *Behinot* was only because of the ascent and the *Hizdakchut Behinat Malchut* that equalized them in her measure of *Aviut*.

    Hence, when the *Masach* rose to *Bina*, it means that it acquired *Behinat Achoraim de Bina* to its *Behinat* detainment on the *Malchut* that rose there. However, afterwards, in the *Partzufim* below this *Partzuf SAG*, the *Behinat Malchut* already mingled with the *Etzem* of the first nine *Sefirot* in a way that the *Behinat Tzimtzum* itself rests on them. In that state the *Masach* does not rely on the *Achoraim de Bina*, but the force of the *Tzimtzum* itself rests on it, even in *Masach de Behina Aleph*.

201. **Why are the *Eser Sefirot de Rosh* always called GAR, and the *Eser Sefirot de Guf* named "The Seven Lower *Sefirot*"?**

    You see in the order of the concatenation of the *Partzuf* that the *Ohr Keter* of the *Partzuf Elyon* remains concealed in the *Rosh*. it does not return to the *Partzuf Tachton*. This is so because the *Ohr Keter* of *Partzuf Keter de AK* did not return to *Partzuf AB de AK* and *Keter de Partzuf AB* received only *Behinat VAK* from it.

    Also, the *Keter de Partzuf AB* remained concealed and did not return to *Partzuf SAG de AK*. *Keter de Partzuf SAG* receives only *VAK* from it, and so on in all the *Partzufim*.

It is known the gist of the *Partzuf* is discerned only by the Upper *Sefira*. since the *Partzuf Tachton* has only *VAK* of the Upper *Sefira*, all of it is therefore considered as *VAK* with respect to the *Elyon*.

Also, you know that these *GAR* of the Upper *Sefira* that are missing to the *Tachton* remained standing in the *Rosh* under *Malchut* of the *Rosh*. *Ohr Keter* that is missing in *Partzuf AB* remained there under the *Malchut* of the *Rosh*, and *Ohr Keter de AB* that did not return to *Partzuf AB* remained standing under the *Malchut* of the *Rosh*.

Thus, the whole difference between the *Rosh* and the *Guf* is only in the *GAR*, as *VAK* reach the *Guf* by the *Keter de Guf* that receives *VAK* from the *Ohr Keter* that remains in the *Rosh*. For this reason we called every *Rosh*, *GAR*, and the *Guf*, *VAK* or *ZAT*, since that is the whole difference between them.

202. **Why is every *Partzuf Tachton* considered Behinat *VAK* with respect to its *Elyon*?**

This has already been explained above in answer 201.

Each *Tachton* lacks the *GAR* of the Upper *Sefira de Elyon*. For this reason it is considered *VAK de Elyon*, as the gist of the *Partzuf* is the highest *Sefira* in it. This is with respect to the *Elyon*, but in itself, it has the entire *Eser Sefirot*.

For example, *Partzuf AB* has *He'arat VAK de Keter* of the *Partzuf Keter*, hence it is considered *VAK*. However, for itself, the highest *Sefira* in it is *Hochma*, not *Keter*, and he has complete *GAR de Hochma*. Also, *Partzuf Bina* has *VAK* of the Upper *Sefira de Partzuf AB*, which is *Hochma*, but it has complete *GAR* from its own highest *Sefira*, and it is likewise in all of them.

Table of Questions for the Meaning of the Words

1. What is A Thin and Frail *Ohr*?
2. What is a Selected *Ohr*?
3. What is a Renewed *Ohr*?
4. What are First *Orot*?
5. What is *Achor*?
6. What are *Alephin*?
7. What is *Et*?
8. What are Two Distances?
9. What is Only *He'arah*?
10. What is *Habata*?
11. What are *Hey* ה *Hey* ה?
12. What are the *Heyin*?
13. What is a Preparation to Receive?
14. What is a *Histaklut* through *Achor*?
15. What is *Histalkut Aleph*?
16. What is *Histalkut Bet*?
17. What is Inversion of the *Panim* Downward?
18. What is *Hitkalelut*?
19. What is *Hitpashtut Aleph*?
20. What is *Hitpashtut Bet*?
21. What are *Yodin*?
22. What are Ten Exits and Ten Entrances?
23. What are *YV*?
24. What is The Descent of the Degree?
25. What is Generality?
26. What is *Keter de Shorashim*?
27. What is *Keter de Anafim*?
28. What is *Matei ve Lo Matei*?

29. What is A Filling?
30. What is *Malchut de Shorashim*?
31. What is A Giving of *Orot*?
32. What is the meaning of *Histalkut*?
33. What are the *Anafim* of the *Peh*?
34. What are *Panim*?
35. What are *Panim* and *Achor de Kli*?
36. What are *Panim* and *Achor de Masach*?
37. What is *Pashut* (lit. Simple) without Filling?
38. What Needs its Mother?
39. What is *Reiah* of the *Eynaim*?
40. What are the *Shorashim* of the *Sefirot*?
41. What is *Shoresh* Above?
42. What are *Shorashim Elyonim*?

1. **What is A Thin and Frail *Ohr*?**

   The *Komat Ohr* extending on a *Masach* of *Aviut de Behina Aleph* is called "A Thin and Frail *Ohr*", as it does not extend anything of *Behinat GAR*.

   (Item 29 and *Ohr Pnimi* there)

2. **What is a Selected *Ohr*?**

   Two *Behinot Orot* are contained in each *Reshimo*: the first is a residue of *Ohr Yashar*; the second is a residue of *Ohr Hozer* that a residue of *Ohr Yashar* is clothed in it. The part of the *Ohr Yashar* of the *Reshimo* is called "Selected *Ohr*", and the part of the *Ohr Hozer* of the *Reshimo* is called the "Inferior *Ohr*" in it.

   (Item 50 and *Ohr Pnimi* there)

3. **What is a Renewed *Ohr*?**

   The *Ohr* extended by a *Zivug de Hakaa*, which comes to the *Partzuf*, is called "Renewed *Ohr*". The *Orot* that exist in the *Partzuf* from the time of *Hitpashtut Aleph*, being the *Reshimot* that the *Orot* left there after their departure, are called "First *Orot*".

   (Item 52)

4. **What are First *Orot*?**

   See answer No. 3.

5. **What is *Achor*?**

   A *Behina* that does not operate in the *Kli*, whether for bestowal or for reception, is called *Achor*, or *Achoraim*.

   (Item 15 and *Ohr Pnimi* there)

6. **What are *Alephin*?**

   A measure of *Koma* educed primarily on *Aviut de Behina Aleph* is called *HaVaYaH de Alephin*.

   (Item 56 and *Ohr Pnimi* Sub Header "**In *Yodin***")

7. **What is *Et*?**

   Malchut is called *Et*. It implies that it contains the alphabet from *Aleph* to *Tav*. It is so because the *Malchut* is the *Shoresh* of the twenty-two *Otiot*, and for this reason they are called *Otiot*.

   (Item 30 and *Ohr Pnimi*)

8. **What are Two Distances?**

   If there are two distances without *Ohr* between a *Kli de Hesed* and a *Kli de Keter*, meaning when *HB* are empty of *Ohr*, the *He'arat GAR* is prevented from the *Partzuf*.

   (Item 40)

9. What is Only *He'arah*?

A giving of *Orot* in the *Sefirot* from one to another is through the *Hizdakchut* of the *Masach*. First, all the *Orot* contained in *Masach de Behina Gimel* come to *Kli de Keter*.

After the *Aviut de Behina Gimel* is purified to *Behina Bet*, whose *Koma* is unsuitable for *Keter*, it gives it to *Hochma*. Also, after *Behina Bet* purifies to *Behina Aleph*, and that *Koma* is unfit for *Hochma*, it gives it to *Bina*, etc. similarly.

There is a *Behina* of giving of *Orot* from *Sefira* to *Sefira* through a *Zivug* and procreation, and this is called *He'arah*, not "Giving of *Orot*".

(Item 35)

10. What is *Habata*?

Receiving or giving of a *Sefira* from another is called *Habata*, since they look at each other.

(Item 15 and *Ohr Pnimi*, sub header "**Parts**")

11. What are *Hey* ה *Hey* ה?

The general *Histalkut de Hitpashtut Aleph* is called "The First *Hey*" of the name *HaVaYaH*, and the general *Histalkut* of *Hitpashtut Bet* is called "The Last *Hey* de HaVaYaH".

(Item 25 and *Ohr Pnimi*, par. "We understand")

12. What are the *Heyin*?

The measure of the *Koma* of *Behinat Malchut* is called *HaVaYaH* in filling of *Heyin*.

(Item 56 and *Ohr Pnimi* Sub Header "**In Yodin**")

13. What is a Preparation to Receive?

When there is a corrected *Masach* in the *Partzuf* at a suitable measure of *Aviut* fit for a *Zivug* and to extend the *Ohr Elyon*, the *Partzuf* is then considered to have a "Preparation to Receive" the *Ohr Elyon*.

(*Ohr Pnimi*, item 6, sub header "**Preparation**")

14. What is a *Histaklut* through *Achor*?

When the *Kli de Panim* is cancelled and still receives through its *Achoraim*, such as after the *Aviut de Behina Dalet* has been cancelled, and it receives *He'arah de Behina Gimel* from its upper *Behina* into its *Behina Gimel*, it is considered to be looking at the *Ohr Elyon* through its *Achoraim*. This is because *Behina Gimel* is considered *Achor* with respect to *Behina Dalet*.

See *Panim* and *Achor de Masach*.

(*Ohr Pnimi*, item 15, sub header "**It looks**")

15. **What is *Histalkut Aleph*?**

    It is the *Histalkut Orot* to the *Maatzil* that was made in the *Olamot* for the first time, which is in *Partzuf Keter de AK*.

    (Item 60)

16. **What is *Histalkut Bet*?**

    It is the second *Histalkut* that was made in the *Olamot*, which is *Partzuf Hochma de AK*.

    (There)

17. **What is Inversion of the *Panim* Downward?**

    The more *Av* in the wall of the *Kli* is called *Panim* because the *Zivug Elyon* is made on it and the *Ohr* extends through it, but the part that is not so *Av*, is called *Achor* since it does not operate in the *Kli*. If the *Ohr Pnimi* departs from the *Kli* and the *Kli* receives *Ohr* from a low *Koma*, and this *Koma* is suitable to the measure of the *Aviut* in this *Kli*, that *Ohr* will be received in the part that is not so *Av*, suitable for that *Koma*.

    It turns out that it now turned its *Panim* downward, the *Av* part in the *Kli* has been cancelled and its *Achoraim* are upward, as the *Achor* part of the *Kli* has now become the receiver of the *Ohr*.

    If, for example, the *Kli* is of *Behina Dalet*, the *Ohr Pnimi de Behina Dalet* has departed, and the *Kli* receives *Ohr* from its adjacent *Behina Gimel*. Thus, the *Kli* receives only in the part that is not so *Av*, called the *Achor* of the *Kli*, meaning in the *Aviut de Behina Gimel* found there.

    You find that the *Achor* has become the *Panim* of the *Kli*, and the previous measure of *Panim* in it is cancelled. It is now completely inoperative in the *Kli*; and this is considered turning its *Panim* downward.

    (*Ohr Pnimi*, item 15, sub header "**At that time**")

18. **What is *Hitkalelut*?**

    Sometimes, two *Orot* from two *Behinot* can incorporate and unite with one another and receive *He'arah* from one another like one *Behina*. It can be depicted in three ways:

    - Either they are both without *Kelim*, meaning ZON that rise to the *Rosh* and incorporate there in both *Zivugim*;

- or they are both in two *Kelim*, meaning in *Hitpashtut Bet* when ZON are incorporated there in *He'arat Keter* and *Hochma* when they are in two *Kelim de Behinat Keter*;
- or in the second *Behina* of *Hitpashtut*, called *Partzuf Bina de AK*, where ZON de Keter have only one *Kli* there and receive *He'arah* from each other.

(Item 25 and *Ohr Pnimi*, par. "However")

19. **What is *Hitpashtut Aleph*?**

Hitpashtut indicates a descent of the *Ohr* from above downward to *Hitlabshut* in the *Kelim*. Any *Hitpashtut* is called *Guf*, and *Hitpashtut Aleph* refers to the *Guf de Partzuf Keter de AK*, which is the first *Guf* in the *Olamot*.

20. **What is *Hitpashtut Bet*?**

This is the *Guf* of *Partzuf Hochma de AK*, called *Partzuf AB de AK*. There is another, second *Behina* of *Hitpashtut Bet*, which is *Partzuf Bina de AK*, called *Partzuf SAG de AK*.

21. **What are *Yodin*?**

The measure of *Aviut* of *Behina Gimel* and *Behina Bet* is named *Yodin*.

(Item 56 and *Ohr Pnimi* Sub Header "**In *Yodin***")

22. **What are Ten Exits and Ten Entrances?**

When the *Orot* entered in the *Kelim* of *Hitpashtut Bet*, they came by way of *Matei ve Lo Matei*. In the beginning they all came to *Keter*. After they are *Lo Matei* in *Keter*, they came in *Hochma*. After they are *Lo Matei* in *Hochma*, they came in *Bina* etc. similarly. Thus, the *Orot* made ten exits and ten entrances until the *Ohr* reached *Malchut*.

(Item 22)

23. **What are YV?**

Yod implies the *Behinat Nekudim* of *Hitpashtut Aleph*, meaning the *Hitpashtut Orot* from *Hochma* down, which is found there. The *Vav* implies the *Behinot Nekudim de Hitpashtut Bet*, which is also from *Hochma* downward. However, there is no insinuation for the *Ohr Keter de Hitpashtut Aleph* and *Hitpashtut Bet* in the four *Otiot HaVaYaH*.

24. **What is The Descent of the Degree?**

In *Hitpashtut Bet*, *Ohr Keter* did not return there, but remained in the *Peh*. Hence, *Ohr Hochma* came and clothed in *Kli de Keter*, and *Ohr Bina* in *Kli de Hochma* etc. It follows, that *Keter* descended to the degree of *Hochma*, and *Hochma* descended to the degree of *Bina* etc.

(Item 10)

25. **What is Generality?**

    When the *Zachar* and *Nekeva* receive *He'arah* from each other, it is called "Generality". There are three kinds of Generality:

    1. When they are without *Kelim*, meaning when they ascend to *Malchut de Rosh*;
    2. When they are in two *Kelim*, when he is in *AB*;
    3. When they are in one *Kli*, which is in *SAG*.

    (See *Hitkalelut*)

26. **What is *Keter de Shorashim*?**

    The *Eser Sefirot* of the *Rosh* are considered *Shorashim* of the *Eser Sefirot* of the *Guf*, and *Keter de Rosh* is *Keter de Shorashim*.

    (Item 3)

27. **What is *Keter de Anafim*?**

    The *Ohr Keter* of the *Eser Sefirot de Guf* is called *Keter* of the *Anafim*.

    (There)

28. **What is *Matei ve Lo Matei*?**

    Matei indicates the *Hitpashtut Ohr Elyon* to the *Sefira*; *Lo Matei* indicates *Histalkut* of the *Ohr* from the *Sefira*.

29. **What is A Filling?**

    The measure of the *Aviut* in the *Masach* in the *Kli*, that the *Zivug Elyon* is made on is called "Filling", since it is the cause of the filling of the *Kli* with *Ohr*.

    (Item 56)

30. **What is *Malchut de Shorashim*?**

    The *Malchut* of the *Rosh* is called *Malchut* of the *Shorashim*, since every *Eser Sefirot de Rosh* are called *Shorashim*.

    (Item 3)

31. **What is A Giving of *Orot*?**

    The matter of the giving of *Orot* from *Sefira* to *Sefira* is through the *Hizdakchut* of the *Masach*. First, all the *Orot* came to *Kli de Keter*. When *Behina Gimel* of the *Keter* purified to *Behina Bet*, she gave the *Orot* to *Hochma*.

    When *Aviut de Hochma* purified from *Behina Bet* to *Behina Aleph*, she gave the *Orot* to the *Kli de Bina* etc. similarly, until the *Ohr* reached *Malchut*.

    There is another matter of the administration of the *Orot* born by a *Zivug* and given from one *Sefira* to another. These are called "Only *He'arot*" (see Only *He'arah*).

    (Item 37 and *Ohr Pnimi*, sub header "**Any**")

32. **What is the meaning of *Histalkut*?**

    There is a *Behinat Reshimo*, whose *Ohr* is going to return to the *Partzuf*, and there is *Behinat Reshimo*, whose *Ohr* will never again return to the *Partzuf*. For this reason it is considered to be in the form of *Histalkut*, meaning that the *Ohr* that departed from it will not return to the *Partzuf*.

    (Item 59)

33. **What are the *Anafim* of the *Peh*?**

    Eser Sefirot de Guf are a *Hitpashtut Malchut* of the *Rosh*. This is because *Malchut de Rosh* expands from her and comes to the *Eser Sefirot* from above downward, which are called *Guf*. Hence, the *Sefira de Guf*, are found to be the *Anafim* of the *Peh*, which is *Malchut de Rosh*.

    (Item 1)

34. **What are *Panim*?**

    The place of the designated *Kli* for bestowal or reception is called *Panim*.

35. **What are *Panim* and *Achor de Kli*?**

    Each *Kli* is designated for dispensing of GAR, or dispensing of VAK. If the *Kli* dispenses GAR, then the place of the administration of GAR is its *Panim*, and the place of the administration of VAK is its *Achor*. If the *Kli* dispenses VAK, the place of the administration of VAK is its *Panim*, and the administration of GAR is its *Achor*.

    (*Ohr Pnimi* item 40, par. "The meaning of")

36. **What are *Panim* and *Achor de Masach*?**

    The thickest *Behina* in the *Masach* is the side of its *Panim*, and the *Behina* that is not so *Av* is the *Behinat Achor* in it.

    (*Ohr Pnimi* item 15, par. "You already know")

37. **What is *Pashut* (lit. Simple) without Filling?**

    When the *Masach* purifies from its *Aviut*, the *Zivug* stops from it, the *Ohr* departs from the *Kli*, and the *Otiot* are considered to be without filling. This is because the *Kelim* are the *Otiot* and the filling is the measure of the *Aviut* in the *Masach*. Since it purified from the *Aviut*, it lacks the filling.

    (Item 58)

38. **What Needs its Mother?**

    Ohr Hesed in *Kli de Bina* is considered a "Thin and Frail *Ohr*". This is because it is from *Behinat Zivug de Aviut de Behina Aleph*, in which there is no *He'arat* GAR, being the *Atzmut* and sustenance of any *Ohr*.

Hence, it must remain in the *Kli de Bina* as long as it does not attain *He'arat Hochma*, so as to suck GAR from *Behinat Kli de Bina*. This is why it is considered needing its mother, meaning *Bina*. When it attains *He'arat Hochma*, it is considered to have attained its *Gadlut* and does not need its mother *Bina* anymore.

(Item 39 and *Ohr Pnimi*, sub header "**The seven sons**")

39. **What is *Reiah* of the *Eynaim*?**

The *Ohr Elyon* that expands for *Zivug de Hakaa* is called *Reiah*, from the verse, "And God saw the light, that it was good." It implies to *Ohr Hochma*, which is the *Atzmut* of the *Ohr Yashar* that expands from *Ein Sof*.

(Item 30)

40. **What are the *Shorashim* of the *Sefirot*?**

The *Reshimo* that her *Ohr* will not return to the *Partzuf*. For example, the *Ohr Keter* remains concealed under the *Malchut* of the *Rosh* and does not descend back to the *Guf* in *Hitpashtut Bet*, but only its *Reshimo* operates in *Kli de Keter* in its place. That *Ohr Keter* that remained above is considered a permanent *Shoresh* there, shining from there to its *Reshimo*.

(Item 59)

41. **What is *Shoresh* Above?**

Eser Sefirot de Rosh are considered the *Shorashim* of the *Eser Sefirot de Guf*.

(Item 9)

42. **What are *Shorashim Elyonim*?**

These are the *Eser Sefirot de Rosh* (see item 40).

(Item 40)

PART SIX

The Eser Sefirot of Olam ha Nekudim

1.	*3	28.	39
2.	6	29.	41
3.	7	30.	41
4.	9	31.	*42
5.	10	32.	*45
6.	10	33.	46
7.	*14	34.	47
8.	17	35.	*47
9.	*17	36.	47
10.	18	37.	*47
11.	*19	38.	*47
12.	19	39.	48
13.	20	40.	*49
14.	21	41.	*50
15.	23	42.	51
16.	23	43.	52
17.	*24	44.	*52
18.	24	45.	55
19.	25	46.	56
20.	26	47.	56
21.	28	48.	57
22.	29	49.	59
23.	29	50.	59
24.	32	51.	60
25.	*33	52.	60
26.	34	53.	61
27.	39	54.	61

1. *AK contains **AB SAG MA BON** in its *Atzmut*. Each of these four consists of all four and *Orot* stem from it, which are its *Anafim*. The AB is in its *Mochin* and corresponds to AA and *Abba de Atzilut*.

   It contains a model of *Behinat Atik de Atzilut* Above its *Galgalta*.

   Its SAG is from *Awzen* down to its *Tabur*, corresponding to *Bina de Atzilut*, and its MA and BON are from its *Tabur* down, corresponding to ZON *de Atzilut*.

Ohr Pnimi

1. **AK contains.**

   This study that I've begun with is the most profound of all the Rav's lessons regarding *Olam ha Nekudim*, and should have been presented at the end of the part. However, in this section the Rav gave us the key by which he explains all the future issues before us in the *Eser Sefirot de Nekudim*. Hence, the reader must know and remember it well before examining the concepts themselves.

   First, we must know which of the *Partzufim* of AK the Rav refers to in this case, as we know that there are five *Partzufim* in AK. However, the Rav has already notified us that in the first two *Partzufim* of AK, namely *Partzuf Keter de AK* and *Partzuf AB de AK*, we have no permission to speak.

   The study begins only in *Partzuf SAG*, from *Behinat Awzen* down, meaning its *Koma* (level) is only up to *Bina*, as *Bina de Rosh* is called *Awzen*. That teaches us that the Rav speaks of *Partzuf SAG de AK* here, and the details and matters elucidated before us revolve only around that *Partzuf*.

   He says that it contains AB SAG MA BON in its *Atzmut*, which are the four *Komot* that come out over the above four *Behinot*. These are *Behina Gimel*, extending *Komat* (*Koma* of) *Hochma*, called *HaVaYaH de AB*, *Behina Bet*, extending *Komat Bina*, called *HaVaYaH de SAG*, *Behina Aleph*, extending *Komat ZA*, called *HaVaYaH de MA*, and *Komat Malchut*, called BON. Each of them contains all four, as he explains henceforth.

   Orot stem from it, which are its branches.

   They are called *Se'arot Reisha* and *Se'arot Dikna*, emanated from this *Rosh de SAG de AK*. Indeed, know that everything said here is but *Shorashim* to the items in *Olam Atzilut*. Although they are not operative here, they are nonetheless rooted here.

   The AB is in its *Mochin*.

   Here we must remember everything that's been explained regarding the emanation of the first three *Partzufim* of AK, very briefly explained in the Rav's words in Part Five. He calls the first *Partzuf* of AK "*Hitpashtut Aleph*", *Partzuf AB de AK* "*Hitpashtut Bet*", and *Partzuf SAG de AK* "The second *Behina* of *Hitpashtut Bet*". We must generally remember all the words brought by the Rav there, and everything explained there in *Ohr Pnimi*, for I will not repeat anything here, only use the names.

You already know that every *Tachton* clothes its *Elyon* only from the *Peh* down, meaning from the place it is rooted and where it emerges, which is the *Malchut* of the *Rosh* of its *Elyon*. This is where the *Tachton* emerges.

Hence, *Keter* of *Rosh de SAG* is called *Awzen* because *Ohr Bina*, called *Awzen* clothes the *Kli de Keter*. He, in turn, clothes his *Partzuf Elyon*, called *AB*, from the *Peh* down.

Know, that this *Guf de AB*, clothed in *Rosh de SAG*, becomes a *Neshama* and *Mochin* to the *Rosh de SAG*. It is written, "**The AB is in its Mochin, and corresponds to AA and Abba de Atzilut.**" It is so because *Guf AB*, clothed in *Rosh de SAG*, are *Behinat Mochin* to the *Rosh de SAG*.

Corresponds to AA and Abba de Atzilut.

AA is AB de MA in *Atzilut*, and *Abba* is AB de BON in *Atzilut*, where the five *Partzufim de MA* and the five *Partzufim de BON* join together. It is written that *Behinat Guf de AB* clothed in *Rosh de SAG* is equivalent to AA and *Abba de Atzilut*.

Know, that this study explains the equivalence of the five *Partzufim de SAG de AK* with the five *Partzufim* in *Atzilut*. This is in order to know how to deduce from one regarding the other, and how the branches connect and concatenate from their *Shorashim*. It is also to study the *Elyon* through the *Tachton*, and this is immeasurably beneficial.

A model of Behinat Atik de Atzilut.

Partzuf Keter de Atzilut is called *Atik*. He says that above *Partzuf AB de AK* there is another (first) *Partzuf*, meaning *Partzuf Keter de AK*, corresponding to *Partzuf Atik* in *Atzilut*.

Its SAG is from Awzen down to its Tabur.

Partzuf SAG de AK, whose *Koma* reaches *Bina*, is called *Awzen*. Everything spoken here stems from it, and completes and ends on the *Tabur*. We must thoroughly understand the essence of that *Tabur*, upon which *Partzuf SAG* ends. This *Tabur* is the entire axis upon which all the items in *Olam ha Nekudim* revolve.

Know, that in fact, SAG stretches down to the *Sium Raglaim* of the inner AK, called *Partzuf Keter*. However, after the *Tzimtzum* of NHY (to be explained later), it rose and ended at the *Tabur*.

However, only the *Raglaim* of *Partzuf AB* ended there. This is because from there down is the place of *Malchut* of the inner AK, namely *Behina Dalet*. Since *Malchut de Partzuf AB* had only *Aviut de Behina Gimel*, it could not shine for *Behina Dalet* of *Malchut de* inner AK, whose place is called *Tabur*. For that reason the *Raglaim* of *Partzuf AB* ended above *Tabur*.

However, the *Koma* of *Partzuf SAG* only reaches *Bina*. It is known that the *Tzimtzum* was only on the *Ohr Hochma*, not on the *Ohr Bina*. For that reason *Partzuf SAG* could expand and shine below *Tabur* too, though it doesn't have *Masach de Behina Dalet*.

You already know that *Partzuf AB* is *Hitpashtut Bet* of the inner AK, expanding and filling the *Kelim*, emptied in *Histalkut Aleph*. This is the meaning of *Hitpashtut Bet*, as has been written, and thus *Behinot ZON* of the inner AK below *Tabur* remained without *Ohr*.

This is so because *Hitpashtut Bet*, meaning AB, cannot shine for them, as it doesn't have the *Masach* needed for *Kelim de Behina Dalet*. For that reason, the *Orot de Partzuf SAG* came and filled in for the absence of AB. They expanded to the same *Kelim de ZON* below *Tabur*, which could not be filled by AB.

It turns out that the *Histalkut* of the *Orot* of the *Kelim de Partzuf Keter de AK*, called "Inner AK", could not be fulfilled once more, only through the two *Partzufim AB* and *SAG*. AB filled it to the *Tabur*, and SAG filled it from *Tabur* down to its *Sium Raglaim*.

SAG itself is divided into *Taamim* and *Nekudot*, being *Keter de Guf*, and the lower nine *Sefirot de Guf* from *Hochma* down (see Part 5, item 24, and *Ohr Pnimi* there). Only the first *Hitpashtut* of the *Partzuf*, before it begins to diminish, is the *Ohr Yashar* of that *Partzuf*, called *Ohr Rachamim*.

However, from the moment the *Masach* begins to purify and diminish its *Koma*, they are no longer *Behinot Ohr Rachamim*. It is so even though the *Ohr Elyon* does not stop mating with it on the four *Behinot* of its purification as it generates the four levels of *Hochma*, *Bina*, *ZA* and *Malchut* on its way. This is the reason they are called *Nekudot*.

The *Orot* clothed the *Sefirot* of the first three *Partzufim GAS de AK* by way of *Matei ve Lo Matei*. Thus, first the *Ohr* expanded only to *Kli de Keter*. Then it is *Lo Matei* in *Keter*, meaning its measure of *Aviut* in the *Masach* has been purified. In that state the *Ohr* is *Matei* in *Hochma*.

This is so because the *Ohr* expanded in *Behinat Rachamim*, called *Taamim*, only in *Kli de Keter*. However, the *Ohr* reached *Kli de Hochma* only after the *Hizdakchut* of the *Masach* and the diminution of the *Koma*, and likewise in the rest of the *Sefirot*.

For that reason, all the *Sefirot* below *Keter* are called *Nekudot*, as they are already from *Behinot Ohr Hozer* and *Din*. It is written at length in the words of the Rav above (Part 4, Chap 3).

It's been explained above (Part 5, item 47, *Ohr Pnimi*) that the two *Orot* that came down and clothed *Kli de Keter*, are called ZON. The *Zachar* has *Behina Gimel de Hitlabshut* and his *Koma* reaches *Hochma*. The *Nekeva* has *Aviut de Behina Bet* and her *Koma* reaches *Bina*.

Hence, *Kli de Keter* too was forced to end on *Tabur*, evened with the *Raglaim* of *AB*, for the same reason as *AB*'s. The *Zachar* has *Komat* (*Koma* of) *Hochma* there in *Kli de Keter*. For that reason the *Tzimtzum* is implemented on him as on *Partzuf AB*, and he must end above *Tabur* because he cannot shine to the *Kelim de* ZON *de Behina Dalet*.

You find that the Rav's words that *Partzuf SAG* expands to the *Raglaim* of *AK* refer only to *Behinot Nekudot de SAG*, which are the nine lower *Sefirot* from *Hochma* down. However, *Taamim de SAG*, being the *Keter de Guf de SAG*, stop at the *Tabur*. It is so because it cannot shine from *Tabur* down due to the *Ohr Hochma* in it.

Only after ZON *de Keter* are purified from *Behina Gimel* and *Behina Bet* in them into *Behina Bet* and *Behina Aleph*, which is given to the *Kli de Hochma de SAG*, these *Orot* no longer have any *Koma* of *Hochma*. Then these *Orot de SAG* expand to the *Kelim de* ZON in the inner *AK* below *Tabur*, as do the *Orot* in the other *Komot*, *Bina*, *ZA* and *Malchut*.

It has been explained in the Rav's words above that these four *Komot HB*, *ZA* and *Malchut de SAG* that expanded below *Tabur*, rose once more to the place of the *Taamim de SAG* above *Tabur*. They did not expand from *Tabur* down any longer.

It is written here, that *SAG* ends on the *Tabur*, meaning after the ascent of these *Orot* above *Tabur*. The ascents of these *Orot* are henceforth called *Tzimtzum NHY*.

Understand all the above thoroughly and repeat it until it is seemingly placed in a box, for you will need all the above in every single word in the explanation of the *Nekudim* and the breaking of the vessels, and it is impossible to always repeat such lengthiness.

And its MA and BON are from its *Tabur* down, corresponding to ZON *de Atzilut*.

It refers to the *Eser Sefirot de Nekudim*, considered MA and BON of this *SAG*. They correspond to the ZON *de Atzilut*, which also clothe *Partzuf AA* from *Tabur* down, and the reason for these words will be explained henceforth.

2. As in its *Pnimiut*, so in the *Orot* that stem from it, which are its branches. The *Se'arot* of its *Rosh* are opposite the braches of **AB**, and the *Se'arot Dikna* are from the **AHP**, corresponding to the branches of **SAG**.

AVI are contained in them, and between the two of them, they took *Bina de MA* after the correction. It is the name **SAG**, that contains the both of them, and they are incorporated in *Mazla de Dikna de AA*. Study it thoroughly for so it is here, but then **SAG** still expanded to the *Raglaim* of **AK**.

Ohr Pnimi

2. **The *Se'arot* of its *Rosh* are opposite the braches of AB, and the *Se'arot Dikna* are from the AHP, corresponding to the branches of SAG.**

These *Se'arot Rosh* and *Dikna* did not come out immediately with the emanation of the *Partzuf*, but after the *Tzimtzum* of NHY and the ascent of the lower *Hey* to the *Eynaim*. It will be explained henceforth that the lower *Hey*, which is the joint *Masach* for *Behina Bet* and *Behina Dalet* together, rose to *Hochma de Rosh de SAG*, called *Eynaim*. There it mated with *Ohr Elyon* and raised *Ohr Hozer* from *Hochma* to *Keter*, meaning from *Eynaim* to *Galgalta*, extending only *Komat* ZA.

In that state the *Eser Sefirot de Rosh SAG* divided into *Galgalta* and *Eynaim* and to *Awzen, Hotem, Peh*. Since the place of the *Zivug* became the *Eynaim*, and the *Eynaim* operated instead of *Peh de Rosh*, the three *Sefirot AHP* became *Behinat Guf*.

They receive from this *Malchut* that stands at the *Eynaim*, pouring to them from above downward, and only two *Sefirot Galgalta* and *Eynaim* remain there in *Behinat Rosh*, meaning in *Behinat* from below upward. Thus, the *Eser Sefirot de Rosh* are divided into two *Behinot*: *Rosh* and *Guf*. It is so because only their *Keter* and *Hochma* remain as *Behinat Rosh*, but *Bina*, ZA and *Malchut* in them departed from *Behinat Rosh* and became *Sefirot de Guf*.

This *Zivug*, which divides the *Eser Sefirot de Rosh* into two *Behinot*, *Rosh* and *Guf*, is made in the *Hochma de Rosh SAG* itself. However, for itself, it remains unchanged, as it is known that there is no absence in spirituality. There is only an addition here, for they are considered *Eser Sefirot* of the branches of *Rosh de SAG*, called *Eser Sefirot de Se'arot*.

They are the ones that were divided on the two above *Behinot Rosh* and *Guf*. The *Keter* and *Hochma* in them, which remained in *Behinat Rosh*, are considered the branches of AB, in the form of *Se'arot Rosh*. The three *Sefirot AHP* in them, which became the *Behinat Guf*, are considered *Se'arot Dikna*, the branches of SAG.

It is written, "**The *Se'arot* of its *Rosh* are opposite the braches of *AB*, and the *Se'arot Dikna* are from the *AHP*, corresponding to the branches of *SAG*.**" It means that that division of the *Eser Sefirot* of the *Rosh* into two *Behinot* GE and AHP that occurred in *Rosh de SAG*, this renewal is called *Se'arot*. Also, *Behinot Galgalta* and *Eynaim* that remained in *Behinat Rosh* is considered the branches of AB, and *Behinot Awzen, Hotem, Peh* in them that went outside the *Rosh*, are considered the branches of SAG. The reason for it will be explained henceforth.

AVI are contained in them, and between the two of them, they took Bina de MA after the correction. It is the name SAG, that contains the both of them, and they are incorporated in Mazla de Dikna de AA.

He tells us that as *AVI de Atzilut* were incorporated and came out of the *Eser Sefirot de Dikna de AA*, so the *Eser Sefirot de Nekudim* emerged from the *Se'arot Dikna de Rosh SAG*.

Know, that there are three *Behinot AVI*: the Inner *AVI*, Upper *AVI*, and YESHSUT. All of these three are contained in *Se'arot Dikna*, as there are thirteen *Tikkunim* of *Dikna*, which are three *HaVaYot*, meaning three *Behinot* of *Eser Sefirot*.

The first *Eser Sefirot* are considered the first four *Tikkunim*, ending at *Shibolet ha Zakan*. The Inner *AVI* emerged from this *Shibolet ha Zakan*, being GAR de *Nekudim*. The Upper *AVI* emerged from the middle four *Tikkunim*, ending on the Upper *Mazal*, called *Notzer Hesed*. Israel and ST *de Atzilut*, emerged from the last *Eser Sefirot*, being the five lower *Tikkunim*, ending at the bottom *Mazal*, called *ve Nakeh*.

It is written, "**they are incorporated in Mazla de Dikna de AA.**" The above-mentioned *AVI* are called *Abba* together, and the above-mentioned YESHSUT are called *Ima* together. *Abba* is incorporated in the Upper *Mazal*, and *Ima* is incorporated in the Lower *Mazal*, and both are incorporated in *Mazla*.

However, the four Upper *Tikkunim*, that end on *Shibolet ha Zakan* belong to the Inner *AVI*. Only GAR *de Nekudim* emerged from them, which are *Behinat* inner *AVI*. Remember these things for you will need them in every single word that follows.

Then SAG still expanded to the Raglaim of AK.

This has already been clarified above (*Ohr Pnimi* item one, in the paragraph beginning with "**Its SAG**").

3. **In the beginning, AK was thus: its first three are AB – Keter, SAG – Hochma and Bina. This SAG was clothing with its lower half, which are**

its **Nekudot**, over *Tabur de AK* down, inside *MA* and *BON de AK*, and all this is **Pnimiut AK: Atzmut, Orot** and **Kelim**.

Ohr Pnimi

3. **In the beginning, AK was thus: its first three are AB – Keter.**

The words here are about the same issue presented above, only in different wording. I copied them only because there are some small innovations here. Here too it revolves around *Partzuf SAG de AK* and connects it with *Partzuf AB de AK* that's clothed in it.

You already know that *Partzuf SAG* clothes from *Peh de Rosh de AB* down, meaning the *Behinat* three *Sefirot HGT de Guf de AB*. It is written, "**Its first three are AB – Keter.**" This is so because *HGT de AB* become *GAR de Partzuf SAG*, where *Rosh de SAG* clothes them from without. The *Peh*, being *Malchut de Rosh de AB*, is *Behinat Keter de Rosh SAG* above it, and *HGT de AB* are the inner *Mochin* in it.

SAG – Hochma and Bina.

It means that there is *Hochma* and *Bina* in *Partzuf SAG* itself. Even though the entire *Koma* of *SAG* is only *Komat Bina*, it still contains *Zachar* and *Nekeva*. It means that the *Masach* that rose to *Malchut de Rosh AB* for the *Zivug* for *Partzuf SAG* consists of two Upper *Reshimot*, being *Reshimo de Behina Gimel de Hitlabshut* (only, without *Hamshacha*) and a complete *Reshimo de Behina Bet*.

For that reason two *Zivugim* were made on them: the first in *Komat Hochma*, and the second in *Komat Bina*, and they are called ZON. The *Reshimo de Behina Gimel de Hitlabshut* that *Komat Hochma* extended on is called *Zachar*, and the *Reshimo de Behina Bet*, which is complete with *Behinat Hamshacha* too, is called *Nekeva*. The principal *Ohr de Partzuf SAG*, which is *Komat Bina*, came out over her.

These ZON were clothed only in *Kli de Keter* of the *Guf de SAG* and do not extend from them to the lower nine *Sefirot de SAG*, though ZON de *Kli de Keter* were purified into *Behina Bet* and *Behina Aleph* (see Part 5, *Ohr Pnimi*, item 47).

It is written, "**SAG – Hochma and Bina.**" this is so because the *Partzuf* is always named after its Upper *Sefirot*. Since the above *Sefirot* of ZON have *Komat Hochma* and *Bina* in them, SAG is called *Hochma* and *Bina*.

He tells us that so as to understand the following text, that this SAG later became *Behinat AB*, though it is known that AB's *Koma* is up to *Hochma*. How then could SAG be turned into AB? For that reason he mentions here that there is *Hochma* and *Bina* in this SAG, for the *Zachar* is *Behina Gimel de Hitlabshut*, being *Behinat AB*, which is why it later turned into *Behinat AB*, and remember that.

Its lower half, which are its *Nekudot*, over *Tabur de AK* down, inside MA and BON *de AK*.

You must remember the meaning of *Taamim* and *Nekudot*, presented above in the Rav's words (Part 4, Chap 3, item 11). The first *Hitpashtut* to the *Partzuf*, before the *Masach* begins to purify, is called *Taamim*. This is *Ohr Yashar* and *Rachamim*.

However, when the *Masach* begins to purify, *Ohr Elyon* stretches from the *Maatzil* and mates with the *Masach* during the gradations of its *Hizdakchut*. The four *Komot* emerging at that time, being *Hochma*, *Bina*, ZA and *Malchut*, are called *Nekudot*, as they are *Behinat Ohr Hozer* and *Din*.

At the same time you must understand that only the *Orot* in *Kli de Keter de Guf de SAG* are called *Taamim*, but all nine lower *Sefirot* below *Keter de Guf de SAG* are called *Nekudot*. You should also know that *Kli de Keter de Guf de SAG* expands to the *Tabur*, meaning to the *Sium Raglaim* of the *Guf de AB*, and that place of *Sium* is called *Tabur*.

It is written, "Its lower half, which are its *Nekudot*, over *Tabur de AK* down, inside MA and BON *de AK*." It refers to its lower nine *Sefirot* because all lower nine *Sefirot* are called *Nekudot* here, for they all descended below *Tabur* and clothed the inner MA and BON *de AK*.

And all this is *Pnimiut AK*.

It means that all this is *Behinat Partzuf* SAG in its own structure, and not at all the braches that stem from it outwardly, which he will explain later.

4. **After that it generated the exterior *Behinot* to clothe it. First it generated *Orot* from the general, interior AB, which is the *Se'arot* of the *Keter*, surrounding its *Rosh* from without to the *Metzach* and to the *Awznaim*.**

Afterwards it generated the *Se'arot* of the *Zakan* that extend from the general SAG called *Nekudim*, from which the collective three *Mochin* in it were made.

Ohr Pnimi

4. **The *Se'arot* of the *Keter*, surrounding its *Rosh* from without to the *Metzach* and to the *Awznaim*.**

It has already been explained that the *Se'arot* divide into two *Behinot*: *Rosh* and *Guf*. Until the *Awznaim*, which is *Bina*, it is considered *Rosh*, because the place of the *Zivug* was in *Nikvey Eynaim*, being *Hochma de Rosh*. For that reason the *Orot* expanded from there down to the *Awzen Hotem Peh*, to *Behinat Hitlabshut*, called *Guf*.

You already know that there is a great difference between the *Rosh* and the *Guf*. This is the reason it is written that the *Se'arot* extend until the *Awznaim*, because until there it is regarded as *Rosh*. However, from the *Awznaim* down it is already considered *Guf*.

Se'arot of the Zakan that extend from the general SAG called Nekudim.

You must know that these *AHP* that came out from *Behinat Rosh* to *Behinat Guf* are always called "The General SAG". The reason is, as the Rav writes in the following, that this entire *SAG de AK* we deal with, is considered all *AB*, except for the *Nekudot* in it, which are its bottom half, to be called *YESHSUT*.

Only that is considered SAG, for only that came out through the *Nikvey Eynaim* into *Behinat AHP de Guf*. This *YESHSUT* is called the "General SAG" in every place; it is the *Rosh* of the *Eser Sefirot de Nekudim*.

It's been explained above that the beginning of the *Zivug* in *Nikvey Eynaim*, which came out of the *AHP* into *Behinat Guf*, was made in *Rosh de SAG* itself, but as *Se'arot*. The *Se'arot Rosh* until the *Awznaim* are considered *Behinat* from below upward, which is *Rosh*. Hence, it is still considered *AB*, as no change is apparent in it yet, due to the ascent of the lower *Hey* to *Nikvey Eynaim*.

However, from *Nikvey Eynaim* down, which are *Se'arot Dikna*, they are already considered *AHP* that came out of the *Rosh* and became *Behinat Guf*. Hence the *AHP de Se'arot* alone, called *Se'arot Dikna*, are regarded as the General SAG, which is *Behinat Nekudim*. This will be explained elaborately in its proper place.

It is written, "**Afterwards it generated the Se'arot of the Zakan that extend from the general SAG called Nekudim.**" That means that from the *Behinat Awznaim* down the *Se'arot* of the *Zakan* extended in the *Behinat* general SAG, called *Nekudim*. However, these *Se'arot* that extend from the *Nikvey Eynaim*, meaning from *Malchut* in *Hochma* from below upward, are still considered *AB*; they are not branches of the general SAG.

Thus, the *Se'arot Rosh* are branches that extend from *AB*, and *Se'arot Dikna* are branches extending from the general SAG, and remember that.

The collective three Mochin in it.

It means that the first three *Sefirot KHB de Nekudim* are made of these *Se'arot Zakan*, though not from itself, but from them in general, grouped in the fourth correction of the *Se'arot Zakan*, called *Shibolet ha Zakan*. As it is written elaborately afterwards. It is written, "**from which the collective three *Mochin* in it were made.**"

5. First the *Taamim de SAG* extended, which is **AHP** through its *Tabur*. It did not bring the other *Behinot* out afterwards, for they are clothed inside **MA** and **BON** as the *Orot* of the collective **AB**, of which only the *Se'arot* that extend from the **AB** of the general **AB** appeared. The rest of them are concealed inside the general **SAG**.

Ohr Pnimi

5. First the *Taamim de SAG* extended, which is **AHP** through its *Tabur*.

It means that in the beginning, *Taamim de SAG* came out before the branches of the general *SAG* came out, meaning the *Se'arot Rosh* and *Dikna*, occupying *Komat AHP* through its *Tabur*, which are *Behinat Ohr Yashar* and *Rachamim* (see *Ohr Pnimi*, item 1). He says there, that there is also *Behinat Zachar* there, whose *Koma* is up to *Hochma*, but he still calls the *Partzuf AHP*.

This is so because the primary *Ohr* and the *Koma* is considered *Behinat Nekeva*, which has *Behinot Aviut de Hamshacha*. The *Nekeva* has only *Komat AHP*, namely *Komat Bina*, and the reason it ends on the *Tabur* has already been explained there elaborately.

For they are clothed inside MA and BON.

The matter of this *Hitlabshut* has already been explained (*Ohr Pnimi*, item 1). The *AB* did not return to fill the *Kelim* that were emptied from *Tabur* down in the inner *AK*. It is so because the *AB* doesn't have a *Masach* of *Behina Dalet*, and therefore cannot shine from *Tabur* down, which is the place of *Behina Dalet*.

Thus, the *Kelim de ZON* in the inner *AK* from *Tabur* down remained without *Ohr*. Afterwards, when *Partzuf SAG* expanded, its nine lower *Sefirot*, having only *Komat Ohr Bina*, which is an *Ohr* that was not restricted, descended below *Tabur de AK* and there filled the *ZON* with *Ohr*.

It is written, "**It did not bring the other *Behinot* out**" below *Taamim de SAG*, being the lower nine *Sefirot de SAG*, because they are clothed in *MA* and *BON*. It means that the lower nine *Sefirot de SAG* that clothe in *ZON* below *Tabur* of the inner *AK*, are called *MA* and *BON*.

Remember these words for this matter of *Hitlabshut* of the lower nine *Sefirot de SAG* in the inner *MA* and *BON* is fundamental for every incident in *Olam ha Nekudim*.

6. Then it wanted to bring the *Hitzoniut* of the inner MA and BON in it outwardly. In that state all the inner *Behinot* SAG, concealed in the inner MA and BON rose, and the inner MA and BON rose along with them. Thus these MA and BON are their MAN, to the *Taamim de* SAG themselves, which are not clothed inside MA and BON.

They are in the role of AVI to YESHSUT, because as Upper AVI mate for ZON, and YESHSUT are contained in them, so here the *Taamim de* SAG mate with the entire AB.

Moreover, the *Nekudot, Tagin* and *Otiot de* SAG join them and annul before them. Consequently, they do not bear a name, as the above-mentioned YESHSUT. Then they procreate *Behinat* BON *de Hitzoniut* and their *Levush* outwardly. Thus, the *Nekeva* was now born first.

Ohr Pnimi

6. **All the inner *Behinot* SAG, concealed in the inner MA and BON rose.**

This issue of ascent is as the ascent of the *Orot* in *Histalkut Aleph* in the inner AK, and as the ascent of the *Orot de Histalkut Bet* in *Partzuf* AB. It implies a complete *Hizdakchut* of the *Masach* from its entire *Aviut* until it equalized with *Behinat Masach de Rosh*. This *Hishtavut* means that the *Masach* and all the *Reshimot* contained in it rose to *Malchut de Rosh* and incorporated in her in the *Zivug* of the *Rosh*.

The same occurred in this *Partzuf* SAG, for after it is *Matei* in *Malchut de* SAG, meaning when the *Masach* had been purified into *Komat Malchut*, it too came from there and was completely purified from its *Aviut*. It equalized entirely with *Malchut de Rosh*, the *Zivug* stopped from the *Partzuf*, and all the *Orot* left to the *Maatzil*, as has been explained above (Part 4, Chap 4, *Ohr Pnimi*, item 50).

It's been explained there that the *Orot* leave *Reshimot* after their departure. It has also been explained that the as the *Masach* passes from *Sefira* to *Sefira* during the *Hizdakchut*, until it is completely purified and comes to the *Rosh*, becomes contained in those *Reshimot*.

It follows, that the *Orot de* SAG that clothed in the inner ZON, these *Orot* that have already mixed with the *Aviut de Behina Dalet* in the *Kelim* below *Tabur*, left *Reshimot* behind them although they have departed. These *Reshimot de Behina Dalet* mingled in the *Masach* that rose to *Malchut de Rosh*, so that when the *Masach* rose to *Malchut de Rosh*, it brought those *Reshimot* of the inner ZON along with it, called the inner MA and BON.

It is written, "**In that state all the inner *Behinot* SAG, concealed in the inner MA and BON rose.**" This applies to the *Reshimot* of the lower nine *Sefirot de SAG* itself, clothed and concealed inside the *Reshimot* of the inner MA and BON from *Aviut de Behina Dalet*.

The *Reshimot de Orot de SAG* are contained and mixed in *Reshimot de MA* and *BON*. Because of that they rose and mingled together with the *Masach de SAG* to the *Malchut de Rosh*, and there incorporated in the Upper *Zivug*, as he will explain henceforth.

We might ask: but it has been explained that *Partzuf SAG* remained in *Behinat* permanent *Matei ve Lo Matei*. How then, does he say here that in SAG there is also the *Histalkut* of all the *Orot* to the *Rosh*.

Indeed, you already know that there is no absence in the spiritual, and all the changes we discern in the spirituals are but additional forms, without the former *Tzura* ever being canceled. It is the same here, for though there is a matter of *Histalkut Orot* here too, after the *Orot de SAG* mixed with the inner MA and BON, the perpetual *Tzura* of *Matei ve Lo Matei* still remains in tact.

And the inner MA and BON rose along with them.

It has already been explained above that the *Reshimot de SAG* mingled with the *Reshimot* of MA and BON, and all were incorporated in the *Masach* and rose along with it to the *Rosh*.

MA and BON are their MAN.

The *Masach* ascends to *Malchut de Rosh* to mingle there in the *Zivug* of the *Rosh*, to be renewed and expand from there to a new *Partzuf* as in the previous two *Partzufim*, AB and SAG. This *Masach* has now acquired a new name, which is MAN, the initials for *Mayin Nukvin* (Aramaic – Female Waters).

It is so for the reason explained above that two kinds of *Reshimot* mingled here in one another: the *Reshimot de Orot de SAG*, being *Behinat Aviut de Behina Bet*, with the *Reshimot* of the *Orot* that clothed the inner MA and BON. Those are, in turn, *Behinat Aviut de Behina Dalet*.

It is known that *Behina Bet* is the first *Hey* of *HaVaYaH*, and the *Aviut de Behina Dalet* is the last *Hey* of the name *HaVaYaH*, which are two females. When the *Masach* rises to mingle in the *Zivug* of the *Rosh*, it mingles with these two females together. For that reason it is now called *Mayin Nukvin*, in plural tense, since it is incorporated of both females.

Know, that this connection caused the making of ten *Kelim* in the ten *Sefirot*, and the *Tikun* of two *Kavim*. This is the meaning of the association of *Midat ha Rachamim* with *Din*: the first *Hey* is *Midat ha Rachamim*, and the last *Hey* is *Midat ha Din*. Now they came together in the *Masach*, in a single *Zivug*.

It is written, "**these MA and BON are their MAN.**" it means that they induced the matter of the MAN that was renewed from here on in the *Olamot*, because they are the ZON of the inner AK, reaching up to *Keter* due to the *Behina Dalet* in it.

They were incorporated and came in the *Reshimo de Behina Bet* which come from the *Orot de SAG*, and were brought together in the *Aviut* in the *Masach*. At that time they were called MAN.

Know, that from the moment they were joined, they never again parted. The only differentiation in them is in the *Pnimiut* and *Hitzoniut*. Sometimes *Behina Dalet* is inside and *Behina Bet* or *Behina Aleph* is on the outside, and sometimes *Behina Bet* is in the inside and *Behina Dalet* is exposed without, as was here the first time they joined.

The Rav writes here, "**the inner *Behinot* SAG, concealed in the inner MA and BON.**" Thus, *Behina Bet* is concealed inside, while *Behina Dalet* is uncovered outwardly. This will be explained further in its place.

Their MAN, to the *Taamim de SAG* themselves, which are not clothed inside MA and BON.

It has been explained above that the *Taamim de SAG*, being the *Orot* in *Kli de Keter de Guf de Partzuf* SAG, must end evenly with the *Sium Raglaim* of AB, meaning above *Tabur*. This is because the *Zachar* clothed in *Kli de Keter* has *Komat Hochma*, as does AB.

It follows, that the *Orot* of *Taamim de SAG* are not clothed in MA and BON below *Tabur*. This is why it says that they became MAN to the *Taamim de SAG* themselves, which are not clothed in MA and BON, namely the ZON in *Kli Keter de Guf de SAG*, ending above *Tabur*. The matter of it being made here and the *Ohr* that was drawn because of it will be explained later in its proper place.

AVI to YESHSUT.

This syllogism must be thoroughly understood, as there are two very different halves of SAG here. Those are the Upper half of SAG, which is *Kli de Keter de Guf de SAG*, called *Taamim*, ending above *Tabur* and not descending and mixing with the inner MA and BON. It remains in its *Aviut* of *Behina Bet*, and *Behina Gimel* of *Hitlabshut*.

The lower half of SAG, meaning the lower nine *Sefirot* from *Hochma* down is called *Nekudot de SAG*. It descended and mingled with the inner MA and

BON and two kinds of *Aviut* were mingled in it: that of *Behina Bet* and that of *Behina Dalet* together.

He says that its Upper half, which did not mix with *Behina Dalet*, is called Upper *AVI*, and its lower half, which was mixed with *Behina Dalet* as MAN, is called *Israel Saba ve Tvuna*. Remember these names well for the Rav uses them all throughout the rest.

Know, that this is the root of the division of *AVI* to two *Partzufim*, called *AVI* and *YESHSUT*. Both emerge as *AHP* that came out, meaning *Se'arot Dikna*, and these *AHP* already receive from the lower half of *SAG*, corrected with MAN. However, because they are ten complete *Sefirot* of *Rosh*, where *AVI* are from *Behinat Nikvey Eynaim* and up, they are still not considered incorporated in the MAN.

This is so because the *Masach de MAN* is erected below them, meaning in *Nikvey Eynaim*, and the *Aviut* does not operate at all from below upward. However, since *YESHSUT* is considered the *AHP* of the *Partzuf*, extending from *Nikvey Eynaim* down, where *Masach de MAN* already operates on them, *YESHSUT* are ascribed to the lower *Partzuf de SAG*, that's already mixed with *Behina Dalet*.

Upper AVI mate for ZON and YESHSUT are contained in them.

The matter of *AVI* and *YESHSUT de Atzilut* has already been explained. They are considered a single *Rosh* of *Eser Sefirot GE* and *AHP*. They were divided into two halves of the *Rosh* through the ascent of the lower *Hey* to *Nikvey Eynaim*. The Upper part, *Galgalta ve Eynaim*, is not considered connected with *Behina Dalet* in the Lower *Hey* yet, since she is below the *Eynaim*. It is called *AVI*.

The other half of the *Eser Sefirot de Rosh*, which are the *AHP* below the lower *Hey* in the *Nikvey Eynaim*, is considered connected with the *Behina Dalet* in the lower *Hey*. Hence, they are regarded as *Guf*, which receives from the *Nikvey Eynaim* of the *Rosh* from above downward.

These two halves of the *Rosh* join together into a single *Partzuf* for the procreation of *ZON*. It is so because that lower *Hey* in *Nikvey Eynaim* returns and descends to the place of the *Peh*, to *Malchut* of the *Rosh*. Then the *AHP* return to the *Rosh* as well and unite with *AVI* into a single *Behina* of *Eser Sefirot de Rosh*. Then they beget *Mochin* for *ZON de Atzilut*.

It is written, **"As Upper AVI mate for ZON and YESHSUT are contained in them, so here the Taamim de SAG mate with the entire AB. Moreover, the Nekudot, Tagin and Otiot de SAG join them and annul before them."**

Explanation: the issue of the birth of *Mochin de ZA* has been explained above. *AVI* join with *YESHSUT* into a single *Rosh*, and the *Zivug* is done on *Masach de Behina Bet* in the general *Peh* of this *Rosh*. The *Eser Sefirot* that come out on this *Masach* have *Komat GAR de Bina*, which become *Mochin* and *GAR* for *ZA*.

However, it is not so for the purpose of *Ibur ZA*, meaning the *Katnut* of *ZA*. Although this *Zivug* should be made in *AVI* too, which are always *Behinat Rosh*, here *YESHSUT* are mixed with *AVI* because the drop of *ZA* contained in *NHY de AA* ascends and mingles in *Masach de YESHSUT*.

YESHSUT, in turn, are incorporated in *AVI*, and the *Zivug* takes place in the *Masach de YESHSUT*, incorporated as *MAN* in *Masach de AVI*. The *Koma* emerging on this *Zivug* is close to *Behina Aleph*, lacking *GAR*, and then *ZA* comes out without *Mochin*, but only as *Behinat Guf* without a *Rosh*.

In the beginning, only *Behinat Katnut de Nekudim* emerged, like the above *ZA de Atzilut*. Hence, *Nekudot de SAG*, mixed with *Behina Dalet*, rose and mingled within the *Taamim de SAG*. Those, in turn, did not mix with *Behina Dalet* and are regarded as Upper *AVI*.

The *Taamim de SAG* rose to *Rosh de SAG* with the *MAN* of the *Nekudot* and the *Zivug* was made on the *MAN de Nekudot*, incorporated in the *Taamim*, not on the *Behinat Masach* of the *Taamim*. Then *MAN* rose to the *Eynaim*, which are *Behina Aleph*, because the *Ohr Hozer* ascending from *Hochma* to *Keter* extends only *Komat ZA*, and it is this *Koma* which descended from *Tabur* down once more to the *Eser Sefirot de Nekudim*.

It is written, "**Moreover, the *Nekudot*, *Tagin* and *Otiot de SAG* join them and annul before them.**" This is so because the lower nine of *SAG*, which are *Hochma*, *Bina*, *ZA* and *Malchut*, are called *Nekudot*, *Tagin*, *Otiot*. *Nekudot* are *HB*, *Tagin* are *MA*, meaning *ZA*, and *Otiot* are *BON*, which is *Malchut*. They became *MAN* and rose to the *Taamim de SAG*, where they joined with them and incorporated in those *Taamim*. Hence the *Zivug* took place there in the *Eynaim de Rosh* of the *Taamim*.

BON de Hitzoniut and their Levush outwardly.

Do not err in interpreting that *Komat Malchut* (always referred to as *BON*) was born here, because the *Zivug* performed in *Nikvey Eynaim* is from *Behinat Aviut de Behina Aleph*, which is *Komat ZA*. Moreover, there is *Behina Bet* from *Behinat Hitlabshut* here, which is close to *Komat SAG*.

Indeed, you shall see that the Rav calls it by the name *BON de Hitzoniut*, and not merely *BON*, as it is actually *Behinat SAG*. This *Koma* is actually called *YESHSUT*, which is *SAG*. However, *Behinat* exterior *AHP* of this *YESHSUT* descended to *Behinat Nekudim* below *Tabur*, where the root *Nekeva* of all the *Olamot* is built, whose value is actually *SAG*, not *BON*.

This is so because the inner *BON*, *Behina Dalet*, remained entirely in the inner *AK*, and not a single *Behina* of it appeared in all the *Olamot*. Thus, *Malchut* of *YESHSUT* that emerged through *Nikvey Eynaim* is called *BON*, as she inherited the place of the inner *BON*, as he says, "**Then they procreate Behinat BON de Hitzoniut.**"

Thus, the *Nekeva* was now born first.

As it says above, *Malchut de YESHSUT* that emerged through the *Eynaim*, from which the *Eser Sefirot de Nekudim* were emanated, is the root *Nekeva* in all the *Olamot*.

7. *When the *Maatzil* wanted to emanate *Olam ha Nekudim*, His intention was to make them *Kelim* so as to have strength in the lower *Olamot* to receive the *Ohr Elyon*. The *MaatzilI*, *Ein Sof*, saw that there is still no strength and ability in the *Tachtonim* to receive these *Orot* that exit through the *Nikvey Eynaim* and expand from the place of *Tabur de AK* to its *Raglaim*.

Consequently, before He emanated these *Orot*, there was another, second *Tzimtzum* in *AK*, as the above-mentioned *Tzimtzum* in *Ein Sof*: He brought all the *Ohr* that expanded in the *Pnimiut* of this *AK* from the place of its *Tabur* down, above the place of the *Tabur* into its Upper half of the *Guf*. As a result, the aforementioned place from *Tabur* down remained without *Orot*.

Ohr Pnimi

7. There is no strength and ability in the *Tachtonim* to receive these *Orot* that exit through the *Nikvey Eynaim*.

It is so because the *Ohr Hozer* that comes out on *Behinat Aviut de Behina Aleph*, is only a fine *Ohr*; it does not reach *Behinat Guf*, meaning *Hitlabshut*, as has been explained in previous parts. You also know, that the *Eynaim* are a name for *Sefirat Hochma* of the *Rosh*, which is *Behina Aleph*, being the reason that he writes that there was still no strength and ability to receive the *Orot de Nikvey Eynaim*.

There was another, second *Tzimtzum* in AK, as the above-mentioned *Tzimtzum* in *Ein Sof*.

This is seemingly perplexing, for in the two previous *Partzufim* there was the same *Histalkut Orot* from the *Guf de Elyon* to emanate to the *Tachton*, which the Rav calls *Histalkut Aleph* and *Histalkut Bet* (see Part 5, item 60). But how is this *Histalkut* of *NHY de AK* different that gives it the name *Tzimtzum Bet*, and even resembles it to the first *Tzimtzum* in the *Olamot*?

The thing is that there is indeed something completely new here, unlike the *Histalkut Ohr* that was in *AB* and *Galgalta de AK*. Here there is a new point of *Tzimtzum*, added to the first point of *Tzimtzum* that was in the *Tzimtzum* of *Ein Sof*.

This is so because of the mixture of the *Reshimot de SAG* and the *Reshimot de Behina Dalet* in one another. Because of that the place of the *Tzimtzum* on *Sium de Behina Dalet* rose to the place of *Sium de Behina Bet*, which is *Behinat Tabur de Olam ha Nekudim*.

In this manner, the matter of the ascent of the *Orot de NHY* to *HGT de AK*, generated the new point of *Tzimtzum* and *Sium* to the *Olamot*, exactly like the first *Tzimtzum* in *Ein Sof*, as the Rav says. You should also know, that from the place of the new *Tzimtzum*, being the *Tabur* of the *Nekudim*, to the place of the first *Tzimtzum*, being *ha Olam ha Zeh*, is where the three *Olamot* below *Atzilut* stand, called *BYA*.

The *Ohr* that expanded in the *Pnimiut* of this AK from the place of its *Tabur* down, above the place of the *Tabur* into its Upper half of the *Guf*. Consequently, the aforementioned place from *Tabur*.

It has already been explained that the Rav speaks of two *Partzufim* here: the first *Partzuf* of AK, called in Inner AK, where *Aviut de Behina Dalet* operates, and the third *Partzuf* of AK, called *SAG*, where *Aviut de Behina Bet* operates. It is written about it in item 1 *Ohr Pnimi*; study it well there for it is impossible to go to that length again.

Tabur means the place of the *Sium Raglin de Hitpashtut Bet de AK*, called *AB*. This is because it's been explained there that this *AB* has only *Masach de Behina Gimel*. For that reason it cannot shine below *Tabur* of the inner AK, being the place of *Kelim de Behina Dalet*.

AB doesn't have *Masach de Behina Dalet*, and it is therefore considered to end on the *Tabur*, and the *Kelim* of the inner AK remain empty, without *Ohr*, from *Tabur* down, as they were during the first *Histalkut* before AB expanded.

However, after the third *Partzuf* expanded, called *SAG*, its *Behinot Nekudot* expanded, which are its lower nine *Sefirot*, having only *Ohr Bina*. They clothed and filled the empty *Kelim* from *Tabur de* Inner AK down.

Thus, these *Orot* from *Tabur de AK* down are two *Partzufim*: the Inner *AK*, and *SAG de AK*. It is so because the nine lower *Sefirot de SAG* clothe half *Tifferet* and *NHY* of the Inner *AK*, meaning the place from its *Tabur* down.

It is written, "all the *Ohr* that expanded in the *Pnimiut* of this *AK* from the place of its *Tabur* down," meaning the two kinds of *Ohr*, being the lower nine of SAG and ZON *de Behina Dalet de* Inner *AK* Himself.

"He brought all the *Ohr* that expanded in the *Pnimiut* of this *AK* from the place of its *Tabur* down, above the place of the *Tabur* into its Upper half of the *Guf*." This means that these two kinds of *Orot* departed from that place below *Tabur*, called TNHY, and rose to the place above the point of *Tabur*, which is *Taamim de SAG*.

He brought all the *Ohr*... ...above the place of the *Tabur*.

This raising of the *Orot* from below, from *Tabur de AK*, to the place above *Tabur*, is the most fundamental issue in this wisdom; hence, we must thoroughly understand it. This is actually a very long issue, clarified only through the understanding of all the Rav's teachings regarding the emanation of *Nekudim*.

However, its axis revolves primarily around the association of *Midat ha Rachamim* with *Din*, namely the joining of *Behina Bet*, which is *Bina*, with *Behina Dalet*, which is *Malchut*. This is brought in the Zohar (Ruth), regarding the verse, "And they both went," explaining that the two *Heys* in the Name *HaVaYaH*, meaning the first *Hey*, *Bina*, and the second *Hey*, *Malchut*, fused and became as one.

This thing is rooted here in the ascent of the *Orot* of *NHY de AK* below *Tabur* to *HGT* above *Tabur*. It is so because in the beginning, the *Ohr* of the lower nine of *SAG*, which are *Behina Bet* below *Tabur de AK*, expanded, clothed and connected with ZON *de Behina Dalet* there.

In that, *Behina Dalet* received strength so that afterwards she would be able to ascend along with the lower nine of SAG, meaning *Ohr Yashar Rachamim* of *Hitpashtut SAG*, called *Nikvey Eynaim*. Thus, *Behina Dalet*, the lower *Hey*, came and clothed in the *Masach* in *Nikvey Eynaim*. She was incorporated there in the Upper *Zivug* on this *Masach* that raises *Ohr Hozer* from *Hochma* to *Keter*, extending *Koma* of *Behina Aleph*, being *Komat ZA*.

However, since there is also *Behinat Hitlabshut* of *Behina Bet* there, it is considered *Komat Israel Saba ve Tvuna*. It turns out that there is *Behina Dalet* incorporated in this YESHSUT that emerges from the *Zivug de Eynaim*, which is the lower *Hey* of *HaVaYaH*. Thus, the two *Behinot*: *Midat ha Rachamim*, which is *Behinat* YESHSUT, and *Midat ha Din*, namely *Behinat* Lower *Hey*, joined here in a single *Partzuf*.

Thus you find that this connection and association of *Behina Bet* with *Behina Dalet* was made by the ascent of the *Orot NHY de AK* to its *HGT* above *Tabur*. This is because *Behina Bet* and *Behina Dalet* rose from there, mingled in one another, until they came to the place of the *Zivug* together with the *Ohr Elyon*, called *Nikvey Eynaim*, where they were actually made into one *Partzuf*.

This *Partzuf* is called *Olam ha Nekudim*. Remember that concept, as it is the basis of all the following teachings. The details of this issue and the reason for the *Histalkut* of the *Orot de NHY* has already been explained (*Ohr Pnimi*, item 6).

8. The learned one shall understand and will conclude one thing from another, how in all the *Olamot*, the *Ne'etzalim* that shine in the *Olam* below them are always *Behinat* lower half *de Tifferet* and *NHY*. It is so because we've found how half *Tifferet* and *NHY de ZA* shine in its *Nukva*, *NHY de AA* and *AVI* shine for *ZA*, and *NHY de Atik Yomin* to *AA*.

Also, this *Tifferet* and that *NHY de AK* shine to *Atik Yomin* and to the entire *Olam Atzilut*, as will be explained. Furthermore, you shall see that the *Tzimtzum* is necessary for every elicitation of *Orot* to emanate them. It shall be clarified how *AA* too restricted its *Orot NHY* to emanate *ZA* and its *Nukva* later in its place.

9. *Thus, after He restricted Himself, He placed one *Parsa* in the middle of its *Guf*, inside its place of *Tabur*, to separate between the two. This is the meaning of the verse, "Let there be a firmament in the midst of the waters, and let it divide the waters from the waters."

It is also mentioned in the Zohar (Bereshit): "There is one membrane in the middle of one's intestines; it stops from above downward, draws from above, and gives below." Then the entire *Ohr* remains above this *Parsa* and it is there squeezed tightly. Then it breaches this *Parsa* and comes down to shine in the rest of the *Guf* from *Tabur* down.

Ohr Pnimi

9. He placed one *Parsa* in the middle of its *Guf*... ...draws from above, and gives below.

Parsa means the ending of the *Masach* of the *Partzuf*, like the toes of the *Raglaim*. The difference is in the values of the *Pnimiut* and the *Hitzoniut*. The *Parsa* is the *Behinat Sium* for the *Hitzoniut* of the *Partzuf* as well.

This *Parsa* was made after the *Zivug Elyon* performed in *Nikvey Eynaim*. It means that the place of the *Zivug* ascended from the place of the *Peh*, being *Malchut* of the *Rosh*, to the place of *Nikvey Eynaim*, which is the *Hochma de Rosh*.

In that state the *Eser Sefirot* of the *Rosh* were divided into two degrees *Rosh* and *Guf*, with a great distance between them, as in the *Rosh* there are as yet no *Kelim* and actual *Hitlabshut*. This is so because the *Ohr Hozer* operates there from below upward, not from above downward, which means *Hitlabshut*.

Malchut of the *Rosh* expanded into *Eser Sefirot* from her and within her by the force of the *Zivug* performed in the *Masach* in her, and then the *Ohr* clothed in her from above downward, meaning in complete *Hitlabshut*. Now the place of the *Masach* and the *Zivug* rose to *Nikvey Eynaim*, which is *Hochma de Rosh*.

Consequently, the *Ohr Hozer* ascends, clothes the *Ohr Yashar* from *Hochma* up to *Keter*, and *Malchut* in that *Hochma* is then found to expand with the *Ohr Yashar* in her from above downward to the three *Sefirot Bina* and ZON *de Rosh*.

These *Bina*, ZA and *Malchut*, called AHP, then become *Behinot Sefirot de Guf*, meaning vessels of reception for that *Ohr* that stems from the *Zivug* in *Nikvey Eynaim*. Thus, a whole *Partzuf*, *Rosh* and *Guf*, was made here of *Eser Sefirot* of a single *Rosh*, where only the *Galgalta ve Eynaim* remained in it as *Rosh*, and the *Awzen*, *Hotem*, *Peh* that were in it, became *Behinat Guf* to that *Rosh*.

To the same extent that the root *Malchut* of the *Rosh* ascended from the *Peh* to *Nikvey Eynaim*, so were the *Eser Sefirot de Sium* of that *Partzuf* SAG divided. It is so because the ending *Eser Sefirot of the Partzuf* begin in the SAG, from the place of the *Chazeh* to *Sium Raglin*. *Behinot Keter* and *Hochma* in it expand from the *Chazeh* to *Tabur*, and the three *Sefirot*: *Bina*, ZA and *Malchut* in it expand from *Tabur* to *Sium Raglin*.

It turns out that now, as *Bina*, ZA and *Malchut de Rosh* departed from *Behinat Rosh* and became *Behinat Guf*, so *Bina*, ZA and *Malchut de Sefirot* of the *Sium* completely departed from the *Atzilut* of the *Partzuf*.

Thus, that ending *Masach* of the *Partzuf*, which stood at the *Malchut* of the ending *Eser Sefirot*, which is the place of the toes of the *Raglaim*, now rose to *Hochma* of these *Eser Sefirot*, being the place of the *Tabur*. The three *Sefirot*: *Bina*, ZA, and *Malchut* below *Tabur* went completely outside the *Partzuf* and *Behinat Atzilut* of the *Partzuf* was completely canceled in them.

Now you can thoroughly understand that those nine lower *Sefirot de* SAG that previously expanded from *Tabur* to *Sium Raglin* of the Inner AK, rose to *Behinat* MAN to the *Taamim de* SAG and to *Behinat Nikvey Eynaim*. They did not come back down afterwards, to their first place, meaning to *Sium Raglin de AK*, as the place of the point of *Sium* of *Partzuf* SAG had already changed to the place of the *Tabur*. A *Masach* that ends SAG was spread there, and they remained above *Tabur* and the *Parsa*. Only ZON of AK *ha Pnimi* that was incorporated in them came down below *Tabur*.

The matter of "**draws from above, and gives below**" and the breaching of the *Parsa* by the *Ohr* will be explained later.

10. Certainly, through the *Histalkut Ohr* above *Tabur*, it was sufficient for *Olam Atzilut* to be able to receive their *Ohr*. However it was insufficient to give strength to *Olam Beria*, so that it too would be able to receive its *Ohr*. For that purpose He added another *Behina*, to place that *Masach* and *Parsa* there.

It turns out that they are two things, the *Tzimtzum* of the *Ohr* above, so that *Atzilut* might receive its *Ohr*. The reason that new *Ohr* emerged through its ascent is certainly that this *Ohr* came diminished. Thus, although it comes from SAG Himself, they could receive it. The matter of the *Parsa* occurred so that *Beria* too would be able to receive His *Ohr*.

Ohr Pnimi

10. The *Tzimtzum* of the *Ohr* above, so that *Atzilut* might receive... ...a new *Ohr* elicited.

This refers to the *Ohr* that emerged by the *Zivug* in *Nikvey Eynaim*, whose point has been explained above. Only *Behinat Atzilut* was corrected through this *Ohr*, meaning *Behinat Nekudim* through the *Tabur de Nekudim*, and until there is the place of the *Atzilut*, to be after this *Olam*. However, nothing of that *Ohr* came to the place below *Tabur de Nekudim*.

New *Ohr* emerged through its ascent is certainly that this *Ohr* came diminished. Thus, although it comes from SAG.

SAG diminished from *Komat Bina* to *Komat ZA* by the ascent up to the place of the *Nikvey Eynaim*, which is *Hochma* and *Behina Aleph*. Hence, the *Kelim* can receive it as *Behinat Atzilut*.

Know, that this new *Ohr* is the *Ohr de Kelim de Panim de* GAR; it is the *Atzmut* of the *Ohr de* GAR and *Nekudim*. However, that new *Ohr* that was later emanated by *Zivug AB* SAG, which descended, breached the *Parsa* and illuminated for *Nekudim*, is not *Behinat Atzmut Ohr* of *Nekudim*. Rather, it is considered an addition of *Ohr* and *Behinat Gadlut*.

It is written, "new *Ohr* emerged through its ascent is certainly that this *Ohr* came diminished. Thus, although it comes from SAG Himself, they could receive it." This refers to the *Kelim de GAR de Nekudim*, and he calls them *Olam ha Atzilut*, because they are the *Shorashim* to *Olam ha Atzilut*.

11. *We should provide the reason why these two things were needed: first, the *Tzimtzum*; second, the laying down of the *Parsa*. The thing is that for the *Tachtonim* to be able to receive the *Ohr*, it must be diminished and come through *Masachim*.

    In *Olam ha Nekudim* there was the main outset of the uncovering of the *Kelim*. For that purpose, the aforementioned *Tzimtzum* had to diminish the *Ohr* so that the *Kelim* of *Nekudim* could tolerate it. Also, since they are restricted there, they are squeezed tightly, and thus come out intensely through the *Eynaim* and expand below.

12. It was also necessary to place the *Parsa* and diminish the *Orot* that come out through the *Parsa*. The reason for the additional diminution through the *Parsa* is not for *Olam ha Nekudim* itself, which is *Olam Atzilut*, but for *Olam Beria* below it, so it would be able to receive the *Ohr* elicited for it. Now you can understand how there is *Masach* and *Parsa* between *Beria* and *Atzilut*.

    However, from *Atzilut* to what is above it there is no need for an actual *Masach*, only remoteness of location, which is the above *Tzimtzum*. This is because the *Ohr* rose above *Tabur* and drew far from the point opposite the *Tabur* and down from without.

Ohr Pnimi

12. **Parsa is not for *Olam ha Nekudim* itself, which is *Olam Atzilut*, but for *Olam Beria* below it.**

    It has already been explained above that the matter of the *Parsa* is the *Masach* that ends *Partzuf SAG*, like the toes of the *Raglaim* before. However, there is a big correction in it, which the Zohar calls "draws from above and gives below."

    This is because it is considered a double *Masach*, made of two *Behinot*: *Behina Bet* and *Behina Dalet* together. Hence, when *Beria* should receive the *Ohr* from *Atzilut* there is the matter of the fissuring of the *Parsa* in it. This fissuring means annulment of the *Gevul* of the *Sium* in it and the *Hitpashtut Orot de SAG* below *Parsa*, though it is only a temporary annulment, which is afterwards blocked once more.

    Thus, it is like an opening that closes and opens. It depends on the descent of *Behina Dalet de Parsa* from within *Behina Bet de Parsa*. When the two *Behinot* are tightly connected to each other, the *Parsa* is closed like the *Masach* that stands at the *Etzbaot* (toes) *Raglaim*, where there is no *Hitpashtut* of the *Partzuf* past its *Etzbaot Raglaim*.

When *Behina Dalet* leaves the *Parsa* and comes down to the place of the *Etzbaot Raglaim* of the *Partzuf*, as was before, the force of the *Sium* of the *Parsa* is then revoked. This is called the "Fissuring of the *Parsa*". Then the *Orot* pass from there down to *Olam Beria*, and this is what the Zohar means by the words, "draws from above and gives below."

Masach and Parsa between Beria and Atzilut.

By the force of the *Parsa* that's been corrected here under *Partzuf* SAG de AK, the *Gevul* of *Olam ha Nekudim* was set on its *Behinat Tabur*. It is on this *Tabur de Nekudim* that that *Parsa* was made between *Atzilut* and *Beria*, and this inference helps understand the *Parsa* between *Atzilut* and *Beria*, for they are one issue.

Atzilut

What is above it does not need an actual *Masach*, only remoteness of location. It means that the *Sium Raglaim* of SAG on the *Parsa* is because of ascent of the *Orot* below *Tabur* to MAN to *Nikvey Eynaim*. Hence, the AHP of the *Rosh* came out of the *Rosh*, and *Bina*, ZA and *Malchut de Eser Sefirot* of the *Sium*, went outside the *Guf* of *Atzilut*.

Therefore, it seems that *Parsa* comes to correct the emanation of the *Orot* of *Nekudim* because they emanate from the *Orot* of the *Eynaim*. That is the reason he says that it is true that the matter of the *Sium* itself *de Partzuf* SAG on the *Parsa*, came along with attribute of *Atzilut* in *Nikvey Eynaim*.

However, this is still not considered *Masach* and *Parsa*, but only remoteness of location. It is so because before that, the *Sium* of *Partzuf* SAG was even with the *Raglaim* of AK ha Pnimi. Now, however, owing to the *Zivug* that rose in the *Ohr Eynaim*, the *Sium* of the *Partzuf* ascended to the place of *Tabur*, and this new *Gevul* is referred to as merely remoteness of location.

The *Parsa*, however, is a different matter, which is added to the remoteness from *Tabur* up, for the purpose of *Beria*, because there is a special *Tikun* in the *Parsa*, because of which *Orot Atzilut* pass into *Beria*.

13. The learned one shall thus understand what is written, that any emergence of renewed **Orot** and additional **Olamot** is only by **Tzimtzum Ohr**. This is because so was **Tzimtzum Ein Sof** to elicit **AK**, and **AK** to elicit **Nekudim**, which is **Atzilut**. All this is very close to the abolition of the **Melachim** (kings), and prohibited to elicit in the **Peh**, as it is a high place.

Ohr Pnimi

13. **Renewed *Orot* and additional *Olamot* is only by *Tzimtzum Ohr*.**

    No *Hidush* occurs in the *Olamot* but only because of *Hidush Kelim*. However, in the *Ohr*, there is never any change. As it shines in the *Rosh* of the *Kav*, so the *Ohr* shines at the end of *Assiya*.

    The matter of the formation of the *Kelim* is as the Rav says above (Part 4, Chap 1, item 9): "**because the reason for the *Hitpashtut* of the *Ohr* and its *Histalkut* later caused the *Kli* to be.**" Thus, the *Tzimtzum* and the *Histalkut* of the *Ohr* is the essence of the existence of the *Kli*. The reason for this is explained in detail in Part 4 and *Histaklut Pnimit* item 58.

    Tzimtzum Ein Sof to elicit AK.

    This is explained in *Histaklut Pnimit* Part 4 item 63.

    close to the abolition of the *Melachim*.

    This has been explained above (Part 4, Chap 4, item 7, and *Ohr Pnimi* there, item 400). The comparison between the *Tzimtzum* of *Ein Sof* to produce the *AK*, which is the first *Kav* that *Ein Sof* illuminated into the place of the *Tzimtzum* and the second *Tzimtzum*, which is *Tzimtzum NHY de AK*, has already been explained. They are both *Behinat Sium* and cessation to *Orot Atzilut*.

    The difference is that the point of cessation made by *Tzimtzum Aleph* and the point of *Sium Raglin de Partzuf AK* was in *Olam ha Zeh*. This is because the *Raglaim* of AK end in *Olam ha Zeh*, as it says, "And His feet shall stand upon the Mount of Olives."

    Tzimtzum Bet made the place of the *Sium* and cessation of *Atzilut de SAG*. This point of new cessation is called *Parsa*. It is also the *Sium Raglin* of all the *Partzufim* of *Atzilut* that come after *Partzuf SAG*. This is because any innovated force in the *Elyon* necessarily controls its *Tachtonim* as well. This is the place of the severance and the cessation between *Olam Atzilut* and the three *Olamot BYA*.

14. After the above-mentioned *Tzimtzum* and *Parsa*, it is found that there are many *Orot* there in the place of the *Chazeh*, and their ascent for *Mayin Nukvin* was beneficial there. You will understand that from what's been written regarding AVI: each were divided into two - *Abba* and *Israel Saba*; *Bina* and *Tvuna*. The learned one shall understand that so was here.

    This is so because the name *AB* of *AK* are the *Mochin* inside *Galgalta*, and the name *SAG* is from *Awzen* down to the *Tabur* in its *Pnimiut*, not in the *Behinat* exiting *Orot*, but the inner *Orot* of AK themselves. Thus, AB, which is *Dechura*, which are its *Mochin*, mated with the *Taamim* of SAG from the inner AHP. Those, in turn, are the *Shorashim* for the exiting *Orot* and branches, and these inner *Taamim* of SAG, *Nukva*, mated together.

Ohr Pnimi

14. **And their ascent for *Mayin Nukvin* was beneficial there. You will understand... ...AVI: each were divided into two.**

The issue of the MAN has already been explained above (*Ohr Pnimi* item 6), and there is no need to repeat the words. The matter of AVI that were divided into two has already been explained (*Ohr Pnimi* item 6), and study it there for it is impossible to repeat all that.

You will find that two *Zivugim* were made there for the *Eser Sefirot de Nekudim*: first by the ascent of NHY de AK, incorporating both *Behina Dalet* and *Behina Bet* together to MAN de *Taamim* de SAG, and from there to *Nikvey Eynaim de Rosh* SAG. This generated a division of the *Eser Sefirot de Rosh* SAG there into two *Behinot Rosh* and *Guf*: GE became the *Rosh*, and AHP departed as *Behinat Guf*. This is so because the same division of *Galgalta* and *Eynaim* and AHP was not done in the *Etzem* of *Rosh de* SAG, but in the *Behinat Eser Sefirot de Se'arot*.

However, the *Rosh de* SAG cannot bestow upon its *Tachton* except through this *Partzuf* of the *Se'arot*, because any force renewed in the *Elyon* necessarily controls its *Tachton*. Thus, all the *Orot* bestowed upon the *Tachtonim* come out by the *Zivug* in *Nikvey Eynaim* and receive from the *Behinat* AHP *de Se'arot*. Also, they must be divided into GE and AHP, like the *Eser Sefirot de Se'arot*.

The *Koma* that emerged by the ascent of MAN to *Nikvey Eynaim* has already been shown to be only *Komat* ZA, with the GAR missing, called YESHSUT, because *Behina Bet de Hitlabshut* remains there, as in the previous *Partzufim*. It is divided into two *Behinot*: GE to *Behinat Rosh*, and AHP to *Behinat Sof*. Their place is from *Chazeh de* SAG down, where the *Rosh*, which is *Behinat* GE, expands from *Chazeh* to *Tabur de* SAG. In and of itself, it is named YESHSUT, and AHP *de Nekudim*, which are GAR *de Nekudim*, expand from the *Tabur* down.

It is written, "**After the above-mentioned *Tzimtzum* and *Parsa*, it is found that there are many *Orot* there in the place of the *Chazeh*, and their ascent for *Mayin Nukvin* was beneficial there.**" it means that after YESHSUT departed from *Nikvey Eynaim*, descended and expanded from the place of the *Chazeh* to *Tabur*, the *Orot* increased there in the place of the *Chazeh*.

You already know that *Parsa* consists of two *Behinot*: *Behina Dalet* and *Behina Bet*. It has been explained above that sometimes *Behina Dalet* descends from the *Parsa*, the *Parsa* is fissured and the *Gevul* is canceled.

This *Hitpashtut* of YESHSUT from the place of the *Chazeh* to *Tabur* caused the descent of *Behina Dalet* from the *Parsa*, because it became MAN to the *Taamim de SAG*. Then, the Inner AB inside the *Rosh de Taamim de SAG* mated with *Rosh de SAG*, called AHP (see *Ohr Pnimi* item 1), as *Ohr de Awzen* is clothed in *Galgalta de SAG*.

The lower *Hey* came back down from *Nikvey Eynaim de SAG* to the place of the *Peh* through this *Zivug de AB and SAG*, meaning *Malchut de Rosh*, as it was in the beginning. Then the *Zivug* was made in *Peh de Rosh* on *Behina Dalet* there, and a new *Koma* emerged from *Peh de Rosh SAG* up to *Keter*.

This new *Ohr* came down from there to YESHSUT in the place of the *Chazeh*, and lowered *Behina Dalet* in *Behinat Nikvey Eynaim* too, which is the place of *Tabur*. It lowered her to the place of the *Peh*, being *Malchut de Rosh* in the *Sium* of GAR *de Nekudim*. Because of that, GAR *de Nekudim*, which are originally AHP *de YESHSUT*, joined with YESHSUT in the *Chazeh*, which is their GE, and together they became *Behinat Eser Sefirot* of one *Rosh* in *Komat Keter*.

This is so because now the *Zivug* is made on *Behina Dalet* that descended to *Malchut* at the *Sium* of GAR *de Nekudim*. This is the meaning of the new *Ohr* that fissured that *Parsa* that the Rav presents afterwards.

Now we have thoroughly clarified the two *Zivugim* for the purpose of *Nekudim*. From the first *Zivug* came only *Behinat Katnut* of the *Nekudim*, meaning only *Komat ZA*, without GAR. This *Zivug* was made in the *Nikvey Eynaim*, taking AHP *de Rosh* out into *Behinat Guf*.

Similarly, two *Behinot Rosh* and *Guf*, called YESHSUT also came out in the *Koma* that came out of there on its *Behinat Nikvey Eynaim*. From *Nikvey Eynaim* up it is called YESHSUT, and the point of *Tabur* is *Behinat Nikvey Eynaim* where YESHSUT ends.

Also, from *Nikvey Eynaim* down, meaning from *Tabur* down, the *Awzen Hotem Peh* of YESHSUT expanded, which are the GAR *de Nekudim*. Know, that although the new *Ohr* that came out of this first *Zivug* lacks GAR, it is still the essence and the *Atzmut* of the *Ohr* of the *Nekudim*.

The second *Zivug* made for the purpose of *Nekudim* extended the GAR and the *Mochin* to them. This *Zivug* was made by two *Partzufim*: AB and SAG. The separation caused by the *Tzimtzum* of NHY and their ascent to *Nikvey Eynaim* was reunited through this *Zivug*.

In other words, the GE and AHP that were separated from each other into *Rosh* and *Guf*, were reunited by the *Zivug de AB SAG* and became *Eser Sefirot* of one *Rosh* once more. This is so because the lower *Hey* was removed from the *Nikvey Eynaim* to the place of *Peh* as in the beginning. Thus the *Parsa* broke, which is the place of the new *Sium* for SAG in the place of *Hochma* of the ending *Eser Sefirot*, being the origin of the *Tabur*.

Now this new *Gevul* has been canceled, because as *Behina Dalet* came down from *Nikvey Eynaim* to the place of the *Peh* in *Rosh de SAG*, so *Behina Dalet* came down from the place of *Tabur* and the *Parsa* to the place of *Sium Raglin de AK*, as in the beginning.

15. Then these *Orot* from its *Tabur* down that rose in the place of the *Chazeh* were there as *Mayin Nukvin* to the *Nukva*, which are *Taamim de SAG*, and through these MAN was the aforementioned *Zivug*.

    A new *Ohr* was procreated by this *Zivug* and this new *Ohr* came down and fissured that *Parsa*. This is so because above her, in the place of the *Chazeh* there are now many *Orot*, and the place hasn't the strength to tolerate them.

    Thus, the *Parsa* fissured and the *Ohr* descended through there from *Tabur* down, and filled that entire place that was empty of this newborn *Ohr*. This is the meaning of the verse in the Zohar (Bereshit): "draws from above, and gives below."

16. Indeed, the *Ohr* that was first down and ascended, remained after that forever in the *Chazeh* and did not come down in the *Parsa*. However, since they are tight up there, they elicited branches from them, through the *Eynaim*, which are the *Nekudim* that expanded outside AK from *Tabur* to *Sium Raglin*, and this is their essence.

    However, that new *Ohr* that descended in its *Pnimiut* through the *Parsa* too, fissured the *Kli* and the *Guf* of AK and illuminated in these *Nekudim*, both through holes in the hair, and through the *Tabur* and the *Yesod*. It turns out that this new *Ohr* fissures twice: once through the *Parsa* and a second time through the walls of the *Kelim* of AK.

Ohr Pnimi

16. Fissures twice: once through the *Parsa* and a second time through the walls of the *Kelim* of AK.

The first fissuring was made for NHY de AK themselves, because *Parsa* limited and ended *Atzilut de SAG* so that no *Ohr* descend from the *Parsa* down anymore, and the *Kelim de ZON* in these NHY were emptied of *Ohr*. Now, through the second *Zivug de AB SAG*, this *Gevul de Parsa* has been lifted.

Consequently, the *Orot* extending from this *Zivug* into the *Kelim de ZON* there, expanded once more, which is called the first fissuring. The second fissuring was made for *Nekudim*, meaning through the *Tabur* and *Yesod* that these *Orot de ZON de AK ha Pnimi* illuminated to the *Eser Sefirot de Nekudim*.

17. *However the first **Ohr** that was down in the beginning and then ascended, did not descend again. It remained there from **Tabur** up and laid its **Shoresh** there for good.

From there it expanded and went out through the **Eynaim**, and these are the **Nekudim**. It continued to expand and stretch from without until the **Sium Raglin** of AK.

Thus, all the **Ohr** extending through **Tabur**, though it is from **Behinat Eynaim**, is all swallowed and incorporated in **Akudim**, hence becoming indistinguishable. However, only the **Ohr** that extends below **Tabur** to its **Raglaim** is called **Nekudot**, as now it stands alone.

Ohr Pnimi

17. **The first Ohr that was first down and then ascended did not descend again.**

    It has been clarified in the above item that through the *Zivug* of AB with SAG, the lower *Hey* descended from the place of the *Tabur* to *Bina de* Nekudim, being the general *Peh de Rosh de YESHSUT* and *Nekudim*. Then GE in YESHSUT and the AHP, which are KHB de Nekudim, became one *Rosh*, by which *Mochin de GAR* extended to the *Nekudim*.

    The Rav tells us here that despite that, the actual *Orot* of YESHSUT did not connect and join with their AHP, namely *Nekudim*. It is written that the first *Ohr* that was there never descended again. It remained there from *Tabur* up even after the second *Zivug*.

    This occurred for two reasons:

1. That then YESHSUT too rejoined with the *Taamim de SAG* into a single degree. It is so because the whole division of SAG into two halves – *Taamim* (considered AB de SAG with the value of AVI), and *Nekudot* (being the first *Ohr*, called YESHSUT, below *Tabur*, considered SAG de SAG).

    Thus, this entire division was because of the association of YESHSUT with *Behina Dalet*. Hence, now that *Behina Dalet* descended back to her place, the difference between *Taamim* and *YESHSUT* is no longer there and they both return to the same degree as before.

2. This is because the matter of the cancellation of the *Gevul de Sium* from the *Parsa* was only for the time being, hence the name fission. After the *Orot* came down, it immediately was blocked once more.

Hence, *YESHSUT* cannot come down below the *Parsa*, even after the descent of the lower *Hey* from there, because she did not come from there permanently. Because of that, the *Parsa* remained as strong as before and *YESHSUT* remained permanently above the *Tabur*, and only its *He'arah* reaches, to complete the *GAR de Nekudim*.

18. Also, that *Ohr* that comes down through the *Parsa* a second time, by this above *Zivug* fissures the *Guf* and the *Kli de Adam Kadmon* as well, then exits and shines in these *Nekudim*. Thus we have to kinds of *Ohr* for *Nekudim*.

19. There is yet another, necessary, third *Ohr*. When the *Ohr Ayin* comes down through the *Akudim*, it looks at these *Orot AHP*; it sucks from there and takes the *Ohr* to make the *Kelim* of the *Nekudot* from them. It takes from three *Orot, Orot Awzen Hotem Peh*.

Ohr Pnimi

19. **It looks at this *Orot AHP*... ...to make the *Kelim* of the *Nekudot*.**

Here the Rav speaks from the perspective of the *Eser Sefirot de Se'arot*, for you already know that because of the ascent of the lower *Hey* to *Nikvey Eynaim*, the *Rosh de SAG* was instantly divided into two *Behinot*, *Rosh* and *Guf*. GE remained in *Behinat Rosh*, and *Awzen Hotem Peh* came out and became a *Guf* and a *Kli* for reception of the *Ohr Eynaim*.

It's been explained above that this great change did not actually occur in *Rosh de SAG*, but in the branches that come out of it. In fact, only *Behinat AHP* of the *Se'arot* departed and became *Behinat Guf* and a *Kli* for reception of the *Ohr Eynaim*.

It is written, "**When the *Ohr Ayin* comes down through *Akudim*, it looks at these *Orot AHP*.**" This means that the *Ohr Eynaim* is poured and clothed in the *Behinat AHP* below the *Eynaim* because *Histaklut* means bestowal and reception. Since these *AHP* receive *Ohr Eynaim* from above downward, they stop being *Behinat Rosh* and become *Behinat Guf*. You already know that they are not *AHP de Rosh SAG* itself, but merely branches of it, called *Se'arot Dikna*.

These *Se'arot Dikna* are also regarded as two *Behinot*, because they necessarily contain *Eser Sefirot*, as they are a complete *Koma*, called *Ohr Eynaim*. Hence, they too are divided into GE and AHP, as their *Shoresh* from which they came.

Therefore, there are three *Behinot* in them:

1. This is the *AHP* in their exit place. In *AA de Atzilut* they are called, "the tips of the hair under the side-locks of the head on the right and on the left, under the ears through the angles in the cheeks below.

   From there the *Dikna* begins to expand, and this is the *Behinat Awzen* in the place of its exit. The *Behinat Hotem* is called *Se'arot* that surround the upper lip on the right and on the left in its exit place. The *Behinat Peh* (in its exit place) is called a path in the middle of the upper lip, under the *Hotem* where there is no hair.

   All these three *Tikkunim* of *Dikna* are considered *Behinat Rosh* and only *Behinat Galgalta ve Eynaim*. They are the first *Behina* of the *Dikna*.

2. The second *Behina* is *Behinat AHP* that went out of the *Rosh de Dikna*, originally considered *Behinat Rosh*. However, they are *Ohr Eynaim*, and the act of this *Ohr* is to have only GE in the *Rosh*, and the *Awzen Hotem Peh* in it are not in its *Rosh*, but exit to become *Behinat Guf*.

   Also, from this perspective the second *Behina* of *AHP de Dikna* is considered *Behinat Guf*, and these *AHP* outside *Dikna* are called *Shibolet ha Zakan*. They are the fourth *Tikun* of *Dikna de AA*, which are the *Se'arot* hanging in the middle of the lower lip.

   It is considered the place where the three corrections gather in *Behinat GE*, regarded as the *Rosh de Dikna*. It is called the gathering place because this *Shibolet* is the vessel of reception to the *Orot* in *Rosh de Dikna*. Everything in the *Rosh*, which are *AHP* in its exit place, is poured and gathered in this *Shibolet*.

3. The third *Behina de Dikna* is all the other *Tikkunim* of *Dikna*, extending through the *Chazeh*, meaning through its completion. These are its actual *Behinat ZAT*, meaning they are originally *Behinat Guf* and vessels of reception.

   It is written, "**When the Ohr Ayin comes down, it looks at these Orot AHP.**" This means that *Ohr Eynaim* is poured into the *AHP*, for which they become *Behinat Kelim*, receivers. By that they move from being *Behinat Rosh* to *Behinat Guf*.

   It is written, "**and takes the Ohr to make the Kelim of the Nekudot from them.**" In other words, the *Kelim de Nekudim* receiving from them must also be as their attribute, as he will explain henceforth.

20. **The thing is that in this manner it's been explained that the Orot of the Awzen expanded to Shibolet ha Zakan, and Orot Hotem Peh pass through there as well. Hence, when Ohr Eynaim de AK extends through there, it must mingle with them and take their Ohr.**

Ten *Nekudot* are they: the first three among them take *Ohr* from what extends from the *Histaklut Ayin* in *AHP*, from their place to the place of the joining of *Shibolet ha Zakan*. They only receive them in *Shibolet ha Zakan* because that is where they begin, and not from what is in *Shibolet ha Zakan* upward.

However, the seven lower *Nekudot* take only what extends from the *Histaklut* in the *Orot* of the *Hotem* and *Peh* from *Shibolet ha Zakan* down. It is known that the *Hotem* reaches the *Chazeh*, and the *Peh* through *Tabur*, and not from *Shibolet ha Zakan* up.

Ohr Pnimi

20. **Ohr Eynaim de AK extends through there, it must mingle with them and take their Ohr.**

    As said above, the forces in the *Elyon* are necessarily enforced in the *Tachton*. It is written, "**Hence, when Ohr Eynaim de AK extends through there, it must mingle with them and take their Ohr.**" This means that the *Nekudim* that receive the *Ohr Eynaim* necessarily passes through the *AHP*.

    Hence, the *Ohr Eynaim* must take their *Ohr* because it will operate in the order of their *Kelim* and divide by the same three *Behinot* that exist in *AHP de Dikna*. Then it will pass them to *Behinat Kelim de Nekudim*.

    You should also remember that any *Elyon* is considered a *Maatzil* to the *Tachton*, the cause of the *Tachton*. Accordingly, the *AHP de Dikna* are considered *Maatzil* to the *Eser Sefirot de Nekudim*.

    The first three among them take Ohr from what extends from the Histaklut Ayin in AHP, from their place to the place of the joining of Shibolet ha Zakan.

    You already know that three *Behinot* are determined in each *Partzuf* that extends from the *Ohr Eynaim*. Two are *Behinot Rosh* and *Guf*, found in the *Eser Sefirot de Rosh* itself, being *Galgalta* and *Eynaim* to the *Rosh*, and *AHP* to the *Guf*. The third *Behina* is the *Guf* itself, called the "Lower Seven *Sefirot*", as has been explained in the previous item regarding *Se'arot Dikna*, and the *Nekudim* are divided by the exact same way.

    The first *Behina* of *Nekudim*, being the *Behinat Galgalta ve Eynaim* in them, meaning the *Rosh* of the *Eser Sefirot de Rosh* is called *Israel Saba ve Tvuna*. Its place is above *Tabur*, until the *Chazeh*. The Rav says about it (item 17) "**all the Ohr that extends through Tabur, though it is from Behinat Eynaim, it is all swallowed and incorporated in Akudim, hence becoming indistinguishable.**"

Note, that the Rav emphasizes that even though it is from *Behinat Eynaim*, it is still considered *Akudim*, and not *Nekudim*. The reason for it is that the *Aviut* in the *Masach* is inactive when operating from below upward. That YESHSUT is the true *Behinat Rosh de Nekudim*, meaning *Galgalta ve Eynaim*, where the *Masach* on the joint *Aviut* from *Behina Bet* and *Behina Dalet* stands below *Nikvey Eynaim de YESHSUT*, which is the place of *Tabur's* point.

Hence, no distinction of the association with *Behina Dalet* operates in it, extending from the *Ohr Eynaim*. This is the reason it's considered *Behinat Akudim*, like the SAG, where only *Behina Bet* is apparent, and where there is no distinction of the *Aviut* of *Nekudim*.

It is written, "**it is all swallowed and incorporated in Akudim, hence becoming indistinguishable.**" Thus, the first *Behina* of *Partzuf Nekudim* has been explained, called *Israel Saba ve Tvuna*, which is incorporated in *Akudim*.

The second *Behina* of *Partzuf Nekudim* is the *Behinat AHP* departing from the *Rosh*, which is considered its *Guf*. This is because they receive and clothe the *Ohr* extending from *Nikvey Eynaim*, as in *Behina Bet* of the *Dikna*, called *Shibolet ha Zakan*, the place of the accumulation of the *Orot de AHP* in their exit place.

Remember and understand these external AHP, for in fact, they are originally *Bina* and *ZA* and *Malchut* of the *Rosh*, joined with *Keter* and *Hochma* found in the first *Rosh* called YESHSUT. Just because they receive the *Ohr Eynaim*, they stopped being *Rosh*, and became *Guf*, hence the name "The Second Rosh", whereas YESHSUT is called "The First *Rosh*". This second *Rosh* is the *Rosh* of the *Nekudim*, called GAR *de Nekudim*, but the first *Rosh*, YESHSUT, is considered *Akudim*, not *Nekudim*, as the Rav says above.

The third *Behina* of *Nekudim* is the real *Guf* of the *Nekudim*, meaning below the *Peh de Rosh*, like the previous *Gufim* in the *Partzufim* of AK. They are called the seven lower *Sefirot* of *Nekudim*, like the *Tikkunim* of *Dikna* found below *Shibolet ha Zakan* extending through the *Chazeh* to the *Tabur*.

The upper area of *Dikna Nimshach* through the *Chazeh*, and the lower area of *Dikna Nimshach* through the *Tabur*. This is so because they are considered the seven lower *Sefirot* of *Dikna*, being ZA that contains six *Sefirot* HGT NHY, and *Malchut* is the seventh.

The upper area of *Dikna* is six *Sefirot*, called ZA, extending from the *Hotem de Rosh*. For that reason it ends at the *Chazeh*, because the place of ZA is from the *Chazeh* to *Shibolet ha Zakan*. The lower area of *Dikna* is *Malchut*, whose *Kli* is from *Chazeh* to *Tabur*, hence ending at the *Tabur*. The seven lower *Sefirot* of *Nekudim* are similar, being ZA that contains six *Sefirot*, and *Malchut* being the seventh.

It is written, "**The first three among them take Ohr from what extends from the Histaklut Ayin in AHP, from their place to the place of the joining of Shibolet ha Zakan.**" It explains that GAR *de Nekudim* are *Behinat AHP* coming out of the *Rosh*. They become vessels of reception on the *Ohr* that descends from above downward from *Nikvey Eynaim* of the first *Rosh* like *Shibolet ha Zakan* that receives from *Behinat Nikvey Eynaim* of the first *Rosh de Dikna*.

These are *AHP* in their place, meaning three *Tikkunim Elyonim* of *Dikna* that depend on the *Etzem* (bone) of the *Rosh* above the *Peh*, on the right and on the left. The path without the hair in the middle of the upper lip and these three are called *AHP* in their place, meaning they are above the *Peh*. The *Malchut* in them is still regarded from below upward, as the upper cheek, and they are *Behinat Galgalta ve Eynaim*.

The *Masach* in the *Eynaim* is the upper lip, but *Shibolet ha Zakan*, connected to the lower lip, is already *Behinat Guf*, though from *Behinat AHP* that went outside to the *Rosh*.

It is known that the entire amount of *Ohr* found in the *Rosh* of the *Partzuf* descends and pours to the *Guf*. It turns out that all the *Orot* of the three upper *Tikkunim* of *Dikna*, being *Behinat AHP* in their place, come down and pour and connect to *Shibolet ha Zakan*.

This is why he says that in *Shibolet ha Zakan* the rest of the *Orot AHP* in their place through the *Shibolet*, connect. Also, from it, they are the GAR *de Nekudim*. Remember these words for the rest of the Rav's words.

They only receive them in Shibolet ha Zakan because that is where they begin.

It has already been explained elaborately that GAR *de Nekudim* are not the actual *Behinat Rosh* of *Nekudim*. Rather, they are considered the second *Rosh*, which are the *Behinat AHP* that exit the first *Rosh*, being *Behinat Shibolet ha Zakan*.

It is written, "because that is where they begin, and not from what is in **Shibolet ha Zakan upward.**" This is so because above *Shibolet ha Zakan* it is *Behinat* first *Rosh*. Also, the first *Rosh de Nekudim*, being YESHSUT, receives from there. However, GAR *de Nekudim* have no hold there, for they are evaluated as *Guf*.

The seven lower Nekudot do not take but only what extends from the Histaklut in the Orot of the Hotem and Peh from Shibolet ha Zakan down.

It's been explained that the seven points are the real *Behinat Guf* of *Partzuf Nekudim*, meaning the above third *Behina*. Hence they receive from below, from *Shibolet ha Zakan*, being from the two areas of *Dikna*, through the *Chazeh* and through the *Tabur*, regarded as the Seven Lower *Sefirot*.

21. We therefore find that three points take **He'arah** for their **Kelim** from the three **Orot AHP**, specifically in the **Shibolet**. However, **ZAT** take only from two **Orot, Hotem** and **Peh**, from the **Shibolet** down to the **Tabur**. This is so because the **Ohr** of the Upper **Awzen** has already ended and was blocked at **Shibolet ha Zakan**, and thus the **He'arah** of the three upper points is greater than the seven lower ones.

Ohr Pnimi

21. **The Ohr of the Upper Awzen has already ended and was blocked at Shibolet ha Zakan.**

    Three *Kelim* are distinguished from *Tabur* up, made by the *Histalkut Orot* (see Part 5, item 27). *Kli Malchut* from *Tabur* to *Chazeh* was made in the *Histalkut Ohr Malchut* to ZA, and when *Ohr ZA* departed, *Kli de ZA* was made from *Chazeh* to the *Shibolet*. When *Ohr Bina* departed, *Kli de Bina* was made in the place of the *Shibolet*.

    It turns out that *Ohr Bina* ends in the place of the *Shibolet* because she doesn't have a *Kli* below *Shibolet ha Zakan*, *Ohr ZA* ends at the *Chazeh* and *Ohr Malchut* at the *Tabur*. This is why it is written that the *Ohr* of the Upper *Awzen* ended and was blocked at *Shibolet ha Zakan*.

    There is yet another reason for the blocking of the *Ohr de Awzen* in the place of *Shibolet ha Zakan*: indeed, *Shibolet ha Zakan* and *Parsa* are one. They are both made of the force of *Tzimtzum NHY* and the ascent of the lower *Hey* to the *Eynaim*. After all, the AHP departed into *Behinat Guf*, and consequently, *Behinat Peh* descended and became *Behinat Tabur*, where the *Parsa* was placed.

    The difference is that the *Peh* originates in *Malchut de Rosh*, and descended to *Behinat Tabur* only because of its reception into the *Ohr Eynaim*. *Parsa*, on the other hand, is in the place of the original *Tabur*, which was *Behinat Tabur* in the *Partzufim* preceding the *Ohr Eynaim* too.

    It turns out that just as there is *Parsa* in the original *Tabur* of the general AK, above its NHY, which are ZON, so there is *Parsa* above *Mazla*, which are *Behinat NHY* and *ZON de Dikna*. The upper area is ZA and the lower area is *Malchut*, and both together are called *Mazla*.

This *Parsa* above *Mazla* is *Shibolet ha Zakan*. As *Parsa* ends SAG and stops above *Tabur* and the *Parsa*, so *Shibolet ha Zakan* ends the *Ohr Awzen*, being *Behinat* SAG in the *Rosh*. It does not shine below the *Shibolet*, but only *Hotem Peh de Rosh*, which are ZON, as in NHY of the general AK. Hence, the *Ohr* of the Upper *Awzen* is blocked at *Shibolet ha Zakan* in such a way that there is no *He'arat* GAR there, namely *Ohr de Awzen*, but only VAK, without GAR, namely only *Behinat Hotem Peh*.

22. For this reason, the first three *Melachim* did not die, since they have a great *He'arah* and their *Kli* is very fine, as it is made of *Behinat* Upper *Awzen*, the *Hotem* and the *Peh*. Their *Kelim* were made in *Histaklut Ayin* in *Orot de Awzen Hotem Peh*, because they took their *Kelim* from a place were *Orot de Awzen*, which are *Behinat Neshama*, are still drawn, being *Shibolet ha Zakan*. However, the Seven Lower *Melachim* died because their *Kelim* were made only of *Histaklut Ayin* in *Hotem Peh*, lacking the Upper *Awzen*.

Ohr Pnimi

22. It is written (item 22), "**For this reason, the first three *Melachim* did not die.**" It is so because they had *Ohr de* GAR from the beginning of their creation, meaning *Ohr Awzen*, which is *Ohr Bina*.

"**However, the Seven Lower *Melachim* died**" because they do not have from the *Ohr* GAR in the beginning of their creation. For that reason they could not tolerate the *He'arat* GAR that came to them from *Yesod de* AK.

23. Thus, even in GAR themselves there is a division between this and that. It is so because not even the *Achoraim* descended from *Keter*, but only the *Achoraim* of NHY. However, in AVI of *Nekudim*, their *Achoraim* descended alone, and their *Panim* remained in their place.

The reason for it is that these *Orot*, extending through *Shibolet ha Zakan*, were divided into three: *Keter* took from *Behinat Awzen* herself, from what the *Reiah* elicits in the *Histaklut* in the *Ohr Awzen*, especially that two other *Orot* mingle with it. From that the *Kli* for *Keter Nekudim* was made. *Abba* took from what the *Reiah* elicits from the *Orot Hotem*, and the *Ohr Peh* was also incorporated in it.

Ohr Pnimi

23. *Keter* took from *Behinat Awzen* herself, from what the *Reiah* elicits in the *Histaklut* in the *Ohr Awzen*, especially that two other *Orot* mingle with it.

In order to thoroughly understand the attribute of these three *Sefirot Keter, Hochma, Bina*, that the Rav explains here, we must understand the order of the creation of this *Partzuf* called *Nekudim*.

You must remember the Rav's words above (Part 5, items 6-14) regarding the creation of *Partzuf AB* from the two upper *Reshimot* of *Partzuf Galgalta de AK*, including everything explained in *Ohr Pnimi* there. We shall only mention the headlines here, as it explained there that the emanation of each *Tachton* is because of the *Histalkut Orot* from the *Guf de Elyon*.

In that state, the *Reshimot* of the *Sefirot* of the Upper *Guf* incorporate in the *Masach de Tabur Elyon*, purified to its *Shoresh*, called *Peh*, which is then incorporated in the Upper *Zivug* in the *Rosh*. The *Koma* elicited by that *Zivug* is regarded as the *Partzuf Tachton*.

It has also been explained that the last *Behina* does not leave a *Reshimo* of her *Aviut* after her, but only from *Behinat Hitlabshut*. Thus, the *Reshimot* that rose to *Peh* of the first *Partzuf* lacked the *Reshimo de Behina Dalet* from *Behinat Hamshacha*. It is left with only *Reshimo de Behinat Hitlabshut*, unfit for *Zivug* with the *Ohr Elyon*, as it lacks the *Aviut*.

This is where the *Shoresh* for the *Behinat Zachar* and *Nekeva* in the *Olamot* is made. The *Reshimo de Behinat Hitlabshut* that always remains after the *Histalkut Orot de Guf Elyon* is considered *Zachar*. It means that it is a part of the *Guf* unfit to draw *Ohr Elyon*, except by collaboration with the *Nekeva*, which complements what it lacks.

That was also the case with *Reshimo de Behina Dalet de Hitlabshut*, which associated with *Behina Gimel*. Thus, the *Zachar* was completed in *Behinat Hamshacha* too, by the force of *Aviut de Behina Gimel*. At that point, the Upper *Zivug* emerged on it, meaning on the *Masach* that's made of the two *Reshimot*: *Behina Dalet de Hitlabshut* and *Behina Gimel de Hamshacha*.

The Rav explains there, that they perform two *Zivugim* by way of *Hitkalelut*. In the first *Zivug*, the *Nekeva*, being *Behina Gimel*, is incorporated in the *Zachar*, being *Behina Dalet*. At that time they elicit *Komat Keter Elyon*, because the *Zivug* on *Aviut de Behina Dalet* elicits *Komat Keter*.

However, since it lacks *Behina Dalet de Hamshacha*, it cannot come down to the *Guf*, meaning to *Behinat Hitlabshut* in the *Kelim*. This is because there is no *Hitpashtut Kelim*, but only in *Behinat Aviut*, meaning by the force of the *Hamshacha*. This is what *Behina Dalet* lacks and hence its need a second *Zivug*.

This is done by the *Hitkalelut* of the *Zachar* in the *Nekeva*, meaning in *Behina Gimel*, where there is *Behinat Hamshacha*. However, the *Koma* emanated by that *Zivug* is merely *Komat Hochma*. After these two *Zivugim* are made, they can come down and clothe in the *Guf*, and they clothe in *Kli de Keter* of the *Guf*.

It is the same in all the *Partzufim* because so also was the order of the creation of *Partzuf SAG* from *AB*. There too the last *Behina* that remained after the *Histalkut Orot de Guf de AB* was only in *Behinat Hitlabshut*, called *Zachar*, meaning *Behinat Hitlabshut de Behina Gimel*.

This is so because the last *Behina de AB* is *Behina Gimel*, and it too must connect with the *Nekeva* to complete its *Behinat Hamshacha* and be suitable for *Zivug* with the *Ohr Elyon*. Hence, it joined with *Behina Bet*, which remained complete in *Behinat Hamshacha* too. At that time they were both incorporated in two *Zivugim*, as has been explained in *Rosh de Partzuf Galgalta*.

The same occurred in the creation of *Partzuf BON*, being *Olam ha Nekudim*, which was emanated and emerged from *Rosh de SAG*. After *Orot NHY de AK* departed with the lower nine *Sefirot de SAG*, the last *Behina* disappeared here too. She did not leave behind a *Reshimo de Hamshacha*, but only from *Behinat Hitlabshut*, called *Zachar*, which is unfit for *Zivug* with the *Ohr Elyon*, except when associated in the *Behinat Hamshacha* of the *Nekeva*, which is merely *Behina Aleph* here.

This is so because the last *Behina de Partzuf SAG* is *Behina Bet*, of which nothing remained but *Behinat Hitlabshut*. It turns out that the complete *Reshimo* is *Behina Aleph*.

These *Zachar* and *Nekeva* rose to *Nikvey Eynaim* and incorporated there in the two above *Zivugim*, as with the *AB* and the *SAG*. In the first *Zivug*, the *Nekeva* was incorporated in the *Zachar*, which is *Behina Bet de Hitlabshut*. Then *Komat Bina* was elicited on them, as it is known that *Behina Bet* extends *Komat Bina*.

It turns out that the *Nekeva* too, which is *Komat Behina Aleph* gained *Behinat GAR* in her *Hitkalelut* with the *Zachar*. However, they still could not descend to the *Guf*, for lack of the *Aviut* of *Hamshacha* from *Behina Bet*. They made the second *Zivug*, and the *Zachar* was incorporated in the *Nekeva*, which is *Behina Aleph*, and extended *Komat ZA*. Afterwards they descended to *Behinat Hitlabshut* in the *Guf*, as the Rav explained regarding *Partzuf AB* (see Part 5, item 14).

Now you can thoroughly understand the property of *GAR de Nekudim*. *Keter de Nekudim* is the *Zachar*, being *Behina Bet de Hitlabshut*, and *Hochma* and *Bina de Nekudim* are both *Nekeva*, which are *Behina Aleph*. They were incorporated in one another in the two *Zivugim de Rosh de SAG*.

From there they came down through *Dikna* to their place below *Tabur* and expanded into their own *Partzuf*, meaning to the above three *Behinot*, made of two *Roshim* (pl. for *Rosh*) and *Guf*. The first *Rosh* is YESHSUT, only in *Behinat* GE, and the second *Rosh* is GAR *de Nekudim*, which are the AHP that came out of the first *Rosh*. These are the ZAT *de Nekudim*.

You can therefore understand *Partzuf Dikna* too. It's been explained that every *Tachton* emerges by the force of the *Reshimot* ascending from the *Histalkut Orot de Elyon* to *Malchut de Rosh* of the *Elyon* itself. These are *Behinat Zachar* and *Nekeva*, and in the beginning they incorporate in the *Masach de Rosh de Elyon* and make two *Zivugim* there, in two kinds of *Hitkalelut*.

There they extend two *Komot*: the first *Koma* on the measure of the *Zachar*, and the second *Koma* on the measure of the *Nekeva*. All this takes place in the *Rosh* of the *Elyon* itself. After that they expand and descend to their correct place.

Know, that these two *Komot* that the *Zachar* and the *Nekeva* of *Partzuf Nekudim* extended when they were in *Rosh de SAG* are the entire *Partzuf Dikna* in the *Rosh de SAG* itself. Despite that, they are indistinguishable in *Rosh de SAG* itself, only in the branches that come out of it, being the *Se'arot*.

Now you see that the first *Tikun* of *Dikna*, being the two straits of the *Zakan*, extending under the *Awznaim*, is the *Zachar*. In other words, it is the *Koma* that emerged in the *Hitkalelut* of the *Nekeva* that emerged in the measure of the *Zachar*, whose *Koma* reaches *Bina*.

The two lower *Tikkunim* are the *Se'arot* on the upper lip under the *Hotem* on the right and on the left. After that there is the path without the hair in the middle, extending in a straight *Kav* in the middle of the lip, under the *Hotem*, to the *Peh*. Both are the *Nekeva* of the *Rosh*, meaning *Koma de Behina Aleph* that emerged in the *Hitkalelut* of the *Zachar* with the *Nekeva*.

It has already been explained that the *Nekeva* too has *Komat Bina*, for she mingled in the first *Zivug* in the measure of the *Zachar*. However, there is still a great difference between them. This is so because the *Zachar* itself is *Behina Bet*, and thus has *Ohr Bina*, while the *Nekeva* is only *Behina Aleph* in and of herself, which is *Ohr ZA*. Consequently, she has *He'arah* only from *Ohr Bina*, but not the *Atzmut* of *Ohr Bina*.

Thus, all the *Orot de Zachar* and *Nekeva* in these three *Tikkunim* come in *Hitlabshut* in *Shibolet ha Zakan*, which is the AHP that came out into *Behinat Guf*. Hence, these two above-mentioned *Komot* are discerned in the three upper *Tikkunim* of *Dikna* in *Shibolet ha Zakan*.

It is written, "**Keter** took from **Behinat Awzen** herself, from what the **Reiah** elicits in the **Histaklut** in the **Ohr Awzen**." This is because *Keter de Nekudim* is *Behinat Zachar*, having *Koma de Behina Bet*.

For that reason it extends from the *Histaklut* in the *Ohr de Awzen*, meaning from the *Zivug* that emerged on *Komat Bina*, which is the *Ohr* of the *Awzen*. From there it extended to the *Zachar* in *Behinat Shibolet ha Zakan*, and from *Shibolet ha Zakan* it descended to its place below *Tabur*, to *Behinat Keter de Nekudim*. Thus, *Keter* has the *Etzem* of the *Ohr Awzen*.

It is written, "**Abba** took from the **Reiah** elicits from the **Orot Hotem**, and the **Ohr Peh** was also incorporated in it." *Abba de Nekudim* is *Behinat Nekeva*, having only *Behina Aleph*. *Ima de Nekudim* is also incorporated in *Abba*, for both are considered *Behinat Nekeva* to the *Keter*.

Hence, for itself, it has only *Ohr Hotem*, which is *Ohr ZA*, as *Behina Aleph* elicits only *Komat ZA*. In addition, the *Ohr Peh*, which is *Malchut*, was also incorporated in the *Ohr* of the *Hotem*, because they are one *Koma* that came out in the second *Zivug*, on the measure of the *Nekeva*.

24. The *Kli* of *Keter*, which took its great *He'arah* from the *Awzen*, did not break. However, AVI, which take only from the *Hotem* and the *Peh*, the *Achoraim* of their *Kelim* broke.

If *Abba ve Ima* had received this *Ohr Hotem* and *Peh* of AK when they were above, close to the place of the *Nikvey Awzen*, though they only received a little *He'arah* from the *Orot Awzen* itself, the *Achoraim* of their *Kelim* would have endured.

However, because they receive only from the *Sium* of the *Awzen*, being the place of *Shibolet ha Zakan*, though they take some *He'arah*, it doesn't help them, and hence the *Achoraim* of their *Kelim* break. However, *Keter* takes the actual *Ohr Awzen*. Although it takes it at its *Sium*, since it takes its *Atzmut*, it is still enough. Consequently, even its *Achoraim* do not break.

Conversely, AVI take only a general *He'arah*, and even that in remoteness of location. Thus we have clarified these three *Behinot*, which are: *Keter*, that remained entirely; AVI, which broke and their *Achoraim* fell; ZON, whose *Achoraim* and *Panim* fell.

Ohr Pnimi

24. It is written, "If **Abba ve Ima** had..." but since they only receive from the *Sium* of the *Awzen*, the place of *Shibolet ha Zakan*, even though they take some *He'arah*, it doesn't help them. That is why the *Achoraim* of their *Kelim* break.

In fact, they were incorporated in the first *Zivug* on the measure of the *Zachar*, at which time they also acquired the *Ohr Koma de Behina Bet* of the *Zachar*, in which case *AVI* too have *He'arat Awzen*, like the *Zachar*. However, as has been explained above, in and of themselves they are merely *Reshimo* of *Behina Aleph*. Hence, this *Hitkalelut* with the *Zachar* is merely *Behinat He'arah de Ohr Awzen*, not *Atzmut*, as the *Zachar*.

Had they received this *He'arah* **"when they were close to the place of the Nikvey Awzen,"** meaning if *AVI de Nekudim* were *Behinat Nekeva* in the first *Rosh de Dikna*, which are the two *Tikkunim* called *Se'arot* of the lip, and the *Orcha* (Path), then their *Achoraim* certainly wouldn't have broken, like the first *Rosh* of *Nekudim* called YESHSUT, which endured entirely.

However, because they are *Behinat* second *Rosh*, and take only from the *Behinat Shibolet*, and also have no *Atzmut Ohr Awzen*, but only *He'arah*, their *Achoraim* break.

It is written, **"However, Keter takes the actual Ohr Awzen. Although it takes it at its Sium, since it takes its Atzmut, it is still enough. Consequently, even its Achoraim do not break."** It means that *Keter* is the *Zachar*, having *Koma de Behina Bet* by itself. Hence the *Ohr Awzen* is considered its *Atzmut*. The matter of the difference between the *Achoraim* and the *Panim* will be explained in its place.

Now you can thoroughly understand the matter of the *Ohr Awzen* that was blocked on the *Shibolet*, brought in the Rav's words above (Part 6, item 21). The two reasons in the *Ohr Pnimi* have already been explained there. Here we find, regarding the *Zachar* and *Nekeva* in the *Ohr* of the *Eynaim*, that even the *Zachar* does not have a complete *Behina Bet*, only half this *Reshimo*, meaning only the *Behinat Hitlabshut* in it.

Hence, there was no *Behinat Hitpashtut* in the *Kelim* from the first *Zivug* that emerged on *Komat Bina* (see Part 6, *Ohr Pnimi*, item 23). Even after the second *Zivug* in the *Hitkalelut* of the *Zachar* with the *Nekeva*, they descended and expanded to the *Guf*, which are the exterior *AHP*, called *Shibolet* in the *Dikna*, and GAR *de Nekudim* in *Partzuf Nekudim*. However, then too they could not shine the *Ohr Bina* into the *Kelim* below them, because of the absence of *Behinat Aviut de Hamshacha* that exists in *Behina Bet*.

For that reason the *Ohr Awzen* was blocked in the *Shibolet*, which is the *Kli* of these ZON, as they cannot give from their *Ohr Bina*. Similarly, in GAR *de Nekudim* the *Ohr Awzen* was blocked in the *Bina*, and they cannot give anything outside them.

This has been explained in detail above (Part 5, *Ohr Pnimi*, item 40). Here too it is considered that *Ohr Bina* remains in the *Rosh* under *Malchut de Rosh*, as the *Ohr Keter* in *AB*, and as *Ohr Hochma* in *SAG*, because the whole issue there applies here too.

25. *These *Nekudim* expanded from *Tabur de AK* to its *Sium Raglaim*, as in the arrangement of *ZON*, clothing *AA*. However, there *ZON* clothes *AA* all around its sides and surroundings, whereas here, their primary *He'arah* is only through *Panim de AK*.

Yet, some *He'arah* expands from these *Nekudim*, whether in their *Behinat Orot*, or in their *Behinat Kelim*, clothing this *AK* on every side, as we've explained above in the *AHP*. Still, their primary *He'arah* is through the *Panim*.

Ohr Pnimi

25. Their primary *He'arah* is only through *Panim de AK*. Yet, some *He'arah* expands from these *Nekudim* etc.

This matter has already been explained in detail (Part 4, Chap 5, *Ohr Pnimi*, item 2) and study it there. The gist of it is that the sides are *Behinat* right and left in the *Partzuf*. In other words, multiplicity of *Hassadim* is called "Right" and scarcity of *Hassadim* is called "Left".

The place of the reception of *Hochma* and *GAR* is called *Panim*, and the place unfit to receive *GAR* is called *Achor*. Hence, the *Rosh* and *Toch* of every *Partzuf* through the *Tabur* is called *Panim* because until the *Tabur* it is fit to receive *Ohr GAR*, and the place from *Tabur* down is called *Achor* because it cannot receive *GAR* there.

You already know of the new *Tzimtzum* that occurred by the ascent of *MAN* to *Nikvey Eynaim*. *AHP de Rosh* departed from there and became *Behinat Guf*, and the *Peh* became *Behinat Sium* on *He'arat GAR*, like the *Tabur*. This is why the *Ohr de Awzen* was blocked at the *Shibolet*.

This is also the reason that *He'arat Ohr Eynaim* is called *Panim*, as they do not shine for *Kelim de Achor* from the *Peh* down, but only *Behinat* small *He'arah*, through the sides, extending from *Behinat* "right and "left", meaning *He'arat Hassadim*.

26. The place of *Keter* from the *Nekudot* is from *Tabur de AK* through the *Sium* of the *Guf*. *HBD* are in the first three *Prakin de NHY de AK*, *HGT* in the three middle *Prakin*, and *NHY* in the three lower *Prakin*, as in *ZON* that clothes over *AA*.

26. HBD are in the first three *Prakin de NHY de AK, HGT* in the three middle *Prakin* etc.

There are four divisions that you find here: *Keter, Hochma Bina Daat, Hesed Gevura Tifferet, Netzah Hod Yesod*. In order to understand that we must first know the two changes here regarding the *Partzufim Galgalta AB SAG* preceding *Partzuf Nekudim*.

The first is the matter of *Kli de Daat*, which did not exist in the *Eser Sefirot*. Thus, where did it come from here in the *Eser Sefirot de Nekudim*? The second is the matter of the *Guf* of *Partzuf Nekudim*. The Rav says about the *Gufim* of the three preceding *Partzufim* that they begin from *Keter*, as in Part 5 regarding *Matei ve Lo Matei*.

However, here he says that the *Guf* begins from *Kli de Daat*, not from *Keter*. He counts only the seven lower *Sefirot* as the entire *Guf*, and not the *Eser Sefirot*, meaning only *Daat, HGT* and *NHYM*.

The thing is that you already know that the GAR of *Nekudim* are *Behinat AHP de Israel Saba ve Tvuna*, being the first *Rosh* of *Nekudim*. Because of the lower *Hey* that rose to the *Eynaim*, and the place of the *Zivug* that ascended to *Nikvey Eynaim*, the AHP of this *Rosh* became a vessel of reception and *Guf*. This *Guf de AHP* are the GAR of *Nekudim*.

Thus, the two *Kelim, Keter* and *Hochma de Rosh* remained in YESHSUT as *Behinat Rosh Aleph*, and the three *Kelim Bina, ZA* and *Malchut*, came in GAR *de Nekudim* and were made into the second *Rosh*. They are the *Rosh* of *Nekudim*.

You already know that the entire amount in the *Rosh* passes and clothes in the *Guf* as well. It turns out that since there are only three *Kelim Bina, ZA* and *Malchut* in *Rosh de Nekudim*, the *Guf* too has no more than these three *Kelim*, since everything that exists in the *Guf* must be received from the *Rosh*.

Hence, *Guf de Nekudim* has only the seven lower *Sefirot*, which are *Bina* and the five *Kelim* of ZA, as *Netzah* and *Hod* are for one *Kli* here, and *Kli Malchut* is the seventh. However, in the three previous *Partzufim Galgalta AB SAG*, meaning before the *Eser Sefirot* were divided into two degrees and the *Eser Sefirot* were complete in the *Rosh*, this entire amount passed to the *Guf* too. Hence their *Gufim* had *Eser Sefirot* from *Keter* to *Malchut* as well.

The matter of the renewal of *Sefirat Daat* in the *Eser Sefirot* has also been explained: it comes from *Behinat* misplacement of the *Orot*. In *Partzuf AB, Ohr Hochma* clothed in *Kli de Keter, Ohr Bina* in *Kli de Hochma*, and *Ohr Hesed* in

Kli de Bina etc. This *Ohr Hesed*, clothed in *Kli de Bina*, became *Sefirat Daat*, which is the *MAN de Bina*.

The matter of *Hitlabshut Ohr Hesed*, which is *Komat ZA* in *Kli de Bina*, considers that *Bina* descended to the degree of *ZA*. As brought in the Rav's words above regarding the *Zivug de Komat Hochma* (Part 5 item 12), due to the misplacement of the above *Orot*, there was a decline in all the degrees. *Keter* came down to the degree of *Hochma*, and *Hochma* to the degree of *Bina*.

We find that because of *Hitlabshut Ohr ZA* in *Kli de Bina*, *Bina's* name was changed into *Sefirat Daat*. You can therefore understand the matter of the exit of *Ohr ZA* from inside *AK* to the outside, which the Rav speaks of henceforth.

You will find that in the inner *Partzuf*, called *Galgalta de AK*, there was *Ohr ZA* in *Kli de ZA*, as it should have been. However, in *Partzuf AB de AK*, *Ohr ZA* rose and clothed *Kli de Bina*, and in *Partzuf SAG de AK*, *Ohr ZA* rose and clothed *Kli de Hochma*. In *Partzuf Nekudim*, *Ohr ZA* rose to *Kli de Keter*.

It is written above that a *Partzuf* that exits the *Ohr Eynaim* has only *Komat Behina Aleph*, being the *Komat Nekeva de Keter*, which is the primary *Ohr*. However, *Komat Bina* in the *Zachar* does not expand below *GAR de Nekudim*.

We could therefore say that since its been shown that *Behinat Keter de Nekudim* is merely *Kli de Bina*, because *Rosh Aleph* took *Keter* and *Hochma*, *Keter de Nekudim* should have been called *Sefirat Daat*. Also, it's been written that *Ohr ZA* in *Kli de Bina* is called *Daat*.

The answer is that since it is *Behinat Rosh*, it is called *Keter* in and of itself. However, it also consists of a second *Zivug* in *Komat Behina Aleph*, which is *Ohr ZA*. Therefore, this is still not considered here that *Ohr ZA* came out, but only in *Olam Atzilut*, for there it clothed in *Kli de Keter*, and is considered to have come outside.

Now you will see that since the *Kli de Bina* of the *Guf* has nothing of the *Ohr Bina*, as *Ohr Bina* ends and is blocked at the *GAR*, its name is therefore changed to *Daat*, as it has none of the *Ohr Bina*. Thus, the reason that *Sefirat Daat* came out in *Olam ha Nekudim*, is because here the *Kli de Bina de Guf* was made completely empty of her own *Ohr*. Also, you find that the reason the *Guf* of *Nekudim* has only the lower seven *Sefirot* is because only these three are also at the *Rosh*, namely *Bina*, *ZA* and *Malchut*.

This is the root for the division of *NHY* into three thirds. They follow the three *Sefirot Bina*, *ZA* and *Malchut* of *Partzuf Nekudim*, clothing *Netzah Hod Yesod de AK*. The *Rosh* of the *NHY* are *Behinat Bina*, and the *Toch* of the *NHY*, which are the middle *Prakin*, are *Behinat ZA*, and the *Sof* of the *NHY*, which are the lower *Prakin*, are *Behinat Malchut*.

The reason for the division is that because in this entire *Partzuf* that shines in *NHY de AK*, there are no more than these three *Sefirot*. This is because *Keter* and *Hochma* in them remained above *Tabur*, in *YESHSUT* above the *Parsa*, considered *Akudim* and is not counted among the *Sefirot de Nekudim*.

However, the Rav counts four divisions here: *Keter, HBD, HGT, NHY*. This is because there were two times in this *Partzuf* of *Nekudim*: *Katnut* and *Gadlut*. In the beginning of their creation, they emerged in *Katnut*, because they came out of *Nikvey Eynaim*, on *Komat Behina Aleph*, which is merely *Ohr ZA*. However, afterwards there was a second *Zivug* of the *AB* and *SAG*, as the Rav says, and the *Mochin de Gadlut de Nekudim* came out, being the *GAR*.

That is why the Rav divides them now by an order of *Tikun Kavim*. ZA that clothes *AA de Atzilut*, meaning *Hochma, Hesed, Netzah* is in the right line, *Bina, Gevura* and *Hod*, on the left line, and *Keter, Daat, Tifferet, Yesod* in the middle line.

Yet, in the beginning of their emanation, the lower seven only came out in one line, one by one, as the Rav writes henceforth. It turns out that the Rav speaks of the *Gadlut de Nekudim* [a second version: emendation from the manuscript of the author Baal HaSulam: This is perplexing since there was no *Tikun Kavim* in *VAK*, but here he gives an example from *ZA de Atzilut* and *NHY de AA*].

It is written that *Keter* from the *Nekudot* clothes from *Tabur de AK* to *Sium* of the *Guf*, and *HBD* are in the first three *Prakin de NHY de AK*. It turns out the one *Rosh*, meaning *GAR de Nekudim*, were separated from one another because the *Keter* clothes *Tifferet de AK* and *HB* clothe the *Roshim de Yarchin de AK*, and we must understand that.

Moreover, where did *Sefirat Daat* come to *Rosh de Nekudim* from? After all, the Rav will count it henceforth among the seven lower *Sefirot* of ZA. The thing is that you know that *GAR de Nekudim* are *Behinat AHP* that came out of the *Rosh*. *Keter* is *Behinat Awzen* and *Bina*, *HB* are *Hotem* and *Peh*, meaning ZA and *Nukva*. ZA in *Behinat Tikun Kavim* is in *Behinat Hesed Gevura Tifferet*, and the *Nukva* is *NHY*.

It's been explained above that through the *Zivug de AB SAG*, *Behina Dalet* descended from the *Nikvey Eynaim* to the *Peh* as in the beginning, the *AHP* rose to the *Rosh* once more, and *Ohr GAR* came down to them (see Part 6, item 14 and *Ohr Pnimi*, item 17). It explains there that despite that, no change was made in the previous situation, and YESHSUT did not return and descended below *Tabur* because of that, only its *He'arah*.

Hence, this *Behinat GAR* is *Behinat HGT* that became *HBD*. It means that *Hotem Peh* that were on *Komat ZA* and *Malchut* first, which are ZAT, the *Hesed* in them returned to *Behinat Rosh* and now became *Hochma*.

The *Gevura* in them that returned to the *Rosh* has now become *Bina* and the rest of the *Sefirot TNHYM* now became *Daat*. Also, the *Behinat Awzen*, which is *Bina* that returned to the *Rosh*, now became *Keter*.

Thus you find how the AHP that were in GAR de Nekudim became KHBD during the *Gadlut*: *Awzen* became *Keter*, and the *Hochma* and *Gevura* in *Hotem* and *Peh* became *Daat*.

Know, that from here on in *Atzilut* there were two *Behinot HGT NHY* made in each *Partzuf*. This is because of the AHP that went out of the *Rosh* and became the *Guf*, being *Komat ZA*.

Afterwards there is *Behinat* genuine HGT NHY that were never in *Behinat Rosh*. These two *Behinot* divide on the *Tabur* of each *Partzuf* because HGT NHY, which are AHP that become the *Guf*, their place is above *Tabur*, regarded as *Behinat AVI* of that *Partzuf*.

The genuine HGT NHY are considered ZON of that *Partzuf* and their place is below *Tabur*. Also, HGT NHY below *Tabur*, which are the real ZON, they too have that same discernment when they expand in a *Partzuf* of their own, whose HGT end at the *Tabur*. They are considered *Behinat AHP* that came out as the *Rosh* of that *Partzuf*, meaning the real ZA. Its NHY below *Tabur* is its genuine *Behinat HGT*, meaning that were never in its *Behinat Rosh*.

Now the order of the *Halbasha* of *Partzuf Nekudim* to NHY de AK that the Rav explains here is thoroughly clarified. It has already been explained that in its SAG de AK there was the beginning of raising of MAN to *Nikvey Eynaim*, causing the exit of the AHP from the *Rosh*.

However, in itself there was no change, and the AHP of Rosh de SAG did not come out of its *Rosh*, but is considered to have elicited a special *Partzuf* of *Se'arot* there, where this great change occurred (see Part 6, *Ohr Pnimi* item 19). For that reason we do not discriminate *Behinat* HGT NHY above *Tabur* de AK here, as in the *Partzufim* that follow.

Rather, it is *Behinat Akudim* from its *Tabur* up, its *Eser Sefirot* beginning from the *Keter*. Also, that entirely new *Partzuf*, where the AHP became HGT, are considered in him as merely HGT NHY below the *Tabur* of its lower *Partzufim*.

Thus, its *Halbasha* resembles ZON *de Atzilut* clothing below *Tabur de AA de Atzilut*. Therefore, *Keter de Nekudim*, which is *Behinat Awzen* when first emanated, namely *Bina*, is found clothing the lower third of *Tifferet* because *Sefirat Tifferet* is *Behinat Bina* of the *Hey Ktzavot* on the part of its *Kli* (see Part 6, *Ohr Pnimi*, item 41). It clothes only below *Tabur* of *Tifferet de AK* and not above its *Tabur*, because there it is *Behinat Akudim*, and *Keter de Nekudim* has no hold in *Behinat Akudim*.

"HBD are in the first three *Prakin de NHY de AK*." It's been explained in *Ohr Pnimi* items 42, 43, that *Sefirat Netzah* is the *Behinat ZA* of the five *Ktzavot* on the part of the *Kli*, and *Sefirat Hod* is the *Behinat Malchut* of the *Hey Ktzavot*.

Hence, the *Hotem* and *Peh* in GAR *de Nekudim* are ZA and *Malchut* that returned to the *Rosh* and became *Hochma* and *Bina*. They clothe the upper thirds of *Netzah Hod de AK*, which are *Behinat Rosh de ZA* and *Malchut*, where *Rosh ZA* is in *Netzah* and *Rosh Malchut* in *Hod*.

However, now these ZA and *Malchut* became actual *Hochma* and *Bina* because they returned to the *Rosh*, as in the beginning. Thus, *Hochma* and *Bina de Nekudim* are proportional to the Upper *Prakin* of *Netzah* and *Hod*, as from the beginning of their creation they are *Behinat ZA* and *Malchut*, as they are.

The *Daat de Nekudim* clothes the Upper *Perek* of *Yesod de AK*, interred between the *Roshim de Yarchin* inside the *Guf*, meaning in *Tifferet*, which is the *Kli de Bina* of the five *Ktzavot*. This is so because *Daat* is *Behinat Ohr Hesed* clothed in *Kli de Bina*.

You already know that these *Hotem Peh* consist of the seven lower *Sefirot*, because the *Hotem* contains HGT NHY and the *Peh* is *Malchut*. You also know that only HG in them became *Hochma* and *Bina*, while the five *Sefirot* from *Tifferet* down became *Behinat Daat*.

It is so because *Sefirat Hesed* is *Behinat Hochma* of the five *Ktzavot* from the perspective of the *Ohr* in it. Hence, its power is good when it returns to *Behinat Rosh*, when it once more receives *Behinat Hochma*. *Sefirat Gevura* is *Behinat Bina* of the *Hey Ktzavot* from the perspective of her *Ohr*, hence she now returned to being *Bina*.

Sefirat Tifferet is *Behinat Ohr ZA* in the *Hey Ktzavot*. Thus, now that it is clothed in *Tifferet de AK*, which is *Bina*, from the perspective of the *Kli*, it became *Sefirat Daat*, clothing the Upper *Perek* of *Yesod de AK*, clothed in *Pnimiut Tifferet de AK*. However, from the viewpoint of *Halbasha*, it clothes only up to *Yesod*.

The reason is that the *Behinat Kli* of *Yesod* is from the *Behinat Malchut* in the *Hey Ktzavot*. It is known that the *Masach* mating with the *Ohr Elyon* is in *Kli Malchut*, thus having three *Prakin* in the *Yesod*. These are the three places of *Zivug*: *Peh*, *Chazeh*, *Yesod*. For that reason *Behinat Daat* in the *Rosh*, over which the *Zivug* was made, clothes the Upper *Perek* of *Yesod*, which is *Behinat Malchut de Rosh*.

"HGT in the three middle *Prakin*, and NHY in the three lower *Prakin*." You already know that these HGT NHY are ZAT *de Nekudim*, being *Behinat* true ZA that were never *Behinat Rosh*.

It has also been clarified that the real ZON are also divided on the two *Behinot* on the *Tabur*. Above *Tabur* they are *Behinat AHP* of itself, exiting from the *Rosh*, called HGT, and below *Tabur* they are its ZON, where there was never *Behinat Rosh*, called NHY. In that proportion the three middle *Prakin* and the three lower *Prakin* divide as well; HGT clothe the middle *Prakin* and NHY the lower *Prakin*.

There is yet another reason, truer in this place. You already know that HGT *de Hey Ktzavot* are the *Behinat* GAR in them, and *Behinat* ZA in the *Hey Ktzavot* begins in *Netzah* from the perspective of the *Kelim* and begins in *Tifferet* from the perspective of the *Orot*.

Hence, *Rosh*, *Toch*, *Sof de* NHY *de* AK are divided thus: the *Rosh* in them is *Behinat* AHP that actually returned to the *Rosh*, the *Toch* in them is *Behinat* GAR *de Hey Ktzavot*, meaning HGT, and the *Sof* in them are VAK *de* VAK, being ZA and *Malchut de Hey Ktzavot*.

Thus we have clarified the four divisions in the *Eser Sefirot de Nekudim* in them during the *Gadlut*. The first is *Keter de Nekudim*. It is not counted here in the *Partzuf*, as it is *Behinat Zachar* of the *Rosh de Nekudim*, being *Behinat Bina* and the *Etzem Ohr Awzen*, for it has *Behinat Bet de Hitlabshut*.

The second are *Hochma*, *Bina* and *Daat*, who from the beginning of their creation are but *Ohr* ZA *de Rosh*, called *Hotem Peh* that came out of the *Rosh* and turned into *Behinat* ZA *de Guf*. However, during the *Gadlut* they became *Behinat Rosh* once more, having *He'arah* from the *Ohr Awzen* through their *Hitkalelut* with the *Zachar*.

The third are HGT *de Nekudim* who were never *Behinat Rosh*, but from the stand point of the *Hey Ktzavot*, they are considered KHB. The fourth are NHY of *Nekudim*, being *Behinat* ZA and *Malchut de Hey Ktzavot*.

One might ask: Since AHP returned to the *Rosh* and became one with the *Galgalta ve Eynaim* in it, the *Hotem Peh*, which are *Hochma* and *Bina*, became one with the *Keter*, which is *Awzen*. Thus, there are only three *Behinot* here.

Indeed, you should remember that there was no change performed on the Upper *Sefirot* again, meaning because of their return of *AVI* to the *Rosh*. YESHSUT, which is *Behinat GE* of that *Rosh*, remained above *Tabur* in itself as in the beginning. *Keter de Nekudim* too, which is *Behina Bet*, remained for itself as in the beginning, but only their *He'arah* reached HB when they returned to the *Rosh*.

27. Two kinds of *Ohr* come out of the *Guf de AK*: the first from the *Tabur*, and the second from the *Yesod*. Also, two *Havalim* come out through there. It should have said that there should have been three *Havalim* there, opposite the GAR that received from the AHP, but since *Ohr Awzen* is absent from *AVI*, the *Behinat Hevel* opposite the *Awzen* is absent too. Hence, only two *Havalim* come out, opposite the *Hotem* and *Peh* alone, from which *AVI* received above, and here below they also receive from them.

Ohr Pnimi

27. The *Behinat Hevel* opposite the *Awzen* is absent too. Hence, only two *Havalim* come out, opposite the *Hotem* and *Peh*.

It means that only two *Havalim* came out of *Peh* of *Yesod*, opposite the *Hotem Peh*. Those are *Vav* to *Ima* and *Nekuda* to *Abba*, as the Rav says above. However, the *Hevel* of the *Tabur*, being opposite the *Ohr de Awzen*, did not reach *AVI*, as they only have a hold on the *Hotem Peh*, as the Rav says above.

28. However, the *Ohr* of the lower seven that took only from the *Guf* down is from the *Sium* of *Shibolet ha Zakan* downward. Hence, they too don't have *Havalim* to shine for them, but they are implied in the words, "and the arms of his hands were made supple," which is the meaning of the ten additions thrown off from among the *Tzipornaim*, as mentioned in *Tikun* 69.

It is so because they are *Behinat Melachim* in and of themselves, for the annulment of the *Melachim* was because he was not yet corrected as one *Adam*, male and female.

Ohr Pnimi

28. The *Ohr* of the lower seven that took only from the *Guf* down is from the *Sium* of *Shibolet ha Zakan* downward.

It's been written (*Ohr Pnimi* item 20), that ZAT take from the *Behinat Tikkunim* of *Dikna* under the *Shibolet*, where the *Ohr* of *Awzen* does not reach because it ends at *Shibolet ha Zakan* (see *Ohr Pnimi* item 21).

"And the arms of his hands were made supple," which is the meaning of the ten additions thrown off from among the *Tzipornaim*.

Even though he says that the ten *Havalim* came out through the *Tzipornaim* of the *Raglaim*, why does he say that they are from the hands here? Indeed, when it says that the ZAT took from the *Havalim* that come out through the *Tzipornaim* of the *Raglaim*, it means that they took from the *Behinat Parsa ha Mesayemet* to the *Raglaim* of SAG. It turns out that he took from the *Tzipornaim* of the *Raglaim*.

You must remember what is written above (*Ohr Pnimi* item 12) that the meaning of this *Parsa* is *Behinat* new point of *Tzimtzum* that moved from the place of *Malchut* of the *Eser Sefirot de Sium* to the place of *Bina* of the *Eser Sefirot de Sium*.

The place of the *Sium* of the *Kav* in *Tzimtzum Aleph de Ein Sof* was in *Malchut* of the *Eser Sefirot de Sium*, which is the actual *Olam ha Zeh*, as it says "And His feet shall stand upon the mount of Olives." Similarly, the same occurs now in *Tzimtzum Bet*, called *Tzimtzum NHY de AK*, the point of *Sium* in the *Bina* of these *Eser Sefirot*, called point of *Olam ha Ba*.

A *Parsa* was placed here, ending the new *Gevul* set up in the *Olamot*, where the *Raglaim* of *Partzuf SAG de AK* end, and *Parsa* is regarded as the *Tzipornaim* of the *Raglaim de SAG de AK*.

It has been explained (*Ohr Pnimi* item 21) that the *Parsa* and *Shibolet ha Zakan* are one matter. That is why the Rav writes here that from *Yesod de AK* **"only two Havalim come out, opposite the Hotem and Peh,"** from which AVI received, and the *Hevel* opposite the *Ohr Awzen* is absent. This is why the ZAT took from the *Tzipornaim* of the *Raglaim*, since they took for the *Sium* of the *Shibolet*, ending the *Ohr de Awzen*.

Understand, that because of the new point of *Sium*, three *Behinot Sium* emerged in SAG, in its *Rosh, Toch, Sof*: the point of *Sium* of the *Rosh*, is called *Nikvey Eynaim*, the point of *Sium* of the *Toch*, being in the place of the previous *Tabur*, is called *Shibolet ha Zakan*, and the *Behinat Sium* of the *Sof*, is called *Parsa*. Thus, the *Parsa* is the *Behinat Etzbaot Raglaim* of SAG de AK.

However, everything we discern in SAG doesn't change *Partzuf SAG* itself in any way, as you already know that there is no absence and change in the spiritual. Everything we discern in it is but a general *Behinat Shoresh* (see *Ohr Pnimi* item 2).

However, all these changes that occur by the force of the new point of *Tzimtzum* is only in that same new *Partzuf* that emerged because of the connection of *Behina Dalet* with *Behina Bet* through the *Nikvey Eynaim*, called *Partzuf Nekudim*. Also, only in the *Rosh, Toch, Sof* of that *Partzuf* did the three *Parsas* emerge and were made in its *RTS* de facto, and remember that.

You already know that there is a great *Tikun* in this *Parsa* that "**draws from above, and gives below,**" because it is *Behinat* double *Masach* from two *Behinot*: *Behina Bet* and *Behina Dalet* together. This is done by the ascent of *NHY* to *HGT*, and the mingling of *Behina Bet* that operates in the *HGT* of *Partzuf SAG* with *Behina Dalet* that operates in *NHY* of the Inner *AK*.

Hence, the *Parsa* stands diagonally from *Chazeh* to *Tabur*, as it contains within it *NHY* and *HGT* together. Thus, during the *Gadlut*, the lower *Hey*, being *Behina Dalet*, descends from the *Parsa* and the *Parsa* is split. In other words, the ending *Gevul* is canceled and the *Orot de SAG* pass below the *Parsa*.

Afterwards, the *Parsa* immediately returns to its place, and in that manner it draws *He'arat SAG* from above, and gives below, to *Partzuf Nekudim* below the *Tabur*. It is similar in the *Partzufim* of *Atzilut* as well.

The above seven lower *Sefirot* of *Nekudim* could not receive any *Ohr* from the SAG because of the *Sium* of the *Parsa*. However, now, during the *Gadlut*, after the *Parsa* has been fissured, they too are found to be receiving *Ohr* from the place of the *Parsa*, the place of *Behinat SAG* and *HGT* of the general *AK*.

Thus, the same *Orot* that the seven lower *Sefirot de Nekudim* received from the *Parsa* is *Behinat HGT*, being the arms of the hands. That is why it says, "and the arms of his hands were made supple."

We find that before the *Zivug de Gadlut*, *Parsa* is considered the *Etzbaot Raglaim* of *Partzuf SAG*. This is so because *He'arat SAG* ends there and the *Sof* of the *He'arah* is called *Raglaim*. However, when the *Parsa* fissures, at which time the *Gevul* returns to the point of *Sium de Olam ha Zeh* as before, the *Behinat HGT* expands as before.

29. The fitting *Havalim* for these seven *Melachim* came out through the *Tzipornaim* of the *Raglaim*. Although the *Tzipornaim* are ten, and the *Nekudot* that broke are only ZAT, the thing is that there are also two kinds of *Achoraim de Ima* that broke, being the nine *Behinot*, and the tenth.

This is so because in *Keter* too there was some flaw, and it is its *Behinat NHY* that came inside as *Mochin* to AVI, and they too broke. Thus, there are ten *Behinot*, for ten *Havalim* that came out of the *Tzimtzum* of his *Raglaim*.

The discriminations of the exit of these ten *Havalim* through his *Tzipornaim* were all the absence of their reception from the *Ohr* of the Upper *Awzen*. Hence it is this reason that caused the annulment of the *Melachim*.

30. Regarding the *Akudim*, the *Behinat Taamim Nekudot, Tagin, Otiot* in them has already been explained above. Here we shall explain them in the *Behinat Nekudim*.

It is written that *Behinat Nekudim* are the first *Orot* that came out in the beginning, and the *Otiot* are the *Kelim*. Then, when the *Kelim* broke and were separated each from its dead, the *Orot* remained as *Tagin* on the *Otiot*, which are the *Kelim*. The *Taamim* is the new name MA, that later came out from the *Ohr* of the *Metzach* for the *Tikun* of the *Melachim*.

Ohr Pnimi

30. Regarding the *Akudim*, the *Behinat TNTO* in them has already been explained above.

It is written (Part 4, Chap 3, item 11) that *Hitpashtut Aleph* of the *Partzuf*, which is *Ohr Yashar, Rachamim*, is considered the *Taamim* in it. When it begins to diminish by the power of the *Hizdakchut* of the *Masach*, at which time the other four *Komot* of *Katnut* from *Hochma* to *Malchut* emerge, they are considered *Behinat Nekudot* in it. Also, The *Reshimot* that remain from the *Behinat Nekudot*, from the *Behinot Nitzotzin* that fall off them into the *Kelim* are called *Otiot*.

Nekudim are the first Orot that came out in the beginning.

By that he tells us that the order is changed here, compared to the way it was in the previous three *Partzufim* of AK. There the *Gadlut* came out first, which are the *Taamim*, and then the degrees of *Katnut* emerged, meaning the *Nekudot*.

However, here in *Olam ha Nekudim*, the *Katnut* came out first, and then the *Gadlut*. This is so because at first, only the GAR came out, in *Orot de Ruach Nefesh*, namely *Komat ZA*. Then AB and SAG mated, the *Parsa* fissured, and the *Orot de GAR* went down to the *Nekudim*, and to the seven lower *Sefirot*.

It is written, "**Nekudot are the first Orot that came out in the beginning,**" meaning the opposite of the previous *Partzufim Galgalta, AB, SAG*, where the *Taamim* came out first. Here the *Behinot Nekudot* came out first, meaning the *Katnut*, and then the *Gadlut*. Notwithstanding, *He'arat Gadlut* is not called *Taamim*, because they were not in *Behinat Rachamim*, as in these *Orot* and in what caused them was the matter of the breaking of the vessels.

And the Otiot are the Kelim.

They also contain the *Nitzotzin* that fell into them during the *Histalkut* of the *Orot* from them, as it was in *Akudim*.

The Taamim is the new name MA.

Those *Taamim* that emerged in *Olam ha Nekudim*, meaning the *Gadlut* that emerged by *Zivug AB SAG*, being the *Taamim de Nekudim*, did not exist in *Nekudim*, but only after the new *Taamim de MA* corrected them. Hence, they are called after the name of the MA.

31. *We shall repeat that we have explained that the *Nekudot* were divided into three parts: The *Elyonim* above the *Otiot*, such as the *Holam*, in the middle, like the *Shuruk*, and the *Tachtonim* like the rest of the *Nekudot*.

    The *Nekuda* of the *Holam* is the *Hevel* that exits from *Tabur*, where the *Keter* stands. This is because *Keter* is the *Holam* on the *Tifferet*, as *Holam* is mainly in *Tifferet de AK*.

    However, *Keter* became *Nekudot*, as it says in the fifth *Tikun*, that *Holam* is *Keter* in the *Otiot*. The *Nikud* (punctuation) of *Shuruk* in the *Vav*, called *Melafom*, being in the middle, is the *Hevel* emerging from *Yesod* to AVI.

    It is divided into two because that *Nekuda* of *Shuruk* is *Vav*, the *Yod* in the middle, and the *Yod* of *Shuruk* is for *Abba*, called the first *Yod* of the Name. Also, the *Vav* of *Shuruk* is for *Ima*, to produce and generate the VAK de ZA. This is the *Behinat Vav* that *Ima* takes.

    There is yet another reason that the *Nekuda*, which is like a *Yod* in the *Shuruk*, is higher, and *Abba de Nekudim* sucks from it. It is known, that the *Vav* of the *Shuruk*, being the letter *Vav*, *Ima de Nekudim* sucks from that. This is because the *Nekudot* of *Hochma*, the *Otiot Bina*, and the seven lower *Nekudot* with the three *Behinot*, are: one - NHY of *Keter*, and two - *Achoraim de AVI*.

    Thus, these ten came out through the *Tzipornaim* of the *Raglaim*. We do not mean to say that these are the *Nekudot* themselves, only that *Ohr* came out of all these *Havalim* to the ten *Nekudot* that came out through the *Ayin*, and remember that.

Ohr Pnimi

31. The *Nekudot* were divided into three parts:

    By the three *Orot Bina*, ZA and *Malchut* that shine in *Nekudim* (see *Ohr Pnimi* item 23). This is so because there is *Ohr Bina* there from *Behinat Hitlabshut* called *Zachar*, being *Keter de Nekudim*. There is also *Koma de Behina Aleph* there, being the *Nekeva de Nekudim*, called *Hochma* and *Bina*, where *Ohr ZA* is in *Hochma* and *Ohr Malchut* in *Bina*.

    It is written that the *Nekudot* are divided into three parts *Bina*, ZA and *Malchut*, clothed in *Keter*, *Hochma* and *Bina* of the *Nekudot*. However, know that ZA and *Malchut* found in *Hochma* and *Bina* are both considered as one part, since they are *Behinat Ohr* of one *Koma*, *Koma de Behina Aleph*.

For that reason the seven lower *Sefirot* are considered the third part. In this way, that *Keter* that has *Bina* from *Behinat Hitlabshut*, is the upper part, and *Hochma* and *Bina* together are the second part, while the ZAT are the third part.

The *Holam* is the *Hevel* that exits from *Tabur*, where the *Keter* stands.

It is *Ohr Bina* from *Behinat Hitlabshut*. It's been explained above (*Ohr Pnimi* item 23) that no *Hitpashtut Kelim* came out of this *Zivug* of *Behina Bet de Hitlabshut*, but from a *Masach* that has *Behinat Hamshacha*. Hence, the *Kelim* only came out from *Behina Aleph* of the *Nekeva*, being *Hochma* and *Bina*.

This is why it is written that the *Hevel* comes out of the *Tabur* to the *Keter* of *Nekudim*. This *Hevel* is the *Ohr Bina* (item 27), *Behinat Holam* above the *Otiot* (see item 17). This is so because the *Otiot* are the *Kelim* and this *Ohr Bina* that only came out from *Behina Bet de Hitlabshut* has no *Hitpashtut* for *Kelim*. Consequently, it is *Behinat Holam* above the *Otiot* and does not touch them, for it cannot clothe within them.

Shuruk in the Vav, called *Melafom*, being in the middle.

It is written above that only AVI, which are the *Nekeva de Nekudim*, have *Hitpashtut Kelim* and can clothe within them. Hence AVI are implied in the *Shuruk*, meaning a *Melafom* in the middle of the *Otiot*.

Yod of Shuruk is for Abba, called the first Yod of the Name.

Meaning the *Yod* of the Name HaVaYaH, which is *Behinat AB*, being *Abba*. He implies the *Behinat* five *Hassadim* of the *Yesod* that *Abba* took. This is because it is known that the influence of *Yesod* is only the *Hassadim* and *Gevurot* and *Abba* takes the five *Hassadim*, since AB is *Hassadim*.

The Vav of Shuruk is for Ima, to produce and generate the VAK de ZA.

Ima is the first *Hey* of the Name HaVaYaH. Hence she received the *Behinat* "truncated *Vav* inside the *Hey*" from the *Yesod*, which is her MAN and is the ZA in the intestines of *Bina*.

The Nekuda... ...and Abba de Nekudim sucks from it.

Nekuda implies the lower *Hey* that rose to *Nikvey Eynaim* from which came AVI *de Nekudim*. Now she became *Behinat* MAN for *Abba* for the great *Zivug* of *Histaklut Eynaim de* AVI.

The Vav of the Shuruk, being the letter Vav, Ima de Nekudim sucks from that.

It is as he wrote in the Tree of Life, that through the force of the raising of MAN to *Nikvey Eynaim*, it splits the *HaVaYaH de SAG* there, where the *Vav* in the *Peh* is *Ima*.

Nekudot of Hochma, the Otiot Bina.

Because *AVI* have only *Komat ZA* from the beginning of their creation. *Abba* is considered *Ohr ZA*, and *Ima* the *Kli*, which is *Otiot*. This *Ohr* in the *Katnut* is called *Ohr Nekudot*, as the Rav says in item 30 here. This is why it is written *Nekudot* – *Hochma*, and *Otiot* – *Bina*.

And the seven lower Nekudot... ...these ten came out through the Tzipornaim of the Raglaim.

It means that they are the *Nekudot* under the *Otiot*, which are the nine *Nekudot*. In the first two *Nekudot*: *Kamatz*, *Patach*, there was no breaking, as they are *Keter* and *Hochma*. In the seven lower *Nekudot* there was a breaking of the vessels, as the Rav says in the Tree of Life.

These nine *Nekudot* are *Tachtonim* under the *Otiot* because they received the *Behinat Havalim* coming out through the *Tzipornaim* of the *Raglaim*, which are under the *Kelim* of the *Partzuf*.

We might ask: He says above that *Holam* and *Shuruk* are the *Keter* and *Hochma*, meaning the Upper and Middle *Nekudot*. However, here he considers them *Kamatz* and *Patach*. It turns out that *Keter* and *Hochma* are also Lower *Nekudot*.

The thing is that we must distinguish in them the *Etzem* of their emanation, as they first emerged through the *Nikvey Eynaim*, when only two *Orot* came out of there, *Zachar* and *Nekeva*. The *Keter* was the *Zachar*, reaching up to *Bina*, from the *Behinat Hitlabshut*, and the *Nekeva* is both *Hochma* and *Bina* together, in the *Koma* of *Behina Aleph*.

Hence they are considered *Holam* and *Shuruk* here, implying that the *Zachar*, which is *Keter*, has no *Hitpashtut* for *Kelim*, and he is above the *Partzuf* as a *Nekuda* of *Tabur* above *Partzuf Nekudim*, as *Behinat Holam*. He is *Keter* to the *Otiot* and does not participate in the *Hitpashtut* of the *Partzuf*. Opposite that the *AVI* are implied in the *Shuruk*, inside the *Otiot*, meaning inside the *Partzuf*, as they are the *Behinat Nekeva*, having complete MAN from *Behinat Hamshacha* too.

However, the *Nekudot* below the *Otiot* imply the time of *Gadlut* of the *Nekudim* after the *AB* and *SAG* mated and the *Koma* that emerged by their *Zivug* descended and fissured the *Parsa*. It means that the *Gevul* of the *Sium Raglin de SAG* was canceled, and then the entire *Partzuf* of *Nekudim* that stands under the *Parsa* received from the *Raglaim de SAG* above the *Parsa*.

This means that the *Eser Sefirot de Sium* of the *SAG* that the *Parsa* rides on now acquired *Behinot Hitpashtut* and illuminated for the *Nekudim*. Thus, the *Nekudim* are now found to be receiving from the *Orot* below the *Partzuf* in its previous form. These are called the *Nekudot* under the *Otiot*.

Study that well for that *Behinat Holam* above the *Otiot* of *Partzuf de Nekudim* during its creation descended from there during the *Gadlut* and clothed in *Nekudim*, meaning inside the *Otiot*. We refer to them as under the *Otiot* only compared to the state of the giver, not with respect to the state of the receiver.

Thus we have learned that these *Keter* and *Hochma* too received from *Sium Raglin de SAG* as the *ZAT*. Moreover, they are the prime receivers, and they are the ones that gave them to the *ZAT*.

In that sense they are called *Kamatz Patach*, for they are under the *Otiot*. Thus, in order to indicate the *Behinat Keter* and *Hochma* from their very creation, they are marked with *Holam* and *Shuruk*. Conversely, when indicated with respect to what they received by the *Gadlut de Nekudim*, they are then called *Kamatz Patach*.

However, when the Rav writes that *Kamatz Patach* did not break, he refers to what they have from their very creation, not to what they received from *Sium Raglin de SAG*. This is because these *He'arot* were canceled from both *Keter* and *Hochma*, and they are called *Orot Achoraim* of *AVI*.

We do not mean to say that these are the Nekudot themselves.

It means that these *Orot* and *Havalim* that came out of the *Tzipornaim* of his *Raglaim* are not the *Atzmut* of the *Nekudot*. Rather, they are considered as mere additions, because the *Behinat Atzmut* of the *Nekudot* came out of the *Ohr Eynaim*.

32. *In the beginning of my studies with my teacher, he would hide, cover and clothe the matters, as I did not yet know the beginning of things, as I have presented them in the previous gates. Hence, when he began to explain to me the matter of *Atik Yomin*, he explained one study, and we shall write it here.

I could not connect it with what I have written thus far, yet I do wish to write it, and perhaps the reader will be able to connect it with the above, for the matters seem to contradict the above. This is its matter:

It is known that there were ten *Nekudim* first, where the first three did not break, and the *Kelim* and the *Orot* remained, but the seven lower *Nekudot* broke and the *Kelim* descended to *Beria*. Consequently, the *Orot* remained in their place in *Olam Atzilut* without any clothing.

Know, that the first three *Nekudot*, both in the *Behinat Orot* and in the *Behinat Kelim*, are the only ones *Partzuf Atik Yomin* is made of. No other force is involved in them.

However, there are many forces involved in the seven lower *Nekudot*: there is an upper *Behina* from *Behinat Atik* in each of the seven *Nekudot*, and there is a second *Behina* of *AA* in each of the seven *Nekudot* as well. There is also *Behinat AVI*, and there is the lowest amongst them, that of *ZON*.

Ohr Pnimi

32. **The first three *Nekudot*... ...are the only ones *Partzuf Atik Yomin* is made of.**

Meaning: *Partzuf Keter*, called *Atik*, has *Eser Sefirot* called Inner *HaVaYaH*. The tip of the *Yod* is the *Keter* in it, meaning *Keter de Keter*; the *Yod* in it is *Abba* and *Hochma*; the first *Hey* in it is *Ima* and *Bina*, and the *Vav* in it is ZA. The last *Hey* in it is *Malchut*.

Complete *HaVaYaH* emerges as *Malbush* out of every single *Ot* in the Inner *HaVaYaH* in *Partzuf Keter* itself. *Partzuf AB* comes out of its *Yod*, and *Partzuf SAG* comes out of its first *Hey*. AB is called *Abba* and the SAG is called *Ima*. *Partzuf ZA* comes out of the *Vav* in it, clothing it from *Tabur* down, and *Partzuf Malchut* comes out of the last *Hey*.

Know, that so it is in every complete *Partzuf*. *Partzuf Keter* is considered the *Pnimi*, also containing inner *AB, SAG, MA, BON*, called Inner *HaVaYaH*. Besides those, it has Outer *AB, SAG, MA, BON*, which are *Malbushim* to it. The AB and SAG clothe above *Tabur*, and MA and BON, being ZON, clothe below *Tabur*, as the Rav says (Part 6, item 1).

Thus, in *Partzuf Nekudim* only *Behinat Partzuf Keter* in it came out with the *AB, SAG, MA, BON* in its *Pnimiut*. It did not have time to produce the outer *AB, SAG, MA, BON*, because the seven lower *Sefirot* in it broke, and the *Achoraim* of the GAR in it were also canceled.

However, the *Behinat Panim* of its First Three remained. It means that everything that was in these GAR from the beginning of their creation is called *Panim*; all of it remained and not a thing of them was canceled.

It is written, "**The first three *Nekudot*, both in the *Behinat Orot* and in the *Behinat Kelim*, are the only ones *Partzuf Atik Yomin* is made of.**" It is so because the outer *AB, SAG, MA, BON* have no hold on the GAR *de Partzuf Keter*.

This is the meaning of the words, "**no other force is involved in them.**" This is because even *Partzuf AB* begins to emerge from *Peh de Partzuf Keter* downward, which is below *Malchut* of its *Rosh*; much less in the rest of the *Partzufim*.

There are many forces involved in the seven lower Nekudot.

It refers to those *Behinot* from which the four *Partzufim* outer ASMB that clothe it should emerge. It is so because they haven't emerged from it in *Olam ha Nekudim*. He will explain henceforth that there is *Behinat AA* that should come out of it.

33. It turns out that the *Partzufim AA, AVI* and *ZON* after the *Tikun,* came out of these *Behinot* in the seven lower *Nekudot,* both from the *Behinat Orot,* and from the *Behinat Kelim.* Indeed, those *Behinot* that have the *Atik Yomin* in them rose and mingled with the first three *Nekudot,* all of which are *Behinat Atik Yomin,* and *Partzuf Atik* was made of all these *Behinot* as we've explained.

Ohr Pnimi

33. **The Partzufim AA, AVI and ZON after the Tikun, came out of these Behinot in the seven lower Nekudot.**

Meaning by the selections in the association of the new MA with them. Even *Partzuf AA* was made of *Behinat NHY de Keter* that was sorted and corrected through the new MA because of the annulment of the *Achoraim* that were there during the breaking of the vessels.

Know, that these *NHY de Keter* from which *AA de Atzilut* was made is considered the seven lower *Sefirot de Keter*. The rule is that any thing that was in *Partzuf Nekudim* from the beginning of creation, meaning as it came out of the *Nikvey Eynaim*, is considered GAR.

This is because *Ohr Eynaim* illuminated only to the *GAR de Nekudim* in the beginning of its creation. Nevertheless, only *Behinat Rosh* without a *Guf* came out of the *Ohr Eynaim*, for *Behina Aleph* doesn't shine to the *Guf*, as the Rav says (Part 3, Chap 1, item 6). Hence, all that the *ZAT de Nekudim* had was *He'arat Kelim* from *Behinat Histaklut Eynaim* in AHP.

Now you can see that the entire *Behinat Gadlut* that reached them as addition to what they had from the beginning of their creation is considered *Behinat ZAT* and *Kelim de Achoraim*. This is because they took them from the *Behinat Tzipornaim* of the *Raglaim de SAG*.

34. It is known that the *Elyon* expands in any *Tachton* to sustain it, but the *Tachton* does not expand in its *Elyon*. Hence there is the force of *Atik*

Yomin in the seven lower *Nekudot*, but no force of AA, AVI and ZON is involved in the first three *Nekudot*, as they are all *Behinat Atik*.

35. *However, the Upper *Maatzil* wanted to create that *Behinat Melachim* in that manner to begin with, consisting of *Behinat Kedusha*, but she is *Dinim* and *Gevurot* and the *Shmarim* and the *Klipot* are mixed in them. He created them like that deliberately so that there would be reward and punishment in the world, to punish the wicked and reward the righteous.

    This is not the place to elaborate, but He created them like that deliberately, in order to abolish and exterminate them. Thus the holy *Nitzotzot* would be sorted out from among them, rise up, and the *Klipot* mixed in them would remain below, as *Sigim* of gold and *Shmarim* of wine.

36. Know, that these seven *Melachim* are ten, but they are like the seven *Heichalot*, which are ten that are called seven. It is so because the top *Heichal* contains the first three *Heichalot*, and the bottom *Heichal* contains the last two *Heichalot*.

    It is exactly the same in these seven *Melachim*, for they are ten, but are called only seven. Since these *Melachim* are *Behinot Dinim* and *Gevurot*, you find that they are all in the form of *Nekeva*, as the *Nekeva* is all *Din*.

37. *He wrote, "Come and see the very beginning of faith etc." "trampled over the black *Nitzotz*," which is the *Shoresh* of the *Din*, "concealed in the intestine of *Ima*," as mentioned in the Zohar (Idra Zuta), "and threw *Nitzotzin* in 320 directions."

    Since these *Melachim* are *Dinim* and strong *Gevurot*, they are called *Nitzotzin* of *Esh* that came out of the *Butzina de Kardinuta* (Candle of Darkness). They numbered 320 *Nitzotzin*, each *Nitzotz* separated from the other, and they each turned their own way. They were thrown until they went below *Olam Atzilut*, and being there, they sorted out the offal from within the thought.

    It turns out that since they are hard *Dinim* the offal of the *Klipa* was mixed with them, and when they were thrown down, they were sorted and corrected. The good and the holy among them returned to be corrected by the eighth *Melech*, called *Hadar*, rose up, and the offal in them became the *Behinot Klipot* and they remained below.

38. *Indeed these ten *Nekudot* were one atop the other. The measure of their *Koma* was as the current measure and *Koma* of *Atzilut*, this is because the place where those *Nekudot* reached, until that place it is now *Olam Atzilut*, and from there down, *Olam Beria*.

Ohr Pnimi

38. Ten Nekudot were one atop the other.

He is uneasy with interpreting the ten *Nekudot* he mentions here. Though only the seven lower *Nekudot* were one above the other, only the first three among them were in *Tikun Kavim*, as it is known in all the places.

The reason the seven lower *Nekudot* were in one *Kav* one below the other is that the matter of the *Tikun Kavim* came out by the ascent of *NHY* to *HGT*, where *Behina Bet* and *Behina Dalet* were mixed together (*Ohr Pnimi* item 1). This is because then *Malchut* was incorporated in every single *Sefira* through *Hochma*.

Consequently, a *Kav* of *Hesed* and a *Kav* of *Din* were created in every single *Sefira*. Thus, through the *Zivug* that raises *Ohr Hozer* they were united with each other as *Rachamim*.

The beginning of this *Tikun* was made in *Partzuf Nekudim* that came out of *Nikvey Eynaim de SAG*, though this *Ohr* reached only *GAR* of *Nekudim*, and not the lower seven. Hence, the seven lower *Kelim* remained without *Tikun Kavim*.

You should know here that the *Kelim* of every *Partzuf* were made of the same *Kelim* in the *Partzuf* above it after the *Histalkut* of their *Orot* from within them. Now you can see that the *Kli* of the *Eser Sefirot de Nekudim* was made of the lower nine *Sefirot de SAG*, which extended below *Tabur*, and the *Ohr* departed from them during *Tzimtzum NHY de AK*.

Hence, since there was still no *Tikun Kavim* in *SAG*, the seven lower *Kelim* came out in one *Kav*. However, the *GAR* that received from the *Zivug* in *Nikvey Eynaim* came out in *Tikun Kavim*. Even though the seven lower *Kelim* took from the *Histaklut Eynaim* in *AHP* as well, this minute *He'arah* is insufficient for them for *Tikun Kavim*.

The measure of their Koma was as the current measure and Koma of Atzilut.

The new point of *Tzimtzum* in the *Olamot* was made of the association of *Behina Dalet* and *Behina Bet* and mixing them together, in the place of *Behina Bet* of the *Eser Sefirot de Sium*. The first *Partzuf* to come out in the new measure of *Sium* is *Partzuf Nekudim*, and all other *Partzufim* of *Atzilut* follow it.

That place from the old point of *Tzimtzum*, being *Olam ha Zeh*, and the new point of *Tzimtzum*, is called the place of the three *Olamot*, *BYA*. Since they stand in that place after the new point of *Tzimtzum* that's been renewed, these three *Olamot* are called the three *Olamot* of separation. That is why it is said that the *Koma* of *Nekudim* and the *Koma* of *Olam Atzilut* have the same length, and from there down, *Olam ha Beria*.

39. However, the *Ohr* of these ten *Nekudim* was great indeed. Also, the *Ohr Elyon* was added to them, and they did not have the strength to receive. It is then that these *Kelim* died, meaning went below, to the place that is now *Beria*, and this descent was their death.

    Indeed, this is only in the seven lower *Nekudot*, because the GAR had power in their *Kelim* to receive their *Ohr*, and they did not die. However, the seven *Kelim* of the lower seven are the ones that died and descended to the place that is now *Beria*, and this is their death.

    Indeed, the time of their death was when they emerged as *Nekudim*. It is so because when they came out of *Akudim*, where they were mixed in the *Keter* together, from which they came out and divided into *Yod Nekudim*. Then they came out and died instantaneously, as it is written in the Zohar, "The craftsman crushes the iron and *Nitzotzin* come out, and quench instantaneously."

Ohr Pnimi

39. **Also, the *Ohr Elyon* was added to them.**

    Besides what they had in the beginning of their creation, from *Zivug Nikvey Eynaim*, another *Partzuf* came to them, complete in *Gadlut*, by the *Zivug de AB SAG*, where the first *Ohr* is called the "essence" of their emanation.

    And they didn't have the strength to receive.

    The *Kelim* were too small to contain the great *Ohr* that came as an addition because that *Ohr* was in *Behinat* GAR, and their *Kelim* began from *Bina* down (*Ohr Pnimi* item 26). Hence, they did not exist until the new MA came and connected them with it; then the *Kelim* grew and existed.

    GAR had power in their *Kelim* to receive their *Ohr*.

    Meaning precisely their own *Ohr*, which they had in the beginning of their creation, meaning the above first *Ohr*. However, the second *Ohr*, called "additions" did not exist in GAR too, meaning the annulment of *Achoraim de AVI* and the blemish of *NHY de Keter* that the Rav introduces.

    When they came out of *Akudim*... ...and divided into *Yod Nekudim*. Then they came out and died instantaneously.

    In the beginning, all the *Orot* came and mingled in *Kli de Keter de Nekudim*. This is still considered *Akudim*, meaning *Behinat Partzuf* SAG, because it has *Behina Bet de Hitlabshut* (*Ohr Pnimi* item 23). There are the *Atzmut Ohr*

Awzen in it, though afterwards, by the *He'arat Yesod de AK*, *NHY* of this *Keter* expanded into *AVI*, and *AVI* returned to be *Panim be Panim* (face to face).

They mated on the MAN of the lower *Hey* as a *Nekuda* that *Abba* took and the great *Zivug* was made as *Histaklut Eynaim de AVI* in each other. This great *Ohr* expanded from above downward to the *Kelim de Nekudim*, meaning to divide into ten *Nekudim*. Because each and every *Kli* consisted of *Yod*, as it is known regarding the 320 *Nitzotzin*, they instantly broke and died.

It is written, "**The craftsman crushes the iron and Nitzotzin come out, and quench instantaneously.**" They are 320 sparks, because each *Melech* consists of four *Behinot HB TM*. Each *Behina* contained ten *Nekudot*, thus forty sparks for every *Melech*. Since they are eight *Melachim*, thus eight times forty is 320, and this is the meaning of the 320 *Nitzotzin* mentioned in all the places.

40. *In the beginning the ten were simple *Atzmut*, consisting of *Yod*, indiscernible in them. The GAR, which were *Rachamim*, could receive the *Ohr Ein Sof*, and when it reached the seven *Nekudot*, they would be canceled.

    Also, these are the *Melachim* that died. Since they are *Din*, while the *Ohr* that comes is *Rachamim*, they could not receive it, and since they did not receive the sustenance, they died. Hence it was necessary to correct where *Kelim* would be made for the *Keter*. Thus the *Ohr* that comes and passes through the *Masach* was corrected and even these *Yod* became apparent in it.

    These *Melachim* are below *Malchut de Atzilut*, and only *Hadar* was left of them, since they were *Dechar* and *Nukva*, and they are *Tifferet* and *Malchut*.

Ohr Pnimi

40. The ten were simple *Atzmut*, consisting of *Yod*, indiscernible in them.

    It means that they are *GAR de Nekudim*, even though *Tikun Kavim* and *Behinat Yod Kavim* were already in them. This means that *Malchut* incorporated in each and every *Sefira* and the ten *Kelim* became *Orot*.

    However, since they are *Behinat Rosh*, and the *Masach* operates in them from below upward, all the *Orot* are therefore still considered to be contained in *Kli de Keter*, as in *Akudim*. Also, the matter of the *Yod Kelim* is indiscernible in them, because the *Behinat Aviut* is unapparent from below upward, meaning before the *Ohr* clothes in the *Kelim*.

    The GAR, which were Rachamim, could receive the Ohr Ein Sof.

    As it says in the previous item, the *Behinat Aviut*, which is *Midat ha Din* from the *Hitkalelut Malchut* in each and every *Sefira*, is not apparent in the GAR just yet. This is because there is no actual *Behinat Hitlabshut* in them, but only in potential, hence they are *Rachamim*.

Since they are Din, while the Ohr that comes is Rachamim, they could not receive it.

It's been written above that the *Kelim* were small, because the great *Kelim* in the *Gufim* of the three previous *Partzufim* of AK, being *Kli de Keter* and *Kli de Hochma*, were absent here in the *Guf* of *Nekudim*. This is because they began from *Sefirat Daat* down, being *Kli de Bina* (see *Ohr Pnimi* item 26).

The *Ohr* that came to them was *Rachamim*, meaning *Orot* of GAR, called *Ohr* of *Rachamim*, they need to clothe in the *Zach Kelim* of *Keter* and *Hochma*. This is the reason they could not receive it.

Kelim would be made for the Keter. Thus the Ohr that comes and passes through the Masach.

He refers to the *Masach de Yesod de Atik* that was corrected in *Atzilut*, by which the *Ohr* was corrected, as written above.

These Yod became apparent in it.

It is so because they were corrected in *Tikun Kavim* and *Yod Kelim* in the ZAT too through the *Ibur* and *Yenika*, and then the *Atzmut* clothed in the *Kelim*.

Below Malchut de Atzilut.

Meaning they expanded below *Parsa de Atzilut* and came out of the *Gevul* of the new point of *Tzimtzum* that was in *Nekudim*, and this was their death.

Since they were Dechar and Nukva.

Meaning his *Nukva* was corrected, as she should have been; therefore he remained. This is the meaning of the name New MA, which will be explained in its place.

41. *Each of these ten *Sefirot* certainly consisted of all the ten *Sefirot*, but that was by way of admixture. [Let us make an allegory such as this: it is as if water and wine, oil, honey and milk were all mixed together in the same pot.]

The lower seven were in *Behinat Dinim* because it is impossible for the world to exist and be conducted except through the *Dinim* and the *Klipot*, as it is written in the Mishna, to punish the wicked and reward the righteous, etc.

Ohr Pnimi

41. **Consisted of all the Eser Sefirot, but that was by way of admixture.**

This means that the *Tikun* of the ten *Kelim* was made by *Tzimtzum* NHY. It means that *Behina Dalet* incorporated in each and every *Sefira* because of her connection with *Behina Bet*, and the *Masach* and *Zivug* were corrected in each and every *Sefira* through *Hochma* and through the *Nikvey Eynaim*.

However, that *Tikun* was only on the GAR *de Nekudim*. The connection of *Behina Bet* with *Behina Dalet* dominated in the ZAT *de Nekudim*, as these *Kelim* are *Behinat Kelim* of the lower nine *Sefirot de SAG*. That connection was primarily in them, and there the *Behina Bet* became AB, by the force of their *He'arah* in the inner ZON *de AK* (see *Ohr Pnimi* item 1).

Hence the ZAT received that doubled *Behinat Aviut* first, but it was in them without a *Tikun*. Instead, they were mixed together in one another like the mixture of moist with moist that the Rav brings. It means that the *Behinot Dinim* themselves and *Behinot Rachamim* themselves were not apparent, but everything was mixed together beyond recognition. Also, from this mixture formed the *Behinot Klipot*, as *Sigim* of gold and *Shmarim* of wine, and they too mixed with those *Kelim* beyond recognition.

You must perceive in this matter that although the *Behinat Aviut* in the *Kelim* is their entire magnitude and merit, the height of their *Koma* is measured by it. Indeed, this is provided they have a *Tikun* of the *Masach* equivalent to that measure of *Aviut*.

However, if they do not have that *Tikun* of the *Masach* that should be with respect to that *Aviut*, the *Aviut* turns into hard and bitter *Dinim*, since *Shinui Tzura* is separation in the spiritual. For that reason they cannot suck their sustenance off the *Ohr Elyon*, for then the *Aviut* turns into *Behinot Dinim* and *Klipot*, meaning to incorrigible nocuous, until they receive their complete *Tikun*.

It is impossible for the world to exist and be conducted except through the *Dinim* and the *Klipot*.

Since the world is conducted according to the thought of creation, which is to delight His creatures, meaning give a good reward to the righteous. Such a leadership cannot exist except by the work in the form of "God hath made even the one as well as the other," hence, the place was prepared for the existence of the *Dinim* and *Klipot*.

42. However, the *Din* was below in the lower seven, but everything was mixed together. Because of that there wasn't any correction in the *Yod Sefirot* at all. Hence, when *Ohr Ein Sof* descended and fissured in them from above downward the *Ohr* descended from *Keter* to *Hochma* and from *Hochma* to *Bina*, which is the third *Sefira*.

However, when that *Ohr Elyon* expanded, being complete *Rachamim* and complete *Hesed,* and when it reached the lower seven, being *Dinim,* and *Dinim* are awakened by them, they could not receive it. This is because they are opposites, one is *Hesed* and one is *Din*, and they were canceled by the *Ohr Elyon* and died, as it says, "And Bela died, And Husham died" etc.

Ohr Pnimi

42. *Ohr Ein Sof* descended and fissured in them from above downward.

    This refers to the new *Ohr* that came down and fissured the *Parsa* and the *Ohr* for *Nekudim*, as the Rav says. Also, fissuring means the annulment of the *Gevul*.

43. Then these seven lower *Melachim* descended below in *Olam Beria*, completely under the place of *Malchut de Atzilut*. Their place under *Sefirat Bina* remained vacant, and in that space between *Sefirat Bina* and these seven *Melachim* another seven *Sefirot* emerged, mingled together in the image of *Adam*, consisting of *Zachar* and *Nekeva*.

    This is ZON, called the eighth *Melech*, whose name is *Hadar*, and the name of his wife, Mehetabel. This is because *Hadar* is ZA and Mehetabel is *Nukva*.

Ohr Pnimi

43. Completely under the place of *Malchut de Atzilut*.

    Under the place of the new *Tzimtzum* where *Behinat Atzilut* ends and the place of the Separated *Olamot* begins.

    Their place under *Sefirat Bina* remained vacant.

    This is so because the GAR, which are KHB, remained, and only the *Melachim* from *Bina* down broke and left a vacant space. After the *Tikun*, that will be the place where *Olam Atzilut* will stand.

44. *Thus, when you count the Name from AB, each *Behinat AB* will be *Yod* from HaVaYaH, and SAG, the first *Hey* of HaVaYaH, MA is the *Ot Vav*, and BON is the last *Ot Hey*. When we count the Name only from *Behinat SAG*, the *Taamim* of SAG will be the *Ot Yod*, the *Nekudot*, the first *Ot Hey*, the *Tagin Ot Vav*, and the *Otiot* the last *Hey*.

    When we divide the *Taamim* too, the *Ot Yod* will be in the *Awzen*, the first *Ot Hey* in the *Hotem*, *Ot Vav* in the *Peh*, and the last *Ot Hey* in the *Eynaim*. This is because the *Ayin* has *Behinat* last *Hey* and first *Hey*.

Ohr Pnimi

44. When you count the Name from AB... ...When we count the Name only from *Behinat SAG*.

You must know that the *Taamim, Nekudot, Tagin, Otiot* relate to the four-letter Name differently than the *Eser Sefirot* or the five *Partzufim* in the four-letter Name. It is so because in the *Eser Sefirot* the tip of the *Yod* is regarded as the *Keter*, the *Yod*, *Hochma* and the *Hey*, *Bina*. The *Vav* is considered *ZA* and the last *Hey* is ascribed to *Malchut*.

However, in the *TNTO*, the *Yod* is considered *Taamim* and *Keter*, the first *Hey Nekudot* and *Hochma*, the *Vav Tagin* and *Bina*, and the lower *Hey Otiot* and *ZON*.

The reason for it is that the four degrees of *TNTO* are but four denominations appearing in the order of the *Histalkut* of the *Orot* of the *Partzufim* prior to the *Tikun*. As the Rav writes above (item 9), the first *Hitpashtut* of *Malchut de Rosh* to the *Guf* is called *Taamim*, since it is *Ohr Yashar, Rachamim*.

That *Kli* is called *Keter* because the beginning of the coming of the *Orot* to the *Guf* is always in *Kli de Keter*. It is called *Yod* of *HaVaYaH* since it is the beginning of the *Hitlabshut* of the *Guf* and the *Kelim*, and it is therefore ascribed to the *Yod*, being the beginning of the *HaVaYaH*.

When the *Masach* in *Kli de Keter* purifies and the *Koma* gradually diminishes on the four *Behinot* until it disappears entirely from the *Maatzil*, all these *Komot* are named *Nekudot*. This is so because they are created during the *Histalkut* of the *Orot* to the *Maatzil*, and they are therefore considered *Ohr Hozer* and *Din*.

Also, they are called *Hochma* because the Upper *Sefira* in them is *Hochma* and the three *Komot Bina, ZA* and *Malchut* are incorporated in the Upper One. They are also called the first *Hey* of *HaVaYaH* since they are *Behinat Din* and *Behinat Din* is always considered *Nukva*, which is *Hey de HaVaYaH*.

In the *Reshimot* remaining after the *Histalkut Ohr*, the *Taamim* are called *Tagin*, since they overlie the *Kelim* during the *Histalkut* of their *Orot* like *Tagin* over the *Otiot*. They are called *Bina* because they come from *Behinat Ohr Yashar* and *Rachamim* and are *Behinat GAR*.

However, since they are in *Behinat Histalkut*, they are considered *Bina*, which is *Behinat Nukva de GAR*.

After their *Histalkut* from the *Ohr Nekudot*, the *Reshimot* are called *Otiot*, meaning *Behinat Kelim*. This is because they come from *Ohr Hozer* and *Din*, and also because they are from *Behinat Histalkut*. For that reason they are also called *Kelim*. They are also considered *Behinat ZON* since the *Ohr* of ZON, which are VAK, is *Behinat Ohr Kelim*.

You find that both the *Reshimot de Taamim*, called *Tagin* and *Bina*, and the *Reshimot de Nekudot*, called *Otiot*, are *Behinat Histalkut* and *Achoraim*. However, since the *Reshimo de Taamim* is *Behinat GAR*, it is therefore called *Bina*. It is also *Behinat Vav de HaVaYaH*, meaning *Vav* in the *Rosh*. Conversely, since *Reshimot de Nekudot* are *Behinot VAK*, they are called *ZON* and *Otiot* and are *Behinat* last *Hey de HaVaYaH*.

Here the Rav means to show the state and the degree of the position of *Partzuf Nekudim* between the *Partzufim* of AK as well as the order of its concatenation from them and its connection with them. Hence, he first arranged for us the five *Partzufim* according to the four-letter Name, and says that AB which is *Partzuf Hochma de AK*, is *Partzuf Yod de HaVaYaH*, and the SAG, which is *Partzuf Bina de AK*, is *Hey de HaVaYaH*.

After we know that the SAG is *Behinat Hey de HaVaYaH*, he elaborates on the SAG itself, regarding its TNTO, whose order is different than the order of the five *Partzufim*, though they are closely related, as we've explained above.

When we divide the *Taamim* too.

This division is done after the ascent of the *Orot* from NHY de AK to MAN to the *Taamim de SAG* and to *Behinat Nikvey Eynaim de Rosh* of the *Taamim* (see item 14). This caused the division of the *Eser Sefirot de Rosh SAG* to two *Behinot* on the *Nikvey Eynaim* because of the *Masach* and the place of the *Zivug* that rose there.

Hence, from *Nikvey Eynaim* up it became a *Rosh*, and from *Nikvey Eynaim* down it became the *Guf*. The *Awzen*, *Hotem* and *Peh* there, are found to have departed from the degree of *Rosh* into the degree of *Guf*.

Ot Yod will be in the Awzen, the first Ot Hey in the Hotem, Ot Vav in the Peh, and the last Ot Hey in the Eynaim.

As has been explained above, all this was caused by the ascent of *Orot NHY de AK* to the *Nikvey Eynaim*. It is so because then the *Nekudot de SAG*, being the four *Komot Hochma*, *Bina*, *ZA* and *Malchut* emerging out of SAG after the *Hizdakchut* of the *Masach* of *Keter de Guf de SAG*, called *Taamim*, expanded below *Tabur* of the Inner AK, where they illuminated to the Inner ZON there.

Two kinds of *Orot* are found there, *Nekudot de SAG*, and the Inner ZON, mixed with each other. *Behinat SAG* is *Behina Bet* and the first *Hey de HaVaYaH*, and *Behinat* Inner ZON are *Behina Dalet* and the lower *Hey de HaVaYaH* (see *Ohr*

Pnimi item 6). There it explains the reason for the ascent of the two *Heys* to MAN to *Nikvey Eynaim* and the matter of their division into two degrees.

It is written that the last *Hey* rose to *Nikvey Eynaim*, meaning through its association with the first *Hey*. In other words, the *AHP* went outside the *Rosh*, as these *AHP* are *Yod Hey Vav*, considered *Behinat Rosh Tachton* containing *Eser* complete *Sefirot*, except the last *Hey*, which is absent there because she remained in the *Nikvey Eynaim*.

It is written, *YHV (Yod Hey Vav)* in the *AHP* and the last *Hey* in the *Eynaim*. It is so because now the *Rosh* of the *Taamim* has been divided into two *Roshim*. The last *Hey* remained in the first *Rosh*, which is *Galgalta ve Eynaim*, and the second *Rosh* contains not more than *YHV*. The *YH* are *KHB*, *Vav* is *HGT NHY*, and *Malchut*, which is the lower *Hey*, is absent in the second *Rosh*.

In order to understand these above-mentioned two *Roshim*, we have to study them from *Partzuf Nekudim* that emerged through that *Zivug de Nikvey Eynaim*. This is because in this place, where the *Zivug* was formed, which is the *Rosh de SAG*, it did not change by the division made on *Nikvey Eynaim* (see *Ohr Pnimi* item 2).

Instead, only that *Koma*, which came out of this *Zivug de Nikvey Eynaim*, accepted all those changes branching from the ascent of the lower *Hey* to *Nikvey Eynaim*. This *Koma* that emerged from there is called *Olam ha Nekudim*.

You should know that three *Roshim* must be discerned in that *Olam de Nekudim*, and three *Roshim* are merely *Eser Sefirot* of a single *Rosh*, relating to what they were prior to the ascent of MAN to the *Nikvey Eynaim*. You should remember the order of the ascents of the *Orot* to the second *Zivug* in the *Rosh de Elyon*, from which the *Tachton* was born.

They are considered *Zachar* and *Nekeva* since they first make two *Zivugim* in the *Rosh* of the *Elyon*, they mingle in one another, and from there descend and expand to their own place in their related *Guf de Elyon*. There they expand once more to *Rosh* and *Guf* (see Part 3, Chap 4, item 50, and Part 6, *Ohr Pnimi* item 6).

It turns out that after the *Reshimot* of *Nekudim de SAG* rose along with the lower *Hey* to *Nikvey Eynaim de Rosh SAG*, and were mingled there in the two *Zivugim*, they returned to their place, the *Tabur de AK*. There they expanded in *Rosh* and *Guf* as the image of the *Zivugim* they made in the *Rosh*, meaning in the place of *Nikvey Eynaim*.

It has already been explained that the *Masach de Nikvey Eynaim* stands at the *Tabur* (see *Ohr Pnimi* item 9), meaning in the place of the *Parsa* that's been erected there. Thus, it turns out that the *Rosh* of this *Partzuf* came out from the *Tabur* up to *Chazeh de SAG*, having only the two *Sefirot Galgalta* and *Eynaim*, and the lower *Hey* is in these *Nikvey Eynaim*.

This is the first *Rosh* in *Partzuf Nekudim*, considered to have the value of *RADLA de Atzilut*, as it does not join *Partzuf Nekudim* at all, but is *Behinat Shoresh Elyon* to the *Partzuf* of *Nikvey Eynaim* (see *Ohr Pnimi* item 20).

The three *Sefirot de Rosh*: *Awzen, Hotem, Peh*, which came out of the degree of the first *Rosh*, consist of two *Roshim*, since they are below its *Masach*. It is so because they are considered the three *Sefirot AHP* compared to what is missing from the first *Rosh*, called YESHSUT. However, they do have *Eser* complete *Sefirot* in themselves, GE and AHP.

They are called GAR *de Nekudim*, standing from *Tabur de AK* down, and they are the actual *Nekudim* where these two *Zivugim de Katnut* and *Gadlut* occur. In *Katnut*, the lower *Hey* is in the *Eynaim* of that *Rosh*, and the three *Sefirot AHP* are considered the lower *Rosh* and *Behinat HGT* compared to the *Elyon*, which is the second *Rosh*, as it is below its *Nikvey Eynaim*.

In *Gadlut*, the lower *Hey* descends to the *Peh*, meaning to *Malchut* that contains all three *Roshim*. Then the GE, being the second *Rosh*, join their AHP, which is the third *Rosh*, and they become one *Rosh*.

Thus, three *Roshim* are made from *Eser Sefirot* of one *Rosh*. The first *Rosh*, which is GE, is called YESHSUT. It is still regarded as *Taamim*, and not *Behinat Nekudim*. The second *Rosh* is the GE of GAR *de Nekudim*, being AHP that were taken off YESH and *Tvuna*, having *Eser Sefirot* in and of themselves. The third *Rosh* is the AHP that were taken off the second *Rosh*, becoming a third *Rosh* in itself.

The second *Rosh* is *Keter de Nekudim* and the third *Rosh* is *Hochma* and *Bina de Nekudim*. The lower *Hey* is in the *Eynaim* of the second *Rosh*, and the YHV is in the third *Rosh*. In the *Zivug* of *Gadlut* that brings them together, when the lower *Hey* descends to the *Peh* of the third *Rosh*, and the two lower *Roshim* become one *Rosh*, the Name *HaVaYaH* is found in its order YH VH, as the lower *Hey* returned to her place.

The *Ayin* has *Behinat* last *Hey* and first *Hey*.

This is so because the entire *Partzuf Nekudim*, called *Ohr Eynaim*, is from *Behinat Nekudot de SAG* that rose and departed from NHY *de AK* and became MAN in *Nikvey Eynaim*. Thus, the *Eynaim* are like the first *Hey de HaVaYaH* because *Nekudot de SAG* are the first *Hey*.

The last *Behinat Hey* that rose along with them to *Nikvey Eynaim* also became *Behinat Eynaim*, and thus the *Eynaim* are regarded as the last *Hey de HaVaYaH*.

We thus learn that the *Masach* in *Nikvey Eynaim* is a double *Masach* from the two *Heys* together. It has already been explained that this is the *Shoresh* for the association of *Midat ha Rachamim* with *Din*, the beginning of which was made in the connection of the two *Heys*, the first *Hey*, and the lower *Hey* in *Nikvey Eynaim*.

45. This is the meaning of what is written in the *Tikkunim* (Zohar), "I sleep" opposite the last *Hey*. In the annulment of *Ohr Nekudim*, "I sleep", meaning "sleep" (הניש), and also "I sleep", the letters of "second" (הינש). This is because *Hochma* is the First *Hey*, and second to *Keter*. It is known that *Taamim* are *Keter*, *Nekudot* are *Hochma*, *Tagin* are *Bina*, and *Otiot* are the lower seven.

It turns out that the *Ayin* is *Behinat Hochma*, which are *Nekudot*. This is the reason the sages of the congregation were called "The Eyes of the Congregation", as it says, "then it shall be, if it be done in error by the congregation, it being hid from their eyes."

Ohr Pnimi

45. "I sleep" opposite the last *Hey*. In the annulment of *Ohr Nekudim*, "I sleep".

The breaking of the vessels was primarily in the *Behinat* last *Hey*, and that's where the sleeping comes to her. That is why sleep is implied in the last *Hey*.

Hochma is the First Hey... ...Nekudot are Hochma.

It is written above (*Ohr Pnimi* item 44) that the *Orot* that rose to MAN from NHY de AK contain all the *Nekudot de SAG*, which are from *Hochma* down, with the ZON de AK. It is known that the *Partzuf* is named after its highest *Sefira*, hence the *Nekudot* are called *Hochma*.

46. These *Nekudot* are *Behinat Melachim* that ruled in *Eretz* (land of) Edom and died. This is also the meaning of "*ve ha Aretz Haita Tohu ve Bohu*" (Now the earth was unformed and void). *Aretz* is the last *Hey*, which is the *Behinat Ayin*. She is the one who was *Tohu ve Bohu*, which is the matter of the death of the *Melachim*, until their *Tikun* came, at which time it is said "Let there be light. And there was light." It is also the meaning of "open Thine eyes, and behold our desolations."

47. In order to understand that verse, we shall explain the matter of the *Ayin*. It is said that there are nine *Nekudot*: *Kamatz, Patach, Tzere, Segol, Shva, Holam, Shuruk, Hirik, Kubutz*. However, they also contain Upper *Behinot*, such as *Holam*, and Middle, such as *Shuruk*. All the rest are below, and their place is under the *Otiot*. All this will be explained later.

Ohr Pnimi

47. Upper *Behinot*, such as *Holam*, and Middle, such as *Shuruk*. All the rest are below.

This is because three *Orot* operated in the first *Nekudim*: the *Hevel* of the *Tabur*, which is *Behinat Peh* of the first *Rosh*, called YESHSUT. This *Ohr* is called *Holam*, for it shines above the *Otiot*, because the first *Rosh* is not considered actual *Ohr Nekudot*, but only a *Shoresh*. Moreover, even during the *Gadlut*, it does not unite into one with its AHP, which are GAR *de Nekudim* (*Ohr Pnimi* item 31).

The second *Ohr* is *Hevel ha Yesod*, which is *Behinat* Inner ZON that shine to GAR *de Nekudim*, *Vav* for *Ima*, *Yod* for *Abba*, as the Rav says in item 31. Also, this *Ohr* is called *Shuruk* because it shines inside the *Kelim de AVI*.

The third *Ohr* is *Ohr* that is poured from *Peh de Nekudim* down to the ZAT *de Nekudim*, which extend from the *Parsa* by the *Zivug de Gadlut* (see *Ohr Pnimi* item 31). Hence, these are *Behinot* lower *Nekudot* below the *Otiot*, meaning extending from under the *Kelim de Elyon* because *Parsa* is the end of *Sium Etzbaot Raglaim de SAG de AK*.

48. Now, all the last seven *Nekudot* are in the form of *Yodin* (pl. for *Yod*), except the first two *Nekudot*, *Kamatz Patach*. These are two *Vavin* (pl. for *Vav*), and *Yod*.

The thing is that when we count all the *Yodin* in these seven *Nekudot*, they are thirteen *Yodin*, *Gimatria* 130, same as *Ayin* (עי"ן). This indicates that the *Nekudot* come out of the *Ayin*, and *Kamatz Patach*, which are *Yod* and two *Vavin* remain. Their *Gimatria* is 22, implying the twenty-two *Otiot* from which the *Kelim de Nekudim* were made.

Ohr Pnimi

48. All the last seven *Nekudot* are in the form of *Yodin*, except the first two *Nekudot*.

It is so because the *Kamatz Patach* are the *Shoresh* of all the *Nekudot*, as the Rav writes here. The *Kamatz* is *Keter* and *Patach* is *Hochma*. You already know that the GAR *de Nekudim* are divided into *Galgalta ve Eynaim*, called *Keter*, and AHP that have departed from this *Keter*, called HB.

This division is because of the two *Heys* that were joined together and rose to the *Eynaim*. As a result, the *Eser Sefirot de Rosh de Nekudim* divided by way of lower *Hey* in the *Eynaim*, and YHV in the AHP.

Interpretation: the *Masach de Behina Bet de Hitlabshut*, which is the first *Hey*, is named *Vav* here, since it is *Behinat Zachar*. The last *Hey*, having joined with this *Vav* in the *Nikvey Eynaim*, is the *Behinat Nekuda* inside the *Vav*. This is because *Nekuda* indicates *Midat ha Din*, as a "black *Nekuda* without any whiteness at all."

However, the connection of the *Nekuda* with the *Vav* in the *Nikvey Eynaim* does not make a *Behinat Shuruk* there, but only *Behinat Kamatz*. This is because the *Vav* is laid down and the *Nekuda* under her is as a *Rakia* and *Nitzotz*.

The reason for it is that the *AHP* are found to be departing because of this connection of the *Rakia* and the *Nitzotz*. Hence, they are called *Kamatz*, from the words *Kimutz* (thrift) and *Situm* (blockage) that occurred by the ascent and connection of the lower *Hey* in the *Eynaim*.

The *YHV* that now shine in *AHP* are in a state of *Kimutz* and *Situm*, as they suffer from two:

1. Their entire *Koma* is *Behina Aleph*, since they are *Behinat Nekeva de Keter* (see *Ohr Pnimi* item 23). They need to get *He'arat GAR* from the *Zachar*, being *Keter*. However, because of the *Kamatz* in *Kli de Keter* they are no longer considered *Behinat Rosh*, and cannot incorporate in the *Zachar* in *Keter*.

2. They have become *Behinat Guf*. Hence, these *HB* are in *Behinat Achor be Achor*.

However, in and of themselves they are *YHV*, as the Rav says that *YHV* is in the *AHP*. This is very interesting since he thus tells us that *Behinat* lower *Hey*, which is the *Nekuda* under the *Patach* in the *Nikvey Eynaim* makes the *Kamatz* there. It is written that it did not come down to *Behinat AHP*.

Only the *Behinat Rakia*, being the *Kav* above the *Nekuda*, which is like a *Patach*, descended by itself to the *AHP*. It did not take with it anything of the *Nekuda*, meaning the lower *Hey*, but the *Masach* in the *Peh* is only *Vav* without the *Nekuda* incorporated in it in the *Nikvey Eynaim*.

Thus, it becomes clear that the *Masach* in *Kli de Keter de Nekudim* contains within it a *Patach* and a *Nekuda*, which are *Rakia* and *Nitzotz*, meaning the form of *Kamatz*. The *Masach* in *Kli de HB de Nekudim* is but *Hitpashtut* of the *Patach* contained in the *Kamatz* in the *Nikvey Eynaim*, meaning in *Kli de Keter*, having nothing of the *Nekuda*.

However, during the *Zivug de AB SAG*, causing the lowering of the lower *Hey* from the *Nikvey Eynaim* to the place of *Peh* as in the beginning (see *Ohr Pnimi* item 14), the *Kamatz* in *Kli de Keter* descends and connects with the *Kli de HB* that was only a *Patach* there.

That causes the opening of the *Eynaim* because the place of the *Zivug* that was in the form of *Kamatz* in the *Nikvey Eynaim*, blocking the *Orot*, has now opened widely, as the *AHP* returned to the *Rosh*. This is because then the *Ohr* descended to the lower seven *Sefirot de Nekudim*, and you can therefore see how all the *Nekudot* emerged from the *Zivug* of *Kamatz* and *Patach*.

It turns out that the seven lower *Sefirot* came out after the descent of *Kamatz* to the place of *Peh* by the *Zivug de Gadlut*. It turns out that these seven *Nekudot* emerged from the *Nekuda* inside the *Kamatz*, for as long as the *Nekuda* was incorporated in the *Nikvey Eynaim*, the *Peh* of *Nekudim* there was only the *Patach*. At that point the seven *Nekudot* could not expand from the *Peh* down for the *AHP* themselves were in *Behinat Guf* and the *Patach* in the *Peh* was in *Behinat Malchut de Malchut*, called *Tabur*.

However, after the descent of the lower *Hey* to the place of the *Peh*, the *Orot* of the seven lower *Sefirot* opened and came out to their place. Thus, the entire merit of the lower seven extended from the *Nekuda*, which is why they were implied in the form of *Yodin*, meaning only *Nekudot*. This is because they do not extend from the *Rakia*, which is a *Patach*, but rather from the *Nitzotz*.

It is written, "**All the last seven Nekudot are in the form of Yodin, except the first two Nekudot, Kamatz Patach. These are two Vavin, and YHV**," for the above reason. The *Vavin*, being *Patach*, are incorporated only in *Keter* and *Hochma*, *Vav* and *Nekuda* in *Keter*, which is the form of *Kamatz*, and *Vav* alone in *Hochma*, which is the form of *Patach*. However, there is only *Behinat Nekuda* in the seven lower *Sefirot*, since this is where they emerge.

The *Nekudot* come out of the *Ayin*.

Meaning that through the descent of the lower *Hey* from the *Eynaim* all the *Nekudot* came out.

The twenty-two *Otiot* from which the *Kelim de Nekudim* were made.

The *Kelim* are called *Otiot* and the number twenty-two contains all the *Behinot Kelim* in reality. It has already been explained how all the ZAT emerged from the *Zivug* of *Kamatz* and *Patach*. They also produced *Behinat* knew *Kelim*, called *Kelim de Achor*.

49. It is not surprising that the *Kelim* were registered and implied in the first two *Nekudot*, the best among them. The thing is that the *Kelim* for the rest of the *Nekudot* were made of these first two *Nekudot*, namely *Keter Hochma*. These are also the ones that procreated and elicited *Kelim* for the *Sefirot* below them.

There is yet another reason: it is known that the seven lower *Nekudot* are the seven *Melachim* that died. However, the first did not die. It is also known that *Behinat* death is the breaking of the *Kli*, hence the seven other *Nekudot* remained without a *Kli*, but only *Ohr*, which is the *Behinot* of the *Nekudot*.

However, the first ones did not die; they remained with their *Kelim*. Thus, the *Orot* conceal and clothe within the *Kelim*. They are named after the *Kelim*, which are the twenty-two *Orot*, implied in the *Kamatz* and *Patach* as we have mentioned.

Ohr Pnimi

49. **The first did not die.**

    Rather, the *Kamatz* returned to the *Nikvey Eynaim* as it was before. Also, the *Patach* remained alone once more in *Kli de Hochma*. It is so because when they are in their place as they were when they were first created, they are considered *Kelim de Panim*, where annulment and breaking do not apply.

50. The **Kamatz** indicates the **Keter**, and the **Keter** is **Taamim**. The **Patach** indicates **Hochma**, and they are the **Nekudot**. Hence, these two **Nekudot** are called **Kamatz** and **Patach**, as they imply the above matter.

    As long as only **Taamim de SAG** elicit, being the **Behinat Orot AHP**, the **Orot** were still blocked and stint. When **Behinat Nekudot** came, which are **Hochma – Patach**, being the **Behinat Ayin**, then they opened in the "opening of the eyes," as mentioned in the **Tikkunim**. This is the matter of the point of **Patach**. However, in the **Behinot Taamim**, which are **Keter**, it is **Kamatz**, because the **Orot** were blocked and stint.

Ohr Pnimi

50. **The *Patach* indicates *Hochma*.**

    This means that the *Nekudot*, meaning the seven lower *Sefirot* came out of this *Zivug de Kamatz Patach*, which are *Keter* and *Hochma*. Then the *Nekudot de SAG* emerge and appear, as will be written henceforth.

    Taamim de SAG elicit, being the Behinat Orot AHP... ...When Behinat Nekudot came... ...opened in the "opening of the eyes."

    You must understand the oppositeness that occurred because of the ascent of the lower *Hey* to the *Eynaim*, where the *Nekudot* preceded the *Taamim*. The primary difference between *Taamim* and *Nekudot* is that *Taamim de SAG*, reaching the *Tabur*, did not connect with the lower *Hey*, meaning the Inner ZON de AK.

However, the *Nekudot de SAG*, which are the lower nine from *Hochma* down, connected with the lower *Hey* and rose to MAN to the *Eynaim* (item 6). Thus, the opposite occurred here in the *Partzuf* that came out of this *Zivug de Nikvey Eynaim*.

The *Behinot Nekudot*, meaning the connection of the first *Hey* with the lower *Hey* was made in the *Nikvey Eynaim*. Hence, the *Behinat Taamim*, meaning the *Behinat* first *Hey* that did not connect whatsoever with the lower *Hey*, came out in the *AHP* (see *Ohr Pnimi* item 48).

Thus, the *Nekudot* were found to be above *Nikvey Eynaim* and *Taamim* below, in the *AHP*. This is the opposite of their stance in *SAG* where the *Taamim* are above *Tabur* and the *Nekudot* below *Tabur*.

However, this is still not considered departure to the *Nekudot*. As long as the *Behinot Nekudot* are in *Nikvey Eynaim*, they are not disclosed outwardly, as they are there as *Kamatz* (see *Ohr Pnimi* item 48).

Afterwards, by the *Zivug de AB SAG* where the *Nekudot* come out from the *Eynaim* to the *Peh* under the *Taamim*, it is considered that the *Nekuda* departed and separated from there. The *Eynaim* remain as a mere *Patach*, without a *Nekuda*, and then the *Eynaim* open, the *AHP* return to the *Rosh*, and the *ZAT* come to their place.

It is written, "**As long as only Taamim de SAG elicit, being the Behinat Orot AHP, the Orot were still blocked.**" Meaning, as long as the lower *Hey* was in the *Eynaim* and the *Nekudot* could not come out, but only the *Taamim* as YHV cleaned from the lower *Hey*, "the **Orot** were still blocked and stint."

"**When Behinat Nekudot came, which are Hochma - Patach, being the Behinat Ayin, then they opened in the 'opening of the eyes'.**" At that time the *Nekuda* that was attached to the opening of the *Eynaim* came down and the *Ohr* of *Nekudot de SAG* appeared outwardly, which are *Behinat Hochma* (see *Ohr Pnimi* item 45).

51. Now we shall return to the matter of the verse "open Thine eyes." When the **Behinat Ayin** comes, which are the **Nekudot**, it is then said, "open Thine eyes." This is because then it is with open eyes.

It has already been explained that all these *Behinot* are in the name SAG. This name implies *Bina*, which is Upper *Gevura*, upon which the *Dinim* are dependent; hence the matter of the annulment of the *Melachim* was in that **Behina** of **SAG**.

In *SAG* itself too there is *Behinat Taamim*, which are also called *AB*, although they are in *SAG*. Yet, the *Nekudot de SAG* are the essence of *SAG* itself, which are *SAG de SAG*, and there was the annulment and the death.

This is the meaning of "they are together become impure," for all the annulment was in the name *SAG*. *SAG* itself, however, is indicated to come from the words "*Nasogu Achor*" (they are turned away back), which is the annulment of the *Melachim*.

52. The *Ayin* is also named after *SAG*, like the above *AHP*. This is because when there were the above three *Behinot AHP*, which are the *Taamim*, their name *SAG* was *Behinat HaVaYaH*, which is *SAG*: Yod, Hey, Vav, Hey. However, in the *Ayin*, which is *Behinat Nekudot*, it is the *SAG* of three times *Ekie*, which is also *SAG* in *Gimatria*, and this is the *SAG* in the *Ayin*.

53. Now, all these *Ekie* from these three, take all the *Behinot* twenty-two *Otiot*, implied in the *Kamatz Patach*, to make of them *Kelim* through the *Histaklut Ayin* in them. Thus, each of their names *Ekie* consists of all the *Behinot* twenty-two *Otiot*.

Thus, the three names *Ekie* with the three times twenty-two *Otiot*, with the *Kolel* (included), amount to 130, which is *Ayin* in *Gimatria*. This is how the name *SAG* is implied in the *Ayin* too.

54. This is the meaning of "open Thine eyes, and behold," because in *AHP* there are three times *SAG*, which is *Pekach* (open) in *Gimatria*, with the *Kolel*, and after them comes *Behinat Eynaim*. This is the meaning of "open Thine eyes," because these three *Ekie* in the *Eynaim* are *Behinat Ekie* in *Yodin*, *Gimatria* 161, the same number as *Einecha* (Thine eyes), with the *Kolel*. This is also the meaning of "and behold our desolations," for here was a great desolation, and annulment of the *Melachim*.

Ohr Pnimi

54. "open Thine eyes, and behold," because in *AHP* there are three times *SAG*, which is *Pekach* in *Gimatria*, with the *Kolel*, and after them comes *Behinat Eynaim*.

This means that the prayer is to straighten the order and make the *YHV*, which are the *Taamim*, above, and the *SAG* in the *Eynaim*, which is the *Behinat* connection of the two *Heys* there come down past the place of the *Taamim*.

It is so because after the *Nekuda* attached to the *Patach* in the *Eynaim* comes down, and the *Patach* remains without the connection with the lower *Hey*, the *Eynaim* open and form a *Patach* . This is the meaning of **"and after them comes *Behinat Eynaim*,"** meaning after the *Taamim* implied in the *Gimatria* "open".

"and behold our desolations," for here was a great desolation, and annulment of the *Melachim*.

This is because through the returning of the order to its place as in the previous item, the lower *Hey* will come down and the *YHV* will return up. Hence, the entire great desolation, which occurred because of the breaking of the vessels, will be corrected with the entire *Tikun Kelim* we have in *Olam ha Tikun* today.

HISTAKLUT PNIMIT

Bear in mind that *Olam ha Nekudim* is the first *Shoresh* that *Olamot ABYA* stem from. It is here that the association of *Midat ha Rachamim* with *Din* is erected and rooted; it is the first beginning. This is the meaning of the ten utterances from which the world was created, referring to the ten *Kelim* for the *Hitlabshut* of the *Ohr Elyon*, as we have already elaborated on above (*Ohr Pnimi*, beginning of Part 4).

However, in the previous three *Partzufim* of AK there was only one utterance. In other words, the *Ohr Elyon* clothed only one *Kli*, called *Malchut*, but the nine *Sefirot* prior to *Malchut* were clean from any *Behinat Kli*.

Hence, we should thoroughly understand the evolution of matters brought in the Rav's words in this part, and how they come and connect by way of cause and consequence from the three previous *Partzufim*. We shall begin in explaining the order of the creation of this *Partzuf Nekudim* from its *Partzuf Elyon*, called *SAG de AK*.

1. It has already been explained that the primary factor in the creation of any new *Partzuf* is the *Bitush de Ohr Makif* and *Ohr Pnimi* on each other. This *Masach* and *Ohr Hozer* that it raises, extend and clothes the *Ohr Pnimi* of the *Partzuf*. To the extent that it clothes and extends the *Ohr Pnimi*, it rejects the *Ohr Makif* from the *Partzuf*, the *Ohr Makif* that belongs to the *Partzuf* (see Part 4, Chap 1, *Ohr Pnimi* item 7).

This *Bitush* of the *Ohr Makif* purifies the *Masach* from its *Aviut* until it raises it to its *Shoresh*, meaning purifies it entirely from its *Behinat Aviut de Guf* until it equalizes with the *Malchut de Rosh* of that *Partzuf*. This is considered that the *Masach* rose and was incorporated there in the *Masach* in *Malchut de Rosh*, in the *Zivug* from below upward.

Then the *Masach de Guf* was renewed with a new *Aviut*, raising a new *Koma* of *Eser Sefirot* in *Rosh, Toch, Sof*. This new *Koma* is considered a new *Partzuf*, the son of the previous *Partzuf*, where the new *Hizdakchut* and *Zivug* are made (see Part 3, Table of Questions, item 210).

That *Ohr* of the newly born *Partzuf* is *Behinat* part of the *Ohr Makif* of the *Partzuf Elyon*. This is because the *Ohr Makif* appears only by the creation of the *Neshamot* and the *Partzufim* of the *Tachtonim*, as our sages have written, "The Son of David doth not come before all the *Neshamot* in the *Guf* end." This refers to the entire well of the *Neshamot* contained in the inclusive *Ohr*

Makif Elyon. This is also the meaning of the *Bitush de Ohr Makif* in *Ohr Pnimi*, as this is the entire manner of its appearance.

You find that the *Masach de Guf*, which is the *Masach de Tabur*, is the primary operator in the emanation of the *Tachton*. This is because it ascends to mingle in the *Zivug Elyon* of the *Rosh* and raises the *Reshimot* of the *Eser Sefirot* that remain after the *Histalkut Orot* of the *Guf de Elyon* to the *Maatzil*, being *Malchut de Rosh* (as written in Part 4, Table of Topics, item 210).

The reason for it is that concealment and revelation always come as one in *Kedusha*. Know, that where you find concealment, this is also the place of the revelation. They cling to one another as the wick to the candle.

Moreover, the covering and the concealment is the only preparation for its appearance. Thus, if it weren't for the concealment, the appearance would never be, as there is no existence for the candlelight without the wick.

You already know that the first appearance of this *Masach de Tabur*, in its first appearance, meaning in the first *Partzuf* of AK, was the sole generator of the existence of the darkness and the vacant *Halal* in the *Olamot*. Also, the entire difference between *Olam Ein Sof* that filled the entire reality and *Partzuf AK*, which is only *Behinat* thin *Kav* of *Ohr*, occurred because of this *Masach de Tabur*.

This *Masach* detained the *Ohr Elyon*, did not let it expand and fill the entire reality as it would, and put a *Sof* and *Sium* on the *Ohr Elyon* in the middle point, as has been written elaborately in previous parts.

Even though the *Masach* in *Malchut de Rosh* set up the matter of the detainment and the *Hakaa* on the *Ohr Elyon*, it is done only in potential. This is because there is no conduct of *Halbasha* in the *Rosh*; all the more so detainment on *Halbasha*. Rather, anything marked as "potential", manifests and appears in the *Guf* "in actual".

The *Behinat Halbasha* made in the *Ohr Hozer de Rosh*, meaning on the first nine *Sefirot*, appears in the first nine *Sefirot* of the *Guf*, whose place is called "from *Peh* to *Tabur*". The detainment and the rejection made in the *Rosh* appear in the *Malchut de Guf*, whose place is called "from *Tabur* to *Sium Raglin*".

Thus it is made completely dark from *Sium Raglin* down, for the *Kav* of *Ohr* extending from *Ein Sof* stops there. It is known that that ending point is in the *Behinat Olam ha Zeh*, meaning our very earth, as it says, "And His feet shall stand upon the mount of Olives."

2. We've learned that the entire *Behinat Din* in reality is packed and sealed in the *Masach de Tabur* in its first appearance, which is the first *Partzuf de AK*.

Hence, a strong *Bitush* took place there between the *Ohr Makif* and the *Ohr Pnimi*. This is because the *Ohr Pnimi* that clothed in *Akudim* of this *Partzuf* was very small compared to the *Ohr Elyon* that remained without, which is all the previous *Ohr* that filled the entire reality, called *Ohr Makif* with respect to that *Partzuf*. Also, the place of the *Bitush* was in the *Masach de Tabur*. Had it not been for that *Masach*, the *Ohr Makif* would have entered the *Pnimiut* of the reality as before.

This generated the *Hizdakchut* of the *Masach* and the *Histalkut Orot* of the *Akudim* of the first *Partzuf de AK*, called *Partzuf Galgalta*. The *Masach* with all the *Reshimot* that remained of the *Eser Sefirot* rose and incorporated in the *Zivug* of the *Malchut de Rosh* of this *Partzuf*, except the last *Behina*, which does not leave a *Reshima*.

This *Zivug* occurred there on the *Reshimo* of the Upper *Behina* contained in the *Masach*, which is the *Reshimo de Behina Gimel*, because the *Reshimo de Behina Dalet* disappeared, as it is the last *Behina*. Hence, the *Zivug* was made there on *Behina Gimel*, eliciting *Komat Hochma* by the power of the ascent of *Malchut* to the *Hotem* since she was incorporated in the *Masach de Tabur* consisting only of *Behina Gimel* (see Part 3, Table of Topics, item 210).

It explains there that after the *Aviut* was recognized in the *Reshimot de Masach de Tabur*, which come from *Aviut de Guf*, they are found to descend from the *Rosh* to the *Guf* instantaneously, meaning to *Behina Gimel* of the *Guf*, called *Chazeh*. From the *Chazeh* up it elicits *Eser Sefirot de Rosh* through a *Zivug* with the *Ohr Elyon*, up to the *Peh* of the Upper *Partzuf*. From the *Chazeh* down, it expands in *Eser Sefirot de Rosh, Toch, Sof* of the *Guf*, ending in the place of *Tabur de Elyon*. It is so because it cannot expand below *Tabur*, as it lacks *Behina Dalet*, and under the *Tabur* it is the place of *Behina Dalet*.

3. You find that this *Masach de Tabur* obstructed the *Ohr Makif* of the first *Partzuf de AK* and did not let it expand from *Tabur* down. Now, by the force of the *Bitush* that the *Ohr Makif* made in it, it has been qualified to extend and clothe a complete *Partzuf* in RTS. Thus, it is precisely the force of concealment that overturned and became a force of revelation.

Moreover, the *Masach de Tabur* of this second *Partzuf de AK*, is also purified by the force of the *Bitush of Ohr Makif* on it. Finally, it ascends and mingles in the *Zivug de Rosh* of that *Partzuf*, and it too is renewed there with a new *Aviut de Behina Bet*. This is because here too the last *Behina*, namely *Behina Gimel*, disappeared and did not leave a *Reshima*.

After the *Aviut* of the *Guf* in the *Masach* had been recognized, it descends to the place of *Behina Bet de Guf*, having the same value as its *Chazeh de Elyon*, because *Tabur* of this *Partzuf AB* is *Behina Gimel*. Since there is no *Behina Dalet* at all in the second *Partzuf de AK*, the *Chazeh* is considered its *Behina Bet*.

Hence, the new *Koma*, emanated from it, descends to the place of its *Chazeh* and produces *Eser Sefirot de Rosh* from the *Chazeh* upward, and *Eser Sefirot de Guf* with *Toch* and *Sof* from the *Chazeh* downward. This *Partzuf* is the third *Partzuf de AK*, called *SAG de AK*.

Thus we find once more that the force of concealment has turned into a force of revelation. This is because the *Masach de Tabur*, which obstructed the *Ohr Makif de Partzuf AB* and did not let it expand below even a bit, has now been renewed and expanded into a new *Partzuf* with *RTS*.

4. The matter of *Masach de Tabur* does not refer solely to the point of *Tabur*, but to the entire *Eser Sefirot* in it. Also, the point of *Tabur* is but the force of *Sium* on *Keter Hochma* and *Bina*, after which there are two more points: the point of *Yesod*, and the point of *Sium Raglin*. The force of the *Sium* on ZA is at the point of *Yesod* and the force of the *Sium* on the *Malchut* is at the point of *Sium Raglin*. They are all contained in *Masach de Tabur*, and remember that.

This entire place called "from *Tabur* to *Sium Raglin*", is but a single *Sefira*, the bottom *Sefira* of the *Guf*, called *Malchut*. The first *Tzimtzum* was on her and the existence of the *Masach*, detaining and rejecting the *Ohr Elyon* from clothing in her, had been erected in her.

Since the *Ohr Elyon* contains *Eser Sefirot*, this *Masach* in *Malchut* contains ten forces of *Sium* for these *Eser Sefirot* too. The extension of ten forces of *Sium* is called "from *Tabur* down". Now you can see that the whole issue of the above *Bitush* of the *Ohr Makif* in *Ohr Pnimi*, expanding the *Gevul* of the *Masach de Tabur*, as has been explained above, all this refers to that place from *Tabur* down.

5. We have yet to understand what is brought in several places, that the place of MA and BON is from *Tabur* of the *Partzuf* downward, as well as the matter of the five *Sefirot* TNHYM of the *Partzuf*, whose place is from *Tabur* of every *Partzuf* downward. According to the above, there is only one *Sefira* there, *Sefirat Malchut*.

The thing is that the Rav has already noted in several places that there is no *Malchut* without NHY, as it is written, "three flocks of sheep lying there by it." The reason for it has already been explained in Part 5, *Ohr Pnimi* item 45. It states that the three *Sefirot Hod, Yesod, Malchut*, are all but an expansion of the *Kli Malchut*. Thus, in *Kli Malchut* itself there are three *Sefirot* HYM.

It is also known that in *Behinat Achoraim*, the *Netzah* and *Hod* are considered one *Sefira*, and they are mingled in one another indistinguishably. Hence, all these four *Sefirot* NHYM are only considered *Sefirat Malchut*, but when the *Ohr* reaches them from the *Behinat Panim*, the *Netzah* is then separated from the *Hod*, and the merit of *Hod* becomes apparent. Then they are considered two separate *Sefirot*.

However, even then, since the four *Sefirot* were once connected, they no longer part. Rather, it is considered that *Netzah* contains the four *Sefirot* NHYM from the *Behinat* "right", and *Hod* contains the four *Sefirot* NHYM from the *Behinat* "left".

You can therefore see how there are always four *Sefirot Netzah, Hod, Yesod, Malchut* in the *Malchut*. Thus, you should know that even though the place from *Tabur de AK* down is indeed only *Sefirat Malchut*, still there are four *Sefirot* NHYM there.

We have yet to explain the issue of MA and BON, which are always from *Tabur* down. This is a completely different matter, for it is not considered among the *Sefirot* of the five *Behinot de Ohr Yashar*, when the place from *Tabur* down is considered the four *Sefirot* NHYM. Rather, it is by measurements of *Koma*, of the five *Partzufim Galgalta, AB, SAG, MA and BON*.

Know, that from the perspective of the measurement of the *Koma*, MA and BON are considered as one *Koma* that comes out by *Zivug de Hakaa* in the *Masach*, whose *Aviut* is from *Behina Aleph*, extending only *Komat ZA*. The reason is that here there are but four *Behinot* of *Aviut* in the *Masach*: *Komat Keter* comes out on *Masach de Behina Dalet* etc. and *Komat ZA* on *Masach de Behina Aleph*.

However, on a *Masach* that is already purified, such as *Behinat Keter*, from which *Komat Malchut* should stem, there is no *Hakaa* between that and the *Ohr Elyon*, in such a way that a *Komat Partzuf* would emerge off it in *Rosh, Toch, Sof*. This is because it is not in *Shinui Tzura* from the *Ohr Elyon*. Hence, there is only *Zivug de Hakaa* until the measure of *Aviut de Behina Aleph*.

Moreover, even *Behina Aleph* is considered a very frail *Aviut*, and in *Masach de Behina Aleph* the *Zivug de Hakaa* is called *Histaklut Dak*, from which there is no *Hitpashtut Partzuf* in *Behinat RTS* (see Part 3, Chap 11, item 6, and *Ohr Pnimi* there).

This *Partzuf* MA and BON that came out on *Masach de Behina Aleph* was only through a special *Tikun*, meaning by the ascent of the lower *Hey* to the *Eynaim*, where the two *Heyin* connected together, the First *Hey* with the Last *Hey* (this Part, item 44). The association of this *Aviut* with *Behina Aleph* induced a sufficient *Zivug de Hakaa* to produce a *Partzuf* in RTS, called MA and *BON*. However, without the association of the last *Hey*, *Behina Aleph* too is unfit for *Zivug* on producing a *Partzuf*.

6. It's been explained that the very cause of the elicitation of the *Koma de Behina Aleph*, called MA and BON, is the last *Hey*, meaning *Malchut de AK*. Thus, two *Partzufim* are related to the last *Hey*, being *Behina Dalet*: the first is *Partzuf Galgalta de AK*, whose level reaches *Keter*, and the second is *Partzuf Nekudim de AK*, which are MA and BON.

   The *Koma* of the latter reaches ZA, which in turn elicited because of the ascent of the lower *Hey*, which is *Behina Dalet*, to *Nikvey Eynaim*. The reason *Behina Dalet* did not produce *Komat Keter* here, as in *Partzuf Galgalta de AK*, will be explained below.

   Thus you find that the force of *Tzimtzum* in *Masach de Tabur* of *Partzuf Galgalta* broadens through the *Bitush* of *Ohr Makif* in *Ohr Pnimi* (see item 4 here). It is so because once it had purified into *Behina Gimel*, RTS of the second *Partzuf de AK* had expanded from it, called AB.

   After it had purified into *Behina Bet*, a third *Partzuf*, called *Partzuf SAG*, expanded from it in RTS. Finally, after it had purified into *Behina Aleph*, *Partzuf Nekudim* expanded from it, called MA and BON *de AK*.

7. We must thoroughly understand, that the *Masach* had already been purified into *Behina Aleph*, meaning the measure of *Aviut* found in *Kli de Hochma*. Thus, how can *Behina Dalet* participate with her *Aviut* here too, generating the *Koma de* MA and BON through the both of them?

   Furthermore, if *Behina Dalet* really has joined with *Behina Aleph* here, there should have been a *Partzuf* in *Komat Keter* here, like *Partzuf Galgalta de AK*. Thus, why did only *Komat ZA* come out here, meaning at the measure of *Komat Behina Aleph*, and not *Komat Behina Dalet*?

   The thing is that it is known that there is no issue of *Hizdakchut* in the *Kelim*. Hence, even though the *Masach* of *Behina Dalet* that operated in *Partzuf Galgalta de AK* has been purified when emanating AB, the *Kelim* themselves were not changed by that in any way. The *Aviut de Behina Dalet* remained in them as in the beginning, before the *Hizdakchut* of the *Masach*.

   However, after the *Ohr* departed from them, no operation manifested off them, since a *Kli* without an *Ohr* is like a body without a soul. Therefore, after *Nekudot de Partzuf SAG* expanded and illuminated from *Tabur* to *Sium Raglin de Partzuf Galgalta de AK* (see *Ohr Pnimi* item 1), because of this *He'arat SAG*, the *Aviut de Behina Dalet* came back to life in the *Kelim* from *Tabur de AK* down.

In that state the *Aviut* of *Behina Dalet* in the *Kelim* from *Tabur de AK* down, mixed with the *Masach* in the *Kelim* of *Nekudot de SAG*. This is because during the ascent of the *Masach* to the *Maatzil*, it was incorporated in all the *Reshimot* in the *Sefirot* from which the *Orot* had left (see *Partzuf* 4, Chap 4, *Ohr Pnimi* item 50).

Thus, as it is incorporated of the *Reshimot de Sefirot de SAG*, which are *Behina Bet*, it was also incorporated of the *Reshimot* in the *Kelim* from *Tabur* down, being *Behina Dalet*. It raised those two *Behinot* to the *Maatzil* together, which is *Malchut de Rosh de SAG*.

You already know that this *Masach* consists solely of *Aviut de Behina Aleph*, because *Behina Bet* is the last *Behina* here, which does not leave a *Reshimo* after her, only from *Behinat Hitlabshut*. Thus, the *Masach* consists of two *Reshimot* that remained after the *Histalkut Orot* from the *Sefirot de SAG*, being *Behina Bet de Hitlabshut* and *Behina Aleph de Hamshacha*, called *Zachar* and *Nekeva*.

Thus, *Malchut de Rosh* too rose to *Behina Aleph de Rosh*, meaning according to the measure of *Aviut* contained in the *Reshimo* that remained in the *Masach*, being *Behina Aleph*, as the Rav wrote concerning *Partzuf AB* (Part 5, item 6 and *Ohr Pnimi* there). However, the *Reshimo de Behina Dalet* is also incorporated in the *Masach* that remained in the *Kelim* below *Tabur de Galgalta de AK* after the *Histalkut Nekudot de SAG* from within them.

Thus, since the *Masach* is primarily *Behina Aleph* and *Behina Dalet* is subordinate to it, and is not at all from its *Behina*, it is therefore drawn with it to the *Nikvey Eynaim*, which is *Behina Aleph de Rosh*. For that reason the *Zivug* was not made on *Aviut de Behina Dalet*, extending *Komat Keter*, but only on *Behina Aleph*, extending *Komat ZA*.

8. With all that is explained above, you will see that the *Tikkunim* depend primarily on MA and BON, standing from *Tabur* of every *Partzuf* downward. This is so because that is the place of the *Din* and lack of every *Partzuf*, as in the *Tabur* of the first *Partzuf de AK* (see items 1, 2), and in all the *Partzufim* through the end of *Assiya*.

Also, every *Partzuf Tachton* comes only to fulfill and complement the place of this lack in the *Elyon*, because of the rejection and detainment force, found in the *Masach* of that *Tabur* on the *Ohr Elyon*. It is as he writes above, that any *Tachton* uncovers a part of that *Ohr* which was rejected by the *Masach de Tabur de Elyon*.

Thus, the more the *Partzufim* and *Neshamot* increase, the more that *Gevul* from *Tabur* down will expand, broaden and become fit for the reception of the *Ohr Elyon*. Finally, the comprehensive *Ohr Makif*, called *Ohr Makif de Ein Sof*, will appear, and then there will be the *Gmar Tikun*.

Hence, the *Tikkunim* depend primarily only on *Partzufim* MA and BON that stand from *Tabur* down. Remember that, as this is an elementary concept in the entire scope of the wisdom.

Thus, this *Olam ha Nekudim* that the Rav deals with here, is the first MA and BON that appeared in the *Olamot*. It is cold merely BON, because there are no remains of it for *Olamot* ABYA, but only the *Behinat Nekeva*, called BON. This is because the *Zachar* that extends the *Mochin*, meaning the GAR, is called MA, and the *Nekeva* that receives the *Mochin* is called BON.

9. Now we shall come the actual words of the Rav. We shall begin by explaining the matter of the *Kelim* of *Partzuf Nekudim*. The Rav says (Part 6, item 19) that the *Kelim* came out by the *Histaklut Eynaim* in AHP.

We must understand why the emergence of the *Kelim de Nekudim* is different from the other *Partzufim*. It is known that *Malchut de Rosh* expands from her and within her into ten *Kelim* from above downward in the entire measure that her *Ohr Hozer* clothed the *Eser Sefirot de Rosh*.

Accordingly, *Malchut de Eynaim* should expand as *Kelim* from *Nikvey Eynaim* down to the extent that she clothed from *Nikvey Eynaim* up. Hence, there should have been a *Histaklut* in the *Nikvey Eynaim*, not in the AHP.

Indeed, there is a profound matter here. We have learned in item 7 that the lower *Hey*, being *Behina Dalet*, rose to *Nikvey Eynaim*, which is *Behina Aleph*. However, there was still no *Zivug* on *Behina Dalet*, but on the *Reshimo de Behina Bet de Hitlabshut*, called *Awzen*, *Behinat Zachar*, and on the *Reshimo de Behina Aleph de Hamshacha*, called *Hotem Peh* (see elaborately *Ohr Pnimi* item 44).

Thus, it turns out that the *Kelim de Nekudim* do not have anything of *Behinat* lower *Hey*, namely *Behina Dalet*. This is because the lower *Hey* remained in the *Nikvey Eynaim* and her *Behina* did not expand downward.

We might therefore ask: "How were GAR *de Nekudim* divided into two *Roshim*, GE, being *Keter*, and AHP, being HB, as it is known that the Lower *Hey* is in the *Eynaim* and the YHV in AHP?"

We must remember that after the *Reshimot* rose to *Zivug* in the *Nikvey Eynaim de Rosh* SAG, they were incorporated in the *Zivug de Rosh*, and their *Aviut* was renewed. Then they instantaneously descended from there to their appropriate place in the *Guf*, namely *Tabur*.

Then the *Ohr Elyon* descended once more on the *Masach* and its *Reshimot* in *Zivug de Hakaa*, eliciting *Eser Sefirot de Rosh* from the *Tabur* upwards, and *Eser*

Sefirot de Guf from the *Tabur* downwards, as in all the *Partzufim*. Hence, the Lower *Hey* became incorporated once more in the *Masach* at the place of the *Tabur*, and the AHP descended outwardly once more as in the *Rosh*.

Similarly in GAR *de Nekudim* themselves, after they divide into GE and AHP, the Lower *Hey* is found in the *Eynaim* once more. However, from the *Eynaim* down the Lower *Hey* does not expand whatsoever, because the *Histaklut*, namely the *Zivug*, is not done in *Behina Dalet*, meaning the Lower *Hey*, but in *Behina Bet* and *Behina Aleph*, being the AHP. Thus we see that the *Kelim de Nekudim* are only from *Behina Bet* and *Behina Aleph*, and have nothing of *Behina Dalet* even though *Malchut de Rosh* is incorporated of the Lower *Hey*.

Thus, you can see, regarding the matter of the association of *Midat ha Rachamim* with *Din*, which are the connection of the two *Heyin*: the First *Hey* and the Lower *Hey*, that association remains fixed and existing in *Nikvey Eynaim*. It is not so in *Behinat AHP*, which came out, because in the AHP that came out there is only *Behinat Vav*, which is only the *Masach* of the First *Hey*. This was so because *Behinat* Lower *Hey* did not extend to them from the *Nikvey Eynaim*.

Now you can understand the matter of the two kinds of NHY that illuminated in HB *de Nekudim*, which are NHY *de Keter* and NHY *de AK*, meaning *Yesod de AK* (Part 6, item 16). Also, the matter of the *Daat de Elyon* in GAR *de Nekudim* (Part 6, item 26), and the issue of the *Daat de Tachton*, which is the *Rosh* of the ZAT and the first *Melech de Nekudim*, to be brought below in Part 7.

10. In order to understand that we must have thorough knowledge about the emergence of the seven lower *Sefirot* through the connection of the lower *Hey* in the *Nikvey Eynaim*.

    Know, that this Lower *Hey* made four steps before coming to her place in the lower seven of *Nekudim*.

    First she came to the *Nikvey Eynaim* as *Holam*, meaning after her descent from her *Hitkalelut* in *Rosh de SAG* to her place in *Tabur de AK*. *Histaklut Aleph* took place on her double *Masach* and *Eser Sefirot* came out from *Tabur* up to the *Chazeh*, called *Rosh ha Aleph*, or YESHSUT. In that place the lower *Hey* in the *Masach* is in *Behinat Holam* above *Otiot* YHV, called GAR *de Nekudim*. This is the first step.

    After that, she expanded from *Tabur* down to *Behinat Guf* from the *Behinat* AHP that come out from the *Rosh*. These AHP are the GAR *de Nekudim*. It is known that they are also considered *Behinat Rosh* in and of themselves, in complete *Eser Sefirot*, which also divide into *Galgalta* and *Eynaim* and AHP (see *Ohr Pnimi* item 48). GE is the *Keter de Nekudim* and AHP are the *HB de Nekudim*.

After that the lower *Hey* comes once more in the *Nikvey Eynaim*, meaning in *Masach de Kli de Keter*, called *Yesod de Keter*, or *NHY de Keter*. This is because the place of the *Zivug* is called *Yesod*, or *NHY*, and here the lower *Hey* is called "the point of *Kamatz*", meaning *Rakia* and *Nitzotz*, or a *Kav* and a *Nekuda* below it. This is the second step.

Here is where it is most noticed that the lower *Hey* is above, in the *Eynaim*, and *YHV* are below, in the *AHP*. This means that these *AHP* have nothing of the lower *Hey*, connected in the *Nikvey Eynaim*, because the *Zivug* and the *Histaklut* were made only in the *AHP*, being only *Behinat* First *Hey*. Thus, only *Keter* carries the lower *Hey* inside it, but the *HB* are clean from the lower *Hey*.

11. The difference between *Behinat Holam* and *Behinat Kamatz* is that the point of *Holam* (being the lower *Hey* incorporated in the *Masach de Rosh ha Aleph* that stands at the place of *Tabur*) remains permanently there. She does not move from there because the first *Rosh* is not considered *Behinat Nekudim* at all (*Ohr Pnimi* item 20).

    However, there are ascents and descents in the point of *Kamatz*, which is the *Behinat* lower *Hey* incorporated in *Keter* of *Nekudim*. This is because during the *Zivug AB SAG* this lower *Hey* is found to be descending from the *Nikvey Eynaim* to the place of *Peh*, meaning below the *Otiot YHV*, when *HB de Nekudim* return to *Behinat Rosh*.

    This is because these *HB de Nekudim* were not rejected from the *Rosh* to *Behinat Guf*, but only because of the lower *Hey* that came in the *Nikvey Eynaim*, meaning *NHY de Keter*, where she was like the *Holam* above the *Otiot YHV*. Hence, the *Otiot YHV*, which are *HB de Nekudim* came out to *Behinat Guf*.

    Now, however, when the lower *Hey* descended from there below the *Otiot YHV*, meaning as a point of *Kamatz*, whose conduct is to come under the *Otiot*, the *HB* return once more and join the *Keter* to *Behinat Rosh*.

    This matter is considered as *Netzah, Hod, Yesod de Keter* having clothed inside *Hochma* and *Bina*, becoming a *Mochin* for them. It means that it brought them back to *Behinat GAR* and *Rosh*. This is because when *NHY de Keter* were above them, they were rejected from the *Rosh* and became *Behinat Guf*. Now, however, that *NHY de Keter* have stretched and the lower *Hey* in them descended under their *Otiot*, they acquired the *Behinat GAR* once more. This is why it is called *Hitlabshut* for *Mochin*. This is the third step of the lower *Hey*, since she descended under the *Otiot*.

12. Now you can see what is always brought in the Rav's words, that *Yesod de Elyon* is *Daat* to the *Tachton*, as here is where it is rooted. When *NHY de Keter* are above *HB* like the *Holam* above the *Otiot*, these *YHV de HB* are considered *Behinat HGT*, meaning a *Guf* where *Yod* is *Hesed*, *Hey* is *Gevura*, and *Vav* is *Tifferet*.

However, after *NHY de Keter* stretched and clothed in the *HB* as *Kamatz* under *Otiot YHV*, and the *HB* returned to the *Rosh*, the *YHV* have now become *Behinat Hochma, Bina, Daat* in the *Rosh*. The *Yod* became *Hochma*, the *Hey*, *Bina*, and the *Vav*, *Daat*.

Thus, it is considered that *Netzah de Keter* raised *Hesed de HB* to *Hochma* by clothing in them, the *Hod de Keter* raised *Gevura* to the degree of *Bina*, and the *Yesod de Keter* raised the *Tifferet de HB* to the degree of *Daat*. You find that through *Hitlabshut Yesod de Keter* in *Tifferet de HB*, the *Tifferet* became *Sefirat Daat*. This is the meaning of *Yesod de Elyon* becoming *Daat* through *Hitlabshut* in the *Tachton*.

You should know that there are two *Behinot* of *Daat*: Upper *Daat*, and *Lower Daat*. This is because the *Tifferet de HB* that has now become *Behinat Daat de HB* is called Upper *Daat*, since these *Kelim de HB* have nothing of the lower *Hey*, only from *Behinat* First *Hey* (*Histaklut Pnimit* here, item 9).

For that reason it has no connection with the *ZON*, which are mixed with the lower *Hey* (*Histaklut Pnimit* here, item 6). Know, that this *Daat* that shines in the *Kelim* that have *Hitkalelut* with the lower *Hey*, is called Lower *Daat*.

13. Thus we have clarified that the *Zivug* and *Hitlabshut NHY de Keter* in *HB de Nekudim* is useful only to *HB*, since it returned them to *Behinat Rosh*. However, for the *ZAT de Nekudim*, these *GAR* do not illuminate at all because of the lower *Hey* in the *Peh de Nekudim*. These *GAR* cannot shine to her because they are not incorporated in her at all.

Therefore, we need a second *Zivug* for *GAR* to shine for *ZAT* as well, and this is the *Zivug* of *NHY de AK* to *HB de Nekudim*. From this *Zivug* the *ZAT* extend with the *Daat Tachton*, as will be explained.

First we must thoroughly understand the matter of *NHY de AK*. You already know that these *NHY* are the *Shoresh* of this whole connection of the two *Heyin* and their ascent to *Nikvey Eynaim*. First, the *SAG* expanded to the *Sium Raglin de AK*, and clothed the Inner *NHY de AK*, meaning the first *Partzuf de AK*.

After that, *Ohr SAG*, being *Behina Bet*, mixed with the *Behina Dalet* in the Inner *NHY de AK*. Therefore, when the *Masach* rose to *Rosh de SAG* to be renewed in a new *Zivug*, it raised with it the *Reshimo de Behina Dalet*, incorporated in it. By that the lower *Hey*, which is *Behina Dalet*, rose to *Nikvey Eynaim* (see *Ohr Pnimi* item 6), and this ascent is called *Tzimtzum NHY de AK*.

The *Zivug* made in the *Nikvey Eynaim* took *Bina* and *ZON* of each degree out, *AHP de Rosh* became the *Guf*, and *HGT*, *Bina* and *ZON de Guf* became *NHY*. *Bina* and *ZON de NHY* departed from the *Atzilut* of the *Partzuf* completely, meaning to *Behinat* Separated *BYA*. For that reason *Partzuf SAG de AK* ended in the place of *Tabur de AK*, and the *Parsa* was stretched below it (see *Ohr Pnimi* item 6).

14. We must thoroughly understand what the Rav has written above (Part 6, items 11, 12), that the *Tzimtzum* and *Parsa* are two separate matters. This is because *Tzimtzum NHY de AK* was to diminish the *Ohr* for the purpose of *Nekudim*, and the *Tikun* of the *Parsa* is not for *Olam ha Nekudim* itself, which is *Olam ha Atzilut*, but for *Olam Beria* below it.

    This means that here is the beginning and the *Shoresh* of the three *Olamot Beria*, *Yetzira*, *Assiya*, called "Separated *Olamot*". This is done by *Tzimtzum NHY de AK*, where the *Reshimot* rose from the two *Heyin*: the First *Hey*, and the lower *Hey*. They connected in *NHY de AK* and came in *Nikvey Eynaim*, and from this *Zivug* came the core of the *Eser Sefirot de Nekudim*, as lower *Hey* in the *Eynaim* and *YHV* in the *AHP*.

    It is known that the *Reshimot de ZON* that came from *NHY de AK* returned to their place below *Tabur* like the *GAR de Nekudim*, meaning also through the division of the degree, where *Bina* and *ZON* departed from the degree. It turns out that that *Ohr de ZON* that returned to its place after the *Zivug de Nikvey Eynaim* in *Rosh de SAG*, did not fill the entire *Eser Sefirot* from *Tabur de AK ha Pnimi* down, but only the *Keter* and *Hochma* in it. *Bina*, *ZA* and *Malchut* in it went completely out of *Atzilut* and became the *Behinat* three *Olamot Beria*, *Yetzira*, *Assiya*, and all this was done through *Tzimtzum NHY de AK*.

    However, the *Parsa* is a special *Tikun* for the purpose of *Beria*, meaning for the purpose of the three Separated *Olamot* that were separated from *Ohr Atzilut* because of the division of the degree. However, they are all named after *Bina*, meaning *Olam Beria*, because this is the highest *Sefira*.

    This matter of the *Tikun* is truly a profound matter, since in fact, the *Parsa* too is a division of the degree on the *Nikvey Eynaim* that extends from *Tzimtzum NHY*. However, there is a matter of "draws from above and gives below" in it, as the Rav brought from the Zohar (Part 6, item 9).

    It means that there is a matter of ascent and descent in it. On the one hand, it is the *Rakia* that separates between the Male *Mayim Elyonim*, and the Female *Mayim Tachtonim*. This is done by force of the division of each degree, bringing *Bina* and *ZON* outside, turning *Keter* and *Hochma* of the degree into Male *Mayim Elyonim*. *Bina* and *ZON* of the degree were separated and departed as Female *Mayim Tachtonim*, which is the reason that *Parsa* is called a "Separating *Rakia*".

On the other hand, there is a matter of drawing from above and giving below in her, meaning by the *Zivug Elyon de AB SAG*, the lower *Hey* descends from the *Eynaim* to the place of *Peh de Rosh*, and then the *Parsa* splits. It means that the difference between *Keter* and *Hochma*, to *Bina* and *ZON*, is canceled because they return to their degree as before (see *Ohr Pnimi* item 12).

15. This *Tikun* of the return of *Bina* and *ZON* to the degree is named only after *Parsa*. However, this was done only because of the *Zivug de AB* and *SAG*, and how would *Parsa* help in that, to merit this *Tikun* being named after it?

The thing is that anything that manifests does not change after its emanation. Hence, after the lower *Hey* came in the *Nikvey Eynaim* once, she never descends from there again. Thus, a second *Rosh* was erected for the matter of the ascent and the descent of the lower *Hey* from the *Nikvey Eynaim*, which receives from the first *Rosh*.

Thus, the lower *Hey* in the *Nikvey Eynaim* of the second *Rosh* is in *Behinat* ascending and descending. Also, that difference in the *Nikvey Eynaim* of the second *Rosh* between the *Keter* and *Hochma* in it and the *Bina* and *ZON* in it is called the *Tikun* of the *Parsa*, since it is in *Behinat* ascending and descending.

This is so because only this is corrected in this way, in the lower *Hey* descending to her place to *Assiya* and *Bina* and *ZON* that departed from all the degrees returning. However, the difference that was made in the *Nikvey Eynaim* of the first *Rosh*, called *YESHSUT*, is never canceled with respect to the *Bina* and *ZON* that departed from it. This is because there it is considered the beginning of *Atzilut*, which is not subject to change.

Besides the above there is yet another special *Tikun* in *Parsa*: it hides and conceals the force of the lower *Hey* in the *Nikvey Eynaim* of the first *Rosh*, so it does not bestow below when the *AHP* return to the *Rosh*. Had it not poured down to the second *Rosh*, the lower *Hey* of the second *Rosh* would have been unable to descend from the *Nikvey Eynaim* to *Peh*. This is because the force of the *Elyon* always dominates its *Tachton*. However, the *Parsa* conceals it, and its power is not dispensed below at that time, and remember that.

From the above you will understand the differentiation between *HaVaYaH de AB* and *HaVaYaH de SAG*. As *HaVaYaH de AB* is fulfilled with *Yodin*, so *HaVaYaH de SAG* is fulfilled with *Yodin*. The only difference between them is in the fulfillment inside the *Vav*: the filling of the *Vav de HaVaYaH de SAG* is with *Aleph*, like this: אֿ.

This is so because the meaning of the *Tzura* of the *Aleph* is explained regarding the *Tikun* of the *Parsa*: its *Tzura* consists of two *Yodin*, an upper *Yod* and a lower *Yod*, with an inclined *Kav*, which is the *Parsa*, diagonally separating between them. This implies the division of the degree that occurred because of *Tzimtzum NHY* and the ascent to the *Nikvey Eynaim*. The upper *Yod* is *Behinat Keter* and *Hochma* of the degree from *Nikvey Eynaim* up, called Male *Mayim Elyonim*.

The lower *Yod* is the *Bina* and ZON of the degree from *Nikvey Eynaim* down, which departed from it, called Female *Mayim Tachtonim*. The *Parsa* between these *Yodin* is the *Rakia* that separates between waters and waters. This matter is discerned as the association of *Midat ha Rachamim* with *Din*, which is the first beginning of the *Olamot*. Hence the *Aleph* is the *Rosh* and the beginning of the twenty-two *Otiot* from which the *Olamot* were created.

16. It has been clarified that the *Tikun* of the *Parsa* is not in the first *Rosh*, which is YESHSUT from the *Tabur* up, but in the second *Rosh*, which is from *Tabur* down. In the *Pnimiut* they are NHY de AK, and in *Hitzoniut* they are the GAR de Nekudim, the place of MA and BON de AK, which the *Vav* of the Name HaVaYaH implies.

Hence, in the YH de HaVaYaH de SAG, which are from *Tabur* up, there is no issue of *Parsa* and lower *Hey* there. They are equal to *Partzuf AB*, filled with *Yodin* equally with *Partzuf AB*. However, the *Vav de HaVaYaH de SAG* from *Tabur* down is filled with *Aleph*, for there is the place of the *Tikun* of the *Parsa* and the division to *Mayim Elyonim* and *Mayim Tachtonim*.

Know, that because of that, HaVaYaH de MA is found to be filling all four *Otiot* with filling of *Alephin*. This is because it was primarily emanated in the form of the *Parsa* and the association of the lower *Hey* (*Histaklut Pnimit* here, item 6).

However, in HaVaYaH de AB there is no fulfillment with *Aleph* whatsoever, because the entire differentiation between AB and SAG refers to the association with the lower *Hey* performed in *Partzuf SAG*, not in *Partzuf AB*. Even in the SAG the connection is unapparent, but only from *Tabur* down in its ZA, and not from the *Tabur* up.

17. Now you can understand the matter of the *Zivug de AB and SAG* by which the lower *Hey* descends from the *Nikvey Eynaim* and returns to her place as in the beginning. You already know that the *Rosh* of the SAG clothes the HGT

de AB from *Chazeh de AB* to its *Peh*, since it is its *Behinat Hitpashtut Bet*, as written in the previous parts.

After the *AB* dispenses its *Orot* to the *SAG*, and since the *Ohr de AB* hasn't any *Behinat Hey Tata'a* in the *Eynaim*, when *Orot AB* come in *SAG* they lower the *Hey Tata'a* in the *Nikvey Eynaim de SAG* to the place of the *Peh* too, being her real place, as she is in *AB*.

Below, in *Olam ha Tikun*, this *Zivug* is performed by the ascent of MAN from the *Tachtonim*. Here, however, there is still no conduct of raising MAN, but the *Zivug* is done by itself, namely by *SAG*'s suction of sufficient amount of *Orot de AB*. These *Orot* lower the lower *Hey* to her real place.

18. After the above-mentioned *Zivug de AB SAG* is performed, two operations occur: one in *Pnimiut AK*, meaning the inner ZON from its *Tabur* down, and one in *Hitzoniut AK*, meaning in GAR *de Nekudim* clothing without, from *Tabur* down. This is because in *Hitzoniut AK*, the *Keter de Nekudim* lowers its NHY and clothes them to *Mochin* in *Hochma* and *Bina de Nekudim*.

It means that it lowers the lower *Hey* from its *Nikvey Eynaim*, separating it from the HB *de Nekudim*, which took them out to *Behinat Guf*. Now it lowered the lower *Hey* to her real place, to *Peh de Nekudim*, as a *Kamatz* under the *Otiot YHV* (see *Histaklut Pnimit* here, item 12), and the YHV that were as HGT returned and became *Behinat HBD*, meaning *Behinat GAR* and *Rosh*.

However, this is enough only for *Behinat HB de Nekudim* themselves, but no *He'arah* extends to ZAT *de Nekudim* any longer, because these HB have nothing of *Behinat* lower *Hey*. Hence, they have no connection to the ZON that are incorporated of the lower *Hey*, as he wrote there in item 12, and item 9 here.

The second act extended from the above-mentioned *Zivug de AB* and *SAG* to the inner ZON *de AK* below its *Tabur*. This is because this *Ohr* descended and fissured that *Parsa* in *Pnimiut de AK* that separates the inner ZON and brings them outside the *Atzilut* of *SAG*. Now it is canceled and *Ohr SAG* returns and expands to the inner ZON as before the *Tzimtzum* NHY, meaning through *Sium Raglin de AK*.

This is so because then *Bina* and ZA and *Malchut* too, which came outside NHY *de AK*, and became the three *Olamot Beria Yetzira Assiya*, have now returned to *Behinat Atzilut*, meaning NHY *de AK*, as in the beginning. Now you can understand the Rav's words above, who says that the *Parsa* is a *Tikun* for the purpose of *Beria*, mentioned in item 14. It is so because through the *Tikun* of ascent and descent in the *Parsa*, *Beria Yetzira* and *Assiya* were returned to NHY *de AK*, and returned to *Behinat Atzilut*.

19. Since *GAR de Nekudim* clothe *NHY de AK*, here too there is a *Zivug* of *NHY de AK* with the *HB de Nekudim*, as in *AB* and *SAG*. It dispenses them the *Ohr* of the *Melafom*, being the *Vav* with the *Nekuda*, which means that it is *Behinat* lower *Hey* that shines inside the *Otiot de YHV*. The lower *Hey* is called *Nekuda* and *Behinat Peh de Nekudim* is the *Vav*, which the *Nekuda* comes inside the *Vav*, incorporated in the *Vav* of the *HB*.

    Before they received the *Melafom* from *NHY de AK*, they could not dispense *ZAT* anything because they were not mingled with the lower *Hey* (see item 9). This is because the lower *Hey* remained in the *Nikvey Eynaim*, meaning *NHY de Keter* of the *Nekudim* and *YHV*, which means a lack, for the lower *Hey* descended to *HB*, being *AHP de Keter*.

    However, now that the *Vav* of the *YHV* received the lower *Hey*, being the *Nekuda* inside the *Melafom*, from *Yesod de AK*, and *Hochma* and *Bina* mingled with the lower *Hey*. Also, *HB* returned and mated on her, meaning extended *Ohr Elyon* on that *Masach* mixed with the lower *Hey*, and extended *Komat Keter*. This *Ohr* returned and poured also from above downward to the *ZAT*, to *Behinat Guf*, as it is written in its place, in Part 7.

    This is the fourth step that the lower *Hey* made, meaning when she came inside the *Otiot de YHV*, which are *HB de Nekudim*, as a *Nekuda* inside the *Vav*. From here she can expand into the *Guf de Nekudim*, called the "seven lower *Sefirot de Nekudim*".

    Delve deep into the matter of these four steps that the lower *Hey* made from the time of her connection with the First *Hey* inside the *Kelim* of the inner *NHY de AK*, until she came inside the *Otiot*, being the *Kelim de HB de Nekudim*. From there she could come to her place, meaning *ZAT de Nekudim*.

    This is because she made the first step from *NHY de AK* to *Nikvey Eynaim* as *Holam*. There are three degrees in this step: the first in *Nikvey Eynaim de Rosh de SAG*; the second, in *Nikvey Eynaim* of *YESHSUT*, being the place of the *Tabur*; the third, in *Nikvey Eynaim de Keter de Nekudim*.

    In all of these, she was as *Holam* above the *Otiot YHV*, meaning as lower *Hey* in the *Eynaim* and *YHV* in the *AHP*. In this *Behina* there were the *YHV*, which are the *AHP*, completely clean from the lower *Hey* (see item 10).

    She made the second step from the *Nikvey Eynaim de Keter Nekudim* to *Peh de Nekudim* as *Kamatz* under the *Otiot de YHV*. By that the *HB* returned to *Behinat Rosh* because *YHV* that were in *Behinat HGT* departed and came to *Behinat HBD de Rosh*. They are still clean of lower *Hey* since she is below them as *Kamatz*.

She made the third step by the *Zivug* of *Yesod de AK*, at which time she came to receive inside the *Kelim de HB*, meaning inside *Otiot YHV*. Through the *Zivug de AVI* she descends to her place to *ZON de Nekudim*, and this is the fourth step.

Know, that this fourth step is called *Psia le Bar* (lit. Stepping Outside). It means that here she stepped outside of *Atzilut* because the *Kelim* of the seven lower *Sefirot*, where the lower *Hey* expanded, illuminate outside *Atzilut* first by the force of the *He'arat Yesod de AK* that returned the *BYA* to *Atzilut*.

However, the *ZAT* could not exist like that, and their *BYA* returned, departed and were separated from *Atzilut*. This is called "the breaking of the vessels", and for that reason this last step is called *Psia le Bar*.

We have explained two *Psi'ot* (pl. for *Psia*) in the *Behinat Holam* itself (item 10 above). This is because there is *Behinat Holam* that does not have *Tikun* of the *Parsa*, meaning it can expand under the *Otiot*, which is the lower *Hey* in the *Nikvey Eynaim de YESHSUT*. Also, there is *Behinat Holam* that does have the matter of ascent and descent, which is the lower *Hey* in *Nikvey Eynaim de Keter de Nekudim*. We considered them two *Psi'ot*, so there are five *Psi'ot* here: four *Psi'ot* until it comes inside the *Kelim de HB*, and one *Psia le Bar*.

20. We must thoroughly understand the difference between the two *Behinot* in the above-mentioned *Holam*. The *Behinat* lower *Hey* in the *Nikvey Eynaim* on the first *Rosh* does not descend form her place any longer and the lower *Hey* of the second *Rosh*, which is the *Keter de Nekudim*, descends below through the *Zivug* of *AB* and *SAG*.

The reason for it is that it's been explained above (here, item 15) that the primary *Tikun* in *Parsa* is to conceal and hide the force of the lower *Hey* found in the *Nikvey Eynaim de Rosh de Elyon* when the lower *Hey de Rosh de Tachton* descends to the place of the *Peh*.

The matter of this *Tikun* will not be portrayed in the first *Rosh* itself, since there, in the place of her first creation, the lower *Hey* is in association with the First *Hey*. Had she descended from there, she would have had no way of ascending any longer. Moreover, the whole issue of the *Parsa* is nothing but an upshot of this lower *Hey* that rose to *Nikvey Eynaim* of the first *Rosh*.

Hence, she cannot descend from her place, as there is no one to conceal her force. However, after the *Parsa* is born under the first *Rosh*, and the *AHP* that went outside the First *Rosh* also divided into *GE* and *AHP* by themselves, it became possible for the lower *Hey* to descend from these *Nikvey Eynaim* of that *Rosh*.

This is because the *Parsa* conceals the First *Hey* in the *Nikvey Eynaim* of the first *Rosh* in a way that the primary association of *Midat ha Rachamim* with *Din*, is made in *Nikvey Eynaim* of the First *Rosh* into a fixed, existing *Shoresh*. However, the *Parsa* can conceal her force on occasion, not permanently. This act of association, meaning the above-mentioned ascent and descent is placed in the second *Rosh*.

21. You should also remember the need for two *Behinot Zivugim* made in *Hochma* and *Bina de Nekudim* that were explained above. They are the matter of *Hitlabshut NHY de Keter Nekudim* to *Mochin* in *HB*, and the matter of the *He'arat Yesod de AK* of the point to *Shuruk* to *HB de Nekudim*.

    This is because the *Zivug de NHY de Keter* helped only *HB*, meaning the *Behinat Rosh de Nekudim*, as by the descent of the lower *Hey* to the place of the *Peh*, the *HB* returned to *Behinat Rosh*. However, that did not help at all to the *Behinat Guf de Nekudim*, being the seven lower *Sefirot*, as it is written in item 10.

    Thus, the *He'arah* of the inner *NHY de AK* was necessitated, being *Behinat* lower *Hey* in and of themselves (see *Ohr Pnimi* item 7). After the *HB* received the *He'arat* lower *Hey* from *Yesod*, as *Vav* with the *Nekuda* inside it, meaning the lower *Hey*, because the *Nekuda* came inside the *Kelim de HB*, that *Ohr* is the core of *ZAT* that came to *Bina de Nekudim*. She procreated them and they came down to their place.

22. We must still clarify, that it is known that any *Partzuf Tachton* clothes its *Elyon* from *Peh de Rosh* down, as it is thoroughly written in the previous *Partzufim de AK*. Thus, why doesn't that *Partzuf de Nekudim*, emanated from *Partzuf SAG*, clothe it whatsoever? After all, *Keter de Nekudim* begins below the *Sium* of the entire *Partzuf de SAG*, but it clothes the *NHY* of the first *Partzuf de AK*, called *Partzuf Galgalta de AK*.

    We must also ask: what happens with the *Reshimot de Taamim de SAG* that remained after the *Histalkut* of these *Orot*? After all, all the *Orot de Guf* depart and rise to their *Maatzil* because of the *Hizdakchut* of the *Masach*.

    What is even more perplexing, where does the fulfillment to the *Guf de SAG* from *Tabur* up to the *Peh* come from after the *Histalkut* of the *Ohr* from there? In all the *Partzufim* the *Tachton* fills and clothes to its *Guf de Elyon* after its *Histalkut*. However, the *Partzuf Nekudim* doesn't clothe its *Elyon*, being SAG, as it stands below its *Sium Raglin*. Thus, who fulfills it after the *Histalkut* of its *Orot* to the *Maatzil*?

    To understand that we must be precise with the Rav's words here (Part 6, item 17). He writes, "**all the Ohr extending through Tabur, though it is** from *Behinat Eynaim*, is all swallowed and incorporated in *Akudim*, hence becoming indistinguishable. However, only the *Ohr* that extends below *Tabur* to its *Raglaim* is called *Nekudot*, as now it stands alone."

This we must understand: why is the *Ohr* from *Behinat Eynaim*, being *Ne'etzal* from *Partzuf SAG*, swallowed and mingled in *Akudim de SAG* and is unapparent whatsoever through the *Tabur*? After all, any *Partzuf Tachton* clothes the *Elyon* above *Tabur* too. Also, it is still quite apparent, and is not contained in it and swallowed in it.

23. Here you must remember all the elements in the creation order of a *Partzuf Tachton* from the *Elyon*, explained in the previous parts. We will mention just a few:

The primary factor in the birth of a *Partzuf* is the *Hizdakchut* of the *Masach* until it equalizes with the *Maatzil*. By that it raises all the *Reshimot de Sefirot Guf* to the *Maatzil*, which remain after the *Histalkut Orot de Guf*. There the *Masach* mingles with them in the *Masach de Malchut de Rosh*, called *Maatzil*, and then the *Reshimot* are renewed by the *Zivug Elyon de Rosh*.

When the *Aviut* in their *Guf* is recognized, they must exit the *Behinat Rosh* and return to *Behinat Guf* as they were in the beginning. However, not to *Behinat Tabur de Elyon* as they first were, but one *Behina* higher than the *Tabur de Elyon*. This is because the last *Behina* always disappears during the *Hizdakchut*, until it leaves no *Reshimo*.

The *Tabur de Elyon* is always the last *Behina* to disappear. Hence its corresponding *Behina* in the *Guf de Elyon* is found to be one degree above the *Tabur de Elyon*. This is the conduct in all the *Partzufim*, (see above Part 4, Table of Topics, item 210).

Partzuf Nekudim, which is MA and BON *de AK*, emanates from its *Elyon*, being *Partzuf SAG de AK*, according to the above order. By the *Hizdakchut* of the *Masach de Guf de Partzuf SAG de AK*, it equalized its *Tzura* with the *Maatzil*, being *Malchut de Rosh SAG*, and raised all the *Reshimot* that the *Orot* left after their *Histalkut* from the *Guf* to the *Maatzil*.

After their renewal there in *Zivug de Rosh*, and after their *Aviut* had been recognized, they came out of the *Rosh* and descended to their corresponding *Behina* in the *Guf*, being one degree above *Tabur de SAG*. That place is called *Chazeh de SAG*, and from the *Chazeh* up emerged the *Eser Sefirot de Rosh* by a *Zivug* with the *Ohr Elyon*. From the *Chazeh de SAG* down the *Eser Sefirot de Guf* came out in *Toch* and *Sof* through *Tabur*, meaning through *Sium Raglin de SAG*, and this is the order in all the *Partzufim*.

24. It is known that this *Masach de Guf SAG* purified and rose to *Malchut de Rosh SAG*, meaning to *Nikvey Eynaim*, to *Behina Aleph de Rosh*. It also contains all the *Reshimot* that remained from *Orot de ZON de AK ha Pnimi* after the *Histalkut* of their *Orot* from them (see *Ohr Pnimi* item 1).

It turns out that in this *Hizdakchut Masach de Guf de SAG* there is a great difference from all the *Partzufim*, as it consists of two *Behinot Reshimot* from two separate *Partzufim*: the first is the *Reshimot* that remain from the ZON de *Partzuf Galgalta de AK*. These are distant from one another because the *Reshimot* of itself come from *Masach de Behina Bet*, and the *Reshimot* of ZON de *AK ha Pnimi* come from *Masach de Behina Dalet*.

Hence, when they were mingled with the *Masach* and rose to the *Zivug de Elyon* in *Rosh de SAG*, two kinds of *Zivugim* came out on them: the first on its own *Reshimot*, from which the *Ohr Eynaim* that expanded to *Tabur* came out (here item 22). He says about it that it was swallowed and incorporated in *Akudim* and is unapparent, and its order of *Halbasha* is as mentioned above. This is because after its *Aviut* had been recognized, and the *Masach* descended from *Rosh* to *Chazeh*, it generated *Eser Sefirot de Rosh* from the *Chazeh* to *Peh de SAG*, and *Eser Sefirot de Guf* from the *Chazeh* down to the *Sium Raglin* of SAG, meaning the place of *Tabur de AK*.

The second *Zivug* was made on the *Reshimot* incorporated from *Behina Dalet*, meaning *Ohr de Nekudot de SAG* that clothed that ZON de *Partzuf Galgalta de AK*. The *Behina Dalet* connected in them there (*Ohr Pnimi* item 6), and this is the *Ohr* that descended from the *Eynaim* and expanded below *Tabur de AK*. The Rav says about it that only it is named "*Nekudot*" because it came out in *Behinat* lower *Hey* in the *Eynaim* and *YHV* in the *AHP*.

25. Indeed, the above division of the two *Partzufim* from *Tabur* up and from *Tabur* down has been rooted in *Partzuf SAG* itself even before its *Histalkut*. This is because then too the Rav states (Part 6, item 6) that it divides by *Taamim* and *Nekudot*. The *Taamim de SAG* are that part of SAG that is not mixed with the inner MA and BON, which he compares to AVI, extending through *Tabur de AK*. The *Nekudot de SAG* are that part of SAG that clothed and connected in the inner MA and BON, which he compares to YESHSUT, beginning from *Tabur* down.

Thus, back in *Partzuf SAG* before the *Histalkut* of its *Orot*, two separate *Partzufim* have been rooted in it, by the force of the connection with the *Behina Dalet* of the inner MA and BON. Its *Partzuf Elyon* is called *Taamim*, being *Behinat AVI*, and its *Partzuf Tachton* is called *Behinat YESHSUT*, called *Nekudot*.

Thus we have learned that the outer *Partzuf* MA and BON *de* AK, emanated from the outer *Partzuf* SAG *de* AK is divided into two *Partzufim*: the *Elyon* through *Tabur*, and the *Tachton* from *Tabur* down. When you regard both as one *Partzuf*, like the *Taamim* and *Nekudot de* SAG, then the *Elyon* will be considered GAR, and the *Tachton* as VAK, which are as AVI to ZON *de Atzilut*.

26. Now you can understand what is presented in several places, that GAR *de* ZA remain in *Ima* during its *Atzilut*, and do not depart with it. It has been explained above (here item 8) that *Olam ha Nekudim* is the first ZON that appears in the *Olamot*, meaning MA and BON.

    It also explains that the core of MA and BON is its connection with the *Behina Dalet* (here item 6). It is always emanated from *Partzuf* SAG, meaning *Partzuf Bina*, because as it is here, so it is in all the *Olamot*. Hence, SAG is called *Ima*, since she is the *Maatzil* of ZON, meaning MA and BON.

    In the first MA and BON you find that the *Ne'etzal* from the SAG *de* AK had to come out in two *Partzufim*: *Partzuf* GAR from *Peh de* SAG to *Tabur*, not incorporated with the lower *Hey*, and *Partzuf* VAK from *Tabur* down, incorporated in the lower *Hey*.

    The *Partzuf Elyon* above *Tabur* was mixed and swallowed in *Akudim de* SAG because it hasn't any of the *Behinat Nekudim*, meaning the connection with the lower *Hey*. Only the *Partzuf* from *Tabur* down is considered *Partzuf Nekudim*, meaning MA and BON. Thus, the GAR *de* MA and BON remain and are swallowed in *Guf de Ima*, meaning the SAG, and do not leave with the MA and BON.

    In other words, they do not connect with them whatsoever since they are an entirely separated *Partzuf*, as the Rav says, that the *Ohr* from *Peh* to *Tabur* is swallowed and incorporated in *Akudim de* SAG.

    It is known that all the forces in the *Elyon* must be in all its *Tachtonim*. Hence, the matter of the division of MA and BON into two *Partzufim* GAR and VAK that appeared in the first MA and BON, applies in all the *Partzufim de* MA and BON from here on. The GAR remains adhesive and is swallowed in its *Maatzil*, meaning *Ima*, and only the VAK come out with the name MA and BON.

Cause and Consequence

We shall now explain the order of all the operations made in the *Olamot* through cause and consequence thus far, meaning how every operation is necessarily generated in all its conditions by its original cause.

1. We shall begin with *Olam ha Tzimtzum*. The *Tzimtzum* was primarily on *Behina Dalet*, which is *Behinat Malchut de Ein Sof*, called the "Middle Point". However, the *Histalkut* of the *Ohr* was from all *Eser Sefirot*, and these *Reshimot* that the *Ohr* left after its *Histalkut* are called *Eser Sefirot de Igulim*.

   Afterwards a *Masach* was erected in the *Malchut* of the *Eser Sefirot de Igulim* and the *Ohr Elyon* expanded once more, until it struck that *Masach* in *Kli Malchut*. From the *Hakaa* of the *Ohr Elyon* in the *Masach*, a great *Ohr* appeared, called *Ohr Hozer*.

   This *Ohr Hozer* rose and clothed the *Ohr Elyon* up to *Keter*, from below upward, and those *Eser Sefirot* are called the *Rosh* of the *Kav*. After that the *Ohr Hozer* expanded once more with the *Ohr Elyon* inside it from above downward, in the same amount it clothed from below upward before in the *Rosh* of the *Kav*.

   That *Hitpashtut* from above downward is called *Toch* and *Sof* of the *Kav*, and these *Rosh, Toch, Sof* of the *Kav* are called "the first *Partzuf* of Adam Kadmon", or "*Partzuf Galgalta de AK*".

2. Thus we have before us ten operations:

   1. The place where the *Tzimtzum* occurred.
   2. The *Eser Sefirot* that the *Reshimot* laid called *Eser Sefirot de Igulim*.
   3. *Eser Sefirot* called *Igulim*.
   4. The *Masach* in *Kli Malchut*.
   5. *Hitpashtut Ohr Elyon* once more.
   6. *Zivug de Hakaa* of the *Ohr Elyon* with the *Masach*.
   7. *Ohr Hozer* that becomes a *Levush* and *Behinat* reception for the *Ohr Elyon*.
   8. *Eser Sefirot de Yosher*, the *Rosh* of the *Kav*.
   9. *Hitpashtut* of the *Malchut* with the *Ohr Hozer* into *Eser Sefirot* from above downward. The first nine *Sefirot* of those *Eser Sefirot* are called "the *Toch* of the *Kav*", and the *Malchut* of those *Eser Sefirot* is called "the *Sof* of the *Kav*".
   10. *Nekudot ha Sium* of the *Kav*. From there down it is darkness and not *Ohr*.

3. Now we shall explain the connections of cause and consequence among them: First, the place where the *Tzimtzum* is made is caused by the *Histalkut Ohr Ein Sof* from there. Thus, the first thing to know is that there is no absence in the spiritual. Hence, any slight change in the spiritual does not mean that the first *Tzura* is absent from its place, as in corporeality. Rather, it means that the first *Tzura* remains in its place unchanged in any way, and the change in the *Tzura* refers to an addition to the previous *Tzura*. Thus, now there are to forms instead of one.

   We must also remember that the law of separation in the spiritual is nothing more than the disparity of *Tzura*. As the ax separates in the corporeal, so disparity of *Tzura* separates in the spiritual. Thus, if the spiritual acquires some change within, it divides and becomes two. The distance between them is as the measure of the difference of form between them. If it is a slight difference, they are still considered close, but if the disparity is great, they are considered far from one another.

4. The reason for the *Tzimtzum* and the *Histalkut Ohr* is that *Malchut de Ein Sof*, which is *Behina Dalet*, wanted a more complete *Hishtavut Tzura* with the *Ohr Elyon*, as explained above in Part 1 *Ohr Pnimi* and *Histaklut Pnimit*. It explains there that there was not even a slight change made in *Ein Sof* itself by the *Tzimtzum* that was made, but that this *Olam Tzimtzum* is only an addition, renewed over the *Ohr Ein Sof*.

   The thing is that *Malchut de Ein Sof* wanted greater *Dvekut*. Hence, a change of form occurred in her, for that yearning did not manifest in her in *Ein Sof*. Thus, it is considered that a new *Tzura* was added here, and she departed from *Malchut de Ein Sof*, and acquired her own name, which is *Behinat Keter de Olam ha Tzimtzum*.

   This *Keter* itself expanded into four *Behinot*, and when *Behina Dalet* in it appeared, wanting greater *Hishtavut Tzura* with the *Ohr Elyon*, she diminished the will to receive in her and all the *Ohr* that was there immediately departed. This is because the entire vessel of reception in the spirituals is the will to receive. Without the will to receive there is no *Ohr*, because coercion applies only in the corporeal, of course.

   Thus we have explained the operations, which are the place where the *Tzimtzum* was made and the *Eser Sefirot* that the *Reshimot* made into *Eser Kelim de Igulim* left. The yearning for equivalence of form in *Malchut de Ein Sof* activated both of them together, meaning the *Hitpashtut Ohr* and its *Histalkut* from there.

From them came the third act, the ten *Kelim de Igulim*, because these *Reshimot* that remain after the *Histalkut* are the *Igulim*. Thus, these three acts are necessary and stem from one another.

5. The fourth act is the *Masach* in *Kli Malchut de Igulim* extending by the *Histalkut Ohr* from all four *Behinot*. This is because the *Tzimtzum* was only on *Behina Dalet* while the *Histalkut* was from all *Eser Sefirot*, for at that time, *Behina Dalet* was the entire receptacle for the *Ohr*.

    Thus, there immediately awakened in her a *Ratzon* to extend the *Ohr* over only the first three *Behinot*, and not on *Behina Dalet*, for she couldn't tolerate the darkness. Because of the manifestation of that *Ratzon*, the fundamental *Gevul* was elicited and born in the *Olamot*, as it says, "Thus far shalt thou come, but no further."

    This refers to the limitation on receiving only in the first three *Behinot*. This form of reception is called "*Tikun Masach* in *Kli Malchut*". It extended by the *Hamshacha* of *Ohr* from the *Maatzil* once more after the *Tzimtzum*.

    Thus the fourth act and the fifth act have been explained. They are: *Masach* in *Kli Malchut*, and the *Hitpashtut* of the *Ohr Elyon* once more. This is because the *Histalkut Ohr* activated both the *Masach* and the *Hamshacha* of *Ohr Elyon* once more, on the first three *Behinot*, for she couldn't tolerate the darkness.

6. The sixth operation is the *Zivug de Hakaa* of the *Ohr Elyon* with the *Masach*, extending by the force of the *Ohr Elyon* itself. The *Tzimtzum* and the *Masach* made on *Behina Dalet* came out by the force of the *Ne'etzal* itself, and the *Ohr Elyon* extending from *Ein Sof* that filled the entire reality there without any *Gevul* does not tolerate the *Gevul* imprinted in the *Masach*.

    Quite the contrary, it wants to come into *Behina Dalet* as well, and fill the entire reality as is its custom, but the *Masach* pushes it back by the force of its *Gevul*. This is called *Zivug de Hakaa*. Thus, the *Zivug de Hakaa* extends from the *Ohr Elyon* itself.

7. The seventh operation is that the *Ohr Hozer*, which becomes a *Levush* and receptacle for the *Ohr Elyon*, extends by the force of the *Hakaa* of the *Masach* in the *Ohr Elyon*, to the extent that it pushes it back. This is because that full measure of the *Ohr Elyon* that was fitting to come in *Behina Dalet* and did not come there because of its detainment on the *Masach* that pushed it back, is called *Ohr Hozer*.

    Thus, the *Ohr Hozer* extends from the *Hakaa* of the *Masach* on the *Ohr Elyon*. Remember, that from the *Tzimtzum* onward, from the time *Behina Dalet* stopped being a receptacle for the *Ohr Elyon*, the *Ohr Hozer* took its place. In other words, the *Ohr Hozer* became the vessel of reception instead of *Behina Dalet* before. Other than that, there is no vessel of reception.

8. The eighth operation is the *Eser Sefirot de Yosher* in *Behinat Rosh* of the *Kav*. It extends by the *Histalkut* of the *Ohr* during the *Tzimtzum* (see item 5), for it is the fifth operation. However, they do not connect and clothe to be *Shorashim* to the *Partzuf* except through the *Ohr Hozer* in the above-mentioned seventh operation, relating to its *Halbasha* on them from below upward.

9. The ninth operation is the *Hitpashtut* of *Malchut* with the *Ohr Hozer* in her from above downward into *Toch* and *Sof*. It extends from the *Masach* in *Malchut* of the *Rosh*.

   She is considered moving from "potential to actual" because the same measure of rejection and measure of *Hitlabshut* that emanated by the force of the *Masach* in the *Eser Sefirot de Rosh*, were only in "potential". In fact, there are neither rejection nor *Hitlabshut* there. Rather, everything that is done in the *Eser Sefirot de Rosh* in potential manifests later in the *Toch* and *Sof*, called *Guf*, in actual fact.

   The measure of the *Ohr* that the *Ohr Hozer* clothed in the *Rosh* in "potential", in that same measure the *Ohr Elyon* is found to clothe in the *Guf* de facto. This *Hitlabshut* is called "the *Toch* of the *Guf*" from *Peh* to *Tabur*.

   The *Behinot Sium* that the *Masach* made in the *Eser Sefirot de Rosh* in potential, meaning the *Behinat Hakaa* it made on the *Ohr Elyon* not letting it expand into *Behina Dalet* appears in the *Guf* de facto, from *Tabur* down to *Sium Raglin*. This is called the *Sof* part of the *Partzuf*.

   Thus, from *Sium Raglin* of the *Partzuf* downward, the middle point appears in actual fact, as the *Masach* stops the *Ohr Elyon* there altogether, and leaves a vacant *Halal* without *Ohr*. Hence, the *Behinat Toch* of the *Guf* is considered the position of the first nine *Sefirot*, and the *Behinat Sof* of the *Guf* is regarded as *Sefirat Malchut* alone, meaning the *Behinat* limitation and power of *Sium* in her.

   Thus the ninth operation and the tenth operation have been explained. These are the *Hitpashtut Malchut* from above downward to *Toch* and *Sof*, called *Guf*, and the point of the *Sium* of the *Kav*, under which it is darkness and not *Ohr*, both activated by the *Masach de Rosh*.

10. Thus the cause and consequence through the elicitation of *Partzuf ha Aleph de AK* has been explained, called *Partzuf Galgalta de AK*. Now we shall explain the elicitation of the five *Partzufim de AK* from one another by way of cause and consequence.

First we shall explain the causes for the birth of a *Partzuf* in general, meaning as it is in all the *Partzufim* equally, and then we will explain the particular *Partzufim*.

The first cause in the birth of a *Partzuf* is the *Bitush de Ohr Makif* and *Ohr Pnimi* on one another, by which the *Masach de Guf* of the *Partzuf* purifies and becomes as *Zach* as the *Masach* in *Malchut de Rosh*. This is considered ascending and mingling in the *Zivug Elyon de Rosh*, along with the *Reshimot de Eser Sefirot de Guf* contained in it.

Its two Upper *Reshimot*, called *Zachar* and *Nekeva*, generate two kinds of *Zivugim* in the *Masach de Rosh*. Through this *Hitkalelut*, the *Masach* and the *Reshimot* renew, until it becomes apparent that its *Shoresh* is from the *Aviut de Guf*, except the last *Behina*, which disappears from them.

Then they descend to the *Guf* once more, in its *Hitzoniut*, to the place of the *Chazeh*, and the *Ohr Elyon* expands in *Zivug de Hakaa* on this *Masach*, raising *Ohr Hozer* from the *Masach* upward. It extends *Eser Sefirot de Rosh*, whose *Koma* reaches the *Peh* of the previous *Partzuf*.

After that *Malchut* expands from the *Chazeh* downward with the *Ohr Hozer* in her into *Eser Sefirot de Guf* in *Toch* and *Sof*. These *Rosh, Toch, Sof* are considered an upshot, a son to the former *Partzuf*, clothing it from *Peh de Rosh* through its *Sium*.

11. Thus there are fourteen operations before us:
    1. *Bitush de Ohr Makif* in *Ohr Pnimi*.
    2. *Hizdakchut* of the *Masach*.
    3. *Hitkalelut* of the *Masach* in *Reshimot de Eser Sefirot de Guf*.
    4. Two Upper *Reshimot*: *Zachar* and *Nekeva*.
    5. Two kinds of *Zivugim* in the *Masach* of the *Rosh*.
    6. Renewal of the *Aviut* in the *Masach* and the *Reshimot*.
    7. The manifestation of the *Aviut de Guf* in them.
    8. The concealment of the *Reshimo* of the last *Behina* in them.
    9. Their exit from the *Rosh*.
    10. Their arrival at the *Hitzoniut* of the *Guf* of the previous *Partzuf* in the place of the *Chazeh*.
    11. *Zivug de Hakaa* performed on the *Masach* in the place of the *Chazeh* extending *Eser Sefirot de Rosh*.
    12. *Hitpashtut* of the *Malchut de Rosh* from the *Chazeh* down to *Behinat Guf* in *Toch* and *Sof*.

13. Clothing the previous *Partzuf*.

14. Its *Koma* begins from the *Peh* of the previous *Partzuf*.

12. Now we shall explain the cause and consequence connections in them. The first operation is the *Bitush de Ohr Makif* in *Ohr Pnimi* extending from the *Masach*. To the extent that the *Masach* extends and clothes the *Ohr Pnimi* in the *Partzuf*, it rejects the *Ohr Makif* that belongs to the *Partzuf*.

    This is so because its ability to clothe the *Ohr Elyon* comes entirely by its *Hakaa* on the *Ohr Elyon* that pushes the full measure of *Ohr* that should expand in *Behina Dalet* back, not letting it expand in the *Partzuf* from its *Tabur* down. It is known that this *Ohr* that cannot clothe in the *Partzuf* is the *Ohr Makif* of the *Partzuf*.

    Hence, the *Ohr Pnimi* and *Ohr Makif* are found to be contradicting one another because the measure of the clothing *Ohr Pnimi* is as the measure of *Aviut* of the *Masach*. Conversely, the measure of the *Ohr Makif* depends on the *Zakut* of the *Kelim*.

    Thus, the *Ohr Makif* purifies the *Masach* and the *Ohr Pnimi* departs from the *Partzuf*. For that reason the *Masach* is the reason for the *Bitush de Ohr Makif* in the *Ohr Pnimi*.

13. The second operation, which is the *Hizdakchut* of the *Masach*, extends from the *Bitush de Ohr Makif* in the *Ohr Pnimi*, as in the first operation.

    The third operation, being the *Hitkalelut* of the *Masach* in the *Reshimot de Eser Sefirot de Guf*, comes together with the *Hizdakchut* of the *Masach* extending from the *Bitush de Ohr Makif* in the *Ohr Pnimi*. Since the *Masach* is purified gradually, according to the *Sefirot*, it passes and comes within each and every one, mingling with it during its ascent.

    When it purifies into *Behina Gimel* it comes and mingles in *Sefirat ZA*, and when it purifies into *Behina Bet*, it comes and mingles in *Bina* etc. similarly. Finally, it comes to the *Maatzil* and mingles with all.

14. The fourth operation, which is the two Upper *Reshimot Zachar* and *Nekeva*, extends by the force of the concealment of the last *Behina* because of the *Hizdakchut* in each and every *Partzuf*.

    For example: after the *Hizdakchut* of *Partzuf Galgalta*, *Behina Dalet* disappears, and after the *Hizdakchut* of *Partzuf AB*, *Behina Gimel* disappears, etc. meaning precisely to that part of *Aviut* in her that stands for *Hamshacha* and *Hakaa*. However, the part *de Hitlabshut* in her does not disappear, and this is called the *Zachar*. It is unfit to mate with the *Ohr Elyon*, except when it connects with its closest *Behina* that has a complete *Reshima*, which is called its *Nekeva*.

For instance, after the *Hizdakchut* of *Partzuf Galgalta*, the last *Behina* remains with only half of the *Reshimo* of *Behina Dalet*, meaning only from *Behinat Hitlabshut*, called the *Zachar*. In order to mate with the *Ohr Elyon*, it must connect with the *Behina Gimel*, which becomes its *Nekeva*, and then it can mate with the *Ohr Elyon*. Thus, the matter of *Zachar* and *Nekeva* appears because of the concealment of the last *Behina* of each *Partzuf* after its *Hizdakchut*.

15. The fifth operation is two kinds of *Zivugim* in the *Masach de Rosh*. It comes together with the *Zachar* and *Nekeva* that were made by the concealment of the last *Behina*. This is so because at first, the *Nekeva* mingles with the *Zachar*, and by the *Zivug* with the *Ohr Elyon* they extend *Ohr* in the *Koma* of the *Zachar*. From this *Zivug* it is still not extended to *Hitlabshut* in the *Kelim*, due to the absence of *Behinat Hamshacha* in the *Zachar*.

    Hence, a second *Zivug* is needed, where the *Zachar* will be mixed with the *Nekeva*, at which time *Eser Sefirot* at the *Koma* of the *Nekeva* will be drawn. From this second *Zivug* the *Ohr* is qualified to clothe in the *Kelim*. Thus, the two kinds of *Zivugim* made on the *Zachar* and *Nekeva* in the *Masach de Rosh* extend because of the concealment of the last *Behina* after the *Hizdakchut* of the *Partzuf*.

16. The sixth operation, which is the renewal of the *Aviut* in the *Masach* and the *Reshimot*, extends by their unification in the *Masach* of the *Rosh*, until they operate together with it in the *Zivug de Hakaa* on the *Ohr Elyon*. This is because the *Tachton* that comes in the place of the *Elyon* truly becomes one with it.

    Thus, immediately as they come to the *Rosh*, they mingle with the *Aviut* from below upward operating in the *Rosh*, hence their own *Aviut* is renewed, meaning the *Behinat* "potential" *Aviut*, which is destined to appear *de facto* and turn into *Aviut* from above downward.

17. The seventh operation is the recognition of the *Aviut de Guf* in the *Masach* and the *Reshimot* that rose. It comes along with the renewal of the *Aviut* that they have acquired during their unification with the *Masach* of the *Rosh*.

    With the renewal of their *Aviut*, the *Behinat* from above downward in them immediately becomes apparent in the *Reshimot*, meaning the *Aviut de Guf* that they have already used before the ascent.

    In the beginning, before they purified from the *Aviut* in them, it was not at all apparent that they are *Sefirot de Guf*, for they were completely silent. Hence, they equalized with *Behinat Rosh* and rose and united with the *Masach de Rosh*. However, after they acquired the *Behinat* "potential" *Aviut* in the *Masach de Rosh*, and the *Reshimot* were revived, along with it a certain measure of *Aviut de Guf* became instantly apparent, imprinted in them since they were in the *Guf*. This thing is considered *Shinui Tzura* with respect to *Malchut de Rosh*.

18. The eighth operation is the concealment of the *Reshimo* of the last *Behina* in them. It extends by the force of the *Bitush de Ohr Makif*, whose operation is discernible primarily on the last *Behina*, and no *Reshimo* remains of her.

    The ninth operation is their exit from the *Rosh*, extending by the discerning of their *Aviut* (see item 17). This is considered *Shinui Tzura* from *Malchut de Rosh* because the *Shinui Tzura* and the exit is the same.

19. The tenth operation is their emergence to the *Hitzoniut* of the *Guf* of the previous *Partzuf* at the place of the *Chazeh*, extending form the concealment of the last *Behina*. For example, after the *Hizdakchut* of *Partzuf Galgalta de AK* its *Masach* and *Reshimot* rose to the *Rosh*, and their *Aviut* returned except for the last *Behina*. Thus, they have only *Behina Gimel* of the *Aviut de Guf* that they had before the purification, called *Chazeh*.

    Behina Dalet is the last *Behina* to disappear from them because of the purification. Hence, this *Koma*, which comes out on the *Aviut de Behina Gimel*, is considered *Hitzoniut* over the previous *Partzuf*, as it is known that the more *Av* is considered the more *Pnimi*, and more *Elyon*. For this reason they are *Hitzoniut* to *Partzuf Galgalta*, which is *Behina Dalet*.

20. The eleventh operation is the *Zivug de Hakaa* performed on the *Masach* in the place of the *Chazeh*. It extends from the *Hitkalelut* of the *Masach* in the *Malchut de Rosh*, which was incorporated and acquired the *Aviut* of *Behinat* "potential" from *Masach de Rosh* (see item 16).

    It was compelled to descend from the *Rosh* because of the *Aviut de Guf* discerned in the *Reshimot* that were incorporated in it. However, it is still not enough for actual *Aviut de Kelim*, but only when it first elicits *Eser Sefirot de Rosh* from below upward in "potential" through the *Zivug Elyon*. Afterwards *Malchut* expands in *Eser Sefirot* from her and within her from above downward in *Behinat Kelim* for actual *Hitlabshut* in *Toch* and *Sof*.

    Thus the eleventh operation has been clarified, which is the *Zivug de Hakaa*. The twelfth operation is the *Hitpashtut* of *Malchut de Rosh* from the *Chazeh* down to *Behinat Guf* in *Toch* and *Sof*. Both extend from the ascent and *Hitkalelut* of the *Masach* in *Malchut de Rosh*.

21. The thirteenth operation is the clothing over the previous *Partzuf*, extending and connected with the *Histalkut Orot de Guf* of the previous *Partzuf*. This is because the new *Partzuf* fill the *Kelim* that have been emptied of their *Orot* with its *Ohr* during the *Hizdakchut* of the *Masach* and its ascent to the *Rosh*. It is considered that it clothes with its new *Orot*.

22. The fourteenth operation is when its *Koma* begins from the *Peh* of the previous *Partzuf*, extending by its birth and emergence from there, as is the

nature of the branch that is attached where it exits and sucks off the *Shoresh*. Similarly, the entire *Shoresh* of the new *Partzuf* is from the *Hitkalelut* of the *Masach de Guf* in the *Malchut de Rosh*, called *Peh*. Hence its *Koma* is attached there, and from there it begins.

23. Thus we have explained the fourteen operations that cause the birth and emanation of a *Partzuf* from *Partzuf* in general, as it is in all the *Partzufim* equally; how each causes and is caused by its prior cause in utter necessity. Now we shall explain the sequence of the five *Partzufim de AK* by cause and consequence.

    The ten operations that were made for the emanation of *Partzuf Galgalta de AK* through cause and consequence have already been explained (item 1). After *Partzuf Galgalta* had been completed, the *Bitush de Ohr Makif* in *Ohr Pnimi* began, and following it all the above fourteen operations until *Partzuf AB de AK* emanated from it in *Rosh, Toch, Sof*.

    Thus, *Peh de Partzuf AB* is AB at the place of *Chazeh de Partzuf Galgalta*, for *Behina Dalet*, called *Tabur de Galgalta*, was not included in the *Masach de AB*, as it is the last *Behina*, which disappears along with the *Hizdakchut*. Hence, the *Eser Sefirot de Rosh AB* stand from the place of the *Chazeh* to the *Peh de Partzuf Galgalta*, and its *Sium Raglin* is above *Tabur de Galgalta*, as it is *Behina Dalet* there. Also, AB has nothing of *Behina Dalet*, hence it cannot expand below *Tabur de Galgalta*.

24. After the *Rosh, Toch, Sof de Partzuf AB* is completed, the *Bitush de Ohr Makif* in *Ohr Pnimi* also returns on it. This activates all fourteen operations, until *Partzuf SAG de AK* is emanated from it in *Rosh, Toch, Sof*, namely the third *Partzuf de AK*.

    There too the *Masach* of its *Rosh* did not stand in the place of *Tabur de AB*, meaning in *Behina Gimel de Guf*, which is *Tabur* for the AB, but at its *Chazeh*. This is because the last *Behina de AB* is not included in the *Masach de SAG*, as it disappears with the *Hizdakchut* of the *Masach*.

    From the *Chazeh* to *Peh de AB* stand the *Eser Sefirot de Rosh SAG*, and from the *Chazeh* down the *Eser Sefirot de Guf SAG* come out in *Toch* and *Sof* through the *Sium Raglin* of the first *Partzuf de AK*, called *Galgalta*.

25. Here, in *Partzuf SAG*, two operations that weren't in *Partzuf AB* were added:
    1. It extended below *Tabur de Galgalta de AK* as well, clothed and illuminated in the *Kelim de Galgalta de AK* from *Tabur* downward.
    2. It divided into two *Partzufim* on the *Tabur de Galgalta de AK*. From *Tabur* upwards it is called *AB de SAG*, or *Taamim de SAG*, and from *Tabur de Galgalta*

downward, SAG is called SAG, MA, BON de SAG, or Nekudot, Tagin, Otiot de SAG.

The first operation, meaning what extends below *Tabur de Galgalta* as well, extends because there still wasn't a *Tzimtzum* on the *Ohr Bina*, obstructing it from illuminating to *Behina Dalet*. This is because *Tzimtzum Aleph* was only on *Ohr Hochma*, hence *Partzuf AB*, whose *Koma* is up to *Hochma* could not expand below *Tabur de Galgalta*, the place of *Behina Dalet*. However, the *Koma* of *Partzuf SAG* is only up to *Bina*, and thus it could shine also into *Behina Dalet*.

The second operation, meaning its division into *Taamim* and *Nekudot*, extends from the first operation, from the force of the *Zachar de Partzuf SAG*. The *Zachar de SAG* is *Behina Gimel de Hitlabshut*. In the *Zivug ha Aleph* of the *Rosh*, it extended *Komat Hochma*, which clothes the *Kli de Keter de SAG* (see *Ohr Pnimi* item 1).

Thus, *Keter de SAG* that extends through the *Tabur* is called *AB de SAG*, or *Taamim*. However, the *Ohr Zachar* cannot expand below *Keter*, therefore the rest of the lower nine *Sefirot de SAG* expand from *Tabur* of *Galgalta* downwards. This is so because there is no *Ohr Hochma* in them, but only *Ohr Bina*, upon which the *Tzimtzum* does not apply. Thus, this part is called *SAG de SAG*, indicates that there is nothing of *AB* there.

26. After the *Rosh, Toch, Sof* of *Partzuf SAG* were completed, the *Bitush de Ohr Makif* in *Ohr Pnimi* returned on it, and the rest of the fourteen operations related to it. Finally, the fourth *Partzuf de AK* was emanated from it, called *MA* and *BON de AK*. *MA* and *BON* too came out in two separate *Partzufim* from one another on the *Tabur de Galgalta de AK*, as *Partzuf SAG*, from which they extend.

However, there are several very important operations added in the order of the emanation of *Partzuf MA* and *BON*. This is because they implanted the matter of the association of *Midat ha Rachamim* with *Din*, considered the beginning of the *Olamot*, as the *Olamot* would not have existed whatsoever were it not for them.

The fundamental cause of all these additional operations is the *Hitpashtut* of *Nekudot de SAG* from *Tabur de AK* downwards, meaning into the *Kelim de NHY de Galgalta*, which are from *Behina Dalet*. In this manner the *SAG*, being *Behina Bet* and the First *Hey*, became cohesive with the *NHY* of *Partzuf Galgalta*, which are *Behina Dalet*, the lower *Hey de HaVaYaH*.

This caused the *Tzimtzum Bet* in *AK*, as was the *Tzimtzum Aleph* in *Ein Sof* (Part 6, item 7). As *Tzimtzum Aleph* was on *Behina Dalet*, so here the *Tzimtzum* was made on *Behina Bet*. Also, *Tzimtzum Aleph* pushed the *Ohr* away from all four *Behinot*, and then returned and extended only the first nine *Sefirot*. Here too the *Tzimtzum* was made on *Behina Bet*, pushed the *Ohr* from the entire *Guf de SAG*, and then returned to clothe only the two *Sefirot Keter* and *Hochma* in the entire *Rosh, Toch, Sof* in this *Partzuf* MA and BON.

In *Tzimtzum Aleph* the *Kav* of *Ohr Ein Sof* on *Malchut de NHY de AK* stopped at the place of *Olam ha Zeh*, and remained without *Ohr*. Here too, in *Tzimtzum Bet*, the *Ohr* stopped on the *Kav* from *Ein Sof* on *Bina de NHY de AK*. Thus, *Bina ZA* and *Malchut* remained below the point of *Tzimtzum*, without *Ohr*.

Know, that here is where *Bina* acquired the name *Beria* in all the degrees, from the word "*Bar*" (lit. outside), such as "*Batei Barai*" (lit. outskirts), meaning outwardly.

It is so because through *Tzimtzum Bet* here, *Bina* in all the degrees went outside the degree. Thus, *Bina* of the *Rosh* became *Behinat Guf*; *Bina* above *Tabur* became *Behinat* below *Tabur*; and *Bina* of the *NHY* went completely outside the *Atzilut* of the *Partzuf*, remaining without *Ohr*, like the *Nekuda de Olam ha Zeh* during *Tzimtzum Aleph*.

27. However, there is a great difference between the *Tzimtzum* here and *Tzimtzum Aleph*, as there the *Tzimtzum* on *Behina Dalet* was absolute, and can never change. However, here in *Tzimtzum bet*, it is not so definite, and might change by a *Zivug Elyon*.

Hence, from here on there are two states in each *Partzuf*: a state of *Katnut*, and a state of *Gadlut*. Consequently, two *Roshim* were erected here: *Rosh Aleph*, where the two *Heyin* are connected to each other permanently, which can never be separated. After that, a second *Rosh* was erected, where their connection is not permanent, but ascends and descends.

The *Parsa* was set up between them. During the *Katnut*, the two *Heyin* are connected in the *Nikvey Eynaim de Rosh ha Bet* by the force of the dominion of the Upper *Rosh*. Then the *Tachton* is considered to be without a *Rosh*.

During the *Gadlut*, performed by the *He'arat AB*, the *Parsa* conceals the *Rosh Aleph* and its dominion is unapparent. At that time the lower *Hey* descends from place of the *Eynaim de Rosh Bet* below *Peh de Rosh ha Bet*, and the three *Sefirot AHP* return to the *Rosh*. Then the *Tachton* acquires *Behinat Rosh* and GAR.

28. Know, that *Katnut* and *Gadlut* apply only in the *Partzufim* MA and BON in all the degrees, where the lower *Hey* is already in the *Nikvey Eynaim* of their *Rosh*. They are considered the *Behinat Guf* of that *Rosh*.

Thus you see that the *Eser Sefirot de Nekudim* are considered the first MA and BON in the *Olamot*. Even though half of the *Partzuf* Upper MA and BON clothes from *Peh de SAG* downwards to the *Tabur* of *Partzuf Galgalta de AK*, it also stemmed form the *Nikvey Eynaim de Rosh de SAG*. However, because the lower *Hey* is connected to the First *Hey* in it, it is no longer considered *Behinat* MA and BON.

This is so because the *Masach* in it consists of the lower *Hey* when it came out of *Nikvey Eynaim de Rosh SAG*, and descended to its corresponding *Behina*, which is the *Tabur*, being the place of the lower *Hey*, and not above *Tabur*. Thus, only the *Eser Sefirot de Nekudim* are considered MA and BON, and only in them does the above matter of *Katnut* and *Gadlut* apply.

Moreover, even the GAR *de Nekudim* are not considered actual MA and BON, because the lower *Hey* remains in the *Nikvey Eynaim de Rosh ha Bet*, which are the GAR *de Nekudim*. Also, YHV are without any manifestation of the lower *Hey* descended in the AHP of this *Rosh Bet*, which are the HB in it.

Thus, the lower *Hey* is only at the *Keter de* GAR *de Nekudim*, which is this *Galgalta ve Eynaim* of this *Rosh*. However, in these HB *de* GAR, there is only *Behinat* First *Hey*. Thus, they too are not considered actual MA and BON. Despite that, the matter of *Gadlut* and *Katnut* does operate in them because there is still the lower *Hey* in them, as *Holam* over their *Otiot* YHV, meaning in the *Keter*.

The real MA and BON are the seven lower *Sefirot de Nekudim*, which are the real *Guf de Nekudim*. They are the first *Shoresh* of MA and BON in the *Olamot* from now on, though *Behinat* MA does not exist in them for there was the breaking of the vessels in them (see Part 7). Only the *Behinat* BON was left of it, hence these MA and BON are only referred to as BON in the Rav's words.

29. The lower *Hey* made four steps from the time she connected with the First *Hey* and came in the *Nikvey Eynaim de Rosh SAG*, until she came to her place, which is *Guf de Nekudim*, called ZAT *de Nekudim*.

The first step from *Nikvey Eynaim de Rosh SAG* to the place of *Tabur de Guf de AK ha Pnimi*, which is the *Nikvey Eynaim de Rosh ha Aleph*, called YESHSUT. There she permanently connected with the First *Hey* and became a fixed *Shoresh* to *Partzuf* MAN and BON in its *Behinat Katnut*.

A second step to *Nikvey Eynaim de Rosh ha Bet*, where there is the *Tikun* of the *Parsa*. The lower *Hey* is separated from the place of *Nikvey Eynaim* by the *Zivug de AB SAG*, and descends to the place of this *Peh de Rosh*.

The third step is the descent of the lower *Hey* from *Nikvey Eynaim* below the *Peh*. It is called *Hitlabshut* NHY *de Keter* to *Behinat Mochin* and GAR in

Hochma and *Bina de Nekudim*. Through the descent of the lower *Hey* under the *YHV*, they return to *Behinat Rosh*, and where they were previously only HGT, they have now become HBD. They clothe the three Upper *Prakin de NHY de AK*: *Hochma* on *Perek Elyon de Netzah*; *Bina* on *Perek Elyon de Hod*; *Daat* on *Perek Elyon de Yesod*.

A fourth step is from *Yesod de AK* to *Daat de HB*, as *Nekuda* inside the *Otiot de YHV*. Then *AVI* mate on the collective MAN from *Vav* and *Nekuda*, and beget the MA and BON to their place.

30. Thus the main operations added to the emanation of MA and BON were explained here. Let us briefly explain them in an orderly manner:

    Because of the *Hitpashtut* of the lower nine of SAG below *Tabur de AK ha Pnimi*, illuminating to the *Kelim de NHY de AK ha Pnimi*, the two *Heyin* became cohesive and connected. This is because the *Ohr SAG* is *Behinat* First *Hey*, and *NHY de AK ha Pnimi* is the lower *Hey*.

    Thus, when the matter of the *Hizdakchut* of the *Masach* returned to *Partzuf SAG* as well, the *Masach* was found to be consisting of two *Partzufim* here: *Partzuf SAG* and *Partzuf Galgalta*, raising them together to the *Rosh de SAG*, to *Nikvey Eynaim*, meaning to *Behina Aleph* from there.

    Because the lower *Hey* is not in its place, but was incorporated and united with the First *Hey*, meaning the First *Hey* received and became *Behinat* lower *Hey*, hence the *Zivug* was made on the First *Hey* alone. Consequently, two *Zivugim* were made there: one for the *Zachar*, and one for the *Nekeva*. However, the primary *Zivug* occurred in the *Behinat Nekeva*, which is *Behina Aleph*. This is because she is complete with *Behinat Hamshacha* too, from which there is *Hitpashtut* to *Kelim*.

    When the *Aviut de Guf* in the *Masach* was recognized, it departed from the *Rosh de SAG* and descended to its corresponding *Behina* in the *Guf*, being *Tabur de AK ha Pnimi*. This is because there begins the place of the lower *Hey*, contained in the *Masach*, and there it mated with the *Ohr Elyon* and the *Eser Sefirot de Rosh* called YESHSUT elicited from *Tabur* upwards.

    Bina, ZA and *Malchut* of that *Rosh* already stand below *Tabur* because the lower *Hey* stands at its *Hochma*, which is also the place of *Tabur*, and the *Sefirot* below *Hochma* stand from the *Tabur* down. Also, they are the GAR *de Nekudim*, meaning the core of the *Rosh de Nekudim*. This is because the first *Rosh* is not at all considered *Nekudim*, as the lower *Hey* in the *Masach* is below it, and the *Aviut* doesn't operate whatsoever from below upward. Hence, it is considered *Akudim de SAG*. For that reason GAR of *Nekudim* remain the *Behinat Rosh* of the *Nekudim*, named *Rosh ha Bet*.

This *Rosh ha Bet* has *Eser Sefirot* too, divided by the GAR. GE are incorporated in the *Keter*, and AHP are in *Hochma* and *Bina*. The lower *Hey* is in *Keter*, which is *Behinat Rosh ha Bet*, and *Hochma* and *Bina*, which are AHP, departed from *Rosh ha Bet* into *Behinat HGT*, meaning *Behinat Guf*.

You find in them that the lower *Hey* in the *Eynaim* and the YHV in these AHP, meaning the lower *Hey* does not shine anything in these AHP, which are *Hochma* and *Bina*. Instead, they are only *Behinat* First *Hey*.

The *Tikun* of the *Parsa* is on this *Rosh ha Bet*, where there are two *Tikkunim*:

1. The first is that the two *Heyin* contained in it are diagonal, meaning that a fissuring of the *Parsa* is sometimes possible there. At that time the two *Heyin* separated from one another and the lower *Hey* descended from there downward below *Malchut* of this *Rosh*, as *Kamatz* under *Otiot* YHV.

2. The second is to hide and conceal at that time the force of the lower *Hey* that stands at the *Nikvey Eynaim* of the first *Rosh* with a tight connection with the First *Hey*. It is so because had it not been for that concealment, it would have been impossible for the lower *Hey* of the second *Rosh* to descend below the *Otiot*.

Here was the *Shoresh* for the state of *Katnut* of the *Partzufim* made, meaning a possibility of ascent and *Gadlut*. However, it can never be that it would also diminish more than the *Komat Katnut* that was in it. This guard extends by the force of the lower *Hey* in the *Nikvey Eynaim* of the First *Rosh*, tightly connected there with the First *Hey*. Also, the state of *Gadlut* extends from the lower *Hey* in the *Nikvey Eynaim* of the second *Rosh*.

Two operations were made in order to beget the *Gadlut de Nekudim*: the first for the *Rosh* of the *Nekudim*, where by the *Zivug de AB SAG* the lower *Hey* in the *Eynaim* that stood above HB, which are YHV, descended and went under these *Otiot* YHV. In that the HB returned to the second *Rosh*, and the YHV that were HGT rose and became HBD.

This is called *Hitlabshut NHY de Keter* in *Hochma* and *Bina*. The second operation was for the ZAT, which are the true *Guf de Nekudim*. *Yesod de AK* illuminated the point of the lower *Hey* inside the *Otiot*, within the HB *de Nekudim*, as *Melafom*, which is a point in the *Vav*. They became MAN in HB and mated on them, begetting the ZAT *de Nekudim*. This will be explained in the next part.

31. We find thirteen operations here:

1. The connection of the two *Heyin*, the First *Hey* and the lower *Hey*.
2. *Hitkalelut* of the *Masach* in the *Reshimot* of the two *Partzufim* from *Partzuf* SAG and from *Partzuf Galgalta de* AK.

3. The *Zivug* was made only on the *Behinat* First *Hey*.
4. The descent of the *Masach* after its *Hitkalelut* in the two *Zivugim* of the *Rosh*, its arriving at the place of *Tabur de AK ha Pnimi*.
5. *Rosh ha Aleph*, called YESHSUT.
6. *Rosh ha Bet*, called GAR *de Nekudim*.
7. The exit of *Bina* and ZON outside the degree in all the degrees.
8. The preparation of the place for the three separated *Olamot*, called *Beria*, *Yetzira*, and *Assiya*, and the *Kav* of *Ein Sof* that previously stopped at the middle point, being the point of *Olam ha Zeh*. Also, *Behinat Malchut de NHY de AK ha Pnimi* rose above the new point of *Tzimtzum* to the place of *Bina de NHY de AK ha Pnimi*.
9. The division of *Rosh ha Bet* itself into GE and AHP, where the lower *Hey* is in the *Eynaim* and YHV in the AHP.
10. The correction of the *Parsa*.
11. The correction of *Gadlut* and *Katnut*.
12. The lowering of the lower *Hey* below *Otiot* YHV, which was for the purpose of *Gadlut* and *Panim be Panim de* GAR of the *Nekudim*.
13. The arriving of the lower *Hey* into the *Otiot* for the purpose of the emanation of ZAT *de Nekudim*.

32. Now we shall explain the connections of cause and consequence in them:
   1. The first is the connection of the two *Heyin*. They extend from the *He'arat* lower nine *de* SAG, which are *Behina Bet* and lower *Hey*, into the *Kelim* of the Inner NHY *de* AK, being *Behina Dalet* and lower *Hey*.
   2. The second is the *Hitkalelut* of the *Masach* from the *Reshimot* of the two *Partzufim*, SAG and NHY *de* AK. They too extend from the *He'arah* of SAG to the *Kelim de AK ha Pnimi*.
   3. The third is the *Zivug* that was only on *Aviut* of the First *Hey*. It extends because the *Reshimo de* SAG is the principle, and the lower *Hey de* NHY *de* AK is subordinate to it, connected to SAG through its illumination to NHY.
   4. The fourth is the descent of the *Masach* to the place of *Tabur*. It extends by the force of the lower *Hey* contained in that *Masach*, and the connection of the *Heyin* being from the *Tabur de* AK downwards because of the *Hitpashtut Ohr* SAG there, and not from *Tabur* upwards.
   5. The fifth is *Rosh ha Aleph*. It extends from the *Hitkalelut* of the *Masach* in the *Aviut* of the *Rosh*. Hence, as it descends below as well, it first elicits the *Behinat* from below upward, which is like all the *Partzufim*.

6. The sixth is *Rosh ha Bet*, called *GAR de Nekudim*. It extends from the *AHP* that departed from *Rosh ha Aleph*.

7. The seventh is the exit of *Bina*, *ZA* and *Malchut* from all the degrees. It extends by the force of the lower *Hey* that was connected with the First *Hey*, and the First *Hey* receiving the *Tzura* of the lower *Hey*. That creates a *Zivug* in the *Nikvey Eynaim*, and *Bina* and *ZON* exit from the *Rosh*, and similarly so from all the degrees.

33. 8. The eighth is the place that became the three separated *Olamot BYA* and the *Kav* of *Ein Sof* that stopped at *Bina de NHY de AK*. It too extends from the ascent of the lower *Hey* in *Nikvey Eynaim* because *Bina*, *ZA* and *Malchut de NHY* came out below the point of the *Tzimtzum*, which has now risen above *Bina de NHY*. This *Bina* became *Olam Beria*, the *ZA*, *Olam Yetzira*, and *Malchut*, *Olam Assiya*.

9. The ninth is the division of the second *Rosh* into lower *Hey* in the *Eynaim* and *YHV* in the *AHP*. It extends from the division of *Partzuf SAG* on *Taamim* and *Nekudot*, called *AB* and *SAG* (see above item 25). Hence, the *Masach* that rose from there to *Rosh de SAG* elicited two *Behinot Rosh* there:

27. One from *Behinat Taamim* and *AB*, from which *Partzuf Elyon de MA* extends, beginning [another version from the manuscript of Baal HaSulam: in that] in *Peh de SAG* and ending in *Tabur*.

28. And a second *Rosh* from the *Behinat Nekudot* and *SAG de SAG*, from which the *Partzuf Tachton de MA* and *BON* extends, beginning from *Tabur de AK* downward, which are the *Eser Sefirot de Nekudim* (see here items 24, 25).

The first *Rosh* is from *Behinat* lower *Hey* in the *Eynaim*, whose branches are *Se'arot Rosh*, and the second *Rosh* is from *Behinat YHV* in the *AHP*, whose branches are *Se'arot Dikna* (*Ohr Pnimi* items 2 and 19).

It explains there that although the second *Rosh* is *AHP* of the first *Rosh*, still it is a complete *Rosh* in and of itself. The reason is that the *Masach* descended to its *Behinat Nikvey Eynaim* and made the *Zivug* with the *Ohr Elyon* on the *Aviut de Behinot Nekudot* in it, generating *Eser Sefirot* from below upward.

It is so because in every place where the *Tzura* of *Aviut* was renewed in the *Masach*, a new *Zivug* was made. Hence, there are three *Behinot* discerned in *Rosh ha Bet*:

1. *Bina*, *ZA* and *Malchut* that came out of *Rosh ha Aleph*.

2. *Behinat* complete *Rosh*, meaning that a new *Zivug* was made on the *Behinat Nekudot* in it, mixed with the lower *Hey*.

3. It is necessarily divided into GE and AHP, since the new *Zivug* made in it was only in the *Nikvey Eynaim*, meaning *Behina Aleph*. It is also regarded that its lower *Hey* is in the *Eynaim* and YHV in the *AHP*, and the *AHP* came out of the *Rosh*.

It is known that the *Masach* displays all the *Zivugim* it consists of in the *Rosh de Elyon* after it comes down to its place in the *Guf de Elyon*. Hence, these two *Roshim* appear below as well:

1. The first *Rosh* from *Tabur* upwards, called YESHSUT, considered *Taamim* and AB.

2. The second *Rosh* from *Tabur* down.

They contain the same three above *Behinot*, which are a complete *Rosh* in and of themselves. Also, the *AHP* from the *Behinat Rosh ha Aleph*, and the *Behinat* division of the lower *Hey* in the *Eynaim* and YHV in the *AHP*, where these *AHP* depart from this second *Rosh*.

34. 10. The tenth is the correction of the *Parsa*. It too extends from the division of *Partzuf de MA* and *BON* into two *Partzufim* on the *Tabur*, imprinted and generated by the force of SAG's division into *Taamim* and *Nekudot* (see here item 33).

It is so because originally they are one *Partzuf*, as the *Taamim* and *Nekudot* of SAG extend from one *Rosh*: the *Taamim* are *Keter de Guf* SAG and the *Nekudot* are the lower nine of that *Guf*. Hence, the MA and BON too come from their *Masach*. Although they have two *Roshim*, they are also considered one *Guf*.

Thus, this division is similar to the *Parsa* inside the intestines of a person, where this *Parsa* divides a single *Guf* and makes it be like two separate *Gufim*.

On the one hand, the *Gevul* in the *Parsa* is similar to the *Gevul* in the *Tzipornaim* of the *Raglaim* of the *Partzuf*, since it too stands and ends the Upper *Partzuf* of MA and BON. It is related to *Partzuf AB de SAG* and *Taamim* and is considered *AVI de MA* and *BON*, where the *Tzipornaim* of the *Raglaim* end on the *Parsa*.

On the other hand it is in the middle of the *Partzuf*, since on the part of the *Shoresh* the *Taamim* and *Nekudot* are only one *Partzuf*. Thus, the middle and the *Sium* are mixed in it together. Consequently, two corrections shine in it:

1. The force of the connection of the two *Partzufim*. It is helped by the primary *Zivug AB SAG*, when the *AB de SAG* and *SAG de SAG* became one and the lower *Hey* descended from the *Eynaim* under the *Otiot YHV*, and the *AHP* in all the degrees return to their degree as in the beginning.

2. The second correction is the concealment of the permanent lower *Hey* in *Rosh ha Aleph*, so that it doesn't manifest its force when the *AHP* return to the *Rosh*. In that regard, she distinguishes the first *Rosh* above her as a separate *Partzuf*, not connected whatsoever with the second *Rosh*.

35. 11. The eleventh is the correction of *Gadlut* and *Katnut*.

12. The twelfth is the lowering of the lower *Hey* below the *YHV*, sufficient for the returning of *HB de Nekudim Panim be Panim*. It extends by the *Zivug de AB* and *SAG* by the force of the two *Tikkunim* in the *Parsa*.

13. The thirteenth is the permeation of the lower *Hey* into the *Otiot* for the purpose of the creation of the *ZAT de Nekudim*, being the real *Guf*. It extends from the *He'arat Yesod de AK* to the *Rosh de Nekudim*, of the *Behinat Shuruk*, which is a *Nekuda* inside the *Vav*. This matter will be explained in completeness in Part 7.

Table of Questions and Answers for the Meaning of the Words

1. *Aleph* in the *Vav de SAG*?
2. What are *Otiot*?
3. What are *AHP* in their Place?
4. What is *Butzina de Kardinuta*?
5. What is the Fissuring of the *Parsa*?
6. What is One Over the Other?
7. What is *Holam*?
8. What is *Taffel*?
9. What is "Coming out Strongly"?
10. What are Twenty-two *Otiot*?
11. What are Male *Mayim Elyonim*?
12. What are Female *Mayim Tachtonim*?
13. What is *Melafom*?
14. What is *Mazla*?
15. What is *Mayin Nukvin*?
16. What is Death?
17. What is Upper *Nekudot*?
18. What are *Nekudot* Under the *Otiot*?
19. What is *Nitzotz de Kardinuta*?
20. What are *Nikvey Eynaim*?
21. What are *Nikvey Awzen*?
22. What is the Opening of the *Eynaim*?
23. What is *Parsa*?
24. What is *Tzimtzum Bet*?
25. What are *Tzipornaim* of the *Raglaim*?
26. What is Separating *Rakia*?
27. What is *Shuruk*?
28. What are *Se'arot Rosh*?
29. What are *Se'arot Dikna*?
30. What is *Shibolet ha Zakan*?

1. **What is *Aleph* in the *Vav de SAG*?**

   There are two *Shorashim* for the *Otiot Yod* and *Aleph*. Indeed, the *Yod* is considered the genuine *Shoresh* of the *Otiot*, since when we want to write any *Ot*, we begin with *Yod*, meaning with a point. When we stretch the point sideways and down, the desired *Ot* appears. Thus, the *Yod* is the *Shoresh* of each and every *Ot*. Despite that, the *Aleph* heads all twenty-two *Otiot*.

   The thing is that the *Otiot* in their Upper *Shoresh* are *Kelim* for the reception of the *Shefa*. It is known that *Hitpashtut Ohr* and its *Histalkut* cause the making of the *Kelim*. This is so because the *Kelim* are made of the *Reshimot* that remain after the *Histalkut Ohr*.

   From that you will understand that the *Shoresh* of all sorts of departures is the *Shoresh* to the *Kelim*, being the *Otiot*. It is known that the first *Tzimtzum* is the *Shoresh* of any *Histalkut* in the *Olamot*. Hence, the *Nekuda* of *Tzimtzum*, being the *Yod*, is considered the *Shoresh* of all the *Otiot*.

   However, it is known that *Tzimtzum Aleph* is still not considered the *Shoresh* of the *Olamot*, only the *Shoresh de Shoresh*, because the real *Shoresh* of the *Olamot* is *Tzimtzum Bet*. The difference between them is that *Tzimtzum Aleph* was only on a single *Nekuda*, namely *Behina Dalet*, which is *Malchut*, the lower *Hey*. *Tzimtzum Bet*, however, was also on *Bina*, meaning the two *Nekudot* joined in this *Tzimtzum*, the *Nekuda* of *Malchut* and the *Nekuda* of *Bina*, which is the association of *Midat ha Rachamim* with *Din*.

   It is known that connecting two *Nekudot* together creates a *Kav*, longitudinally or across. Hence, *Tzimtzum Bet* is called a *Kav*, because of the two *Nekudot* that joined in this *Tzimtzum*, as it says, "and they two went." Because of that it is called *Rakia*, or *Parsa*, which is like a *Kav* laid across, separating the *Elyonim* from the *Tachtonim*.

   It has been explained inside the book that the primary innovation that occurred in *Tzimtzum Bet* is the matter of the division of the *Eser Sefirot* into two *Behinot* in all the degrees. This is because *Bina*, *ZA* and *Malchut* of every degree went out of the degree and acquired the value of its inferior degree. Thus, from a single degree, an upper and lower were made, where *Keter* and *Hochma* became the upper, and *Bina*, *ZA* and *Malchut* became a lower degree to *Keter* and *Hochma*.

   These two innovations, which are the connection of the two points together like a line and the division of the degree into upper and lower manifest in the shape of the *Aleph*(א): the connection of the two points in the *Tzimtzum* is the line of the *Aleph* in this manner - (). The upper *Behina* of each degree is the *Yod*(י) over the *Kav*, containing *Keter* and *Hochma* of the degree, as *Mayim Elyonim*, like this (). The lower *Behina* of each degree is the lower *Yod* below the *Kav*, containing *Bina*, ZA and *Malchut*, which became the *Tachtonim*, meaning *Mayim Tachtonim*, like this ().

Thus, you can see how there are two *Shorashim* to the *Olamot*: the *Yod* is the first *Shoresh*, made in the first *Tzimtzum* only on the point of *Malchut*, and the *Aleph* is the second *Shoresh*, made in *Tzimtzum Bet* on the two points *Bina* and *Malchut* together.

The first *Tzimtzum* is a far *Shoresh* from the *Olamot*, and only *Tzimtzum Bet* is considered the *Shoresh* of the *Olamot*. Hence, the *Yod* is not considered the *Shoresh* of the *Olamot*, until it is fit to head all the twenty-two *Otiot*.

Only the *Ot Aleph* is considered the *Shoresh* of all the *Otiot*, since it is regarded as *Tzimtzum Bet*, being the true *Shoresh* to the *Olamot*. Hence, the *Aleph* is at the head of the twenty-two *Otiot*, and the *Yod* is considered a primordial *Shoresh*, serving the *Otiot* in hiding.

Now you can understand the meaning of the four fulfillments operating in the Name *HaVaYaH*. They are: AB - *Yod, Hey, Viv, Hey*; SAG - *Yod, Hey, Vav, Hey*; MA - *Yod, He, Vv, He*; BON - *Yod, Heh, Vav, Heh*.

The primary difference is whether the *Kelim* come from *Tzimtzum Aleph*, or from *Tzimtzum Bet*. Fulfilling the *Otiot* with *Yodin* indicates that they come primarily from *Tzimtzum Aleph*, and fulfilling the *Otiot* with *Alephin* indicates that they come from *Tzimtzum Bet*.

Now you can see that if all the *Otiot de HaVaYaH* are fulfilled with *Yodin*, being *HaVaYaH de AB*, then the *Kelim* of that *Partzuf* have nothing of *Behinat Tzimtzum Bet*, only *Tzimtzum Aleph*. Conversely, if the *Otiot* are filled with *Alephin*, which is *Gimatria MA*, then the *Kelim* of that *Partzuf* have nothing of *Behinat Tzimtzum Aleph*, only *Tzimtzum Bet*.

However, in *HaVaYaH de SAG* the *Otiot* are not filled equally, as they are all with *Yodin* except for the *Vav de HaVaYaH*, which is with *Aleph*.

The reason for it is that *HaVaYaH* is also divided into four *Partzufim*, which are: *Hochma, Bina, ZA* and *Malchut*, by the order of her *Otiot*. Thus, the *Vav* in her is *Behinat ZA de Partzuf SAG*.

It is known that *Tzimtzum Bet* was only in *Partzuf SAG*, not in the first two *Partzufim* in her, being YH, meaning *Hochma* and *Bina* in her, but only in ZA in her, standing below *Tabur de SAG* (see *Histaklut Pnimit* item 15).

Thus, the beginning of the *Shoresh* of the *Aleph*, meaning *Tzimtzum Bet*, was not in YH *de SAG*, only in the *Vav de SAG*. Hence the YH *de SAG* are filled with *Yodin* as in *HaVaYaH de AB*, but the *Vav de SAG* is filled with the *Aleph*, as *Tzimtzum Bet* is unapparent at all before ZA *de SAG*.

The matter of *HaVaYaH* fulfilled with *Heyin* indicates that she lacks the fulfillment, but receives from her Upper *Partzuf*. Hence she is only double *HaVaYaH*, for two *HaVaYot* are BON in *Gimatria*.

The reason for it is that the fulfillment indicates the measure of the *Koma* extending by the *Zivug* of the *Ohr Elyon* on the *Masach* there. The *Masach* in *Partzuf* ZA, being in *Aviut de Behina Aleph*, extends the *Ohr* for *Malchut* too, whose *Masach* is very frail. It doesn't have sufficient *Aviut* for *Zivug de Hakaa* with the *Ohr Elyon*, hence she lacks the fulfillment of her *Behina*. All she has is double *HaVaYaH*, indicating the part of ZA in her.

Now you can see why *Hochma* and *Bina* are not considered the *Shoresh* of the *Olam*, and the *Olam* begins only in ZA. This is the meaning of the six days of creation, as their *Kelim* contain only from *Behinat Tzimtzum Aleph*. Thus, only ZA, being *Behinat HaVaYaH de* MA with fulfillment of *Alephin*, meaning *Tzimtzum Bet*, is the *Shoresh* for all the *Olamot*.

2. **What are *Otiot*?**

See answer No. 1.

3. **What are AHP in their Place?**

The first three *Tikkunim* of the thirteen *Tikkunim* of *Dikna* are called "AHP in their Place". It means that they did not come out from the *Behinot Rosh*, and they are *Behinot GE de Rosh* of the *Dikna*. They are named AHP only with respect to *Rosh de SAG*.

(Part 6, item 20)

4. **What is *Butzina de Kardinuta*?**

Butzina means illumination and *Kardinuta* means hardness or darkness. It implies the lower *Hey*, meaning *Behina Dalet*. This is the meaning of the lower *Hey* in the *Eynaim* in *Keter de Nekudim*, whose *He'arah* is uncovered. It is the *Nekuda* inside the *Vav*, meaning the *Melafom* that poured *Yesod de AK* to HB *de Nekudim*. Only the *Vav* actually appeared, but the *Nekuda* is concealed in it. This means that *Butzina de Kardinuta* is concealed in *Yesod de Ima*.

(Part 6, item 37)

5. **What is the Fissuring of the *Parsa*?**

The fissuring of the *Parsa* implies the annulment of the *Gevul* in her, separating between *Keter Hochma*, and *Bina* and ZON inside the *Toch* of the degree. Through the fissuring, *Bina* and ZON return to the degree as in the beginning.

(Part 6, item 15)

6. **What is One Over the Other?**

   One Over the Other means that the *Sefirot* stand by themselves and cannot receive or bestow upon each other. This is due to the disparity of form between each and every one of them, separating them from one another. In that state they stand one over the other according to the order of degrees; the *Panim* of the *Tachton* in the *Achor de Elyon*.

   For instance: ZA, whose *Panim* is *Behina Aleph*, equalizes with the *Achor de Bina*, who is also *Behina Aleph*. Also, *Panim* of *Bina*, being *Behina Bet*, equalizes with *Achor de Hochma*, which is also *Behina Bet*, etc. similarly. In that state they are opposite from one another and separated from one another.

   (Part 4, Chap 3, *Ohr Pnimi* item 30)

7. **What is *Holam*?**

   The *Nekudot* indicate primarily the *He'arat Zivug* emerging by the force of the connection of the lower *Hey* with the first *Hey*, called *Nekudot*.

   There are three *Behinot* in that:

1. When the lower *Hey* is in *Keter de Nekudim* in the form of Lower *Hey* in the *Eynaim* and *YHV* in the *AHP*. In that state she is called *Holam*, which is above the *Otiot YHV*.

   It is so because *Ohr Keter* is not poured to the *HB* from *Behinat* lower *Hey*, but only from *Behinat* first *Hey*.

2. As *Nekudot* under the *Otiot YHV*, which are the *Kelim* of *HB*. This is by the Upper *Zivug* of *AB* and *SAG*, lowering the lower *Hey* from the *Eynaim* to the *Peh* in the form of *Kamatz* under the *Otiot*.

   Even now the lower *Hey* is concealed in the *Kamatz*, which is *Behinat Yesod de Keter*, and the *YHV* still have no *He'arat* lower *Hey*.

3. In the form of *Nekudot* inside the *Otiot de YHV*. This is by the *He'arat Yesod de AK* on the *Behinat Melafom*, where the *Nekuda de* lower *Hey* is inside the *Vav*.

   This *He'arah* comes inside the *Otiot de YHV*, which are *HB*, from which elicit the Lower Seven *de Nekudim*.

   (Part 6, item 31, and *Histaklut Pnimit* item 19)

8. **What is *Taffel*?**

   The first *Sefira* in every degree contains all the *Behinot* below it. Hence, the Upper *Behina* is always considered the kernel of the degree, compared to which all other *Behinot* are secondary, and do not merit a name.

   (Part 6, item 8)

9. **What is "Coming out Strongly"?**

The greater the *Aviut* in the *Masach*, the more strongly the *Ohr* comes out. If the *Aviut* is frail, the *Ohr* does not come out strongly, meaning there is little *Ohr Hozer*, and the *Komat Ohr* it extends does not expand downward. Since the lower *Hey* connected with the *Nikvey Eynaim*, the *Orot* there are found to be coming out forcefully, expanding downward.

(Part 6, item 11)

10. **What are Twenty-two *Otiot*?**

The *Otiot* are the *Kelim* where the *Atzmut* clothes. They contain twenty-two heads of discernments, from which all the *Partzufim* are built. They are called, twenty-two *Otiot*. See answer No. 1.

(Part 6, item 53)

11. **What are Male *Mayim Elyonim*?**

See answer No. 1.

It explains there that *Keter* of the *Nekudim* is the *Mayim Elyonim* above the *Rakia*, which is the *Parsa*. HB de *Nekudim* is the *Mayim Tachtonim* under the *Rakia*.

It is known that *Keter* is the *Zachar*, and HB is its *Nekeva* (*Ohr Pnimi* item 23). Thus, *Mayim Elyonim* are considered *Zachar*, and *Mayim Tachtonim*, being HB, are *Behinat Nekeva*.

(Part 6, item 9)

12. **What are Female *Mayim Tachtonim*?**

See answers No. 11 and answer No. 1.

13. **What is *Melafom*?**

See answer No. 7.

14. **What is *Mazla*?**

Se'arot Dikna are called *Mazla*, as it is written, "Water shall flow from his branches etc." This is because their *Shefa* flows bit-by-bit until they join the greater *Orot* in the *Olamot* (see below answer No. 29).

(Part 6, item 2)

15. **What is *Mayin Nukvin*?**

It is known that two *Behinot Reshimot* were joined in the *Masach* through the *Hitpashtut* of *Nekudot de SAG* to MA and BON de AK ha Pnimi: *Behinot* first *Hey* in SAG, and the lower *Hey* in AK ha Pnimi. You find that the *Masach* consists of two females, *Bina* and *Malchut*, hence the name of the *Masach*

"Mayin Nukvin". From here on these two females are incorporated in it in every *Zivug* it makes with the *Ohr Elyon*.

(Part 6, item 15)

16. **What is Death?**

    Life is until the place where *Kav Ohr Ein Sof* reaches. After the *Sium* of the *Kav*, meaning below the point of *Tzimtzum*, the Light of life ceases. This is *Behinat* Death.

    Hence, the *Kelim* that fell to BYA, below the new point of *Tzimtzum*, are considered to have died there, as they were departed from the Light of life.

    (Part 6, item 39)

17. **What is Upper *Nekudot*?**

    See answer No. 7.

18. **What are *Nekudot* Under the *Otiot*?**

    See answer No. 7.

    Three *He'arot* operated in *Nekudim*: *Hevel ha Tabur*, *Hevel ha Yesod*, and *Hevel de Tzipornaim* of the *Raglaim*. The *Hevel Tabur* is the *Behinat Nekudot* above the *Otiot*, meaning *Holam*. *Hevel ha Yesod* is *Behinat Nekudot* inside the *Otiot*, being the *Melafom*, and *Hevel de Tzipornaim* of the *Raglaim* is the *Behinot Nekudot* under the *Otiot*.

    (Part 6, item 28, and *Ohr Pnimi* there)

19. **What is *Nitzotz de Kardinuta*?**

    See answer No. 4.

20. **What are *Nikvey Eynaim*?**

    Behina Aleph in the *Rosh* is called *Nikvey Eynaim* because *Hochma de Rosh* is called *Eynaim*, and because of the ascent of the lower *Hey* there, *Behinat Nukva* was also made in *Hochma*, called *Nikvey Eynaim*.

    (Part 6, item 7)

21. **What are *Nikvey Awzen*?**

    See answer No. 20.

    The two *Heys* joined in the association of *Midat ha Rachamim* with *Din*, and the lower *Hey* rose to the *Eynaim*. From then on a *Behinat Nukva* was made in all the *Sefirot* up to *Hochma*. These are the *Nekavim* (foramens) made in *Hotem*, *Awzen*, and the *Eynaim*. However, before they were connected, *Behinat Nukva* was only in the *Peh*.

22. **What is the Opening of the *Eynaim*?**

    He'arat Hochma is called "Opening of the *Eynaim*" because *Eynaim* are *Hochma*. (Part 6, item 51)

23. **What is *Parsa*?**

    Parsa is the premises of the liver (diaphragm) separating the breathing organs, which are the sustenance, from the feeding organs. It seemingly creates two *Gufim* within a single *Guf*. Similarly, when *Partzuf* MA and BON came out of the *Nikvey Eynaim*, it was divided into two *Partzufim* on the *Tabur* and the *Parsa*.

    From *Peh de Rosh SAG* to *Parsa* it is *Behinat* GAR *de* MA and BON, considered a complete *Partzuf* in and of itself. Its *Sium Raglaim* is on the *Tabur*, because it came out from the *Behinat Reshimot de Taamim de SAG* that didn't connect with the lower *Hey*.

    From *Parsa* down came out the lower BON, being the *Eser Sefirot de Nekudim*. They came out from *Behinat Nekudot de SAG*, and connected with the lower *Hey* below *Tabur*. Thus, the *Parsa* divides a single *Partzuf* of MA and BON into two *Partzufim*.

    (Part 6, item 9, and *Histaklut Pnimit* item 34)

24. **What is *Tzimtzum Bet*?**

    Tzimtzum NHY *de* AK is called *Tzimtzum Bet*. This is because similarly to *Tzimtzum Aleph* on *Behina Dalet* in *Ein Sof*, so here there was a *Tzimtzum* on *Behina Bet*.

    As *Kav Ohr de Ein Sof* stopped at the *Malchut* of NHY *de* AK, so *Kav Ohr Ein Sof* stopped here on *Bina de* NHY *de* AK. Thus *Bina*, ZA and *Malchut* remained under the point of *Tzimtzum* without *Ohr*, forming the three separated *Olamot*, called BYA: *Beria* from *Bina*, *Yetzira* from ZA and *Assiya* from *Malchut*.

    (Part 6, item 7)

25. **What are *Tzipornaim* of the *Raglaim*?**

    The *Behinot Sium* of every *Partzuf*, which is *Malchut de* NHY of the *Partzuf*, is called *Etzbaot Raglaim*. From the time of the *Tikun* of *Parsa* on, another force was made on the *Behinat Sium* of the *Partzuf*, relating to the association of the point of *Bina* in the *Tzimtzum*.

    When this additional force is in the place of *Tabur*, it is called *Parsa*; when it is in the place of *Sium* NHY, it is called *Tzipornaim*, namely *Tzipornaim* of the *Raglaim*.

    (Part 6, item 29)

26. **What is Separating *Rakia*?**

    The "Separating *Rakia*" is the *Parsa* placed in the *Eser Sefirot* of each degree by the connection of the two points, *Bina* and *Malchut*. It distinguishes *Keter* and *Hochma* in it as Male *Mayim Elyonim*, from the *Bina*, ZA and *Malchut* in it, being *Behinat* Female *Mayim Tachtonim*, See answer No. 11 and answer No. 1.

    (Part 6, item 9)

27. **What is *Shuruk*?**

    The *Melafom* is also called *Shuruk*, explained in above in answer No. 7.

    (Part 6, item 31)

28. **What are *Se'arot Rosh*?**

    The first *Zivug* for *Partzuf Nekudim* was in *Nikvey Eynaim* of *Rosh de SAG*. It did not take out the *AHP* of *Rosh de SAG* outwardly, since there is no absence in the spiritual.

    The matter of the division of the degree did not affect in *Rosh SAG* itself whatsoever, only as an addition to the *Partzuf*, being the *Partzuf Se'arot*. From *Nikvey Eynaim* up came out the *Se'arot Rosh*, and from there down the *Se'arot Dikna* in *Behinot AHP*.

    (*Ohr Pnimi* item 2)

29. **What are *Se'arot Dikna*?**

    See answer No. 28.

30. **What is *Shibolet ha Zakan*?**

    Shibolet ha Zakan is *Behinot AHP* that came out of the first *Rosh de Dikna* because the first three *Tikkunim de Dikna* are *Behinot GE*, meaning *Rosh de Dikna*. *Shibolet ha Zakan* is the *AHP* that came out of *Rosh de Dikna* into *Behinat Guf*, where the *Shefa* of the first three *Behinot Tikkunim* of *Dikna* accumulates.

    (Part 6 item 9, and *Ohr Pnimi* item 23)

Table of Questions for Topics

31. How are the ascents of the *Orot* to the *Rosh* of SAG different than in all the other *Partzufim*?
32. How many *Orot* rose from below, from *Tabur*, for MAN?
33. What is the new *Ohr* that emerged by the *Tzimtzum* NHY and their ascent upward?
34. Is the *Ohr* that came out of *Nikvey Eynaim Atzmut* or additions?
35. What is the *Koma* that came out of *Nikvey Eynaim*?
36. How many *Zivugim* were there for the purpose of *Nekudim*?
37. What is the gist and the *Atzmut* of *Nekudim*?
38. What is the first *Behina* of *Nekudim*?
39. What is the second *Behina* of *Nekudim*?
40. What is the third *Behina* of *Nekudim*?
41. Where do GAR de *Nekudim* take *Ohr*?
42. Why did GAR de *Nekudim* not die?
43. Why is there no cancellation in the *Keter*, but only in the *Achoraim* of AVI?
44. Why is the primary *He'arah* of *Nekudim* only through *Panim*?
45. Why does the *Guf de Nekudim* begin from *Daat* and not from *Keter*, as in every other place?
46. Why is *Keter* not called *Daat*?
47. From which place in *Dikna* do GAR de *Nekudim* extend?
48. What caused the ascent of the *Nekudot* from MA and BON?
49. Which renewal occurred in the ascent of the *Masach de SAG* compared to the other *Partzufim*?
50. How did *Behina Dalet* connect in the *Masach de SAG* after it had already been purified into *Behina Aleph*?
51. Why did *Komat Keter* not come out of the lower *Hey* in *Nikvey Eynaim* as in *Partzuf Galgalta*?
52. Why did the *Masach* rise to *Nikvey Eynaim* and not to *Peh*?
53. Why are all the *Tikkunim* dependent primarily on MA and BON?
54. Why is *Olam ha Nekudim* called BON only?

55. Which *Partzuf* of AK does the Rav deal with?
56. Where are the *Mochin de SAG* from?
57. Why does *SAG* begin from the *Awzen*?
58. Where does *SAG* end?
59. Where does *AB* end?
60. Where do *Taamim de SAG* end?
61. Where was the place of *Nekudot de SAG* prior to the *Tzimtzum*?
62. Why is only *Keter de SAG* called *Taamim*?
63. Why are the lower nine called *Nekudot*?
64. What is the *SAG de SAG de AK*?
65. Is the division of the degree apparent also in the *Rosh de SAG*?
66. What caused the division of MA and BON into two *Partzufim*?
67. What is the merit of MA and BON above *Tabur* compared to MA and BON below *Tabur*?
68. What caused the division of AVI and YESHSUT into two *Partzufim*?..
69. Did YESHSUT and GAR *de Nekudim* connect after the fissuring of the *Parsa*?
70. How many *Behinot* are there in *Partzuf Dikna*?
71. Why was the *Ohr Awzen* blocked at *Shibolet ha Zakan*?
72. What are the four divisions of *Nekudim*?
73. What is the meaning of "and the arms of his hands were made supple," and not his legs?
74. Where is the distinction of the lower *Hey* in the *Eynaim* and the *YHV* in the *AHP* most noticed?
75. What does it mean that the *Tzimtzum* was to diminish the *Ohr de Atzilut*?
76. What is the *Parsa*?
77. What is the correction of the *Parsa* for the purpose of *Beria*?
78. What is the difference between *Parsa* and *Sium Raglin*?
79. When was the *Parsa* made?
80. What is the fissuring of the *Parsa*?
81. Why is the return of the *AHP* to the *Rosh* named after the *Parsa*?
82. Why does the Difference between *HaVaYaH de AB* and *HaVaYaH de SAG* depends entirely on the filling of *Aleph* in the *Vav*?

83. Is the connection of the two *Heyin* permanent?
84. In which *Behina* of SAG was the *Zivug* for the *Nekudim*?
85. What is the primordial *Nekeva* of the *Olamot*?
86. Where do BYA stand?
87. How many fissures were caused by *Zivug* of AB and SAG?
88. What is the *Shoresh* for ABYA?
89. Where is the beginning of the association of *Midat ha Rachamim* with *Din*?
90. Where is the *Sium Raglin de AK ha Pnimi*?
91. Which is the fundamental action of all the innovations made in *Nekudim*?
92. What is the association of *Midat ha Rachamim* with *Din*?
93. What is the reason for the association of *Midat ha Rachamim* with *Din*?
94. What is the name *Mayin Nukvin*
95. Why is *Bina* called *Beria*?
96. What is the difference between *Tzimtzum Aleph* and *Tzimtzum Bet*?...
97. In which *Partzuf* is there *Katnut* and *Gadlut*?
98. When was *Zivug de AB* and SAG made?
99. Why is the new MA the *Taamim* of *Nekudim*?
100. Why is *Yesod de Elyon, Daat* to the *Tachton*?
101. Why does the lower *Hey* descend from the *Eynaim* through *Zivug* AB SAG?
102. What are the two operations that emerge by *Zivug de AB* and SAG?...
103. Through what were the correction of *Tikun Kavim* and ten *Kelim* in ZAT too?
104. What are the four steps of the lower *Hey* before it comes into the *Otiot*?
105. How many kinds of *Orot* operated in *Nekudim*?
106. What is the difference between *Daat Elyon* and *Daat Tachton*?
107. What is the difference between *He'arat NHY de Keter* and NHY de AK?
108. Where does the *Halbasha* of YESHSUT begin?
109. Why don't the *Nekudot* clothe any of the SAG, from which they stem?
110. Where does SAG clothe AB de AK?
111. Why do *Nekudim* clothe NHY de AK?

112. Why is the *Holam* on top of the *Otiot*?
113. Why is the *Shuruk* in the middle?
114. Why did *Abba* take the point of *Shuruk*?
115. Why are *Keter* and *Hochma* once called *Holam* and *Shuruk*, and once *Kamatz* and *Patach*?
116. Why are *Kamatz Patach* from the *Nekudot* under the *Otiot*?
117. Which *Behina* of *Kamatz Patach* did not break?
118. Why are the seven *Nekudot* in the shape of *Yodin*?
119. What is the difference between the *Nekuda* of *Holam* and *Kamatz*, as they are both *Keter*?
120. What is the main cause for the emergence of *Partzuf* MA and BON?...
121. What is the primary cause of a birth of a *Partzuf*?
122. How does *Ohr Makif* appear in the birth of *Partzufim*?
123. What mainly operates to emanate a second *Partzuf*?
124. How many *Nekudot* of *Sium* from *Tabur* to *Sium Raglin*?
125. How are there *Eser Sefirot* from *Tabur* down, which is only *Malchut*?.
126. How are there TNHYM below *Tabur*?
127. Why are MA and BON below *Tabur*?
128. Why must MA be associated with the lower *Hey*?
129. Why isn't there lower *Hey* in HB de *Nekudim*?
130. What is the reason that GAR de ZA de *Atzilut* remain in *Ima*?
131. What are the *Achoraim* de AVI that were cancelled?
132. Why are the lower seven in one *Kav*?
133. Where were ZON made?
134. Where were the *Kelim de Nekudim* made?
135. What does it mean that the *Kelim* were small?
136. What is the need for *Dinim* and *Klipot*?
137. What does it mean that the lower Seven are *Din* and the *Ohr* that comes to them is *Rachamim*?

Questions Regarding Cause and Consequence

138. What eventuates from the yearning of *Malchut de Ein Sof* for greater *Dvekut* with the *Ohr Elyon*?
139. What eventuates from the *Histalkut Ohr* from all four *Behinot*?
140. What eventuates from the *Masach*?
141. What eventuates from the *Ohr Hozer*?

    [For the Creation of *Partzuf AB de AK*]

142. What eventuates from the *Masach de Tabur de Galgalta*?
143. What eventuates from the *Bitush de Ohr Makif* in *Ohr Pnimi* in *Partzuf Galgalta*?
144. What eventuates from the disappearance of the last *Behina*?
145. What eventuates from of the two *Reshimot Zachar* and *Nekeva* that rose from the *Guf de Galgalta*?
146. What eventuates from the two *Zivugim* of ZON that the *Masach* makes in its *Hitkalelut* in *Hotem* in *Rosh de Galgalta*?
147. What eventuates from the manifestation of the *Aviut de Guf* in the *Masach* and the *Reshimot*?
148. What eventuates from the two *Zivugim* that the *Masach* makes in the place of *Chazeh de Galgalta*?

    [For the Creation of *Partzuf SAG de AK*]

149. What eventuates from the *Masach de Tabur de AB*?
150. What eventuates from the *Bitush de Ohr Makif* in *Ohr Pnimi de AB*?...
151. What eventuates from the disappearance of the last *Behina de AB*?...
152. What eventuates from the two *Reshimot Zachar* and *Nekeva* that rose from *Histalkut AB*?
153. What eventuates from the two *Zivugim de ZON* that the *Masach* made in its *Hitkalelut* in *Awzen de Rosh AB*?
154. What eventuates from the manifestation of the *Aviut de Guf* in the *Masach*?
155. What eventuates from the two *Zivugim* that the *Masach* makes in the place of *Chazeh de AB*?

    [For the Creation of *Partzuf* MA and BON *de AK*]

156. What eventuates from the *Masach de Tabur de SAG*?
157. What eventuates from the *Bitush de Ohr Makif* in *Ohr Pnimi de SAG*?

158. What eventuates from the concealment of the last *Behina de SAG*?
159. What eventuates from the two *Reshimot ZON* that rose in the *Nikvey Eynaim de Rosh de SAG*?
160. What eventuates from the *Hitkalelut* of the *Reshimot* in the *Zivugim* in the *Nikvey Eynaim de Rosh de SAG*?
161. What eventuates from the manifestation of *Aviut de Guf* in the *Masach* and the *Reshimot*?
162. What eventuates from the descent of the *Masach* to its corresponding *Behinot* in the *Hitzoniut de Guf de SAG*?
163. What eventuates from the elicitation of the *AHP* from all the degrees?
164. How are the actions connected to one another through cause and consequence from *Tzimtzum Aleph* to the end of *Olam ha Nekudim* in *Katnut*?
165. What ten actions were taken through the completion of *Partzuf Galgalta de AK*?
166. How are these ten actions connected by cause and consequence?
167. What are the fourteen actions generally executed in the creation of a *Partzuf*?
168. How are the fourteen actions of the creation of the *Partzuf* interconnected?
169. What are the two actions added in *Partzuf SAG*?
170. What are the thirteen actions added in *Partzuf Nekudim*?
171. How are the thirteen actions interconnected by the above order of cause and consequence?

31. **How are the ascents of the *Orot* to the *Rosh* of *SAG* different than in all the other *Partzufim*?**

    The *Reshimot de SAG* connected with the *Reshimot* of the Inner MA and BON. This caused a new *Tzimtzum* in the *Nekuda de Behina Bet*.

    (*Ohr Pnimi* item 7)

32. **How many *Orot* rose from below, from *Tabur*, for MAN?**

    Two kinds of *Orot*: the lower nine *de SAG*, and ZON *de AK ha Pnimi*.

    (*Ohr Pnimi* item 7)

33. **What is the new *Ohr* that emerged by the *Tzimtzum* NHY and their ascent upward?**

    By the *Tzimtzum* of NHY, the *Reshimot* contained in it, rose to the *Rosh de SAG*, to *Nikvey Eynaim*, which are *Behina Aleph*, and a *Koma de Behina Aleph* extended, called MA and BON. When the *Aviut de Guf* in the *Masach* was recognized, it descended from there to its place in the *Guf*, which is *Tabur*. In addition, it is *Behinat Katnut de Nekudim*.

    (*Ohr Pnimi* item 10)

34. **Is the *Ohr* that came out of *Nikvey Eynaim Atzmut* or additions?**

    It is the *Atzmut* of the *Ohr de Nekudim* because what appears in the beginning of the creation is the *Atzmut*.

    (*Ohr Pnimi* item 10)

35. **What is the *Koma* that came out of *Nikvey Eynaim*?**

    The *Koma* is primarily *Behina Aleph*, which is *Komat ZA*. However, there is also *Behinat Zachar* there, having a *Koma* of *Behina Bet* as *Hitlabshut* that remains from the last *Behina*.

    (*Ohr Pnimi* item 14)

36. **How many *Zivugim* were there for the purpose of *Nekudim*?**

    Two kinds of *Zivugim*:

    - The first *Zivug* was by the ascent of the *Masach* and the *Reshimot* to the *Rosh de SAG* to *Nikvey Eynaim*, from which came the *Behinat Katnut de Nekudim*.
    - The second *Zivug* was by the *Zivug de AB* and *SAG* and the fissuring of the *Parsa*. Consequently, the AHP returned to *Behinat Rosh*, and from here emerged the *Gadlut de Nekudim*.

    (*Ohr Pnimi* item 14)

37. **What is the gist and the *Atzmut* of *Nekudim*?**

    The *Ohr* that came out of the *Nikvey Eynaim* is considered the *Atzmut* of the *Nekudim*.

    (*Ohr Pnimi* item 14)

38. **What is the first *Behina* of *Nekudim*?**

    The first *Rosh* that came out of *Tabur de AK ha Pnimi* and up to the *Chazeh*, called YESHSUT, is the first *Behina* of the *Nekudim*. However, it is considered *Akudim* since the *Aviut* in the *Masach* that stands in the place of *Tabur* is completely inactive from below upward, hence this *Rosh* has nothing of *Behinat Nekudim*.

    (*Ohr Pnimi* item 20)

39. **What is the second *Behina* of *Nekudim*?**

    AHP that came out of *Rosh* ah *Aleph* and were considered and valued as *Behinat Guf* and receiving from it, are the second *Behina* of the *Nekudim*. Also, they are the *GAR de Nekudim*.

    (*Ohr Pnimi* item 20)

40. **What is the third *Behina* of *Nekudim*?**

    The *Behinot* of the actual *Guf* of *Nekudim*, below the AHP, are the third *Behina de Nekudim*. They are called "the seven lower *Sefirot* of the *Nekudim*".

    (*Ohr Pnimi* item 20)

41. **Where do GAR *de Nekudim* take *Ohr*?**

    GAR *de Nekudim* receive from the first three *Tikkunim* of *Dikna* in their gathering place, called *Shibolet ha Zakan*. This is because the three *Tikkunim* of *Dikna* in their place in the *Rosh* are *Behinat Rosh ha Aleph* of the *Dikna*.

    (*Ohr Pnimi* item 20)

42. **Why did GAR *de Nekudim* not die?**

    Because they received their *He'arah* from *Shibolet ha Zakan*. However, the lower seven received their *He'arah* only from the *Hotem Peh* and therefore died.

    (Item 23)

43. **Why is there no cancellation in the *Keter*, but only in the *Achoraim* of AVI?**

    Because the *Keter* is the *Behinat Zachar* of the MA and BON, having *Behina Bet de Hitlabshut*, while *Hochma* and *Bina* are the *Behinat Nekeva*, having only *Aviut de Behina Aleph*. Hence the *Zachar* has *Komat Bina*, which is *Ohr Awzen*, and he also has *Behinot GAR* from the beginning of its creation.

For that reason even its *Achoraim* were not canceled, whereas the *Nekeva*, which is *HB*, has only *Komat Behina Aleph*, which is *ZA*. Thus, she could not receive *Komat GAR* and their *Achoraim* were canceled.

(*Ohr Pnimi* item 23)

44. Why is the primary He'arah of Nekudim only through Panim?

Because the *Ohr Eynaim* does not shine to the *Kelim de Achor* but to the *Kelim de Panim*, above *Tabur*, which are here through the *Peh*. The lower seven are considered from *Tabur* down because the *AHP* came out and became *Behinot HGT*. However, some *He'arah* does come to them through the sides as *Ohr Hassadim*.

(*Ohr Pnimi* item 25)

45. Why does the Guf de Nekudim begin from Daat and not from Keter, as in every other place?

Because *Rosh ha Aleph* took the two *Sefirot Keter* and *Hochma*, called *GE*, and the second *Rosh* has only *Bina* and *ZON*, meaning *AHP de Rosh ha Aleph*. It is known that *Rosh ha Aleph* does not join *Partzuf Nekudim* in any way; only *Rosh ha Bet* is considered the *Rosh* of the *Nekudim*.

It is also known that the entire amount in the *Rosh* travels through and clothes in the *Guf*. Thus, since there are no more than three *Kelim Bina*, *ZA* and *Malchut* in the *Rosh*, there are also not more than these three *Kelim* in the *Guf*, lacking *Keter* and *Hochma*.

(*Ohr Pnimi* item 26)

46. Why is Keter not called Daat?

Because there is *Ohr Awzen* in *Keter* too, since there is *Behinat Zachar* there, having *Behina Bet de Hitlabshut*.

(*Ohr Pnimi* item 26)

47. From which place in Dikna do GAR de Nekudim extend?

From *Shibolet ha Zakan*.

(*Ohr Pnimi* item 4)

48. What caused the ascent of the Nekudot from MA and BON?

Because the *Masach* had been purified of its entire *Aviut* and equalized with *Malchut* of the *Rosh*, as it is known in the other *Partzufim*.

(*Ohr Pnimi* item 6)

49. **Which renewal occurred in the ascent of the *Masach de SAG* compared to the other *Partzufim*?**

   Here in SAG, the *Masach* consists of *Reshimot* of two *Partzufim*: its own *Partzuf*, and *Partzuf Galgalta de AK*.

   (*Ohr Pnimi* item 6)

50. **How did *Behina Dalet* connect in the *Masach de SAG* after it had already been purified into *Behina Aleph*?**

   Behina Dalet is primarily from *Tabur de Partzuf Galgalta de AK* downward. Even though the *Masach* has already been purified from there, it still does not relate to the *Kelim* in any way, as there is no *Hizdakchut* in the *Kelim*.

   However, when the *Kelim* are emptied of *Ohr*, they are quiet, inactive. Thus, when *Ohr SAG* reached there, *Behina Dalet* returned and reappeared as in the beginning.

   (*Histaklut Pnimit* item 7)

51. **Why did *Komat Keter* not come out of the lower *Hey* in *Nikvey Eynaim* as in *Partzuf Galgalta*?**

   Because the First *Hey* is the principal, since the *Masach* is from *Partzuf SAG*. The lower *Hey* is subordinate to it, having connected in it through *He'arat SAG* below *Tabur*.

   (*Histaklut Pnimit* item 7)

52. **Why did the *Masach* rise to *Nikvey Eynaim* and not to *Peh*?**

   Because the last *Behina* does not leave a *Reshima*, except from *Behinat Hitlabshut*, from which there is no *Hitpashtut Kelim*. Also, nothing remains from the *Behinat Hamshacha* but *Behina Aleph*, hence it rose to its corresponding *Behina* in the *Rosh*, which is the *Eynaim*.

   (*Histaklut Pnimit* item 7)

53. **Why are all the *Tikkunim* dependent primarily on MA and BON?**

   Because the lower *Hey* only connected with MA and BON, and not in its previous *Partzufim*. She comes from the below *Tabur de AK ha Pnimi*, being the *Shoresh* of any *Tzimtzum* and *Din* in the *Olamot*.

   (*Histaklut Pnimit* item 8)

54. **Why is *Olam ha Nekudim* called BON only?**

   Because everything that is considered MA broke in the breaking of the vessels, and only its *Behinat* First *Hey* remained, being ascribed to BON.

   (*Histaklut Pnimit* item 8)

55. **Which *Partzuf* of AK does the Rav deal with?**

    Partzuf SAG de AK. This is because it is forbidden to engage in the first two *Partzufim Galgalta de AK* and *AB de AK*.

    (*Ohr Pnimi* item 1)

56. **Where are the *Mochin de SAG* from?**

    HGT de AK are *Neshama* and *Mochin* to the *Rosh de SAG*.

    (*Ohr Pnimi* item 1)

57. **Why does *SAG* begin from the *Awzen*?**

    Because *Partzuf SAG* comes out on a *Masach* of *Aviut de Behina Bet*, which raises *Ohr Hozer* and clothes only up to *Bina*, whose name in the *Rosh* is *Awzen*.

    (*Ohr Pnimi* item 1)

58. **Where does *SAG* end?**

    Before *Tzimtzum Bet* expanded to the *Sium Raglin* of AK, and from *Tzimtzum Bet* onward, it rises and ends above *Tabur de AK*.

    (*Ohr Pnimi* item 1)

59. **Where does *AB* end?**

    Above *Tabur de AK ha Pnimi*. This is because the lower *Hey* is not contained in the *Masach de AB*, hence it cannot expand below *Tabur*, where *Behinot* lower *Hey* is, meaning *Malchut de AK ha Pnimi*.

    (*Ohr Pnimi* item 1)

60. **Where do *Taamim de SAG* end?**

    They end equally with *Sium Raglin de AB de AK* because the *Zachar* clothed in *Kli de Keter*, which is *Taamim*. It has *Komat Hochma*, like the *AB*, and it too, like *AB*, cannot shine to the lower *Hey* below *Tabur*.

    (*Ohr Pnimi* item 1)

61. **Where was the place of *Nekudot de SAG* prior to the *Tzimtzum*?**

    They begin from *Tabur de AK ha Pnimi* and end at its *Sium Raglin*.

    (*Ohr Pnimi* item 1)

62. **Why is only *Keter de SAG* called *Taamim*?**

    Because first all the *Orot* come in *Kli de Keter*. Only after the *Masach* begins to purify and diminish do the other *Komot Hochma*, *Bina* and *ZON* begin to emerge during the degrees of its purification. It is known that before the *Masach* begins to purify, it is *Ohr Yashar* and *Rachamim*. This is only *Kli de Keter*, hence the name *Rachamim*.

However, the rest of the lower nine come out along with the *Hizdakchut* of the *Masach*; that is why they are called *Nekudot*. It indicates that they are *Ohr Hozer* and *Din*.

(*Ohr Pnimi* item 3)

63. **Why are the lower nine called *Nekudot*?**

    See above answer No. 62.

64. **What is the *SAG de SAG de AK*?**

    That part of SAG incorporated in the lower *Hey* is called *SAG de SAG*, meaning the *Nekudot* of SAG that came out as lower *Hey* in the *Eynaim* and YHV in the *AHP*. However, that part of SAG not incorporated in *Behinat* lower *Hey* is called *Taamim de SAG*, or *AB de SAG*, or *AVI*.

    (*Ohr Pnimi* item 4)

65. **Is the division of the degree apparent also in the *Rosh de SAG*?**

    No division of the degree is apparent in the *Rosh* of SAG, although it is where the *Zivug* of the lower *Hey* in the *Eynaim* is rooted. Instead, a new *Partzuf* is added there, in the form of *Se'arot*, whose *AHP* departed, called *Se'arot Dikna*.

    (*Ohr Pnimi* item 2)

66. **What caused the division of MA and BON into two *Partzufim*?**

    The *Masach* that purified and rose from the SAG consists of two *Behinot*: *Reshimot de Taamim*, and *Reshimot de Nekudot*. Thus, two kinds of *Zivugim* were made on it:

    1. From the *Zivug* on the *Reshimot de Taamim* came out the MA and BON *Elyon*, clothing the place of *Taamim*, which is from *Peh de SAG* to *Tabur*.

    2. From the *Zivug* on the *Reshimot de Nekudot de SAG* came out the MA and BON *Tachton*, clothing the place where *Nekudot de SAG* stood, from *Tabur* down. This MA and BON *Tachton* is the one called *Eser Sefirot de Nekudim*.

    (*Histaklut Pnimit* item 24)

67. **What is the merit of MA and BON above *Tabur* compared to MA and BON below *Tabur*?**

    As GAR compared to VAK, or as AVI compared to ZON.

    (*Histaklut Pnimit* item 24)

68. **What caused the division of AVI and YESHSUT into two *Partzufim*?**

    The issue of the *Hitpashtut* of the lower nine below *Tabur de AK ha Pnimi* to the place of the lower *Hey* and *Behina Dalet* caused the division of SAG into two *Partzufim*. This is because the *Taamim* that did not mix with the lower

Hey and end above *Tabur*, are considered the same as AVI compared to the *Nekudot* that descended below *Tabur* and mixed with *Behina Dalet*. Also, the *Nekudot* to the *Taamim* are as YESHSUT to AVI.

(Item 6)

69. **Did YESHSUT and GAR de Nekudim connect after the fissuring of the *Parsa*?**

    The issue of the cancellation of the *Gevul* of the *Parsa* was only for the time being. Hence the lower *Hey* in YESHSUT is considered permanent and not as descending below *Tabur* to connect with the GAR de *Nekudim*. Only its *He'arah* alone descends to the GAR de *Nekudim*.

    (Ohr Pnimi item 17)

70. **How many *Behinot* are there in *Partzuf Dikna*?**

    There are three *Behinot* in *Dikna*:

    1. The first three *Tikkunim* of *Dikna*, connected at the *Rosh* in the Upper *Lechi* (cheek).
    2. *Shibolet ha Zakan*, which is the *Behinat AHP* that exit from the *Rosh*.
    3. The other *Tikkunim* of *Dikna*.

    (Ohr Pnimi item 19)

71. **Why was the *Ohr Awzen* blocked at *Shibolet ha Zakan*?**

    Because the entire *Ohr Awzen* in the *Ohr Eynaim* is merely the *Behinat Zachar*, having *Behina Bet de Hitlabshut*. It is known that *Behinat Zachar* has no *Behinat Hitpashtut* to *Kelim*. Hence, the *Behinat Kli de Zachar* is blocked at *Shibolet ha Zakan*, which is the *Behinat Keter de Shibolet*.

    Also, in HB de *Shibolet*, being its *Behinat Nekeva*, its *He'arah de Zachar* reaches, but it does not expand at all below the *Shibolet*, as it lacks *Behinat Hamshacha*.

    (Ohr Pnimi item 24)

72. **What are the four divisions of *Nekudim*?**

    There is the *Keter* of *Nekudim* here, where the *Etzem* of the *Ohr de Awzen*, being *Behinat Zachar*, has *Behina Bet de Hitlabshut*, being *Behinat GE de Rosh* of the *Nekudim*. There is also *Behinat HB*, which are *Behinat AHP* that went outside and became HGT, though they are *Behinat Rosh* at their *Shoresh*.

    After that there is the *Behinat* actual *Guf* of the *Nekudim*, which is ZAT. There are two *Behinot* there too: HGT, considered GAR de VAK, and NHY, which are the ZON de VAK.

    (Ohr Pnimi item 26)

73. **What is the meaning of "and the arms of his hands were made supple," and not his legs?**

    The *Parsa* consists of *Behina Bet* and *Behina Dalet* because of the ascent of *NHY* to *HGT*, since *Behina Bet* that operates in *HGT*, which are the *SAG*, with *Behina Dalet*, operating in *NHY de AK ha Pnimi*. Then the *Ohr de Eynaim* did not reach *ZAT de Nekudim*, only the *GAR* alone.

    However, by the force of the *Zivug de AB* and *SAG*, a new *Ohr* came, fissuring the *Parsa*. It canceled the *Gevul* because it lowered the lower *Hey* to her place and *Ohr HGT* returned and illuminated to *NHY* as in the beginning. At that time the lower seven of *Nekudim* received *He'arat SAG* too, thus the *Ohr* itself is considered *Ohr de HGT*, meaning of the *SAG*.

    It is said about that, "and the arms of his hands were made supple," but the reception place is considered the *Tzipornaim* of the *Raglaim*. This is *Behinat Gevul* in the *Parsa*, ending the *SAG* from the lower seven, received because of its fissuring. Thus, from the perspective of the reception, it is considered *Raglaim*, and from the perspective of the *Ohr* itself, it is considered hands.

    (*Ohr Pnimi* item 28)

74. **Where is the distinction of the lower *Hey* in the *Eynaim* and the *YHV* in the *AHP* most noticed?**

    It is most noticed in the *GAR de Nekudim*, called *Rosh ha Bet*.

    (*Histaklut Pnimit* item 10)

75. **What does it mean that the *Tzimtzum* was to diminish the *Ohr de Atzilut*?**

    All the degrees were divided by two through *Tzimtzum NHY*, to *GE* and *AHP*. Only *GE* remained in the *Atzilut* of the degree, and the *AHP* became the *Beria* of the degree.

    This is what happened in all the degrees until *Bina* and *ZON* of *Eser Sefirot de NHY* became *Behinat* "separated *Beria*". Thus the *Atzilut* was diminished in all the degrees through *Tzimtzum NHY*.

    (*Histaklut Pnimit* item 14)

76. **What is the *Parsa*?**

    See answer No. 23 and Answer 79.

77. **What is the correction of the *Parsa* for the purpose of *Beria*?**

    Through the *Tikun* of *Parsa* in such a way that the lower *Hey* can descend to her place, the *AHP* that came out and became the *Beria* of the degree return to the *Atzilut* of the degree.

    (*Histaklut Pnimit* item 14)

78. **What is the difference between *Parsa* and *Sium Raglin*?**

    The *Parsa* is considered the *Sium Raglin* of the inner *Partzuf*. Like the *Parsa* inside the intestines of a person separates the breathing, vitality organs, from the feeding organs, so the *Parsa* separates SAG above *Tabur* from the other half of the *Partzuf* below *Tabur*. This is so even though these two halves are one *Partzuf*, but the *Etzbaot Raglaim* are *Behinot Sium* for a whole *Partzuf*.

    (*Ohr Pnimi* item 9)

79. **When was the *Parsa* made?**

    The *Parsa* was made after the *Masach* was incorporated in the *Zivug de Rosh* SAG in the *Nikvey Eynaim* from which it descended to the place of *Tabur*. It generated *Eser Sefirot de Rosh* from *Nikvey Eynaim* upward, meaning from *Tabur* up, called YESHSUT, and the two *Heyin*, the First *Hey* and the lower *Hey* connected in these *Nikvey Eynaim* at the *Peh* of *Tabur*.

    Then a *Behinat Parsa* expanded by that connection, generally considered the *Behinat Sium* on the GAR. However, she particularly ends three *Partzufim*:

    1. She ends *Nekudot de SAG* so that they do not expand to shine below *Tabur* once more as prior to *Tzimtzum* NHY. This is because the point of *Sium de SAG* was in her because of the incorporation of the lower *Hey* in her.

    2. She has the point of *Sium* on the MA and BON *Elyon*, which also came out of the *Nikvey Eynaim*, though she came out of the *Behinot Reshimot de Taamim de SAG* that are not mixed in the lower *Hey*. Thus, they too ended on the *Parsa*.

       Because there is *Behina Bet de Hitlabshut* in them, meaning the *Zachar*, whose *Koma* reaches the *Awzen*, they are considered SAG, *Behinat AVI*.

    3. The third is that *Rosh ha Aleph*, the *Behinat GE* of the *Nekudim*, considered *Akudim* because the lower *Hey* in its *Eynaim* cannot act at all from below upward.

    Thus, the *Parsa* ends three *Partzufim*, and the *Ohr* that descends below *Parsa* is but *Ohr Achoraim*, meaning VAK without GAR. Hence, the HB de *Nekudim* are devoid of GAR.

    (*Ohr Pnimi* item 9)

80. **What is the fissuring of the *Parsa*?**

    Canceling the partition between the GE of the degree and its AHP is considered the fissuring of the *Parsa*, meaning the canceling of the *Gevul* in it. This is done by lowering the lower *Hey* to her actual place.

    (*Histaklut Pnimit* item 14)

81. **Why is the return of the *AHP* to the *Rosh* named after the *Parsa*?**

    The diminution of the *Ohr de Atzilut*, which is the erection of the degree on the two *Sefirot Keter* and *Hochma* alone, and the removing of the *AHP* from there, is done by the ascent of the lower *Hey* to the *Nikvey Eynaim de Rosh ha Aleph*. This is because the lower *Hey* was associated with the First *Hey* there, and never descends from there.

    However, there are two *Tikkunim* in the *Parsa*, extending from this connection: lowering the lower *Hey* from the *Behinat* First *Hey*, and returning the *AHP* to the *Atzilut* of the degree.

    Aleph א is the *Behinat* "diagonal" in her, meaning the connection is not fixed in her, but turns this and that way. This is because she is a branch off the Upper connection in the *Nikvey Eynaim de Rosh ha Aleph*, and the branch is not as strong as the *Shoresh*, making such a separation in her possible.

    The second: there is a concealment force in her, over the lower *Hey* in the *Nikvey Eynaim de Rosh ha Aleph*, so that it does not manifest its force during the descent of the lower *Hey* to her place.

    (*Histaklut Pnimit* items 15, 34)

82. **Why does the Difference between *HaVaYaH de AB* and *HaVaYaH de SAG* depends entirely on the filling of *Aleph* in the *Vav*?**

    See answer No. 1 here.

83. **Is the connection of the two *Heyin* permanent?**

    The connection of the two *Heyin* is permanent, but the difference in them is only regarding the concealment and the revelation, where at one time the lower *Hey* is disclosed, and another time the lower *Hey* is concealed, not manifesting its power.

    (*Ohr Pnimi* item 6)

84. **In which *Behina* of *SAG* was the *Zivug* for the *Nekudim*?**

    The *Masach* that was purified from the *Guf de SAG* consists of two *Behinot Reshimot*: *Reshimot de Taamim* and *Reshimot de Nekudot*. For the purpose of *Nekudim* there was a *Zivug* on the *Behinot Nekudot* incorporated in the *Masach*, which are the *Behinot* lower nine *de SAG* (see answer No. 66).

    (*Ohr Pnimi* item 6)

85. **What is the primordial *Nekeva* of the *Olamot*?**

    Malchut de YESHSUT that the *Eser Sefirot de Nekudim* emanated from is the primordial female to the *Olamot*.

    (*Ohr Pnimi* item 6)

86. **Where do BYA stand?**

   From the place of the new point of *Tzimtzum* in *Bina de Eser Sefirot de NHY*, being the place of *Tabur de Nekudim*, down to the place of the point of *Tzimtzum Aleph*. This is the *Malchut* of the *Eser Sefirot de NHY de AK*, the place of the separated BYA. It is so because *Bina* is the place for *Olam Beria*, the ZA for *Olam Yetzira* and *Malchut* for *Olam Assiya*.

   (*Ohr Pnimi* item 7)

87. **How many fissures were caused by Zivug of AB and SAG?**

   Two fissures:

   - The first whereby the *Zivug* of AB and SAG a new *Ohr* descended and fissured the *Parsa*, meaning lowered the lower *Hey* from there and the *Gevul* was canceled.

   - The second split the walls of the *Kelim de AK* through the *Peh de Yesod* and that new *Ohr* came to the *Eser Sefirot de Nekudim* as well.

   (*Ohr Pnimi* item 16)

88. **What is the Shoresh for ABYA?**

   The *Shoresh* for the four *Olamot* ABYA is *Olam ha Nekudim*. However, prior to that, there is no *Shoresh* to the *Olamot* there since there hasn't been the association of *Midat ha Rachamim* with *Din* there.

   (Beginning of *Histaklut Pnimit*)

89. **Where is the beginning of the association of Midat ha Rachamim with Din?**

   In *Olam ha Nekudim*.

   (Beginning of *Histaklut Pnimit*)

90. **Where is the Sium Raglin de AK ha Pnimi?**

   At *Nekuda de Olam ha Zeh*.

   (*Histaklut Pnimit* item 1)

91. **Which is the fundamental action of all the innovations made in Nekudim?**

   The *Hitpashtut* of *Nekudot de SAG* into the inner MA and BON *de AK* where they connected with the lower *Hey*. This is the fundamental action for all the innovations made in *Olam ha Nekudim*.

   (*Ohr Pnimi* item 5)

92. **What is the association of *Midat ha Rachamim* with *Din*?**

    The connection of the two *Heyin*, the First *Hey* and the lower *Hey*. This is called "the association of *Midat ha Rachamim* with *Din*", because *Bina* is *Rachamim* and *Malchut* is *Din*.

    (*Ohr Pnimi* item 6)

93. **What is the reason for the association of *Midat ha Rachamim* with *Din*?**

    The *Hitpashtut* of the lower nine *de SAG* inside the Inner MA and BON *de* AK caused the connection of the two *Heyin* together, which is the association of *Midat ha Rachamim* with *Din*.

    (*Ohr Pnimi* item 6)

94. **What is the name *Mayin Nukvin***

    After the two *Heyin* were connected in that *Masach*, it was called *Mayin Nukvin*. It is named after the *Nukvin* (females) connected in it, namely *Bina* and *Malchut*.

    (*Ohr Pnimi* item 6)

95. **Why is *Bina* called *Beria*?**

    Since the ascent of the lower *Hey* to *Nikvey Eynaim* onward, when *Bina* departed from the degree, *Bina* acquired the name *Beria*, from the word *Batei Barai* (outskirts).

    (*Histaklut Pnimit* item 26)

96. **What is the difference between *Tzimtzum Aleph* and *Tzimtzum Bet*?**

    Tzimtzum Aleph was only on *Behina Dalet*, and *Tzimtzum Bet* was on *Behina Bet* too. Also, *Tzimtzum Aleph* was absolute, while in *Tzimtzum Bet* there is the *Tikun* of the *Parsa*, which sometimes returns *Behina Bet* to *Atzilut*.

    (*Histaklut Pnimit* item 27)

97. **In which *Partzuf* is there *Katnut* and *Gadlut*?**

    Only in *Partzuf* BON is there *Gadlut* and *Katnut*. The *Katnut* is when the lower *Hey* is in the *Eynaim*, and the *Gadlut* is when the lower *Hey* descends to her place. However, that matter cannot be seen in the three *Partzufim* Galgalta, AB and SAG, where the lower *Hey* is not involved.

    (*Histaklut Pnimit* item 28)

98. **When was *Zivug de AB* and SAG made?**

    After the *Ohr* that came out of *Nikvey Eynaim* expanded to its place and the *Atzilut* was diminished into merely *Keter* and *Hochma*, the *Nekudot de SAG* remained above *Tabur* and couldn't come down below *Tabur*. This whole diminution caused *Behinat* MAN, and awakening of the *Zivug* of AB and SAG, whose *Ohr* returned and lowered the lower *Hey* to her place, splitting the *Parsa*, and *Ohr* SAG expanded below *Tabur* once more.

(*Ohr Pnimi* item 14, and *Histaklut Pnimit* item 17)

99. **Why is the new MA the *Taamim* of *Nekudim*?**

Because those *Taamim*, meaning the *Gadlut* that came out on *Olam ha Nekudim* was not kept there. Only afterwards the new MA came and corrected them, and then they existed. That is the reason the *Taamim* are named after the new MA.

(*Ohr Pnimi* item 1)

100. **Why is *Yesod de Elyon, Daat* to the *Tachton*?**

The place of the *Masach* and the *Zivug* is called *Yesod*. Hence, the *Behinat* lower *Hey* in the *Nikvey Eynaim de Keter de Nekudim* is called *Yesod* of the *Keter*.

When *Yesod de Keter* is above HB, their YHV became *Behinat* HGT. However, when *Yesod de Keter*, which is the lower *Hey*, extend below YHV, as *Kamatz*, then HB return to the *Rosh*, and YHV that were HGT now become HBD.

It turns out that through *Yesod de Keter*, *Tifferet*, which is *Vav*, becomes *Behinat Daat*. Thus, *Yesod de Elyon* becomes *Daat* in the *Tachton* because *Tifferet* is turned into *Daat* through *Yesod de Keter* which extends to the place of the *Vav de HB*, which is *Tifferet*.

(*Ohr Pnimi* item 30)

101. **Why does the lower *Hey* descend from the *Eynaim* through *Zivug* AB SAG?**

Because AB never connected with the lower *Hey*. Hence, when *Mochin de AB* are poured to SAG, they lower the lower *Hey* from the *Eynaim* of SAG to the *Peh*, as the lower *Hey* is not found in the *Eynaim de AB*.

(*Histaklut Pnimit* item 17)

102. **What are the two operations that emerge by *Zivug de* AB and SAG?**
    1. Lowering the lower *Hey* from the *Keter* of the *Nekudim* to her place to *Peh de Nekudim*, and returning the YHV to *Behinat* HBD *de Rosh*.
    2. A new *Ohr* that extends and fissures the *Parsa*, expanding to the Inner NHY de AK and returning *Bina* and ZON to *Atzilut*.

(*Histaklut Pnimit* item 18)

103. **Through what were the correction of *Tikun Kavim* and ten *Kelim* in ZAT too?**

Through *Ibur* and *Yenika* (to be explained in the next part).

(*Ohr Pnimi* item 40)

104. **What are the four steps of the lower *Hey* before it comes into the *Otiot*?**
   1. From *Nikvey Eynaim de Rosh de SAG* to *Nikvey Eynaim de YESHSUT*, where they permanently connect to *Behinot Shoresh* to MA and BON in their *Katnut*, which is their primary self and *Atzmut*.
   2. From *Nikvey Eynaim de YESHSUT* to *Nikvey Eynaim de Keter de Nekudim*, where there is the *Tikun* of the *Parsa* for the *Gadlut* of MA and BON.
   3. From *Nikvey Eynaim de Keter* to *Peh de Nekudim*, as *Kamatz* under the *Otiot* YHV. This is because then the *HB* return to *Behinat Rosh* and YHV become HBD. This is enough for the correction of the *Rosh*, but not yet for the ZAT.
   4. Its coming from *Yesod AK* as *Nekuda* inside the *Otiot*, meaning *Melafom*, which is a *Nekuda* inside the *Vav* ו into the *HB de Nekudim*, by which the *HB* mate and beget the lower seven of *Nekudim*.

   (*Histaklut Pnimit* item 29)

105. **How many kinds of *Orot* operated in *Nekudim*?**

   Three *Orot*:
   1. *Ohr* that came out through the *Eynaim*, from which comes the primary *Atzmut* of the *Nekudim*, though it is *Behinat Katnut de Nekudim*.
   2. The *Ohr* that extends through the *Zivug de AB SAG* that fissured the *Parsa* and illuminated to the *Nekudim* through *Yesod de AK*. From here comes the *Gadlut de Nekudim*. It is considered a mere addition; it is not considered the *Atzmut* of the *Ohr* of the *Nekudim*.
   3. That which extends by *Histaklut Eynaim* in AHP, which is merely for the purpose of the *Kelim* of the *Nekudim*.

   (Items 17, 18, 19)

106. **What is the difference between *Daat Elyon* and *Daat Tachton*?**

   The *Behinat Vav* ו *de HB* that became the *Daat Elyon* because the *Kelim de HB* are clean from the lower *Hey*. However, regarding the *Melafom* that came to them from *Yesod de AK* as a *Nekuda* inside the *Vav*, the *Daat Tachton Nimshach* from there, as it contains the entire lower *Hey*, being the *Nekuda* inside the *Vav*.

   (*Histaklut Pnimit* item 12)

107. **What is the difference between *He'arat NHY de Keter* and *NHY de AK*?**

   NHY de Keter return only the *HB* that are clean from lower *Hey* into *Behinat Rosh*. This does not help the lower seven mixed with the lower *Hey* whatsoever. However, *NHY de AK* illuminates the *Behinat Nekuda* inside the *Otiot*, which is the *Hitkalelut* of the lower *Hey*, and from there the lower seven *de Nekudim* extend.

(*Histaklut Pnimit* item 13)

108. **Where does the Halbasha of YESHSUT begin?**

It begins from *Tabur de AK ha Pnimi* because there is the place of the descent of the *Masach* mingled with the lower *Hey*, extending from below upward to the *Chazeh*.

(*Ohr Pnimi* item 14)

109. **Why don't the Nekudot clothe any of the SAG, from which they stem?**

Since the *Masach* that purified and rose from the *Guf de SAG* consists of two kinds of *Reshimot*: *Reshimot de Taamim*, having no *Behinat* lower *Hey* since they did not descend below *Tabur de AK*, and *Reshimot de Nekudot*, mingled with the lower *Hey* because of their expansion below *Tabur de AK* through its *Sium Raglin*.

Hence, two kinds of *Zivugim* were made on the *Masach*. MA and BON *Elyon* came out of the *Zivug* on the *Reshimot de Taamim*, extending from *Peh de Rosh SAG* through *Tabur*, meaning in the place where *Orot de Taamim de SAG* stand. The *Eser Sefirot de Nekudim* that clothe from *Tabur de AK* down came out of the *Zivug* on the *Reshimot* of the *Nekudot de SAG*, meaning in the place where *Nekudot de SAG* stood before they purified. Thus, the *Eser Sefirot de Nekudim* clothe and fulfill the *Kelim de Nekudot de SAG* that were emptied of their *Orot*.

(*Histaklut Pnimit* item 24, and item 31)

110. **Where does SAG clothe AB de AK?**

Rosh de SAG clothes AB from its *Peh* down to the *Chazeh*. Thus, HGT *de AB* are *Neshama* and *Mochin* in *Rosh SAG*, and the *Taamim de SAG* clothe from *Chazeh de AB* through *Sium Raglin* of AB. The *Nekudot de SAG* extend below the *Sium Raglin* of AB, which is below *Tabur de AK ha Pnimi* through *Sium Raglin de AK ha Pnimi*.

(*Ohr Pnimi* item 1)

111. **Why do Nekudim clothe NHY de AK?**

See answer 109.

112. **Why is the Holam on top of the Otiot?**

The lower *Hey* in the *Eynaim de Keter* in the form of lower *Hey* in the *Eynaim* and YHV in the AHP. The lower *Hey* is there as *Holam* on top of *Otiot* YHV.

This is because its *He'arah* does not expand into the *HB*, which are *Behinot YHV* because the *Zivug* was not made on this lower *Hey*, but only on the First *Hey*.

(*Histaklut Pnimit* items 9, 10)

113. **Why is the *Shuruk* in the middle?**

    The *Shuruk*, called *Melafom*, is the *Ohr* of *NHY de AK*; it is completely *Behinat* lower *Hey*. There is a new *Ohr* inside it that came out through *Zivug de AB* and *SAG*, which fissured the *Parsa*. This *Ohr* is *Behinat Vav* ו, which is a son to the *YH*, being *AB* and *SAG*. It turns out that here the lower *Hey* is mixed together with the *Vav*, meaning they shine together.

    (Item 31)

114. **Why did *Abba* take the point of *Shuruk*?**

    First the *Zivug* was made as *Histaklut Eynaim de AVI* on the *Behinat Nekuda*. This *Zivug* is named after *Abba*. Afterwards the *Masach* purified and there was a *Zivug* on the *Vav* that *Ima* took.

    (Item 31)

115. **Why are *Keter* and *Hochma* once called *Holam* and *Shuruk*, and once *Kamatz* and *Patach*?**

    Holam is considered the beginning of the creation of *Keter*, which is the lower *Hey* in the *Eynaim de Keter*, above the *Otiot* (see answer 112). The *Shuruk* is the *Ohr Yesod* that *AVI* took from *Yesod de AK* for the purpose of their *Zivug*.

    However, the *Kamatz Patach* are *Behinot Gadlut de Keter* and *Hochma*. This is because the descent of the lower *Hey* from *Nikvey Eynaim de Keter* under the *HB de Nekudim*, which returns them to *Behinat Rosh*, the *Keter* is called *Kamatz* here, being under *Otiot YHV*. Also, *Hochma* is called *Patach* here, because through its arriving at the *Rosh*, the *Ohr Hochma* opens, called "the opening of the *Eynaim*", and that is why *Hochma* is called *Patach*.

    (Item 31)

116. **Why are *Kamatz Patach* from the *Nekudot* under the *Otiot*?**

    See answer 115.

117. **Which *Behina* of *Kamatz Patach* did not break?**

    This refers to what they have from their beginning, not to what they received from *Sium Raglin*.

    (*Ohr Pnimi* item 32)

118. **Why are the seven *Nekudot* in the shape of *Yodin*?**

    Because the lower seven come out from *Behinot Hitkalelut* of the lower *Hey*, called *Nekuda*. Hence the seven *Nekudot* are in the shape of *Yodin*.

    (*Ohr Pnimi* item 48)

119. **What is the difference between the *Nekuda* of *Holam* and *Kamatz*, as they are both *Keter*?**

    Holam means that the *Nekuda*, which is lower *Hey*, is above the *Otiot YHV*. Then they are considered *AHP* that come out to *Behinat Guf*, meaning HGT.

    The point of *Kamatz* means that the lower *Hey* descended from the *Nikvey Eynaim* and came to her place under the *Otiot YHV*. At that time the YHV return to the *Rosh* and become HBD.

    (*Histaklut Pnimit* item 11)

120. **What is the main cause for the emergence of *Partzuf* MA and BON?**

    The ascent of the lower *Hey* to the *Eynaim*, meaning the connection of the two *Heyin* together is the primary cause for the elicitation of *Partzuf* MA and BON.

    (*Histaklut Pnimit* item 6)

121. **What is the primary cause of a birth of a *Partzuf*?**

    The *Bitush de Ohr Makif* in *Ohr Pnimi*.

    (*Histaklut Pnimit* item 1)

122. **How does *Ohr Makif* appear in the birth of *Partzufim*?**

    All the *Partzufim* and the *Neshamot* that emanate and come in the *Olamot*, all are parts of the *Orot Makifim*. When all of them manifest it will be *Gmar Tikun*.

    (*Histaklut Pnimit* item 1)

123. **What mainly operates to emanate a second *Partzuf*?**

    The *Masach de Tabur* which purifies until it ascends to *Hitkalelut* of the *Zivug* in the *Rosh*. This is the primary operator in the creation of a second *Partzuf*.

    (*Histaklut Pnimit* item 3)

124. **How many *Nekudot* of *Sium* from *Tabur* to *Sium Raglin*?**

    There are three points of *Sium*: the point of *Tabur* ends the KHB; the point of *Yesod* ends on ZA; the points of *Sium Raglin* are the force of *Sium* of *Malchut*.

    (*Histaklut Pnimit* item 4)

125. **How are there *Eser Sefirot* from *Tabur* down, which is only *Malchut*?**

Since they are ten forces of *Sium* on the ten *Sefirot*.

(*Histaklut Pnimit* item 1)

126. **How are there TNHYM below *Tabur*?**

The three *Sefirot Hod*, *Yesod* and *Malchut*, are all merely the *Hitpashtut* of *Malchut*. *Netzah* and *Hod* are considered one *Sefira*. Hence, the four *Sefirot* NHYM are all the *Hitpashtut* of *Malchut*.

(*Histaklut Pnimit* item 5)

127. **Why are MA and BON below *Tabur*?**

Since they consist of the lower *Hey*, and the place of the lower *Hey* is below *Tabur*.

(*Histaklut Pnimit* item 1)

128. **Why must MA be associated with the lower *Hey*?**

Since *Komat ZA*, which is MA and BON, comes out on *Masach de Behina Aleph*, and it is known that the *Aviut* of *Behina Aleph* is frail, and the *Ohr Zivug* that comes out on it has no *Hitpashtut* below.

(*Histaklut Pnimit* item 1)

129. **Why isn't there lower *Hey* in HB de Nekudim?**

Since they extend from *Behinat Histaklut Eynaim* in AHP, which are YHV without the lower *Hey*, and the lower *Hey* remains concealed in the *Eynaim*.

(*Histaklut Pnimit* item 9)

130. **What is the reason that GAR de ZA de Atzilut remain in *Ima*?**

As the *Partzuf Elyon de* MA and BON remains adhesive with the SAG and is not considered *Nekudim*, so it has a *Partzuf Elyon* to the ZA that remains attached to *Ima*, not regarded as ZA.

(*Histaklut Pnimit* item 26)

131. **What are the *Achoraim de AVI* that were cancelled?**

The *Orot* that came during the *Gadlut* as additions and are not from their primary essence, are called *Achoraim*.

(*Ohr Pnimi* item 32)

132. **Why are the lower seven in one *Kav*?**

Because the matter of the *Tikun* of the three *Kavim* emerged by the association of the lower *Hey* with the First *Hey*. The beginning of this *Tikun* occurred in the *Ohr* that came out of the *Nikvey Eynaim*, and this *Ohr* did not reach the lower seven *de Nekudim*, only the GAR. Hence the lower seven remained without *Tikun Kavim*, but in a single *Kav*, like the previous *Partzufim*.

(Ohr Pnimi item 38)

133. **Where were ZON made?**

    The lower seven *de Nekudim* came out by the *Zivug de HB* on the *He'arat Melafom* that they received from *Yesod de AK*, which are ZON.

134. **Where were the *Kelim de Nekudim* made?**

    The *Kelim* of every *Partzuf* are made of the *Kelim* of the *Partzuf Elyon* after the *Histalkut* of their *Orot* from them. Similarly, the *Kelim de Nekudim* were made of the *Kelim* of the lower nine *de SAG* that the *Ohr* departed from during the *Tzimtzum NHY*.

(Ohr Pnimi item 38)

135. **What does it mean that the *Kelim* were small?**

    The two *Kelim Elyonim* are missing in the *Kelim de Guf de Nekudim*, being *Keter* and *Hochma*, and they only have *Behinat ZAT*. However, the *Ohr* that reached them had *Eser* complete *Sefirot*. Hence, the *Kelim* were found to be small and thus broke.

(Ohr Pnimi item 39)

136. **What is the need for *Dinim* and *Klipot*?**

    Since the thought of creation is to delight His creatures, and this thought is not executed except through a conduct of one opposite the other.

(Ohr Pnimi item 41)

137. **What does it mean that the lower Seven are *Din* and the *Ohr* that comes to them is *Rachamim*?**

    Because the *Kelim* were from *Behinat ZAT*, which are *Din*, and the *Orot* were of GAR, which are *Rachamim*.

(Ohr Pnimi item 40)

Questions Regarding Cause and Consequence

138. **What eventuates from the yearning of *Malchut de Ein Sof* for greater *Dvekut* with the *Ohr Elyon*?**

    Three actions eventuate from that:
    1. The departure of the *Ohr* from all four *Behinot*;
    2. A place was made for the *Olamot*;
    3. *Kelim de Eser Sefirot de Igulim*.

    (*Histaklut Pnimit* item 4)

139. **What eventuates from the *Histalkut Ohr* from all four *Behinot*?**
    1. *Ohr* of *Kav de Ein Sof* on only three *Behinot*;
    2. The *Tikun* of the *Masach* that limits and impedes the *Ohr* from expanding in *Behina Dalet*.

    (*Histaklut Pnimit* item 5)

140. **What eventuates from the *Masach*?**
    1. *Zivug de Hakaa* with the *Ohr Elyon*;
    2. Pushing the *Ohr* that belongs to *Behina Dalet*, called *Ohr Hozer*, backwards.

    (*Histaklut Pnimit* item 6)

141. **What eventuates from the *Ohr Hozer*?**
    1. Potential and actual reception of the *Ohr Elyon*, called *Rosh* and *Guf*;
    2. Rejection of the *Ohr Elyon* from *Behina Dalet* that manifests de facto in *Masach de Tabur*, which expands into ten forces of *Sium*, called *Eser Sefirot de NHY*, or *Eser Sefirot de Sof*.

    (*Histaklut Pnimit* item 9)

[For the Creation of *Partzuf AB de AK*]

142. **What eventuates from the *Masach de Tabur de Galgalta*?**

    Bitush de Ohr Makif and *Ohr Pnimi* on one another.

    (*Histaklut Pnimit* item 12)

143. **What eventuates from the *Bitush de Ohr Makif* in *Ohr Pnimi* in *Partzuf Galgalta*?**
    1. The *Hizdakchut* of the *Masach* until it equalizes with the *Behinat Malchut de Rosh*, for renewal in *Zivug de Rosh*.
    2. *Hitkalelut* of the *Masach* in the *Reshimot de Eser Sefirot de Guf* as it ascends.

3. The concealment of the *Reshima de Hamshacha* from the last *Behina*.

(*Histaklut Pnimit* items 12, 13 and 18)

144. **What eventuates from the disappearance of the last Behina?**
   1. The concealment of *Ohr Keter* and the diminution of the *Koma* up to *Hochma*.
   2. Two Upper *Reshimot* that became *Zachar* and *Nekeva*.

   (*Histaklut Pnimit* items 14, 19)

145. **What eventuates from of the two Reshimot Zachar and Nekeva that rose from the Guf de Galgalta?**
   1. The ascent of *Malchut de Rosh* to *Hotem de Rosh*, which is *Behina Gimel*.
   2. The *Zivug* was made there on *Behina Dalet de Hitlabshut*, meaning on the *Behinat Zachar*, extending *Komat Keter* there, which is not in *Behinat Hitpashtut* for *Kelim*.
   3. The *Zivug* on *Behina Gimel* was made there, meaning on *Behinat Nekeva*, extending *Komat Hochma*, having *Hitpashtut* from above downward to *Behinat Kelim*.

   (*Histaklut Pnimit* item 15)

146. **What eventuates from the two Zivugim of ZON that the Masach makes in its Hitkalelut in Hotem in Rosh de Galgalta?**
   1. The renewal of the *Aviut* in the *Masach* and the *Reshimot* until they are fitting for *Zivug de Hakaa* with the *Ohr Elyon*.
   2. The appearance of the *Aviut de Guf* in the *Masach* and the *Reshimot*.

   (*Histaklut Pnimit* items 16, 17)

147. **What eventuates from the manifestation of the Aviut de Guf in the Masach and the Reshimot?**
   1. Their exit from the *Rosh* and their arriving in their corresponding *Behina* in the *Hitzoniut* of the *Guf de Partzuf Galgalta*, meaning in *Behina Gimel* of the *Guf*, called *Chazeh*.
   2. That two *Zivugim* are made there in the place of *Chazeh de Galgalta*, of the *Zachar* and the *Nekeva*, as is their property in the *Rosh*.

   (*Histaklut Pnimit* item 19)

148. **What eventuates from the two Zivugim that the Masach makes in the place of Chazeh de Galgalta?**
   1. That *Eser Sefirot de Rosh* come out from the *Chazeh* upward to *Peh de Partzuf Galgalta* on *Komat Hochma*.
   2. The *Eser Sefirot* from the *Chazeh* down to *Behinat Hitlabshut*, called *Guf*.

3. The *Eser Sefirot de Sium* expanding from the *Masach de Tabur* downward, and end above *Tabur de Partzuf Galgalta*. This *Hitpashtut RTS* is called *Partzuf AB de AK*.

(*Histaklut Pnimit* items 20, 21, 22)

[For the Creation of *Partzuf SAG de AK*]

149. What eventuates from the *Masach de Tabur de AB*?

    Bitush de Ohr Makif and *Ohr Pnimi* on one another.

    (*Histaklut Pnimit* item 12)

150. What eventuates from the *Bitush de Ohr Makif* in *Ohr Pnimi de AB*?

    1. The *Hizdakchut* of the *Masach* until it equalizes with *Malchut de Rosh* for renewal in the *Zivug de Rosh*.
    2. The *Hitkalelut* of the *Masach* through its ascent in the *Reshimot de Eser Sefirot de Guf*.
    3. The concealment of the *Reshima de Hamshacha* from the last *Behina*.

    (*Histaklut Pnimit* items 12, 13, 18)

151. What eventuates from the disappearance of the last *Behina de AB*?

    - The concealment of the *Ohr Hochma* and the diminution of the *Koma* up to *Bina*.
    - The two Upper *Reshimot* that became *Zachar* and *Nekeva*.

    (*Histaklut Pnimit* items 14, 24)

152. What eventuates from the two *Reshimot Zachar* and *Nekeva* that rose from *Histalkut AB*?

    1. The ascent of *Malchut de Rosh* to the *Awzen*, being *Behina Bet de Rosh*.
    2. The *Zivug* on *Behina Gimel de Hitlabshut* was made there, meaning on the *Behinat Zachar*, extending *Komat Hochma*, which is not in *Behinat Hitpashtut* for *Kelim*.
    3. The second *Zivug* that was made there on *Behina Bet*, which is the *Behinat Nekeva*, extending *Komat Bina*, having *Hitpashtut* to *Behinat Kelim*.

    (*Histaklut Pnimit* item 15)

153. What eventuates from the two *Zivugim de ZON* that the *Masach* made in its *Hitkalelut* in *Awzen de Rosh AB*?

    1. The renewal of the *Aviut* in the *Masach* and the *Reshimot* until they are fitting for *Zivug de Hakaa* with the *Ohr Elyon*.

2. The disclosure of the *Aviut de Guf* in the *Masach* and the *Reshimot*.
(*Histaklut Pnimit* items 16, 17)

154. What eventuates from the manifestation of the *Aviut de Guf* in the *Masach*?

1. Their exit from the *Rosh* and their arriving at their corresponding *Behina* in the *Hitzoniut* of the *Guf de Partzuf AB*, meaning in *Behina Bet de AB*, called *Chazeh*.
2. That they return and make two *Zivugim* there in the place of *Chazeh de AB*, like the attribute of the two *Zivugim* that they made by the *Hitkalelut* in the *Zivug de Rosh AB*.

(*Histaklut Pnimit* items 19, 24)

155. What eventuates from the two *Zivugim* that the *Masach* makes in the place of *Chazeh de AB*?

1. That *Eser Sefirot de Rosh* came out of the *Chazeh* upward to the *Peh de Partzuf AB* on *Komat Bina*, which is the *Behinat Nekeva* where the *Kelim* of the *Partzuf* come from. However, there is also *Komat Hochma* there from the *Behinat Zachar*, who has not *Hitpashtut* for *Kelim*.
2. The *Eser Sefirot* from *Chazeh de AB* downward that expand in *Kli de Keter de Guf* through the *Tabur de Partzuf Galgalta*. It reaches the *Sium Raglin de Partzuf AB*, where this *Hitpashtut* stops because there is *Ohr Komat Zachar* there, which is *Hochma*.
3. The *Hitpashtut* of the nine lower *Sefirot* from *Tabur* down to *Sium Raglin de Galgalta de AK*, called *Nekudot de SAG*.
4. The *Eser Sefirot de Sium* that expand by the *Masach de Tabur*, called *Eser Sefirot de NHY*, or *Eser Sefirot de Sof* of the *Partzuf*. This *Hitpashtut RTS* is called *Partzuf SAG de AK*.

[For the Creation of *Partzuf* MA and BON de AK]

Named *Olam ha Nekudim* or BON

156. What eventuates from the *Masach de Tabur de SAG*?

Bitush de Ohr Makif and *Ohr Pnimi* on one another.

157. What eventuates from the *Bitush de Ohr Makif* in *Ohr Pnimi de SAG*?

The *Hizdakchut* of the *Masach* until it equalizes with *Malchut de Rosh* to receive renewal from the *Zivug de Rosh*.

The second is the *Hitkalelut* of the *Masach* in two kinds of *Reshimot*: *Reshimot* that are not connected with the *Reshimot de NHY de Galgalta*, called *Taamim*, and *Reshimot* that are connected with *NHY de Galgalta*, called *Nekudot*, where the two *Heyin*, the lower *Hey* and the First *Hey*, are connected.

The third is the concealment of the *Reshimot de Hamshacha* from the last *Behina*.

(*Histaklut Pnimit* items 12, 13, 18, and 25)

158. **What eventuates from the concealment of the last *Behina de SAG*?**

    The diminution of the *Koma* to *Behina Aleph*. The second is the two Upper *Reshimot* that became *Zachar* and *Nekeva*.

    (*Histaklut Pnimit* items 14, 15)

159. **What eventuates from the two *Reshimot ZON* that rose in the *Nikvey Eynaim de Rosh de SAG*?**

    The ascent of *Malchut de Rosh* to *Nikvey Eynaim*.

    The second is that the *Zivug* on *Behina Bet de Hitlabshut* was made there, meaning on the *Behinat Zachar* that *Komat Bina* extends on, which is not *Behinat Hitpashtut*. This is performed over the two kinds of the above *Reshimot*: *Taamim* and *Nekudot*.

    The third is the *Zivug* made there in the *Behinat Nekeva*, meaning on *Behina Aleph* that *Komat ZA* extends on. however, she has *Hitpashtut* for *Kelim*, and this is done on two kinds of *Reshimot* too: *Taamim* and *Nekudot*.

    (*Histaklut Pnimit* items 15, 30)

160. **What eventuates from the *Hitkalelut* of the *Reshimot* in the *Zivugim* in the *Nikvey Eynaim de Rosh de SAG*?**

    1. The renewal of the *Aviut* in the *Masach* and the *Reshimot* that rose from the *Guf de SAG* until they are fitting for the *Zivug de Hakaa* with the *Ohr Elyon*.
    2. The exit of the *Dikna* as lower *Hey* in the *Eynaim* and the *YHV* in the *AHP*.
    3. The disclosure of the *Aviut de Guf* in the *Masach* and the *Reshimot*.

    (*Histaklut Pnimit* items 16, 17, and *Ohr Pnimi* item 2)

161. **What eventuates from the manifestation of *Aviut de Guf* in the *Masach* and the *Reshimot*?**

    Their exit from the *Rosh* and their coming to the corresponding *Behina* in *Hitzoniut* of the *Guf de SAG*.

    (*Histaklut Pnimit* item 19)

162. **What eventuates from the descent of the *Masach* to its corresponding *Behinot* in the *Hitzoniut de Guf de SAG*?**

    It elicited three *Roshim* as it came to three places in the *Guf*: *Chazeh*, *Tabur* and the *Sium de Guf*. From the *Chazeh* to *Peh de SAG* it elicited the *Eser Sefirot* de *Rosh* de *MA* and *BON Elyon*, and its *Eser Sefirot de Guf* end at the *Tabur*. From *Tabur* to *Chazeh de SAG* it elicited *Eser Sefirot de Rosh* called YESHSUT, or *Rosh ha Aleph de Nekudim*.

From the *Sium de Guf*, meaning *Tifferet de AK* through *Tabur*, it elicits the GAR *de Nekudim*, and all have *Zachar* and *Nekeva*. The *Komat Zachar* is up to *Bina*, and the *Komat Nekeva* is *Komat ZA*.

(*Histaklut Pnimit* items 20, 21, 22, 24 and 30)

163. **What eventuates from the elicitation of the AHP from all the degrees?**

    The diminution of *Atzilut* on *Keter* and *Hochma* alone, and *AHP* of every degree are considered the *Beria* of that degree.

    Second: a new *Gevul* of the *Sium* of the *Kav de Ein Sof* that rose from *Malchut de NHY de AK*, and the emergence of the three *Sefirot Bina, ZA* and *Malchut de NHY de AK* below the point of *Tzimtzum*. This is called *Tzimtzum Bet*.

    Third: these three *Sefirot* below the point of *Tzimtzum* became the place for the three *Olamot BYA*: *Olam Beria* in the place of *Bina*, *Olam Yetzira* in the place of *ZA*, and *Olam Assiya* in the place of *Malchut*.

    Fourth: the *Tikun* of the *Parsa*.

    (*Histaklut Pnimit* items 33, 34)

164. **How are the actions connected to one another through cause and consequence from Tzimtzum Aleph to the end of Olam ha Nekudim in Katnut?**

    Because of the yearning for greater *Dvekut*, meaning for *Hishtavut Tzura* with the *Ohr Elyon*, *Malchut de Ein Sof* restricted the *Behinat Gadlut* of the will to receive. In other words, she did not want to receive in *Behina Dalet*. Since *Behina Dalet* was the entire vessel of reception for the *Ohr Elyon*, the *Ohr* departed from all four *Behinot*, and there became a vacant place for the *Olamot*.

    From the *Histalkut Ohr* from all four *Behinot* eventuates the *Tikun Masach* on *Behina Dalet* to extend the *Ohr* on the first three *Behinot*, without extending to *Behina Dalet*.

    From the *Masach* erected on *Behina Dalet* comes the *Zivug de Hakaa* with the *Ohr Elyon* returning all the parts of the *Ohr* fitting to come to *Behina Dalet* and to its *Achoraim*, called *Ohr Hozer*.

    Two actions stem from the *Zivug de Hakaa* and the *Ohr Hozer* that ascended:

    1. The potential and actual reception of the *Ohr Elyon*, called *Rosh* and *Guf*, through *Tabur*.
    2. The force of rejection on the *Eser Sefirot de Ohr Elyon* called *Masach de Tabur*, from which expand the ten forces *de Sium*, called *Eser Sefirot de Sof*, or *Eser Sefirot NHY*.

(From *Galgalta* to *AB*)

From the *Masach de Tabur* extends the *Bitush de Ohr Makif* on *Ohr Pnimi* on one another.

Three actions stem from the *Bitush de Ohr Makif* on *Ohr Pnimi* on one another:

1. The *Hizdakchut* of the *Masach* and its coming for renewal in the *Zivug* in the *Rosh*, because of which all the *Orot de Guf* departed.
2. The *Hitkalelut* of the *Masach* in the *Reshimot de Guf* during its ascent.
3. The disappearing of the *Reshima de Hamshacha* from the last *Behina*.

Two actions stem from the concealment of the *Reshima de Hamshacha* from the last *Behina*:

1. The concealment of the *Ohr Keter* and the diminution of the *Koma* to *Hochma*.
2. The two Upper *Reshimot* became *Zachar* and *Nekeva*.

Three actions stem from the two *Reshimot Zachar* and *Nekeva*:

1. The ascent of *Malchut de Rosh* to the *Hotem*, which is *Behina Gimel de Rosh*.
2. The *Zivug* that was made there on *Behina Dalet de Behinat Hitlabshut*, meaning on the *Behinat Zachar*, and the *Komat Keter* that extends there. It is not in *Behinat Hitpashtut* to *Kelim*.
3. The second *Zivug* that was made there on *Behina Gimel*, meaning on the *Behinat Nekeva*, extending *Komat Hochma* there, from which there is *Hitpashtut* for the *Kelim*.

The renewal of the *Aviut* in the *Masach* and the *Reshimot* stems from the two *Zivugim* of ZON that were made in their *Hitkalelut* in the *Rosh de Galgalta*, until they became fitting for *Zivug de Hakaa* with the *Ohr Elyon*. The second is the manifestation of the *Aviut de Guf* in the *Masach* and the *Reshimot*.

Three actions stem from the two *Zivugim* made by the *Zachar* and the *Nekeva* at the place of the *Chazeh*:

1. The elicitation of the *Eser Sefirot de Rosh* from the *Chazeh* upward to the *Peh de Partzuf Galgalta* in *Komat Hochma*.
2. The expansion of the *Eser Sefirot* from the *Chazeh* downward, called *Guf*, to the *Masach* of its own *Tabur*.
3. The *Eser Sefirot de Sium* that expanded from the *Masach de Tabur* and ended above *Tabur de Partzuf Galgalta*. This *Hitpashtut RTS* is called *Partzuf AB de AK*.

(From *AB* to *SAG*)

The *Bitush* of *Ohr Makif* and *Ohr Pnimi* on one another extends from the *Masach de Tabur de AB* (*Histaklut Pnimit* item 12).

Three actions stem from the *Bitush de Ohr Makif* and *Ohr Pnimi*:

1. The *Hizdakchut* of the *Masach* to equalize with *Malchut de Rosh* in order to be renewed in a *Zivug* that the *Orot de Guf* depart with.
2. The *Hitkalelut* of the *Masach* with *Reshimot de Eser Sefirot de Guf* during its ascent.
3. The concealment of the *Reshima de Hamshacha* from the last *Behina*.

The concealment of the *Ohr Hochma* and the diminution of the *Koma* to *Bina* extends from the last *Behina de Hamshacha*. The second is that the two Upper *Reshimot* were turned into *Zachar* and *Nekeva*.

The ascent of *Malchut de Rosh* to the *Awzen* extends from the two *Reshimot Zachar* and *Nekeva*. The second is that the *Zivug* was made on *Behina Gimel de Hitlabshut* there, which is the *Behinat Zachar*. It extends *Eser Sefirot* in *Komat Hochma* there, but has no *Hitpashtut* to *Kelim*. The third is *Zivug Bet* that was made there on *Behina Bet*, being the *Behinat Nekeva*. It extends *Komat Bina*, which expands to the *Kelim*.

From the *Behinat Zachar* and *Nekeva* from the two *Zivugim* made in the *Rosh* extend:

1. The renewal of the *Aviut* in the *Masach* and *Reshimot* to make them fitting for *Zivug de Hakaa* with the *Ohr Elyon*.
2. The manifestation of the *Aviut de* in the *Masach* and *Reshimot*.

Their exit from the *Rosh* and their coming to their corresponding *Behina* in *Guf de AB*, meaning in *Behina Bet*, called *Chazeh*, stems from the manifestation of the *Aviut de Guf* in the *Masach* and *Reshimot*. Two: they return and make two *Zivugim* there in *Chazeh de AB*, like their attribute that they made in the *Rosh*.

Four actions stem from the two *Zivugim de Zachar* and *Nekeva* made in *Chazeh de AB*:

1. *Eser Sefirot de Rosh* emerge from the *Chazeh* upwards to *Peh de Partzuf AB* on *Komat Bina*, which is the *Behinat Nekeva*, from which there is *Hitpashtut* to the *Kelim* of the *Partzuf*. However, there is also *Komat Hochma* there, which is the *Zachar* of the *Partzuf*, which has no *Hitpashtut* for *Kelim*.
2. The *Eser Sefirot* from *Chazeh de AB* downward that expand in the *Kelim de Keter de Guf* through the *Tabur de Partzuf Galgalta*, where that *Hitpashtut* ends.

3. The *Hitpashtut* of the nine lower *Sefirot* through *Sium Raglin de Galgalta de AK*, called *Nekudot de SAG*.
4. The *Masach de Tabur* from which expand the *Eser Sefirot de Sium*. This *Hitpashtut RTS* is called *Partzuf SAG de AK*.

(From SAG to MA and BON)

Bitush de Ohr Makif and *Ohr Pnimi* extends from the *Masach de Tabur de SAG*. The *Hizdakchut* of the *Masach* until it equalizes with *Malchut de Rosh* extends from *Bitush de Ohr Makif* and *Ohr Pnimi* to receive renewal from the *Zivug de Rosh* there.

The second is the *Hitkalelut* of the *Masach* in two kinds of *Reshimot*: *Reshimot* that are not connected with *Reshimot NHY de AK ha Pnimi*, and *Reshimot* that are connected with the inner *Reshimot NHY*, called *Nekudot*. In those the two *Heyin* are connected together, the First *Hey* and the lower *Hey*.

The third is the concealment of the *Reshima de Hamshacha* from the last *Behina*.

The diminution of the *Koma* to *Behina Aleph* extends from the concealment of the last *Behina de Hamshacha*. The second is the turning of the two *Reshimot* into *Zachar* and *Nekeva*.

From the two *Reshimot* that turned into *Zachar* and *Nekeva* extends the ascent of *Malchut de Rosh* to *Nikvey Eynaim*.

The second is the *Zivug* that was made there on *Behina Bet de Hitlabshut*, being the *Behinat Zachar*, extending *Komat Bina* from which there is no *Hitpashtut* for *Kelim*. Hence, the *Zivug* is made both on the *Reshimot de Taamim* and the *Reshimot de Nekudot*.

The third is the second *Zivug* that created a *Behinat Nekeva* there, being on *Behina Aleph*, over which extends *Komat ZA*. There is *Hitpashtut* for *Kelim* from it, and that *Zivug* too was made both on the *Reshimot de Taamim* and the *Reshimot de Nekudot*.

Three actions stem from the *Hitkalelut* of the *Reshimot* in the *Zivugim* of the *Rosh* in the *Nikvey Eynaim*:

1. The renewal of the *Aviut* in the *Masach* and the *Reshimot* that rose from the *Guf de SAG* and became suitable for *Zivug de Hakaa*.
2. The elicitation of the *Dikna* in the form of lower *Hey* in the *Eynaim* and *YHV* in the *AHP*.
3. The manifestation of the *Aviut de Guf* in the *Masach* and the *Reshimot*.

Three *Roshim* extend from the descent of the *Masach* to its corresponding *Behina* in the *Hitzoniut* of the *Guf*, as it comes to three places in the *Guf*: the *Chazeh*, the *Tabur*, and the *Sium de Guf*, meaning *Sium Tifferet de AK*.

It elicits the *Eser Sefirot de Rosh* of the MA and BON *Elyon* from *Chazeh* to SAG, and his *Guf* ends above *Tabur de AK ha Pnimi*, and from *Tabur* to *Chazeh de SAG*, *Eser Sefirot de Rosh* of YESHSUT, being *Rosh ha Aleph de Nekudim*. It elicits a second *Rosh* from the *Sium* of the *Guf* up to *Tabur*, called GAR *de Nekudim*, and from the *Sium de Guf* downward emerged the *Guf de Nekudim*, which is ZAT *de Nekudim*.

All of them contain *Zachar* and *Nekeva*: the *Komat Zachar* is up to *Bina*, and the *Komat Nekeva* is up to ZA.

The second is the departure of the *AHP* from all the degrees. Four actions extend from the departure of the *AHP* from all the degrees:

1. The diminution of the *Atzilut* on *Keter* and *Hochma* alone, since the *AHP* of the degree departed from it, and are considered its *Beria*.
2. The *Tikun* of the *Parsa*.
3. A new *Gevul* for *Sium* of the *Kav de Ein Sof* in the place of *Bina de NHY de AK*, where *Bina*, ZA and *Malchut de NHY de AK* are found below the point of *Sium* of *Kav Ein Sof*. This is called *Tzimtzum Bet*.
4. The three *Sefirot de NHY de AK* that departed below the point of *Tzimtzum Bet* became the place for the three separated *Olamot* called BYA. *Bina* became the place of *Olam Beria*; ZA, the place of *Olam Yetzira*; *Malchut*, for *Olam Assiya*.

165. **What ten actions were taken through the completion of Partzuf Galgalta de AK?**
   1. The place where the *Tzimtzum* was made.
   2. The *Reshimot* that remained after the *Tzimtzum*.
   3. The *Eser Sefirot de Igulim*.
   4. The *Masach* in *Kli Malchut*.
   5. The *Hamshacha* of *Ohr* back.
   6. The *Zivug de Hakaa* with the *Ohr Elyon*.
   7. The *Ohr Hozer* that became a *Levush* and *Kli* for the *Ohr Elyon*.
   8. The *Eser Sefirot de Yosher* from below upward, which are *Rosh de Kav*.
   9. The *Hitpashtut Malchut de Rosh* from above downward in *Eser Sefirot* from her and within her through *Tabur*, which are the *Toch* of the *Kav*.
   10. The *Hitpashtut* of the *Masach de Tabur* in *Eser Sefirot de Sium*, where from *Malchut de Sium* downwards it is darkness, not *Ohr*.

166. **How are these ten actions connected by cause and consequence?**

Four actions extend by the *Histalkut Ohr* on all four *Behinot*: the place for the *Olamot*; the *Reshimot*, which are *Eser Sefirot de Igulim*; the awakening for the *Hamshacha* of *Ohr* back; the *Tikun* of the *Masach*.

The *Masach* causes two actions: *Zivug de Hakaa* and raising *Ohr Hozer*. The *Zivug de Hakaa* and the *Ohr Hozer* cause four actions: *Rosh*, *Toch*, *Sof*, and the point of *Tzimtzum* that ends the *Kav*.

167. **What are the fourteen actions generally executed in the creation of a *Partzuf*?**

    1. *Bitush de Ohr Makif* and *Ohr Pnimi*.
    2. The *Hizdakchut* of the *Masach*.
    3. The *Hitkalelut* of the *Masach* in the *Reshimot de Eser Sefirot de Guf*.
    4. The two Upper *Reshimot*: *Zachar* and *Nekeva*.
    5. Two kinds of *Zivugim* in the *Masach de Rosh*.
    6. The renewal of the *Aviut* in the *Masach* and the *Reshimot*.
    7. The recognition of the *Aviut de Guf* in them.
    8. The concealment of the *Reshima* of the last *Behina* from them.
    9. Their departure from the *Rosh*.
    10. Their arrival at the *Hitzoniut de Guf* of the previous *Partzuf* at the place of the *Chazeh*.
    11. The *Zivug de Hakaa* made in the *Masach* at the place of the *Chazeh*, extending *Eser Sefirot de Rosh*.
    12. The *Hitpashtut* of *Malchut de Rosh* from the *Chazeh* downward.
    13. Its clothing of the previous *Partzuf*.
    14. Its beginning from the *Peh de Elyon*.

    (*Histaklut Pnimit* item 11)

168. **How are the fourteen actions of the creation of the *Partzuf* interconnected?**

    Bitush de Ohr Makif and *Ohr Pnimi* causes three actions: the *Hizdakchut* of the *Masach*, the *Hitkalelut* of the *Masach* in the *Reshimot*, and the concealment of the last *Behina*.

    The concealment of the last *Behina* causes two actions: two *Reshimot ZON*, and two new *Zivugim* in the *Rosh*.

    The *Hitkalelut* in the *Zivug de Rosh* causes the manifestation of the *Aviut de Guf*.

The manifestation of the *Aviut de Guf* causes three actions: the exit from the *Rosh*, the arrival at its corresponding *Behina* in the *Hitzoniut de Guf*, and the new *Zivug* at the place of the *Chazeh*.

Three actions stem from the *Zivug* in the *Chazeh*: *Rosh, Toch, Sof*.

Two actions stem from the *Hizdakchut* of the *Masach* and the *Histalkut* of the *Orot de Guf*: the *Halbasha* of the *Tachton* on the *Elyon*, and the beginning of the *Koma* of the *Tachton* from *Peh de Elyon*.

169. **What are the two actions added in *Partzuf SAG*?**

    The descent of *Nekudot de SAG* below *Tabur de AK ha Pnimi* and the division of the *Partzuf* into *Taamim* and *Nekudot*.

170. **What are the thirteen actions added in *Partzuf Nekudim*?**

    See *Histaklut Pnimit* item 31

171. **How are the thirteen actions interconnected by the above order of cause and consequence?**

    See *Histaklut Pnimit* items 32 through 35.

PART SEVEN

The *Eser Sefirot* of the seven *Melachim* that died

1.	*4	26.	*22	51.	55
2.	4	27.	24	52.	55
3.	6	28.	*25	53.	56
4.	6	29.	27	54.	56
5.	7	30.	29	55.	*56
6.	9	31.	29	56.	56
7.	*9	32.	30	57.	58
8.	9	33.	30	58.	59
9.	10	34.	31	59.	59
10.	11	35.	31	60.	61
11.	12	36.	32	61.	62
12.	13	37.	33	62.	64
13.	13	38.	33	63.	65
14.	13	39.	*33	64.	65
15.	14	40.	35	65.	65
16.	14	41.	38	66.	66
17.	14	42.	41	67.	67
18.	14	43.	43	68.	67
19.	14	44.	43	69.	67
20.	15	45.	44	70.	67
21.	16	46.	49	71.	*68
22.	16	47.	50	72.	68
23.	*17	48.	50	73.	69
24.	21	49.	*51		
25.	22	50.	53		

1. *Know, that the *Shoresh* of these *Melachim* is the name First *BON* that emerged from the *He'arat Eynaim* of *AK*, called *Olam ha Nekudim*. Every *Behinat Malchut* that exists in all the *Olamot* was made of this name *BON*.

    This is so because there is *Malchut* in *Arich*, in *AVI*, and in *ZON*, and they were all sorted by the name *MA* that elicited from the *Metzach* of *AK*, which is the *Behinat Zachar*. You already know that there is not a *Sefira* that does not consist of ten *Sefirot*. Hence, each and every *Sefira* in all the *Olamot* must have *Behinat Malchut*, made of the above *Melachim*.

    Ohr Pnimi

1. **The *Shoresh* of these *Melachim* is the name First *BON*.**

    This means that in *Olam ha Tikun* they are *Behinat* Name *HaVaYaH* filled with *Heyin*, which is *BON* in *Gimatria*, although they are *Behinat HaVaYaH de SAG* in their origin, meaning *Nekudot de SAG*. It is as the Rav wrote (Tree of Life; Gate 10), that in the future, when all these *Melachim* will be completely corrected, the name *SAG* shall be as before and the name *MA* shall be cancelled. This is the meaning of the return of the world to *Tohu ve Bohu* (lit. Unformed and Void). At that time, there will be only two *Orot*, *AB* and *SAG*.

    However, in *Olam ha Tikun*, the *Nekudot de SAG* descended and became the name *BON* there, meaning a *Nukva* of the name *MA* and subordinate to him. Everything she has, she receives from the *Zachar*, which is *HaVaYaH de MA*. This is why we always name the *ZAT de Nekudim*, *BON*, though they are *Nekudot de SAG*.

    In fact, the *Partzuf* that emerged by the *Zivug* in *Masach de Behina Aleph*, called the *Ohr Eynaim*, which is *HaVaYaH de MA*, means *Eser Sefirot* at the level of *ZA*. However, it is called *HaVaYaH de SAG* for two reasons: One, because there is *Ohr Zachar* there, which came out on *Behina Bet de Hitlabshut*, called *YESHSUT* (see Part 6, *Ohr Pnimi* item 14), and *Komat YESHSUT* is called *HaVaYaH de SAG*.

    The second reason is that the *Kelim de Nekudim*, which are *Behinat Nekudot de SAG de AK*, meaning the lower nine *de SAG* that descended below *Tabur de AK*. The *Ohr* departed from them and these *Kelim* moved to the *Eser Sefirot de Olam ha Nekudim* (see Part 6, *Ohr Pnimi* item 38). For this reason they are called *Nekudot de SAG*.

    Behinat Malchut that exists in all the Olamot was made of this name BON.

    Through the ascent of the *Hey Tata'a*, namely *Malchut*, to the place of the *Eynaim*, which is *Hochma*, *Malchut* mixed and connected to each and every

Sefira of the *Eser Sefirot*. From then onward, this *Malchut* is connected with the First *Hey*, incorporated in each *Sefira* and in each *Partzuf* (see Part 6 *Ohr Pnimi* item 38).

2. **When the Upper *Maatzil* began to create the world, He emanated, created, made, and did the four *Olamot* ABYA. He began to sort the four above-mentioned *Melachim* that died. What was sorted from Him, rose in the *Kedusha* of the *Olamot*, and what was not sorted remained a *Klipa* and *Sigim*.**

    However, the essence of these *Sigim* and *Melachim*, their *Shoresh* is the name First BON. It is one *Partzuf Adam* from its *Rosh* to its *Raglaim*, containing corresponding *Klipot* from its *Rosh* to its *Raglaim*.

Ohr Pnimi

2. **These *Sigim* and *Melachim*, their *Shoresh* is the name First BON.**

    We must thoroughly understand what these *Sigim* are and how they were rooted and come from the name BON.

    The thing is that you already know that the *Kelim* of each *Partzuf* come to it from its *Elyon*. This is so because once the *Orot de Eser Sefirot de Guf de Elyon* depart and the *Kelim de Eser Sefirot* remain emptied of *Ohr*, these *Kelim* move to the *Tachton* and fill up with the *Orot* of the *Tachton* (see Part 5, *Ohr Pnimi* item 35, par. "The Rav has already thoroughly explained").

    Accordingly, you see that the *Kelim* of the lower nine of *Partzuf* SAG *de* AK that were emptied of their *Orot* with *Tzimtzum* NHY *de* AK are the very *Kelim* of the *Nekudim de* AK, called BON there. It has been explained in *Ohr Pnimi* (Part 6 item 1, Sub Header "**Its SAG**") that the lower nine of SAG *de* AK mixed there with the *Behina Dalet* that is in the *Kelim de* NHY *de Partzuf Keter de* AK (Part 6 *Ohr Pnimi* item 38).

    Behina Dalet mixed with every single *Sefira* up to *Hochma*, and thus there is a mixture of *Behina Dalet* in the *Kelim de* SAG, in each and every *Behina* in them. It has also been explained above (Part 6 item 1, Sub Header "**Its SAG**") why the *Orot* and *Kelim* of SAG could shine in the place of *Behina Dalet de* AK. This is so because there was no *Tzimtzum* on the *Ohr* SAG, being the *Ohr* of *Bina*; the *Tzimtzum* was only on the *Ohr Hochma*.

    Afterwards, these *Kelim* moved to the ZAT *de Nekudim*, and AVI of the *Nekudim* mated in *Zivug de Gadlut Panim be Panim*, and extended *Komat Hochma* in their place from below upwards in *Behinat Rosh*. After that they dispensed this *Ohr Hochma* to the ZAT of *Nekudim* where the *Behina Dalet* was mixed in each and every one of their *Behinot*.

Thus, that *Ohr* could not clothe in these *Kelim* since the *Behina Dalet* was already restricted to not receive the *Ohr Hochma*. Therefore, when the *Ohr* extended into the *Kli* and struck the *Behina Dalet* that was mixed in the *Kli*, it instantly departed and left all the *Kelim*. Then the *Kli* too broke and died because of *Behina Dalet* in it. It sucked something from the *Ohr* before it left there, and this sucking caused a disparity of form in *Behinat* oppositeness from the *Maatzil*, which is the Light of Life, hence it is called "Death".

You find that this mixture of *Behina Dalet* in the *Kelim de SAG*, which are *Behina Bet*, caused a shattering and death in the *Kelim*. For this reason this mixture is called *Sigim* in the *Kelim*. These are parts in the *Kelim* that cannot receive the *Ohr Elyon* and because of them, the corruption falls into all the *Kelim*, even in the parts that were worthy of receiving the *Ohr*, namely the *Kelim de SAG* that are from *Behina Bet*.

He says that when He "began to create the world etc. He began to sort the four above-mentioned *Melachim* that died. What was sorted from Him, rose in the *Kedusha* of the *Olamot*, and what was not sorted remained a *Klipa* and *Sigim*." This is because after the *Ohr* departed from the *Kelim* and the *Kelim* died and fell to the Separated *Olamot*, to *BYA*, the *Maatzil* returned and sorted the broken *Kelim* of the *Melachim*.

This means that He sorted the *Kelim* that are worthy for *Halbasha* of the *Ohr Elyon*, which belong to the *Kelim de SAG*, which are the *Partzufim* of *Atzilut* in the *BON* part in them. These *Sigim* that are mixed in *Behina Dalet* that were not sorted, remained in *BYA* within the *Klipot*.

Thus, we learn that the *Sigim* are parts of *Behina Dalet* that mixed with the *Kelim de SAG*. That mixture was rooted in the *Kelim de Nekudim*, called *BON*, as he says, "these *Sigim* and *Melachim*, their *Shoresh* is the name First *BON*," meaning in *Nekudim*.

Containing corresponding Klipot from its Rosh to its Raglaim.

This is because in general, *ZAT* are considered one whole *Partzuf* in *Rosh* and *Guf*. This is because they received the *Ohr GAR* and the *Rosh* from the *Zivug* of *Gadlut de AVI*. The entire *ZAT* broke *Panim* and *Achor*, as it is written below in this Part, and because *Behina Dalet* was mixed in every single *Behina* of the *Kelim* of the *Nekudim*. Because of that there are *Klipot* in it from its *Rosh* to its *Raglaim*, meaning *Sigim* that remained inside the *Klipot*.

3. **Even though they are seven Melachim, they are ten, as we say that they are seven Heichalot, when they are actually ten. This is so because the first Heichal consists of the first three Sefirot, called Kodesh Kodashim. The**

last *Heichal* consists of two, *Yesod* and *Malchut*, which is *Livnat ha Sapir*. So it is here, since they are *Yod Sefirot*, called seven *Melachim*.

Ohr Pnimi

3. **Though they are seven *Melachim*, they are ten.**

   This means that not only do ZAT HGT NHYM of the *Katnut* contain *Eser Sefirot* as well, meaning *Eser Sefirot* in each contains HGT NHYM, but they also had a *Zivug de Gadlut* that have actual GAR, meaning HBD too.

4. A more elaborate matter is this: We have learned that from these *Melachim*, the suitable *Behinot* were sorted for *Atik*, *AA*, and *AVI de Atzilut*. However, there was some breaking in their *Achoraim*. Not actual death, which is the *Klipa*, but a lessening of *Ohr*.

   Thus, these *Achoraim* fell below their place in the *Kedusha* itself and do not have actual *Sigim*, which are death. All the *Behinot Malchut* in each *Sefira* were sorted from these *Melachim* of the name BON in the part of ZON *de Atzilut*. However, some *Nitzotzot*, which were not sorted, remained in them and are mixed inside the *Klipot* and the *Sigim*. Hence, in these there is actual death. You find that all the *Klipot* cling solely to ZON, not from *Ima* upwards.

Ohr Pnimi

4. **There was some breaking in their *Achoraim* etc. do not have actual *Sigim*.**

   Interpretation: GAR *de Atzilut* too were not completely sorted, and the *Achoraim* that fell from them during the breaking of the vessels did not rise to their place completely until *Gmar Tikun*. However, that does not give any hold to the *Klipot* since these *Achoraim* never left *Olam Atzilut* at all, but descended from a high degree to a low degree.

   Conversely, ZAT *de Nekudim*, called ZON, have actual *Sigim*, as we have written above. This is why they died and fell to the Separated *Olamot*. Thus, because these *Kelim* were not entirely sorted, but many *Sigim* remained inside the *Klipot*, they have a hold of ZON too, in the extent that they take their authority from these *Kelim de ZAT*.

   The *Klipot* cling solely to ZON, not from *Ima* upwards.

   It is written above in the previous item that unsorted parts remained inside the *Klipot* only from the *Kelim de ZA*, and this is why they have a hold of it. Conversely, nothing fell to the share of the *Klipot* from *Ima* upwards, hence the *Klipot* have no hold at all from *Ima* upwards.

5. You know that the *Shoresh* of ZA is only six *Sefirot*. However, afterwards they grew and became *Eser Sefirot* for it. Similarly, the *Shoresh* of *Malchut* is one *Nekuda*, which is later made to consist *Eser Sefirot*.

Thus, in their first *Shoresh* they are only seven *Melachim*, six in ZA and one in *Nukva*. These cling to the last two *Otiot* of The Name, which are VH, and these two *Otiot* are eleven in *Gimatria*.

This is the meaning of the eleven signs of the incense, ten inner *Sefirot*, and one *Makif*. Although the *Makif* too consists of ten *Sefirot*, it is called one.

Ohr Pnimi

5. **The *Shoresh* of ZA is only six *Sefirot*.**

This is so because when it was born, it had no *Rosh*, which is GAR, called HBD. He had only VAK, being HGT NHY, and *Malchut* has only her *Malchut*, lacking all first nine *Sefirot*. Hence, the *Sitra Achra* do not have any sucking from the *Rosh de* ZA, since during the *Katnut* it has no *Rosh*.

As we shall see, these are very interesting things, but here we shall only elucidate the reason that ZA came out without GAR. Indeed, even during the *Gadlut*, it has no more than six *Kelim* HGT NHY. When the Rav writes that it has *Eser Sefirot*, it does not mean that the first three *Sefirot*, namely KHB, were added to it, only that its HGT of *Katnut* grew to become a HBD, and the NHY *de Katnut* grew to become a HGT. All that was added are the three lower *Sefirot*, being NHY.

Thus, even during the *Gadlut* it does not attain the first three *Kelim* KHB, and because this is a great principle in the wisdom, we must understand it at its source, each with its own reason.

It is known that the *Shoresh* of ZA emerged at *Nekudim*, called *HaVaYaH de* BON. This is *Partzuf* MA, called YESHSUT that came out of the *Nikvey Eynaim*. Also, you find a great innovation in this *Partzuf*, unlike all the previous *Partzufim* of AK.

The *Gufim* emerged in them in *Eser Sefirot* and *Eser Kelim*, and each *Guf* begins with *Kli de Keter*, as it is written in *Matei ve Lo Matei*. However, in this *Partzuf* that came out of the *Eynaim*, the *Guf* begins from *Daat*; there is no memory of the first three *Sefirot Keter Hochma Bina* in them.

Besides that, there is a great difference in the *Eser Sefirot de Rosh* itself. Until here there is only one *Rosh* for each *Partzuf*: the first is YESHSUT that stands from *Tabur de* AK upward to the *Chazeh*; the second is the *Keter* of the *Nekudim*; and the third is AVI *de Nekudim*.

These two changes are interdependent. It has already been thoroughly clarified in Part 6 that all these three *Roshim* are only one *Eser Sefirot de Rosh*. The matter of their division in this manner is because of the ascent of the *Hey Tata'a* in the *Eynaim*, where the *Zivug* was made on the *Masach de Behina Aleph*, called *Nikvey Eynaim*.

The first *Rosh* came out in two *Sefirot Keter* and *Hochma* and in the *Nukva de Hochma*, the *Zivug* was made on the *Hey Tata'a* incorporated there, and this *Rosh* is called YESHSUT. For this reason, the three *Sefirot Bina, ZA*, and *Malchut*, are considered *HGT de Rosh*, as they are below the *Masach* and the place of the *Zivug* and in that they are no longer considered GAR.

Nonetheless, these *HGT* are also considered *Rosh*. Moreover, they are the gist of the *Rosh* of *Partzuf Nekudim* because the above first *Rosh*, called YESHSUT that stands from *Tabur AK* upward through the *Chazeh* does not join the *Partzuf* at all. Instead, it is regarded entirely as *Akudim* (see Part 6, *Ohr Pnimi* item 20), but its *Behinat AHP* that exited to *Behinat HGT* are considered *Rosh de Nekudim*.

Also, these *AHP* are divided into two *Roshim*. This is so because the *Behinat Awzen*, called *Sefirat Keter de Nekudim* is considered *Behinat Keter* and *Hochma* of this *Rosh*, in the form of *Hey Tata'a* in the *Eynaim*.

The *Behinat Hotem Peh* that came out of this *Rosh* too are YHV in the *AHP*. They are considered the third *Rosh*, called *AVI de Nekudim*. Know, that the second *Rosh* too, called *Keter de Nekudim*, is also not considered the *Rosh* of the *Partzuf*. This means that its *Malchut* does not expand from above downward to *Behinat Eser Sefirot de Guf* since it only shines and clothes in the third *Rosh*, meaning *AVI de Nekudim*.

AVI alone are the *Rosh* for the *Partzuf* of the *Nekudim*. This means that they *Malchut* expands from above downward to *Behinat Eser Sefirot de Guf de Nekudim* (see above *Histaklut Pnimit* Part 6, section Cause and Consequence, item 30).

Know, that even during the *Gadlut*, when *Hey Tata'a* descends from the *Eynaim* in the *Keter* to the *Peh de Rosh*, *Keter* itself still does not join *AVI* in such a way that they will literally be made into one *Rosh*. Instead, only *He'arat NHY* of *Keter* clothes *AVI*. This is the meaning of *AVI* becoming *Behinat HBD*, and the second *Rosh* is in *Behinat Keter* above their *Rosh*.

You see how the *Eser Sefirot* of one *Rosh* were divided and made into three *Roshim*. The first *Rosh* took *Keter Hochma*; the second *Rosh* took the *Bina* in them, called *Awzen*; and the third *Rosh*, called *AVI*, took the ZAT in them, called *Hotem Peh*. However, the first two *Roshim* do not join the *Guf* of the *Partzuf*.

You already know that all the *Sefirot de Guf* extend from the *Rosh*. The full measure that *Malchut de Rosh* clothes in her *Ohr Hozer* from below upward in the *Rosh* expands from her and within her in that same amount to *Eser Sefirot de Guf*.

Yet, understand that *Malchut* of the third *Rosh* has no more than the two *Sefirot Hotem Peh*, which are ZAT *de Rosh*. The GAR of *Rosh* are in the two previous *Roshim* because *Keter* and *Hochma* are in the first *Rosh*, called YESHSUT and *Bina* is in the second *Rosh*, called *Keter*. Thus we have thoroughly explained that it is impossible for ZON to have more than seven *Kelim* HGT NHYM, since their *Rosh*, being AVI, have no more than these ZAT, which are *Hotem Peh*.

We might ask about that: Since both lack GAR, what then is the greatness of AVI over ZON? The Rav has already explained that to us above (Part 6 items 21-25). The whole merit of AVI over the ZON is because AVI took a little bit *He'arah* from the *Ohr Awzen*. This is why their *Kelim* did not break, and only their ZON did not receive any *He'arah* from the *Ohr Awzen*, but only from the *Hotem Peh*. This is why all their *Kelim* broke.

In general, we have already learned there thoroughly and we shall explain further in this part that this *He'arah* that AVI received from the *Ohr Awzen* corrected them by means of *Zivug Achor be Achor*. This means that because of that they had *Behinat* GAR of *Bina*, as we shall elaborate below.

6. The essence of how they were seven and became eleven is that the four *Achoraim* broke from HB and YESHSUT. They were joined above with these seven *Melachim* and became eleven. Do not wonder at how *Klipot* were made of HB etc. since this is discerned as what clothes in ZON below to become *Mochin* for them, and that *Behina* is considered actual ZON.

7. *Let us complete the scrutiny regarding the primary reason and what it was. His intention is to create this world, which contains reward and punishment. This is impossible except through an officer, which is the measure of repaying the evil. Also, the evil is the *Shoresh* of the *Sigim* and the *Shmarim* of the *Gevurot* and the *Dinim*, as it is written, "in the place of justice, that wickedness was there."

Ohr Pnimi

7. "In the place of justice, that wickedness was there."

This refers to the sentence of the *Sitra Achra* that is turned into harsh and bitter *Dinim*, as it is written, "His ordinances, they have not known them." Now you can understand the words of the Zohar (Truma, p.164), "The *Sitra Achra* is given an extra count, and it is counted as a deficit, such as eleven."

This is the evil attribute to repay the evil, since the *Sitra Achra* is given more power to hold than they deserve. In that, "a whirling storm; it shall whirl upon the head of the wicked," and this is what our sages imply, "A camel that went looking for horns, its ears were cut off."

8. The *Sigim* and the *Klipot* cannot appear except through a concatenation of *Olamot*. In the end, the *Sigim* will be sorted and manifest, and all this was through the death of these *Melachim*. All of them are strong *Dinim*, named BON, which are *Gevurot*.

   This is so because all these are *Behinot Nekudot*, being *Nekevot* and *Behinot Ohr Hozer, Mayin Nukvin*. The *Tzura* of the *Nekudot* is *Nitzotzot* and they are the strong *Nitzotzin* mentioned in Parashet Pekudei, "Come and see, the *Rosh* of the beginning of the faith inside the thought. It hammered a strong spark and educed *Nitzotzin*."

Ohr Pnimi

8. **Behinot Nekudot, being Nekevot and Behinot Ohr Hozer, Mayin Nukvin.**

   Malchut is called *Nekuda*. This is named after the root *Malchut* over which there was the first *Tzimtzum*, called The Middle Point. Hence, the *Malchuyot* and the *Nekevot* in all the *Olamot* are called *Nekudot*, since they are the subject of the *Tzimtzum* and the *Masach* over which the *Zivug de Hakaa* with the *Ohr Elyon* occurred.

   He writes, "through the death of these *Melachim*. All of them are strong *Dinim*," etc. These are *Behinot Nekudot*, which are *Nekevot* and *Ohr Hozer* and MAN. It is so because these three are one matter, meaning the *Behinot* of the *Masach* that raises *Ohr Hozer* and unite and copulate the *Partzufim Elyonim* when they rise to MAN from the sorting of BYA. The explanation to this matter will be brought below.

9. The thing is that these seven *Melachim* are the *Behinat Gevurot* that emerged in the world first, as it is written, "In the beginning God created." Afterwards He associated *Midat ha Rachamim* with it "in the day that the Lord God made" so that the world could exist and not return to *Tohu ve Bohu*, as it is written, "Now the earth was unformed and void."

   After he says, "In the beginning God created," which are the seven *Melachim*, there are seven words corresponding to them in the verse "In the beginning." The name HaVaYaH is the *Hassadim* and is the eighth *Melech*, called *Hadar*, which is the Upper *Hesed*, as mentioned in the Idra, and this is the name MA.

It is known that the name MA is in *Hassadim,* and the name BON in *Gevurot.* All are hard *Dinim* from which *Sigim* the *Klipot* came out through their death and fall, in the form of the dust of the Upper Earth.

That dust that will be in the ground of the *Mishkan* (lit. Tabernacle), *Olam Beria,* where they were sorted as in a man in the grave. This is because *Beria* under the *Mishkan* is *Malchut de Atzilut* and these strong *Nitzotzin* are thrown there, as it is written in Parashat Pekudei, "Throws *Nitzotzin* in every direction and sorted the waste from within the thought."

Thus, throwing these *Nitzotzin* down to *Beria* is to sort out the waste and the *Klipot* that were in potential in the Upper thought, and have now been executed. As the *Nitzotzin* that the craftsman beats with his hammer instantly quench, so these *Nitzotzin* quenched and died and returned to the dust, and then they were sorted.

Ohr Pnimi

9. the *Behinat Gevurot* that emerged in the world first, as it is written, "In the beginning God created."

This refers to what our sages have written, "In the beginning it came up in the thought to create the world in *Midat ha Din.* Saw that the world does not stand, preceded *Midat ha Rachamim* and associated it with *Midat ha Din.*"

We have already discussed it at length (Part 4, Chap 1, *Ohr Pnimi* item 4), and it explains there that the first three *Partzufim de AK* had only one *Kli* from the *Behinat Malchut,* being *Midat ha Din,* hence they had only one *Kav.* In order for the world to exist according to His wish to do good to His creatures, this can only be depicted in the form of a conduct of reward and punishment, by way of Ten Utterances, and the *Tikun* of the three *Kavim, Hesed, Din,* and *Rachamim.*

This was done by the association of *Midat ha Rachamim* with *Din,* meaning the association of the First *Hey,* called *Midat ha Rachamim,* namely *Bina,* with the *Hey Tata'a,* called *Midat ha Din,* which is *Malchut.* The beginning of this association is made in the *Zivug* of the *Rosh SAG* for *Olam ha Nekudim* in the form of ascent of *Hey Tata'a* to the *Eynaim* and YHV in the AHP.

This is sufficient only for *Tikun Kavim* in GAR, but in ZAT there was still no *Tikun Kavim.* For this reason the *Kelim* of the ZAT broke and fell to BYA, as written there at length.

The association of *Midat ha Rachamim* with *Din* in the GAR was not enough to correct the ZAT entirely, meaning from *Behinat Hassadim* too. Nonetheless, the association in *GAR de Nekudim* did help to correct the *ZAT* in the *Behinot Gevurot*. Although the *Kelim de ZAT* broke and fell to *BYA*, still, *Nitzotzin* came down with them to revive the *Kelim*.

Know, that these *Nitzotzin* mean the *Tikun* of the *Gevurot* to be ready to receive the *Hassadim* afterwards, when they are sorted, and rise from there to *Atzilut* as MAN. He writes, "these seven *Melachim* are the *Behinat Gevurot* that emerged in the world first, as it is written, 'In the beginning God created.'"

This refers to the *Tikun* of the *Gevurot* to be fitting for sorting and to raise them as MAN to receive the *Hassadim* of the new MA. They are implied in the words, "In the beginning God created," as the name God indicates *Gevurot*.

He associated Midat ha Rachamim with it "in the day that the Lord God made."

This refers to the verse, "These are the generations of the heaven and of the earth when they were created, in the day that the Lord God made earth and heaven" (Genesis 2; 4). The name *HaVaYaH* (lit. Lord) implies *Hassadim*, which is *Melech Hadar*, called the new MA.

They cause a *Zivug Elyon* there through raising MAN from the sorting of the *Nitzotzin* and the *Kelim* in *BYA* to the *Atzilut*, and receive the *He'arat Hassadim* of the new MA. At that time the desired association of *Midat ha Rachamim* with *Din* is over, meaning by that the *Tikun Kavim* is completed in *ZAT* too, and all this will be explained elaborately in its place.

10. It is written in Idrat Nasso (p. 131), "Some were corrected and some were not corrected." This does not mean that there are some *Melachim* among them that were corrected and some that were not corrected. Rather, it means that some were sorted and corrected from them, from the actual *Melachim* themselves, from each and every part of them, and that a part of them in each and every one of them was not corrected and remained below.

Ohr Pnimi

10. "Some were corrected and some were not corrected" etc. a part of each and every one of them was not corrected and remained below.

It is a *Partzuf* of one *Adam*, having corresponding *Klipot* from its *Rosh* to its *Raglaim*, meaning opposite all five *Partzufim de ZON de Atzilut*. These five *Partzufim* that were sorted and became *Olam Atzilut*, each of them left parts of it that were still not sorted, but are destined to be sorted by raising MAN from the work of the righteous throughout the six thousand years of *Olam ha Tikun*.

Know, that remains of the above *Partzufim de Atzilut* that remained unsorted are the entire good reward awaiting the righteous because the world was created in ten utterances, meaning the ten *Kelim de Atzilut* in *Behinat* association of *Midat ha Rachamim* with *Din*.

It is by that that the conduct of reward and punishment was made in the world, and this is because of the two states of ZON, *Katnut* and *Gadlut*. By doing good deeds they raise MAN to ZON, by which it attains the *Gadlut* and GAR, and the *Rachamim* appear.

If they do bad deeds, by that they cause ZON to return to the state of *Katnut* and a conduct of *Din* manifests in the world. It is also the same for each and every individual, relating to one's own *Neshama*. Yet, here you should understand that there is no absence in the spiritual, much less in *Atzilut*, where He is One and His name One.

The matter of *Mochin de Gadlut* and *Katnut* that travel back and forth in ZA *de Atzilut* by the actions of the *Tachtonim*, does not mean that when the *Mochin de Katnut* is absent, the previous *Mochin de Gadlut* vanish. Rather, there is only an addition here, as the previous *Mochin de Gadlut* that were extended through the work of the righteous remain for ever, unchanged at all by the bad deeds of the wicked.

Instead, the wicked caused a *Behinat* new *Mochin* to be made, additional to the previous *Mochin*, though the conduct of the world is always through the *Mochin* that is added last. Thus, the chain of time we find in this world, in terms of past and present, extends to us from the *Elyonim*, from the *Pnimiut* and *Hitzoniut*.

The past extends from the *Pnimiut*, and the present extends from the *Hitzoniut*. The *Hitzoniut* is always apparent to us in this world, and the *Pnimiut* is hidden from us and does not serve us at all, but is destined to appear before us in the future, at *Gmar Tikun*.

This is the meaning of "Righteous have no rest, not in this world and not in the next world." This does not refer to the next world after they die, as it is known, "Set free among the dead."

Instead, some righteous are awarded the *Orot* of the next world in their life. Our sages tell us that even those great righteous that have already been awarded the next world in their life have no rest. Instead, they must labour in the Holy Work and always come in *Behinat Achoraim* that precede the *Panim* in order to raise MAN to a new, higher *Mochin*.

This is so because there is sorting in the *Partzufim de GAR de ZA* too, above the *Orot* of the next world. This is the meaning of the *Partzufim* of the *Neshamot* being destined to clothe up to *Komat AK de Assiya*. At that time they will equalize the *Koma* of the *Hey Partzufim de AK*, and this will be explained in its place.

The matter of this *Halbasha*, that the *Neshamot* are awarded clothing the *Partzufim Elyonim* means the good reward, that is hidden for the righteous in the future. Because of all the *Mochin*, extended by raising MAN that they raise by the good deeds that they do, though afterwards they come in *Behinat Achoraim* and cause *Katnut* in ZON again, we see that the previous *Mochin de Gadlut* are not absent. Instead, they come as *Pnimiut*.

Hence, they have a way of always extending new *Mochin*. The first *Mochin* come to them in *Pnimiut*, in a way that they extend a higher *Mochin* every time.

Also, all these *Mochin* that were drawn to the *Partzufim Elyonim* through the MAN that they raised, all these belong to their share. Though in the present they enjoy only the last *Mochin* that they have extended, the previous *Mochin* remain forever. However, they do not use them in the present, so that they will be able to increase strength and go from strength to strength. In the future, they will all acquire all these *Mochin* that were drawn by them at once.

This is the meaning of what our sages said, "The Creator is destined to impart every righteous 310 worlds, as it is said, 'That I may cause those that love Me to inherit substance, and that I may fill their treasuries'" (end of Masechet Okatzin). It means that the *Mochin* that they have extended in the *Olamot Elyonim* is their share in their future.

11. The thing is that of these 288 *Nitzotzin* of the *Melachim* that died and descended to *Olam Beria*, when the *Tikun* of the eighth *Melech, Hadar*, came, he began to sort out the *Nitzotzot* and the *Kelim* from them too. Everything that it sorted of them was only the *Nukva* parts in all the *Partzufim*. In the beginning, the selected and the best of them was sorted and rose in *Atzilut*.

12. There are also degrees in *Atzilut* itself. First, through the above mentioned *Ibur Elyon*, they began to sort the best among them, of which *Nukva de Atik* was made.

    After the *Ohr Nitzotzot* of the 288 *Nitzotzot* was mixed with the *Ohr* of *Nekudat Keter* that remained in *Atzilut* and the *Kelim* of the *Melachim* mixed with the new *Kelim* of the new MA, all that was made into *Nukva de Atik* and *Atik*. It is so in all the others too.

Afterwards, through the *Zivug de Dechura de Atik* with *Nukva,* they raised and sorted *Nitzotzot* that fell below, the fitting part, to *Nukva de Arich* and entered in the place of the *Ibur* in the form *Mayin Nukvin.* There they sweeten and correct by being there for the time of the *Ibur* and become *Behinat Partzuf.*

13. Likewise, *Arich* sorted for *Nukva de AVI* and *AVI* for *ZON,* the entire *Behinat Malchut* in them. This is why these are called *Melachim,* since all the *Malchuyot* were made of them.

    Similarly, every *Yod Sefirot* themselves in each and every *Partzuf* were sorted in the above-mentioned order. What could not be sorted and rise in *Olam Atzilut* even for the bottom *Nukva de ZA,* remained in *Beria.* Later on, all the parts of *Beria* were made of them, in its order of degrees.

    The *Nitzotzot* of *Beria* cannot be sorted by *AVI de Atzilut* since they cannot rise above *ZON.* Instead, they are sorted in *Beten* of *Nukva de ZA* through the *Zivug* of *ZA* with it.

    However, there too only *Behinat Atik de Beria* is sorted, and there *Arich de Beria* is sorted, and *AVI de Beria* are sorted in *Arich,* and likewise always. This is so because it is impossible for any part to be sorted above the place of its degree, not in place and not in time. They are only one after the other in both order of degrees and the order of the time of their *Tikun,* and this is elaborated sufficiently.

14. See regarding *Ibur ZA,* how it is impossible to open the grave without blood when it is born. These are the parts called *Sigim* in comparison with *Atzilut.* These *Sigim* and blood return to be sorted in *Beria,* that which *Beria* evaluates as *Sigim,* returns to be sorted in *Yetzira* etc. similarly in each degree, and this is enough.

    Afterwards it is likewise with the worse in *Yetzira,* and after that with the worst of all in *Assiya,* also according to its degrees. This is so because all the parts of these three *Olamot BYA* are *Behinat Nukva*; there is no *Dechura* among them at all. Even the *Dechurin* (pl. for *Dechura*) among them are but forces of the *Nukva,* since they are all soldiers and armies of the *Malchut,* and all were made of the sorting of the seven *Melachim* as we have mentioned.

15. Also, all the creatures and the *Neshamot* of the righteous are all from the sorting of these *Melachim.* They are sorted daily by our prayers and rise up as *Mayin Nukvin.* Then they are corrected and come to the world.

    This is the meaning of, "All of Israel are children of *Melachim,*" and this is the meaning of, "Messiah Son of David doth not come until all the

Neshamot in the *Guf* perish," being the *Guf* that is mixed of good and evil. Also, all the angels and all the creatures in heaven and in earth, all came from these scrutinies.

16. After every thing that was made to create the four *Olamot ABYA* had been sorted, *Adam ha Rishon* was created to complete and examine through his actions and *Mitzvot*.

    By the power of the *Mitzvot* and the prayers to scrutinize the scrutinies these *Melachim* were joined in the Tree of Knowledge of Good and Bad in their *Sigim*. Then he too died and his entire offspring after him, to sort his parts that were mixed with good and bad like the *Melachim*.

    This is the meaning of reincarnation, as it is explained in its place. For this reason there are angels that die and are renewed every day, as it is written, "created His servants," etc. This is enough for the understanding for the pen fails to specify every thing.

17. After all these scrutinies that was scrutinized during the creation of the *Olamot ABYA*, most of the *Sigim* in them had still not been sorted, as the good leaves and the little good remains with the completely evil. Every day the good is sorted and leaves, and the evil remains.

    Hence, these parts that were not sorted before the creation of *Adam ha Rishon* and had to be sorted by *Mayin Nukvin* that *Adam* will raise through his actions, these were the *Behinat Sigim* and *Klipot*. They were also as it is mentioned in *ABYA* since the better part in them were the constituents of *Sigim* in *Atzilut* of the *Klipot*. This too is according to the degrees *Atik* and *Arich* etc. and the worst in *Beria* of the *Sigim*, and that too through her degrees etc. similarly through *Assiya*.

18. Indeed, you should know that when these *Sigim* were sorted and the *Behinot* four *Olamot ABYA* were made of them, they are complete *Sigim* and *Klipot*. All the *Behinot Melachim* that could not be sorted were placed inside them in *Behinat Neshama* and sustenance in them, reviving them, as mentioned in Parashat Itro p. 69, "There is no *Sitra Achra* that does not have a minute Light."

    This is the meaning of the pursuit of the evil inclination and the *Sitra Achra* to cause the righteous to sin and to cling to *Kedusha*, as they have no sustenance besides that. When *Kedusha* and goodness increase, their lives increase. Now you should not wonder why the evil inclination is in pursuit of *Adam* to cause him to sin.

19. Everything that we always sort in our prayers from the day of *Adam's* creation to the days of the Messiah, everything is from those *Behinot* of the *Melachim* placed inside the *Klipot*. There are *Behinot* that are sorted every day, even now, which concern *Atzilut*, there are for each *Olam* in *BYA*, and there are for the *Neshamot* and so on in every item.

When all the sustenance and goodness completes its exit from them and complete *Sigim* are left, it is then written, "He will swallow up death for ever." These are *Sitra Achra*, called death because they are the *Sigim* of the dead *Melachim*, and keep that. It is as we have written about Son of David, that he doth not come before all the *Neshamot* in the *Guf* perish.

20. Indeed, you should know that as they are four *Olamot ABYA* in *Kedusha* and their *Shoresh* is only *Eser Sefirot* that expand in them sort-by-sort and degree-by-degree, so it is in *ABYA de Klipot*. They are all rooted in the sorting of the *Melachim* that could not be sorted, and they are eleven *Sefirot*.

It is written in the Zohar (Parashat Truma p.164), "The *Sitra Achra* is given an extra count, and it is counted as a deficit, such as eleven." It means that when it is given the extra count, it is a demerit, since they are ten in *Kedusha* and eleven in the *Klipot*.

This is so because while they are eleven, they are only nine, since these eleven are seven *Behinot*, seven *Melachim*, and two *Achoraim de AVI*, which are only nine. However, in the division of *AVI* into two *Behinot* they will have four *Achoraim*, and then they will all be eleven *Behinot*.

Ohr Pnimi

20. "The *Sitra Achra* is given an extra count, and it is counted as a deficit, such as eleven."

He brings evidence to his words above when he says that in general, *ABYA de Klipot* are eleven *Sefirot* vis-à-vis the general *ABYA de Kedusha*, which are *Eser Sefirot*. He explains that the reason they number eleven is because they are from the residue of the *Sigim* that were not sorted.

There are eleven *Behinot* in this matter, which are seven *Melachim* and four *Achoraim*, de *AVI* and *YESHSUT*, which are eleven, as it is written, "Where are their gods, the rock in whom they trusted." These are the very eleven days from Horev through Mt. Seir, and this is the meaning of the eleven signs of the incense. Since they are the entire sustenance in the *Klipot*, when they are burnt, the vitality of the *Klipot* rises upwards, the *Sigim* and the death are cancelled, and the plague stops.

The Rav does not come down to interpret the words of the Zohar here. However, since there is a great secret in their words, the text should be brought complete and be somewhat interpreted. It says, "The *Sitra Achra* is given an extra count, and it is counted as a deficit, such as eleven. It is as we have stated that in every place where letters are added, such as here, it is a demerit, such as your brothers have said, that they said enough, and on the side of *Kedusha*, he reduced a letter, and it is an addition," thus far its words.

Interpretation: The whole of the *Sitra Achra* is from the breaking of the vessels, as the Rav says, that there are eleven *Behinot*. It is known that their *Tikun* is in the form of the twelve *Partzufim* of *Kedusha*, as the entire *Tikun* of the breaking of the vessels is in the twelve *Partzufim* of *Atzilut*. Through them, the *Sitra Achra* is gradually annulled until "He will swallow up death for ever."

He says, "The *Sitra Achra* is given an extra count, and it is counted as a deficit." This is so because a "count" is a name for *Malchut*, and *Malchut de Sitra Achra* is considered an extra count. [Written aside in the manuscript of the author: "Count" means wisdom; "Extra" means adding, by way of "All who adds, subtracts."].

This is the meaning of *Malchut* without a crown, which are nine and not ten since they have no sucking from the *Keter*. A Crown is *Keter*. Hence, they are in impudence, in the form of "*Malchut* without a Crown". They are the evil eye, in the form of, "Ninety nine die of evil eye, and one from other diseases."

He says, "such as eleven," meaning all who adds, subtracts. They add seventy to the eleven [Written aside in the manuscript of the author: and the *Partzuf Elyon* of the twelve departs, which is *Ein Sof* and *Keter*] and are left only in the eleven. [Written aside in the manuscript of the author: eleven because they cancel and break and fall to the authority of the *Klipot*. This is the meaning of the tree shouting, "Do not touch me," because in the touching of the *Ayin* in the eleven it falls to the *Klipot*.] This is so because they have no sucking in *Keter*.

This is the meaning of, "in the side of *Kedusha* he diminished an *Ot* and it is an addition. It means that the *Ayin* is reduced from the eleven and the combination of *Kedusha* comes out in the addition since it becomes twelve. Understand that in addition to the Rav's words and with the rest of the words of the Zohar there.

21. **You find that the *Melachim* that remain from the sorting are the very sustenance of the *Klipot*. They are called "Multimple Authorities" since they are separated and are not connected, as they have not been corrected yet.**

These are eleven days from Horev to Mt. Seir, and they are the *Melachim* that ruled in Mt. Seir, which is Edom.

They are the ones who said, "Where are their gods, the rock in whom they trusted," and these are the eleven signs of the incense that rise upward when they burn. They depart from within the *Sigim*, called death, and then the *Sigim* and the death are cancelled and the plague stops.

22. These eleven signs of the incense are but one *Behina*, which is the *Noga* around it, and corresponds to it in *Yetzira*, in *Beria*, and in *Atzilut*. This *Klipa de Noga* is called "*Ruach Elokim Merachefet*" (lit. the spirit of God hovered). Its *Otiot* are *Mem, Tav – Peh, Reish, Het* (תיתפריימ).

    These are the 288 *Nitzotzin* of the *Melachim* that died and this *Klipa* is made of the 288 *Nitzotzin* that remained inside the *Kelim* and were not sorted. It hovers over the *Klipot* and does not enter them.

Ohr Pnimi

22. **The *Noga* around it, and corresponds to it in *Yetzira*, in *Beria*, and in *Atzilut*.**

    Know, that *ABYA de Klipa* are the opposite from *ABYA de Kedusha*. This is so because in *Kedusha*, all that is higher is more Holy, and every thing that lessens, its *Kedusha* descends to the *Sof* of *Assiya*.

    Conversely, in the *Klipot*, the highest *Klipa* opposite *Atzilut* is weak and not so bad, and the lower it descends the stronger are the impurity and the *Klipot*.

    Also, there is a difference regarding the mixture of good and bad in *Klipat* (*Klipa* of) *Noga*, meaning in the *Behinat Sigim* that were not sorted. In *Assiya* it is mostly bad, where they father every impurity, meaning the impurity of the dead.

    The *Klipot de Yetzira* are mixed good and bad, half each, and she defiles the weekdays too, as *Olam Yetzira* is the pure weekdays. In the *Klipot de Beria* the mixture is mostly good and some bad. It defiles only the *Truma* (lit. Contribution) because *Olam Beria* is *Behinat Truma*.

    Olam Atzilut is mostly good and there is a little bit of *Klipa* in it. However, even that little bit is not mixed with the *Kedusha*. The *Kedusha de Atzilut* has no impurity, but disqualifies the *Kodashim*, as *Atzilut* is *Behinat Kodashim*.

    "*Ruach Elokim Merachefet*" (lit. the spirit of God hovered). Its *Otiot* are *Mem, Tav – Peh, Reish, Het* (ת"תפר"מ).

    It means that the *Nitzotzin* are *Behinot Reshimot* from the *Orot* that fled from the seven *Melachim* and died. The *Reshimot* descended with them so that they would have the strength for the revival of the dead. Also the *Otiot Reish*, *Peh*, *Het* (288) and *Peh*, *Reish*, *Het* (fled) are the same, and understand that.

23. *Know, that there are four *Behinot* in *Olam Atzilut*, in how the *Zachar* and the *Nekeva* are situated there, whether they are in *Behinot Nekudot* prior to the *Tikun*, or when they are in *Behinot* complete *Partzuf* after the *Tikun*.

    This is their arrangement: the worst is both being *Achor be Achor*. Above it is *Achor be Panim*. This means that the *Zachar* will turn its *Achoraim* facing the *Panim* of the *Nekeva*, as now the *Nekeva* can receive the *Ohr* from the *Achoraim* of the *Zachar*, through her *Panim*. However, she still does not have the strength to receive from the *Panim* of the *Zachar*.

    Above it, it is *Panim be Achor*. This means that the *Zachar* turns his *Panim* facing the *Achoraim* of the *Nekeva* and shines in her. There is greater merit in that since the *Ohr* of the *Panim* of the *Zachar* themselves shine in the *Nekeva*, though she still does not have the strength to receive it through the *Panim*. For this reason she turns her *Achoraim* and receives the *Ohr* in the *Panim* themselves through there.

    By so doing, the *Ohr* becomes a little thicker there, and when the *Ohr* passes through the *Achor* and reaches the side of her *Panim*, she will be able to receive it, since it became a little more *Av*. This is the meaning of, "a wise will better her in the back (*Achor*)."

    When the *Panim* of the *Hochma*, being the *Zachar*, look in the *Achoraim* of the *Nekeva* and shine in her, he will better her and shine in her additional *He'arah*, more than if they were the opposite, which is *Achor* in *Panim*, which is the second degree.

Ohr Pnimi

23. Four *Behinot* etc. the worst is both being *Achor be Achor*.

    These four degrees apply both in ZON and in AVI, though they originate in AVI. Since they are the first elements to understand the *Mochin de AVI* and ZON, it is appropriate to elaborate and explain them thoroughly.

    It has been explained (Part 6) that *Rosh de Nekudim*, called AVI, are only *Behinat Hotem Peh de Rosh* compared to the *Eser Sefirot* of the general *Rosh*. From the perspective of the second *Rosh*, they are *Behinat AHP* that went outside the *Rosh* because the *Hey Tata'a* is in the *Eynaim de Keter*. Thus, AVI are found below the *Masach de Rosh*, for which they are considered HGT (Part 6, *Ohr Pnimi* item 44, sub-header "*Ot Yod*").

You must know that even though we have said that these *AVI* are *Behinat HGT*, they are still considered *Behinat GAR* and *Rosh* from the perspective of *Bina*, by the *Tikun de Achor be Achor* in them. This *Tikun* extends from the *Bina de Ohr Yashar* since the *Bina de Ohr Yashar* is *Ohr de Hassadim*, not *Hochma*, by way of "because He delighteth in mercy" (as the Rav has written above, Part 6 item 41 and *Ohr Pnimi* item 40, par. "The *Panim* and *Achor*").

Hence, it is considered that her *Achoraim* reject *Hochma* and her *Panim* is only *Ohr Hassadim*. It follows, that the *Hochma* and *Bina de Ohr Yashar* are in *Achoraim* to each other (see above Part 1, Chap 1, *Ohr Pnimi* item 50).

It has been explained above in the Rav's words (Part 6 item 24) that *AVI* took some *He'arah* from the *Ohr Awzen*, meaning the *Ohr Bina* of the *Eser Sefirot* of the general *Rosh*. Hence, the *Achoraim de Ohr Bina* helped to sustain them in *Behinat GAR*.

Although they are below the *Masach de Rosh* at *Nikvey Eynaim de Keter*, and this *Masach*, which is the *Hey Tata'a*, prevents the *He'arat Hochma* of the *Rosh* from them, it is still not considered a flaw for them at all. It is so because in any case, they do not want to receive *He'arat Hochma* at all, as they specifically crave and want *Hassadim*. They reject *Hochma* by the force of the *Achoraim* that rides on them and imprints that desire in them, in the form of "because He delighteth in mercy."

Now you can thoroughly understand the Rav's words there (Part 6, item 25) that the *ZAT* that did not receive anything from the *He'arat Awzen*, and because of that the *Kelim* broke *Panim* and *Achor*. However, *AVI*, which received some *He'arah* from the *Ohr Awzen* did not break, only their *Achoraim*. Their *Panim* sustained and did not break although they took *He'arat Ohr Awzen* in remoteness of location.

Now you can thoroughly understand the matters. It has been explained that through the *He'arah* that they received from the *Achoraim de Ohr Awzen*, they were not at all blemished from the remoteness of location. This means that they have departed from the *Behinat Rosh*, by the *Hey Tata'a* in the *Eynaim de Keter* that prevents *He'arat Hochma de Rosh* from them.

This is so because they have no wish for *Ohr Hochma*. Even if they had been at a near location, they would still reject the *Ohr Hochma* from them, as they are in *Achoraim* with it. For this reason they still have *Behinat* complete *Rosh* from this *Behina de Bina*, and this is why the flaw of the breaking did not govern them at all in this *Behina*. It means that the *Kelim de Panim* sustained entirely, namely the *Panim de Bina*, which is *Ohr de Hassadim*.

Only what they later received in their *Kelim de Achoraim* through the *Zivug de Yesod AK*, by which *Zivug* they turned their *Kelim de Achoraim* and made them into *Behinat Panim*, meaning received *He'arat Hochma* in them, only these *Kelim* broke (see Part 5, item 40, par. "The *Panim* and *Achor*"). This is because they had already been blemished by the remoteness of location and have become *Behinat Guf*.

The Rav says above that if AVI had not begun in *Behinat Achor be Achor*, they would have broken like the ZAT of the *Nekudim*. It means that through this *Tikun* of *Achor be Achor*, which is the *He'arat Ohr Awzen*, they are considered *Behinat Rosh*, being below the *Masach de Hey Tata'a* in the *Eynaim*. For this reason the breaking does not govern them.

However, if that *Tikun* of *Achor be Achor* had not been in them, they would have been considered actual *Guf*, like the *ZAT de Nekudim*, as both are only *Behinat Hotem* and *Peh* (*Ohr Pnimi* item 5, par. "We might ask").

Thus we have thoroughly clarified the matter of the *Achoraim de Ima* with respect to *Hochma*. Yet, *Abba* too is considered to be with his *Achoraim* toward *Bina* because of the *Hey Tata'a* in the *Nikvey Eynaim* of the *Keter*.

Consequently, *Abba* cannot dispense *Bina* any *Behinat Hochma*, as he is below the *Masach*. This is why it is considered *Achor be Achor*, since *Abba* cannot administer to *Bina* from the *He'arat Hochma*, due to the *Achoraim de Hey Tata'a*, even if *Bina* had returned her *Panim* to the *Hochma*.

Conversely, *Bina* would not have received the *Ohr Hochma* from *Abba*, even if *Abba* had returned his *Panim* to *Bina*, to give her *Ohr Hochma*, "because He delighteth in mercy." Thus we have thoroughly explained the situation of the first degree, called *Achor be Achor*.

Above it is *Achor be Panim*. This means that the *Zachar* will turn its *Achoraim* facing the *Panim* of the *Nekeva*.

You must know that two diminutions occurred in the *Bina* by the ascent of the *Hey Tata'a* in the *Eynaim*: 1 – The *Masach* that was erected in the *Eynaim*, because of which *Bina* came down to the *Behinat* restricted *Malchut*, in which there was a *Zivug de Hakaa* in the *Rosh* and in which the *Partzuf* ended, meaning in *Sefirat Bina de NHY*. The second diminution occurred in her by the force of the *Gevurot*, meaning the blockage of *Hassadim* in the *Kli Malchut* from the source of her emanation.

The matter of these *Gevurot* in *Kli Malchut* was explained above in the Rav's words regarding the *Ohr Malchut* in *Kli de Yesod*, present in *Partzuf AB de AK*, which is *Hitpashtut Bet de AK*. The *Orot* have changed and *Ohr Hochma* came in *Kli de Keter*, *Ohr Bina* in *Kli de Hochma* etc. until *Ohr Malchut* in *Kli de Yesod* (Part 5, item 45 and *Ohr Pnimi* there).

This is the *Ohr Achoraim* that remains of *Sefirat Hod* that no longer has *He'arat Hassadim* of the *VAK de ZA* in it. Hence, it is discerned as *Behinot Hey Gevurot* there in the *Kli de Yesod*.

It has also been explained there that the *Shoresh* of *Malchut* is the *Sefirat Hod*, meaning the fifth *Hesed* of the *Hey Hassadim*, though she has two diminutions in *Yesod* and in *Malchut*. Hence, *Malchut* is discerned as having *Kelim de Panim* from the perspective of her *Hitkalelut* in the ZA, that receive *He'arat Hochma* like the ZA, but with a blockage of *Hassadim*.

Thus, the *Panim* and *Achoraim* found in the *Kelim* of *Malchut* have been explained, and they are both *Behinat Gevurot*. In herself, she is corrected with a *Masach* that rejects *Hochma*. This is discerned as her *Achoraim*. Also, she has *He'arat GAR* from the perspective of her *Hitkalelut* in ZA, which is the fifth *Hesed*, *Hod*, though she is blocked to *Hassadim*. *Bina* received these two diminutions from *Malchut*, by the ascent of the *Hey Tata'a* in the *Eynaim*.

Now you can understand the necessity for these two situations, *Achor be Achor* and *Achor be Panim*. First, the first diminution is erected, being the hard *Achoraim* of the *Malchut* because of the *Masach* and the *Tzimtzum* that lie on *Bina* because of the *Hey Tata'a* in the *Nikvey Eynaim*. This *Tikun* is done by the *Achoraim de Bina*.

After this is corrected, there still remains the second diminution on her, being the blockage of *Hassadim* in the *Kli de Panim* of the *Malchut* that rests on the *Bina* due to the *Hey Tata'a* in the *Eynaim*. This is done by the state of *Achor be Panim*, as the *Zachar*, which is *Hochma*, shines *Ohr Hassadim* in her from his *Behinat Achoraim* into the *Kelim de Panim* of the *Bina*, which suffer from this shortage only, as they do not lack *He'arat GAR*.

Now *Bina* is corrected from the perspective of the *Kelim*, both in her *Achor* part, and in her *Panim* part. However, she still receives only *Ohr de Hassadim* from the *Behinat Achoraim* of the *Hochma*, and she is still unfit to receive the *Ohr Panim*, which is *Ohr Hochma*.

Above it, it is **Panim be Achor**.

The first two *Tikkunim*, *Achor be Achor* and *Achor be Panim*, extended from the *Achoraim de Bina*. The *Tikun* of *Achor be Achor* is the *Achoraim de Bina*, which reject *Hochma*, "because He delighteth in mercy." Hence, the matter of the *Masach* does not diminish her at all, since she rejects *Hochma* anyhow. For this reason she is not blemished by the *Masach* at all.

After the *Achoraim* are corrected, begins the *Tikun* of the *Kelim de Panim* by itself. This is because their entire shortage was from the blockage of *Hassadim*. Now, however, after the *Tikun de Achor be Achor*, they receive abundant *Hassadim* from the *Achoraim de Hochma*.

However, that third degree, which is *Panim be Achor*, meaning the *Panim* of the *Zachar* in the *Achoraim* of the *Nekeva*, comes to him by the *Zivug de AB SAG* that lowers the *Hey Tata'a* from *Eynaim* to *Peh*. At that time *HB* return to the *Rosh*, and the *Zachar*, which is *Hochma*, attains his *Behinat Panim* as in the beginning. However, *Bina* still remains in *Behinat Achoraim*, since she still does not have the power to receive with her *Kelim de Panim*.

She still does not have the strength to receive it through the *Panim*.

In fact, she can receive the *Ohr Pnimi* of *Hochma*, as she is already above the *Masach*, as in the previous *Partzufim* of AK. *Bina* holds to her *Achoraim* due to the previous *Tikkunim*, *Achor be Achor* and *Achor be Panim*, the first being the *Achoraim de Ima* that want *Hesed* and reject *Hochma*, the second being the *Behinat Gevurot* in her *Kelim de Panim* that are thirsty for the *Ohr Hassadim* from their *Shoresh*.

She does not wish to disclose her *Kelim de Panim* to receive *Ohr Hochma* from the *Zachar*, only *Ohr de Achoraim*, namely *Hassadim*. He says, "she still does not have the strength to receive it through the *Panim*," because of the great yearning for *Ohr de Hassadim* that she has.

The *Ohr* becomes a little thicker there etc. she will be able to receive it, since it became a little more *Av*.

It means that this *Ohr Panim*, received in the *Kelim de Achoraim* of *Bina*, greatly improves her *Achoraim*, until the *Achoraim* themselves ascend to complete *Behinat GAR*. Thus, the *Kelim de Panim* become of secondary importance and receive the *Ohr GAR* from the *Kelim* of the *Achoraim*. It follows that the *Kelim de Achoraim* are more important than the *Kelim de Panim*, as they administer them.

The reason for it is that indeed, the *Kelim de Achoraim* receive only a very small *He'arah* from the *Ohr Panim* of the *Zachar* since they are *Kelim* that reject *Hochma* and crave only *Ohr de Hassadim*. However, that diminished *He'arah* that they receive brings the *Achoraim* to be more important than the *Kelim de Panim*.

This is so because when the *Kelim de Panim* received *Hochma*, meaning the *Ohr Malchut* in *Kli de Yesod* in the previous *Partzufim*, they were in great blockage of *Ohr Hassadim*, which is the *Hey Gevurot* in the *Yesod*. However, these *Kelim de Achoraim* have an abundance of *Ohr de Hassadim*, and some diminished *He'arat Hochma* that they receive.

He says, "the *Ohr* becomes a little thicker," meaning it is a small *He'arah* because of the force of rejection found in the *Kelim de Achoraim*. "The *Ohr* becomes a little thicker there, and when the *Ohr* passes through the *Achor* and reaches the side of her *Panim*, she will be able to receive it, since it became a little more *Av*."

In other words, when the *Kelim de Panim* could receive *He'arat Hochma*, they could not receive the *Ohr Hassadim*, but were in *Behinot Gevurot*. Now, however, that they receive *He'arat Hochma* through the *Kelim de Achoraim*, they have both *Hochma* and *Hassadim*.

"A wise will better her in the back (*Achor*)" etc. more than if they were the opposite, which is *Achor* in *Panim*.

This is because now the *Hochma* improves the *Ohr Achoraim* and turns it into *Behinat GAR* and *Ohr Panim*. Before that, when they were in *Behinat Achor be Panim*, though they received in the *Behinat Kelim de Panim*, they only received *Ohr de Achor* from *Hochma*. Now, however, although they receive in the *Kelim de Achoraim*, she receives *Ohr GAR* and *Panim*.

24. Above all is the fourth degree, being the *Zachar* and *Nekeva* in *Panim be Panim* one opposite the other. This is so because then she receives the *Ohr* of the *Panim* of the *Zachar*, which is a wonderful *Ohr*. Moreover, there is no need for it to first thicken in her *Achor*, she can receive it as she is, *Zach*, through her *Panim*.

Ohr Pnimi

24. **The fourth degree, being the *Zachar* and *Nekeva* in *Panim be Panim*.**

    The first two degrees, *Achor be Achor* and *Achor be Panim*, are extended through the *Achoraim de Ima*, and the third degree is extended through the *Zivug Elyon de AB SAG* that lowers the *Hey Tata'a* from the *Eynaim*. This *Tikun* is beneficial only for the *Zachar* to acquire its *Panim* as in the beginning. However, the *Nukva* is still cleaved by the force of her *Achoraim*, choosing *Hassadim* and rejecting *Hochma*.

    Hence, *Bina* needs raising MAN from the *Tachtonim*, which are ZON, as only then is she forced to stop her force of *Achoraim* and return the *Panim* to *Hochma*. She does it only for ZON since she cannot extend them *He'arat Hochma* except by that. For this reason she returns *Panim be Panim* with the *Hochma*, which is the fourth degree.

Know, that the matter of raising MAN that returns to *HB Panim be Panim* is rooted back in *Eser Sefirot de Ohr Yashar*. This is because *Bina de Ohr Yashar* is *Behinat Ohr de Hassadim* and not *Hochma* (Part 1, Chap 1, *Ohr Pnimi* item 50).

Thus, she too is considered to be with her *Achoraim* to *Hochma*. However, when she wishes to emanate the ZA, who is essentially *He'arat Hochma*, she must return her *Panim* to *Hochma Panim be Panim* in order to receive *He'arat Hochma* from him to the *ZA de Ohr Yashar*.

It follows that as long as she does not emanate the ZA, she is in *Achoraim* with the *Hochma*. After she emanates the ZA she is *Panim be Panim* with the *Hochma*, to extend its *He'arah* for it. You find that the original root of the state of *HB Panim be Panim* is the *ZA de Ohr Yashar*.

Now you can thoroughly understand the above words of the Rav (Part 5, item 51), who says that the *Ohr Hesed* placed in *Bina*, which is *Ohr ZA*, remains in her always in *Behinat MAN*. It means that when *Bina* wants to extend the *Gadlut* of the *Ohr Hesed* in order to emanate it to its place, she must then return her *Panim* to the *Hochma*. For this reason this *Ohr Hesed* is considered *Behinat MAN* to the *Bina*, meaning that which causes her *Zivug Panim be Panim* with the *Hochma*.

Thus, the matter of raising MAN has been thoroughly explained, meaning a stimulating element for *Zivug HB*. Without that element, *Hochma* and *Bina* would not have mated *Panim be Panim* because of the *Achoraim de Bina* that reject *Hochma*, "because He delighteth in mercy."

This element is the ZON, as they are the progeny of *Bina* and their essence is only *He'arat Hochma*. This is so because the whole difference between *Bina de Ohr Yashar* and the *ZON de Ohr Yashar* is only in that *He'arat Hochma* that the *Bina* extends for the ZA.

After all, they are both *Ohr* of *Hassadim*, though *Bina* is *Ohr de Hassadim* without any *He'arat Hochma*, and ZA is in *He'arat Hochma* (Part 1, Chap 1, *Ohr Pnimi* item 50). For this reason a *Zivug de Gadlut* cannot be depicted for AVI without ascent of MAN since as long as the ZON do not rise to MAN to *Bina*, it is tied in a craving for *Hamshacha* of *Hassadim*, being the essence of her structure back from the *Ohr Yashar*. Remember these words in all the places that bear any mention of raising MAN.

25. **Know, that in ZON, all four mentioned *Behinot* were in the above order, but in AVI there were only three *Behinot* in them, which are the first, the third and the fourth, though the second *Behina* had no need for them.**

Ohr Pnimi

25. In AVI there were only three *Behinot* in them.

This is so because the second degree of *Achor be Panim* does not apply to AVI. The reason is that the two degrees, *Achor be Panim* and *Panim be Achor*, are erected in them at once, meaning at the lowering of the *Hey Tata'a* from *Eynaim* to *Peh*. At that time *Bina* returns to her previous state and the diminutions of the *Hey Tata'a* do not touch her at all. However, in ZON, the *Nukva* needs two corrections for both her diminutions, one for the *Kelim de Achoraim* and another for the *Kelim de Panim*.

26. *Now we shall explain the matter of *Achoraim de AVI* that fell and broke as well. First, we must explain the introduction of *Panim be Panim* and *Achor be Achor*.

The thing is that the place of the *Klipot* and the exteriors are the *Achoraim* of *Nukva de ZA*, and there they cling. However, there is also some gripping to the *Achor de ZA*.

Before God created *Adam* on earth the *Klipot* had strength to suck *Shefa* from the *Kedusha*, as it is written, "and there was not a man to till the ground." One of the works on the soil is mowing thorns from the vineyard, for which, practical *Mitzvot* are needed.

However, when ZAT were emanated, the lower *Adam ha Rishon* had not been created in the world. ZON emerged *Achor be Achor* for fear of the sucking of the exteriors.

This is because had they stood *Panim be Panim*, the *Klipot* would have had a place to grip in their holding place to suck, which are the *Achoraim*. This is because they cannot suck from the *Panim*, and for this reason they had to cleave *Achor be Achor* so that the exteriors would not be able to suck from there.

Ohr Pnimi

26. The place of the *Klipot* and the exteriors are the *Achoraim* of *Nukva de ZA*, and there they cling.

This is so because the *Klipot* cling only to a place of lack, meaning in a place that does not shine, called *Achoraim*, meaning precisely to the *Achoraim de* ZAT, which are ZON. However, they have no hold at all in GAR.

There is also a division in ZON between the ZA and the *Nukva*. This is because their hold is primarily in *Nukva de ZA*, as she is the ending *Sefira* of the *Partzuf*, which stops the *Ohr* in the *Partzuf* from expanding further by the force of the *Tzimtzum* and the *Masach* in her.

For this reason her *Achoraim* are complete darkness, as it is written, "Her feet go down to death," being the *Klipot*, called "death". He writes, "the place of the *Klipot* and the exteriors are the *Achoraim* of *Nukva de ZA*, and there they cling." It means that the *Klipot* and the exteriors begin from the place of darkness downward, which is from the *Sium* of the *Nukva* downward, because after her begins darkness, as she is *Behinat Sium* on the *Ohr* in the *Partzuf*.

However, there is also some gripping to the *Achor de ZA*.

Meaning in the full amount that does not shine, called *Achoraim*, because the rule is that Tzor is built only over the ruin of Jerusalem. This is so because the entire sustenance and construction of the *Sitra Achra* is on the ruin of the *Kedusha*. Thus, when *Kedusha* is corrected until there is no form of ruin in it, the *Sitra Achra* will be cancelled from the world, as it is written, "He will swallow up death for ever."

Before God created *Adam* on earth the *Klipot* had strength to suck *Shefa* etc.

This means that then ZON could not mate *Panim be Panim* because there is no *Zivug Panim be Panim* without a raising of MAN by their *Tachton*. It is explained there in *AVI*, and so it is regarding ZON, as ZON too are corrected in *Achor be Achor* because of the *Achoraim de Ima*, as we shall see below.

Thus, *Nukva* too does not stop her *Achoraim* before she has an element that compels her to that. This element are the *Neshamot* of the righteous that rise to her for MAN. In order to give them *He'arat GAR*, she must stop her *Achoraim* and return her *Panim* to ZA, and then mate with the ZA *Panim be Panim*.

Hence, before *Adam ha Rishon* was created, there was no one to raise MAN to the *Nukva de ZA*. For this reason they lacked GAR, meaning *Ohr Panim*, which is the primary sustenance of the *Partzuf*. This is why there was power in the *Klipot* to draw *Shefa* from the *Kedusha*, meaning from the *Behinat* lack of this *Ohr GAR*.

ZON emerged *Achor be Achor* for fear of the sucking of the exteriors.

It means that they emerged in the *Tikun* of the *Achoraim de Ima* since they rose above to AVI, ZA was incorporated in *Abba*, and *Nukva de ZA* in *Ima*. By so doing they have acquired *Behinat Achoraim de Ima*, which is as sufficient for them as *He'arat GAR* (*Ohr Pnimi* item 23).

Once they have obtained that, the exteriors can no longer suck from ZON, it is considered for them as *Behinat Ohr GAR*. Since there is *Ohr GAR* in the

Partzuf, there is no place for the exteriors to suck from, as there is grip only in ZAT without GAR.

Had they stood *Panim be Panim*, the *Klipot* would have had a place to grip in their holding place.

This does not mean had they stood in *Zivug Panim be Panim*. On the contrary, then the *Klipot* would have been expelled from ZON entirely. Instead, it means that if they had not had that *Tikun* of *Achor be Achor*, but the *Nukva* had wanted to receive the *Ohr Panim* of ZA, their *Achoraim* would have been exposed. In other words, the lack of GAR in them would have been exposed and sensed. In that state the *Klipot* would have had a place to grip, meaning in the lack in them.

Now, however, when they are corrected in the *Achoraim de Ima*, when they reject *Ohr Hochma*, meaning *Ohr Panim*, no lack is felt in them where the exteriors can grip. This is because now the lack of *Ohr Hochma* is not considered a flaw in them, as they do not want *Hochma* anyhow (see *Ohr Pnimi* item 23).

He writes, "had they stood *Panim be Panim*, the *Klipot* would have had a place to grip in their holding place to suck, which are the *Achoraim*. This is because they cannot suck from the *Panim*." This means that if the *Kelim de Panim* of the *Nukva* had been open to receive the *Ohr Panim*, the lack of *Ohr Panim* would have been exposed in them, and this lack is *Achoraim*, from which the *Klipot* grip and suck.

Remember onward, that *Achoraim* means a place of lack of *Ohr Hochma*. In this manner there is hold and sucking for the exteriors, whose entire sustenance is from the place of lack in the *Kedusha*.

Conversely, *Achoraim de Ima* is *Behinat* GAR, although there too there is a necessary lack of *Hochma*, hence the name *Achoraim*. However, with respect to *Bina*, this is not at all considered a lack since she is so from her *Shoresh* in *Bina de Ohr Yashar*, choosing *Hassadim* and rejecting *Ohr Hochma*.

Because *Bina* is essentially a *Sefira* from the GAR, hence her *Ohr de Hassadim* is also considered GAR. After ZON rise and mingle in AVI too, receiving this *Tikun* of *Achoraim de Ima* from them, they too obtain *He'arat* GAR from these *Behinat Achoraim de Ima*, because of which, this lack of *Ohr Panim* is not considered a shortcoming, even in ZON.

27. **When *Adam ha Rishon* was created and performed practical *Mitzvot* he returned them *Panim be Panim*. In that state there was no longer fear of the *Klipot*, as he had already dug, hoed, removed the stones, and cut the thorns from the vineyard.**

When they are *Achor be Achor*, *ZON* have only one wall for both of them. One wall is enough for both of them and they use one wall, half a wall for *ZA* and half a wall for *Nukva*. When *Adam* returned them *Panim be Panim* through *Mitzvot* and good deeds, one *Achor* was finished and completed, one complete *Achor* for one, and one complete *Achor* for the other, and they can return *Panim be Panim*.

Ohr Pnimi

27. **Practical *Mitzvot* he returned them *Panim be Panim*.**

    This means that through good deeds that he deed, he cleaved further to *Kedusha* and could scrutinize scrutinies in the *Nitzotzin* and *Kelim* that fell to *BYA*, purifying them from the *Sigim* in them, meaning from the mixture of *Behina Dalet* in them (*Ohr Pnimi* item 2).

    In that state he raised them for MAN to the *Nukva*. These *Nitzotzin* and *Kelim* that he raised came from the seven *Melachim de Nekudim* that had already had *Ohr Hochma* before they broke. Also, they are parts of *Nukva*, and hence *Nukva de ZA* feels their absence from the *Ohr Hochma*, and hence stops her *Achoraim*, brings her *Panim* back to *ZA*, and mates *Panim be Panim*.

    In that state there was no longer fear of the *Klipot*, as he had already dug, hoed, removed the stones, and cut the thorns from the vineyard.

    It means that after he sorted the *Nitzotzin* and the *Kelim* from all the *Sigim* in them, called cultivating the vineyard, meaning dug, hoed, etc. they are worthy of rising to MAN to *Nukva*, causing a *Zivug Panim be Panim* there with *ZA*. At that time these *Kelim* are corrected in *Behinat GAR* and there is no more fear that they will break, as had happened to these *Kelim* in the first time in *Olam Nekudim*. This is so because the thorns have already ended in the vineyard, which are the *Sigim* in them, and from here on they remain forever in *Kedusha*.

    One wall for both of them. One wall for both of them is enough and they use one wall.

    A "Wall" means *Achoraim*. This refers to *Achoraim de Ima*, corrected in her in *Behinat Achor be Achor*, which satisfies both of them as *He'arat GAR*. It complements the lack of *Hochma* in them, and for this reason they are defended from the exteriors.

    He writes, "One wall for both of them is enough." It means that it is enough for them to cover and conceal the lack of *Hochma* in their *Achoraim* and the *Klipot* cannot suck from there.

Half a wall for ZA and half a wall for *Nukva*.

It means that both are contained in these *Achoraim* in a way that the *Klipot* can suck from neither the ZA, nor the *Nukva*.

One complete *Achor* for one, and one complete *Achor* for the other, and they can return *Panim be Panim*.

This is so because by the *Hassadim* and the *Gevurot* that they obtain from the *Zivug Elyon* of AVI, by the *Hassadim* the *Achoraim de* ZA are completed in *Behinat* GAR. Also, the *Achoraim de Nukva* are completed in and of themselves in *He'arat* GAR through the *Gevurot*, as written below, and then they are fitting to return *Panim be Panim*.

28. *The reason that now two complete *Achoraim* were made for them was in this manner: Through *Mitzvot* and good deeds of the lower *Adam*, he induced a *Zivug Elyon* in AVI, and they returned to give them, to ZON, *Behinat* another *Mochin*. These are the *Behinat Hassadim* and *Gevurot* of *Daat de* ZA, and this is the essential drop that AVI give in their *Zivug*.

    The reason is that the *Orot* of two *Mochin de* ZA, called HB, do not appear in ZA. This is because they are clothed in the form of *Netzah Hod de Ima*, and only a lessened *He'arah* exits by the force of the *Hakaa* of disclosed *Orot Hassadim*. These strike them and educe some *He'arah* from them outwardly.

    It is not so in *Hassadim* and *Gevurot* that clothe inside *Yesod de Ima* that end at *Chazeh de* ZA because from there they appear in complete disclosure, exit into ZA, and shine in it. For this reason, the most important are the *Hassadim* and the *Gevurot*.

Ohr Pnimi

28. **Induced a *Zivug Elyon* in AVI.**

    This is because when *Adam* raises MAN to ZON, ZON too raise MAN to AVI; then AVI above them, and further up above the *Elyon* to the end of all the degrees. At that time a new *Mochin* come from *Ein Sof* through the degrees until they reach AVI, and from them to ZON, as there is no *Hidush Ohr* in the *Olamot* except from *Ein Sof* alone, and remember that always.

    Another *Mochin*, which are the *Behinat Hassadim* and *Gevurot* of *Daat de* ZA.

    It is written in the Zohar (Mishpatim p. 172), that "the *Rosh* of the *Melech* is corrected in *Hesed* and *Gevura*." However, *Hesed* rose to *Hochma*, *Gevura* to *Bina*, and the Upper third of *Tifferet* from the *Chazeh* upwards became its *Daat*. This is done by the *Hassadim* and the *Gevurot* that it receives from *Zivug de AVI*.

This is the essential drop that AVI give in their Zivug.

You already know that the whole *Zivug de AVI Panim be Panim* is because of the ZON that rose to them for MAN (*Ohr Pnimi* item 24). Thus, first ZON were *Achor be Achor*, meaning without *He'arat Hochma*. Instead, they were corrected in *Achoraim de Ima*, and then they do not need *Hochma* at all.

This is the meaning of, "their hinder parts were inward." This is because the *Behinat NHY de ZON*, which are their *Achoraim*, are not disclosed outwardly since the *Achoraim de Ima* extend from the *Bina de Ohr Yashar* before she emanated ZON outwardly.

It is so because when she emanated the ZON she had already returned *Panim be Panim* to extend *He'arat Hochma* for it (*Ohr Pnimi* item 24, par. "Know"). Hence, since ZON were also corrected in those *Achoraim*, because of that you find that *NHY de ZON* too, are still incorporated in their *HGT*, in their *Pnimiut*, and only the *HGT* is disclosed outwardly.

After *Adam ha Rishon* raised MAN to ZON, these MAN caused ZON to not suffice for *Achor be Achor*, but need to extend *He'arat Hochma*. For this reason they too rise for MAN to the *Bina*. They caused *Bina* to stop her *Achoraim* as well, and mate with the *Hochma Panim be Panim*.

In that state the drop departed this *Zivug de AVI* for the ZON. It refers to that *He'arat Hochma* that is suitable for the *NHY de ZON*, rooted in the *Ohr Yashar*, and in that the lack of the *NHY* of ZON is satisfied.

This drop *de AVI* clothes *Yesod de Ima*. This *Yesod* clothes in *Tifferet de ZA* up to the *Chazeh*, and this is the disclosed *HG* that exit from *Yesod de Ima* from the *Chazeh* downward, meaning the new *NHY*, contained in that drop *de Zivug AVI*.

It has been said, that there is *He'arat Hochma* in them, that they can now appear outwardly, and there is no fear of the *Klipot*, as now they are complete without any dearth. For this reason they are called exposed *Hassadim* and *Gevurot*.

However, prior to that, when the ZON were corrected in *Achor be Achor*, these HB were covered and concealed in the *Masach de Achoraim de Ima* in the form of, "their hinder parts were inward."

HB, do not appear in ZA. This is because they are clothed in the form of Netzah Hod de Ima.

The *Mochin de ZA* are clothed in *NHY de Ima* and *NHY de Ima* are clothed in the *HGT* of ZA. *Hesed* ascends to *Hochma*, *Gevura* ascends to *Bina*, and from the *Chazeh* upwards rises to *Daat*.

Hochma and *Bina* remained in *Rosh de ZA* and have no *Hitpashtut* into the *Guf*. However, *Daat de ZA* in *Yesod de Ima* has *Hitpashtut* from the *Chazeh* downward, which are the new *NHY* that now appear in ZON.

He writes, "HB, their *Orot* do not appear" etc. It is not so in *Hassadim* and *Gevurot* that clothe inside *Yesod de Ima* that end at *Chazeh de ZA* from which they appear in complete disclosure and come out. In other words, they are the *Behinat NHY* that appear outwardly because they received the *He'arat Hochma*, and their *Achoraim* is completed entirely.

29. You find that when *Hassadim* and *Gevurot* expand below in the *Guf de ZA*, the *Hassadim* are given to ZA and in that complete and finish the construction of its *Achoraim* entirely. Also, the *Gevurot* are given to the *Nukva* and thus complete her *Achoraim*.

Thus, he has complete *Achoraim* and she has complete *Achoraim*. In that state they can return *Panim be Panim* since their *Achoraim* are complete and now the exteriors are unable to seize there. It was not so in the beginning, when one had half the *Achoraim* and the other had half, and they could have a hold in them.

For this reason they can now return *Panim be Panim*, as there is no fear of the exteriors, as we say in the explanation of the intention in the blessing of the patriarchs of the stance during the weekdays, and examine that closely.

You find that the benefit from the entrance of the *Hassadim* and the *Gevurot* in ZA was for two reasons, which are one: They increase and complement the *Achoraim de ZON*, and in addition, by that they return *Panim be Panim*.

Ohr Pnimi

29. **The *Hassadim* are given to ZA etc. Also, the *Gevurot* are given to the *Nukva*.**

It has already been explained that the drop of *Zivug* that extends to ZA is *Behinat* new disclosed *NHY*, and it is exposed *Hassadim*; it is *Hassadim* and *Gevurot* that come out of *Yesod de Ima* that stops in the place of *Chazeh de ZA*. This is because their own *Behina* is *Hassadim*, and the part of *Malchut* in them is *Gevurot*.

He writes, "the *Hassadim* are given to ZA and in that complete and finish the construction of its *Achoraim* entirely." This is because now that it acquired NHY in *He'arat Hochma* in *Behinat NHY de Ohr Yashar*, the entire *Gadlut* of its *Achoraim* is completed and there is no lack in them anymore.

For this reason they can now appear outwardly without any fear of the exteriors. "The *Gevurot* are given to the *Nukva* and thus complete her *Achoraim*." This is because the *Gevurot*, which are *Behinat NHY* in *He'arat Hochma*, contained in the drop of *Zivug AVI* from the perspective of the *Gevurot* in them, are dispensed to the *Nukva*.

Now the *NHY de Nukva* too are completed and finished and appear outwardly without any fear of the *Klipot*. Thus, they are now separated from one another as each has his own *Achoraim*.

In that state they can return *Panim be Panim* since their *Achoraim* are complete and the exteriors are unable to seize there. It was not so in the beginning, when one had half the *Achoraim* and the other had half, and they could have a hold in them.

It is written above that when they were *Achor be Achor* it means that they were protected in the *Achoraim de Ima* that choose the *Ohr Hassadim* more, and reject *Hochma*. It is true that that was enough to keep them from the exteriors so that they cannot seize the place of want, meaning the lack of *He'arat Hochma* since when they are corrected in these *Achoraim*, they do not want *Hochma* and do not need it.

Hence, no want is apparent in them where the exteriors could grip. However, they are still regarded as having no NHY because the place of the lack of *Hochma* manifests primarily in their NHY [written aside in the author's manuscript: What is missing in the *NHY de Kelim* is missing in *GAR de Orot* due to the opposite value between the *Kelim* and the *Orot*, and thus it should be said].

It is so because with respect to the *Ohr Yashar*, they are the essence of *ZON de Ohr Yashar*, whose essence is not more than the *He'arat Hochma* in them. This is because the *Bina de Ohr Yashar* is *Ohr de Hassadim* without any *Hochma*, as she wants only *Hassadim*, "because He delighteth in mercy." Thus, the GAR in her are considered HGT, as it is known that KHB in *Behinat Hassadim* are discerned as HGT.

When she emanated the ZON, she saw that *Hassadim* cannot exist without *He'arat Hochma*, and for this reason she extended *He'arat Hochma* into *Hassadim* once more. This *Hamshacha* that has already departed from *Behinat*

Bina de Ohr Yashar acquired her own name, which are ZON, or NHYM *de Ohr Yashar* (see Part 4, Chap 6, *Ohr Pnimi* item 80).

Thus you see that the only difference between the *Bina* and the NHY *de Ohr Yashar* is only in the *He'arat Hochma* that she extended. The *Behinat Hassadim* without the *He'arat Hochma* is originally a part of *Bina* herself, and *Behinat He'arat Hochma* in *Hassadim* are the part of the NHYM, or ZON (see above Part 1, Chap 1, *Ohr Pnimi* item 50).

Now we have thoroughly clarified that the essence of the degree of NHY is only the *Behinat He'arat Hochma* in them. For this reason as long as there is no *He'arat Hochma* in them, they carry that lack. Also, this is why the *Klipot* and the exteriors seize that lack. Because of that too the NHY are called *Achoraim*, since *Achoraim* means a place of lack. This is what the Rav wrote above (item 26), that the place of the *Klipot* and the exteriors is the *Achoraim* of the *Nukva de ZA*, and the *Achor de ZA*.

Because of the fear that the *Klipot* would grip these *Achoraim*, the *Achoraim* were erected *Achor be Achor*, meaning in the *Achoraim de Ima*, called "wall". Through this wall, the NHYM take caution that the lack of *Hochma* will not appear in them, and this is the meaning of, "their hinder parts were inward."

The NHY are concealed in the *Pnimiut*, being inside the wall of *Ima* that defends them, and their *Panim* are disclosed outwardly, meaning the HGT, which they do not need for *He'arat Hochma* in their origin in *Ohr Yashar*. We have said that they extend from the *Behinat Bina* before she extended the *Ohr Hochma*. For this reason they can be disclosed outwardly, as no want appears in them and no place to grip for the outer ones.

He writes, "In that state they can return *Panim be Panim* since their *Achoraim* are complete and the exteriors are unable to seize there. It is unlike it was in the beginning, when one had half the *Achoraim* and the other had half, and they could have a hold in them."

In the beginning, when they were erected in one wall, meaning in *Achoraim de Ima*, they were both adhesive in this wall, which is the wall of HGT, and there was no difference between the ZA and the *Nukva*. This is because now both are *Behinat Hassadim* without *Gevurot* because the whole HGT is now *Hassadim* because of the *Achoraim de Ima*, and this is the meaning of "because He delighteth in mercy."

However, now that they have already obtained the drop of *Zivug de AVI*, which is the NHY in *He'arat Hochma*, their *Achoraim* now grew and were completed. ZA took the NHY from the side of *Hassadim*, and its *Achoraim* were completed and finished until there was no lack in it, as there is already

He'arat Hochma in it. For this reason his *Achoraim*, meaning the *NHY*, can appear outwardly without any fear.

Similarly, the *Nukva* took these *NHY* from the side of the *Gevurot* and her *Achor* was completed. Now she could separate from the *Achor* of *ZA*, as she had a complete *Achor* of her own, namely the *Gevurot de NHY*. For this reason they now mate *Panim be Panim* and dispense *He'arat Hochma* to their *MAN*, which are the *Neshamot* of the righteous.

For two reasons, which are one. They increase and complement the *Achor de ZA*, and in addition, by that they return *Panim be Panim*.

This is because the complete *Achoraim* that they have acquired, meaning the new disclosed *NHY*, raise the *HGT* to *Behinat HBD* and *Mochin*, and they mate *Panim be Panim*. The *Mochin* and the *Zivug* extend from the disclosed *Zivug*, and for this reason they are regarded as one *Behina*.

30. It turns out that as mentioned in the introductions, on the one hand, this *He'arah* that now comes from these *Hassadim* and *Gevurot* that now came anew will be more, and better, and greater than the first *He'arah* that *ZON* had already had. This is because he emanated the first only in *Behinat Achor be Achor*, and this new *He'arah* returned them *Panim be Panim*. Hence, this new *He'arah* will be called *Behinat Panim be Panim*.

    However, on the other hand, this new *He'arah* will be worse than the first *He'arah*. This is so because the first *He'arah* made and emanated all their *Partzufim*, and this new *He'arah* performed only the increase of half their *Achoraim*.

    Their return *Panim be Panim* came anyway, hence the *Behina* of this new *He'arah* shall be called *Achor be Achor*, since its benefit was only to increase half of the *Achor* alone.

Ohr Pnimi

30. **He emanated the first only in *Behinat Achor be Achor* etc. made and emanated all their *Partzufim* etc.**

    The first *He'arah* is the concealed *HGT* and *NHY*, and the second *He'arah* is the disclosed *NHY*. He says that we can call the first *He'arah* both by the name *Panim*, and by the name *Achoraim*.

    The second one can also be called *Panim* and *Achoraim*. This is so because from the perspective of the first *He'arah* being the actual emanation of the entire *Partzuf*, it can be called *Panim*, all the more so since the *HGT* are the *Kelim de Panim* that become *HBD* in *Gadlut*.

It can also be named *Achoraim* because of the situation of *Achor be Achor* in them. Similarly, the new *He'arah* can be called *Panim* although she is only *Behinat NHY*. Because these *NHY* are disclosed, they extended the *Panim be Panim* of the ZON, and can be called *Achoraim* since they are *Behinat* completion and increment of the *Achoraim*, meaning the *NHY*.

31. Regarding this introduction, it will be clarified to you, and you shall understand and learn what will be explained regarding the fall of the *Achoraim de Kelim de AVI* from here on.

Know, that the thing is that these *Behinot* of *Hassadim* and *Gevurot* that increase the *Achoraim de ZON* and return them *Panim be Panim*, is a matter of the *Behinot* of the *Achoraim* of *AVI* that fell. Hence, do not be surprised if at one time we call this *Behina Panim*, and once it is called *Achoraim*.

This and those *Hassadim* and *Gevurot* with the *Behinot* they had enhanced in the *Achoraim*, all fell down. These are the *Behinot Hassadim* and *Gevurot* that take AVI from AA so that they return *Panim be Panim*. This is so because in AVI too, their stance was *Achor be Achor* too, as will be explained.

Ohr Pnimi

31. **These *Behinot* of *Hassadim* and *Gevurot* that increase the *Achoraim de ZON* and return them *Panim be Panim*, is a matter of the *Behinot* of the *Achoraim* of AVI that fell.**

He explains below that the state of *AVI de Nekudim* was first *Achor be Achor* too, like the ZON. For this reason they too were in *Behinat*, "their hinder parts were inward." It means that their *NHY* were concealed and covered in the *Achoraim de Ima*, which is *Behinat* original HGT prior to the exit of the *NHY* from them, meaning the *Bina de Ohr Yashar* before she emanated the *NHY de Ohr Yashar*.

However, afterwards, the *Hey Tata'a* descended from the *Eynaim de Keter* and HB in it returned to the *Rosh*, and then the *Yesod de AK* gave them its drop, which is the *Vav* and *Nekuda* that became MAN in them. At that time *NHY de Keter* clothed in them in the form of *He'arat* disclosed *NHY*, and AVI mated *Panim be Panim* on their MAN.

You find that the *Zivug de Gadlut Panim be Panim de AVI* on the MAN de *Yesod de AK* was also through attaining the new disclosed *NHY* that they have acquired from the *Keter* because that is where their *Zivug Panim be Panim* extends from. Afterwards, the *Behinat Guf* of that *Zivug* is dispensed to ZAT and they break. Consequently, the *Behinat Gadlut de AVI* descends to *Behinat HGT* and *VAK*.

This *Gadlut* is not more and not less than the *Behinat* new disclosed *NHY* that had *He'arat Hochma* and *GAR*, that have now fallen into *VAK*. It means that the *He'arat GAR* departed from them and they have become *Behinat* incomplete *Achoraim*.

32. It is known that the drop that raises and shapes the fetus is the *Behinat Hassadim* and *Gevurot*, as we have mentioned above. This is the meaning of the *Otiot* that make up the fetus.

    Also, the *Otiot* are always the *Behinot Kelim*. These become *Kelim* to AVI in *Behinat Achoraim*. They are also the ones that descended and fell below with the rest of the *Hassadim* that descend to depict the *Kelim* of the fetus. These are the general seven *Melachim* that died, which are incorporated in ZON.

33. All these are the *Behinat* twenty-two *Otiot* of the Torah. The seven *Otiot* are *Kelim* to the ZON, which are seven *Melachim*, and fifteen *Otiot* are *Kelim* to AVI because the *Achoraim* of AVI are greater than any ZON. The sign of the number of *Otiot Kelim de AVI* is fifteen, like the number YH.

    Also, it is known that AVI are the first two *Otiot* YH of the *HaVaYaH*. The *Otiot* of ZON are SATNZ GT צגזנטעש (Shin, Ayin, Tet, Nun, Zayin, and Gimel, Tzadik), and the other fifteen *Otiot* of the alphabet are in AVI. Six *Otiot* of them are BDK HYH הייהקדב (Bet, Dalet, Kof, and Het, Yod, Hey), mentioned in the manuscript of the book of Zohar, being the *Achoraim de AVI*, and the rest of the *Otiot* are *Panim* to AVI.

Ohr Pnimi

33. **The *Otiot* of ZON are SATNZ GT צגזנטעש**

    It implies to *Behina Dalet* that mixed in their *Kelim*. This mixture is called SATNZ, which are the *Sigim* (*Ohr Pnimi* item 2), and the GT implies the *Nitzotzin* that descended to revive the *Kelim*.

    BDK HYH etc. being the *Achoraim de AVI*.

    This implies the *Behinat* exposed NHY, which are the *Achor de AVI*. BDK means correction, from words *Badak* (lit. Checked) the house. HYH means *Ohr Hochma*, since it is known that *Ohr Hochma* is called *Haya*. The entire merit of these NHY is the *He'arat Hochma* in them, hence they are implied in the name BDK HYH, meaning *Tikun Hochma* in *Hassadim*.

There is yet another reason why they are implied in the *Otiot BDK HYH*. It is that these *Achoraim de AVI* fell in the place of *ZON*. Afterwards, at the time of the *Tikun*, ZA sorts scrutinies from these *Achoraim* and raises them for MAN to AVI.

AVI mate *Panim be Panim* through these MAN, and dispense *Mochin* to ZA. Thus, all the *Mochin de ZA* are through the MAN that rise from these *Achoraim*. For this reason they are called *BDK HYH*, named after the *Tikun* of the *Mochin de GAR* of the ZA that comes through them. As we have said above, BDK means *Tikun*, and HYH is *Ohr Hochma* and *Mochin*.

34. Now you will thoroughly understand why there are *Tagin* over these thirteen *Otiot*, more than the other nine, why on seven of them that are SATNZ GT there are three *Tagin* on each and every *Ot* of them, and on the other six, which are BDK HYH there are no *Tagin* on them, but only one *Tag* (singular for *Tagin*) on each of their *Otiot*.

    The thing is that the SATNZ GT are *Behinat* seven *Melachim de ZON*, from whose *Sigim* the *Klipot* called STN AZ were made, hence the name SATNZ. It is a connection of STN, as mentioned in the Zohar, indicating that through the fierce and strong *Din* came out the SaTaN, which is the *Klipot*.

    It is also called GT, to indicate what they said in the book of Zohar, Parashat Pekudei, that these *Melachim* are the 320 *Nitzotzin* that were thrown, like that craftsman that hammered the iron and generated *Nitzotzin*. It is also as our sages said, "A spark that comes from under the hammer is SATNZ GT."

35. It has already been explained above that these seven *Melachim* took their *He'arot* because of the *Histaklut Ohr Eynaim* of AK in the *Orot Akudim* in their *Behinat Hitpashtut* below in the place of the *Guf* of AK. This is why they broke, since they lacked the *He'arat GAR* in it, which are AHP in their place above, hence they broke *Panim* and *Achoraim*.

    Also, for this reason they were tagged with three *Tagin* on each of their *Otiot*, indicating the shortage and absence of the three above-mentioned kinds of *Orot*, which are the *Otiot*. The *Ohr* remained above the *Gufim*, which are the *Otiot*, and not inside them, as will be explained below in the meaning of *Tagin*.

Ohr Pnimi

35. These seven *Melachim* took their *He'arot* etc. in their *Behinat Hitpashtut* below in the place of the *Guf*.

There are four divisions in the *Eynaim*: three *Roshim*, and *Guf*. This is because the *Eser Sefirot de Rosh* are divided into three. The first *Rosh* is *Galgalta ve Eynaim*, the second *Rosh* is *Awzen*, and the third *Rosh* is *Hotem Peh*. After that the *Guf*, which is ZON.

The first *Rosh* is YESHSUT from the *Tabur de AK* upward. It does not join *Partzuf de Nekudim* at all. The second *Rosh* is *Keter de Nekudim*, and the third *Rosh* is AVI *de Nekudim*.

The *Guf* is the ZAT of the *Nekudim*, and it is known that every *Partzuf* is emanated by the *Rosh* in the *Partzuf Elyon*. Also, *Partzuf de Nekudim* that emerged from the *Eynaim* was emanated in its *Elyon*, which is the *Rosh de Partzuf SAG de AK*.

This *Zivug* that was in *Rosh de SAG* for the purpose of the *Nekudim*, where four divisions emerged, is called *Se'arot Dikna de SAG*. The first three *Tikkunim* of *Dikna* that depend on the *Rosh de SAG* itself, are the *Behinat Rosh ha Aleph*, which does not join the *Partzuf*. They are called *Orot AHP* in their exit place, meaning the *Shoresh* of *Partzuf AHP*, which are the *Nekudim*.

The *Shibolet ha Zakan* is the *Behinat Rosh ha Bet*, and *Rosh ha Gimel* is called the *Orot AHP* that are not in their exit place that receive from *Rosh ha Aleph*. The *KHB de Nekudim* receive from these AHP in *Shibolet ha Zakan*. The *Keter* receives from the *Behinat Awzen* in *Shibolet ha Zakan*, HB receive from the *Behinat Hotem Peh* in *Shibolet ha Zakan*, meaning each *Behina* from its corresponding *Behina* in the *Rosh SAG*.

The *Keter*, which is *Rosh ha Bet*, receives from *Awzen* in the *Shibolet*, which is the *Behinat Rosh ha Bet* of *Dikna*. HB *de Nekudim*, which are *Rosh ha Gimel*, receive from HP in the *Shibolet*, which are *Rosh ha Gimel de Dikna*, and the ZAT *de Nekudim*, being *Behinat Guf* of the *Nekudim*, receive from the *Dikna* below the *Shibolet*. These are also the *Behinot Guf* of the *Dikna* [and we have already elaborated on that Part 6, *Ohr Pnimi* item 23].

He says, "these seven *Melachim* took their *He'arot* because of the *Histaklut Ohr Eynaim* of AK in the *Orot Akudim* in their *Behinat Hitpashtut* below in the place of the *Guf* of AK." It means that the seven *Melachim*, which are the *Behinat Guf* of the *Partzuf Nekudim*, receive from the *Behinat Guf* of the *Dikna* from below the *Shibolet*, which is in turn, their corresponding *Behina* in *Rosh ha SAG*.

They are called *Akudim de AK* since they are above *Tabur de AK*, and the *Nekudim* being only below *Tabur*. He says, "This is why they broke, since they lacked the *He'arat GAR* in it, which are AHP in their place above." It means that they do not have a *Shoresh* in the *Rosh*, which are GAR, from the beginning of their creation, and their whole *He'arah* is only from the *Behinat Gadlut de AVI de Nekudim*. When they could no longer tolerate the *Ohr* of the *Gadlut*, they broke *Panim* and *Achor*.

36. Yet, *Otiot BDK HYH*, which are *Kelim de Achoraim de AVI*, of which it has been explained that *AVI* took two *Orot Hotem* and *Peh*, and only the *Ohr Awzen* is lacking in them. For this reason only the *Behinot Achoraim* descended form them.

   To indicate that one *Ohr* of the *Awzen* that is missing from them, we tag one *Tag* only on each *Ot* of them, for it alone departed. It stands hanging above the *Ot*, which is the *Kli*.

Ohr Pnimi

36. He writes, "*AVI*, of which it has been explained that they took two *Orot Hotem* and *Peh*, and only the *Ohr Awzen* is lacking in them. For this reason only the *Behinot Achoraim* descended form them." Because they are essentially *Behinat Rosh* and also had some *He'arah* from the *Ohr Awzen* (Part 6 item 24), hence there is *Behinat GAR* in them from the beginning of their creation, though in *Behinat Achor be Achor*.

   For this reason this whole *Behina* that they have from their very creation is called *Panim*. They sustained and were not cancelled but only the *Behinat Zivug de Gadlut* and *Panim be Panim* that they have attained afterwards as additions, called *Achoraim*, and this alone descended and was cancelled from them.

37. We have already explained that what descended from *AVI* is called by two names, which are *Achoraim* or *Panim*. This is because as it lacks the *Ohr Awzen*, being the more *Elyon Ohr* of all three *Orot*, the want that extends to them through its departure is very great, and this is the *Behina* that makes them return *Panim be Panim*.

38. These *Mochin*, which are the above-mentioned *Hassadim*, extend to AVI with the *Kelim* of NHY de AVI like the *Mochin de ZA* that extend clothed inside NHY de AVI. These NHY de AVI too descended below with the *Achoraim de AVI*.

   In the sense that they come from AA, you find that this matter too shall be called a need for an Upper *Nekuda*, called *Keter*. We have already explained that this too is called *Behinat* want in *Keter*, and it caused it, as it does not take the *Ohr Awzen*, only at its tail, not at its *Rosh*.

   However, with regard to these NHY have already expanded as *Kelim de Mochin* inside AVI, this lack is named after AVI, and not after the *Keter*.

Ohr Pnimi

38. He writes that the *Kelim NHY de Keter* that clothe in *AVI* in *Behinat Levushim* for *Mochin* were also cancelled. However, they are not considered *Keter* since they have already clothed in *AVI*.

    This is because this *Rosh ha Bet*, which is *Keter de Nekudim*, did not take anything from the *Behinat Zivug de Gadlut* of the *Nekudim*, as it is *Behinat Bina de Rosh* and *GAR* from its very creation. Only its *Behinat NHY* that clothe in *AVI* that became *Levushim* for *Mochin* for them, which came at the time of *Gadlut de Nekudim*, only they were cancelled.

39. *We shall return to the intention and say that *AVI* were first *Panim be Panim* since the *Mochin* was made for them from the *Keter*. Hence, their MAN, which causes their erection and sustenance of the *Behina de Panim be Panim*, was the reality of these seven *Melachim* that were in the *Me'i Bina*, and these were its MAN.

    This is how it always is. The sons are MAN *de Ima* while these seven *Melachim* that were inside the *Bina* raised MAN and caused a *Zivug* to *AVI*. The *Mochin* were extended to them, *AVI* were returned *Panim be Panim*, and they mated together in order to educe these seven *Melachim*.

    When these *Melachim* came out, had they not died but existed, they would have situated *AVI Panim be Panim* although they came out below. In addition, they would have been beneficial for their MAN although because they broke and died.

    For this reason the *Achoraim* of *AVI* too, which locate them *Panim be Panim*, went below and then returned *Achor be Achor*, as there is no one to raise MAN for them anymore, and sustain their return *Panim be Panim*.

Ohr Pnimi

39. **AVI were first *Panim be Panim* since the *Mochin* was made for them from the *Keter*.**

    We have written above (*Ohr Pnimi* item 31) that the *Zivug de Gadlut de AVI* was by obtaining the disclosed *NHY* from *Keter de Nekudim*.

    Their MAN, which causes their erection and sustenance of the *Behina de Panim be Panim*, was the reality of these seven *Melachim*.

    It has already been explained above that *AVI* do not return *Panim be Panim* unless through raising MAN *de ZON* (*Ohr Pnimi* item 24) because *Bina* is in the form of "because He delighteth in mercy" at her *Shoresh*, and rejects *Hochma*. However, when *ZON* rise to her for MAN, her *Shoresh de Ohr Yashar* awakens in her since ZON de Ohr Yashar are her sons, which she emanated in He'arat Hochma.

Hence, after ZON rise to her for MAN and Bina awakens to dispense them He'arat Hochma, she then arrests her Achoraim and returns her Panim to Hochma. She mates with him Panim be Panim and renews He'arat Hochma to ZON, and once ZON obtain He'arat Hochma, they come to their place below. From there on Bina is found in a Zivug Panim be Panim with Hochma in order to sustain He'arat Hochma in ZON.

Here [Written aside in the manuscript of the author: "Needs scrutiny. After all ZON were previously emanated from Hotem Peh de Dikna. They only received the Gadlut from the Vav and Nekuda, as it is written in Part 6, Histaklut Pnimit item 19, that lowering the Hey Tata'a to the Peh, which is the Vav, makes the Shuruk] the ZON were not yet emanated to be able to raise MAN to AVI.

This is why this raising of MAN was made by the inner NHY de AK, and the Yesod de AK illuminated the Shuruk for AVI, the Vav ו and Nekuda. It is written in the Rav's words (Part 6 item 31) that the ו is Behinat ZA, and the Nekuda is the Behinat Nukva, and they became MAN in Ima. At that time Ima was awakened to bestow He'arat Hochma in them, stopped her Achoraim, and returned Panim be Panim with Abba.

AVI raise MAN higher up, meaning to Keter, and Keter too above it etc. up to Ein Sof. Then a new Ohr comes down from Ein Sof and cascades through the degrees until the drop of Zivug de AVI that descends on the ו and Nekuda inside them, which are ZON.

They acquire He'arat Hochma, and then expand to their place below, meaning to the bottom seven de Nekudim. In addition, in order to keep the He'arat Hochma in the ZON, Ima must extend the Panim be Panim with Abba.

Now you can thoroughly understand the Rav's words that ZON not only cause the returning of AVI Panim be Panim when they are up in Ima in the form of MAN, but even after they expand downward to their place, they are still considered the causes of the sustenance of the Zivug AVI Panim be Panim. Because of them Ima must be Panim be Panim with Abba, in order to keep their He'arah in ZON.

He writes, "their MAN, which causes their erection and sustenance of the Behina de Panim be Panim, was the reality of these seven Melachim that were in the Me'i Bina, and these were its MAN." It means that in the beginning, the seven Melachim were in Behinat MAN in the Me'i of Bina since they are the ו and Nekuda that Yesod de AK administered them, which caused the return of Panim be Panim with Abba when they came to Me'i Ima.

Afterwards, when the seven *Melachim* expanded and descended to their place, they still induce *AVI* sustenance and existence of the *Behina de Panim be Panim*. This is because *Bina* must extend her *Zivug Panim be Panim* with *Abba* because of them, in order to administer and keep the *He'arat Hochma* in them.

Because they broke and died. For this reason the *Achoraim* of *AVI* too, which locate them *Panim be Panim*, went below.

The whole matter of the *Hamshacha* of the *Zivug Panim be Panim de AVI* is only in order to keep *He'arat Gadlut* in the sons, which are *ZON*. Hence, when the sons died, *Bina* no longer needs to extend the *Panim be Panim* with *Abba*. For this reason they return *Achor be Achor* and all the *Behinat Orot de Gadlut* that were in them descend from their degree and fall to *Behinat Guf* and *ZAT*, meaning they were rejected from the *Rosh de AVI*.

The reason that they descend from the *Rosh de AVI* is that the *Bina* returned to her original degree that appreciates *Hassadim* more than the *Ohr Hochma*. You find, that after the sons died and she no longer has a need to extend *He'arat Hochma* for them, she immediately returns *Achor be Achor*, meaning to her first state, to extend *Hassadim* and reject *Hochma*.

By that she rejected and dropped the *Mochin de Hochma* outside the *Rosh* into *Behinat ZAT*, as it is written, "my princes all of them kings" (Isaiah 10;8). This is because these *Achoraim* that descended from their degree and became ministers, were *Melachim* before, meaning when they were up in *Rosh de AVI* in *Behinat Mochin de Gadlut*. Now that they have descended into *Behinat ZAT*, they have become ministers, meaning subordinate and enslaved to the *Melachim*.

40. It is simple: the *Achoraim de AVI* did not stop descending until the end of the breaking of the seven *Kelim*. Each *Behinat* breaking of one *Melech* caused a descent of some of the *Achoraim de AVI*, and this is the explanation of the matter.

    When we appreciate the existence of these seven *Melachim* in the four *Partzufim* of HB, Israel Saba ve Tvuna, we find that until a third of *Sefirat Tifferet*, being the fourth *Melech*, the *Achoraim de* Upper *AVI* completed their descent. When all seven *Melachim* broke, the *Achoraim de Israel Saba ve Tvuna* came down as well.

Ohr Pnimi

40. These seven *Melachim* in the four *Partzufim* of HB, Israel Saba ve Tvuna etc.

We must understand the matter of the assessment of the seven *Melachim* in the four *Partzufim AVI* and *YESHSUT*. This is the key to understand the reign and the death of the seven *Melachim de Nekudim*, as well as all the *Behinat ZON* in *ABYA* that these seven *Melachim* are their *Shoresh*. We shall explain them here briefly in general. We shall explain them in detail below, in the interpretation of the Rav's words below.

Know, that five *Partzufim* emerged here in *Olam ha Nekudim*, four *Partzufim* that are *Hochma, Bina, Israel Saba* and *Tvuna*. These emerged in *Rosh* and *Guf*. The fifth *Partzuf*, which is *Partzuf Daat*, came out in *Rosh* without a *Guf*.

You should also know that the order of the breaking of the vessels was in the order of the *Hizdakchut* of the *Masach* according to the degree, like the order of the *Histalkut* of the *Orot* from the *Kelim de Guf* of the previous *Partzufim de AK*.

You should also know that the *Kelim de Nekudim* preceded the *Orot* since the *Kelim de Nekudot de SAG* that expanded below from *Tabur de AK*, whose *Orot* departed during *Tzimtzum NHY de AK*, remained empty of their *Orot*. They moved and became the *Kelim de Nekudim* since the *Kelim* that were emptied by the *Histalkut Orot* in the *Guf de Elyon* always became *Kelim* in the *Partzuf Tachton*.

In addition, know that all that this speaks of is only the *Orot de Gadlut* that came to *AVI* as additions. However, the Rav does not deal here with the *Orot de Katnut*, meaning from *Behinat Achor be Achor de AVI*.

It is so because there wasn't any breaking and annulment in the *Behinat Katnut* that emerged in the beginning of its creation. The entire cancellation, the breaking, and the flaw, was only in the *Orot de Gadlut* that came as additions, meaning in the *Zivug de Panim be Panim de AVI*, and remember that.

First, all the *Orot* of the *Gadlut* came out incorporated in *Kli de Keter*, meaning in *NHY de Keter*. This is because *Keter* itself, which is the second *Rosh*, did not take any part in these *Mochin de Gadlut* for itself.

Instead, only because these renewals of *Orot* necessarily come from *Ein Sof*, hence, this new *Ohr* must cascade from *Ein Sof* through all the reasons that precede this *Partzuf* that receives and extends the new *Ohr*. For this reason it is considered descending from *Ein Sof* and hanging down degree-by-degree until it comes to the receiver, being the consequence of all its preceding degrees.

Hence, it is considered that *AVI* too raised to the *Keter*, which is the *Behinat Galgalta ve Eynaim de AVI*, meaning their *Rosh*, and *Keter* to its own *Rosh* as well and so on up to *Ein Sof*. At that time the new *Ohr* extended from *Ein Sof* through the degrees until it came to *Behinat* drop of *Zivug de Galgalta ve Eynaim* in the *Keter*, which are *HB* in the *Keter*.

The drop clothes in the new *NHY de Keter*, meaning complete *NHY* that can be shown outwardly (*Ohr Pnimi* item 29, sub header "**In that state**") and these *NHY de Keter* with the *Ohr* of the drop of *Zivug* that extends from *Ein Sof* descend and clothe in *Mochin de AVI*.

Hence, this above *Ohr*, called drop of *Zivug de HB* in *Keter* clothed in *NHY de Keter* that descended to *Mochin de AVI* is considered the entirety of the *Ohr* that expands in all five *Partzufim* of the *Nekudim*, since all the degrees of the *Nekudim* are but a lessening of this general *Ohr*. It gradually lessens from degree to degree until it disappears and departs to its *Shoresh*.

However, since the *Ohr Elyon* does not stop, it therefore educes new *Komot* as it lessens one below the other until it disappears and rises to the *Maatzil* as has been explained in the *Histalkut Orot* of the previous *Partzufim*. Thus, that same *Ohr* clothed in *NHY de Keter* is the entirety of the *Ohr* of all the *Partzufim* of *Nekudim*.

Yet, after *NHY de Keter* clothed to *Mochin* in *AVI*, they have already departed from *Behinat Keter* entirely and were considered *Kelim de AVI* and *Ohr de AVI*. Know, that this *Koma* that emerged first is considered *Komat Keter de AVI*.

Here in the Rav's words it is called *Histaklut Eynaim* of *AVI* on each other. This is because through *NHY de Keter* that clothed in them for *Mochin* and mated *Panim be Panim*, their *Eynaim* were opened and they looked at each other, meaning a *Zivug de Gadlut* in *Komat Keter de AVI*.

Hitpashtut ha Aleph of *Komat Keter* from above downward is in *Melech ha Daat*, and from here on began the *Hizdakchut Masach de Partzuf AVI*. This is so because after *Melech ha Daat* broke, the *Masach* was purified from *Behina Dalet* into *Behina Gimel* and *Komat Hochma de AVI* emerged from below upward.

The *Eser Sefirot de Guf* expanded from above downward, clothing in *Melech ha Hesed*. When *Melech ha Hesed* broke, the *Masach* was purified from *Behina Gimel* to *Behina Bet* and *Komat Bina* of *AVI* emerged from below upward.

The *Eser Sefirot de Guf* expanded from above downward in *Melech ha Gevura*, and when *Melech ha Gevura* broke, the *Masach* purified from *Behina Bet* to *Behina Aleph*. At that time *Behinat Daat de AVI* emerged, meaning *Komat ZA*. It is also called *Behinat Yesodot de AVI* that emerged from below upward, and its *Guf* expanded in the Upper third of *Melech ha Tifferet*.

After the Upper third of *Melech ha Tifferet* broke, the entire *Masach* was purified and rose to its *Shoresh* to *Peh de Nekudim*. It was incorporated there in the *Zivug de Rosh* and a new *Koma de Behina Bet* emerged on it, since the last *Behina* is always lost during the *Hizdakchut*, and this *Koma* is called YESHSUT.

First emerged the *Taamim* in it, which are the *Rosh* and *Guf de Hitpashtut Aleph*. The *Rosh* is called *Histaklut Eynaim de YESHSUT* on each other, and you already know that the last *Behina de Hitlabshut* remains in the *Masach*, though it only expands in *Kli de Keter*, called *Taamim*.

Know, that this is what is called *Histaklut Eynaim* both in AVI and YESHSUT. In AVI it is always considered *Behina Dalet de Hitlabshut* and in YESHSUT it is considered *Behina Gimel de Hitlabshut*. The *Hitpashtut* from above downward in the *Behinat Taamim de AVI* is called *Melech ha Daat*, and the *Hitpashtut* from above downward *de Behinat Taamim de YESHSUT* is called the two lower thirds of *Tifferet*.

After *Melech ha Tifferet* broke, the *Masach* was purified from *Behina Gimel* to *Behina Bet* and *Behinat YESHSUT* emerged from below upward. Their *Guf* expanded from above downward to the *Melachim NH*.

When the *Melachim* of NH broke, the *Masach* purified from *Behina Bet* to *Behina Aleph* and *Daat de YESHSUT* emerged from below upward, called *Yesodot de YESHSUT*. Its *Guf* expanded and descended to *Melech ha Yesod*, and when *Melech ha Yesod* died, the *Masach* was purified from *Behina Aleph* to *Behinat Keter*.

At that time *Komat Malchut* emerged from below upward and her *Guf* expanded to *Malchut de Nekudim*. When *Kli Malchut de Nekudim* broke, the *Masach* was purified entirely and rose to its *Shoresh* in the *Peh* where it was once more incorporated there in the *Zivug de Rosh*.

However, only *Aviut de Behina Aleph* remained in it since the last *Behina*, which is *Behina Bet*, was lost during the *Hizdakchut*. *Komat* ZA, which is *Behinat Daat*, whose matter will explained below, emerged on it, and this *Koma* of *Daat* has no *Hitpashtut* from above downward, as we shall explain below.

Thus we have briefly explained all the degrees that came out in *Nekudim*: the first degree is AVI on *Masach de Behina Dalet* and *Behina Gimel* together. The *Taamim* in the first *Koma* expanded in *Melech ha Daat*, and the *Nekudot* in her are the three *Komot* that expanded one below the other in the three *Melachim Hesed*, *Gevura*, and the upper third of *Tifferet*.

Then surfaced the second degree, called YESHSUT. Its *Taamim*, which emerged on the two *Reshimot Behina Gimel* and *Behina Bet*, expanded in the two lower thirds of *Tifferet*. Also, the *Nekudot* in it are the three *Komot* that expanded one below the other in the three *Melachim NH*, *Yesod*, and *Malchut*.

Then surfaced the third degree, called *Daat*. It has only *Behinat* from below upward, and you should know that these three degrees, *Hochma*, *Bina*, and *Daat*, are the *Neshama*, *Ruach*, *Nefesh*.

41. The *Daat* is the first *Melech* to come out, and all seven were incorporated in him. You already know that the principal raising of MAN are the *Kelim* that were already born in the *Olam*, hence thus far, raising MAN was primarily through *Daat* that emerged in the *Olam* first.

We have already explained that in the beginning there was no need for MAN to AVI, only the ascension of the desire. When it is written that these seven *Melachim* were MAN, it does not mean that they extended *Hassadim* and *Gevurot*, since they have already been extended in the beginning.

The evidence of that is that they returned AVI *Panim be Panim*, and afterwards *Hochma* placed these seven *Melachim* in *Bina*. Thus, we cannot say that they were MAN to *Bina*, though it means that they were placing them in *Behinat Panim be Panim* to AVI through their raising of MAN, once they were already in *Bina*. In addition, in that state they extended the *Hassadim* and *Gevurot* further as in the beginning.

We shall return to the matter that after the *Ohr Daat* emerged and entered its *Kli*, it raised MAN and extended *Hassadim* and *Gevurot* in AVI. This is because *Daat* consists of *Hassadim* and *Gevurot*, and because the seven *Melachim* were contained in it at that time. For this reason it had the strength to lower *Hassadim* and *Gevurot*.

However, since the other *Melachim* do not raise MAN, since the exit was still not to them, but to the *Daat*, it is therefore impossible to lower complete *Mochin* only through ZON together. Therefore, what *Daat* lowered was *Behinot Hassadim* and *Gevurot* in *Rosh* and Upper AVI in the place of their *Daat*, resembling him, as he does.

Ohr Pnimi

41. After the *Ohr Daat* emerged and entered its *Kli*, it raised MAN and extended *Hassadim* and *Gevurot* in AVI.

It has already been explained in the previous item that this *Daat* does not imply one *Sefira* of *Daat*. Rather, it is the first *Hitpashtut* of the *Zivug de Gadlut de AVI de Nekudim*, which is a whole *Koma* of *Eser Sefirot* that came out on *Masach de Behina Dalet de Hitlabshut* and *Aviut de Behina Gimel*.

Its *Behinat* from below upward is called *Histaklut Eynaim de AVI* on each other and there are *Eser Sefirot* in *Komat Keter* there. The *Behinat Taamim*, meaning the *Hitpashtut* from above downward called *Guf*, is called *Melech ha Daat* that the Rav speaks of here.

Although there is only *Masach de Behina Aleph* here in *AVI de Nekudim*, it has been explained elaborately (Part 6) that they *Hey Tata'a* descended from the *Eynaim* through *Zivug de AB SAG* and came to its place in the *Peh*, meaning *Malchut de Rosh*. This is because in *AB*, the *Hey Tata'a* is in its place, hence, when the *He'arat AB* was drawn there, it lowered the *Hey Tata'a* in *Nekudim* to the place of *Peh* as well, and *AVI* returned to the *Rosh*.

Know, that when the *Hey Tata'a*, which is *Behina Dalet*, came to its lace, it was erected there with a *Masach*, as it is in *Partzuf AB*, which is *Behina Dalet de Hitlabshut* and *Behina Gimel de Aviut*. It is because that *He'arat AB* that lowered her to the *Peh* corrected her with his *Masach* too, hence the *Eser Sefirot* emerged on it in *Komat Keter*.

However, the Rav wrote that *Daat* extended in *Mochin de AVI* only *Hassadim* and *Gevurot*. However, according to the above it should have extended *Eser Sefirot* in *Komat Keter* and *Hochma*, as it extended in *Partzuf AB*.

To understand that we must thoroughly know the matter of *Zivug de Panim be Panim de AVI*. Three degrees in *Abba ve Ima* have been explained in my words above, until the *Zivug de Panim be Panim*: The first is *Achor be Achor*, meaning the state of *AVI de Nekudim* in the beginning. The second is *Panim be Achor*, and the third is *Panim be Panim*.

You find that before *AVI* return *Panim be Panim*, they must first be in a state of *Panim be Achor*. We have already explained there that that state of *Panim be Achor* came by lowering the *Hey Tata'a* from the *Eynaim* to the *Peh*, at which time *AVI* return to the *Rosh* and *Abba* acquires its *Behinat Panim*.

However, *Ima* is still in her *Achoraim*, meaning in *Hamshacha* of *Ohr de Hassadim*, since she chooses *Hassadim* more than *Hochma*, by way of "because He delighteth in mercy" (*Ohr Pnimi* item 23, sub header "**Above it, it is Panim be Achor**").

However, afterwards, when the MAN *de Behinat ZON* comes to her, her *Shoresh* from *Ohr Yashar* awakens to dispense *He'arat Hochma* to these *ZON* that rose to her. At that time she must stop her *Achoraim* and mate *Panim be Panim* with *Abba*, dispensing *He'arat Hochma* to the *ZON* (*Ohr Pnimi* item 24).

Now you can understand why the *Daat* extends only *Hassadim* and *Gevurot*. It is because these MAN that *AVI* received from *Yesod de AK* are the *Behinat*

Daat that mates *AVI*. The *Vav* ו is *Hassadim* and the *Nekuda* is *Gevurot*, which are *Behinot* ZON.

Because they are ZON and must have *He'arat Hochma*, they mate to *AVI*. Hence, this is the meaning of the *Daat de AVI*. Since the whole matter of the must that *Bina* needs to extend *He'arat Hochma* to these MAN extends only from the original connection *de AVI*.

Bina de Ohr Yashar extends *He'arat Hochma* in *Hassadim* during her emanation of ZON *de Ohr Yashar*. Hence, now too she does not receive from *Abba* from his *Behinat* GAR, but from his *Behinat* ZON, which are actual *He'arat Hochma* in *Hassadim*, like the ZON *de Ohr Yashar*, which is in turn the measure that these MAN awakened her to extend from *Abba*.

Thus, the whole drop of *Zivug de AVI Panim be Panim* is not more than *Behinat Hassadim* and *Gevurot*, which are ZON in *Gadlut*, meaning *Hassadim* in *He'arat Hochma*, but not at all the *Atzmut Ohr de Hochma* and *Bina*. Understand and remember that for it is the key for all the *Mochin* of the ZON.

Now you can see that the five *Komot* that emerged here in *AVI* through the *Hizdakchut* of the *Masach* are *Behinat* NRNHY *de Haya de* ZON *de Nekudim*. They are all not more than *Behinat Hassadim* and *Gevurot*, even the *Yechida de Haya*.

It has been explained that the matter of the *Zivug de Panim be Panim de AVI* came in two degrees, which are *Panim be Achor* and *Panim be Panim*. In the beginning, *Abba* is corrected in GAR, by lowering the *Hey Tata'a* from the *Eynaim* to the *Peh*. Thus, *AVI* return to the *Rosh* and this *Tikun* is still insufficient for *Ima* to turn her *Panim* back to *Abba*.

Because of her *Achoraim* in the form of "because He delighteth in mercy" she craves *Hassadim* more than *Hochma*. Hence, at that time *AVI* stand *Panim be Achor*, *Panim de Abba* in the *Achoraim de Ima*.

Only afterwards, when MAN *de Yesod* obtains MAN, she returns her *Panim* to *Abba* for the purpose of correcting the MAN in *He'arat Hochma*. You already know that even now when she mates *Panim be Panim* with *Abba*, she still does not receive of him more than these MAN need.

You also know that the *Zivug de Hakaa* made on the *Hey Tata'a* that descended to the *Peh*, educed *Eser Sefirot* in *Komat Keter*, which is *Ohr Yechida de Hochma*. Hence, it is considered that the drop of *Zivug* that came to the MAN through this *Zivug Panim be Panim* is the *Behinat* measure of ZON *de Yechida* since the *Eser Sefirot de Abba* are in *Komat Keter*, which is *Ohr Yechida*.

Since *Ima* receives from *Abba* only as much as ZON need, which are her MAN, hence, this *He'arah* that she receives is ZON of *Yechida de Abba*. Know, that with respect to ZON itself, she is *Behinat* complete *Yechida* for him, and this is the end of ZON's growth.

That *Koma* that emerged in *Zivug Panim be Panim de AVI* on the *Masach de Behina Dalet* in the *Peh*, which is *Komat ZON de Yechida* is considered *Daat de AVI* since she is the principal element that copulates them. It is not more than *Hassadim* and *Gevurot*: the ZA in it are in the form of *Hey Hassadim*, and the *Nukva* in it is in the form of *Hey Gevurot*.

All this is the *Behinat Rosh*, meaning the *Behinat Eser Sefirot* educed from below upward. Afterwards, they descend and clothe the *Guf* from above downward, meaning in the full amount that they clothed in the *Rosh*, and these *Eser Sefirot* that clothed in the *Guf* are called *Melech ha Daat*. This is the first *Hitpashtut* of the *Nekudim*, and it is the *Behinat Taamim de Nekudim*.

After *Melech ha Daat* broke, *Behina Dalet* purified in the *Rosh* to *Behina Gimel*. It means that *Hey Tata'a* rose from the place of the *Peh* to the place of the *Hotem*, and the *Zivug* on the *Masach de Behina Gimel* emerged, extended *Komat Eser Sefirot* up to *Hochma*, and *Komat Keter* disappeared from *Abba*. For this reason, it is now called *Guf de Abba*.

Thus, you now find that when *Bina* mates with *Abba* she extends only ZON *de Hochma*, since *Behinat Hey Hassadim* and *Hey Gevurot* do not receive the *Ohr Yechida* from *Abba* now, since the *Ohr Keter* has vanished from *Abba*. Instead, they receive *Komat Haya*, which is the measure of ZON *de Hochma*.

For this is reason it is considered that *Hey Hassadim* and *Hey Gevurot* are the MAN, and ZON descended now from *Behinat Rosh de Abba*, which is *Yechida* to the *Behinat Guf de Abba*, which is *Haya*. Also, their *Hitpashtut* from above downward into *Behinat Guf* is called *Melech ha Hesed*, which is *Behinat ZON de Gadlut* in the *Ohr Haya*.

When *Melech ha Hesed* broke, the *Behina Gimel* in the *Rosh* purified into *Behina Bet*, *Malchut de Rosh* rose to the *Awzen*, and *Eser Sefirot* in *Komat Bina* emerged. *Komat Hochma* disappeared, and it is considered that the *Hey Hassadim* and *Hey Gevurot* descended into *Behinat Guf de Ima*, which is *Komat Bina*.

Now they receive only the measure of ZON *de Bina*, and the *Hitpashtut* of the *Eser Sefirot* from above downward from this *Koma* is called *Melech ha Gevura*, being *Behinat ZON de Gadlut* in *He'arat Neshama*. Similarly, after *Melech ha Gevura* broke, the *Masach* purified from *Behina Bet* to *Behina Aleph*, and *Eser Sefirot* in *Komat ZA* emerged from below upward.

This is considered that the *Hey Hassadim* and the *Hey Gevurot* emerged to *Behinot Yesodot de AVI*. It expanded into *Behinat Guf* in the upper third of *Melech ha Tifferet* from above downward, and it is *Behinat Ruach Nefesh de ZA*.

Now we have thoroughly explained how all five *Behinot NRNHY de Nekudim* are only *Hassadim* and *Gevurot*, even the *Neshama*, *Haya* and *Yechida* in them. Even *Daat de AVI* is only *Hassadim* and *Gevurot*, but the *He'arah* that it receives from *Keter de AVI* is *Yechida*, the *He'arah* that it receives from *Hochma de AVI* is *Haya*, and the *He'arah* that it receives from *Bina de AVI* is *Neshama*.

He says, "after the *Ohr Daat* emerged and entered its *Kli*, it raised MAN and extended *Hassadim* and *Gevurot* in *AVI*. This is because *Daat* consists of *Hassadim* and *Gevurot*." It means that in *Daat* in the *Rosh*, meaning the MAN that *AVI* received from *Yesod de AK*, has only *Hassadim* and *Gevurot* because *Ima* extended only *Behinat He'arah* from *Abba* for it.

It is similar to the *He'arah* that there is in *ZON de Abba* itself from the *Ohr Keter de Abba*. For this reason it does not have more than *Hassadim* and *Gevurot* in *He'arat Keter de Abba*, as the *Guf* has only what expands to it from the *Rosh*.

It has also been explained that this *Melech ha Daat* is *Hitpashtut Aleph de Olam ha Nekudim*, called *Taamim*, where all the *Komot* below it are contained in it, and are only a *Behinat* diminution from its *Koma*. He says, "and because the seven *Melachim* were contained in it at that time. For this reason it had the strength to lower *Hassadim* and *Gevurot*."

This is because the greater part of the entirety of the *Hassadim* and *Gevurot* extended by the MAN *de Yesod AK* and because of it returned *AVI* to a *Zivug Panim be Panim*. Hence, even after it expanded from above downward to its place to the *Guf* to *Melech ha Daat*, it is considered the cause for *AVI* to extend the *Zivug de Panim be Panim*.

It is so because *Ima* cannot return to her *Behinat Achoraim* so that the *He'arat Hochma* in it will not be annulled. Hence, *Melech ha Daat* too is considered *Behinat* MAN and the cause of the sustenance and positioning of *AVI Panim be Panim*.

Yet, when *Melech ha Daat* broke and *Behina Dalet* purified, the entire *Zivug* was not cancelled instantaneously, because there still remained the *Aviut de Behina Gimel* in the *Masach* on the path of its gradual *Hizdakchut*. Thus, it educes the rest of the *Komot* to the three *Melachim Hesed*, *Gevura*, and the upper third of *Tifferet*.

For this reason, the entire *Behinat Panim be Panim* did not vanish from *AVI*, but only their *Komat Keter*, called *Histaklut Eynaim de AVI*. However, *Behinat Panim be Panim de Komat Hochma* still remained in it, educed on *Behina Gimel* of the *Masach*, which does not belong to *Komat Daat*.

He writes, "since the other *Melachim* do not raise MAN, since the exit was still not to them, but to the *Daat*, etc. Therefore, what *Daat* lowered was *Behinot Hassadim* and *Gevurot* in *Rosh* and Upper *AVI* in the place of their *Daat*, resembling him, as he does."

It means that the *Behinat Panim be Panim* was not entirely cancelled, only the *Koma* that is attributed to the *Daat*, resembling him as he does. Yet, the *Panim be Panim* attributed to the other *Melachim* still remained in *AVI*, since they have not come out yet.

42. When this *Kli* of the *Melech* called *Daat* broke, *Daat* of Upper *AVI* too descended in the place of *Guf de AVI*, but this *Kli* of *Melech* called *Daat* descended to *Olam Beria* after it broke. The other six *Orot* that were with it entered in the *Kli* of *Melech*, called *Hesed*, and at that time, Upper *AVI* were still *Panim be Panim*.

This is because they do not return *Achor be Achor* until everything completes the descent, as they are adhered *Panim be Panim*. This adhesion must be removed entirely, and then they will return *Achor be Achor*.

However, as long as there is some *Dvekut* left in them, they do not return *Achor be Achor*. We shall explain below the matter of the complete *Dvekut de AVI* when they are *Panim be Panim*, and what it is about.

When *Hey Hassadim* and *Hey Gevurot* descended from *Rosh de* Upper *AVI* to down in the *Guf*, it necessarily caused the lack of *Ohr*, though they did not return completely *Achor be Achor*. Also, the meaning of this lack is the lack of *Histaklut Eynaim* of *AVI* on each other.

Ohr Pnimi

42. He writes, "When this *Kli* of the *Melech* called *Daat* broke, *Daat* of Upper *AVI* too descended in the place of *Guf de AVI*."

The concealment of the *Ohr Keter* is considered, with respect to *Abba*, as the concealment of its *Behinat Rosh*. Therefore, it is considered that the *Behinat MAN* that stands at the *Rosh* of *AVI* descended to their *Behinat Guf*, meaning to *Komat Hochma* without *Keter*. It is so because the *Masach* purified to *Behina Gimel*, which elicits merely *Komat Hochma*, and what is written, that it fell to *Beria*, will be explained below.

The other six *Orot* that were with it entered in the *Kli* of *Melech*, called *Hesed*.

It means that it was done by the *Zivug* on the *Masach* that was purified to *Behinat Hochma*, and the drop of the *Zivug de AVI Panim be Panim* of this *Koma* that descended on the MAN in them. It is regarded as the measure of the illumination of ZON *de Hochma de Abba*, considered its *Behinat Haya* with respect to the *Partzuf de ZON* itself, and it expanded in *Melech ha Hesed*.

It has already been explained that the *Masach* purifies and lessens gradually, degree-by-degree until it elicits six other *Melachim*, except *Hesed*, which are two *Komot* back in Upper *AVI*, *Behina Aleph* and *Behina Bet*. These are the *Melachim Gevura*, the upper third of *Tifferet*, and the four *Komot* in YESHSUT. These are *Behina Gimel*, *Behina Bet*, *Behina Aleph*, and *Behinat Shoresh*, which are the two thirds of *Tifferet*, NH, *Yesod*, and *Malchut*.

All these *Komot* were incorporated in *Behina Gimel* over which *Komat Hochma de Abba* and *Melech ha Hesed* came out, since they gradually lessen from him onward. This is why he says, "The other six *Orot* that were with it entered in the *Kli* of *Melech*, called *Hesed*," as they are all incorporated in it, as we have explained.

Histaklut Eynaim of AVI on each other.

It has already been explained that this is what *Komat Keter* of *Abba* is called. This is the one that vanishes due to the breaking of *Melech ha Daat*, and the resulting *Hizdakchut* of *Behina Dalet*. It is because the *Masach* appears primarily in the *Guf*, as it is only in potential in the *Rosh*, not in actual fact. Thus, when the *Kli* broke, the *Behinat Masach* was cancelled from that *Behinat Aviut* that the *Kli* is from.

43. **When the second *Melech* reigned, which is *Hesed*, he extended the *Hey Hassadim* to expand in *Guf de Abba*. When he died, he descended to *Beria*, and the five *Orot* descended in *Gevura* in the third *Melech*.**

At that time the *Achoraim de Abba* made by the *Hitpashtut* of the above *Hey Hassadim* fell, and now all of them have fallen. The *Hassadim* descended in the *Yesod de Abba*, *Abba* returned his *Achoraim* to the *Panim* of *Bina*, and this *Behina* is called *Achor be Panim*, as the *Panim* of *Bina* are now facing the *Achoraim* of *Hochma*.

Ohr Pnimi

43. ***Hesed*, he extended the *Hey Hassadim* to expand in *Guf de Abba*. When he died, he descended to *Beria*, and the five *Orot* descended in *Gevura* in the third *Melech*. At that time the *Achoraim de Abba*...fell.**

This is because when *Melech ha Hesed* broke, *Behina Gimel* purified to *Behina Bet*, *Komat Hochma* disappeared, and *Eser Sefirot* in *Komat Bina* came out. It is therefore considered that *Hochma* turned her *Panim* to *Achoraim* since *Behinat Bina* is considered *Achoraim de Hochma* although it is the *Panim* of *Bina*. This is the meaning of, "*Abba* returned his *Achoraim* to the *Panim* of *Bina*."

Abba returned his Achoraim to the Panim of Bina, and this Behina is called Achor be Panim, as the Panim of Bina are now facing the Achoraim of Hochma.

This is because the *Panim de Ima* are *Hey Gevurot*, as the Rav wrote above, and they are sweetened by *Ohr de Hassadim de Abba*. The matter of the degree of *Achor be Panim* is written above (*Ohr Pnimi* item 23, sub header "**Above it, it is Panim be Achor**"), and we should not ask about the Rav's words there (item 25) that the degree of *Achor be Panim* is not conducted in *AVI*.

This is so because there it concerns the *Tikun de AVI* in *Olam Atzilut*, and at that time they do not need it, and here it is about the diminution of the *Orot* and their gradual ascent to the *Maatzil*. It is not at all important here if they need it or not, and this is simple.

44. If you say that *Partzuf Abba* does not complete its descent until the third of the *Tifferet*, we must understand that that third of *Tifferet* is like *Yesod* compared to *Abba*. It is like the ZA with its *Mochin* from the perspective of *Bina*, and you need to understand this whole study in the same manner as that study, all in one picture, and then you will understand it.

The entire *Yesod* is *Behinat Panim*, having no *Achoraim* that descended from it. It is not so in the rest of the body, where there is *Behinat Achoraim* that return opposite the *Panim* of the *Nekeva*, though his *Achoraim* are not adhered with her.

Hence, the *Sium Achoraim de Abba* complete descending before there is a blemish and a flaw in *Yesod de Abba*. Afterwards the third *Melech* reigned, which is *Gevura*, and extended the *Hitpashtut* of the *Hey Gevurot* in the Upper *Ima*.

When he died, he descended to *Beria* and the four *Orot* descended in the fourth *Kli*, which is the *Tifferet*, the *Hitpashtut Gevurot* fell in *Yesod de Ima* and her *Achoraim* fell below as well. At that time *Ima* returned her *Achoraim* and *Achor de Ima* were in the *Achor de Abba*.

Ohr Pnimi

44. The entire *Yesod* is *Behinat Panim*, having no *Achoraim* that descended from it.

It means that it has been explained above that only the *Behinat Kelim de Achoraim* were cancelled, being all that reached them as additions to their essential making. This refers to the *Behinat Zivug de Gadlut* that emerged because of the descent of the *Hey Tata'a* from the *Eynaim* and the MAN of *Yesod de AK*.

However, what they had from the very creation, meaning *Behina Achor be Achor de AVI* that they had in the beginning, this is called *Kelim de Panim*. These were not cancelled and did not descend (item 31).

It has also been explained that after the *Masach* purified from *Behina Bet* to *Behina Aleph*, the HG fell to *Yesodot de AVI*, as then *Komat Eser Sefirot de ZA* emerged. This *Koma de Behina Aleph* that came out in *AVI* is entirely *Panim*. In other words, it was incorporated in *Behinat Achor be Achor de AVI* that they had in the beginning, "having no *Achoraim* that descended from it." this is because it has nothing of *Behinat Zivug de Gadlut*, meaning from *Otiot BDK HYH*, which are *Behinat Achoraim de AVI*.

Achoraim that return opposite the Panim of the Nekeva, though his Achoraim are not adhered with her.

It means that all that did not depart from *Behinat Achor be Achor* that they had in the beginning, is considered *Behinat Achoraim* that return opposite the *Panim of the Nekeva*. This is because their *Achoraim* are not cohesive with each other as in the beginning when their *Achoraim* were adhered *Achor be Achor*.

For this reason they are considered *Behinat Gadlut* and addition from the *Behinot Otiot BDK HYH* that descend from *Rosh de AVI*. This includes all three degrees above *Achor be Achor*, which are *Achor be Panim*, *Panim be Achor* and *Panim be Panim*.

Only the first degree of *Achor be Achor* whose *Achoraim* are adhered with each other, since both use the same wall, this alone is considered *Behinat Kelim de Panim* that remained in *AVI* and were not cancelled. From that we hear that *Behina Bet*, which is *Komat Bina* that *Melech ha Gevura* extended from, this *Koma* too is considered *Achoraim*, and it too was cancelled, though in this *Behina AVI* are *Achor be Panim*.

However, *Yesodot de AVI*, which are *Behina Aleph*, are considered *Achor be Achor* and are not counted in the calculation of the annulment of the *Achoraim de AVI*. This is because *AVI* were *Achor be Achor* even before the fourth *Melech* reigned, as the Rav says above.

Gevura, and extended the Hitpashtut of the Hey Gevurot in the Upper Ima.

This is because *Panim de Behina Bet* is *Hey Gevurot*, as the whole of *Ima* is *Gevurot* compared to *Abba*. For this reason they now stand *Achor be Panim*, whose meaning has already been explained above at length (*Ohr Pnimi* item 23, sub header "Above it, it is **Panim be Achor**") and study it there.

45. After that the fourth *Melech* reigned, which is *Tifferet*. When the *Ohr* reached its upper third up to the *Chazeh*, it extended *Behinat* general *Hey Hassadim* in *Yesod Abba* and *Hey Gevurot* in *Yesod Ima*.

It is for this reason that *Yesod* is called "Everything", as it contains *Hey Hassadim* and *Hey Gevurot*. We have already explained that picture; *Daat* contains *Rosh de AVI*, *Hesed* is *Guf de Abba*, *Gevura* is *Guf de Ima*, and the upper third of *Tifferet* is the *Yesod de AVI*.

When the *Ohr* came to the two bottom thirds of *Tifferet*, all the *Achoraim* of the upper *AVI* completed their descent, and the *Hassadim* and *Gevurot* continued in the *Rosh de Israel Saba ve Tvuna* because this is the place of their *Rosh* together.

When he died, three *Melachim* descended in the fifth *Kli*, which is *Netzah*. Then the *Hassadim* descended from *Rosh de Israel Saba*, and *Gevurot* from *Rosh de Tvuna* down to its *Guf*. In addition, the *Behinat Histaklut Eynaim* on each other was deducted from **YESHSUT**, as it was in Upper *AVI*.

Ohr Pnimi

45. When the *Ohr* reached its upper third up to the *Chazeh*, it extended *Behinat* general *Hey Hassadim* in *Yesod Abba* and *Hey Gevurot* in *Yesod Ima*.

It is written above that when the *Masach de Behina Bet* purified after the breaking of the *Kli de Melech ha Gevura* into *Behina Aleph*, being *Komat ZA*, the general *Hey Hassadim* and *Hey Gevurot* appeared in *Yesodot de AVI*. Also, the *Ohr* reached the fourth *Melech*, which is the upper third of *Tifferet* down to the *Chazeh*.

We must still understand the matter of these general *Hey Hassadim* and *Hey Gevurot* in *Yesod de Abba ve Ima*, and what they mean. You will understand the matter in what is written in the Zohar, "*Ima* expands up to *Hod*, but has no *Yesod*."

The thing is that the Rav has already written in Part 5 (item 33) regarding *Matei ve Lo Matei*, that in *Hitpashtut Bet*, *Ohr Hochma* comes in *Kli de Keter*, and *Ohr Bina* in *Kli de Hochma*. Finally, *Ohr Malchut* in the *Kli* of *Yesod*, and *Malchut* remains without *Ohr*.

You find that the *Masach de Behina Aleph* that educed *Komat Ohr Hassadim* expanded only up to *Hod*, where it purified into *Behinat Shoresh* and *Komat Malchut* emerged on it. This *Ohr Malchut* clothed in *Kli de Yesod*, as it is written at length in *Ohr Pnimi* there (Part 5, *Ohr Pnimi* item 45) and study it there for it is impossible to bring this length here.

You find that the *Ohr Yesod* is *Behinat Hochma* that lacks *Hassadim* because all the *VAK* came out there by *Ima* in *He'arat Hochma* in *Hassadim*. After the *Masach de Behina Aleph* purified, there remained *He'arat Hochma* alone without any *Hassadim*, and this is the meaning of, "*Ima* expanded only up to *Hod*," since the entire *Behinat Ima* is only *Ohr de Hassadim*.

Since the *Hassadim* have disappeared, she no longer has any *Hitpashtut* to shine in *Kli de Yesod*, but *Abba*, which is *Ohr Hochma*, still shines in *Yesod*. This is the meaning of *Abba* being long and narrow, because he had expanded more than *Ima*, as the entire *He'arah* of *Ima* has already stopped at *Hod*, but *Abba* still illuminates for *Yesod*, which is the *Ohr Malchut*.

This *He'arat Abba* in the *Kli de Yesod* is considered the *Behinat Hey Gevurot*, as it is written there in *Ohr Pnimi*, because of the lack of *Hassadim* there. The *Yesod Abba* is narrow because of the *Gevurot* from the blockage of *Hassadim*.

Thus, you will understand that after the *Masach* purified from *Behina Bet* to *Behina Aleph*, meaning that the *Hey Tata'a* rose to the *Eynaim* once more, which are *Behina Aleph de Rosh*, the *Bina* incorporated in *Malchut* once more. Hence, *Hey Gevurot de Ohr Malchut* in the *Kli de Yesod* incorporated in her once again (*Ohr Pnimi* item 23, sub header **"Above it, it is *Panim be Achor*"**).

This is the meaning of, "it extended *Behinat* general *Hey Hassadim* in *Yesod Abba* and *Hey Gevurot* in *Yesod Ima*," meaning because of the ascent of the *Hey Tata'a* in the *Eynaim*, where they returned *Achor be Achor* once more. *Hassadim de Abba* have no GAR, because of the *Hey Tata'a* in the *Eynaim*, and this is the meaning of the general *Hey Hassadim* in *Yesod de Abba*. In addition, *Ima* was incorporated in the *Ohr Malchut* in *Kli de Yesod*, which is *He'arat Hochma* without *Hassadim*.

The reason they are called the general *Hey Hassadim* and *Hey Gevurot* and not just *Hey Hassadim* and *Hey Gevurot*, is that it is known that the *Shoresh* of everything is the five famous *Behinot* KHB ZON. However, they are evaluated by three fundamental modes, evaluated as *Rosh, Toch, Sof*.

The five *Behinot* from the perspective of *Ohr Hochma* are called KHB ZON, and the five *Behinot* from the perspective of *Ohr de Hassadim* in *He'arat Hochma* are called HGT, *Netzah* and *Hod*. *Behinat Ohr de He'arat Hochma* without *Hassadim* is called mere *Hey Gevurot*.

Behinat Hassadim without GAR, or the *Behinot Gevurot*, protected in the *Achoraim de Ima* but are in fact without GAR, as here when the *Hey Tata'a* is in the *Eynaim* above *Bina*, are also called the general *Hey Hassadim* or the general *Hey Gevurot*, and remember that.

We have yet to understand the matter of the division of the *Kli de Tifferet* into two halves, which we did not find in any *Sefira*. The thing is that it is known that the three *Kelim*, *Hesed*, *Gevura*, *Tifferet*, are *Behinat* GAR, *Keter*, *Hochma*, *Bina*.

However, they are called HGT since they are *Behinot Ohr de Hassadim*. It follows that *Kli de Tifferet* is *Behinat Bina*, and *Sefirat Bina* is considered two *Behinot*: the first is called Upper *Bina*, and the second is called *Tvuna*.

The reason it is divided is, as has been explained above (*Ohr Pnimi* item 29, sub header "**In that state**"), that *Bina de Ohr Yashar* is *Ohr de Hassadim* without any *Hochma*. Moreover, it rejects *Hochma* since it wants *Hassadim* more, by way of, "because He delighteth in mercy." However, when she emanated to ZON *de Ohr Yashar*, she returned *Panim be Panim* with the *Hochma* in order to extend *He'arat Hochma* to ZON *de Ohr Yashar*.

Thus, there are two situations to the *Bina de Ohr Yashar*: the first is before she emanated to ZON, when she is in *Ohr de Hassadim* and her *Achoraim* to *Hochma*, and the second is after she had emanated to ZON. At that time she is already in *Behinat Panim be Panim* with *Hochma* in order to extend *He'arat Hochma* to her children, which are ZON. Thus, these two situations divide *Bina de Ohr Yashar* into two separate *Behinot*. The first is called *Bina* or Upper *Ima*, and the second is called *Tvuna*.

Now you will thoroughly understand the matter of the division of *Tifferet* into two halves on the *Chazeh*. This is the actual matter of the division of *Bina*: from the *Chazeh* up it is *Behinat* Upper *Ima*, whose *Achoraim* are toward *Hochma*, as she chooses *Hassadim* in the form of, "because He delighteth in mercy"; and from the *Chazeh* down it is in *Behinat Tvuna*, whose *Panim* is toward *Hochma* and she has *He'arat Hochma*.

He says, "When the *Ohr* reached its upper third up to the *Chazeh*." After AVI returned *Achor be Achor* the *Zivug* was made on the *Masach* that rose to the *Ohr Eynaim*, and elicited *Koma de Behina Aleph*, protected in the *Achoraim* of *Ima* that reject *Hochma*.

The *Ohr* of this *Koma* that expanded from above downward to the *Guf*, to the *Kli de Tifferet*, could not expand further there, only up to the upper third of *Tifferet*, meaning the *Chazeh*, where it is the part of *Tifferet* that extends from Upper *Ima* in *Behinat Ohr de Hassadim* and in *Achoraim* on the *Hochma*.

Yet, in the part of *Tifferet* from the *Chazeh* downward, there is the *Behinat Tvuna* that extends *He'arat Hochma* for ZON. Hence, *Ohr Achoraim* of the Upper *Ima* cannot come to clothe there, since it has already stopped at the *Chazeh*.

When the *Ohr* came to the two bottom thirds of *Tifferet*, all the *Achoraim* of the upper *AVI* completed their decent.

It means that the entire *He'arat Partzuf* of Upper *AVI* stopped and they cannot even shine their *Orot Achor be Achor* from the *Chazeh* downward, since they stop at the *Chazeh*.

It has been explained that the entire *Ohr* of *Sefirat Hesed* is *Behinat Guf de Abba*, the *Ohr de Sefirat Gevura* is *Behinat Guf de Ima*, and the *Ohr* of the Upper third of *Tifferet* is *Behinat Yesodot de AVI*. You should know that the matter of the *Hamshacha* of the two *Gufim de AVI* to the place of these three *Sefirot*, is in complete accuracy, as that is their place with respect to the *Kelim*.

You already know that the three *Kelim Hesed, Gevura, Tifferet*, are *Behinat KHB de Hassadim*. You also know that the whole *Komat Gadlut de Nekudim* extends through *Zivug de AB SAG*, and is considered *Komat AB* (*Ohr Pnimi* item 41, par. "Although there is only").

It is known that in *AB*, *Ohr Hochma* clothes in *Kli de Keter*, *Ohr Bina* in *Kli de Hochma*, and *Ohr ZA* in *Kli de Bina*. Hence, *Guf de Abba*, which is *Ohr Bina* in *Kli de Hesed*, being *Behinat Keter de Hassadim*, clothed here too.

Guf de Ima, which is the *Ohr Bina* in *Kli de Gevura*, being *Behinat Hochma de Hassadim*, and *Guf de Yesodot AVI*, which is *Komat ZA*, clothed in the Upper third of *Tifferet*, which is *Behinat* Upper *Ima de Hassadim*. It could not expand to the two bottom thirds of *Tifferet* because it is *Behinat Tvuna de Hassadim* there; hence it stops at the *Chazeh*.

Thus, each *Ohr* comes precisely to its suitable *Kli* in the *Hey Behinot de Ohr de Hassadim*. He writes, "We have already explained that picture; *Daat* contains *Rosh de AVI*, *Hesed* is *Guf de Abba*, *Gevura* is *Guf de Ima*, and the upper third of *Tifferet* is the *Yesod de AVI*." In other words, it is as has been explained that the three *Kelim HGT* are *Behinat GAR* of the *Hey Behinot* in the *Hassadim*.

For this reason they receive from the Upper *AVI* too, and only the upper third of the *Kli de Tifferet* belongs to GAR since from the *Chazeh* down it is already *Behinat Tvuna*.

The *Hassadim* and *Gevurot* continued in the *Rosh de YESHSUT* because this is the place of their *Rosh* together.

This is because the *Masach* was purified from *Behina Aleph* to *Behinat Shoresh* too, and to the *Behinat Masach* of the *Rosh*, and was then incorporated there in the *Zivug* of the *Rosh*, as has been explained in the previous *Partzufim* (Part 6, Histaklut Pnimit item 15). The *Aviut* on the *Masach* returned, except the last *Behina* in it, which is *Behina Gimel*, of which nothing was left but a *Behinat Hitlabshut* (there item 14).

Hence, only *Behina Bet* with *Behina Gimel de Hitlabshut* remained in it, which are *Zachar* and *Nekeva*, and two *Komot* came out on them, *Komat Hochma de Zachar*, and *Komat Bina de Nekeva*.

The principal part of the *Koma* is the attribute of the *Nekeva*, which is *Behina Bet*. This is because *Behinat Hochma* does not have the *Aviut* that could expand from above downward. This *Koma* is called YESHSUT, and it is a son and a *Tachton* to the Upper AVI.

He writes, "and the *Hassadim* and *Gevurot* continued in the *Rosh de* YESHSUT." This is because *Koma de Behina Bet* emerged there on the *Masach* from below upward, in *Peh de Rosh de* AVI.

When the *Aviut de Guf* in the *Masach* was recognized, it is considered that it descended to the place of *Guf* of AVI, meaning the place of the *Chazeh* of the *Guf*. It elicited *Eser Sefirot de Rosh* from the *Chazeh* up to *Peh de* AVI, and the *Eser Sefirot* of their *Guf* came out from the *Chazeh* down, meaning in the place of the two lower thirds of *Tifferet*.

He writes, "because this is the place of their *Rosh* together," meaning the place of their *Rosh* is from the place of the *Chazeh* to the *Peh*, as has been clarified in the previous *Partzufim* (see Part 6, Histaklut Pnimit item 11 concerning all the operations in the birth of a *Partzuf*, as it is impossible to bring here the entire length from there).

Remember what we have explained above regarding the difference between AVI and YESHSUT, which stems from the *Bina de Ohr Yashar*. It is divided into two *Behinot*: 1 - Before she emanated ZON *de Ohr Yashar*, at which time it is only *Hassadim* without *Hochma*; and 2 - after she emanated ZON *de Ohr Yashar*, at which time she is *Panim be Panim* with *Hochma* because she must extend *He'arat Hochma* for ZON.

Hence, the *Eser Sefirot de Bina* are discerned as dividing into GAR and ZAT. Her KHB are *Behinat* the upper half of *Bina*, from *Behinot Hassadim* without *Hochma*, and her ZON are considered the lower half of *Bina*, which is in *He'arat Hochma*.

Thus, YESHSUT, which are *Behinat* lower half of *Bina*, is considered the ZAT of *Bina*, meaning her *Behinat* ZON. They cannot be without *Ohr Hochma* since their quintessence is *He'arat Hochma*, as with ZON (*Ohr Pnimi* item 39).

For this reason only YESHSUT are considered the Rosh of ZON because since Bina extended the He'arat Hochma for ZON, she is considered Behinat Tvuna, and not as Upper Ima, since Upper Ima is discerned only before she emanated to ZON. Remember well that difference between Bina and Tvuna in their origin for you will need it in all the places.

We might argue that here Upper AVI were Rosh to the ZON, because their Guf clothed in HGT de ZA. The thing is that in fact, AVI with YESHSUT are considered one Partzuf, GAR and ZAT.

The issue of their division comes only through the ascent of the Hey Tata'a to the Eynaim. Hence, since the Hey Tata'a descended from the Eynaim through the Zivug Panim be Achor, they were both joined into one Partzuf through the MAN that AVI received from Yesod AK in it Panim be Panim.

For this reason Upper Ima too received He'arat Hochma into her ZAT, which is now considered Behinat Upper Ima too. However, now that the Masach purified into Behina Aleph once more, and the Hey Tata'a returned to the Eynaim, AVI and YESHSUT were divided into two Partzufim once more. Now Upper Ima is considered Behinat Hassadim without Hochma once more, meaning only Behinat Achor be Achor.

The matter of He'arat Hochma does not belong to her, but to the ZAT that have now become a separate Partzuf, being YESHSUT. From here on only YESHSUT are considered the Rosh of ZON, and not Upper AVI.

Regard and see that even when they were in a single Partzuf, before the Hey Tata'a rose to the Eynaim, when Upper AVI were still Rosh to ZON, they still administered only to HGT de ZA, which are as KHB de Hassadim from the perspective of the Kelim, and not the essence of ZON. This is because the essence of ZON are Netzah and Hod from the perspective of the Hassadim; Netzah is ZA, and Hod is Malchut.

Hence, they could only receive from the Rosh of YESHSUT in a way that GAR de AVI, meaning Upper AVI in addition with the ZAT in a single Partzuf, administered to GAR de Hassadim. After ZAT de AVI were cut off from them and became a separate Partzuf named YESHSUT, they dispensed to ZAT de Hassadim, which are NH, which are ZON de Hassadim.

The Hassadim descended from Rosh de YESH, and Gevurot from Rosh de Tvuna down to its Guf.

After the Kli de Tifferet from the Chazeh down died, the Masach de Behina Gimel that is mingled with the Nekeva purified. At that time, the Komat Hochma in them disappeared and Hey Hassadim and Hey Gevurot descended from the *Rosh de YESHSUT* into *Behinat Guf de YESHSUT*. This means that a *Zivug* was made on the remnants *de Aviut* that remained in the *Masach*, which is *Behina Bet* that educes *Komat Bina*, considered *Behinat Guf* with respect to *Komat Hochma*.

However, this does not refer to the actual *Behinat Guf*, which is from above downward, since the entire YESHSUT is *Behinat Rosh*, meaning *Behinat* from below upward, and their *Guf* is TNHYM of the *Nekudim*, as the Rav writes here.

The *Behinat Histaklut Eynaim* on each other was deducted from YESHSUT.

It has already been explained above that the *Koma* of the *Hitkalelut* of the *Nekeva* in the *Zachar*, being *Komat Behina Gimel de Hitlabshut* here, is called *Histaklut Eynaim* on each other, referring to the *Hitkalelut* in one another. This *Komat Hochma* expanded only in *Kli de Tifferet* from its *Chazeh* down since *Kli de Tifferet* is *Behinat Bina de Hassadim*; it is still considered *Behinat* GAR from the *Behinat Kelim de Hassadim*.

For this reason this great *Ohr de YESHSUT* clothed only it, and not the *Kelim de NH*, which are *Behinat ZAT*, even from the perspective of *Hassadim*, which are ZON *de Hassadim*. You already know that the *Ohr* that extends to the *Partzuf* always clothes the more *Zach Kli*, which is most similar to it in *Hishtavut Tzura*.

46. After that *Netzah* reigned and extended *Hey Hassadim* in the *Guf de Israel Saba*. When he died, the rest of the *Melachim* descended in *Hod* and the *Achoraim de Israel Saba* descended, and returned the *Achoraim* facing the *Panim* of *Tvuna*.

After that *Hod* reigned. He extended the *Hey Gevurot* in the *Guf de Tvuna*, and when he died, two *Melachim* came down in *Yesod*. At that time the *Kelim de NH* descended to *Beria* because both are only one *Melech*, "as both or only parts of the *Guf*."

Even though they reigned one after the other, they are still regarded as only one *Melech*. At that time the *Achoraim de Tvuna* descended too and *Israel Saba ve Tvuna* returned *Achor be Achor*.

Ohr Pnimi

46. ***Netzah* reigned and extended *Hey Hassadim* in the *Guf de Israel Saba*.**

It is written above regarding AVI, that the MAN of ZON extend only *Hassadim* and *Gevurot*. It is the same here too since the same MAN that were in Upper

AVI later descended into *Behinat Zivug de YESHSUT*. Also, it has already been explained that *Behinat Eser Sefirot de Guf* that expand from *Guf de Israel Saba*, come in the *Melech* of *Netzah*.

Both are only one *Melech*.

This is so because both extend from the *Behinat Guf de YESHSUT*, meaning *Masach de Behina Bet*, hence they are one *Koma* and one *Melech*.

Achoraim de Tvuna descended too and Israel Saba ve Tvuna returned Achor be Achor.

This is because when the *Melachim* of NH died, the *Masach* purified from *Behina Bet* to *Behina Aleph* and the *Hey Tata'a* returned in the *Eynaim*. At that time they returned *Achor be Achor* meaning to *Behinot Achoraim* of Upper *Ima* in order to protect the lack of GAR in them.

47. After that reigned the sixth *Melech*, which is *Yesod*. He extended the general *Hey Gevurot* in *Yesod Tvuna* and general *Hey Hassadim* in *Yesod Israel Saba*. When he died, these *Behinot* descended too.

    After that reigned the seventh *Melech*, which is the *Malchut*, only in her own *Kli*. She extended general *Hey Hassadim* in *Malchut de Israel Saba* and general *Hey Gevurot* in *Malchut Tvuna*, since *Malchut* too has a generality, as in *Yesod*.

    He too is called *Kala* (lit. Bride), as the *Yesod* is called *Kol* (lit. Everything), and when she died the general *Hey Hassadim* and *Hey Gevurot* descended from *Malchut de Israel Saba* and from *Malchut de Tvuna*, and the *Kli de Malchut* descended to *Beria*. Now all the *Achoraim* of the four *Partzufim de AVI* of *Israel Saba ve Tvuna* completed their descent entirely.

Ohr Pnimi

47. **Yesod. He extended the general *Hey Gevurot* etc. After that reigned the seventh *Melech*, which is the *Malchut*.**

    When the *Zivug* was made in *Behina Aleph*, they expanded in *Kli de Yesod* and extended the general *Hey Hassadim* and *Hey Gevurot* in *Yesodot de YESHSUT*, as has been explained above in *AVI*. After *Melech ha Yesod* died, the *Masach* was purified into *Behinat Shoresh*, and *Komat Malchut* came out in *YESHSUT*, and the *Ohr* descended into *Kli Malchut* from above downward, which is the seventh *Melech*.

48. If you say, "Why were the general *Hassadim* and *Gevurot* not in the general account of the Upper *AVI* as they were counted in *Malchut de Israel Saba ve Tvuna*?" We must understand that it is known that the *Behinat Atara*

is in the Upper third of *Tifferet*, which is the *Behinat Malchut*, and she is incorporated in *Yesod*.

Here, however, she, the *Malchut de Tvuna*, is more revealed than *Malchut de Bina*. This is because *Malchut de Tvuna* is actually *Malchut* with respect to the general *Bina* and *Tvuna* together in one *Partzuf*, but the *Malchut* of the Upper *Bina* is *Behinat Guf* of the generality. It is the place of the *Chazeh* of *Tifferet* of the generality of *Partzuf Bina* and *Tvuna* together, and it is not the actual *Malchut*.

Ohr Pnimi

48. ***Malchut de Tvuna* is actually *Malchut* with respect to the general *Bina* and *Tvuna* together etc. but the *Malchut* of the *Bina* is *Behinat Guf* of the generality.**

Interpretation: Upper *Ima* and *Tvuna* are indeed *Behinat Eser Sefirot* with respect to *Bina de Ohr Yashar*. Upper *Ima* is GAR, and the *Tvuna* is ZAT. However, they were divided because of the ascent of the *Hey Tata'a* in the *Eynaim*, hence *Malchut de Tvuna* is the *Malchut* of both *Ima* and *Tvuna* together.

Yet, *Malchut* of the Upper AVI "is *Behinat Guf* of the generality. It is the place of the *Chazeh* of *Tifferet* of the generality of *Partzuf Bina* and *Tvuna* together, and it is not the actual *Malchut*." It means that afterwards, in *Atzilut*, *Tvuna* clothes from *Chazeh* of Upper *Ima* downward, and the place of the *Chazeh*, *Behinat Guf* of the generality of both, and she is not *Bina*.

According to the above, you will understand the matter thoroughly. It has been explained that Upper *Ima* expands through *Hod*. However, she does not have *Yesod* (*Ohr Pnimi* item 45). This is because the *Hassadim* stop there and there is only *He'arat Hochma* there without *Hassadim*, which is not at all the *Behina* of *Ima*, as she is the opposite, *Behinat Hassadim* without *Hochma*.

Hence, Upper AVI extended only through the *Zivug* of the *Masach de Behina Aleph* where there is still *Ohr de Hassadim* there anyhow. Yet, after the *Masach* of *Behina Aleph* purified, their *He'arah* stopped entirely because she has no *Hitpashtut* without *Hassadim*, and *Komat Malchut* could not come out in Upper AVI. Only in YESHSUT, after it was distinguished as a distinct *Partzuf*, *Komat Malchut* could emerge without *He'arat Hassadim*.

49. *****When the third of *Tifferet* still hasn't died, the descent and fall of the *Achoraim de Abba ve Ima* was not completed. When these *Melachim* entered their *Kli*, they were revealed in a great *Ohr*.**

However, after the Upper third of *Tifferet* died, the *Achoraim de AVI* fell there. When the rest of the remaining *Orot* came out in order to enter in their *Kli*, they were clothed in these *Achoraim* that fell and remained in *Atzilut*, and the last *Melachim* came out clothed in the *Achoraim* of *AVI*.

This remained for them always until all the scrutinies could emerge in the future. This is the meaning of the raising of MAN that ZON raise to *Abba ve Ima*, and it is from these *Achoraim de AVI* that descended there below in *Atzilut* itself that they took.

Ohr Pnimi

49. **When the rest of the remaining *Orot* came out in order to enter in their *Kli*, they were clothed in these *Achoraim* that fell.**

The matter of these *Achoraim* of *AVI* has already been explained. They are all the *Behinot* of *Gadlut* that were in *AVI* with respect to *Panim be Achor* and with respect to *Panim be Panim*. All this came down from *Behinat Rosh* and they were made into *Behinot HGT* without a *Rosh*.

This is so because their *Behina* from above downward, which is the *Guf*, which are the four *Melachim Daat HGT* through the Upper third of *Tifferet*, broke and fell to *BYA*. As a result, the MAN that operated in the *Rosh* were blemished too, fell with their *Orot*, and lost the *He'arat Hochma* in them, obtaining *Behinot HGT* without a *Rosh*.

However, they did not descend outside *Atzilut* because of that, like the *Kelim de ZAT*, because the *Achoraim de AVI* that still remain above the *Behinot Achor be Achor*, meaning from what they'd had prior to the *Gadlut*, all this remains in its full completeness. Hence the *Behinot Gadlut de AVI* that fell to *HGT* were also protected in those *Achoraim* from *Achor be Achor de Rosh*.

Yet, there is a big difference between *AVI Achor be Achor* that remained in the *Rosh*. This is because those that remained in the *Rosh* were never restricted because of the *Hey Tata'a* in the *Eynaim*.

Rather, these *Behinot de Gadlut* already extended *He'arat Hochma*, and departed from them once more due to the ascent of the *Hey Tata'a* in the *Eynaim*, though they received the *Tikun* of the *Achoraim de Rosh* after they had suffered the corruption. For this reason they are discerned as receiving from the *Rosh* and are considered *Guf*.

In spite of that, these *Achoraim* that fell to *HGT* and became *Behinot* new *Kelim*, corrected in *Tikun Kavim*, are considered to be like *AVI* of *Rosh*, since they receive from the *Rosh*. This is because the *Achoraim de Ima* corrects them in *Tikun Kavim* and connects them into one knot. It means that the middle line that extends from Upper *Bina* in *Ohr Hassadim* unites the right and the left, and sentences them in her *He'arat GAR* as well.

All three *Kavim* are united by the influence of *Ohr de Hassadim* because the *Elyonim* too receive their completion through them. Here you must remember that the *Elyonim* are *Hesed* and *Gevura*, which are of the value of *Hochma* and *Bina*.

Tifferet is considered the *Tachton* that receives *Ohr de Hassadim* from Upper *Bina* that have *Behinat GAR* in her *Levush* of *Achoraim*. By so doing, the *Hesed* and *Gevura* that require *He'arat GAR* are completed too.

It has been explained above that *Rosh de YESHSUT* clothes from the *Chazeh de Nekudim* to *Peh de AVI de Nekudim*. Thus, *Rosh de YESHSUT* clothes these *Achoraim de AVI*, which is similar to *AVI de Atzilut* that clothe *HGT de AA de Atzilut*, and these *HGT* administer all their wholeness to *AVI de Atzilut*. Similarly, here the *Achoraim de AVI* that fell to *HGT* became the *Pnimiut* to *Rosh de YESHSUT*, from which it sucks its wholeness.

He writes, "When the rest of the remaining *Orot* came out in order to enter in their *Kli*. They were clothed in these *Achoraim* that fell and remained in *Atzilut*, and the last *Melachim* came out clothed in the *Achoraim* of *AVI*." This is because the *Orot de Rosh de YESHSUT* themselves were clothed in these *Achoraim*, as they clothe them in their *Pnimiut*. Hence, their *Gufim* too, which are the four *Melachim TNHYM* clothe these *Achoraim de AVI* too.

You must know that there is a great difference between the *Achoraim de AVI* that fell and the *Rosh de YESHSUT*. This is because these *Achoraim* come from *Behinat Rosh de AVI*, but because of the blemish of the breaking of the vessels, they descended to *HGT*.

Although the *Orot* came out on the *Masach de NHY de AK*, which are *Behinot ZON*, yet the *MAN* do not act at all in the *Rosh*, since they are there in *Behinat* from below upward. Hence, these *Orot de Gadlut* that came out on the *MAN* are considered *Behinat AVI*, and do not consist of the *Atzmut Hey Tata'a*.

Rosh de YESHSUT came from the *Masach de Guf* of the *Nekudim*, meaning from the *Masach de Chazeh*, which are the *Kelim* and the *Orot* that expanded from the *MAN de NHY de AK* from above downward. Thus, the *Hey Tata'a* is actually mixed in them, and for this reason these *YESHSUT* clothed the *HGT de Nekudim* themselves, these did not break.

Therefore, now these *YESHSUT* gain much since they clothe the *Achoraim de Ima* and they really are a higher degree than they. Yet, because of their fall, it became possible for *YESHSUT* to clothe them.

This remained for them always until all the scrutinies could emerge in the future.

It means that these *Achoraim* are always made *Behinot Levushim* for *Mochin* to the *Orot* of ZON. Through them, ZA can obtain all its degrees and is protected in them. Were it not for these *Levushim*, ZA would not have been able to obtain any *Mochin*, and therefore it needs them until "in the future", meaning until it obtains all its degrees, which is at *Gmar Tikun*.

Raising of MAN etc. from these *Achoraim de AVI* that descended there etc.

The matter of raising MAN when AVI do not mate *Panim be Panim* but through raising MAN has already been explained above (*Ohr Pnimi* item 24). Since Upper *Ima* is in the *Achoraim* to *Abba* in the form of "because He delighteth in mercy," she does not stop her *Achoraim* except by raising MAN *de* ZON that awaken her to administer them *He'arat Hochma*. For them she stops her *Achoraim* and returns *Panim be Panim* with *Abba*.

There was already *He'arat Hochma* of ZON in these *Achoraim* that fell from AVI, which were already *Behinat Yechida, Haya, Neshama* for ZON (*Ohr Pnimi* item 41, par. "It has been explained"). Hence, when ZON rises to MAN, it returns and scrutinizes scrutinies from *Neshama, Haya, Yechida*, that are in these *Achoraim*, and raises them to MAN for him to AVI.

This is because when it raises scrutinies *de Neshama* to MAN, meaning from that part of the *Achoraim* that has already served there in AVI in the form of *Komat Bina*, you find that it causes *Zivug Panim be Panim de Neshama* to AVI. When it raises from scrutinies of *Haya*, meaning from that part of *Achoraim* that has already served there in AVI in *Behinat Komat Hochma*, that causes the return of *Panim be Panim* to AVI in *Behinat Haya*. Also, it raises scrutinies *de Yechida* from them of the needs of *Yechida*.

50. **You find that these *Orot* from the *Chazeh* down come covered and you already know that the concealment of the *Ohr* and its covering is the reality of its *Tikun*. This is because by so doing, there is power in the *Kli* to tolerate the *Ohr*, as it comes clothed.**

Hence, the breaking of the *Kelim* from the *Chazeh* down, which are the two bottom thirds of *Tifferet* and NHY and *Malchut*, is not like the breaking of the *Kelim* of *Daat* and HG and the Upper third of *Tifferet*. This is because the breaking of the *Elyonim* would certainly be greater than the breaking of the *Tachtonim*.

Thus, when the *Tikun* of ZA came, during the *Tikun* of its *Partzuf*, it came the opposite. This is because its *Orot* and the *Hassadim* were disclosed

from the two thirds of *Tifferet* downward, since they have an ability to receive them not through *Masach Bina*, since their breaking was not great.

However, the *Elyonim*, which are from the *Rosh de ZA* through the *Chazeh*, now they came blocked and clothed in the *Tikun* inside *Masach Bina*, which is her *Yesod*. This is because in the beginning they were disclosed and their breaking was great. Though the *NH* are covered and blocked, it has been explained that the disclosed *Hassadim* strike them and their *Ohr* comes out.

Ohr Pnimi

50. **These *Orot* from the *Chazeh* down come covered.**

This means that the *Behinat GAR* in them is covered in the *Achoraim de Ima*. Here you must know that the complete *Tikun de ZON* is that their *GAR* will be covered in the *Achoraim de Ima*, and their *ZAT* will be disclosed. This is because then their *Eser Sefirot* are corrected like the *Eser Sefirot de Bina de Ohr Yashar*, as *Bina de Ohr Yashar* consists of *Eser Sefirot* as well, *Keter* and *Hochma* above her and *ZAT* below her, which are her *Behinot ZON*, called *Tvuna* (*Ohr Pnimi* item 45, par. "We have yet to understand").

It explains there that from the time *Bina* began to extend *He'arat Hochma* for *ZON*, it is already considered *Tvuna*, and as her *ZAT*, meaning the *Shorashim* that remained in *Bina* that *ZAT* left in her after they left to their place. Yet, *Bina* herself is considered as it is in the beginning of its creation, meaning in *Ohr de Hassadim* and her *Achoraim* to *Hochma*.

Thus, *GAR de Bina* are covered with her *Achoraim* and only her *ZAT* manifested in *He'arat Hochma*. Hence, when *ZA* is also corrected like her and his *ZAT* are disclosed in *He'arat Hochma*, it is then in a complete *Tikun*.

He writes, "these *Orot* from the *Chazeh* down come covered and you already know that the concealment of the *Ohr* and its covering is the reality of its *Tikun*." It means that because *Rosh de Tvuna* already clothes the *Achoraim* of the Upper *Abba ve Ima* that are corrected in *Tikun Kavim* (*Ohr Pnimi* item 49, par. "In spite of that"), hence, each of the *Orot de TNHYM* that expanded from them has *Eser Sefirot*.

Also, their *GAR* were covered in the *Achoraim de Ima* and there was only *Behinat He'arat Hochma* in their *ZAT*, which is like the *Eser Sefirot de ZA* during its *Tikun*.

He writes, "the concealment of the *Ohr* and its covering is the reality of its *Tikun*," as thus the *Tikun* rises in *ZA de Atzilut* too. However, the *Orot de HGT* that did not have any *Tikun* from the *Achoraim de Ima*, but their entire *Eser Sefirot* were revealed, and even the GAR in each of them, for that reason their breaking was harder than NHY.

During the *Tikun* of its *Partzuf*, it came the opposite.

It is because in the *Tikun*, you find that its HGT are corrected in *Achoraim de Ima*, which is the *Masach de Yesod Ima*, clothed in its *Tifferet* through the *Chazeh*. Also, from the *Chazeh* down the *He'arat Hochma* in *Hassadim* appears in it, meaning that its GAR, which are HGT, is covered with a *Masach* and NHY, which are ZAT de ZA.

In addition, the *Hassadim* are exposed, which is the opposite of ZA de Nekudim, whose HGT were completely exposed, and whose NHY were covered. This *Tikun* began in NHY de Nekudim that came out clothed in *Achoraim de Ima*, and ended in *Olam Atzilut*.

The disclosed *Hassadim* strike them and their *Ohr* comes out.

This is because the *Hassadim* appear only in the middle line de ZA, which is through *Yesodot de AVI* that are clothed there, though *Achoraim de Ima* control the *Ktzavot*. However, the *Ohr Hozer* rises from below upward, strikes the two *Kavim* right and left, and educes their *Orot* outwardly. Know, that these *Orot* that come out because of the *Hakaa* are the *Orot de NHY* of each and every *Sefira* that were there in each of them in the form of "and all their hinder parts were inward."

It means that they were incorporated in the HGT of each one (*Ohr Pnimi* item 28, sub header **"This is the essential drop"**). Now, through the *Hakaa* of disclosed *Hassadim* from the middle line in the *Sefirot de Ktzavot*, the NHY of each can come out of the *Hitkalelut* of HGT and appear outwardly in *Behinat Achoraim* that are completed in *He'arat Hochma* that no longer have any fear from the sucking of the exteriors.

You already know that *Hakaa* means lessening because when two opposite *Orot* meet each other, they lessen one another, and as a result, a new *He'arah* is born. So it is here, because since the disclosed *Hassadim* in *He'arat Hochma* is opposite to the *Sefirot* in the two *Ktzavot*, where because of the *Achoraim de Ima* they are found to reject *Hochma*, hence they beat on each other. As a result of their *Hakaa*, new NHY in *He'arat Hochma* are born and appear, and the rest of the matter will be explained in its place.

51. **In the death of ZA, the *Achoraim* of AVI descended to its Upper third *de Tifferet*, but the *Achoraim* of Israel Saba ve Tvuna were not completed until the death of Nukva de ZA. Hence, the ZA takes the *Achoraim de***

AVI, and *Malchut* takes the *Achoraim de Israel Saba ve Tvuna*, and their *Orot* clothe in them like the *Mochin de ZA*.

52. Now you will understand what is written, that when the ZON are equal together *Panim be Panim*, then *Netzah* and *Hod de AVI* are *Mochin* to ZA and the *NHY de Israel Saba ve Tvuna* are *Mochin*, and enter in *Rosh de Nukva*.

Ohr Pnimi

52. **Netzah and Hod de AVI are Mochin to ZA and the NHY de Israel Saba ve Tvuna are Mochin, and enter in Rosh de Nukva.**

This does not mean that NHY of the Upper *AVI de Atzilut* become *Mochin* for ZA. This is utterly impossible since no *Partzuf* receives *Mochin* but only from its *Elyon*, not from its *Ali Elyon*.

The *Elyon* of ZA are YESHSUT and not AVI, which are its *Ali Elyon*. Rather, it means that AVI become one *Partzuf* with YESHSUT, as it was here in AVI *de Nekudim*.

At that time NHY *de* YESHSUT that are clothed in it for *Mochin* are discerned as NHY *de* AVI. This is because then YESHSUT became the actual *Guf de* AVI, hence its HGT are considered receiving from their *Behinat Gufim*, such as the reception of the *Gufim de* AVI by HGT *de Nekudim*.

This is through what ZA clothes in the *Achoraim de* AVI that fell to their place, as the Rav says. However, *Nukva de* ZA cannot receive as he does since *Nukva* has no *Shoresh* in HGT, and her entire *Atzmut* begins from *Chazeh de* ZA downward, meaning only NHY.

This too came to her through her *Hitkalelut* in ZA, since she is merely *Behinat Hod* at her *Shoresh*. Yet, the completion of her *Gadlut* is to receive like the reception of NHY *de Nekudim* of the *Behinat Gufim de* YESHSUT, which is the final level of *Partzuf* NHY.

At that time they are the two great Lights that do not need each other since the *Nukva* receives *Partzuf* NHY from *Behinat Guf de* YESHSUT like the NHY *de Nekudim*. Also, ZA receives its *Partzuf* HGT from *Behinat Guf* of the Upper AVI that are connected with YESHSUT like the HGT *de Nekudim*.

As HGT *de Nekudim* and NHY *de Nekudim* did not need each other, so ZA and *Nukva* will not need each other. Hence, ZA will no longer control the *Nukva* and will not be considered greater than her, since she does not need him.

53. You will also understand what is written, that when they were *Panim be Panim*, two *Behinot Ya'akov* come out, one in ZA and one in *Nukva*. It is

so because the one that is from *Mochin de ZA* is from *AVI*, and the other, which is from *Mochin de Nukva* is from *Israel Saba ve Tvuna*.

At that time they are the two great Lights, she is not greater than him, and he is not greater than her, and they do not need each other at all. Nevertheless, the *Achoraim* of *Abba* are on the right hand side, in *Hesed de ZA*, and the *Achoraim de Ima* are on the left hand side, in *Gevura de ZA*, and this study will be addressed in its place.

54. Here in this place is the place of the descent and the fall of the *Achoraim* of *AVI*, as we have said above that they descended in *Atzilut* itself. Even though the *Kelim de ZA* broke, yet the *Orot de ZA* remained clothed in these *Achoraim* of the Upper *AVI*, the entire *Kav Hesed de ZA* in the *Achoraim* of *Abba*, and the entire *Kav Gevura* clothed in the *Achoraim de Ima*, and study this introduction thoroughly.

Ohr Pnimi

54. The *Orot de ZA* remained clothed in these *Achoraim* of the Upper *AVI*.

This is because after the breaking of the vessels through the Upper third of *Tifferet*, when all the *Achoraim* of the Upper *AVI* had descended, they expanded in the place of *Kelim de HGT* and were corrected in *Gimel Kavim*, right, left, and middle. At that time the *Orot de HGT* rose and clothed these *Kelim*; *Ohr Hesed* in the right *Kav*, *Ohr Gevura* in the left *Kav*, and the *Ohr* of the Upper third of *Tifferet* in the middle *Kav*.

55. *Now we shall explain how during the demise of these *Melachim*, their *Kelim* descended to *Olam Beria*, which is not so in the four *Achoraim de AVI*. Now we have explained the division that was between *AVI* and the seven *Melachim*, which are ZON.

We have said that the seven *Melachim* that actually died descended to *Olam Beria*, and their *Kelim* and the *Achoraim* of *AVI* were cancelled and did not die. Instead, they descended below in *Olam Atzilut* itself. We have explained the reason for it there, and said that it became the reason that the seven *Melachim* did not received *Orot AHP de AK*, but only from its *Guf* onward.

56. The reason for this itself was also another difference between GAR, which are KHB, and the seven bottom *Melachim*. It is so because the GAR first came out with a little *Tikun*, since when they first came out, they expanded in an order of *Gimel Kavim*.

It is not so with the ZAT that came out one below the other, and this is the meaning of what is written in the Idra Raba, "How long will we sit in the keeping of one pillar?" He wishes to say, that the *Tikun*, which is through *Kavim*, was made, but prior to that, when they were one atop the other, there existed the one *Kav*.

We have already explained that the *Tikun* of *Atzilut*, since it is made of **VAK**, is made in the form of three *Kavim*, tied and connected to one another, in the form of the third that decides between them. At that time it is called "single authority".

Yet, when they are atop the other and they are separated from one another, at that time it is called "multiple authorities". For this reason, the *Achoraim* of the **GAR** were cancelled and did not die, and the seven *Melachim* died *Panim* and *Achor*, since they came out without any *Tikun* at all.

Ohr Pnimi

56. When they first came out, they expanded in an order of **Gimel Kavim**.

It has already been explained above that the matter of *Tikun Kavim* begins by the force of the *He'arat Achoraim de Ima* (Ohr Pnimi item 49, par. "Yet, there is a big difference").

It is known that *AVI de Nekudim* first came out in *Behinat Achor be Achor*. It means that they were corrected in the *Ohr Achoraim* of the Upper *Bina*, hence they were not blemished by the *Hey Tata'a* that rose to the *Eynaim*, and remained in *Behinat GAR de Bina* (Ohr Pnimi item 23).

This *Tikun* is called *Tikun Gimel Kavim*, where each three, right, left, and middle, come up as one, which is the *He'arat GAR* by the force of the *Achoraim de Bina*. For this reason they are considered connected to one another in one knot.

We must also thoroughly note the matter of their division into two *Ktzavot* and the sentencing between them, since there is a great interest in that. The thing is that through the ascent of the *Hey Tata'a* to the *Eynaim*, which are *Hochma*, *Malchut* was incorporated in each and every *Sefira* of the *Eser Sefirot*. For this reason a *Behinat Nukva* and *Kli* was made in each and every *Sefira*.

Because of that, it is considered that there is *Behinat* right and left in each *Sefira*, meaning *Hesed* and *Din*. This is because the *Sefira* itself is *Behinat Hesed*, and the force of *Malchut* that was mingled in it through the ascent of *Hey Tata'a* to the *Eynaim* is the *Behinat Din* in the *Sefira*.

Hence, *AVI de Nekudim* too are considered right and left, meaning the *Kav* of *Hesed*, which is *Hochma* and *Abba*, and the *Kav* of *Din*, which is *Bina* and *Ima*. *AVI* had no *GAR* with respect to these two *Kavim*. Hence the *Ohr Achoraim* of the Upper *Bina* was drawn to them in *Behinat* deciding *Kav* in the middle of them.

This *Ohr Achoraim* is considered *Behinat* middle, and determining. This is because for itself, there is no distinction between right and left, since the whole difference in the *Ktzavot* is because the left is the *Kav* of *Din*, for lack of *Ohr Hochma* that is fitting for the right *Kav*. This refers to the GAR *de Hochma* that cannot receive because of the mixture of the *Hey Tata'a* inside it since they are two *Ktzavot* that deny one another.

However, this *Kav* that extends from *Bina*, rejects *Ohr Hochma* in any case, meaning even if there had not been *Behinat Din* there. Thus you find that it is in equivalence with the two *Ktzavot* together, and in that the right *Kav* complements the *Behinat* GAR that it lacks, which is *Hochma*.

In addition, it sweetens the left and connects it with the right in complete unification since it no longer contradicts it. Thus, the two *Kavim* right and left are connected and corrected by the *Achoraim de Ima*, which is the middle line (*Ohr Pnimi* item 49, par. "Yet, there is a big difference").

He writes, "the GAR first came out with a little *Tikun*, since when they first came out, they expanded in an order of *Gimel Kavim*." It means that in the beginning, they emerged in correction of *Achor be Achor*, and this *Tikun* means *Tikun Kavim*.

ZAT that came out one below the other.

It is because ZAT did not come out from AVI with respect to their being in *Behinat Achor be Achor*, but they emerged from a *Zivug* of *Panim be Panim de* AVI. Hence, there was no connection between them whatsoever, but each *Sefira* was its own *Guf*. *Hesed* was *Guf de Abba*, and *Gevura* was *Guf de Ima* etc. because they lacked the *Tikun Achoraim de Ima*, which is the tie that connects all the ends together.

VAK, is made in the form of three *Kavim*, tied and connected to one another, in the form of the third that decides between them.

As has been explained in the previous item, the beginning of the *Tikun* was made in HGT, in the form of NHY *de Ima*. At that time the NHY too are integrated in them in the form of, "their hinder parts were inward." Hence, even afterwards, when the *Achoraim* are completed from the perspective of the *He'arat Hochma* too, still the first *Tikun de Achoraim de Ima* remains in them. This is because they come from the essence of the beginning of its creation and does not undergo a change, as every thing that comes from the beginning of its creation never changes, as is known in the Rav's words.

57. Let us explain the order of the emanation of the seven *Melachim*. We shall begin with the first, which is the *Daat*, which emerged first. When the *Kli* could not endure, the *Kli* broke and descended in *Olam ha Beria*, meaning in the place that was to be *Olam Beria* afterwards, since *Olam Beria* was not created yet.

Also, this *Kli* fell in the place of *Daat de Beria*, as it relates to it similarly. However, the *Ohr* of the *Daat* descended too, but remained in *Atzilut* itself, in the place of *Kli Malchut* of the *Atzilut*.

Ohr Pnimi

57. **This *Kli* fell in the place of *Daat de Beria*, as it relates to it similarly.**

The reason for the breaking has already been thoroughly clarified above, and for this reason they were separated from the *Kedusha*.

In the matter of their fall to the three *Olamot BYA* that the Rav mentioned, although they still weren't these three *Olamot* at all, nevertheless, their *Reshimo* was already evident. This is because they are the *Behinat* three *Sefirot Bina*, *ZA*, and *Malchut* of *NHY de Sium* that went outside *Atzilut de AK* during *Tzimtzum Bet* (as written at length in Part 6, *Ohr Pnimi* item 7).

Since each of these *Melachim* consisted of *Eser Sefirot*, which are *Rosh, Toch, Sof*, the *Rosh* fell to *Beria*, their *Toch* fell to *Yetzira*, and their *Sof* fell to *Assiya*. The Rav writes that the *Kli* of *Daat* fell to *Daat de Beria*, meaning its *Behinat Rosh*, which is *KHBD de Daat*, but its *HGT* fell to *Yetzira*, and its *NHYM* fell to *Assiya*. You will understand the matter of the fall of all seven *Melachim* similarly.

As it relates to it similarly.

This is because there are *Eser Sefirot* in each *Olam* of the three *Olamot BYA*, hence the *Kli de Melech ha Daat* fell to *Daat de Beria*, meaning to its corresponding *Behina*.

The *Ohr* of the *Daat* descended too, but remained in *Atzilut* etc. in order to shine from afar in its *Kli* that stands in *Beria*.

Know, that this *Ohr* that the Rav says means the *Reshimo* that remained of the *Ohr Daat* after its *Histalkut* from the *Kli*. This is because every *Ohr* leaves a *Reshimo* after its *Histalkut*, and thus shines to the *Kli* so that it will not be cancelled and not die, as the Rav said (Part 4, Chap 2, items 2, 8).

The Rav tells us that the *Reshimo* of *Daat* did not actually remain in the *Kli*, as it did in the previous *Partzufim*, but remained in *Atzilut*. He writes, "the breaking was in the *Kelim* and not in the *Orot* etc. and it is in *Behinat Tagin* on the *Otiot*." This is because for some reason, the *Ohr* of the *Reshimo* cannot clothe inside the *Kli* and it shines to the *Kli* from afar, called *Tagin*, as the Rav says above (Part 4, Chap 3, item 11).

58. However, it did not come down there because of a flaw in it, as it has been explained above that the breaking was in the *Kelim* and not in the *Orot*, while its descent was there due to a flaw. We should attribute the cancellation to the *Orot*, as we similarly attributed the cancellation to the *Kelim de Achoraim de AVI* that fell in *Atzilut* itself.

    However, their descent was in order to shine from afar in its *Kli* that stands in *Beria*, so that it would not die entirely and would remain hopeless. For this reason it shines in it from afar while it stands in *Atzilut*, and it is in *Behinat Tagin* on the *Otiot*.

59. Afterwards *Hesed* came out, the *Kli* broke and descended in *Bina de Beria*, and the *Ohr* descended in the place of the *Kli* of *Yesod de Atzilut*. This is because the *Ohr Daat* preceded to take the place of *Malchut*.

    After that *Gevura* came out and broke, the *Kli* descended in *Hochma de Beria*, and the *Ohr* descended in *Kli de Netzah Hod de Atzilut*, which are two parts of the *Guf*.

    After that *Tifferet* came out and broke, the *Kli* descended in *Keter de Beria*, and the *Ohr* remained in its place, which is in *Tifferet de Atzilut*.

Ohr Pnimi

59. *Hesed* came out, the *Kli* broke and descended in *Bina de Beria*, and the *Ohr* descended in the place of the *Kli* of *Yesod de Atzilut*. This is because the *Ohr Daat* preceded to take the place of *Malchut*.

    It means that when the *Orot* are clothed in the *Kelim*, it is considered that the one that is more *Av* than the other, is greater than the other. This is because it is known that the one whose *Masach* is more *Av* educes a greater *Koma*. Yet, when the *Kelim* are empty of *Orot*, their *Aviut* is considered a demerit, hence it is considered the opposite, that the purer is more important.

    He writes, "and the *Kli de Hesed* fell to *Bina de Beria*." This is because the *Kli de Daat* extends from a *Zivug* on *Masach de Behina Dalet*, connecting the *Behina Gimel* (see *Ohr Pnimi* item 41), and the *Kli de Hesed* extends from *Zivug* on *Behina Gimel* only.

    You find that the *Kli de Hesed* is more *Zach* than the *Kli de Daat*, hence the *Kli de Hesed* is considered above the *Kli de Daat*, meaning it is more important than it, as it is more *Zach*. He writes, "and the *Ohr* descended in the place of *Yesod*." This is because according to the value of the *Reshimot* that clothe them, hence, the *Reshimot* are also appreciated according to the importance of the *Kelim*.

Gevura came out and broke, the Kli descended in Hochma de Beria.

This means that the one that is purer than the other is more important than the other. It is so because after the *Histalkut* of the *Ohr* from the *Kelim*, the *Aviut* is regarded as lowness. Similarly, the *Kli de Tifferet* too is more important than the *Kli Gevura*, hence it fell to *Keter de Beria*.

Thus, the four *Kelim*: *Daat*, *Hesed*, *Gevura*, and *Tifferet*, fell to KHBD *de Beria*, which are GAR of *Beria* like the *Kelim* DHGT that were the GAR of ZON. However, they fell in oppositeness of degree.

This means that *Daat* is below them all, as it is the most *Av*, hence its breaking is the hardest. *Kli de Hesed* is less than that, as it is only from *Behina Gimel de Aviut*, and *Kli Gevura*, which is only from *Behina Bet de Aviut*, is less than that. The breaking of *Kli de Tifferet* is the least of all, since it is only from *Behina Aleph de Aviut*.

All the *Reshimot* of the *Kelim* fell similarly: the *Reshimo de Daat* in *Malchut de Atzilut*, meaning below everyone at the *Sium* of the *Atzilut*. Atop it is the *Hesed*, in *Yesod de Atzilut*, and atop that is the *Gevura* in *Netzah Hod de Atzilut*. Above all is the *Tifferet*, which remained in its place, meaning in *Tifferet de Atzilut*, meaning with respect to the *Kelim*.

De Netzah Hod de Atzilut, which are two parts of the Guf.

Only while they are still in *Behinat Achoraim*, lacking *He'arat Hochma*. However, when they are in *Behinat Panim*, meaning when there is *He'arat Hochma* in them, they are considered two separate *Sefirot* from one another.

You will find the reason for it in the Rav's words (Part 5 items 42, 43). He says there that *Sefirat Netzah* extends from *VAK de Keter*, at which time *Lo Matei* in *Hochma*. Hence, the *Netzah* is considered not having *He'arat GAR de Hochma*, and *Sefirat Hod* extends from *Behinat Matei* in *Hochma*. For this reason the *Hod* is considered to be shining *He'arat Hochma* in it.

Thus, the whole difference between *Netzah* and *Hod* is in the *He'arat Hochma*, which is absent in *Netzah*, and present in *Hod*. This difference is therefore possible when there is *He'arat Hochma* in the *Partzuf* in general. Yet, when there is only *He'arat Achoraim de Ima* in the *He'arat Partzuf* in general, then there is no longer any difference between *Netzah* and *Hod*, since there is no *He'arat Hochma* in *Hod* too, just like in *Netzah*.

Hence, at that time they are considered one *Sefira*, and for this reason the *Sefirot Netzah* and *Hod de Nekudim* that have only from *Behina Bet de YESHSUT*, and are also clothed in the *Achoraim* that fell form the Upper *AVI*, do not have *He'arat Hochma*, and are thus considered one *Sefira*.

We might say that accordingly, the *Sefirot Hesed* and *Gevura* too should have been regarded as one *Kli*. This is because its been clarified that the only difference between *Hesed* and *Gevura* is in the *He'arat Hochma* too, existing in *Hesed* and missing in *Gevura*, since the disparity between the *Hesed* and *Gevura* and the *Netzah* and *Hod* is great.

This is so because the force of the *Achoraim de Bina* begins primarily from *Bina* downward in all the *Partzufim*, since each *Behina* sucks from its corresponding *Behina* in the *Eser Sefirot de Ohr Yashar*. These *Achoraim* are not incorporated in the two *Sefirot Keter* and *Hochma* at all, only in *Bina*. Hence, *Hesed* and *Gevura* too, which are *Behinat Keter* and *Hochma de Hassadim*, the force of the *Achoraim* does not operate on their own *Behina* with respect to themselves.

The force of the *Achoraim* operates in its fullest measure only from *Tifferet* downward, which is known to relate to *Bina*. Thus, *Hesed* is always considered containing *GAR* even during the *Katnut* of the *Partzuf*, which is not so with *Gevura*. Also, there is a big difference between *Hesed* and *Gevura*, since *Hesed* still contains *GAR* with respect to itself, whereas *Gevura*, which is not so with the *Gevura*, being in *Achoraim* on the *GAR* from its *Shoresh*.

60. Now there is no distance among any of the above *Orot* and their *Kelim* that is more than three degrees. This is because more than three degrees are a complete distance and it cannot shine in it. However, the rest of the *Orot* descended from their place as well, except *Tifferet*, which remained in its place and did not descend.

    You find, that undoubtedly, though we have clarified that the descent of the other *Orot* from their place was for the needs of the *Kelim*, to shine for them, still, being below their place, their force was slightly weakened.

    For this reason they do not have the strength to rise upwards, but the *Ohr Tifferet* that stood in its place, its taste did not change, and its power is strong. Hence when it sees that it has no *Kli*, it can rise to the place it came from because it has no wish to stay bare, disclosed without a *Levush*. It returns to *Bina*, to the place where it first stood. If it does that, you will find that it will be very distant from its *Kli*, and it will die completely.

Ohr Pnimi

60. The *Ohr Tifferet* that stood in its place, its taste did not change etc.

By that he explains the *Hitpashtut Kli de Keter* up to the *Chazeh*. Also, he gave below the reason for the *Hitpashtut* of the *Kli de Bina* up to *Gevura* in order to give room for the reigning of *Netzah* and *Hod*. It is also the reason for the *Hitpashtut Kli de Hesed* in order to give a place for the reigning of *Yesod*. Thus, all these reasons are completely unnecessary according to the Rav's words in several places (Tree of Life, Gate 9, Chap 84, and in Mavo She'arim, Gate 2, Part 2, Chap 6).

He writes there, "When *Tifferet* died and the *Ohr* began to die and depart from the first third through the *Chazeh*, the general *Hey Hassadim* and *Gevurot* descended from the two *Yesodot* of the two *Malchuyot* of the Upper *AVI*. Their *Achoraim* completed their fall and the *Achoraim* of Upper *AVI* were found sitting here below in this manner, since the *Achoraim* of *Abba* sit on the right line, in the place that was *Hesed de ZA*, which is the second *Melech*.

The *Achoraim of Ima* in the place where the third *Melech*, which is *Gevura de ZA* was. It is known that *AVI* were as *Kavim* because they were the *Achoraim* that fell thus far. This is the *Behinat* new *Kli* that *AVI* made, which expanded thus far, and then *Hesed* and *Gevura* rose there.

That *Hitpashtut* is these *Behinat Achoraim* itself, which fell down through there etc. and *Orot Hesed* and *Gevura* clothed these two *Achoraim* as well as *Orot Netzah* and *Hod*. However, it is all above in the place of *Hesed* and *Gevura*, and understand that thoroughly." Similarly, *Kli de Keter* was made of *Behinat Achoraim de NHY* of the *Keter* that were blemished and fell below.

Accordingly, the matter of the *Hitpashtut Kelim de KHB* to *HGT* is one with the fall of the *Achoraim de AVI* and *NHY de Keter*, as the Rav says there. Hence there is no longer a question why three *Kavim* of *KHB* expanded and there is no matter and place for these reasons.

Moreover, these reasons contradict the Rav's words above. This is because according to the reasons that he wrote here about the *Hitpashtut* of the *Kavim*, to be in order to give room for the *Melachim* of *NHYM*, you find that *Kav Bina* expanded first to *Kav Hochma* because *Netzah* and *Hod* reigned before the *Yesod*.

Hence, he says here that first *Kav Bina* expanded and then *Hochma*, but in fact they are *Behinat Achoraim* that fell from *AVI* and *Keter*. Thus, the *Kav Hochma* expanded prior to the *Kav Bina*, since the *Achoraim de Hochma* fell in the death of *Kli de Hesed* and *Achoraim de Ima* fell in the death of *Kli de Gevura*.

It follows that first the *Kav Hochma* expanded to *Hesed*, and then the *Kav Bina* to *Gevura*. This is the opposite of what he wrote here, and perhaps both rumors are from the Rav. It is truer to say that these reasons are from Rav Chaim Vital himself and are not at all the Rav's words.

Besides the above, what also stems from the above reasons is that the *Kelim de Melachim* of *Netzah* and *Hod* fell between the *Kelim* of *HGT* as he will say below. This is hard to hear since *NHY* compared to *HGT* is like *VAK* compared to *GAR*, and how would *Kli de VAK* fall dwell in the middle of the *Kelim de GAR*, between *Hesed* and *Gevura*?

It has been thoroughly clarified in the Rav's words in Mavo She'arim, that at the very death of the upper third of *Tifferet* and the completion of the fall of all the *Achoraim de AVI*, they became three new *Kelim*, *Hesed*, *Gevura*, and *Tifferet* together. The four *Orot* from the four *Melachim Daat, Hesed, Gevura*, and *Tifferet* rose there together, and *Reshimot de Daat* and *Tifferet* clothed in the new *Kli de Tifferet*. Also, the *Reshimo de Hesed* in the new *Kli de Hesed*, and also the *Reshimo de Gevura* in *Kli de Gevura*.

61. For this reason the *Maatzil Elyon* wanted and extended and magnified the *Kli Keter*, which did not break and extended through the middle line. This is because the *GAR* were formed as three lines to begin with, and extended through the middle line up to the place of *Tifferet*, only through its middle, which is up to the *Tabur*.

    At that time the *Ohr Tifferet* rose and vanished inside that *Kli* of *Keter* that expanded up to its place. You find that only half the bottom *Ohr Tifferet* rose, since the upper half stands in its place that has already expanded in it through the *Kli Keter*.

    Then the *Ohr Daat* that descended below in *Malchut de Atzilut*, seeing that it was already a new *Kli* in its place, here its place is also in the middle line between the *Keter* and the *Tifferet*, and then it too rose and ascended to its place.

    At that time, since the *Ohr* had drawn far from its *Kli*, it descended down in *Malchut de Beria*, though the *Kli* of *Tifferet* remained in its place, which is in *Keter de Beria*, since only half its *Ohr* rose, not all of it, and its Upper half remained in its place.

Ohr Pnimi

61. Only half the bottom *Ohr Tifferet* rose, since the upper half stands in its place.

    It means that after the *Masach de Chazeh* was purified and rose to its *Shoresh* to *AVI*, the *Rosh de YESHSUT* came out on it through its *Hitkalelut* in the

Zivug de Rosh from there. Their *Guf* expanded from above downward in the two thirds of *Tifferet* from the *Chazeh* downward from their *Histaklut Eynaim*. Also, after the *Kli de Tifferet* broke and descended to *Keter de Beria*, this *Ohr* that was in the two bottom thirds of *Tifferet* rose and ascended to the new *Kli de Tifferet* that was made of the *Achoraim de Keter*.

The upper half stands in its place.

It means that it did not descend from its degree because of the breaking of its *Kli*, and this is because of what the Rav wrote above (item 44), that *Achoraim de Abba* and *Achoraim de Ima* descended before there was a blemish and deficit in the *Yesodot de AVI*.

This is because after the *Achoraim de AVI* have already descended and returned *Achor be Achor*, the fourth *Melech* began to reign, being the Upper third of *Tifferet*. He wrote the reason there, which is because the *Yesod* is all *Panim* and has no *Achoraim* that descended from it.

It explains there in *Ohr Pnimi* that this entire *Ohr* that descended through the *Zivug Yesodot de AVI* is *Behinat Achor be Achor*. This is because they mated after they'd returned *Achor be Achor*, and *He'arat Achor be Achor* is considered *Behinat Panim de Abba ve Ima*, meaning from what they have from the beginning of their creation, which are not at all harmed by the matter of the breaking of the vessels.

Thus, the *Ohr* of the Upper third of *Tifferet* up to the *Chazeh* that extends from the *Zivug Yesodot de AVI* has no flaw because of the breaking of the vessels, since it extends from *Zivug de Achor be Achor*. He writes here, "but the *Ohr* of the upper half of *Tifferet* that stood in its place, its taste did not change, and its power is strong."

We might therefore ask, why did the *Kli* of the Upper third of *Tifferet* break, since it only had *Behinat Achor be Achor*, which is all *Behinat Panim*? The Rav has already written that the *Behinat Panim* remains only in *AVI*, yet in the *Kelim de ZAT*, the *Behinat Panim* broke in them too.

However, indeed his breaking was not great, but he rather descended from *Behinat Rosh de Tifferet* to *Behinat VAK de Tifferet*, meaning to *Behinat* from the *Chazeh* downward. What the Rav wrote above, that it fell to *Keter de Beria*, it is after the *Guf de Histaklut Eynaim de YESHSUT* expanded in it, and it broke and the *Ohr* ascended to the Upper half of the new *Kli de Tifferet*.

At that time it fell to *Keter de Beria*, meaning to the corresponding *Behina*, since the *Guf de YESHSUT* that it expanded in is *Behinat Keter de YESHSUT* as well. From this you can see that its breaking is not great since all the *Kelim* of the *Melachim* descended to *ZAT de Beria* and only the *Tifferet* fell to the *Keter de Beria*, which is close to *Atzilut*.

Ohr Daat that descended etc. it too rose and ascended to its place.

It has already been explained above (*Ohr Pnimi* item 61, sub header "**Only half the bottom**"), that right after the *Hitpashtut* of the three *Kavim de KHB* to the *Behinot* new *Kelim DHGT*, all the *Orot* of the four *Melachim Daat* and *HGT* rose to their place together, each in his own *Kav*.

The reason for their ascent back to the *Kelim* of the new *HGT* that emerged in their place is because of the new *Zivug* which is the *Rosh de YESHSUT* that came out there in their place, which is *Behinat Hitpashtut Bet* that returns and fills the *Kelim* and the *Reshimot* that remained after the *Histalkut* of the *Partzuf Elyon*, as it was in the previous *Partzufim de AK*.

This is because the *Reshimot* and the empty *Kelim* of the *Partzuf Elyon* always travel to its *Partzuf Tachton*. So it is here with *YESHSUT*, which fills the *Kelim* and the *Reshimot de Guf* of the Upper *AVI*. However, the *Kelim* have already broken and fell, and it fills only the *Reshimot* alone, which are the *Orot DHGT* that previously fell to *NHYM de Atzilut*. Hence, now they returned to their place and are filled with *Ohr de YESHSUT*.

Now you can also understand the reason for the double decline that happened to the *Kelim* of the *Melachim*, those *Daat* and *HGT*. It is that the primary sustenance of these *Kelim* that fell to *KHBD de Beria*, is their *Reshimot*. Since these *Reshimot* were from *Behinat GAR de ZAT*, which are the *Orot Gufim* of the Upper *AVI*, hence they also fell to their corresponding *Behina*, to *GAR de Beria*, meaning in *KHBD de Beria*.

On the one hand, now after their *Reshimot* rose to the place of the new *Kelim* and were renewed in the *He'arat Rosh de YESHSUT*, they gained much, since they have obtained a new *Ohr* under the first *Ohr* of the Upper *AVI* that departed from them. On the other hand, they lost much due to their becoming receivers of the *Ohr de YESHSUT*, in that they have descended from *Behinat GAR* to *Behinat ZAT*.

Thus, *YESHSUT* with respect to *AVI* are only *Behinot ZAT*. Because of that their *Kelim* that are in *Beria* descended from the *Behinat GAR* of *Beria* to *Behinat ZAT* of *Beria* too, and hence fell an even greater fall from the place of *KHBD de Beria* to the place of *NHYM de Beria*.

We might say that according to that, they should have fallen to *HGT de Beria*, and not to *NHYM*. This is because it has already been explained that the *Aviut* is considered lowness in the empty *Kelim*, and the more *Zach* in them is more important. Hence, when HGT NHYM fall to ZAT, they are inverted. The HGT fall to NHYM, and the purer NHYM fall to HGT de Beria, and this is simple.

You should know that this *Ohr Daat* that rose to its place is only the *Reshimot de Hassadim* of the *Daat*, but the *Reshimo de Gevurot* still remained there in *Malchut*, and rose only after the breaking of the vessels of the *Melachim de NHYM*.

62. You might say, that we have said above that there must be a distance of only three *Sefirot* between the *Kelim* and its *Ohr*. Thus, how did the *Kli* of *Daat* descend to *Malchut de Beria*? The answer is that certainly, where it is possible, it is possible.

In the beginning, one enjoyed and the other was not in deficit. This is because in the beginning the *Kli* enjoyed its *Ohr* while *Daat* was below, and the *Ohr* was also not in deficit. Even if it rises to its place in the *Daat* of *Atzilut*, it hasn't any *Kli* there, hence it wished to shine in its *Kli*, and since it descended, it did not rise again.

Yet, when it saw that there is a *Behinat Kli* in its place, it is close to its own pleasure and benefit more than to benefit to its *Kli*. This is because now when it rises upward in its place, it has a *Kli* where it can receive the *Ohr* for itself from above, from the *Maatzil* and from the *Keter* in great proximity, and this is why it rose.

This reason will suffice to the discernment of the benefit of the *Ohr* for itself. However, it is also not such a great loss to the discernment of the demerit of its *Kli* when it descends below in *Malchut de Beria*.

This is because when we say that there must not be a distance between the *Ohr* and its *Kli*, but only of three *Sefirot*, it is the measure of three *Sefirot de Atzilut*, whose measure is great. Yet, in *Beria*, the measure of the entire *Yod Sefirot de Beria* is not even as one *Sefira* of *Atzilut*. Thus, it is as if she stands at the *Rosh* of *Beria* because all the *Yod Sefirot de Beria* are considered one *Sefira*.

Ohr Pnimi

62. **From the *Maatzil* and from the *Keter* in great proximity.**

It is because there it receives from the new *Rosh de YESHSUT*, which is *Keter*, because every *Rosh* is *Behinat Keter*. Also, afterwards when his *Reshimot de Gevurot* ascend in him, a new *Zivug* is made on himself and he receives Ohr from the *Maatzil*. He writes, "where it can receive the *Ohr* from the *Maatzil* and from the *Keter* in great proximity," and this is why he ascended.

63. You might say, but there is a difference of seven *Sefirot de Atzilut* between the *Kli de Daat* and her *Ohr*, as he stands up in *Daat de Atzilut*? We must understand that even in the *Sefirot de Atzilut* themselves there is not so much of a loss, except when there is a measure of three *Sefirot* between the *Ohr* and the *Kli* without any *Ohr* at all, not it, and not any other.

Yet, here, though her *Ohr* itself rose up, there are still other *Orot* standing at the end of *Atzilut*, close to *Beria*, and she can receive the *He'arah* from them. She can also receive *He'arah* from her own *Ohr* through these *Orot* that are close to her.

Remember this rule in all the other *Sefirot* since there are never more than three empty *Sefirot de Atzilut* between the *Kli* and the *Ohr*, and we will never have to return and say this matter in each of them.

64. When *Ohr Daat* rose to its place above, it magnified the *Kli* of *Keter* and extended through opposite the place of *Sium* of the entire *Tifferet*. At that time the bottom half of the *Ohr Tifferet* that rose up now returned in its real place as in the beginning.

The reason for the magnification of *Kli Keter* was because of the *Ohr Daat* that clothed it and magnified it. It is also because the *Daat* contains the entire *VAK* and it is *Neshama* to them. Hence, because it rose, it gave force in its *Kli* and magnified it in order to benefit the *Ohr Tifferet* that descended and would be in its proper place.

Ohr Pnimi

64. It magnified the *Kli* of *Keter* and extended through opposite the place of *Sium* of the entire *Tifferet*.

It means that afterwards, when it rose to it with the *Reshimot de Gevurot* of the *Daat*, as the Rav says below, a *Zivug* was made anew on the *Hassadim* and *Gevurot* of the *Daat*, and then the *Kelim* from the *Chazeh* downward grew.

65. After that *Netzah Hod* reigned. They had to come and reign in their place, in their proper *Kli*, but they did not find their place vacant since the *Ohr Gevura* descended there. For this reason *Bina* had to expand through her *Kav*, which is the left side, to the place that is fitting to later be the real place of *Gevura*, after the *Tikun*, since now they were all one atop the other.

Then, when *Ohr Gevura* saw that it was already *Behinat Kli* in her place, she rose in her place and when her *Kli* departed from it, he too departed and descended down to *Yesod de Beria*. At that time *Netzah Hod* came down in their real place and reigned there in their *Kli*, and broke.

Then their *Ohr* rises up to *Gevura,* because *Hod* rose there, since it too is a left line, and then *Netzah* rose with him there. This is because *Netzah Hod* are two parts of the body, and their *Kli* descended in *Netzah Hod de Beria*.

Ohr Pnimi

65. *Netzah Hod* reigned. They had to come and reign etc. descended in *Netzah Hod de Beria*.

It has already been explained above (*Ohr Pnimi* item 60) that according to the reasoning here about the matter of the *Hitpashtut* of *Gimel Kavim de KHB* to *HGT*, that it is because the *Melachim* of *NHYM* could not come out of their place. This is because they were not vacant, since the *Orot de DHGT* were there.

Thus you find that *Kav ha Bina* expanded at the time of the emergence of the *Melachim de NH*. Since the *Ohr Gevura* rose and drew far from the *Kli*, the *Kli* of *Gevura* fell to *Yesod de Beria*. After that *Netzah* and *Hod* reigned and when they broke, *NH* descended to *NH de Beria*.

At the time of the emergence of *Melech ha Yesod*, which did not find its place vacant, the *Kav* of *Hochma* had to expand. The *Ohr Hesed* rose there from the place of *Sefirat Yesod* to the *Kli de Hesed* that was made of the *Hitpashtut* of *Hochma*.

Also, the *Kli de Hesed* fell to the place of *Tifferet de Beria* through the drifting of the *Ohr Hesed* from the *Kli*, and now you find that the *Kli de Daat* is in *Malchut* of the *Beria*, and the *Kli Gevura* atop it. The *Kli de Netzah* and *Hod* atop it, and atop that, the *Kli de Hesed*.

Yet, it is very puzzling, that the *Kli de NH*, which is from the last *Melachim* whose breaking is not so great, would fall further below the *Kli de Hesed*, which is from the first *Melachim*, whose breaking is great indeed, which were disclosed without any *Hitlabshut* from the *Achoraim de Ima*, as the Rav says above.

We have already elaborated our speech about that above (*Ohr Pnimi* item 60) and from the Rav's words it has been explained there that in most places, the *Hitpashtut* of the *Gimel Kavim KHB*, is the matter of the fall of the *Achoraim de AVI* itself. Also, this whole *Hitpashtut* ended along with the end of the fall of the *Achoraim de AVI*, meaning in the Upper third of *Tifferet*.

After YESHSUT came out and clothed the *Achoraim de AVI*, there immediately rose all the *Orot de HGT* to the new *Kelim de Hitpashtut KHB*. At that time all three *Kelim Daat, Hesed, Gevura*, came down together to the place of *NHYM de Beria, Daat* in *Malchut, Hesed* in *Yesod*, and *Gevura* in *NH*. In other words, the more *Av* it is, the lower it is.

All this was before the exit of the last *Melachim* to *Kelim de NHYM de Atzilut*. Thus, when the *Melachim* of *NHYM* came to reign, their place was already vacant, hence they too fell to *Beria*, according to the order that the more *Av* one is, the lower it falls. For this reason *NH* fell in *Tifferet de Beria, Kli de Yesod* in *Gevura de Beria* and *Kli Malchut* in *Hesed de Beria*.

Now you find the seven *Melachim* in *ZAT* of *Beria* according to the right order that the more *Zach* is above since its breaking is not so great, and the more *Av* is below because its breaking is greater. Thus, the *Kli Malchut* is in *Hesed de Beria*, the *Kli Yesod* is in *Gevura de Beria*, *Kli NH* is in *Tifferet de Beria*, and *Kli Gevura* in *Netzah* and *Hod de Beria*. Also, the *Kli Daat* is in *Malchut de Beria*.

The exception is the *Kli de Tifferet*, which did not descend to *ZAT de Beria*, but only to *Keter de Beria* for the reason explained above (*Ohr Pnimi* item 61, sub header "**The upper half**").

66. Afterwards came out the *Ohr Yesod*. Yet, *Ohr Hesed* was in its place, and so *Kli Hochma* had to expand through the right line up to the fitting place to be the real *Hesed* after the *Tikun*.

    Then *Ohr Hesed* rose there and was integrated in the general *Hochma*, and the *Kli* of *Hesed* descended down to *Tifferet de Beria*. At that time the *Yesod* came out and entered in its *Kli*, and reigned in its place and broke.

    The *Ohr* rose through the middle line and rose up to the place of *Daat Elyon* and its *Kli* descended in *Gevura* of the *Beria*. Afterwards we will explain why the *Ohr Yesod* rose above *Tifferet*, up to *Daat*.

67. Afterwards the *Ohr Malchut* came out to reign in her *Kli*. She reigned there and broke, and then her *Ohr* rose in *Daat* through the middle line too, and her *Kli* descended in *Hesed* of *Beria*. Now *Kli Tifferet* is in the place of *Keter de Beria*, and *Kli Malchut* is in the place of *Hesed de Beria*.

    It follows that the place between *Kli* to *Kli de Beria* is only three degrees, which are *HBD*. In *Atzilut*, however, there is no vacant place, but only two degrees, which are the place of *Yesod* and *Malchut*.

68. Now we should provide the reason that both *Ohr Yesod* and *Malchut* rose up to *Daat*, above *Tifferet*. The reason is etc. that since the conduct of *Yesod* is to rise to the *Daat*, hence now *Ohr Yesod* rose to the *Daat*, above *Tifferet*. All the more so in order to connect all the *VAK* together and bring them *He'arah* from there.

69. Now we shall explain the reasoning of *Malchut*, why she too rose up to *Daat* above *Tifferet*. The thing is that *Malchut* is called "a crown to her husband." She ascends above *Tifferet*, and especially now that she had a *Reshimo* from the *Daat*.

This is because when *Ohr Daat* descended to the place of *Malchut de Atzilut*, when its *Kli* broke, it left its *Reshimo* there. When *Malchut* reigned in her place, she took this *Reshimo* and rose up to the place of *Daat* itself.

There is yet another reason: she connects all the *VAK* from below upward by her ascent there, thus this connection is corrected more. Since both *Netzah* and *Hod* were on the left line in the place of *Gevura*, and now the *Netzah* has separated from the *Hod*, it went and rose with the *Hesed* in the right line in it.

70. Now we shall explain this matter in greater detail: This *Reshimo* that *Daat* left in *Malchut's* place is certainly the *Behinat Malchut* in *Daat*, on the part of *Gevurot*, and understand that well.

Malchut rose up to *Daat* and the above *Reshimo* rose along with her, which is the *Behinat Gevura*. This *Reshimo*, which is the *Malchut* of *Gevurot* in *Daat* connected the *Atara de Gevura de Nukva* with the *Hassadim* in *Daat*, *Atara de Dechura*.

At that time the *Daat* expanded through this connection and illuminated in *VAK*. The *Reshimo*, which is in *Gevura*, illuminated in the left line, and left the *Hod* there in its place. Also, that *Daat* itself, *Atara de Hesed*, illuminated in the right line and extended the *Netzah* there, and thus the *Atzilut* was corrected.

Ohr Pnimi

70. ***Malchut* rose up to *Daat* and the above *Reshimo* rose along with her.**

The matter of the ascent of *Malchut* and the *Reshimo* in *Zivug Hey Hassadim* and *Hey Gevurot* in the *Daat* requires elaborate explanation, and will be interpreted in its place. Here I will present it briefly.

You know that the whole matter of these four *Melachim* that expanded from both *AVI* and from *YESHSUT* are a matter of the *Hizdakchut* of the *Masach* and the *Histalkut* of the *Orot* as has been explained in the previous *Partzufim de AK*.

When the *Masach de AVI* purified until it equalized with the *Shoresh*, which is the *Peh de AVI*, the *Masach* and the *Reshimot* in it returned in the form of *Hitkalelut* of the *Zivug de AVI*. Also, the *Masach* retuned and thickened in

Aviut de Behina Bet, since the last *Behina* was lost, and the *Komat YESHSUT* came out on it.

Thus, *Masach de YESHSUT* too was purified from degree to degree until it reached *Komat Malchut*, and then the seventh *Melech* emerged, which is *Malchut*. After this *Melech* broke, the *Masach* is found to have purified from the *Aviut Malchut* too, and then it is equalized with its *Behinat Shoresh*, which is the *Peh de YESHSUT*.

At that time it made a new *Zivug* there in *Aviut de Behina Aleph*, since the last *Behina* is lost, and for that reason the *Komat Daat*, being *Komat ZA*, came out on it. Not a whole *Partzuf Rosh* and *Guf* expanded from this *Zivug*, since it emerged only in *Hey Hassadim* and *Hey Gevurot*, two *Itrin* (Aramaic: *Ketarim*).

For this reason it came out only in *Behinat* from below upward, in *Behinat Achor be Achor*, and hence tied the *VAK* together, meaning the *Behinat Gufim* that came out in *YESHSUT*, which are from the *Chazeh* down since there is its *Behinat Hitpashtut* from the *Peh* of *YESHSUT* downward.

He writes, "the *Daat* expanded through this connection and illuminated in *VAK*," meaning it expanded from the *Chazeh* down which is the place of the *Peh de YESHSUT*, meaning in the place of *NHY*, as there is its place, meaning below the *Rosh de YESHSUT*. Since it came out in the form of *Achor be Achor*, hence, there was a *Tikun Kavim* in it.

He writes, "The *Reshimo*, which is in *Gevura*, illuminated in the left line, and left the *Hod* there in its place etc. and extended the *Netzah* there." This is because the *Rosh de Tachton* clothes and fills the *Kelim* and the *Reshimot de Elyon*, and thus illuminated in the *Reshimot de Melachim* of *Netzah* and *Hod*. It administered *Tikun Kavim* in them and in that the *Tikun Kavim* expanded from the *Chazeh* down too, and magnified the *Kelim* to the place of *Netzah* and *Hod*.

Thus, the *Tikun Kavim* was completed in all the *ZAT* from the *Behina* of the *Reshimot* in them, since *HGT* were corrected in the *Rosh de YESHSUT* and *NH* were corrected in the *Rosh* of the *Daat*, meaning in *Behinat* from below upward.

71. *Now see and understand how the *Atzilut* was not corrected at one time, but they their correction came slowly, one-by-one, and every time a little more *Tikun* was added in it. This is so because in the beginning, a *Behinat Kli* was not made at all, and it is known that any *Tikun* is only the *Ohr* clothing in the *Kli* so that the *Tachtonim* might receive the *Ohr Elyon*.

72. The making of the *Kli* began only in *Olam ha Akudim*, though only one *Kli* was made for all of its *Eser Sefirot*. Afterwards, in *Olam ha Nekudim*,

before they broke, some *Tikun* was added in them, and this is because ten *Kelim* were added to the *Yod Sefirot* in it.

There is also a second *Tikun*: The GAR came out and were corrected through *Kavim*, which is not so in ZAT that emerged one atop the other and were not connected. Afterwards, when the *Nekudim* broke, another *Tikun* was added in them, which is that the *Orot* of ZAT too clothed through the *Kavim* of KHB.

73. After that when the *Maatzil* wanted to correct them, he raised the *Kelim* in *Atzilut* too, in an order of three *Kavim*. Then when they were made in *Behinat Kavim*, came the *Ibur Aleph* of ZON, and a second *Tikun* was added, as the *Orot* came inside the *Kelim*.

However, it is still only in *Behinat Gimel Kavim*, which we call *Gimel* contained in *Gimel*. Then they expanded in the form of VAK during the *Yenika*, and after that, at the time of the *Mochin* and all *Yod Kelim* were completed, there was another change.

This is because in the beginning, before there was any *Ibur*, there wasn't even the first *Ibur de* ZON, but only a restricted *Ohr* in the *Kli*. Afterwards the *Kli* expanded in the form of a complete *Partzuf* in order to diminish the *Ohr*, since this is the primary intention of the *Tikun*.

Ohr Pnimi

73. **There was another change.**

Here he tells us that two principal *Tikkunim* were necessary to complete the *Kelim* in a manner that the *Tachtonim* can receive the *Ohr Elyon*. The first is the *Tikun* of the *Gimel Kavim*; the second is the enlargement of the *Kelim* in the form of a *Partzuf*.

Now, in the *Gufim* of GAS *de* AK, called *Akudim*, there was only one *Kli* and one *Kav*. Afterwards, when the MA and BON *de* AK, called *Akudim*, or BON *de* AK, came out, ten *Kelim* emerged, as well as *Tikun Kavim* in GAR *de Nekudim*. After HGT broke, and the *Rosh de* YESHSUT came out, there was a *Tikun Kavim* in *Orot de* HGT.

When *Netzah Hod Yesod Malchut* broke and the *Zivug de Hey Hassadim* and *Hey Gevurot* in *Daat* came out, there was a *Tikun Kavim* in the *Orot NHY de Nekudim* as well, and the matter of the *Ibur Yenika Mochin* will be clarified in its place.

Histaklut Pnimit

The matter of the seven *Melachim* explained in this part in the Rav's words is the foundation of the entire wisdom. This is because all four *Olamot ABYA* extend from them, and the whole matter of the *Tikkunim*, the scrutinies and the concatenation of all the degrees come only to complement and to correct them. Hence, they require extra care to thoroughly understand the origin of their emanation and the reason for their breaking and fall to *BYA*.

1. **First** we must discern and distinguish between these seven *Melachim* and *AVI de Nekudim*, because although they extend from *AVI*, they are still very far from each other. This is because they did not extend and concatenate directly from *AVI* through cause and consequence, but reached them through another *Partzuf*, as the Rav says above (Item 31), that *Yesod de AK* administered *Vav ו* and *Nekuda* to *AVI* to elicit and beget the *ZAT*. Thus, *AK* administered the seven *Melachim* to *AVI*.

   We must understand that matter. How is *Partzuf ZAT de Nekudim* different from all the previous *Partzufim*, all of which extended directly through cause and consequence from one another? Only *Partzuf ZAT* does not extend from its *Elyon* directly, but rather three *Partzufim* participated in its emanation, *Yesod de AK*, *Abba*, and *Ima*.

2. **We** should also understand why *Partzuf Nekudim* did not expand *GAR* and *ZAT* at once as in all the previous *Partzufim*. Instead, first only *GAR* expanded, which are *Keter* and *AVI*, and afterwards, through the *Zivug* of *Yesod de AK* that the *Shuruk* administered them, the *ZAT de Nekudim* emerged.

   The reason for it is as has been explained above (*Ohr Pnimi* item 5 par. "You see" and par. "We might ask") that these *AVI* are but *Behinat ZON de Rosh*, which are merely *Behinat HP*. The reason they are considered *Behinat Rosh* is only because of the *He'arat Ohr Awzen* that they received by their *Hitkalelut* in the *Keter* of *Nekudim*.

   As it is written (Part 6, *Ohr Pnimi* item 23, par. "Thus, all the *Orot*"), this *He'arah* corrected them in *Behinat Achor be Achor*. The *Achoraim de Bina*, called *Awzen*, sustain them in *Behinat GAR*, and they are not blemished because of the *Masach de Hey Tata'a* above them, preventing *He'arat Panim de Hochma* from them.

   This is because they crave only *Hassadim* through the *Achoraim de Bina*, in the form of "because He delighteth in mercy" and they reject *Hochma*. Hence, the

Masach de Hey Tata'a does not diminish them at all, as they have no wish for *Hochma* in any case (*Ohr Pnimi* item 23, par. "It has been explained").

However, that *Tikun de Achoraim* is sufficient only to complement AVI themselves, but it is not enough for them to be able to illuminate and elicit the ZON, which are the ZAT.

This is so because the force of the *Achoraim* of *Bina* is only in her GAR, and they are not in her ZAT. This is because when she came to emanate and expand in her ZAT, she must stop her *Achoraim* on *Abba*, and returns *Panim be Panim* with him in order to extend *He'arat Hochma* from him for her ZAT (*Ohr Pnimi* item 24).

From this you know that any *Partzuf* that is corrected in the *Achoraim* of *Bina* is found to be without NHY. This is because GAR *de Hassadim*, which are HGT, can be well corrected in the *Achoraim de Ima*. The NHY, however, cannot even exit and expand from her outwardly even in *Sefirat Bina* except through *Panim be Panim* with *Hochma*.

For this reason they cannot appear in this *Partzuf* that is corrected in her *Achoraim*, and it is considered in it that its NHY are integrated in its HGT, in the form of, "their hinder parts were inward." The NHY, which are *Behinat Achoraim*, are in *Pnimiut* HGT, and their *Panim* are disclosed outwardly, and only their *Panim*, which are HGT, are disclosed outwardly (*Ohr Pnimi* item 29, par. "Now we have thoroughly").

That thoroughly explains that AVI *de Nekudim* that were corrected in *Tikun Achor be Achor* could not have educed the ZON, but only after they obtain *Behinat Panim be Panim*, since *Hitpashtut* ZON does not come out from *Behinat Achoraim* at all. Examine all the places I have mentioned above well for it is impossible to elaborate twice.

3. **The** Rav has already explained above (item 25) that AVI do not return *Panim be Panim* but through three degrees: *Achor be Achor*, *Panim be Achor*, and then *Panim be Panim*. Examine there in *Ohr Pnimi* where the reason for the matters is thoroughly explained.

It explains there (*Ohr Pnimi* item 23, sub header, "**Above it, it is Panim**") that this degree *de Panim be Achor* comes to them through *Zivug de* AB SAG that lowers the *Hey Tata'a* from the *Eynaim*, at which time AVI return to the *Rosh* and obtain their GAR. We must still understand who causes AB SAG to mate in order to lower the *Hey Tata'a*.

The Rav has already explained above (Part 6, item 6) that "all the inner *Behinot* SAG, concealed in the inner MA and BON rose, and the inner MA and *BON* rose along with them. Thus these *MA* and *BON* are their *MAN*, to the *Taamim de SAG* themselves, which are not clothed inside *MA* and *BON*."

Interpretation: *Nekudot de SAG* expanded below *Tabur de AK ha Pnimi* which is the place of the inner *MA* and *BON*, being *ZON de AK ha Pnimi*. Thus you find that after the *Hizdakchut* of the *Masach* and its ascent to *Peh de Rosh SAG*, it is integrated with these inner *MA* and *BON*.

For this reason they became *MAN* to the inner *AVI de Rosh SAG*, called *AB SAG de AK*. At that time these *AB* and *SAG* mated and the *AB* lowered the *Hey Tata'a* from the *Eynaim* of *SAG*, and the *AHP de SAG* returned to the *Rosh*. Hence, all the *AHP* that went outside the degree have now returned to their degree as in the beginning.

It explains there in *Ohr Pnimi* that the *Behinot SAG* that rose from the *MAN BON*, became *MAN* too, though there were two *Zivugim* there: One for the *Katnut de Nekudim* from which *AVI* emerged in the form of *Achor be Achor*, and a second for the purpose of *Gadlut de Nekudim* from which *AVI* obtained their *GAR* (Part 6, *Ohr Pnimi* item 14, par. "Now we have thoroughly clarified").

You should know that the *Katnut de Nekudim*, which are in *Behinat Hey Tata'a* in the *Eynaim* and *YHV* in the *AHP*, emerged from the *Reshimot de SAG* that were mixed in the *MA* and *BON*. Also, the *Zivug de AB SAG* that lowered the *Hey Tata'a* from the *Eynaim* once more and reconnected the *AHP* to the *Rosh* as in the beginning, emerged from the *Reshimot* of the inner *MA* and *BON* themselves.

4. **The** reason for *MA* and *BON* becoming the cause for Upper *AB* and *SAG* to mate to lower the *Hey Tata'a* from the *Eynaim* is that the *Partzuf* that emerged from the *Nikvey Eynaim* would not have expanded to shine for these *MA* and *BON*, being *NHY de AK*.

This is because of the *Tikun* of the *Achoraim de Ima* that lies there. This *Tikun* detains the *Hitpashtut NHY* since they must be incorporated in *HGT* in the form of, "their hinder parts were inward." Hence, once the *Partzuf de Nikvey Eynaim* came out on the *Masach* that consists of the *Reshimot de Nekudot de SAG* and *Hey Tata'a*, it did not suffice for the *NHY de AK*, and the *Reshimot de NHY de AK* were made into *MAN* in the *Rosh SAG*, which is the *Behinat* general *Bina*.

She has a correlation to dispense *He'arat Hochma* to *ZON* on the part of *Bina de Ohr Yashar*, and therefore *SAG* stopped its *Achoraim* and mated with *AB Panim be Panim*. Also, the *Hey Tata'a* was lowered from the *Eynaim de Rosh*

SAG through this *Zivug* since *He'arat AB* does it, as there is no *Hey Tata'a* in the *Eynaim de Rosh AB*.

At that time this new *Ohr* expanded from above downward too and fissured the *Parsa*. This means that it annulled the new *Gevul de Tzimtzum Bet* that took the *AHP* out of all the degrees. This is because this new *Ohr* that comes from *AB* cancels and lowers the *Hey Tata'a* to its place to *Malchut de Rosh* as well as to *Malchut* of all the degrees. The *AHP* of each return to their degree as in the beginning and this new *Ohr* expanded below the *Tabur de AK*, meaning to *NHY de AK*, called *MA* and *BON de AK*.

This new *Ohr* expanded and came out through the *Tabur* to *Keter de Nekudim*, as the Rav says above (Part 6, item 27). It cancelled the *Gevul* and the cessation between *Keter* and *AVI de Nekudim* that was made there because of the *Hey Tata'a* in the *Eynaim de Keter* since it lowered her from *Eynaim* to her place in the *Peh*. Thus, *AVI* returned to the *Rosh* since now the *Masach de Hey Tata'a* is below them, hence they returned to their *GAR* degree as in the beginning.

Besides this exit through the *Tabur*, this new *Ohr* exited through *Yesod de AK* as well, administering them the *Shuruk*, which is the *Vav* ו and *Nekuda*. *Abba* took the *Nekuda* and *Ima* took the ו to elicit and beget the *VAK de ZA*, as the Rav says above (Part 6 item 31).

5. **Know** that the two *He'arot* that we've said to have received *GAR de Nekudim* from the new *Ohr* that fissured the *Parsa*, made two situations in *AVI*. This is because the first *He'arah* that *Keter* received through the *Tabur* lowered the *Hey Tata'a* from *Keter* to *Peh de AVI*, and then *AVI* returned to *Behinat Rosh*, like the *Keter*. This is so because the *Masach* is already below them, and this is considered that *NHY de Keter* clothed in them and *AVI* obtained the *Ohr Panim*.

Yet, it still did not help *Ima* since although she could now return her *Panim* to *Abba* and receive the *Ohr Hochma* because the *Gevul* that was made by the *Hey Tata'a* in the *Eynaim* has now been revoked. Yet, she still does not have a reason that would stop the *Achoraim* that she has from her *Shoresh* in the *Ohr Yashar*. It is so because she always craves *Hassadim*, "because He delighteth in mercy," and she rejects *Hochma*.

You find that only *Abba* enjoys the return to the *Rosh* since he receives his *GAR* and *Panim*. *Ima*, however, still keeps her *Achoraim* in the form of, "because He delighteth in mercy."

For this reason, *AVI* have now come to a state of *Panim be Achor*, meaning the *Panim* of *Abba* in the *Achoraim* of *Ima*. This is because *Abba* has *Behinat Panim*, and *Ima* still keeps her *Achoraim* on *Abba*. Thus, this *He'arah* that the

Keter received to lower the *Hey Tata'a* from the *Eynaim* created only a state of *Panim be Achor* in AVI.

The second *He'arah* through the *Yesod de AK*, which AVI de *Nekudim* received, meaning the *Vav* ו and *Nekuda*, brought AVI to a state of *Panim be Panim*. This is because that *Shuruk* that illuminated their *Yesod* is *Behinat* ZON. The ו is *Behinat* VAK, HGT NHY de ZA, and the *Nekuda* is *Behinat Malchut*, and they have become MAN in AVI (Part 6 item 31).

It caused *Ima* to stop her *Achoraim* and return her *Panim* to *Abba* so as to mate with him *Panim be Panim* and extend *He'arat Hochma* for ZON that rose to her for MAN. Thus we have explained that through the *He'arat* new *Ohr* through the *Tabur* to the *Keter*, AVI received the new state of *Panim be Achor*.

Also, AVI received the state of *Panim be Panim* through the *He'arah* of this new *Ohr* through the *Yesod* to AVI, as well as the rudimentary *Orot de* ZON in the form of MAN, and educed and procreated them to their place through their *Zivug* of *Panim be Panim*.

We might ask, "Since these NHY *de AK ha Pnimi* could not receive from *Taamim de SAG* before *Tzimtzum Bet* (Part 6, *Ohr Pnimi* item 1, sub header "**Its SAG**"), since AB lacks the *Masach de Behina Dalet*, how could they receive the new *Ohr* of *Zivug AB SAG* here?"

Yet, this is not at all a question since it is different here: The *Reshimot de* NHY *de AK* themselves rose to MAN and integrated in the *Zivug de AB SAG*. Hence they can now receive from AB. Yet, in fact, it is not considered reception of the *Kelim de* NHY *de AK*, since they did not extend this new *Ohr* for themselves, but to procreate ZAT *de Nekudim*, like the drop that is extended from the father's brain. Concerning the NHY *de AK* themselves, their reception is considered a mere "in passing".

6. **Now** we have clarified our above question in item 2, why did *Partzuf Nekudim* not expand GAR and ZAT simultaneously as did all the previous *Partzufim*. This is so because there is a necessary distance of three situations here. The GAR *de Nekudim* emerged by the *Zivug* in the *Nikvey Eynaim*, and were therefore forced to be in a state of *Achor be Achor*. In that state, even AVI themselves are considered devoid of NHY, as in item 2, much less elicit the ZAT.

However, when they later rose to AB SAG through MAN *de* NHY *de AK* and begotten the new *Ohr* that fissured the *Parsa*, *Keter* received that *Ohr* first through the *Tabur*, and lowered the *Hey Tata'a* from the *Eynaim*, bringing AVI to a state of *Panim be Achor*. After that AVI received that *Ohr* through *Yesod de AK*, and then obtained the seven *Orot* that belong to the seven lower *Sefirot*, which are ZON, and then came to a state of *Panim be Panim* and could beget the seven lower *Sefirot de Nekudim*.

The matter of the difference between ZAT *de Nekudim* and the ZAT of the previous *Partzufim* has also been thoroughly clarified, that they did not extend directly from their GAR, which we have discerned in item one. It has been explained that AVI have nothing of *Behinat* ZON from the essence of their creation.

This is because besides the fact that they themselves have no NHY, they are also only from *Behinat* First *Hey*, without any *Hey Tata'a* (see Part 6, Histaklut Pnimit item 9). The *Hey Tata'a* remained in the *Eynaim* in *Keter*, and nothing extended from her to AVI *de Nekudim*, hence it is impossible that ZAT *de Nekudim* would extend from AVI directly, but only through AK *ha Pnimi*, whose *Kelim* are from *Behina Dalet*, whose *Koma* is up to *Keter*.

Thus, it was impossible that ZAT *de Nekudim* would emerge but only after NHY *de* AK *ha Pnimi* themselves would rise to MAN to AB SAG. Thus they would extend a new *Ohr* in the form of *Shuruk*, which means *Vav* ו and *Nekuda*, meaning the fundamental *Orot* of the ZON. AK *ha Pnimi* dispensed them to MAN to AVI, at which time they mated on them and procreated them to their place.

We might ask, "Accordingly, why are the *Partzufim de* AVI even necessary? They have a connection to the *Behina Dalet* that is incorporated in ZON, and they should have emerged directly from AK *ha Pnimi*?"

However, according to the gradations, this is impossible. The *Ne'etzal* from AK *ha Pnimi* is *Partzuf* AB, whose *Koma* is up to *Hochma*, and not *Partzuf* ZAT, which are *Koma de Behina Aleph*, lacking GAR from the essence of their creation.

Hence, ZON are compelled to come out through AVI, meaning in the concatenation of the degree up to *Masach de Behina Aleph* (as it is written in Part 6, Histaklut Pnimit item 5, par. "We have yet to explain"). It follows that it needs them both, since the *Atzmut de* ZA that must be incorporated in the *Hey Tata'a* comes out only through NHY *de* AK *ha Pnimi*, and its emanation to come out to its place is only possible through the *Partzufim* of AVI.

7. **Now** you will understand what our sages wrote (Kidushin p. 30), that three partners are in a person: the Creator, his father, and his mother. The father sows the white in him, the mother sows the red in him, and the Creator breathes his soul in him. This partnership extends from the upper degrees, because it is explained that in the first ZON in the *Olamot* there were also three partners: AK *ha Pnimi*, and AVI *de Nekudim*. The white in it, meaning

the *Hassadim*, are from *Abba*, the red in it, meaning the *Gevurot*, are from *Ima*, but the *Etzem* of its *Neshama* is from AK *ha Pnimi*.

The same thing applies in ZA *de Atzilut*, where three participate in its creation, AA and *Abba* and *Ima*. This is because AA in *Atzilut* corresponds to AK *ha Pnimi* here, and there too the gist of its *Atzmut* and *Shoresh* come from AA, and *Hassadim* and *Gevurot* come from AVI.

8. **Thus**, the matter of the two *Zivugim* made for the *Nekudim* on the two kinds of *Reshimot* that the *Masach* that rose to *Rosh* SAG consisted of, has been thoroughly explained. The first *Zivug* was made on the *Reshimot* of the *Nekudot de* SAG, mingled with the *Hey Tata'a*.

This *Zivug* was made in *Behinat Nikvey Eynaim*, meaning in *Behina Aleph* in the *Rosh*, in the form of *Hey Tata'a* in the *Eynaim*. By this the AHP came out of all the degrees and this exit induced three *Roshim* in the *Nekudim*. *Bina* and ZON of *Eser Sefirot de Sium de* AK also came outside of the entire *Atzilut*, and have become the Separated BYA.

AVI *de Nekudim*, being the third *Rosh*, were erected in *Achor be Achor*, and a second *Zivug* was made on the *Reshimot de* NHY *de* AK *ha Pnimi*, meaning it became MAN for *Zivug* AB SAG *de Rosh* SAG. Thus the *Hey Tata'a* was lowered from the *Eynaim* to the *Peh* as in the beginning, and the *Ohr* that came out of this *Zivug* fissured the *Parsa*. In other words, it cancelled the *Gevul* and the *Masach* that separates the *Eynaim* from the AHP.

It retuned the AHP to their preliminary degree and illuminated to the *Nekudim* in two: One – through the *Tabur* to the *Keter de Nekudim*. It lowered the *Hey Tata'a* in the *Nikvey Eynaim de Keter* to the *Peh* of the whole *Rosh* below AVI too. By that AVI returned to the *Rosh* and obtained their GAR. The second *He'arah* through *Yesod de* AK to AVI, which is the *Behinat* ו and *Nekuda*, meaning the *Shorashim* of ZON.

They have become MAN in them that returned them *Panim be Panim*, and they mated and extended *He'arat Hochma* to ZON first, by their *Hitkalelut de* ZON in *Zivug* AVI themselves. In that state, these ZON are considered *Behinat Daat* of AVI, and then they expanded from *Malchut* of AVI downward to *Behinat Guf*, clothing the *Kli* of *Melech ha Daat*. The *Ohr* that expanded in this *Melech* is considered the *Ohr Yechida de* ZA.

9. **You** already know that the first *He'arah* of the new *Ohr* that fissured the *Parsa* that illuminated through the *Tabur* to *Keter de Nekudim* still did not return *Panim be Panim* to AVI, but only *Panim be Achor*. This is because even after *Ima* returned to the *Rosh*, she still did not stop her *Achoraim* except by a reason that compels her to stop.

For this reason she did not return her *Panim* to *Abba*, but only after she received the MAN de ו and *Nekuda* from *Yesod de AK*. These MAN, which are *Behinot ZON* that she has connection with from the part of *Ohr Yashar* to dispense *He'arat Hochma* in, awaken her to stop the *Achoraim* and return *Panim be Panim* to *Abba*.

Thus, these two situations became the reason that ZON would not receive from *Zivug Panim be Panim de AVI*, but only *Hassadim* and *Gevurot* and only in *He'arat Hochma*. This is so because even now, after she returned *Panim be Panim* with *Abba*, she receives from him only that measure of *He'arat Hochma* that *Bina de Ohr Yashar* administers to ZON de *Ohr Yashar*.

This is so because her entire return *Panim be Panim* was only for ZON that she is connected with from the perspective of the *Ohr Yashar*, and not at all for herself. For this reason she administers them in this measure of ZON de *Ohr Yashar*. Also, it is known that ZON de *Ohr Yashar* are themselves merely *Hassadim* in *He'arat Hochma* (Part 1, Table of Topics, item 69).

For this reason we must greatly consider the measure of the *Koma*, whether it is *He'arat Hochma* from *Komat Keter* or *He'arat Hochma* from *Komat Hochma* etc. since the *Hochma* lessens and descends from *Koma* to *Koma*. Also, you should know that the measure of the *Koma* is attributed to the first situation, meaning to the new *Ohr* that shines through the *Tabur* to *Keter de Nekudim* that lowered the *Hey Tata'a* above AVI, below AVI to the *Peh*.

Although he still returned only the *Panim be Achor* to AVI, yet the measure of the *Koma* depends on lowering the *Hey Tata'a*. This is because in the lowering of the *Hey Tata'a* to the *Peh*, when *Behina Dalet* is found in its place in *Malchut de Rosh*, *Komat Keter* emerges on her.

However, if she comes only to *Behina Gimel de Rosh*, called *Hotem*, *Komat Hochma* emerges on her, and if to *Awzen*, *Komat Bina* emerges on her etc. Still, the *Mochin de ZA*, meaning the measure of *He'arat Hochma* that ZA receives, come only in the second state, when AVI come into a state of *Panim be Panim*.

This is because at that time *Bina* dispenses the *Mochin*, meaning *He'arat Hochma* to ZON. Thus, the measure of the *Koma* depends on the first situation according to the place that the *Hey Tata'a* came down to, and *Mochin de ZON* depend on the second situation, as then *Ima* receives *He'arat Hochma* for them.

10. **Now** you shall clearly see the quality of the *Orot NRNHY de Haya* that the four *Melachim* received, *Daat*, *Hesed*, *Gevura*, and the upper third of *Tifferet*. This is because the whole change in the *Orot* and their lessening came only

by the changes that were made in the first state, meaning in the descent of the *Hey Tata'a* from the *Eynaim*.

This is because when she came to the *Peh*, the *Koma de Ohr Yechida* came out to *Melech ha Daat*, and when she rose to *Hotem*, the *Komat Ohr Haya* came out to *Melech ha Hesed*. When she rose to *Awzen*, the *Komat Ohr Neshama* emerged to *Melech ha Gevura*, and when she rose to the *Eynaim*, to the place where she was in the beginning, *Komat Ohr de Ruach Nefesh* came out to the upper third of *Melech ha Tifferet*.

However, no change was made in the second state, meaning in the state of *Panim be Panim*. Instead, when the *Komat Yechida* was in the *Partzuf*, and the *Hey Tata'a* was in the *Peh*, *Ima* received *He'arat Hochma* from *Komat Yechida* in the same measure that ZON *de Ohr Yashar de Keter* receive from *Bina de Keter*. This is also the measure *de Mochin de Yechida de ZA*.

This is so because every *Sefira* consists of *Eser Sefirot*, even the *Sefirot de Ohr Yashar*. When the *Hey Tata'a* was in *Hotem*, *Ima* received *He'arat Hochma* from *Komat Haya*, and this is the measure *de Mochin de Haya de ZA*.

Also, when *Hey Tata'a* was in the *Awzen*, *Ima* received *He'arat Hochma* from the *Komat Neshama* to the extent that ZON *de Ohr Yashar de Bina* receive from *Bina de Bina*, and this is the measure of the *Mochin de Neshama de ZA*. When *Hey Tata'a* returned to the *Eynaim* once more, the second situation changes as well, and she returned *Achor be Achor* with *Abba*. This is because she no longer receives any *He'arat Hochma* from *Abba*, only *Behinat Ruach Nefesh*, and she is completely devoid of *He'arat GAR*, but only in *Behinat Achor be Achor*.

11. **Also**, afterwards it purified entirely and returned to its *Shoresh* to *Peh de AVI*, when its *Aviut de Behina Gimel* returned, meaning when *Hey Tata'a* descended from the *Eynaim* to the *Hotem* once more (*Ohr Pnimi* item 45, sub header "**The Hassadim and Gevurot continued**"). This *Koma* is close to *Komat Haya* and is generally called *Neshama* or *YESHSUT*.

Thus, these two situations that were in *AVI* returned on them. Here too the first situation changes, meaning the lowering of the *Hey Tata'a* from the *Eynaim*. This is because when the *Hey Tata'a* descended to *Hotem*, *Tvuna* receives *Panim be Panim Behinat Yechida Haya de Neshama* to ZON.

At that time the *Ohr* descends from *Malchut de YESHSUT* down to the two lower thirds of *Melech ha Tifferet*. When the *Hey Tata'a* rose to the *Awzen*, *Tvuna* receives *Behinat Neshama de Neshama* to ZON, and the *Ohr* expands to *Melech Netzah* and *Hod* from her *Malchut*.

When *Hey Tata'a* rose to the *Eynaim*, the second situation changes too, since then YESHSUT return *Achor be Achor* and the *Behinat Ruach* dispenses to *Melech ha Yesod*, and then the *Behinat Nefesh* to the seventh *Melech*, which is the *Malchut*. This is so because when it purifies to *Behina Aleph*, she administers *Ruach*, and when it purifies to *Behinat Shoresh*, she administers *Malchut*.

12. **Here** you must discriminate between AVI *de Katnut* in a state of *Achor be Achor*, when they came out of *Nikvey Eynaim* in the first *Zivug*, and AVI *de Gadlut*, when they came out through *Zivug de AB SAG* until they came to a state of *Panim be Panim*. This is so because the differences between them are the most important elements in the wisdom.

    We must especially make the precision of the oppositeness between them from their start to their end. In the beginning they are considered one degree that comes in two situations. With respect to their very creation, they are emanated in a state of *Achor be Achor*, and with respect to the additional Light that they have obtained from the *He'arat Zivug de AB SAG* and from MAN *de Yesod de AK*, they have obtained the state of *Panim be Panim*.

    However, they are one degree, and moreover, the second situation is much more important than the first situation. This is because in the first situation they were devoid of GAR *de Hochma*, and there were only *Behinot* GAR *de Achoraim Bina* in them, that reject *Hochma*. Yet, in the second situation they returned to the *Rosh* and obtained their GAR completely.

    However, in the end, the thing was overturned from end to end, because they were separated from each other and became two degrees. The first state became a *Behinat Rosh* and *Behinat Panim*, and the second situation became *Behinat Guf* and *Behinat Achoraim*.

    The reason for it is because of the breaking of the vessels, meaning their *Gufim* that expanded in the four *Melachim Daat*, *Hesed*, *Gevura*, and the Upper third of *Tifferet*. Yet, there is a very important understanding in the form of the matter, worthy of special attention.

13. **The** thing is that the whole *Partzuf de Nekudim* is regarded like *Partzuf SAG de AK*, because there is *Behina Bet de Hitlabshut* in its *Masach*. Also, the whole SAG is *Behinat Bina*, since the *Bina* is the highest *Behina* in it; hence all the tendencies of *Bina de Ohr Yashar* control it.

    It is known that *Bina de Ohr Yashar* is all *Hassadim*, and *Behinat He'arat Hochma* that receives into the *Hassadim* is already considered an outer *Behina* from it, which obtained its own name, which is ZA. The distance between them is indeed great, as the distance between the *Shoresh* and a tiny *Anaf* that stems from it, as *Bina* is the *Shoresh*, and ZA is the little *Anaf* that stems from her.

Even though there is *Behinat Achoraim* on the *Ohr Hochma* in *Bina*, these *Achoraim* are still not considered any diminution to her. Moreover, they are considered the whole merit of *Bina*, in the form of, "because He delighteth in mercy."

Hence, *Bina* is all *Behinat GAR* without any lessening at all, and because of that *AVI* were not at all blemished in their exit from the *Rosh* due to the *Hey Tata'a* in the *Eynaim de Keter*. This is because that little *He'arah* that they had of the *Ohr Awzen*, which is *Bina*, by their *Hitkalelut* in the *Zivug de Hitlabshut* of the *Zachar*, sufficed to them for *Behinat GAR*. They are not at all blemished by the *Tzimtzum Hochma* that the *Hey Tata'a* in the *Eynaim* detains since they would not have received *Hochma* anyhow because of the *He'arat Ohr Awzen* in them.

Thus you see that the state of *Achor be Achor* of *AVI* is sufficient for them for complete wholeness without any deficit. Hence, they do not have such a great connection with the second state *de Gadlut* that they've acquired from the hew *Ohr* that fissured the *Parsa*.

Had it not been for the *MAN* that *Yesod de AK* illuminated in them, they would not have received this new *Ohr* whatsoever, since their craving cleaves solely to *Hassadim*. Thus, the matter of the annulment of the *Zivug de Gadlut* did not concern them at all, as this whole *Rosh de Gadlut* was as something outside them, which they extended only for the *MAN* that *Yesod* illuminated in them.

Moreover, even afterwards when all *Eser Sefirot de Rosh de Gadlut* were cancelled, they were not cancelled entirely like *ZAT*, but were rather immediately incorporated in the *Achoraim de AVI* of the first situation. These *Achoraim* supported them in *Behinat GAR* and *Atzilut*, and they did not fall to *BYA*.

Cause and Consequence

We shall now explain the order of all the operations made in the *Olamot* through cause and consequence thus far, meaning how every operation is necessarily generated in all its conditions by its original cause.

Table of Questions for the Meaning of the Words

1. What is *Achor be Achor*?
2. What is *Achor be Panim*?
3. What is an Exiting *Ohr*?
4. What is a Thickening *Ohr*?
5. What are *Otiot*?
6. What is the *Achoraim* of ZA?
7. What is *Achoraim* of *Nukva*?
8. What is *Achoraim de Abba*?
9. What is *Achoraim de AVI*?
10. What is *Achoraim de Ima* that fell?
11. What is Complete *Achoraim de ZA*?
12. What is Complete *Achoraim de Nukva*?
13. What is a Grip?
14. What are *BDK HYA*?
15. What is a Cancellation?
16. What are Scrutinies?
17. What are the two lower thirds of *Tifferet*?
18. What are *Gevurot*?
19. What is Grown?
20. What is *Gadlut*?
21. What is *Guf de Abba*?
22. What is *Guf de Ima*?
23. What is *Guf YESH*?
24. What is *Guf de Tvuna*?
25. What the Completion of the Construction of the *Achoraim*?
26. What is Complete *Dvekut*?
27. What are *Dinim*?
28. What are Strong *Dinim*?

29. What is *Habata* of *Panim*?
30. What is Increasing half the *Achoraim*?
31. What are *Hey Hassadim* and *Hey Gevurot*?
32. What is Diminution of *Ohr*?
33. What *Histaklut Eynaim* of AVI?
34. What is *Histaklut Eynaim* of YESHSUT?
35. What is Raisng MAN?
36. What is *Dvekut Panim be Panim*?
37. What is *Dvekut* of the *Klipot*?
38. What is *Hitpashtut Hey Gevurot*?
39. What is *Zach*?
40. What is *Had Samcha*?
41. What is the Sustenance of the *Klipot*?
42. What are the Armies of *Malchut*?
43. What are the Parts of *Nukva*?
44. What is Half the *Achoraim*?
45. What is Half a Wall?
46. What is The Lower Half of *Tifferet*?
47. What is The Upper Half of *Tifferet*?
48. What is a Drop that Raises the Fetus?
49. What is the *Yenika* of the *Klipot*?
50. What are YESHSUT?
51. What is the Force of the *Klipot*?
52. What are the General *Bina* and *Tvuna*?
53. What is the General *Hey Hassadim* and *Hey Gevurot*?
54. What is Disclosed?
55. What is *Mochin*?
56. What is Death?
57. What is the Death of the *Melachim*?
58. What is Covered?
59. What are MAN?
60. What is *Masach Bina*?
61. What are Mingled in the *Klipot*?

62. What is the Place of the Gripping of the *Klipot*?
63. What is the Place of *BYA*?
64. What is the Place of *Rosh*?
65. What is a Minute Light?
66. What are *Nitzotzot* that Quenched?
67. What are *Nitzotzot* that were not Scrutinized?
68. What are Strong *Nitzotzin*?
69. What is a Fall?
70. What are *Sigim*?
71. What is a Thickening in the *Achoraim*?
72. What is *Etz ha Daat* Good and Bad?
73. What is *Panim be Panim*?
74. What are Parts of the *Guf*?
75. What is the *Panim* of the *Zachar*?
76. What is the *Panim* of the *Nekeva*?
77. What is *Panim be Achor*?
78. What is Waste?
79. What is Small?
80. What is *Katnut*?
81. What are Complete *Klipot*?
82. What is *Klipat Noga*?
83. What is Some *Dvekut*?
84. What is Some Breaking?
85. What is Some *Tikun*?
86. What is a Connection?
87. What is *Rosh de AVI*?
88. What is *Rosh de YESHSUT*?
89. What is the Breaking of the Vessels?
90. What is Upper Third of *Tifferet*?

1. What is *Achor be Achor*?

    Tikun Achor be Achor extends from the *He'arat Ohr Awzen*, which is *Ohr Bina de Rosh*, whose *Achoraim* is to *Hochma* by way of "because He delighteth in mercy." When the *Partzufim* are devoid of *GAR de Hochma*, they are corrected in this *Ohr de Achoraim de Bina*, which suffices for them instead of *GAR*. This is the meaning of "their hinder parts were inward."

    (Item 23 and *Ohr Pnimi* there)

2. What is *Achor be Panim*?

    Tikun Achor be *Panim* is applied in ZON, which qualifies the *Kelim de Panim de Nukva* to receive the *Ohr Panim*. This is because the *Kelim de Panim de Nukva* are in *He'arat Hochma* without *Hassadim*, as the entire *Nukva* is *Behinat Gevurot*.

    Since it is so, she too cannot tolerate *He'arat Hochma* since the *Hochma* is not accepted without *Hassadim*. Hence, the *Kelim de Panim* have no correction except by preceding the *Zivug de Achor be Panim*.

    At that time the *Zachar* dispenses *He'arat Hassadim* in those *Kelim de Panim*, and they become suitable for their *He'arat Hochma*. You see that although the *Achor de Zachar* is *He'arah* which is all *Hassadim*, it nevertheless qualifies the *Kelim de Panim de Nukva* to receive *He'arat Hochma*.

    (*Ohr Pnimi* item 23, par. "Now you can understand")

3. What is an Exiting *Ohr*?

    As long as the *Mochin de ZA* are clothed in the *Kelim de Ima*, the *Achoraim de Ima* cover and conceal the *Orot de Hochma*. They do not appear from them outwardly inside ZA, but in the Middle Line *de ZA* from *Chazeh* downward, where *Yesod de Ima* stops and her force of *Achoraim* to hide the *Hochma* stops. In that state the *Orot* that have *He'arat Hochma* in them appear outwardly from the *Yesod de Ima* inside ZA.

    ()

4. What is a Thickening *Ohr*?

    Even when *AVI* are both worthy of *He'arat GAR* and *Ohr Panim*, still only the *Zachar* is completed in *Behinat Panim*. The *Nekeva*, however, craving *Hassadim* in her *Shoresh*, by way of "because He delighteth in mercy," is not yet awakened to return her *Panim* to the *Zachar* and receive *Hochma*, except by what compels her, which is through MAN.

    Hence, as long as she has no MAN they are in *Behinat Panim be Achor*, meaning the *Panim* of the *Zachar* in the *Achor de Nekeva*. At that time the *Orot de Panim* of the *Zachar* pass on to her through her *Achoraim* and thicken there.

They clothe in the cover of her *Ohr Achoraim* and thus reach her *Kelim de Panim*. For this reason these *Orot de Panim* are called "Thickened *Ohr*", as the cover of the *Achoraim* of the *Nekeva* greatly diminish and lessen its value.

(Item 23 and *Ohr Pnimi*, sub header "**Above**")

5. **What are Otiot?**

   Otiot are always *Behinat Kelim*, both the *Otiot* of the alphabet and the *Otiot* of the Holy Names, and we must always remember that.

   (Item 32)

6. **What is the Achoraim of ZA?**

   The *NHY de ZA* are only completed in *He'arat Hochma*. They are considered its *Achoraim*, where the *Klipot* grip as long there is no *He'arat Hochma* in them.

   (Item 26)

7. **What is Achoraim of Nukva?**

   The *Achoraim of Nukva* are *NHY de Nukva*, where there is the principal grip of the *Klipot* as long as they lack *He'arat Hochma*. This is so because it is adjacent to the *Klipot* as it ends the *Ohr Atzilut* and from it downward begin the *Klipot*, by way of "Her feet go down to death." See the word "Grip of the *Klipot*".

   (Item 26)

8. **What is Achoraim de Abba?**

   The *Reshimot* of the *Eser Sefirot de Gadlut* of all the four *Komot* that were in *Behinat Roshim* to the four *Melachim DHGT*, and the *Behinat MAN* that received from *Yesod de AK*, meaning the *Nekuda* that *Abba* took and the *Vav* that *Ima* took, all these are considered *Achoraim de AVI* that fell from *Behinat Rosh de AVI* and became *Behinat Guf*. Each fell to the place of its *Guf*, and the *Roshim* that emerged from *Behinat Ima*, and the *Vav* ו that *Ima* took from *Yesod de AK* are the *Achoraim de Ima*.

   (Item 43)

9. **What is Achoraim de AVI?**

   These are the general Seven *Melachim*, which are the MAN and the *Reshimot* of the *Roshim* of the *Melachim*. See item 8.

   (Item 25)

10. **What is Achoraim de Ima that fell?**

    See above answer 8.

11. **What is Complete *Achoraim de ZA*?**

    When ZA is in *Behinat Achor be Achor*, he has only *Behinat Achoraim de Ima* that shine in his *HGT*, meaning through the *Chazeh*. From there downward *Yesod de Ima* stops, and for this reason the *NHY* cannot appear in it, fearing the grip of the exteriors (see item 6).

    When it obtains the new *HG* in *He'arat Hochma* from *Zivug Panim be Panim de AVI*, the *Achoraim de Yesod de Abba* shine in it from the *Chazeh* downward too, through the end of its *NHY*. At that time it has complete *Achoraim*, as it receives *Achoraim de Ima* in *HGT* and *Achoraim de Yesod de Abba* in *NHY*.

    However, before it obtains the *Hey Hassadim* from *Zivug de AVI Panim be Panim*, the *Achoraim de Abba* cannot appear in it. This is because it is *Behinat He'arat Hochma* without *Hassadim* and there is no existence for *Hochma* without *Hassadim*, since *Yesod Abba* is long and narrow. In other words, it stretches in *He'arat Hochma* below *Yesod de Ima*, but it is narrow since it has no *Hassadim* (see *Ohr Pnimi* item 45).

    For this reason, the *Ohr Achoraim de Yesod Abba* does not shine in NHY de ZA before it obtains the *Hey Hassadim*. This is the meaning of, "He takes *Hassadim* and his *Achor* is complemented," meaning *Achor de NHY*, by the force of the *Ohr Achoraim de Yesod Abba*. This is because when it has *Hassadim*, *Yesod Abba* can illuminate the *He'arat Hochma* in it.

    (Item 29)

12. **What is Complete *Achoraim de Nukva*?**

    The entire construction of the *Nukva* is only of *Gevurot*. This is because she begins from the *Chazeh de ZA* downward, where *Yesod de Ima* has already stopped. Hence, her entire *Behinat Achoraim* is built primarily of *Behinat Yesod Abba*, which is all *Gevurot* (see item 11).

    This is the meaning of, "*Abba* founded a daughter." Yet, when she was in *Behinat Achor be Achor*, she used the *Achoraim de ZA*, and one wall operated between them, meaning the *Achoraim de HGT de ZA* (see item 12).

    However, after ZA obtains the new *HG* from *AVI*, being *Hey Hassadim* and *Hey Gevurot*, the wall *de ZA* is completed with the *Hey Hassadim*, and the *Achoraim de Nukva* are completed with the *Hey Gevurot*. After they are sweetened with *Hassadim* in NHY de ZA, *Yesod de Abba* appears there and the *Gevurot* are sweetened and given to the *Nukva* through a *Zivug*.

    ()

13. **What is a Grip?**

    A Grip is like an *Anaf* that grips to the tree and sucks its *Shefa* through its holding place. Similarly, the *Klipa* grips the place of lack that she finds in the *Kedusha*. This place is her tube by which she sucks her entire force and sustenance, according to the measure of dearth that she finds there, see item 50.

    (Item 26)

14. **What are BDK HYA?**

    They are the *Behinat Achoraim de AVI* that fell in the place of ZON. There is a hint in this combination of *BDK HYA*, where the entire *Behinat MAN de ZA* that it raises to AVI have the power to induce a *Zivug Panim be Panim AVI* to extend *Mochin de Haya* from there, which is the *Ohr Hochma*. They come from the scrutinies that ZA scrutinizes in these *Achoraim de AVI*. BDK refers to *Tikun* and scrutiny, and *HYA* is the *Ohr Hochma*.

    (Item 33)

15. **What is a Cancellation?**

    When the *Kli* is no longer fitting to receive anything from the *Ohr Atzilut*, it is completely cancelled from its erection. It is then considered that the *Kli* has been broken.

    However, when it is fitting to receive from the degree of *Atzilut*, though from a smaller place than itself, and cannot receive from the *Ohr Elyon* that belongs to its own degree, it is considered that the *Kli* has been cancelled. This means that it does not operate in its function in its fitting place, and that *Kli* was cancelled from the degree, though the *Kli* has not been entirely broken, as it still receives *Ohr*. Though it is below its value, it is nonetheless reception.

    (Item 4)

16. **What are Scrutinies?**

    As long as the parts of *Behina Dalet* are mixed inside the *Kli*, the *Kli* is unfit to receive the *Ohr Elyon*. For this reason it needs scrutinies, meaning to sort out the parts of *Behina Dalet* inside the *Kli* and to separate them from there, and then the *Kli* becomes qualified to receive the *Ohr Elyon*.

    (Item 4)

17. **What are the two lower thirds of *Tifferet*?**

    You already know that each *Sefira* of the *Eser Sefirot* has *Eser Sefirot* in itself. When the *Kli de Tifferet* is discerned in itself, it is then divided to *Rosh, Toch, Sof*, which are HBD, HGT, NHYM. They are called "Three Thirds", where the upper third is the place of GAR, and the two lower thirds are the place of ZAT.

()

18. **What are *Gevurot*?**

    Gevurot mean lack of *Hassadim*. Even though it is fitting to receive *Ohr Hochma*, it is still called *Gevurot* since *Ohr Hochma* does not exist in the *Kli* as long as there is no abundance of *Hassadim* in it.

    (Item 30)

19. **What is Grown?**

    The appearance of *Ohr Hochma* in the *Partzuf* makes it grown. This means that it is completed bit-by-bit until it attains its *Gadlut*, which is *He'arat Hochma*. For this reason *He'arat Hochma* is called Great *Ohr*.

    (Item 49)

20. **What is *Gadlut*?**

    Mochin de Abba, meaning *He'arat Hochma*, is called *Gadlut*.

    (Item 19)

21. **What is *Guf de Abba*?**

    The *Eser Sefirot de Rosh* that come out of the *Nikvey Eynaim* are always discerned as three *Roshim*: the GE are considered the first *Rosh*, the *Awzen*, the second *Rosh*, and the *Hotem* and *Peh*, the third *Rosh*.

    Compared to the first *Rosh*, the two lower *Roshim*, are considered AHP, in *Behinat ZAT* and *Guf*. The second *Rosh* is its *Behinat HGT*, and the third *Rosh* is its *Behinat NHYM*.

    Hence, the *Eser Sefirot de Gadlut* too, which came out in *AVI de Nekudim*, are dominated by this arrangement. This is so because they are first emanated from the *Ohr Eynaim*.

    The *Behinat Rosh ha Aleph* came out first, called *Histaklut Eynaim de AVI* on each other. Afterwards, the *Behinat Rosh ha Bet* came out, called *Guf de Abba* and *Guf de Ima*. This is because *Rosh ha Bet* is considered *Guf* compared to *Rosh ha Aleph*. After that the third *Rosh* came out, called *Yesodot* (pl. for *Yesod*) *de AVI*, considered as such with respect to *Rosh ha Aleph*, where the third *Rosh* is *Behinat NHYM de Rosh ha Aleph*.

    You will understand their stature according to their names. The first *Koma*, called *Histaklut Eynaim de AVI* on each other, containing *Behina Dalet de Hitlabshut* and *Behina Gimel de Aviut* are a *Hitkalelut* of the two *Komot Keter* and *Hochma*. For this reason they are called *Galgalta ve Eynaim*, named after the Upper *Behinot*, *Keter* and *Hochma*.

The second *Koma* is called *Guf de Abba*, containing *Behina Gimel de Hitlabshut* and *Behina Bet de Aviut*. It is called *Awzen* after the Upper *Behina* from the perspective of its *Aviut*.

Also, *Guf de Ima* is called *Awzen* because it contains *Behina Bet* of *Aviut*, which is *Awzen*, and *Rosh ha Gimel*, which is *Hotem* and *Peh*, is called *Yesodot de AVI*. Thus, its *Koma* is in *Behina Aleph*, which is ZON *de Rosh*, called *HP*.

It follows, that the names go hand in hand with the *Komot*. Although these *Guf de Abba ve Ima* are not actual *Behinat Guf*, from *Behinat* from above downward, but it is *Behinat Rosh ha Gimel*, and the appellation *Guf* fits *Rosh ha Aleph* only.

(Item 43)

22. **What is *Guf de Ima*?**

    See above answer 21.

23. **What is *Guf YESH*?**

    YESHSUT is also divided into three *Roshim* as in AVI in answer 21. *Rosh ha Bet de YESHSUT* is called *Guf* compared to *Rosh ha Aleph* although in itself, it is a complete *Rosh*. *Rosh* is the *Hey Hassadim* in it from the *Behinat Hey YESH*, and *Rosh ha Bet* is the *Hey Gevurot* in it from the *Behinat Tvuna*, see answer 3.

    (Item 6)

24. **What is *Guf de Tvuna*?**

    See above answer 23.

25. **What the Completion of the Construction of the *Achoraim*?**

    See above answer 11.

26. **What is Complete *Dvekut*?**

    Complete *Dvekut de AVI Panim be Panim* is when *Hochma de Abba* illuminates to *Hochma de Ima*, because *Ima* is cleaved entirely to *Abba*.

    (Item 42)

27. **What are *Dinim*?**

    Two *Behinot Dinim* were made in *Tzimtzum Bet* when *Hey Tata'a* was incorporated in the First *Hey*: the first is the First *Hey* that was mixed with the *Dinim de Hey Tata'a*; this is *Behinat* Weak *Dinim*. The second is the *Hey Tata'a* that is incorporated with the First *Hey* in the place of the *Hey Tata'a*. This is *Behinat* Hard *Dinim*, meaning strong *Dinim*, *Behina Dalet* itself.

    (Item 7)

28. **What are Strong *Dinim*?**

    See above answer 27.

    (Item 8)

29. **What is *Habata* of *Panim*?**

    Habata means bestowal. *Habata* of *Panim* means bestowal of *He'arat Hochma*.

    (Item 23)

30. **What is Increasing half the *Achoraim*?**

    This means increasing the *Achoraim de NHY* that is missing while it is *Achor be Achor*, by way of "their hinder parts were inward."

    (Item 30)

31. **What are *Hey Hassadim* and *Hey Gevurot*?**

    The *Eser Sefirot* are discerned in *Hey Behinot KHB ZON*, meaning the GAR are *Behinat Atzmut*. However, when their whole *Atzmut* is but *Ohr de Hassadim*, the *Hey Behinot* are called *HGT NH*, meaning *Hey Hassadim*.

    If they are in *Behinot Gevurot*, meaning *He'arat Hochma* without *Hassadim*, the *Hey Behinot HGT NH* are called *KHB ZON*.

    If their *Atzmut* is *Hassadim* and they also have *He'arat Hochma*, they are called *Hey Hassadim HGT NH*, and if they lack *Hassadim*, but only *He'arat Hochma* is left in them, they are called *Hey Gevurot HGT NH*.

    (Item 42)

32. **What is Diminution of *Ohr*?**

    If the *Kli* descends below its degree it causes the lessening of the *Ohr* to the *Kli*, since the *Elyon* that descends to the place of the *Tachton* becomes like it.

    (Item 4)

33. **What *Histaklut Eynaim* of AVI?**

    Eynaim is an appellation for *Sefirat Hochma* of *Rosh*. When *Hochma de Abba* dispenses to *Hochma de Ima*, it is called *Histaklut Eynaim* of AVI on each other, and this is *Komat Keter de AVI*. In YESHSUT, when *Hochma de Israel Saba* gives to *Hochma de Tvuna*, it is called *Histaklut Eynaim* of YESHSUT on each other, and this is *Komat Keter de YESHSUT*.

    (Item 42)

34. **What is *Histaklut Eynaim* of YESHSUT?**

    See answer 33.

35. **What is Raisng MAN?**

    MAN means inducing *Zivug*. It is always *Behinat NHY* or *ZON*. This is so because the *Nekeva* is erected in *Ohr Achoraim de Ima* that is cleaved only to *Ohr de Hassadim*, rejecting *Hochma*.

    For this reason she does not bring her *Panim* to the *Zachar* to receive *He'arat Hochma*, except if she has some element that compels her to. This element is the *Behinat ZON* that *Bina* has a connection to, to illuminate it in *He'arat Hochma* through the relation of *Bina* and *ZON de Ohr Yashar*.

    Hence, when ZON rises to her for MAN, she immediately stops her *Achoraim* and brings her *Panim* back to *Hochma*, to receive *He'arat Hochma* from him, mating *Panim be Panim* with him.

    ()

36. **What is *Dvekut Panim be Panim*?**

    When AVI have *Komat Keter*, at which time *Hochma de Abba* gives to *Hochma de Bina*, AVI are found cleaved *Panim be Panim* from their *Rosh* to their *Sof*. It is so because then *Ima* is considered *Behinat Ohr Hochma*, as AVI are in *Hishtavut Tzura*, called *Dvekut*.

    However, when the *Koma* falls into *Behinat Guf*, at which time only *Bina de Abba* administers to *Bina de Ima*, *Ima* is not entirely *Behinat Hochma*, as is *Abba*, as she receives only from his *Bina*. There is an apparent *Shinui Tzura* from *Ima* to *Abba* and thus, *Zivug* of *Hochmot* (pl. for *Hochma*) *de AVI* is called "Complete *Dvekut Panim be Panim*".

    Zivug de Binot (pl. for *Bina*) *de AVI* is called Some *Dvekut de Panim be Panim*, because she still receives from *Bina de Abba*, containing some *He'arat Hochma*, but is not complete *Dvekut*.

    (Item 42)

37. **What is *Dvekut* of the *Klipot*?**

    The *Klipot* cleave to the *Achoraim de Nukva* because the *Nukva* is *Behinat Sium* on the *Ohr Elyon*. From her down it is a place of darkness and not *Ohr*. Hence, there is *Behinat Hishtavut Tzura* at the *Nekudat Sium* of *NHY de Nukva* to the *Klipot* and this is why it is considered that the *Klipot* cleave there, see item 49.

    (Item 26)

38. **What is *Hitpashtut Hey Gevurot*?**

    The *Shoresh* of the *Hey Hassadim* is in *Yesod*, being below all the *Hey Hassadim*. Yet, when they are not in *Zivug*, their *Koma* is even, as there is *Hitpashtut Hey*

Gevurot in them in *Behinat* from below upward to *Behinat* from above downward in all the *Hey Behinot* HGT NH.

(Item 41)

39. What is *Zach*?

He'arat Hochma received in the *Kelim de Panim* of the *Nekeva* which is not first thickened in *Ohr de Achoraim*, is called *Ohr Zach*, see answer 4.

(Item 24)

40. What is *Had Samcha*?

Before the *Tikun Kavim*, when ZAT were in one *Kav* one below the other, they were called *Had Samcha*, meaning One Line.

(Item 56)

41. What is the Sustenance of the *Klipot*?

See below answer 49.

(Item 21)

42. What are the Armies of *Malchut*?

All the *Partzufim* in BYA come from the diminishing of the *Koma* of *Malchut de Atzilut*, and all that is there. For this reason they are considered the soldiers of *Malchut* and her armies.

(Item 14)

43. What are the Parts of *Nukva*?

Only the *Behinat Nekevot* of the *Hey Partzufim* of *Atzilut* were made of these seven *Melachim* that fell to BYA. However, the *Zecharim* were made of the new MA, as will be explained in its place, hence they are named "Parts of the *Nukva*".

(Item 11)

44. What is Half the *Achoraim*?

See below answer 45.

(Item 30)

45. What is Half a Wall?

There are two distances and covers on the *Ohr Hochma*: One – by the force of the *Achoraim de Ima*. This cover is called "The Wall of HGT", as it is present only in HGT until the *Chazeh*.

There is also *Behinat* covering by the force of the *Achoraim de Yesod Abba*. They too cover *Ohr Hochma* as long as there is no *Ohr de Hassadim* in the *Partzuf*.

This cover is called *Achoraim de NHY*, as it operates primarily in the *NHY*, since this is its place.

When the ZON is in *Katnut* and their whole *Tikun* comes to them from the *Achoraim de Ima*, which is the Wall of *HGT*, you find that they both use this wall of *HGT*, half for ZA and half *Nukva*. This is because the wall of *NHY* that belongs to *Nukva* has no place to appear because of the fear from the exteriors, so that they will not suck from it. This is because the Wall of *NHY* appears only when the *Partzuf* is fitting for *He'arat Hochma* (See answer 11)

(Item 47)

46. What is The Lower Half of *Tifferet*?

The two lower thirds of *Tifferet* are called "The Lower Half of *Tifferet*", whose meaning has been explained above (item 17).

(Item 61)

47. What is The Upper Half of *Tifferet*?

This refers to the upper third through the *Chazeh*, which is the *Behinat GAR de Sefirat Tifferet* (see answer 16).

(Item 61)

48. What is a Drop that Raises the Fetus?

The *Behinat Hassadim* and *Gevurot* dispensed from *Zivug Panim be Panim de AVI* that contain *He'arat Hochma*, are the *Behinat* "Drop that Raises the Fetus", which are ZON. It means that through it they attain *He'arat Hochma* and become grown, as there is only *Gadlut* in *He'arat Hochma* (as written in item 20).

(Item 32)

49. What is the *Yenika* of the *Klipot*?

The essence of the substance of the *Klipot* is complete evil. It means that it is unfitting to receive at all, as they are from the *Behinat* Vacant *Halal*, which is from the restricted *Behina Dalet* to receive nothing of the *Ohr Elyon*. You therefore find that it is discerned as substance without any sustenance.

However, after the breaking of the vessels because of the good and evil mixed in them, these *Kelim* fell to those *Klipot*, and became a *Neshama* and sustenance to them. This is so because although the *Orot* departed from the *Kelim*, there still remained remnants of the *Orot* in them, and these remnants became *Behinat* minute *Ohr* that shines and sustains the *Klipot*.

Thus the structure of the *Partzufim* and the *Olamot* was made for them, like the BYA *de Kedusha*. This was enough for them for their essential structure.

However, after the sin of *Etz ha Daat*, and also when people sin, by that they cause proliferation of sustenance and *Shefa* to the *Sitra Achra*, according to the measure of the flaw that they cause in the *Kedusha*.

This is so because the *Guf* of *Adam* is from the *Sigim* of the *Melachim* that were not sorted. It is mingled, good and bad, as it is written, "a wild ass's colt is born a man."

When purifying one's *Guf*, separating the evil from it, then one receives Upper *He'arot* to one's *Neshama* and *Nefesh*, according to the measure of the purification. Afterwards, when one sins, the *Orot* depart and the *Levushim* from these *He'arot* fall to the *Klipot*. It is just as it happened in the breaking of the vessels, where because *Behina Dalet* was mixed in the *Kelim*, the *Ohr* was forced to leave and the *Kelim* fell to the *Klipa* and became sustenance for them.

It is exactly the same when one sins, meaning when one mixes that evil that he has already purified himself from and separated it from his *Guf*. The Upper *He'arot* immediately depart one's *Nefesh*, and the *Levushim* of these *He'arot* fall to the *Klipot* and become sustenance and nourishment for them.

This is the meaning of the pursuit of the evil inclination and the *Sitra Achra* to cause the righteous to sin and cling to *Kedusha*, as they have no sustenance without it. When good and *Kedusha* proliferate, so do their lives. In other words, the greater one is, the more good and *Kedusha* he has.

You find that when the *Sitra Achra* fails one into sinning, causing the good and *Kedusha* to depart and their *Levushim* fall to the portion of the *Klipot*, they receive abundance of *Shefa* and sustenance from it. Hence, "The greater one is from one's friend, the greater is one's desire," because the *Sitra Achra* chases him more.

(Item 18)

50. What are **YESHSUT**?

Behinat ZA de AVI, meaning their *AHP*, is called *YESHSUT*. In the beginning, during the *Zivug de Histaklut Eynaim* on each other, *YESHSUT* and *AVI* are considered united in a single *Partzuf*. Afterwards, when *AVI* return to *Behinat Zivug Achor be Achor*, *YESHSUT* depart from them and exit as a separate *Rosh* in *Komat AHP*, becoming a separate *Partzuf* in themselves (see item 21).

(Item 40)

51. What is the Force of the *Klipot*?

The *Levushim* of the *Orot de Kedusha* leave the *Kelim* because of the mixture of evil in them. These *Levushim* fall into the portion of the *Klipot*, and the remains that were left of the *Orot* that were in them add sustenance and force in the *Klipot* (see above item 49).

(Item 26)

52. **What are the General *Bina* and *Tvuna*?**

    When the *Hey Tata'a* descends from the *Eynaim de AVI* to their general *Malchut*, the *YESHSUT*, which are *AHP de AVI*, reconnect with the *Rosh*, which are *AVI*. Thus, *Bina* and *Tvuna* connect into a single *Partzuf*. This is called the general *Bina* and *Tvuna* together in a single *Partzuf*.

    (Item 48)

53. **What is the General *Hey Hassadim* and *Hey Gevurot*?**

    The General *Hey Hassadim* and *Hey Gevurot* means, as they were when they were rooted in *Yesod de AB*. This is because there the *Shoresh* of the *Hey Gevurot* appeared in the *Ohr Malchut* that clothed in *Kli de Yesod* as well as in *Malchut* (see Part 5, *Ohr Pnimi* item 35). Also, the general *Hey Hassadim* were rooted there in *Behinat* Truncated *Vav* (as written in the above *Ohr Pnimi*).

    Plain *Hey Hassadim* and *Hey Gevurot* means that when they come in a *Zivug*, each has *HGT NH*, both in *Hassadim* and in *Gevurot*, which are actual five *Sefirot*. However, the general *Hey Hassadim* and *Hey Gevurot* are only one *Sefira*, either of *Yesod*, or of *Malchut*.

    (Item 43)

54. **What is Disclosed?**

    The *Orot de Hochma* have a way of appearing when they are covered in *Achoraim de Ima*, but in *Behinat Levush Dak*. When they do not have that *Levush Dak* too, they are too exposed, and *He'arat Hochma* without any *Levush* comes to the first four *Melachim de Nekudim* from *Achoraim de Ima*. This is why their breaking was hard.

    There is also exposed *Hassadim* and *Gevurot*. This is a different matter, because as long as there is no *He'arat Hochma* in *HG*, they are considered covered in the *Achoraim de Ima*, as in this cover they are corrected in *He'arat GAR*. When they have *He'arat Hochma*, they are regarded as appearing outwardly from the covering of *Ima*, as then they have their own stance.

    (Item 49)

55. **What is *Mochin*?**

    The *GAR* are considered *Mochin*, and this appellation applies primarily when the *Atzmut* are *HG*, not having *He'arat GAR*.

    (Item 38)

56. **What is Death?**

Histalkut Ohr Atzilut from the *Kli*, meaning *He'arat Hochma*, is considered a dead *Kli*, as there is no sustenance for the *Kli* except in *He'arat Hochma*. For this reason the *Ohr Hochma* is called *Ohr Haya*, meaning having precisely that corruption, when she is no longer qualified to receive the *Ohr Atzilut* any more, meaning containing that mixture of *Behina Dalet*.

(Item 4)

57. **What is the Death of the *Melachim*?**

After they have been disqualified from receiving the *Ohr Hochma* anymore, they are severed from *Kav Ein Sof*. This is considered that they have fallen to BYA and died, since *Kav Ein Sof* ends in *Atzilut*.

(Item 55)

58. **What is Covered?**

See answer 54.

(Item 3)

59. **What are MAN?**

See answer 35.

(Item 39)

60. **What is *Masach Bina*?**

The *Achoraim de Bina* that cover and conceal the *Ohr Hochma* is called *Masach Bina*.

(Item 50)

61. **What are Mingled in the *Klipot*?**

The *Kelim de SAG* that are mixed in *Behina Dalet*, meaning the *Kelim* of the seven *Melachim* that fell to BYA, are called *Sigim*. The *Nitzotzin* that descended to revive the *Kelim* mixed in these *Sigim*.

(Item 4)

62. **What is the Place of the Gripping of the *Klipot*?**

The place of lack in *Kedusha* is the place of the gripping of the *Klipa* because the *Kelim* and the *Levushim* that belong to that place of lack are in the section of the *Klipot*. For this reason they too suck from the *Shefa* that belongs to those *Kelim* and *Levushim* in their authority.

(Item 26)

63. What is the Place of BYA?

The place for *BYA* was prepared during *Tzimtzum Bet*. This is because the *Hey Tata'a* rose there to the *Eynaim* and the *AHP* departed from the degree in *RTS* and the point of *Sium* that was in *Malchut de NHY* rose to the *Behinat Malchut de Hochma de NHY*.

Bina and *ZON de NHY* went outside, below the *Sium* of *Kav de Ein Sof*. In that, they were separated from the *Atzilut* and became a place for the Separated *BYA*, from which those three *Olamot* were later formed.

(Item 57)

64. What is the Place of Rosh?

From the place of the *Chazeh* to the *Peh* of the *Rosh*, it is always considered to be the place of the *Rosh* of the *Partzuf Tachton*. This is because each *Tachton* comes out from *Masach de Tabur de Partzuf Elyon* that consists of the *Eser Sefirot de Guf* of the *Elyon* that stand in this place from the *Chazeh* to its *Peh*.

After the *Hizdakchut Masach* to the point of *Hishtavut* to the *Masach de Malchut de Rosh*, it rises along with the *Reshimot de Sefirot de Guf* and is renewed in the *Hitkalelut* of the *Zivug Elyon de Rosh*.

The *Koma*, educed in the renewal of this *Zivug* belongs to the *Tachton*. Thus, the *Shorashim* of the lower *Eser Sefirot*, called *Rosh*, extend from the *Eser Sefirot de Guf de Elyon* that stand from the *Chazeh de Elyon* to its *Peh*. For this reason the *Rosh* of the *Tachton* clothes over them, since this is its place and its *Shoresh*.

(Item 45)

65. What is a Minute Light?

The *Kelim de Melachim* that remained in *BYA* after the *Partzufim de Atzilut* were sorted from them, are called *Sigim*. They are in the section of the *Klipot*, which became *Behinat Neshama* and sustenance for them, called "Minute Light" of *Kedusha*. It means a small and fine *He'arah* that sustains the *Klipot* (See answer 49).

(Item 18)

66. What are Nitzotzot that Quenched?

Nitzotzin mean parts of *Ohr Hozer*. The *Orot* that descended from *AVI* from above downward to clothe in the *Melachim* were each clothed in *Ohr Hozer*. When the *Kelim* broke, these *Behinot Ohr Hozer* descended along with them. Since the *Zivug* stopped from them, they are considered to have quenched, been put out, having no more of the *He'arat Zivug*.

(Item 9)

67. **What are *Nitzotzot* that were not Scrutinized?**

   See above answer 66.

   (Item 22)

68. **What are Strong *Nitzotzin*?**

   They are mixed with the *Atzmut* of *Behina Dalet*.

   (Item 8)

69. **What is a Fall?**

   When the degree descends to a lower degree, it is called "A Fall". This is because the *Elyon* that descends to the place of the *Tachton* becomes like it.

   (Item 26)

70. **What are *Sigim*?**

   See answer 61.

   (Item 2)

71. **What is a Thickening in the *Achoraim*?**

   When the *Ohr Panim* is first received in the *Kelim de Achoraim* before it comes to its *Kelim de Panim*, the *Ohr* receives *Behinat* covering of the *Achoraim* as it passes there. By that the *Ohr* thickens and lessens, and does not shine in its fullest measure even after it enters the *Kelim de Panim*.

   (Item 24)

72. **What is *Etz ha Daat* Good and Bad?**

   Etz ha Daat was mixed with good and evil. It means that *Behina Dalet*, called evil, was mixed there. After *Adam ha Rishon* had eaten from *Etz ha Daat*, he lost his first *Guf*, which was all good, and a *Guf* from *Behinat Mishcha de Hivia* (Aramaic: lit. The serpent's skin) came to him, mixed of good and evil too. For this reason he is unfitting to clothe the *Kedusha*, except through purification and separation of the evil from the *Guf*.

   (Item 16)

73. **What is *Panim be Panim*?**

   When the *Nekeva* receives the *Ohr Elyon* from the *Panim* of the *Zachar* into her *Kelim de Panim*, it is called *Zivug Panim be Panim*.

   (Item 24)

74. **What are Parts of the *Guf*?**

   Netzah and *Hod* from *Behinat Achor be Achor* before they have acquired *Behinat Tikun Kavim*, are only one *Kli*, without any apparent difference from one to another.

   (Item 46)

75. **What is the *Panim* of the *Zachar*?**

The administration of *He'arat Hochma* is the *Panim* of the *Zachar*, and the *Kli de Panim*, ascribed to the reception of *He'arat Hochma*, is the *Panim* of the *Nekeva*.

(Item 23)

76. **What is the *Panim* of the *Nekeva*?**

See above answer 75.

77. **What is *Panim be Achor*?**

This refers to the *Panim* of the *Zachar* in the *Achoraim* of the *Nekeva*. This is because even when the *Nekeva* is already fitting to receive the *Ohr Panim* from the *Panim* of the *Zachar*, because she is corrected with the *Achoraim de Ima*, she still craves *Hassadim* more than *Hochma*.

For this reason she does not stop her *Achoraim* to return her *Panim* to the *Zachar* without an element that obligates her. Thus, she receives the *Ohr Panim* of the *Zachar* through her *Kelim de Achoraim*, from which they are administered to the *Kelim de Panim*. This *Zivug* is called *Panim be Achor*.

(Item 23)

78. **What is Waste?**

Waste refers to the *Sigim* that remain after the scrutinies (see *Sigim*)

(Item 9)

79. **What is Small?**

See answer 19.

80. **What is *Katnut*?**

See answer 19.

81. **What are Complete *Klipot*?**

This refers to the actual substance of the *Klipot*, which are the complete evil, unfitting at all to receive the *Ohr Elyon*, which is the restricted *Behina Dalet* that remained in *Behinat* Vacant *Halal*.

(Item 18)

82. **What is *Klipat Noga*?**

The *Behinat Nitzotzin* that have a mixture of good and bad are the *Klipat Noga*. When she receives the *Ohr* in her good part, it is dispensed to her bad part too.

(Item 22)

83. **What is Some *Dvekut*?**

See answer 37.

(Item 62)

84. **What is Some Breaking?**

Some Breaking indicates that the *Kli* has not been disqualified from receiving *Atzilut* altogether, but was disqualified to receive from its own degree. It is still qualified to receive in a lower *Behina* it had been in, and this is also called "Cancellation".

(Item 4)

85. **What is Some *Tikun*?**

Tikun Kavim from *Behinat Achor be Achor* is considered "Some *Tikun*". This is because the *Ohr Achoraim de Ima* connects all the *Sefirot* until there is no oppositeness between them and equalizes their *Tzura* to each other.

(Item 56)

86. **What is a Connection?**

The first *Koma de AVI*, called *Histaklut Eynaim de AVI*, is also called "The *Rosh de AVI*" (see answer 21).

(Item 69)

87. **What is *Rosh de AVI*?**

Rosh ha Aleph de YESHSUT that emerged from the *Chazeh* upwards is called *Rosh de YESHSUT* (See answer 45).

(Item 45)

88. **What is *Rosh de YESHSUT*?**

Rosh ha Aleph de YESHSUT that emerged from the *Chazeh* upwards is called *Rosh de YESHSUT* (See answer 63).

(Item 45)

89. **What is the Breaking of the Vessels?**

When the *Kli* was disqualified from receiving the *Ohr*, it is considered that the *Kli* broke.

(Item 26)

90. **What is Upper Third of *Tifferet*?**

When the *Kli de Tifferet* was divided into *Eser Sefirot*, three thirds are discerned in it: the upper third through the *Chazeh* is the GAR in it, from *Chazeh* to *Tabur* is HGT in it, and from *Tabur* down it is NHYM in it.

(Item 45)

Table of Questions for Topics

91. Why are *Nekudim* called *HaVaYaH de SAG*?
92. Where is the *Malchut* in each *Sefira* from?
93. Why are there *Klipot* opposite the *BON* from its *Rosh* to its *Raglaim*?
94. Why is there no *Yenika* to the *Sitra Achra* from GAR de ZA?
95. Why is *Malchut* called *Nekuda*?
96. What are the four situations until *Panim be Panim*, and where are there three situations until *Panim be Panim*?
97. What causes the state of *Panim be Achor*?
98. What causes the state of *Panim be Panim*?
99. Where are there four situations until *Panim be Panim*, and where are there three situations until *Panim be Panim*?
100. How do the HG complement a complete *Achor* for ZA and a complete *Achor* for *Nukva*?
101. How does the MAN that is raised to ZON extend new *Orot*, if every *Hidush Ohr* should be from *Ein Sof*?
102. What are the GAR de ZA that take from AVI?
103. What are the two reasons in the HG?
104. How many *Partzufim* came out in the *Nekudim*?
105. What is the reason for the breaking of the vessels?
106. Which *Orot* were cancelled from AVI?
107. What is the *Koma* of *Melech ha Daat*?
108. What is the *Koma* of *Melech ha Hesed*?
109. What is the *Koma* of *Melech ha Gevura*?
110. What is *Komat Tifferet* until the *Chazeh*?
111. What is *Komat* Two Lower Thirds of *Tifferet*?
112. What is *Komat NH*?
113. What is the *Komat Yesod*?
114. What is the *Komat Malchut*?
115. How did *Gadlut de AVI de Nekudim* emerge?
116. How did *Komat YESHSUT de Nekudim* emerge?

117. How did the *Zivug* of the two *Ketarim* (pl. for *Keter*) in *Daat de Nekudim* emerge?
118. Why is there only HG in *Daat de AVI*?
119. What are the NRNHY *de ZA*?
120. Why is the *Yesod* entirely *Panim*, and has no *Achoraim* at all?
121. Why is *Tifferet* divided into two halves, more than the other *Sefirot*?
122. Why are the *Gufim de AVI* drawn to the place of DHGT?
123. Why is Upper *AVI* not regarded as the *Rosh* of ZON, but as YESHSUT?
124. Why did the *Achoraim de AVI* not fall to BYA like the ZON?
125. Why did the *Achoraim de AVI* fall to *Behinat Guf*?
126. Where did the *Hitpashtut* KHB to the new *Kelim de HGT* come from?
127. Why were the *Achoraim de AVI* made into *Behinat* MAN that the ZON raise to them?
128. Which *Behinot Kelim* of the Seven *Melachim* fell to *Yetzira* and *Assiya*?
129. Where did the *Orot* of the Seven *Melachim* leave their *Reshimot* after their departure?
130. Why where the *Reshimot* arranged in NHYM *de Atzilut* in an opposite order, *Daat* below, and *Tifferet* above all?
131. Why did the *Reshimot* of the *Dalet Melachim* DHGT fell to NHYM *de Atzilut*?
132. Why did the *Reshimo* of the Upper third of *Tifferet* remain in its place unchanged?
133. Which change was there in the *Reshimo* of the two lower thirds of *Tifferet*?
134. Who brought the *Reshimot* back to the new *Kelim* DHGT *de Atzilut*?
135. Why did the four *Melachim* DHGT descend to GAR *de Beria, Yetzira*, and *Assiya*?
136. Why were there two falls in the *Melachim* of DHGT, one for GAR *de BYA*, and another for NHYM *de BYA*?
137. Who magnified the *Kli de Keter* up to the place of *Chazeh de Tifferet*?
138. Who complemented the new *Kli de Tifferet* from the place of the *Chazeh* to its *Sium*?
139. How do the new *Kelim de HGT* come from *Hitpashtut* KHB *de Nekudim*?
140. How was the *Zivug* of the two *Ketarim de Daat* made after the breaking of the four *Melachim* NHYM?

141. Who reared the *Kelim* of the new *Tifferet, Netzah,* and *Hod*?
142. What are the causes for the elicitation of the *Katnut* and *Gadlut de AVI de Nekudim*?
143. Who raised MAN for the Upper *Zivug AB SAG* for the *Gadlut de AVI*?
144. What did the inner *Orot* that came out through the *Tabur* and the *Yesod de AK* do?
145. Why did the GAR and ZAT *de Eser Sefirot de Nekudim* emerge at once?
146. Since the Seven *Melachim* do not belong to *AVI*, which are only from *Behina Bet*, they had to emerge from NHY *de AK*.
147. What is the essence of the *Achoraim de AVI* that fell?
148. Where is the place of the fall of each of the four *Komot de Achoraim de AVI*?
150. What are the four reasons that preceded the *Zivug AVI Panim be Panim*?
151. What are the twelve actions accustomed in every *Melech* of the four *Melachim* DHGT?
152. What are the four reasons that preceded the *Zivug Panim be Panim de* YESHSUT?
153. What are the eleven operations that were in each of the four *Melachim* TNHYM?
154. Why did the ascent of *Malchut* in the *Zivug* of the two *Ketarim de Daat* tie all the VAK?
155. What are the 103 operations that emerged from one another in an order of cause and effect from after the situation *de Achor be Achor de AVI* until after *Tikun Kavim* of the new *Kelim Tifferet, Netzah,* and *Hod,* made after the breaking of the vessels?

91. **Why are *Nekudim* called *HaVaYaH de SAG*?**

    It is so because there is *Koma* of *Behina Bet* in *Behinat Hitlabshut* there, which is *Behinat Israel Saba*, and YESHSUT is *Behinat HaVaYaH de SAG*.
    ()

92. **Where is the *Malchut* in each *Sefira* from?**

    Through the ascent of the *Hey Tata'a* in the *Eynaim* that was in *Tzimtzum Bet*. It means that when the *Malchut* rose in *Hochma*, *Malchut* mixed and connected in each and every *Sefira* up to *Hochma*.
    ()

93. **Why are there *Klipot* opposite the BON from its *Rosh* to its *Raglaim*?**

    Because the Seven *Melachim*, named BON, emerged in a complete *Partzuf Rosh* and *Guf*, and broke *Panim* and *Achor*. For this reason they have *Klipot* from its *Rosh* to its *Raglaim*, meaning in its entire RTS. All the *Behinot Rosh* of the Seven *Melachim* fell to *Beria*, all the *Behinot Toch* of the Seven *Melachim* fell to *Yetzira*, and all the *Behinot Sof* of the Seven *Melachim* fell to *Assiya*.
    ()

94. **Why is there no *Yenika* to the *Sitra Achra* from GAR de ZA?**

    This is because during the *Katnut*, it lacks GAR, as it is so from its very creation. However, during the *Gadlut* it attains the GAR in *Behinat* addition, and the *Klipot* have no *Yenika* from there.

    This is so because when the *Tachtonim* blemish, before the flaw appears, the GAR immediately leave the ZA. This is so because as long as it does not come with the *Partzuf* from the beginning of its creation, it can leave the *Partzuf* when necessary.
    ()

95. **Why is *Malchut* called *Nekuda*?**

    Malchut is always called *Nekuda*, after the root *Malchut* over which there was the first *Tzimtzum*. Therefore, the actual carrier of the *Tzimtzum* and the *Masach* over which the *Zivug* is made, are called *Nekuda* in every place.
    ()

96. **What are the four situations until *Panim be Panim*, and where are there three situations until *Panim be Panim*?**

    The four situations are *Achor be Achor*, *Achor be Panim*, *Panim be Achor*, and *Panim be Panim*. It means that when the *Zachar* and *Nukva* lack GAR because of the ascent of the *Hey Tata'a* in the *Eynaim*, the first *Tikun* that suffices to support them in *Atzilut* is *Achor be Achor*. It means that they obtain the

Ohr Achoraim of Upper *Ima*. Because she craves *Ohr de Hassadim*, by way of "because He delighteth in mercy," you find that she rejects the *Ohr Hochma*.

Thus, when they are incorporated in this *Ohr* and in these *Achoraim*, they are not at all blemished due to the lack of *Hochma* in them because of the *Hey Tata'a* in the *Eynaim*. This is because even if they could receive *Hochma*, they would still reject its reception due to the craving for *Hassadim* imprinted in the *Achoraim* of Upper *Ima*. Hence, the *Achoraim de Ima* serves them as *He'arat* GAR, and this is the first *Tikun*, called *Achor be Achor*.

The second situation is *Achor be Panim*. Besides the diminution of the lessening of *He'arat Hochma* by the *Hey Tata'a* in the *Eynaim*, there is lessening and diminution of *He'arat Hochma* in the *Kelim de Panim* of the *Nekeva* as well.

Because of the blockage on *Ohr de Hassadim* that there is in her *Kelim de Panim*, she is unfit to receive *He'arat Hochma*, as there *He'arat Hochma* is not received in the *Partzuf* without *Hassadim*.

Thus, after the lessening because of the *Hey Tata'a* in the *Eynaim* was corrected by the above *Zivug de Achor be Achor*, the *Zivug* of *Achor be Panim* was made. The *Zachar* gives her *Ohr de Hassadim* abundantly and corrects the *Kelim de Panim* of the *Nekeva*, thus qualifying her to be fit to receive *He'arat Hochma* in them.

The third situation is *Panim be Achor*. This comes to them by the *Zivug Elyon de AB SAG* that lowers the *Hey Tata'a* from the *Eynaim* and returns the HB to the *Rosh*. At that time the *Zachar* acquires his *Ohr Panim* as in the beginning, prior to the lessening.

However, the *Nekeva* does not return her *Panim* to the *Panim de Zachar* to receive *He'arat Hochma* without a reason that compels her to it. This is so because her *Achoraim* are in the form of *Bina de Ohr Yashar*, by way of, "because He delighteth in mercy."

Thus, at that time the *Nekeva* receives the *Ohr Panim* from the *Zachar* through her *Achoraim*. The *He'arat Hochma* is greatly diminished by that, and this *Zivug* is called *Panim be Achor*. The *Panim* of the *Zachar* dispense to the *Nekeva* through her *Achoraim* and the *Kelim de Panim* receive from the *Kelim de Achoraim*.

The fourth situation is *Panim be Panim*. This comes to them only through raising MAN from *Behinat ZON*, since *Bina* is connected with the ZON by way of the *Eser Sefirot de Ohr Yashar*, where *Bina* dispenses them *He'arat Hochma*.

Thus, when ZON rise to her to MAN, she stops her *Achoraim* and returns her *Panim* to the *Hochma* to receive *He'arat Hochma* from him for the ZON, and in that state she mates with the *Hochma Panim be Panim*.

(Items 23-25 and *Ohr Pnimi* there)

97. **What causes the state of *Panim be Achor*?**

   The *Zachar* acquires his *Behinat Panim* through the *Zivug Elyon de AB SAG* that lowers the *Hey Tata'a* from the *Eynaim* and returns the *HB* to the *Rosh*. However, the *Nekeva* is still in need of raising MAN, hence their *Zivug* is made in *Behinat Panim be Achor*.

   ()

98. **What causes the state of *Panim be Panim*?**

   Raising MAN to the *Bina* from the *Behinat ZON* awakens the *Bina* to return *Panim* to *Hochma* (see answer 96).

   ()

99. **Where are there four situations until *Panim be Panim*, and where are there three situations until *Panim be Panim*?**

   All the situations, *Achor be Achor*, *Achor be Panim*, *Panim be Achor*, and *Panim be Panim*, are implemented in ZON. However, *Behinat Achor be Panim* does not apply in AVI, only *Achor be Achor*, *Panim be Achor*, and *Panim be Panim*.

   ()

100. **How do the HG complement a complete *Achor* for ZA and a complete *Achor* for *Nukva*?**

   When the ZON are in *Behinat Achor be Achor*, there is only the wall of HGT in them, being the *Behinat Achoraim de Ima* (See answer 96). You find, that they both use this *Achoraim*, half for ZA and half for *Nukva*.

   The *Achoraim* of the NHY are absent in both, as they are in the form of, "and all their hinder parts were inward." This is because the *Achoraim de NHY* are from *Behinat Yesod de Abba*, which appears only through *Hassadim* and new *Gevurot*, which are in *He'arat Hochma*.

   Hence, when HG come from the *Zivug Panim be Panim de AVI*, the *Achoraim de NHY* are completed for both, ZA takes the *Hassadim* for itself, and gives the *Gevurot* to the *Nukva* (see above answer 45).

   ()

101. **How does the MAN that is raised to ZON extend new *Orot*, if every *Hidush Ohr* should be from *Ein Sof*?**

   As the lower *Adam* raises MAN to ZON through good deeds, so the ZON scrutinize from the *Achoraim de AVI* that fell to their place and raise MAN for AVI. Also, AVI extend *Mochin* from *Ohr Ein Sof* above them through all the degrees until the first *Partzuf Elyon*, and lowers them to the one below it, and so they are passed to ZON.

Thus, any raising of MAN from the righteous induces a new descent of the *Ohr* from *Ein Sof* itself, as there is no *Hidush* of *Ohr* in all the *Olamot* that does not extend from *Ein Sof*, and remember that.

()

102. **What are the GAR *de* ZA that take from AVI?**

    They are primarily *Hassadim* and *Gevurot*, though there is *He'arat Hochma* in them according to the measure of *Koma* present in AVI at that time. If they are in *Komat Keter*, these *Mochin* are from *Behinat He'arat Hochma de Partzuf Keter*. If they are in *Komat Hochma*, the *Mochin* are found to be from *Behinat He'arat Hochma de Partzuf Hochma* etc.

    ()

103. **What are the two reasons in the HG?**

    The first is that these new HG where there is *He'arat Hochma* rear and complete the *Achoraim de* ZON (See answer 100). The second is that they acquire the *Mochin de Panim*, which are their GAR, and then mate *Panim be Panim*.

    (Item 29)

104. **How many *Partzufim* came out in the *Nekudim*?**

    Three *Partzufim* came out in *Nekudim*: AVI in four *Komot*, whose *Gufim* are *Daat, Hesed, Gevura*, and the upper third of *Tifferet* until the *Chazeh*.

    The second *Partzuf* is YESHSUT in four *Komot*. Their *Gufim* are the two lower thirds of *Tifferet*, NH, *Yesod*, and *Malchut*.

    The third is the *Zivug* of the two *Ketarim* in *Daat* that came out a *Rosh* without a *Guf*.

    ()

105. **What is the reason for the breaking of the vessels?**

    There were many causes there, but what caused their death and descent to BYA was the mixture of *Behina Dalet*, which is unfit to receive from the *Ohr Elyon*, that mingled in these *Kelim* of the Seven *Melachim*. Thus, when the *Ohr* came to meet *Behina Dalet*, it immediately departed and separated itself from the entire *Kli*, and the *Kli* died and fell to BYA, meaning below the line of *Ein Sof* that ends with the *Karka de Atzilut*.

    They fell there into the *Klipot*, and after they are sorted and the mixtures of *Behina Dalet* are separated from them, they are returned to *Atzilut* by way of the revival of the dead, and this is done by the new MA.

    ()

106. **Which *Orot* were cancelled from *AVI*?**

    Only the *Orot* that came out of *Zivug de Gadlut de AVI* were cancelled, but what was present in *AVI* from the beginning of their creation was not cancelled at all.

    (Item 31)

107. **What is the *Koma* of *Melech ha Daat*?**

    His *Rosh*, meaning the *Behinat* from below upward, is the *Rosh de AVI*, called *Histaklut Eynaim de AVI* at each other. He emerged on *Behina Dalet de Hitlabshut* and *Behina Gimel* from the *Aviut*, which were incorporated in one another, eliciting *Komat Keter*. The *Guf* of this *Komat Keter*, which is its from above downward, expanded in *Melech ha Daat*, and it is *Behinat Yechida de ZON*.

    ()

108. **What is the *Koma* of *Melech ha Hesed*?**

    His from below upward is called *Guf de Abba*, which came out on *Behina Gimel de Hitlabshut* and *Behina Bet* from the *Aviut*, whose *Koma* is up to *Hochma*. The *Guf* of this *Koma* expanded in *Melech ha Hesed* and it is *Behinat Haya de ZA*.

    (Items 42, 43)

109. **What is the *Koma* of *Melech ha Gevura*?**

    His from below upward is called *Guf de Ima*, which came out on merely *Aviut de Behina Bet*, whose *Koma* is up to *Bina*, and the *Guf* expanded in *Melech ha Gevura*, and it is *Behinat Neshama de ZA*.

    (Item 43)

110. **What is *Komat Tifferet* until the *Chazeh*?**

    His from below upward is called *Yesodot* (pl. for *Yesod*) *de AVI*. He came out on *Aviut de Behina Aleph*, whose *Koma* is up to *ZA*, and from above downward of this *Koma* expanded in *Melech ha Tifferet* until his *Chazeh*, and it is *Behinat Ruach de ZA*.

    (Item 45)

111. **What is *Komat* Two Lower Thirds of *Tifferet*?**

    His from below upward is called the *Rosh* of *YESHSUT* and *Histaklut Eynaim de YESHSUT* at each other. He emerged on a *Masach* from *Behina Gimel de Hitlabshut* and from *Aviut de Behina Bet* whose *Koma* is up to *Hochma*. His *Guf* expanded in *Melech ha Tifferet* in his lower two thirds of the *Chazeh* down to his *Sium*, and it is *Behinat Haya de Neshama de ZA*.

    (Item 45)

112. **What is Komat NH?**

His from below upward is called *Guf de YESHSUT*. He emerged on *Masach de Behina Bet*, and his *Guf* expanded in the *Melech de Netzah* and *Hod*, and he is *Behinat Neshama* from the *Neshama de ZA*.

(Item 46)

113. **What is the Komat Yesod?**

His from below upward is called *Yesodot de YESHSUT*, which came out on *Aviut* of *Behina Aleph*. His *Koma* is up to *ZA*, his *Guf* expanded in *Melech ha Yesod*, and he is *Behinat Ruach de ZA* of the *Neshama*.

(Item 47)

114. **What is the Komat Malchut?**

His from below upward is called *Malchut de YESHSUT*. He emerged on *Masach de Behinat Shoresh*, whose *Koma* is up to *Malchut*. His from above downward expanded in the seventh *Melech*, which is *Malchut*, and he is *Behinat Nefesh de Neshama de ZA*.

(Item 47)

115. **How did Gadlut de AVI de Nekudim emerge?**

See below answer 150.

116. **How did Komat YESHSUT de Nekudim emerge?**

See below answer 152.

117. **How did the Zivug of the two Ketarim (pl. for Keter) in Daat de Nekudim emerge?**

See below answer 154.

118. **Why is there only HG in Daat de AVI?**

The whole return of *Panim de Ima* to *Panim de Abba* was primarily in order to dispense *He'arat Hochma* to the *ZON* by the force of the connection that she has to administer *He'arat Hochma* to the *ZON* from the relation of *Ohr Yashar*. Hence, after her *Zivug Panim be Panim* with *Abba*, she still receives from him only as much as *Bina de Ohr Yashar* administers *Hochma* to the *ZON de Ohr Yashar*.

It is known that the essence of *ZON de Ohr Yashar* is *Ohr de Hassadim*, but in *He'arat Hochma* that *Bina* dispenses it. Hence, here too she gives it primarily only *Hassadim* and *Gevurot*, but only with *He'arat Hochma*.

For this reason, *Ima* does not receive *Ohr Hochma* in *Keter* from *Abba* even in *AVI*, which are in *Komat Keter*, but only *He'arat Hochma* in the *ZON de Keter*.

This is a measure of a *Koma* from below upward in *AVI*, called *Daat de AVI*, and discerned as *Behinat Rosh* of *Melech ha Daat*.

(Item 41 and *Ohr Pnimi* item 9)

119. **What are the NRNHY *de ZA*?**

    Two factors operate together in the values of the five *Komot de NRNHY de ZA*: the first is the measure of the *Koma de AVI* itself. This extends from the state of *Panim be Achor de AVI*, meaning according to the place of the descent of the *Hey Tata'a*.

    If up to the *Peh*, they have *Komat Keter*; if up to the *Hotem*, they have *Komat Hochma*; and if up to the *Awzen*, they have *Komat Bina*. If returning back to the *Eynaim*, they have *Komat ZA*.

    The second element is the *Behinat MAN* that rose to *Ima*, awakening her to the *Zivug Panim be Panim*, when they do not extend from the entire *Koma de AVI*, but only from the *He'arat Hochma de ZON* in the same *Koma AVI de ZON* are. Thus, if *AVI* are in *Komat Keter*, *He'arat Hochma* in *ZON de Keter* extends, and it is *Yechida de ZA*. If *AVI* are in *Komat Hochma*, only *He'arat Hochma* extends in *ZON de Hochma*, which is *Haya de ZA*. If *AVI* are in *Komat Bina*, *He'arat Hochma* is extended in *ZON de Bina*, and she is *Neshama de ZA*.

    ()

120. **Why is the *Yesod* entirely *Panim,* and has no *Achoraim* at all?**

    Because the *Achoraim de AVI* fell and were cancelled, meaning only what came to them in *Behinat* addition to their actual creation is *Behinat Achor be Achor*. Hence, the *Achoraim* did not fall from the *Behinat Yesodot de AVI*, as *AVI* have already returned *Achor be Achor*, even before the *Zivug Yesodot de AVI* emerged, meaning right after the *Guf de Ima* was cancelled. For this reason the *Orot* of *Yesod* are entirely *Panim* from the *Behinat* beginning of their emanation, and it contains no *Behinat Achoraim* that descended from it at all.

    (Item 44)

121. **Why is *Tifferet* divided into two halves, more than the other *Sefirot*?**

    Because *Tifferet* relates to the *Hey Hassadim* as *Bina* to the *Hey Behinot*. Thus, *Bina* is divided into two halves, *Bina* and *Tvuna*. *Bina* is *Ohr Hassadim* without *Hochma* and it is *Behinat GAR*, meaning before she emanated the *ZON de Ohr Yashar*. *Tvuna* is in *He'arat Hochma*, and she is *Behinat ZAT de Bina*.

    When she emanated *ZON de Ohr Yashar* in *He'arat Hochma*, she came out from *Behinat Atzmut* of *Bina*, which is mere *Ohr Hassadim*, and acquired a new name, *Tvuna*. She is *Behinat He'arat Hochma* that remains in the *Shoresh Bina* even after she emanated to *ZON*, hence *Tvuna* is considered *ZAT de Bina*.

Since the *Tifferet* is *Behinat Bina* of the *Hey Hassadim*, it is therefore divided as *Bina* is, into GAR until the *Chazeh*, and to ZAT, from the *Chazeh* down to its *Sium*. It too, like the *Bina*, only *Ohr de Hassadim* illuminate in its GAR until the *Chazeh*, and the *He'arat Hochma* disappears there in *Yesod de Bina*. In its ZAT from the *Chazeh* down, it is in disclosed *He'arat Hochma* since the *Yesod de Ima* has already stopped in the place of the *Chazeh*.

()

122. **Why are the *Gufim de AVI* drawn to the place of DHGT?**

    Because the *DHGT* in the *Hey Hassadim* are like the *KHBD de Hey Behinot KHB ZON*. For this reason their *Orot* were drawn from their corresponding relation in the *Hey Behinot*. *Ohr Yechida* extends to the *Daat*; *Ohr Haya* extends to the *Hesed*, which is *Behinat Hochma de Hassadim*. *Ohr Haya* extends to the *Hesed*, which is *Behinat Hochma de Hassadim*, *Ohr Neshama* extends to the *Gevura*, which is *Behinat Bina de Hey Hassadim*, and *Ohr Ruach* extends to the *Tifferet*, which is *Behinat Daat de Hey Hassadim*.

    ()

123. **Why is Upper AVI not regarded as the *Rosh* of ZON, but as YESHSUT?**

    You already know the division of *Bina* and *Tvuna* into two halves, GAR and ZAT. The GAR are *Behinat Bina* before she emanated the ZON, at which time she is only *Ohr de Hassadim*. This is *Behinat* Upper AVI.

    The ZAT, which is *Behinat Bina* after she emanated the ZON, has *He'arat Hochma* too, called *Tvuna*, and this is *Behinat YESHSUT*. Now you can understand that Upper AVI are not at all designated to be *Rosh de ZON*.

    Moreover, the whole essence of the Upper AVI, is because they are *Behinat Bina* before they emanated the ZON. They have only *Ohr de Hassadim*, which is not at all from the *Behinat ZON*, which are only *Behinat Hassadim* in *He'arat Hochma*.

    Hence, only the YESHSUT, which are *Behinat ZAT de AVI* that emanated the ZON *de Ohr Yashar*, and have *He'arat Hochma* in them, which is the entire degree of ZA, are always considered *Rosh de ZON* in all the *Partzufim*.

    ()

124. **Why did the *Achoraim de AVI* not fall to BYA like the ZON?**

    This is because the cancellation *de Achoraim de AVI* was not due to a mixture of the *Dinim*, which are the *Behina Dalet*, but only because of the *Hizdakchut* of the *Masach*. Hence, they were not entirely disqualified from *Behinat Atzilut*, but were only cancelled temporarily.

In other words, as long as they have no one to dispense to, they are cancelled. But when the *Kelim* return from *BYA* to *Atzilut*, they too return to bestow upon them as in the beginning. For this reason they are only in *Behinat* temporary cancellation, not in *Behinat*, breaking and death like the seven *Melachim*.

Behinat He'arat Achor be Achor de AVI too reached the above-mentioned *Achoraim*, called *Hitpashtut Gimel Kavim KHB* to the *Achoraim* that stand in HGT.

(Item 14)

125. **Why did the *Achoraim de AVI* fall to *Behinat Guf*?**

    Because all these four *Komot* that emerged in the *Gadlut de AVI* came out on the MAN *de Vav* ו and *Nekuda de Yesod AK*, which are the general *Behinat* ZON and *Behinat Guf*, and are not at all from *Behinat AVI*.

    Instead, when they were incorporated in the *Zivug de AVI* itself and operated there in *Behinat MAN*, extending *He'arat Hochma* for the seven *Melachim*, they had a place in *Rosh de AVI*. However, after the *Zivug* on them has been cancelled, they no longer have a place there, and they must return to their place in the *Guf*.

    (Item 14)

126. **Where did the *Hitpashtut KHB* to the new *Kelim de HGT* come from?**

    The four *Komot* emerged in *AVI de Gadlut* and in *NHY de Keter* and served them as *Mochin*, which were in *Behinat KHB de Nekudim*, corrected in *Tikun Kavim*. Now, after they were cancelled and fell to their *Behinat Gufim*, they drew the *Behinat Tikun Kavim de KHB* with them into the places they fell to, and these *Achoraim* too were corrected in *Tikun Kavim* like the KHB.

    ()

127. **Why were the *Achoraim de AVI* made into *Behinat MAN* that the ZON raise to them?**

    Because those *Achoraim* that fell from *AVI* are the *Behinat MAN* that *AVI* received from the *Yesod de AK*. Hence, once they have fallen to the place of ZON, the ZON raises them back to *Behinat MAN* to *AVI* from all the *Komot* in them, which are NRNHY.

    ()

128. **Which *Behinot Kelim* of the Seven *Melachim* fell to *Yetzira* and *Assiya*?**

    The *Behinat Toch* in all the *Kelim* fell to *Yetzira*, and the *Behinat Sof* in all the *Kelim* fell to *Assiya*.

    ()

129. **Where did the *Orot* of the Seven *Melachim* leave their *Reshimot* after their departure?**

The *Reshimot de Dalet Melachim DHGT* first descended to *Behinat NHYM de Atzilut*. Afterwards they clothed in the new *Kelim DHGT* that were made of the *Achoraim de AVI de Nekudim*. The *Reshimo de Dalet Melachim TNHYM* first rose to the new *Kelim de DHGT*, and then descended from there and clothed the new *Kelim de Tifferet, Netzah*, and *Hod*, made of the *Achoraim de YESHSUT*.

()

130. **Why where the *Reshimot* arranged in *NHYM de Atzilut* in an opposite order, *Daat* below, and *Tifferet* above all?**

During the *Hitlabshut* of the *Orot* in the *Kelim*, the more *Av* is considered more important and more *Elyon*. It is inverted after the *Histalkut Orot* from the *Kelim*, as then the more *Av* is lower.

Thus, since the *Daat* was the highest during the *Hitlabshut*, you find that during the *Histalkut*, he is the lowest. *Hesed*, whose *Aviut* is less than him, is above it, and the *Gevura*, whose *Aviut* is less than *Hesed*, is above *Hesed*. The *Tifferet*, whose *Aviut* is less than all, is the highest.

(Histaklut Pnimit item 19)

131. **Why did the *Reshimot* of the *Dalet Melachim DHGT* fell to *NHYM de Atzilut*?**

Their *Kelim* broke and fell to *BYA*. Hence, they came as close to them as they could in order to illuminate them in *Behinat Tagin* over the *Otiot*.

(Histaklut Pnimit item 20)

132. **Why did the *Reshimo* of the Upper third of *Tifferet* remain in its place unchanged?**

Its *Kli*, which is the upper third of *Tifferet*, fell only to *Behinat* from the *Chazeh* downward. Hence, it did not have to descend at all, as it was cleaved to it from its place in *Behinat Tagin* over it.

(Item 28)

133. **Which change was there in the *Reshimo* of the two lower thirds of *Tifferet*?**

It did not stay in its place, but rose and clothed the new *Kli* of the upper third of *Tifferet* that was made of the *Achoraim de AVI*. Regardless, it is not a great change since in the end, they are two halves of one *Kli*.

(Histaklut Pnimit item 30)

134. **Who brought the *Reshimot* back to the new *Kelim DHGT de Atzilut*?**

    The *Rosh de YESHSUT* clothed the entire place of the four *Melachim DHGT* from below upward. It is *Behinat Hitpashtut Bet*, whose conduct is to fill the empty *Kelim* and the *Reshimot* of the *Guf de Elyon*.

    Hence, he illuminated to these *Reshimot* of the four *Melachim* of *DHGT*, which are *Behinat* its *Guf* of the *Elyon*, meaning *de AVI*, and drew them to their place in the new *Kelim* in order to clothe them.

    ()

135. **Why did the four *Melachim DHGT* descend to *GAR de Beria, Yetzira*, and *Assiya*?**

    The *Melachim* of *DHGT* are *Behinot GAR de ZAT*, and are therefore ascribed to *GAR de BYA*.

    ()

136. **Why were there two falls in the *Melachim* of *DHGT*, one for *GAR de BYA*, and another for *NHYM de BYA*?**

    When the *Reshimot* were close to them in *Behinat Tagin* over the *Otiot* in the place of *NHYM de Atzilut*, they could sustain themselves in *GAR de BYA* since they too are *Behinat GAR de ZAT*. However, after the *Reshimot* had distanced and clothed in the new *Kelim* and in the *Rosh de YESHSUT*, their *He'arah* stopped from the *Kelim*. For this reason they fell to the last level *de BYA*, which is the place of *NHYM de BYA*.

    (Histaklut Pnimit item 25)

137. **Who magnified the *Kli de Keter* up to the place of *Chazeh de Tifferet*?**

    The *Achoraim de Daat de AVI* that was clothed in *NHY de Keter de Nekudim* expanded in the middle line and became the new *Kelim de Daat* and *Tifferet*.

138. **Who complemented the new *Kli de Tifferet* from the place of the *Chazeh* to its *Sium*?**

    Behinat Achoraim that fell from the *Rosh de YESHSUT*, which fell from the place from the *Chazeh* up to the place from the *Chazeh* downward. They were corrected in *Behinat* middle line through the *He'arat Rosh* from the *Zivug* of the two *Ketarim* in *Daat* and increased the *Kli de Tifferet* through its *Sium*.

    (Histaklut Pnimit item 32)

139. **How do the new *Kelim DHGT* come from *Hitpashtut KHB de Nekudim*?**

    These *Achoraim de AVI* come from *Behinat AVI* and *NHY de Keter*, being *KHB de Nekudim*, corrected in *Tikun Kavim* at their very creation in *Behinat Achor be Achor* through the luminescence of the Upper *Ima*. Hence, after they'd fallen from the *Rosh* to the place of *DHGT*, they are also given from *Behinat Achor be Achor de AVI* that were not cancelled, and their *Tikun Kavim* extends on the *Achoraim* too.

(Histaklut Pnimit item 22)

140. **How was the Zivug of the two Ketarim de Daat made after the breaking of the four Melachim NHYM?**

    After *Kli Malchut* was also broken and the *Masach de YESHSUT* purified from every *Behinat Aviut* that it had, you find that it rose and incorporated in the *Zivug* of *Rosh de YESHSUT*. *Behina Bet* disappeared, being the last *Behina*, and only the *Aviut de Behina Aleph* remained. Hence, only *Komat ZA* emerged on it, which is *Behinat Hesed* and *Gevura*, called *Bet Ketarim de Daat*.

    (Histaklut Pnimit item 32)

141. **Who reared the Kelim of the new Tifferet, Netzah, and Hod?**

    The new *Kelim Tifferet, Netzah*, and *Hod*, were made through the *Achoraim de YESHSUT* that fell to the place of *TNHY*, and through their clothing in the new *Rosh*.

    (Histaklut Pnimit item 32)

142. **What are the causes for the elicitation of the Katnut and Gadlut de AVI de Nekudim?**

    The *Katnut de Nekudim* until *Behinat Achor be Achor de AVI* emerged from the *Reshimot de SAG*, contained in the *Masach*. Also, the *Gadlut de Nekudim* and the seven *Melachim* emerged from the *Reshimot de NHY de AK* contained in the *Masach*.

    ()

143. **Who raised MAN for the Upper Zivug AB SAG for the Gadlut de AVI?**

    MA and BON *de AK*, which are *NHY de AK*, rose to MAN to the Upper *AB SAG*, mated *Panim be Panim*, and lowered the *Hey Tata'a* from the *Eynaim*, returning all the *AHPs* to their preliminary degree.

    (Histaklut Pnimit item 4)

144. **What did the inner Orot that came out through the Tabur and the Yesod de AK do?**

    The new *Ohr* that fissured the *Parsa* and came out through the *Tabur*, lowered the *Hey Tata'a* from the *Eynaim de Keter*, and *AVI* returned to the *Rosh* and came to a state of *Panim be Achor*. The *Ohr* that came out through *Yesod de AK* to *AVI* became MAN for *AVI*, brought them to a state of *Panim be Panim*, and elicited the Seven *Melachim de Nekudim*.

    (Histaklut Pnimit item 5)

145. **Why did the GAR and ZAT de Eser Sefirot de Nekudim emerge at once?**

    When GAR de Nekudim emerged, AVI were in Behinat Achor be Achor, where there is no Hitpashtut to the Guf from them. For this reason they needed the Zivug de AB SAG and the MAN de Yesod de AK, and then they came in a Zivug Panim be Panim and expanded to their Gufim, which are the seven Melachim.

    (Histaklut Pnimit item 6)

146. **Since the Seven Melachim do not belong to AVI, which are only from Behina Bet, they had to emerge from NHY de AK.**

    This is because according to the order of degrees, Komat ZA emerges only from AVI, which are Behinat SAG, and not from NHY de AK, which is Behinat Galgalta.

    ()

147. **What is the essence of the Achoraim de AVI that fell?**

    They are the Behinat Vav ו and Nekuda de Yesod de AK, meaning the general ZON, and all the Reshimot of the four Komot de Gadlut with their dresses.

    (Histaklut Pnimit item 15)

148. **Where is the place of the fall of each of the four Komot de Achoraim de AVI?**

    Each Rosh of the four Komot fell into Behinat its own Guf.

    (Histaklut Pnimit item 15)

150. **What are the four reasons that preceded the Zivug AVI Panim be Panim?**

    - The first is the ascent of MAN from NHY de AK to the Upper AB SAG, which mates them together.

    - The second, a new Ohr that came out of Zivug de AB SAG that fissured the Parsa.

    - The third, the descent of that new Ohr below Tabur and its exit to Keter de Nekudim, which lowered the Hey Tata'a from Eynaim de Keter to the Peh de Nekudim.

    - The fourth, the He'arah that emerged through the Yesod to AVI and became a MAN to the seven Melachim, which returned AVI Panim be Panim.

    (Cause and Consequence item 2)

149. **What are the twelve actions accustomed in every Melech of the four Melachim DHGT?**

    - The first is the Zivug on the Masach that measures the height of the Koma according to the place of the Hey Tata'a.

- The second is the *Zivug de AVI Panim be Panim*, measuring the *He'arat Hochma* for the *ZON*.
- The third, the *Koma* that elicits from below upward in *AVI* themselves.
- The fourth, the *Koma* that expands from above downward into *Behinat Guf*, called *Melech*.
- The fifth, the *Histalkut Ohr* to its *Shoresh* because of the mixture of the *Behina Dalet* in the *Kli*.
- The sixth is the fall of the *Kli* to the *GAR de BYA*.
- The seventh is the remaining of the *Reshimo* of the *Orot* that departed.
- The eighth is the descent of the *Reshimo* to *NHYM de Atzilut* in *Behinat Tagin* over the *Otiot*.
- The ninth is the fall of the *Achoraim de AVI* to the places of their *Gufim*.
- The tenth is *Tikun Kavim*, made in these *Achoraim de AVI* that fell.
- The eleventh is the ascent of the *Reshimot* from *NHYM de Atzilut* to the new *Kelim de HGT* that were made of the *Achoraim de AVI*.
- The twelfth is the descent of the *Kelim* from *GAR de BYA* as well, to *NHYM de BYA*.

(Cause and Consequence item 4)

150. **What are the four reasons that preceded the *Zivug Panim be Panim de* YESHSUT?**

    - The first is the ascent of the *Masach* that purified to *AVI*.
    - The second is its *Hitkalelut* in *Zivug Achor be Achor de AVI*.
    - The third is *Hitkalelut* in *Zivug Panim be Achor de AVI*.
    - The fourth is *Hitkalelut* in *Zivug Panim be Panim de AVI*.

(Cause and Consequence item 7)

151. **What are the eleven operations that were in each of the four *Melachim* TNHYM?**

    - The first is the *Zivug* on the *Masach* that measures the height of the *Koma* according to the place of *Tifferet*.
    - The second is the *Zivug de Panim be Panim* that measures the *He'arat Hochma* for the *ZON*.
    - The third is the *Koma* from below upward.

- The fourth is the *Koma* from above downward in the *Guf*, called *Melech*.
- The fifth is the *Histalkut* of the *Ohr*.
- The sixth is the fall of the *Kli* to BYA.
- The seventh is the *Reshimot* that remained of the *Orot*.
- The eighth is the ascent of the *Reshimot* to the new *Kelim de Achoraim de AVI*.
- The ninth is the fall of the *Achoraim de YESHSUT* into *Behinat Guf*.
- The tenth is the *Tikun Kavim* in the *Achoraim de YESHSUT* that were thus made into *Kelim de Tifferet*, *Netzah*, and *Hod*, to the new *Kelim* from the *Achoraim de YESHSUT*.

(Cause and Consequence item 17)

152. **Why did the ascent of Malchut in the Zivug of the two Ketarim de Daat tie all the VAK?**

    The ascent of *Malchut* means the ascent of the *Masach* after its *Hizdakchut* from all the *Aviut de Guf* in it, to the *Masach de Rosh de YESHSUT*. A new *Zivug* was made on it in *Koma de Behina Aleph*, and only the *Behinat* from below upward did not come out in it. It corrected the *Achoraim de YESHSUT* in *Kavim* and completed the *Tikun Kavim* in all the VAK.

    ()

153. **What are the 103 operations that emerged from one another in an order of cause and effect from after the situation de Achor be Achor de AVI until after Tikun Kavim of the new Kelim Tifferet, Netzah, and Hod, made after the breaking of the vessels?**

    This answer of cause and consequence is a continuation of the answer of cause and consequence presented in Lesson Six, answer 164. It explained there the necessity of cause and consequence from *Tzimtzum Aleph* down to the *Katnut de AVI de Nekudim* in a state of *Achor be Achor*.

    Here we shall continue to explain from the *Gadlut de AVI de Nekudim* to the *Tikun Kavim* of the new *Kelim*, namely the two lower thirds of *Tifferet* and NH that emerged after the end of the breaking of the vessels. We shall explain how there are a 103 actions here, and how they emerge from one another in complete necessity of cause and consequence.

    You already know that in general, the *Orot* are divided by two discernments: *Ohr Hochma* and *Ohr Hassadim*. Both contain five *Behinot*. The five *Behinot* de *Ohr Hochma* are called *KHB ZON*, and the five *Behinot de Ohr Hassadim* are called *HGT NH*.

The two above discernments emerged and hung from *AK ha Pnimi* until they came to *Komat* MA and BON. Three *Partzufim* emerged from *AK* in the beginning: *AB, SAG, MA,* and *BON,* until *AVI de Nekudim,* that were *Achor be Achor*. All these are from the first discernment *de Ohr Hochma*.

Afterwards, three *Partzufim* came out similarly in the second discernment from the *Ohr de Hassadim*. These are *AB, SAG, MA,* and *BON,* called *AVI, YESHSUT,* and *Daat*. All of them came out in *Olam ha Nekudim*, as is written in this part, and from them we shall begin our explanation here.

1) The first cause of the elicitation of the three *Partzufim* in *Behinat Ohr de Hassadim* are the *Reshimot de* MA and BON *de* AK that rose to MAN to the Upper AB SAG, and mated *Panim be Panim* (see Cause and Consequence item 1).

   b) Through this *Zivug*, a new *Ohr* emerged and fissured the *Parsa*.

   c) That new *Ohr* fissured the *Parsa* and came out through the *Tabur* to the *Keter de Nekudim*, and lowered the *Hey Tata'a* from the *Eynaim de Keter* to the general *Peh de Nekudim*. It returned *AVI* to the *Rosh*, and they obtained their GAR and thus came to a state of *Panim be Achor*.

   d) This new *Ohr* descended and illuminated to the *NHY de AK*. At that time *Yesod* illuminated the *Vav ו* and *Nekuda* to *AVI* in *Behinat* MAN, causing them the state of *Panim be Panim*.

Thus, the two operations, the third and the fourth, join *Panim be Panim*. *Panim de Abba* is a resultant of the third act, meaning of the new *Ohr* that illuminated through the *Tabur*, and *Panim de Ima* extends from the new *Ohr* that illuminated the MAN through the *Yesod*, causing the *Panim de Ima*.

It follows, that these four operations stem from one another and cause one another: The fourth and the third, which the two situations *Panim be Panim* and *Panim be Achor*, extend from the new *Ohr* that fissured the *Parsa*, which is the second operation, extended from the *Zivug de AB SAG*, which is the first operation. The cause for this *Zivug* is the raising of MAN from *NHY de AK*.

You must remember that the cause for raising MAN *de NHY de* AK is the *Hizdakchut* of the *Masach de Guf de SAG* that consisted of two kinds of *Reshimot*: *Reshimot de NHY de* AK, and its own *Reshimo*, meaning *de SAG*.

After it purified from its entire *Aviut*, it is considered to have risen and mingled in the *Rosh* SAG. Thus, first there was a *Zivug* on the *Reshimot de* SAG, contained in the *Masach*. From this *Zivug* rose the *Hey Tata'a* in the *Eynaim*, and the *AHP* of all the degrees were expelled outside the degree. Ultimately, the *AHP de Eser Sefirot de Sium*, meaning *Bina*, *ZA*, and *Malchut de Eser Sefirot de NHY de AK*, were expelled below the *Kav* of *Ein Sof* to the place of *BYA*.

This is the last consequence, in which we ended the answer of Cause and Consequence in Part Six. It is also the last operations that hung down from the *Hey Partzufim GASMB*, from the discernment of *Ohr Hochma*.

After that the *Zivug* of the Upper *AB* and *SAG* was made on the *Reshimot* contained in the *Masach* from the *NHY de AK* that returns and brings the *AHP* of all the rejected degrees back. This is because a new *Ohr*, elicited from *Zivug de AB SAG*, lowers the *Hey Tata'a* from the *Eynaim* to its *Peh* as in the beginning, and thus fissures and cancels the *Gevul de Parsa*, returning the *BYA* to *Atzilut*.

There are two things you must learn here:

- That the two above *Zivugim*, *Katnut* and *Gadlut*, contradict one another though they are both resultants of the same cause, being the *Hizdakchut Masach de SAG* that raised the two kinds of *Reshimot* to the *Zivug*.

The first *Zivug de Katnut*, which emerged on the *Reshimot de SAG*, raised the *Hey Tata'a* to the *Eynaim* and expelled the *AHP* from all the degrees. The second *Zivug de Gadlut*, made on the *Reshimot de NHY de AK*, lowered the *Hey Tata'a* from the *Eynaim* once more and returned the *AHP* to their degree. It follows, that they contradict each other.

- We must learn here that between the above two *Zivugim*, there is the intersection of the two above kinds of *Hey Partzufim*, from a discernment of *Ohr Hochma*, and from a discernment of *Ohr Hassadim*.

The *Zivug* that emerged from the *Hey Tata'a* in the *Nikvey Eynaim* on the *Reshimot de SAG* is the last *Partzuf de Hey Partzufim GASMB* from the discernment of *Ohr Hochma*. The second *Zivug de Gadlut* that emerged on the *Reshimot de NHY de AK* through the *Zivug de AB SAG* is the beginning for the *Hey Partzufim GASMB* from the discernment of *Ohr de Hassadim*.

From here on the *Partzufim* are discerned as primarily *Ohr Hassadim*, though there is only *He'arat GAR* in them, as the *ASMB de Nekudim* called *AVI*, *YESHSUT*, and *Daat*, were explained, which are *Behinat NRNHY de ZA*. Thus, the intersection of the two kinds of *Hey Partzufim* is found between the two above *Zivugim*.

1) Now we have thoroughly explained the four necessary operations to bring *AVI* to a state of *Panim be Panim*. These are raising MAN from *NHY de AK* to *Zivug AB SAG* and the new *Ohr* that fissured the *Parsa*, which came out of the *Zivug*, and the elicitation of the new *Ohr* through the *Tabur*. It lowered

the *Hey Tata'a* and brought *AVI* to a state of *Panim be Achor*, and its *He'arah* elicited through the *Yesod* in *Behinat MAN* that brought *AVI* to a state of *Panim be Panim*.

Now we shall explain the nine operations extending from that *Zivug Panim be Panim*, how they result from one another by way of cause and consequence. Also, all these nine operations were made in *Melech ha Daat* from the beginning of its making in the *Rosh de AVI* up to the cancellation of its *Zivug*.

There are two principal factors here, connecting into one action. The first of them measures the height of the *Koma*, and the second measures and receives only the *He'arat Hochma*.

The first factor is the measure of the *Aviut* in the *Masach*, evaluated according to the place of the *Hey Tata'a*. Here, it is *Behina Dalet de Hitlabshut* and *Behina Gimel de Aviut*, eliciting *Eser Sefirot* from below upward in *Komat Keter*. It is so because the place of the *Hey Tata'a* is in the general *Peh de Rosh de Nekudim*. This element is affected by the third action, the lowering of the *Hey Tata'a* from the *Eynaim*.

The sixth operation is the second cause, which is the return of the *Panim de Ima* that depends on the MAN, which is the *Behinat* general *ZON*, rooted in the *Vav* ו and *Nekuda* that received from *Yesod de AK*.

Thus, she does not receive from the *Panim de Abba* more than the measure of *He'arat Hochma de ZON de Ohr Yashar* that receives from *Bina de Ohr Yashar*. This measure is called *Halon* (lit. Window). Also, that second factor results from the fourth operation, which is the *MAN de Yesod de AK*.

Thus, the fifth operation, which is the measurement of the *Koma*, and the sixth operation, which is the measure of the *He'arat Hochma*, are caused by operations three and four.

Eser Sefirot de Rosh in *AVI* from below upward called *Daat de AVI* extend from the above fifth and sixth operations, whose *Atzmut* is *Hey Hassadim* and *Hey Gevurot*, but in *He'arat Hochma*. Its *Koma* is measured like *ZON de Komat Keter*, since the fifth operation measures *Komat Keter*, and the sixth operation limits it to *He'arat Hochma de ZON de Keter*.

This is the seventh operation, meaning the *Eser Sefirot de Rosh* in *Komat ZON de Keter*. Also, the *Malchut* of this *Rosh* expands in the full measure of *Koma* that is in the *Rosh*, descends and clothes *Melech ha Daat*, and this is the eighth operation, caused by the sixth operation.

Two operations extend from the eighth operation, being *Komat Keter* that clothed in *Melech ha Daat*: the ninth - the *Histalkut Ohr*, and the tenth - the death of the *Kli* and its fall to *BYA*. It is so because had that *Koma* been received in the *Kli de Daat*, it would have returned the *BYA* to *Atzilut*, as the *Zivug* came out on the *Hey Tata'a* that descended to her place as in the beginning, before *Tzimtzum Bet*, since the *Parsa* had already been fissured.

However, because of the mixture of the *Sigim* in the *Kli* the *Ohr* could not fully clothe in it. This is so because when the *Ohr* encountered the *Behina Dalet* that was mixed in it, it immediately departed to its *Shoresh*.

Thus, the *Kli* fell to the Separated *BYA*. Because there was the completion of *BYA* in it, it had to connect them to *Atzilut*. Since it did not connect them because the *Ohr* departed from it, it remained in the Separated *BYA* itself.

Therefore, you see that the measure of the *Ohr* itself, which is the eighth operation, caused its departure, as the *Kli* could not receive it, and this caused its fall to *BYA*. Because its measure would have placed it in the place of *BYA* in order to connect them to *Atzilut*, it thus caused the *Kli* itself to separate from *Atzilut* and fall to *BYA*, which is death to the *Kli*.

Two operations extend from the tenth and ninth operations, which are the *Histalkut* of the *Ohr* and the fall to *BYA*. The eleventh is the remaining of the *Reshimot* from the *Ohr* that departed, as that is the conduct of the *Orot*, that after their departure, they leave *Reshimot* after them in the place where they were. Thus, the eleventh operation is a consequence of the ninth.

The twelfth operation, which is the descent of the *Reshimot* to the bottom of *Atzilut* as much as they could, is a resultant of the tenth operation, which is their fall to *BYA*. For this reason they could not be inside the *Kelim* as they usually are, and were forced for shine on them from above, as *Tagin*. Hence, they descended to the bottom of *Atzilut* to come as close as they could to their *Behina*, to revive them.

The thirteenth operation is the cancellation of the *Zivug* in the *Rosh de AVI* and the fall of the *Reshimot* and the *MAN* to the place of its *Guf*. It is called "the cancellation of *Achoraim de AVI*," and it too is a result of the tenth operation.

This is so because when the *Kli* broke and fell to *BYA*, her *Masach* was cancelled and no longer received to the *Orot de Rosh*. It is known that any return of *Panim de Ima* was not at all for herself, but for the connection *de Ohr Yashar* that she has to administer *He'arat Hochma* to the *ZON*.

Hence, once the receiver broke, this whole *Zivug* was cancelled since all she wants for herself is *Hassadim*, by way of "because He delighteth in mercy."

Thus we have explained how the eleventh operation, being the leaving of the *Reshimot*, results from the ninth, which is the *Histalkut* of the *Ohr*, and how the two operations, the twelfth and the thirteenth, result from the tenth operation, which is the fall to *BYA*.

2) From the thirteenth operation, which is the cancellation of the *Zivug* from the *Masach* in the *Rosh de Komat Keter*, the *Hey Tata'a* leaves the place of the *Peh* and rises to the *Hotem*. This is because the *Histalkut* is executed gradually, from *Behina Dalet* to *Behina Gimel*, and from *Behina Gimel* to *Behina Bet* etc. until it leaves entirely.

You find, that when the *Zivug de Behina Dalet* leaves, which is the *Behinat Hey Tata'a* in the place of the *Peh*, she rises to *Behina Gimel*, which is the *Hotem*. Hence, two new operations are educed here, meaning the factors implemented in the *Hey Partzufim de Hassadim*: the first, to measure the *Koma*, resulting from the above thirteenth operation, and this is the fourteenth operation.

The second is to extend *He'arat Hochma*, extending from the remains of the *MAN de Yesod AK*. It is so because in the annulment of the *Zivug de Komat Keter*, only one part of the MAN ascribed to *Komat Keter* was cancelled, while the remnants still remained in *Ima*. They had returned her *Panim be Panim* in the new *Zivug* on the *Masach de Behina Gimel*, and this is the fifteenth operation.

Thus we have seen how the three operations, the fourteenth - the measurement of the *Koma de Behina Gimel*, the fifteenth - the *Hamshacha* of *He'arat Hochma* from *Koma de Behina Gimel*, both result from the thirteenth operation, being the annulment of the *Zivug de Komat Keter*. This is because they are the remnants that remained in the *Aviut* and in the MAN, after the annulment of *Komat Keter*.

The *Eser Sefirot* from below upward, called *Guf de Abba*, extend from the two operations fourteenth and fifteenth. The fourteenth measures the *Komat Hochma* in it, and the fifteenth extends the *He'arat Hochma* from this *Koma*, and this is the sixteenth operation.

Also, the *Eser Sefirot* extend from above downward to the *Guf*, called *Melech ha Hesed*, and this is the seventeenth, a resultant of the sixteenth.

Two operations of *Histalkut Ohr* from the *Kli de Hesed* extend from the seventeenth operation. This is the eighteenth operation, and its fall to *BYA* is the nineteenth operation, as we have explained above in the ninth and tenth operations.

The twentieth operation, which is the leaving of the *Reshimo*, extends from the eighteenth operation, which is the *Histalkut* of the *Ohr*, as this is the nature of any departing *Ohr*.

Also, two operations result from the nineteenth operation. These are the 21st operation, being the descent of the *Reshimot* to the bottom of *Atzilut*, and the 22nd operation, the cancellation of the *Zivug de Rosh de Komat Hochma*. It is in the same manner as in the twelfth and thirteenth operations that result from the tenth operation.

3) Two operations stem from the 22nd operation, being the cancellation of the *Komat Hochma*: the 23rd, which is a new cause for *Komat Bina*. This is because due to the cancellation of the *Zivug* from the *Hotem*, the *Hey Tata'a* rose to the *Awzen*, which is *Behina Bet*. The 24th is a *Hamshacha* of *He'arat Hochma* from *Komat Bina*, which is the second factor, as we have said in the fourteenth and the fifteenth that extend from the thirteenth.

The *Eser Sefirot* from below upward in *AVI*, called *Guf de Ima*, result from the two operations, the 23rd and the 24th. This is the 25th operation, where the 23rd measures the *Koma de Bina*, and the 24th extends the *He'arat Hochma* from this *Koma*.

The *Hitpashtut* to the *Guf* extends from the 25th operation, from the *Malchut* in her, the *Melech ha Gevura*, and this is the 26th operation.

The *Histalkut Ohr* extends from the 26th operation. This is the 27th operation, and the fall of the *Kli* to *BYA*, which is the 28th operation, similar to the eighteenth and nineteenth that result from the seventeenth.

The 29th operation, which is the leaving of the *Reshimo*, stems from the 27th operation, which is the *Histalkut Ohr*.

Two operations stem from the 28th operation, which is the fall to *BYA*. These are the descent of the *Reshimo* to the bottom of *Atzilut*, which is the 30th operation, and the cancellation of the *Zivug de Komat Bina*, which is the 31st operation, similar to operations twelve and thirteen that result from the tenth.

4) Two operations, the 32nd and the 33rd, are caused by the 31st operation, which is the cancellation of the *Zivug de Komat Bina*. These are the measurement of *Komat ZA*, as after the *Zivug* was cancelled from the *Awzen*, the *Hey Tata'a* rose to the *Eynaim*, which is *Behina Aleph* once more, and this is the 32nd operation, extending this *He'arah* to ZON, which is the 33rd operation.

The *Eser Sefirot de Komat ZA* from below upward in *AVI*, called *Yesodot de AK*, result from the two operations, the 32nd and the 33rd, and this is the 34th operation.

From the 34th operation stem the *Hitpashtut* to the *Melech* of the upper third of *Tifferet*, and this is the 35th operation. From that results the 36th operation, being the *Histalkut Ohr*, as well as the 37th, which is its fall to *Behinat* two lower thirds of *Tifferet*. This is similar to the two operations, the ninth and the tenth, that result from the eighth.

The resultant of the 36th operation, which is the *Histalkut Ohr*, is the leaving of the *Reshimo*, being the 38th operation.

From the 37th operation, which is the fall to BYA, extends from the cancellation of the *Zivug de Behina Aleph*. This is because through the breaking of the *Kli*, the receiver is cancelled, and the *Zivug de Rosh* stops, as it has no one to bestow to, and this is the 39th operation.

One operation is missing here, meaning the descent of the *Reshimo*, since the *Reshimo* remains in its place, as its *Kli* did not fall to BYA now, but to its two bottom thirds from the *Chazeh* downward, and the *Reshimo* can shine to it from its place form the *Chazeh* upward, without any descent.

YESHSUT and the *Melachim* of TNHYM

5) The ascent of the *Masach de Guf* with the *Reshimot* in it to AVI stems from the 39th operation, being the cancellation of the *Zivug de Behina Aleph* because of the *Hizdakchut* of the *Masach*. This is so because after the *Masach* has been purified from the *Aviut de Behina Aleph* to the *Shoresh*, and after all its *Aviut de Guf* has stopped from it entirely, it is considered that it rose and was incorporated in the *Masach of Rosh de AVI* (see Cause and Consequence item 5). This is the 40th operation.

The 41st operation, which is its *Hitkalelut* and renewal there in *Zivug Achor be Achor* that remains in AVI, stems from the 40th operation, being the ascent of the *Masach* to AVI.

From the 41st operation stems the 42nd operation, being the elicitation of the *Zivug de Panim be Achor* in AVI on the *Masach* and the *Reshimot de YESHSUT* contained in it. This is so because through the renewal of the *Aviut* in the *Masach* through its *Hitkalelut* in *Zivug Achor be Achor de AVI*, the *Aviut* returned over all the *Reshimot* contained in the *Masach*, except the last *Behina*, *Behina Gimel*, as only *Behinat Hitlabshut* was left of it.

Hence, a new *Zivug* over the *Aviut de Behina Gimel de Hitlabshut* and *Behina Bet de Aviut* was made there in the *Hitkalelut* in AVI. This is considered that the *Hey Tata'a* in AVI descended once more from *Eynaim* to *Behinat Awzen* and *Hotem*, contained in one another, and *Komat Hochma* came out there, which is the *Behinat Panim de Abba*.

However, *Ima* still does not return her *Panim* to *Abba* without MAN. For this reason they have now come to a state of *Panim be Achor*.

The 42nd operation, which is *Panim be Achor*, causes the 43rd operation, which is the state of *Panim be Panim*. This is because once the *Reshimot* contained in the *Masach* have thickened, they have become MAN for *Ima* too, as these *Reshimot* are from ZON, that always awaken MAN in *Ima*. For this reason she has returned *Panim be Panim* with *Abba*.

The 43rd operation, namely the state of *Panim be Panim*, causes the 44th operation, being the descent of the above *Komat Panim be Panim* that emerged in AVI to the *Guf de Nekudim*, to the place of *Chazeh* in *Tifferet*.

This is so because once the *Aviut* in the *Masach* with the *Reshimot* contained in it was recognized, it appeared in it that it is *Behinat Masach de Guf*, different from the *Behinat Rosh*. For this reason it descended to its *Shoresh*, from which it ascended, which is the place of the *Chazeh*.

It educed *Koma Eser Sefirot* there from the *Chazeh* upward to the *Peh de AVI*, as the measure of its *Koma* that it had in the *Hitkalelut* in AVI.

6) Four simultaneous operations, meaning up to the 48th operation, stem from the 44th operation, which is the descent of the *Koma* to the place from the *Chazeh* up to the *Peh*, called YESHSUT.

This operation, namely the clothing of YESHSUT on the place of *Guf de Nekudim* from the *Chazeh* to the *Peh de Rosh de AVI* where the four *Komot de AVI* fell after their *Zivug* has been cancelled (Cause and Consequence item 3), is called, "the fall of the *Achoraim de AVI*".

This, in turn, induced a *Hitpashtut* of *Gimel Kavim de KHB* in these *Achoraim*, from which four new *Kelim de DHGT* were erected in the place of *Rosh de YESHSUT*.

The *Rosh de YESHSUT* clothed them as any *Rosh de Partzuf Tachton* clothes the *Guf de Elyon*: A *Kli de Hesed* was made in the right line, a *Kli de Gevura* in the left line, and a *Kli de Tifferet* in the middle line, up to the *Chazeh*, meaning up to the place where the *Rosh de YESHSUT* begins to clothe.

By that, operations 45, 46, 47, and 48, were made. The 45th is the new *Kli de Daat*. The 46th is the new *Kli de Hesed* on the right. Operation 47 is the new *Kli de Gevura* on the left. Operation 48 is the new *Kli de Tifferet* in the middle up to the *Chazeh*, meaning only the upper third.

Four other operations result from these four operations: 49th, 50th, 51st, and 52nd. The 45th operation, which is the new *Kli de Daat*, causes the ascent of the *Reshimo de Daat* that was in the place of *Malchut de Atzilut*, and has now risen to the new *Kli* that was made in her place, and this is the 49th operation.

From the 46th operation extends the ascent of the *Reshimo de Hesed* to the new *Kli de Hesed*, and this is the 50th operation. From the 47th operation extends the ascent of the *Reshimo de Gevura* to the new *Kli de Gevura*, and this is the 51st operation. In addition, from the 48th operation stems the *Hitlabshut* of the *Reshimo de Tifferet* in the *Kli de Tifferet*, and this is the 52nd operation.

Three other operations stem from them, the 53rd, 54th, and 55th. The descent of the *Kli de Daat* that was in *Daat de BYA* stems from the 49th operation, namely the *Hitlabshut Reshimo de Daat* in the new *Kli de Daat*.

Now, because of the removal of the *Reshimo* from it, she descended to the bottom of *BYA*, meaning to their *Malchut*, and this is the 53rd operation.

The 54th operation is the descent of the *Reshimo de Hesed* from *Bina de BYA* to *Yesod de BYA*, resulting from the 50th operation, and the descent of the *Reshimo de Gevura* from *Hochma de BYA* to *NH de BYA*, which is the 55th operation, stems from the 51st operation.

7) Nine operations stem from the 44th operation, which is the *Rosh* of YESHSUT, from the 56th operation to the 64th operation, until that *Koma* is completely revoked. Two elements were extended there in the beginning. The first is that which measures the height of the *Koma*, extending from the *Hey Tata'a* that descended into *Behina Gimel*. This is the 56th operation. The second is the measure of *He'arat Hochma* from this *Koma*, being the 57th operation.

The measure of the *Koma* called *Histaklut Eynaim de YESHSUT*, which is *Behinat HG* in *He'arat Hochma* extends from the two operations, the 56th and the 57th, and this is the 58th operation.

A *Hitpashtut* to the *Guf*, to the *Melech* of the two lower thirds of *Tifferet* extends from the 58th operation, from the *Malchut* in it, and this is the 59th operation.

Two operations extend from the 59th operation: one is the *Histalkut Ohr* from the *Kli*, being the 60th operation, and the second is their fall to *BYA*. It is similar to the above explanation regarding the two operations, the ninth and the tenth, that extend from the eighth.

The leaving of the *Reshimo*, which is the 62nd operation, extends from the 60th operation, which is the *Histalkut Ohr*. It is so because the nature of the *Ohr* is to leave a *Reshimo* after its departure.

Two operations result from the 61st operation, which is their fall to *BYA*: the ascent of the *Reshimot* and their *Hitlabshut* in the new *Kelim*, since they cannot clothe in their *Kelim* as they have fallen to *BYA*. This is the 63rd operation.

The second is the cancellation of the *Zivug* and the fall of the *Koma* to the place of her *Guf*, called "the fall of the *Achoraim de YESHSUT*". It is so because after the *Kelim* were broken, its *Masach* purified, the *Zivug* of the *Rosh* was cancelled, and the *Koma de Rosh* fell to BYA. This is the 64th operation.

8) Two operations, the 65th and the 66th, stem from the 64th operation, which is the cancellation of the *Zivug de Rosh de YESHSUT* that was in *Komat Hochma*. Because the *Zivug de Behina Gimel* was cancelled and only the *Aviut de Behina Bet* remained in the *Masach*, the *Zivug* came out on it in *Komat Bina*, and this is the 65th operation.

The second is the *Hamshacha* of *He'arat Hochma* from this *Koma*, and this is the 66th operation. It is in the same manner that operations twelve and thirteen stem from the tenth.

The *Eser Sefirot* from below upward in *Komat Bina*, called *Guf de YESHSUT*, stem from the two operations, the 65th and the 66th, and this is the 67th operation. The 65th measures the *Koma* of *Bina*, and the 66th extends the *He'arat Hochma*.

The *Hitpashtut* to the *Guf*, to *Melech NH* results from the 67th operation, from the *Malchut*, and this is the 68th operation.

From the 68th operation extends the *Histalkut Ohr*, which is the 69th operation, and the fall to BYA, which is the 70th operation. It is in the same manner as the ninth and the tenth result from the eighth.

The 71st operation, which is the leaving of the *Reshimo*, results from the 69th operation, which is the *Histalkut* of the *Ohr*. Also, two operations stem from the 70th operation, which is the fall to BYA: the ascent of the *Reshimo* to the new *Kli de Gevura*, being the 72nd operation, and the annulment of the *Zivug de Komat Bina* of the *Rosh* and its fall to the *Guf*, which is the 73rd operation.

9) Two operations stem from the 73rd operation, which is the annulment of the *Zivug de Komat Bina*: it causes *Komat ZA*, which is the 74th operation. This is so because after the annulment of *Aviut de Behina Bet*, there still remains *Aviut de Behina Aleph*. The second is *Hamshacha* of *He'arat Hochma* from this *Koma*, which is the 75th operation.

The 76th operation is the *Eser Sefirot* from below upward in *Komat ZA*, called *Yesodot de YESHSUT*, caused by the two operations, the 74th and the 75th.

The 77th operation is the *Hitpashtut* to the *Guf*, to *Melech ha Yesod*, resulting from the 76th operation, form the *Malchut* in it.

Two operations stem from the 77th operation: the first is the *Histalkut Ohr* from the *Kli de Yesod*. This is the 78th operation. The second is the fall to BYA, and this is the 79th operation.

From the 78th operation, being the *Histalkut Ohr*, stems the leaving of the *Reshimo*, which is the 80th operation. In addition, two operations stem from the 76th operation, which is the fall to *BYA*: The first is the ascent of the *Reshimo* and its *Hitlabshut* in the *Kli de Daat*, which is the 81st operation. The second is the annulment of the *Zivug* and the fall of the *Koma* to the *Guf*.

10) There are operations that stem from the 82nd operation. These are the measurement of the *Komat Malchut*, being the 83rd operation, and the *Hamshacha* of the *He'arah*, which is the 84th operation.

The *Eser Sefirot de Rosh* in *Komat Malchut*, called *Malchuyot de YESHSUT*, stem from the two operations, the 83rd and the 84th, and this is the 85th operation. Also, from that operation stems the *He'arah* to the seventh *Melech*, being *Malchut*, and this is operation 86.

Two operations stems from the 86th operation, which are the *Histalkut Ohr*, being the 87th operation, and the fall to *BYA*, which is the 88th operation, as with the ninth and the tenth that stem from the eighth.

From the 87th operation, which is the *Histalkut Ohr*, stems the leaving of the *Reshimo*, being the 89th operation. Two operations stem from the 88th operation: the first is the ascent of the *Reshimo* and its *Hitlabshut* in the new *Melech de Daat*, being the 90th operation. The second is the annulment of the *Zivug* of the *Rosh*, and the fall of the *Koma* to the *Guf*. This is the 91st operation.

11) The ascent of the general *Masach de Guf de YESHSUT* with the *Reshimot* contained in it to the *Rosh de YESHSUT* for the renewal of the *Zivug* stems from the 91st operation, which is the cancellation of the *Zivug de Rosh* because of the *Hizdakchut Masach* in *Kli de Malchut*.

It is so because after the *Masach* had purified from *Malchut* too, the entire *Aviut de Guf* that was in it had completely stopped, and equalized with the *Masach de Rosh*. This is the 92nd operation.

The 92nd operation is the ascent of the *Masach de Guf de YESHSUT'* to its *Shoresh* to the *Masach de Rosh*. From it stems the renewal of the *Aviut* of the *Reshimo de Behina Aleph* in it, and the elicitation of the *Zivug de Komat ZA* in *Hitkalelut* in YESHSUT, and this is the 93rd operation.

The 93rd operation is the new *Koma* that came out on *Behina Aleph* in *Hitkalelut* in the *Rosh de YESHSUT*. From that stems the descent of the *Rosh* to the place of *Chazeh de Guf de YESHSUT*. This is from the upper *Perek de Yesod* up to *Peh de YESHSUT* at the upper third of *Tifferet* in the place of the three *Kelim*: the two thirds of *Tifferet*, *Netzah*, and *Hod*. In other words, it clothes its *Guf de Elyon*, as any *Partzuf Tachton*, and this is the 94th operation.

The 95th operation is the *Tikun Kavim* in the *Achoraim de YESHSUT* that fell to the *Guf* in this place, which the new *Rosh* clothes there, as mentioned above in item 7 in the *Rosh de YESHSUT*. It stems from the 94th operation, namely the *Halbasha* of the *Rosh de Komat ZA* to the place from *Yesod* upwards.

Three simultaneous operations stem from the 95th operation: these are the new *Kli* in the two thirds of *Tifferet* through its *Sium*, meaning up to the place of the new *Peh de Rosh*. This is the 96th operation. The new *Kli de Netzah* on the right is the 97th operation, and the *Kli de Hod* on the left is the 98th operation.

Five operations stem from these three operations: from the 96th operation, which is the new *Kli de Tifferet*, stems the descent of the *Reshimo* to the new *Kli de Tifferet*, and this is the 99th operation.

From the 97th operation, the new *Kli de Netzah*, results the descent of the *Reshimo de Netzah* from the place of *Gevura* to the new *Kli de Netzah* in its own place, and this is the 100th operation. From the 98th operation, being the new *Kli de Hod*, stems the descent of the *Reshimo de Hod* from *Gevura* to the new *Kli de Hod* in its own place, and this is the 101st operation.

Two more operations stem from the above-mentioned 96th operation, which is the new *Kli de Tifferet* that has been made: the first is the descent of the *Reshimo de Yesod* to the *Kli de Tifferet*, which is the 102nd operation, and the second is the descent of the *Reshimo de Malchut* to this *Kli de Tifferet*, being the 103rd operation.

Abbreviation for Cause and Consequence, without Explanations

1) The *Masach de Guf de SAG* rose to the *Reshimot de NHY de AK* to MAN to AB SAG and they mated *Panim be Panim*. This is the first operation.

   A new *Ohr* that fissured the *Parsa* and returned the AHP came out by the *Zivug de AB SAG*.

   Two operations stem from the new *Ohr*: it illuminated through the *Tabur* to the *Keter* and lowered the *Hey Tata'a* from the *Eynaim*, returned AVI to the *Rosh*, and brought them in a *Zivug Panim be Achor*. This is the third operation. The second is that through *Yesod AK* it illuminated MAN to AVI, and they came *Panim be Panim*. This is the fourth operation.

2) Two operations stem from the two operations three and four: the first measures the height of the *Koma*, which is the fifth operation, and the second extends *He'arat Hochma*, and this is the sixth operation.

From the two operations five and six stem the *Eser Sefirot de Rosh*. The fifth operation measures its *Komat Keter*, and the sixth operation extends *He'arat Hochma* from this *Koma*, which is the seventh operation.

The *Eser Sefirot de Guf* that expand to *Melech ha Daat* stem from the *Malchut* of the seventh operation, and this is the eighth operation.

Two operations stem from the eighth operation: The first is *Histalkut Ohr* from the *Kli de Daat*, being the ninth operation, and the second is the fall to BYA, which is the tenth operation.

The leaving of the *Reshimo* is caused by the ninth operation, and this is the eleventh operation. Also, two operations stem from the tenth operation: the first is the descent of the *Kli* to *Daat de BYA*, being the twelfth operation, and the second is the cancellation of the *Zivug Rosh* and the fall of the *Achoraim*. This is the thirteenth operation.

3) Two operations stem from the third operation, which is the cancellation of the *Zivug de Komat Keter*: that which measures the height of *Komat Hochma*, which is the fourteenth operation, and the second extends *He'arat Hochma* from this *Koma*. This is the fifteenth operation.

The two operations, the fourteenth and the fifteenth, cause the *Eser Sefirot de Komat Hochma*, called *Guf de Abba*. This is the sixteenth operation from the *Malchut* of the sixteenth operation, causing the *Eser Sefirot de Guf* that expand to *Melech ha Hesed*, and this is the seventeenth operation.

Two operations stem from the seventeenth operation: this first is the *Histalkut* of the *Ohr*, which is the eighteenth operation, and the second is the fall to BYA, which is the nineteenth operation.

The leaving of the *Reshimo* is a resultant of the eighteenth operation, and this is the twentieth operation. In addition, two operations stem from the nineteenth operation. The first is the descent of the *Reshimo de Kli de Hesed* to *Bina de BYA*. This is the 21st operation. The second is the cancellation of the *Zivug* and the fall of the *Achoraim*, which is the 22nd operation.

4) Two operations stem from the 22nd operation, which is the cancellation of the *Zivug*: the first, which measures for *Komat Bina*, being the 23rd operation, and the second, which extends *He'arat Hochma* from this *Koma*, which is the 24th operation.

The *Eser Sefirot de Komat Bina*, called *Guf de Ima*, stem from the two operations 23 and 24. The 23rd measures the *Koma*, and the 24th extends the *He'arah*, and this is the 25th operation. From *Malchut* of the 25th operation stems the *Hitpashtut* to the *Guf* to *Melech ha Gevura*, and this is the 26th operation.

Two operations stem from the 26th operation: The first is the *Histalkut Ohr* from the *Kli de Gevura*. This is the 27th operation. The second is the fall to *Hochma de BYA*, and this is the 28th operation.

The leaving of the *Reshimo* stems from the 27th operation, being the 29th operation. In addition, two operations stem from the 28th operation: the first is the descent of the *Reshimo* to *NH de Atzilut*, being the 30th operation, and the second is the cancellation of the *Zivug*, and this is the 31st operation.

5) Two operations stem from the 31st operation, that which measures *Komat ZA*, being the 32nd operation, and the second, which extends *He'arah*, being the 33rd operation. The *Eser Sefirot* called *Yesodot de AVI* stem from these two, and this is the 34th operation.

From *Malchut* of the 34th operation stem the *Eser Sefirot* to *Melech* Upper Third *de Tifferet*, and this is the 35th operation. Also, two operations stem from operation 35: the *Histalkut Ohr*, which is the 36th operation, and the descent of the *Kli* to the two lower thirds of *Tifferet*; this is the 37th operation.

The 36th operation induces the leaving of the *Reshimo*, which is the 38th operation, and the 37th operation induces the cancellation of the *Zivug de Rosh* and the fall of the *Achoraim*, being the 39th operation.

6) The ascent of the *Masach* and the *Reshimot* in it to the *Masach de Rosh* to *AVI* is the 40th operation, resulting from the 39th operation. The *Hitkalelut* of the *Masach* in the *Zivug Achor be Achor* is the 41st operation, resulting from the 40th operation, and its *Hitkalelut* in *Panim be Achor* in *AVI*, being the 42nd operation, stems from the 41st operation. Also, its *Hitkalelut* in *Panim be Panim de AVI* is the 43rd operation, resulting from the 42nd operation.

The descent of the *Koma* from the *Rosh* from *AVI* to the place of *Chazeh de Guf de Nekudim* stems from the 43rd operation, and this is the 44th operation.

7) Four simultaneous operations stem from the 44th operation. This is because its *He'arah* connects all four *Komot de Achoraim de AVI* that fell to the *Guf* and became four new *Kelim*. The first is *Daat*, which is the 45th operation; the second is *Hesed* on the right, which is the 46th operation; the third is *Gevura* on the left, being the 47th operation; and the fourth is the upper third of *Tifferet*, in the middle, and this is the 48th operation.

Four other operations stem from these four above operations:

The ascent of the *Reshimo de Daat* from *Malchut de Atzilut* clothes the new *Daat*. This is the 49th operation, a resultant of the 45th operation. Operation 50 is the ascent of the *Reshimo de Hesed* there, resulting from the 46th operation.

From the 47th stems the ascent of the *Reshimo de Gevura* there, and this is the 51st operation. Also, from the 48th operation stems the ascent of *Tifferet* there, and this is the 52nd operation.

Three other operations stem from them: From the 49th operation stems the descent of the *Kli de Daat* to *Malchut de BYA*, being the 53rd operation; from operation 50 stems the descent of *Kli de Hesed* to *Yesod de BYA*, which is the 54th operation, and from the 51st operation stems the descent of *Kli de Gevura* to *NH de BYA*, being the 55th operation.

8) Nine operations stem from one another from the 44th operation, which is the *Rosh de YESHSUT*, up to the cancellation of its *Koma*. Two operations are caused first: the first is the measurement for *Komat Hochma*, which is the 56th operation; and the second extends *He'arat Hochma* from the *Koma*, and this is the 57th operation.

The *Eser Sefirot de Rosh* called *Histaklut Eynaim de YESHSUT* result from these two operations, being the 58th operation. From the 58th operation stems the *Hitpashtut* to *Melech* of the two thirds of *Tifferet*, and this is operation 59. Two operations stem from the 59th operation: the first is the *Histalkut* of the *Ohr*, which is the 60th operation, and the second is the fall to *BYA*, which is the 61st operation.

The leaving of the *Reshimo* is the 62nd operation, resulting form the 60th operation. Also, two operations stem from the 61st operation: the first is the ascent of the *Reshimo* to the new *Kli* of the upper third of *Tifferet*, which is the 63rd operation, and the second is the cancellation of the *Zivug* and the fall of the *Achoraim* to the *Guf*. This is operation 64.

9) Two operations stem from the 64th operation: the first measures *Komat Bina* and extends *He'arah*, which are the 65th and 66th operations.

From these two operations stem *Eser Sefirot de Komat Bina*, called *Guf de YESHSUT*, and this is the 67th operation. From the 67th operation stem the *Eser Sefirot de Guf* to *Melech NH*, and this is the 68th operation.

Two operations stem from the 68th operation: the *Histalkut Ohr*, and the fall of the *Kli* to *BYA*, which are the 69th and the 70th operations. From operation 69 stems the leaving of the *Reshimo*, which is the 71st operation. Also, from operation 70 stem two operations, the ascent of the *Reshimo* to a new *Kli de Gevura*, which is the 72nd operation, and the cancellation of the *Zivug* and the fall of the *Achoraim*, being the 73rd operation.

10) Two operations stem from the 73rd operation: measuring the *Komat ZA*, and extending the *He'arah*, which are the 74th and 75th operations. From them stem *Eser Sefirot de Rosh*, called *Yesodot de YESHSUT*. This is the 76th operation.

The *Hitpashtut* to *Melech ha Yesod* stems from the 76th operation, and this is the 77th operation. Two operations stem from the 77th operation: the first is the *Histalkut* of the *Ohr*, which is the 78th operation, and the second is the fall to *BYA*, being the 79th operation.

The 78th operation causes the leaving of the *Reshimo*, which is the 80th operation, and two operations stem from operation 79: the ascent of the *Reshimo* to the new *Kli de Daat*, being the 81st operation, and the annulment of the *Zivug*, being the 82nd operation.

11) Two operations stem from operation 82: it measures the *Komat Malchut*, which is the 83rd operation, and extends *He'arah*, which is the 84th operation. From them stem the *Eser Sefirot de Rosh*, called *Malchuyot de YESHSUT*, which is the 85th operation. From that stems *Hitpashtut* to the seventh *Melech*, which is the 86th operation.

Two operations result from the 86th operation: the *Histalkut Ohr* and the fall to *BYA*, which are operations 87 and 88. The leaving of the *Reshimo* stems from the 87th operation, and this is the 89th operation. In addition, two operations stems from the 88th operation: the ascent of the *Reshimo* to the *Daat*, which is the 90th operation, and the annulment of the *Zivug*, which is 91st operation.

12) The ascent of the *Masach* and the *Reshimot* to *YESHSUT* stems from the 91st operation, and this is the 92nd operation. From the 92nd operation stems the elicitation of *Komat ZA* in *Hitkalelut* in *YESHSUT*, and this is the 93rd operation.

From operation 93 stems the descent of this new *Rosh* to the place of *Chazeh de Guf YESHSUT*, being the 94th operation. From the 94th operation stems a *Tikun Kavim* in the *Achoraim de YESHSUT*, and this is the 95th operation.

In addition, three simultaneous operations stem from the 95th operation: a new *Kli* in the two lower thirds of *Tifferet*, which is the 96th operation, a *Kli* in *Netzah* on the right, which is the 97th operation, and a *Kli de Hod* on the left, which is the 98th operation.

Five operations stem from these three operations: from the 96th operation stems the *Hitlabshut* of the *Reshimo* of the two lower thirds of *Tifferet* there. This is operation 99. Also, from operation 97 stems the *Hitlabshut* of the *Reshimo de Netzah* there, which is the 100th *Reshimo*.

The *Hitlabshut* of the *Reshimo de Hod* there stems from the 98th operation, and this is the 101st operation, and from the above 96th operation, two other operations stem: the first is the *Hitlabshut* of *Reshimo de Yesod* there, being operation 102, and the second is the *Hitlabshut Reshimo de Malchut* there, and this is operation 103.

PART EIGHT

The Eser Sefirot of Olam ha Atzilut

1. * When the **Maatzil** wanted to revive the dead and correct these broken **Melachim** that were fallen into **Olam Beria**, He sentenced and raised MAN from below upward. Thus, there was a **Zivug Elyon de HB de** Inner AK, generating the new MA there, and the **Melachim** were corrected.

Ohr Pnimi

1. **Revive the dead.**

   Meaning the first seven fallen *Melachim* that fell into the separated *BYA*. This fall is considered death since they are separated there from the Light of life, meaning the *Ohr Hochma*, as it says, "wisdom preserveth the life of him that hath it." This is the reason that *Ohr Hochma* is called *Ohr Haya* (Light of life).

   Also, the three *Olamot BYA* are called The Separated *Olamot*, since the *Ohr Hochma* cannot expand in these places and everything in them will die without *Hochma*. They cannot be corrected except through ascent to *Atzilut*, meaning to the place where there is *Hochma* that can expand in them.

   Hence, when they rise to *Olam ha Atzilut* they are considered to have been revived, having been granted the *Ohr Haya*. It is written, **"When the Maatzil wanted to revive the dead,"** meaning to raise them from *BYA* to *Atzilut*, which is the revival of the dead. This is the meaning of the correction of the seven *Melachim*.

   He sentenced and raised MAN from below upward.

   Meaning from ZON to *Keter*. The matter of raising MAN has already been explained (Part 7, *Ohr Pnimi* item 24) and study it there. However, here we should understand another principal issue: These MAN are the seven *Orot* that remained of the seven *Melachim*, meaning the *Reshimot* that the *Orot de* ZAT left after their departure.

   This is so because once the *Masach de Nekudim* purified from its *Aviut* entirely, it returned and rose to its *Shoresh* in *Rosh de Nekudim* with all the *Reshimot* contained in it. Since it has already come there, in *Behina Aleph* in the *Zivug* of *Daat de Nekudim* (see *Ohr Pnimi* item 70), you find that its last *Behina* is *Behina Aleph*.

   Hence, the *Masach* did not become *Av* because of its *Hitkalelut* in the *Rosh*, but only to the extent of the *Aviut de Keter*, since the last *Behina* was lost.

Thus, only *Komat Malchut* could have come out on it. Thus, you find that the *Hey Tata'a* (lower *Hey*), incorporated in the *Masach*, rose from the *Eynaim* to the *Keter*, and the *Zivug* was made on *Sefirat Keter*. It turns out that the above rising of MAN is to the place of *Keter*.

2. It has already been explained that the seven *Orot* of the *Melachim de BON* rose, mingled and clothed the three *Kavim HB* and *Keter*, which expanded to the end of the above-mentioned place, being HGT.

Now that above *Hitpashtut* returned to be collected upward and became as it first was, when only three were in their place above. It raised the seven lower *Orot* with them to their place, and now all seven lower *Orot* were up in *Bina*'s place. This is because she is the Mother of the sons, and there is the place of the *Herayon* and *Ibur*.

Ohr Pnimi

2. Now that above *Hitpashtut* returned to be collected upward etc. It raised the seven lower *Orot* with them to their place etc. all seven lower *Orot*.

This above-mentioned *Hitpashtut* was entirely from *Behinat Hey Tata'a* (lower *Hey*) in the *Eynaim*. Now, that the *Masach* has been purified entirely from all the *Aviut de Guf* of *Behinat Hey Tata'a* in the *Eynaim*, they too rose and departed with the *Masach* and the *Reshimot* to their *Shoresh* in the *Rosh*.

[Written aside by the author: this is where the *Zivug de Katnut de Hey Tata'a* in the *Eynaim* comes from. However, it is insufficient from *Zivug de Gadlut* in GAR since GAR too are not corrected for *Gadlut*. They must raise MAN for *Zivug AB SAG de AK* that lowers the *Hey Tata'a* from the *Eynaim*. Thus, when it says that He sentenced and raised MAN, and hence there was the *Zivug de HB*, it is only for the descent of the *Hey Tata'a* from the *Eynaim*, like the new *Ohr de Nekudim* that fissured the *Parsa*.]

Here we must remember what the Rav has written above (Part 7 item 49), that these *Achoraim* that fell to HGT are the *Behinat* MAN *de AVI*, which ZON always raise for them until *Gmar Tikun*.

Also, you know that the *Hitpashtut* of the three *Kavim KHB* to HGT are the *Achoraim de Keter* and AVI that fell to HGT (see Part 7 *Ohr Pnimi* item 60). It follows, that the *Reshimot* that rose, meaning the seven *Orot*, are the MAN for ZON *de Atzilut* of all *Hey Partzufim*.

The *Achoraim de Keter* and AVI, which are the *Hitpashtut* of the three *Kavim KHB*, are the MAN for GAR of all the *Partzufim de Atzilut*, and remember that. You will also learn here how ZON, which are the seven *Orot*, raised the

MAN *de AVI*, which are their *Achoraim*. This is because the *Hizdakchut* of the *Masach* of ZAT raised the above-mentioned *Hitpashtut* above, to their *Shoresh*, to GAR, as the Rav explained (Part 7 item 49).

In *Bina*'s place. This is because she is the Mother of the sons, and there is the place of the *Herayon* and *Ibur*.

This is because the matter of raising MAN applies only to *Sefirat Bina*. Even raising MAN to *Malchut* is only after it was corrected with the corrections of *Ima*. The reason is that the entire connection of raising MAN is by *Bina*'s correlation with ZON *de Ohr Yashar* (see Part 7, *Ohr Pnimi* item 24). Hence it does not apply to the other *Sefirot*, which are not in possession of this correlation.

3. When the seven *Orot* rose upward, the *Kelim* that descended into *Beria* rose upward to *Atzilut* as well. However, they did not join together. The seven *Orot* were in a state of *Ibur* and "*Gimel* contained in *Gimel*", and the *Nekudat* (*Nekuda* of) *Malchut* was their seventh, in the form of *Psia le Bar*. Likewise, the seven *Kelim* were also in that manner, *Gimel* contained in *Gimel*, and *Malchut* along with them.

Ohr Pnimi

3. **The *Kelim* that descended into *Beria* rose upward to *Atzilut* as well.**

   He tells us that the ascent of the *Orot*, meaning the *Reshimot* in the correction of the MAN, correct their *Kelim* along with them to the extent that the *Reshimot* were connected in this ascent. This is because the *Reshimot* always receive the *Tikun Kelim*. This is what he means when he says that when the seven *Orot* rose upward, the *Kelim* that descended to *Beria* rose up in *Atzilut* as well.

   However, they did not join together.

   This means that although the place of the *Reshimot* is in their *Kelim*, and although the *Kelim* have already been connected by them to rise into *Atzilut*, the *Reshimot* are still unable to clothe in their *Kelim*. This is because the *Reshimot* themselves still haven't received their complete correction through that ascent of MAN; they still need *Zivugim*, called months of *Ibur* (will be explained in their place). By the *Reshimot* being in the intestines of *Bina*, they acquire all the MAD from the *Zivugim de Ibur* and become completely corrected, and then clothe their *Kelim*.

4. **However, the *Behinat* MAN we have mentioned above, when they rose for the *Zivug Elyon*, is in itself the matter of the ascent of the seven *Orot* above in *Bina*. Remember this forward regarding the meaning of the topic of raising MAN.**

In this *Zivug*, all *Eser Sefirot* from *Keter* to *Malchut* must be corrected because even GAR are not corrected. Hence, this *Behinat* "raising" of these MAN was above in AB SAG de AK.

Ohr Pnimi

4. **Even GAR are not corrected.**

   This because nothing of the *Mochin de Gadlut* that they'd received in *Nekudim* remained in them, but only what was in them when they were first created by the *Zivug de Hey Tata'a* in the *Nikvey Eynaim*. Hence they lack all the *Behinot Gadlut*. This is why it is written that even the GAR are not corrected.

   Hence, this *Behinat* "raising" of these MAN was above in AB SAG de AK.

   This means that there is no raising of MAN but only from the *Tachton* to its *Elyon* by one degree, meaning from ZON to AVI, from AVI to AA etc. but not to the one higher than it by two degrees.

   It is written that since GAR also need *Tikun*, and they too need raising MAN, it is necessary that the Upper *Behina* of raising MAN will be the *Rosh* SAG. This is because the MAN de ZAT are corrected in AVI de *Nekudim*, MAN de AVI in *Keter de Nekudim*, MAN de *Keter* in *Rosh ha Aleph de Nekudim*, and MAN de *Rosh ha Aleph de Nekudim* are corrected in *Rosh* SAG, meaning every *Tachton* in its *Elyon*.

   He says above that all the MAN together, meaning both ZAT de *Nekudim* and GAR de *Nekudim*, rose to GAR de *Nekudim*, which are seven *Reshimot* of seven *Orot de* ZAT being the *Achoraim de* HB and *Keter*. However, that does not mean that all were corrected there together, but only gradually. Each *Tachton* raised the MAN of its *Elyon* to its *Ali Elyon*, which in turn, corrects them for the *Elyon*.

   Thus, each sorted out a part of the general MAN and raised them to its *Ali Elyon*, until they ascended to the Upper AB SAG.

5. *****Thus, by raising this above MAN, which are the aforementioned *Orot*, the *Behinat HaVaYaH de AB de Yodin* mated, namely the collective *Behinat Mochin de AK* with *Behinat Taamim de SAG*, which are AHP.**

   This is because these *Taamim de SAG* did not have any breaking in them, and hence mated along with the *Behinat AB de AK*. This does not refer to the departing *Orot* from the *Hevel AHP*, only to the *Behina* of their actual self and *Pnimiut*.

Ohr Pnimi

5. *Mochin de AK* with *Behinat Taamim de Ruach*.

Though all the *Nekudim*, even *Rosh ha Aleph* in them, extend from *Nekudot de SAG*, for which the MAN should have risen only up to the *Nekudot* in *Rosh de SAG*, in fact, they rose to *Nekudot de SAG*. However, because with this ascent, the *Zivug de AB SAG* occurred, during which the *He'arat AB* that reached *SAG* lowered the *Hey Tata'a* from the *Eynaim de SAG* to *Peh de SAG*, this connected the *AHP* that came out of *Rosh de SAG*. They return to *Behinat Rosh*, and the *Nekudot* connect with the *Taamim de SAG* into a single degree.

In that state, the *Nekudot de SAG* do not merit a name any longer, as they are annulled in the Upper *Behina* in them, being the *Taamim*. Hence, the ascent of MAN is also considered to have risen to the *Taamim*, for the *Nekudot* do not bear a name, as they are nullified before them, as the Rav has written (Part 6 item 6).

Know, that from here comes the rule that every ascent of MAN is from the *Tachton* to the *Ali Elyon*, and the *Ali Elyon* corrects them from the *Elyon*. This is because ZON raise the MAN their *Elyon*, which are YESHSUT, to the *Ali Elyon*, which are AVI. AVI correct them for YESHSUT, and so it is in all the degrees.

It is so because any ascent of MAN induces the lowering of the *Hey Tata'a* from the *Nikvey Eynaim* down, by which it acquires the GAR. Hence, when ZON raise the MAN de YESHSUT, they induce the lowering of the *Hey Tata'a* from the *Eynaim de AVI* downward. In that state YESHSUT connect with AVI into a single degree and YESHSUT acquires its GAR, meaning *Behinat AVI*. You see that the MAN that ZON raised for YESHSUT rose to *Behinot AVI*, meaning to the *Hey Tata'a* in the *Eynaim de AVI*, which in turn, lowered it, thus correcting the *Mochin de YESHSUT*.

Thus, the *Tachton* raised the MAN for its *Elyon*, which are AVI. AVI mated together on the MAN and lowered the *Hey Tata'a* from their *Eynaim* downward, and thus connected YESHSUT to their own degree, and YESHSUT acquired its GAR. Now you can understand the Rav's comparison (Part 6 item 6) of AB SAG to AVI and YESHSUT there.

This matter began in the first ascent of MAN in the *Olamot*, being the ascent of MAN of the Inner NHY de AK to the *Taamim de Rosh SAG* in the Rav's words above (Part 6 item 6), which lowered the *Hey Tata'a* from *Eynaim* to *Peh de SAG*.

However, since here the *Hey Tata'a* rose to *Keter*, which is the *Metzach*, hence, the *Hey Tata'a* descended from *Metzach* to *Peh*. It is written, "**By raising this above MAN, which are the aforementioned *Orot*, the *Behinat HaVaYaH* de AB de Yodin* mated, namely the collective *Behinat Mochin de AK* with *Behinat Taamim de SAG*, which are AHP.**" This is because *Rosh SAG* is called *Awzen, Hotem, Peh*, because the Upper *Behina* in it is the *Ohr* of the *Awzen*, meaning *Bina*.

It clothes *Partzuf AB de AK* from the *Chazeh* upward to *Peh de AB*. Hence, *HGT de AB de AK* are considered *Behinat Mochin* to *SAG*, and also as the general *Mochin* that extend from *AK*. this is because the first *Partzuf de AK* is higher than the *Olamot* and they only shine through *HGT de AB*, which are the *Mochin de SAG de AK*. After the *He'arat Mochin* from these *AB* extends to *Rosh SAG*, meaning to the *Taamim*, the *Hey Tata'a* descends from *Metzach* to *Peh*.

These *Taamim de SAG* did not have any breaking in them.

You must know here, that the breaking begins even before *Olam ha Nekudim*, meaning in the lower nine *de Partzuf SAG de AK*, called *Nekudot de SAG*, which expanded from *Tabur de SAG* down to its *Sium Raglin* (Part 6 item 3). Because they expanded from *Tabur* downward in the place of *NHY de AK ha Pnimi*, they mixed with *Behina Dalet*, which caused the *Tzimtzum* in both *Olamot*, called *Tzimtzum NHY de AK*.

Because of the mixing of *Behina Bet*, which is *Bina*, in *Behina Dalet*, which is *Malchut*, *Bina* acquired the *Behinat Tzimtzum* of *Malchut*. Hence, *Bina* and *ZON* departed from all the degrees outside, where *AHP de Rosh* came out into *Behinat Guf* and *Bina* and *ZON de Guf* came out to *Behinat NHY* below *Tabur*. *Bina* and *ZON* of the *Eser Sefirot de NHY* went completely out of *Atzilut* and became the Separated *BYA*.

Thus, in *SAG* too, *Bina* and *ZON de NHY* came out and fell to *BYA* as in the breaking of the vessels. However, this occurred only in *Nekudot de SAG* that expanded from *Tabur* down and mixed with *Hey Tata'a*. It does not concern the Upper half of *SAG* at all, called *Taamim*, which end above *Tabur de AK*. this is the meaning of the words, "The ascents of MAN were to the *Taamim de SAG*, which did not have any breaking in them."

Departing *Orot* from the *Hevel AHP*, only to the *Behina* of their actual self and *Pnimiut*.

There are two kinds of *AHP*:

1. *Rosh de SAG*, called *Taamim de SAG*. Because its *Koma* is up to *Bina*, it is named *AHP*.

2. The *Havalim* of *AHP*, which departed from the degree. They are considered branches that come out of *SAG*, which are *Se'arot Dikna de SAG* that become *Shorashim* to the *GAR de Nekudim* (Part 6 item 4). That is why it is written that the *Zivug de AB* was with the *AHP*, being the *Taamim de SAG*, and not with the *Partzuf Se'arot*, which came out, being *Behinot Nekudot de Rosh SAG* that were broken.

Although the *Elyon* is related to the *Eser Sefirot de Nekudim*, it is only the *Nekudot de SAG*, meaning the *Se'arot Dikna*. However, they are nullified in *Taamim de SAG* and do not bear a name at all, since the *Zivug de AB* connects them to the degree of *Rosh de SAG* during the *Zivug* (Part 8, *Ohr Pnimi*, beginning of item 5).

6. **When they mated together, a new *Ohr* was born from them, through this *Zivug*. This new *Ohr* is called *MA de Alephin*. It too is divided into four *Behinot TNTO*, containing the entire *Atzilut* in this manner: *Taamim de MA* is *Behinat Atik Yomin*; *Nekudot de MA* are *AA*; *Tagin de MA* are *AVI*; *Otiot de MA* are *ZON*. This *MA de Alephin* comes out from the *Metzach de AK*.**

Ohr Pnimi

6. ***MA de Alephin.***

Meaning *HaVaYaH* filled with *Alephin*, like that: Yod He Vav He (יו״ד ה״א וא״ו ה״א). The filling with *Alephin* indicates the correction of the breaking because this new *Ohr* that comes out of the *Zivug de AB* and *SAG* returns the *AHP* that were broken from the degree, to the degree as before.

This matter is implied in the shape of the *Aleph* (א), because it contains two *Yodin* and a *Parsa* in between. The first *Yod* is *Keter* and *Hochma* that remained in the degree. This is the *Mayim Elyonim*. The bottom *Yod* is the *AHP*, meaning *Bina* and *ZON* that were broken from the degree, and went out. This is the *Mayim Tachtonim*.

The *Kav* that separates between them is the *Parsa*, and the *Rakia* that separates between the *Mayim Elyonim* and the *Mayim Tachtonim*. A new *Ohr* emerges by the *Zivug Elyon de AB SAG*, fissuring that *Parsa* and connecting the *AHP* back to the degree.

Even though the matter of the breaking of the *AHP* happened back in *Partzuf Nekudot de SAG*, *HaVaYaH de SAG* is still filled with *Yodin*, not with *Alephin*. The breaking was at the bottom half of *SAG*, which are *Nekudot*. This is because there weren't any breaking in the Upper half, as the Rav said, that there weren't any breaking in *Taamim de SAG*. Hence, its Upper half, which are *Yod Hey*, are filled with *Yodin*, while its bottom half is already filled with א in its *Vav*.

This א implies the breaking of the *AHP* that occurred there. Know, that this א in the filling of *Vav de SAG* is considered the *Shoresh* of the name MA *de Alephin* (see Part 6, Table of Questions, item 1).

TNTO, containing the entire *Atzilut*.

The *Taamim* are *Keter*, *Nekudot* are *Hochma*, the *Tagin* are *Bina*, and the *Otiot*, ZON. The *Taamim de* MA, which are *Keter*, is *Atik Yomin de Atzilut*, AA is *Hochma de* MA, AVI are *Bina de* MA, and ZON are ZA *de* MA, called *Otiot*.

Comes out from the *Metzach de* AK.

It means that the ascent of MAN was to the *Metzach*, meaning to *Sefirat Keter de Rosh*, called *Galgalta*, where the *Metzach* is. The reason for it is the last *Behina* of the *Nekudim* is *Behina Aleph*. Hence, all that remains in the *Masach* is the *Behinat Aviut* of the *Keter* (see Part 8, *Ohr Pnimi* item 1).

We must remember that there is no ascent of MAN but to *Bina*. Hence, it does not mean that these MAN rose to *Keter de Keter*, but to *Bina de Keter*. Indeed, *Galgalta*, is regarded as merely *Bina de Keter*. You will also learn that *Galgalta* is divided like *Bina* and like *Tifferet*. Its Upper third is always covered and concealed in the *Achoraim de Bina*, but only in the two bottom thirds, which are *Behinat ZAT de Bina*.

The *Behinat* from *Chazeh de Tifferet* downward is where *He'arat Hochma* appears (Part 7, *Ohr Pnimi* item 45). Know, that this is the meaning of *Panim* and *Achoraim de Galgalta*. It is so because from the *Metzach* upward it is *Behinat* Upper third of *Tifferet*, concealed and covered in the *Achoraim de Ima*. For that reason the *Se'arot Reisha* cover there.

From the place of the end of *Se'arot* down to the *Eynaim* is a place called *Metzach*. It is considered the two revealed thirds of *Tifferet* from the *Chazeh* downward where *Yesod de Ima* has already stopped.

It is written, "**This MA *de Alephin* comes out from the *Metzach de* AK.**" This is so because the existence of the manifestation of the *He'arat Hochma* begins there. However, above there it is covered with *Se'arot Reisha* for it is *Behinat GAR de Bina* and the Upper part of *Tifferet*, where *He'arat Hochma* cannot appear.

7. We have already explained above that things advance gradually: The *Hevel* of the *Awzen* is unfelt. A little bit of *Hevel* comes out of the *Hotem*, and the *Hevel* of the *Hotem* is less than the *Hevel* of the *Peh*, though they are all equal in that they raise *Hevel*.

However, the *Ayin* has no *Hevel*, only *Histaklut*. The reason for this difference is that the three are *Behinat Taamim*, but the *Ayin* is *Behinat Nekudot SAG*, which is below the degree of *Taamim*.

Ohr Pnimi

7. Things advance gradually.

    It means that the sequence follows the gradual order of the *Aviut* in the *Masach*, as it contains five *Behinot Aviut*, discerned according to the *Sefirot de Ohr Yashar*. The first three *Behinot*, which are *Behina Dalet*, *Behina Gimel*, and *Behina Bet*, called "Peh", "Hotem", "Awzen", are actual *Havalim*.

    This is because they raise *Ohr Hozer* called *Hevel* in a manner sufficient for the emergence of *Partzuf* in RTS. They are the three *Partzufim*, Galgalta, AB, SAG de AK. However, *Behina Aleph de Aviut* does not raise sufficient *Hevel* for the *Hitpashtut* to the *Guf*. Hence, it is named *Histaklut Dak*.

    Behinat Aviut de Shoresh, called *Keter*, does not have *Hevel* for *Hitpashtut* in the *Guf*. However, by the ascent of *Hey Tata'a* to the *Eynaim*, *Behina Aleph* too becomes capable for the emergence of a *Partzuf*, which is the *Partzuf* called *Nekudim*, or BON.

    Also, by the ascent of *Hey Tata'a* to the *Keter*, meaning to the *Metzach*, *Behinot Shoresh de Masach* also become worthy of the emergence of a *Partzuf*. This *Partzuf* is called the new MA, which is the *Eser Sefirot de Atzilut*.

    Hence, this *Ohr Hozer* that comes out on the *Hey Tata'a* that rose to *Metzach*, is only called manifestation of *He'arah*, or *Ratzon*, and not as *Hevel*, or *Histaklut*. This indicates that it does not have actual *Aviut*, but *Behinat Shoresh* of the *Aviut*, hence the name *Ratzon*.

    The four *Behinot Aviut* are gradual magnifications in the will to receive. However, their *Behinat Shoresh* is only a *Behinat* will to bestow, without any will to receive, except that it is a *Shoresh* for them. For that reason it is named a mere *Ratzon*, or "*Ratzon* of the *Metzach*".

8. This new *Ohr MA* that comes out of the *Metzach* is the very last, hence it has no *Behinat Hevel*, like the three, and no *Behinot Histaklut*, like the *Nekudot* of the *Ayin*. It has only *Behinat He'arah*.

    This is the meaning of what is written in the Zohar (Idra Zuta): "Appearing in the *Metzach*." This is because there is only a separate manifestation of *He'arah*.

    It is also the meaning of what is written in many places in the Zohar, "When the *Re'uta* came to create the *Olam* of *Atzilut*." it means that

Metzach of the *Ratzon de AK* came up in His will to create *Olam ha Atzilut* by the new *Ohr MA* that comes out of Him, by which the entire *Atzilut* was corrected. Thus, the meaning of *Ratzon* is the aforementioned *Metzach* of the *Ratzon*, because the translation of the *Ratzon* is *Re'uta*.

9. *Behinat AB* is in the *Rosh* of *AK*, which are *Behinat Mochin*, and their place is inside, opposite the place of the *Metzach*, where the *Mochin*, which are *Behinat AB*, mate with *Behina SAG*, being *AHP de Taamim de SAG*. These are below the *Mochin*, at the end of the *Rosh*. Because of the great *Ohr* there at the *Metzach*, due to that *Zivug*, a new *Ohr* extended from it downward, named "The New *MA*".

10. When this new *Ohr* came out, named *MA de Alephin*, it sorted out what it could sort out from the *Nekudot de SAG* that had the breaking in them. These joined and participated with Him, and then the *MA* became *Behinat Dechura* and *SAG* became *Behinat Nukva*.

However, since this *SAG* has become *Nukva* to *MA*, it now acquired a different name, which is *BON de Heyin*, like this: *Yod, Heh, Vav, Heh* (יוד הה וו הה). It is no longer called *SAG*, but *BON*.

Ohr Pnimi

10. It sorted out what it could sort out from the *Nekudot de SAG* that had the breaking in them.

This examination begins at *Rosh ha Bet de Nekudim*, which is *Keter de Nekudim*. However, *Rosh ha Aleph de Nekudim* that stands above *Tabur* did not connect with this new *MA* because there wasn't any breaking in it. This is because the *Masach* stands below it and the *Aviut* in the *Masach* cannot blemish above its location.

SAG became *Behinat Nukva*.

This does not refer to *SAG de AK*, only to the *Eser Sefirot* of the *Nekudim*, which the Rav calls *SAG* because their *Kelim* are from the *Behinat* lower nine of *SAG*, called *Nekudot de SAG*.

11. The thing is that the name *SAG* is the general *TNTO*. Though these are only *Nekudot de SAG*, it is not called *SAG*, like the rest of it, because they are but a single item in the name *SAG*. Hence, when this item, being the *Nekudot*, connected with the name *MA* and became *Nukva* to it, it is now called *BON*.

Ohr Pnimi

11. Only *Nekudot de SAG*, it is not called *SAG*, like the rest of it.

As it is written in the previous item, the *Eser Sefirot de Nekudim* are sometimes called *SAG*, because their *Kelim* are from *Nekudot de SAG*, meaning its lower half. It is written, **"Though these are only Nekudot de SAG, it is not called SAG, like the rest of it, because they are but a single item in the name SAG."**

The essence of *SAG* is the *Taamim* in it. This means that before the *Masach* in it began to purify, there is *Komat Hochma* there. However, once it begins to purify from this *Koma*, there is no longer *Komat SAG* in it (see Part 6, *Ohr Pnimi* item 1).

12. Though it is necessarily so, that although they are only **Behinot Nekudot**, there is a **Behina** in them that joins with the **Taamim de MA**, and a **Behina** that joins with the **Nekudot de MA**. The same applies for the other divisions, though all together, they are only **Behinot Nekudot de SAG**.

    Through this connection of **MA** with it, these **Nekudot** have now connected and became **Nukvin** (pl. for **Nukva**) to them. That reason they are called **Melachim**, from the word **Malchut**, indicating that they've become **Nukva** to **MA de Alephin**.

Ohr Pnimi

12. There is a *Behina* in them that joins with the *Taamim de MA*.

    This is because the *Eser Sefirot de Nekudim* came out in five *Partzufim GASMB*. Hence, there is also *TNTO* in them, where each *Behina* connects in its opposite *Behina* in the *TNTO* of the new *MA*, though there are some changes in them that will be explained below.

13. *The realization of the place of the *Hitpashtut* of these male and female *Partzufim* was made of the joining of **MA** and **BON**. Their place is the place where the *Nekudot* that came out through the *Nikvey Eynaim* were at first, meaning from *Tabur de AK* to the *Sof* of its *Raglaim*.

    The *Ohr Metzach* is called **MA** there. Though it came out above the *Metzach*, it expands from there downward and begins its existence from *Tabur* to the *Sof* of its *Sium Raglin*.

Ohr Pnimi

13. The **Ohr Metzach** etc. and begins its existence from **Tabur** to the **Sof** of its **Sium Raglin**.

    This is because all *Eser Sefirot* of the new MA are an upshot of the *Eser Sefirot de Nekudim*, since they came out on the *Behinat Masach de Guf de Nekudim* that purified and rose to the *Metzach* (Part 8 *Ohr Pnimi* item 1). Hence, it cannot clothe *Rosh ha Aleph de Nekudim*, standing from *Tabur de AK* upward, but begins at the *Peh de Rosh ha Aleph*, which is at the place of *Tabur de AK*. Its existence necessarily begins from the *Tabur* to its *Sium Raglin*.

14. What has changed now from the beginning, when the **Nekudot** of the **Eynaim** came out, is that then the **Nekudat Keter** was by itself, alone in its place. After it was the **Nekudat Hochma** alone by itself, and similarly were all ten **Sefirot**.

   However, a great *Tikun* was added now. The point of *Keter* extended and expanded from its place down to close to the *Sium Raglin* of AK. This entire measure of *Hitpashtut* is called *Olam ha Atzilut*, and that point is called **Nukva de Atik Yomin**.

   Likewise, *Atik Yomin Dechura* that was made of the *Taamim de MA* expanded similarly too, and so did all the rest, AA and *Nukva*, AVI and ZON. They clothed one another up to *Behinat ZON* so that the *Raglaim* of all the *Partzufim de Atzilut*, whether *Atik*, AA, AVI, or ZON, all ended equally. They end together, slightly above *Sium Raglin* of AK, and this is the *Sium* of the entire *Atzilut*.

   By so doing, they became *Neshama* to one another, one clothing the other. Also, by that the creatures can receive the *Orot Elyonim*, which are now covered and clothing one within the other. Their *Kelim* grew too by expanding all the way down. Since they are big *Kelim*, they have the strength to receive their *Orot*.

Ohr Pnimi

14. **The point of *Keter* extended and expanded from its place down etc.**

   This means that one *Sefira* of *Keter* expanded into a complete *Partzuf Rosh* and *Guf* in itself. It is called *Partzuf Atik de Atzilut*, whose place begins at *Tabur de AK* and expands to *Sium de Atzilut*.

   The reason for this *Hitpashtut* is the ascent of the *Hey Tata'a* to the *Keter*. In *Nekudim*, when *Hey Tata'a* rose to the *Eynaim*, it caused each degree to divide in two: GE became the *Elyon*, and AHP became the *Tachton*, as in the division of AVI and YESHSUT.

   Now the *Hey Tata'a* rose to the *Keter* and all lower nine came out of the degree of *Keter*. Hence, *Keter* was divided and made into a complete degree in itself. From the *Metzach* upward they are the GAR in it, and the *Rosh* in it. From the *Metzach* down it is *Behinat Guf* and ZAT in it. It is called *Atik de Atzilut*.

Similarly, each and every *Sefira* of the *Eser Sefirot de MA* was divided into a whole *Partzuf* in itself, *Rosh* and *Guf*.

They clothed one another up to Behinat ZON.

This is because each *Partzuf* is born and comes out of the *Peh* of the *Rosh de Elyon*, hence clothing the ZAT *de Elyon* from the *Peh* down.

Slightly above Sium Raglin of AK, and this is the Sium of the entire Atzilut.

The *Sium Raglaim* of AK is at the actual *Nekuda de Olam ha Zeh*, as it is written, "And His feet shall stand upon the mount of Olives." However, the *Sium* of *Atzilut* is made in *Tzimtzum Bet de AK*, where *Bina* and ZON *de Eser Sefirot de NHY* from *Behinat SAG de AK* came out of *Olam Atzilut* and became the Separated *BYA*.

Thus, the distance between the *Sium* of the *Atzilut* and the *Sium Raglaim* of AK is as the measure of the above *Bina* and ZON *de Eser Sefirot de NHY*. It is written that the *Sium* of the *Atzilut* is slightly above *Sium Raglaim* of AK.

Their Kelim grew too by expanding all the way down. Since they are big Kelim, they have the strength to receive their Orot.

This is because the *Gadlut* of the *Kelim* means multiplicity of *Masachim*. The *Masachim* diminish the *Orot* to expand in measure and weight so that the *Orot* can exist in the *Kelim*.

15. This *Ohr* of the new MA that comes out of the *Metzach* is the eighth *Melech*, called *Hadar* (mentioned in Parashat Vayyishlach), where death is not mentioned in the Torah, since he did not die like the others. On the contrary, he corrects and sustains the first seven *Melachim* that died before him.

16. When he came out, he immediately began to sort these *Behinot Melachim* out, to make *Behinot Nukva* to him, called BON *de Heyin*. Hence, it is said about him, "and Hadar reigned in his stead; and his wife's name was Mehetabel." This is as the Zohar says, "Until now, the male and female were not mentioned at all. Now, however, because of them they all exist, for now there are visible male and female," as mentioned in Idra Raba.

17. *This above-mentioned *Behinat Ibur* was forced to wait and be delayed for twelve months, as it is written in the *Tikkunim* in an article called "The Measurement Line". The reason was to correct the entire *Atzilut*, which are the twelve *Behinot Atik* and *Nukva*, AA and *Nukva*, Upper AVI, YESHSUT and ZON, Yaakov and Leah. These are twelve complete *Partzufim*, hence the reason this *Ibur* had to last twelve months.

17. This above-mentioned *Behinat Ibur* was forced to wait and be delayed for twelve months.

Komat Malchut, which is the most restricted *Katnut* possible, is called *Ibur*. This comes from the word *Avara* (impregnation) and *Dinim*, as it is written "But the LORD became pregnant in me for your sakes."

However, here we should understand, that they are three *Sefirot* in thickness, in the form of *Gimel Kavim*, called NHY. This is because a lesser measure than that is not called a *Partzuf*, as it is written, "and behold a well in the field, and, lo, three flocks of sheep lying there by it," which are NHY.

Even though the *Koma* is but one *Sefira* of *Malchut*, still, because there is *Tikun Kavim* there, it contains three *Behinot*: right, left, and middle. These three *Behinot* in *Komat Malchut* are called *Netzah*, *Hod*, *Yesod*, hence we discern them as standing thickwise one within the other.

This indicates that although there are three *Sefirot* there, they do not increase *Komat Malchut* in any way. Instead, all those three are on a *Koma* of a single *Sefira*.

The issue of the months of pregnancy refers to renewals of *He'arot* that the *Partzuf* generates and manifests during the situation of *Behinot Ibur*. These are seven months, nine months, or twelve months. Any *Hidush He'arah* is called "Month", and here the Rav says that this *Ibur* consists of twelve months, to manifest twelve *Partzufim*.

The reason was to correct the entire *Atzilut*, which are the twelve *Behinot*.

It means that through the ascent of this MAN to the *Metzach*, which is *Behinat Bina de Keter*, where the *Eser Sefirot* on *Komat Malchut* came out, called *Ibur*, this *Ibur* needs to fully correct the entire *Atzilut*, all the way. Also, because they are twelve *Behinot*, they need twelve months.

The reason for that is because all the *Behinot* diminished, fell and broke during the breaking of the vessels *de Nekudim*, all together rose to MAN to this *Ibur*. The Rav said above (item 2) that they contain all the *Partzufim* from *Olam Atzilut* and BYA, all of them (see *Ohr Pnimi* item 4). This is because all four *Achoraim* of the Upper AVI and YESHSUT, contained in the three *Kavim* KHB, rose and regrouped above (*Ohr Pnimi* item 2), as well as the seven *Orot* of the *Reshimot* that remained of the seven *Melachim* that fell to BYA.

The four *Achoraim de* AVI and YESHSUT contain all the *Partzufim de* GAR that came out in *Atzilut*. Also, the seven *Orot* contain the ZON, four *Olamot*

Atzilut and *BYA*. Thus, all the *Olamot* contained in the *MAN* that rose to the *Zivug* to *Keter*, and thus must all be corrected by this *Zivug de Ibur*.

You already know that there is an opposite value between the *Orot* and the *Kelim*. In the *Kelim*, the *Elyonim* grow first, and in the *Orot* it is the opposite, the *Tachtonim* clothe first. Hence, *Komat Ibur*, called *NHY* clothes *Kelim de KHB*.

It turns out that by the above-mentioned general *Zivug*, all twelve *Partzufim* came out from the *Behinat Ibur*, one below the other, *KHB de Atik* and *Nukva*, and afterwards *KHB de Arich Nukva*. After that *KHB de AVI*, then *KHB de YESHSUT*, then *KHB de ZON*, and then *KHB de* Yaakov and Leah. All of them came out by the single *Zivug Elyon*, though they came one below the other in a gradual order.

18. *This **Behinat Ohr Metzach** is sometimes mentioned in the book of Zohar in that manner, which is "When the Upper *Metzach* appeared etc." The thing is that the profusion of *Ohr* in that place causes *He'arah* to expand and extend below.

    Reisha de AK is the place of the *Mochin* in it, being *HaVaYaH de AB*. Their place is inside the *Rosh* and the *Metzach* coats and covers opposite them. That was the place of the *Zivug* of the *Orot Mochin*, called *AB*, with **Orot de Awzen Hotem Peh,** called *SAG*.

    Hence, from that place itself, which is the *Metzach*, standing opposite the *Mochin*, came this new *Ohr MA* that was born out of the above *Zivug*. This *Ohr* that came out of the *Metzach* expanded from there down, and its primary existence stood from *Tabur de AK* down until close its *Sium Raglin*.

Ohr Pnimi

18. The profusion of *Ohr* in that place causes *He'arah* to expand and extend below.

    We have learned that all four *Achoraim de AVI* and *YESHSUT* and all seven *Orot* of the seven *Melachim*, all rose to *MAN* to the *Metzach*. It has also been explained that first there was a *Zivug* on the *Masach* only on *Komat Malchut*, called *Ibur*. That corrected only a very small portion of the general *MAN* that rose there, only the *Behinot NHY* in each *Partzuf* from the *Partzufim* of *Atzilut*.

    Accordingly, most of the *MAN* remained there without any *Tikun*. Also all these four *Komot Rosh* and *Guf*, contained in the *Achoraim* of the Upper *AVI* and the four *Orot DHGT*, the four *Komot Rosh* and *Guf* contained in the *Achoraim de YESHSUT*, and the four *Orot NHYM*, all these remained there without *Tikun*.

It is written, "**the profusion of Ohr in that place causes He'arah to expand and extend below.**" It is so because thus they became MAN to the Upper AB SAG. It is as he wrote that by this Zivug from the He'arat AB, the Hey Tata'a descends from the place of Metzach to the place of the Peh. Then the Zivug is made on the Hey Tata'a in the place of Peh, and Komat Keter de MA extends on it. This is the Behinat Zachar de Atik, meaning the first Koma of the new MA.

This Ohr that came out of the Metzach expanded from there down.

This is because this new Ohr that came out of the Zivug de AB SAG expanded and came to Rosh ha Aleph de Nekudim, standing from Tabur de AK upward, and from it to Rosh de Atik, standing in the place of GAR de Nekudim. Also, Rosh de Atik came out from the place of Peh de Nekudim upward to the Tabur de AK, and Eser Sefirot de Guf from Peh de Nekudim downward to Sium of the Atzilut.

We must thoroughly understand the difference between here and the previous Partzufim. In all the previous Partzufim the ascent of the Masach was after the completion of its Hizdakchut to the Rosh of its Partzuf Elyon, meaning its Shoresh.

Here, the Masach rose to the Ali Elyon since the Elyon of the new MA is Partzuf Nekudim. It had to rise to the Peh of GAR de Nekudim and not to AB SAG, which are the Partzuf Elyon of Nekudim. However, this thing was already explained by the Rav above (item 4), where he says that the reason is that GAR de Nekudim themselves are not corrected, hence the Behinat raising MAN there was to AB SAG.

GAR de Nekudim did not break, nor were they even touched by the cancellation of the Achoraim, since they are only Behinot additions to what they received through He'arat NHY de AK. However, their own Behina, meaning everything that came out at the beginning of their creation, was not cancelled from them even a bit.

Yet, since the Masach rose to them with all the Reshimot in it, their ascent caused the manifestation of the absence in them. This is because the whole issue of the correction of GAR de Nekudim was by the Achor be Achor, meaning the small He'arah that they received from the Ohr of the Awzen (Part 7, Ohr Pnimi item 5).

It is so because through the He'arah of the Achoraim de Bina, they are not blemished at all by the Hey Tata'a in the Eynaim, which is at Keter de Nekudim above them, preventing He'arat Hochma from them. Without it, they would not receive Hochma too, because of the He'arat Bina in them, which has no wish for Hochma, but for Hassadim, "for she delights in Mercy."

The *Masach* and the *Reshimot* rose to them, as all these *Reshimot* are *Behinot* ZON that require *He'arat Hochma*. They had already had *He'arat Hochma*, for even the four *Achoraim de AVI* and *YESHSUT* are also *Reshimot* from the *Komot* that emerged on the MAN of *Yesod de AK*, called *Vav* and *Nekuda*, which are *Behinot* ZON.

Then, *Ima de Nekudim* had to stop her *Behinat Achoraim*, and could not do so because of the *Hey Tata'a* above her. For that reason the deficit appeared because of the *Tzimtzum Hochma* by the force of the *Hey Tata'a* over her. Because the deficit appeared, they too had to rise to MAN to their *Elyon* to receive *Tikun*.

Thus, GAR *de Nekudim* were forced to rise with the *Masach* and the *Reshimot* to their *Rosh de Elyon*, which is *Rosh de SAG de AK*, and all of them became *Behinat* MAN to the *Rosh de SAG*. in the beginning, the *Masach* was incorporated in the *Zivug de Rosh SAG* itself. By that it did not become more *Av* from the *Behinat Aviut* in the *Keter de Masach* because the last *Behina* it had as a *Masach* in *Partzuf Nekudim* is *Behina Aleph*, and it is known that the last *Behina* is always lost by the past *Hizdakchut*.

It turns out that the *Masach* cannot become more *Av* now, but only in *Behinat Shoresh*, which is *Behinat Aviut de Keter*. It is therefore considered that the *Masach de Rosh SAG* rose for that *Zivug* to its *Behinat Metzach*, meaning *Galgalta*, which is *Keter de Rosh*.

The *Metzach* is a part of the *Galgalta*, but it is its *Behinat Bina*. The *Ohr Elyon* mated with the *Masach* and *Eser Sefirot* came out on it on *Komat Malchut*. This is so because even though the *Hey Tata'a* is also incorporated in this *Masach*, yet because she stands at *Keter*, only *Aviut de Keter* can manifest in her, producing only *Komat Malchut*. You already know that this *Zivug* is called *Behinat Ibur* and has three *Kavim*, called NHY.

However, this is still not all of it. In this *Zivug* the *Reshimot* are not corrected in the *Masach*, only the smaller part in them. Thus, there was still great pressure there, due to the abundance of *Ohr* of all the *Reshimot* that need correction. It is known that the *Reshimot de* ZON have a great connection with *Behinat Bina*, being SAG, to receive *Behinat He'arat Hochma* from her through the connection of *Bina* and ZON *de Ohr Yashar*.

Hence, he rose a second time to MAN to SAG *de AK*. Then *Rosh* SAG returned the *Panim* to the *Mochin* in it, meaning *Behinat HGT de AB*, clothed in its *Rosh* in *Behinot Mochin* and *Neshama*. The AB SAG are found to be mating and the new *Ohr* that comes out of this *Zivug* lowers the *Hey Tata'a* that rose to *Metzach* there, when reaching *Rosh* SAG.

This is because *Orot de AB* are always complete and there is no breaking in them, for which it lowered the *Hey Tata'a* to the place of the *Peh*, meaning in the place of the *Zivug*, operating in *AB* itself. Because the *Hey Tata'a* came to its place in the *Peh*, the *Masach* received *Behina Dalet de Hitlabshut* from her, and *Behina Gimel de Aviut* in her.

In that state the *Ohr Elyon* that mated with the *Masach* generated *Eser Sefirot* on *Komat Keter*. This *Koma* emerged on the *Masach* and *Reshimot* now contained in *Rosh SAG* itself. From there the *Masach* descended to the place of *Tabur de AK*, meaning to the *Tachton de SAG*, and the same *Eser Sefirot* came out in *Komat Keter*, which is *Behinat Rosh ha Aleph de Nekudim*.

The *Masach* descended from there to the place of *Peh de Nekudim* and there too *Eser Sefirot* came out in *Komat Keter*. These *Eser Sefirot* are *Behinat Rosh de Atik Dechura*. From *Peh de Nekudim* down, *Eser Sefirot de Guf* expanded from above downward, which are called *ZAT de Atik*.

In fact, the *Masach* should have come down to the place of *Chazeh de Nekudim* for there is its true *Shoresh*. This is because this *Masach* was from *Behinat Guf de Nekudim*, meaning from the *Hitpashtut* of the seven *Melachim*.

However, *GAR de Nekudim* needed it, for they receive *Komat Keter* from it, and hence hold it in their place. Moreover, it is considered their *Behinat Zachar* [another version from the manuscript of Baal HaSulam, requires scrutiny: It is truer to say that *Atik* clothes the *Guf de Rosh ha Aleph de Nekudim*. This is because *Atik* is *Rosh ha Aleph de Atzilut*. We can also answer that even though *GAR de Nekudim* actually stand below *Tabur de AK*, because of *Behina Dalet* that mixed in them, yet in fact, they clothe from *Peh de Rosh SAG* downward, and the *Atzilut* below *Tabur de SAG*.], meaning because it gives them *GAR*, which they do not have when they are first created.

19. *When the **Tikun** of the eighth **Melech** came, called **Hadar**, he first sorted out the **Nitzotzot** and the **Kelim** from among them too. Every thing he sorted from them was but the female parts in all the **Partzufim**. It is so because in the beginning, it started to sort out the purest among them through the **Ibur Elyon**.

    From that **Nukva de Atik** was made, after the **Ohr** of the 248 **Nitzotzin** mixed with the **Ohr** of the **Nekudat Keter** that remained in **Atzilut**. Also, the **Kelim** of the **Melachim** mixed with the new **Kelim** of the new MA. **Nukva de Atik** and **Atik** were made of all of that, and it follows similarly in all of them.

Ohr Pnimi

19. He first sorted out the Nitzotzot and the Kelim from among them too.

It means that besides sorting the *Orot de BON*, which are the *Reshimot*, he also sorts the *Nitzotzin* and the *Kelim* because by sorting the *Orot* and the *Reshimot*, the *Kelim* receive their correction too. This is so because the *Reshimot* correct and raise to themselves the *Kelim* that are related to them.

This matter of sorting out means that he gives them from his *He'arah*, as we've explained above. The *Rosh de Eser Sefirot* of the new MA that came out by the *Zivug Elyon de AB SAG* clothes the place of GAR *de Nekudim*, and they receive *Komat Keter* from him.

This is considered that the new MA sorted GAR *de Nekudim* and corrected them to be *Behinat Nukva* to him, meaning receive his bestowal. It is called "sorting" because each degree of the new MA sorted precisely those parts of BON related to his degree because all the *Reshimot* of BON from the GAR and ZAT rose to MAN at once (*Ohr Pnimi* item 17).

The new MA sorted them gradually, one by one, meaning according to the appearance of his own degrees. This is because when *Atik de MA* was created, it sorted the better among the general MAN, meaning the GAR *de Nekudim*. He added them to himself, to *Behinat Nukva de Atik*, and then when AA *de MA* was created, it sorted the part that belongs to his degree. He added it to himself, to his *Behinat Nukva* and so on similarly. It is for this reason that it is called sorting.

The female parts in all the Partzufim.

All the males were made of the new MAN, and all the females were made of the *Orot* and the *Nitzotzin* and the *Kelim* that remained of *Nekudim* after the breaking of the vessels. However, in AVI and ZON there is *Hitkalelut* of the BON in the males, and the *Hitkalelut* of MA in the females too. This will be explained in its place.

It started to sort out the purest among them through the Ibur Elyon.

The beginning of the sorting is during the first *Zivug* of the ascent of MAN to *Metzach de SAG* that was in *Rosh SAG* itself. At that time only *Komat Malchut* came out (*Ohr Pnimi* item 17).

Since that *Koma* and *Ibur* of the new MA had just come out, he immediately sorted for himself the *Orot, Nitzotzin* and *Kelim* that belong to him from the general MAN, in the same quantity and quality of the *Behinot Ibur*. They rose from BYA to *Atzilut* and were corrected there in the form of *Gimel* within

Gimel, and we have already explained that the *Komat Ibur* is the three *Sefirot* NHY.

They clothe the three *Kelim Elyonim KHB* because of the opposite value between *Kelim* and *Orot* (*Ohr Pnimi* item 17). You find, that now they were sorted and only the best, highest *Kelim* among the *Kelim* and *Nitzotzin* that fell to BYA, meaning *Kelim de KHB*, rose from BYA by the *Koma de Ibur*. That is the meaning of the words, "**in the beginning, it started to sort out the purest among them through the Ibur Elyon.**"

Nukva de Atik and Atik were made of all of that.

He wishes to say, ZAT *de Nukva de Atik*. However, GAR *de Nukva de Atik* were not sorted even a little bit from the *Nitzotzin* and *Kelim de BYA*. Rather, she is made of GAR *de Nekudim* from the same *Behinot* that the breaking did not touch at all.

20. **Aferwards, through Zivug de duchra de Atik with its Nukva, they brought up and sorted Nitzotzot that were fallen below, the suitable part for Nukva de Arich. They entered the place of the Ibur as Mayin Nukvin, where they sweeten and correct by spending the time of the Ibur, becoming Behinat Partzuf.**

Ohr Pnimi

20. **Through Zivug de duchra de Atik etc. the suitable part for Nukva de Arich.**

    The Rav was very brief here, relying on other places. Between the above *Zivug de Ibur* and the *Zivug Dechura* with *Nukva de Atik*, between them was the *Zivug de Gadlut* through AB SAG. It ejected the *Hey Tata'a* from the *Metzach* to the *Peh*, and *Eser Sefirot de Rosh* and *Guf de Atik* came out on *Komat Keter* (*Ohr Pnimi* item 18).

    This is so because a *Zivug* is not performed when the *Partzuf* is in *Behinat Ibur*. Only after the *Zivug de Gadlut de AB SAG*, when *Atik* and *Nukva* acquired *Komat Keter*, did they mate and sorted the *Nukva de AA*. He also does not explain here how the *Zachar de AA* is emanated here, for he only comes to clarify the sorting out of the females of *Atzilut*, and how they are all made of the name BON.

    Indeed, the matters of MA and BON, and how they connect, are generally quite scattered in the Rav's words, and they are also very brief. There is a great need to gather the essentials in a single place to make it possible to interpret all the many details that the Rav introduces before us.

First we must understand the difference between the new *MA* and the *BON*. Know, that the entire difference is the matter of the ascent of *Hey Tata'a*. In *BON*, all its *Kelim* are from *Behinat Hey Tata'a* in the *Eynaim*, as they so emerged at their creation, and in the new *MA*, all its *Kelim* are considered as *Behinat Hey Tata'a* that rose in *Galgalta*. It is so because this is how it emerged in the beginning of its creation, and anything that comes out in a *Partzuf* in the beginning of its creation never changes.

Even though it later receives additional *Gadlut*, the *Kelim* of the *Katnut* do not change by that, much less multiply. Instead, the same *Kelim* he had during the *Katnut*, in quantity and quality, grow in *Koma* and *Aviut* during his *Gadlut*, and remember that.

The *Zivug de Ibur* of the new *MA* has already been explained. Its origin is the *Masach de Guf* of the *Nekudim* that purified and rose to *Rosh de SAG*. By force of its *Hitkalelut* in the *Zivug* there, it became *Av* only in the measure of the *Aviut* of the *Keter*.

Hence, when it mated with the *Ohr Elyon*, it did not raise *Ohr Hozer*, but only on *Komat Malchut*. This is because the last *Behina* he had in *Guf de Nekudim* is *Behina Aleph*, and that disappeared with the *Hizdakchut* of the *Masach*.

However, you should remember that *Behinat Hitlabshut* always remains, even from the last *Behina*. Hence, here too there is *Behina Aleph de Hitlabshut*. It turns out that *Komat Behina Aleph*, which is *Komat ZA*, came out here as well. However, it is *Komat Zachar*, having *Zivug* only in the *Hitkalelut* with the *Nekeva*, which has *Aviut*, as there is no *Zivug* but only from *Behinat Aviut* (Part 6, *Histaklut Pnimit* item 14).

Thus, there really is *Komat ZA* here, but considering the *Behinat Kelim*, there are only *Kelim* from *Komat Malchut* here. For that reason it is only named *NHY*, being the three *Sefirot* in *Komat Malchut*.

Nevertheless, of course there is *Komat ZA* there as well, being *HGT*, meaning the three *Sefirot* thickwise from *Komat ZA*, but they are clothed inside *NHY*. This is because this *Koma* comes from *Reshimo de Hitlabshut*, from which there are no *Kelim*.

Know, that the name *MA* is primarily *Komat ZA* because *Komat Malchut* is never called by the name *MA*. Hence, *MA* is always considered half of the *Partzuf* of the *Zachar*. Because there is no *Zivug* from its own *Behina*, as there is only *Behinat Hitlabshut* in it, it cannot be corrected except by joining and mixing with the *Aviut* of the *Behinat Nekeva*. Thus we have explained the *Zachar* and *Nekeva* from the *Behinat* new *MA* itself, being the *Reshimo de*

Behina Aleph de Hitlabshut and the *Behinat Hey Tata'a* in *Galgalta*, which is *Komat Malchut* from the *Behinat Aviut*.

We might ask: "How then is there *Behinat MA* in all the *Partzufim*, since MA is only *Behinat Hitlabshut*, unfit for *Zivug* with the *Ohr Elyon*? For that reason it joins with the *Aviut* in the *Reshimot* of *Kelim de BON*. That is also the reason that *BON* is considered the *Nekeva* of MA, since his own *Nukva* operates only in *Rosh de RADLA*, which is the first *Rosh* of the new MA. From there downward it takes the *Reshimot de Aviut* of the *BON* for itself, as its *Behinat Nukva*, and remember that.

However, we have already explained that the MA of the first *Rosh*, though it too has its own *Behinat Malchut* there, it still sorted GAR *de BON* for itself as *Behinat Nukva*. Indeed, that *Zivug* is very hidden, and there are also doubts regarding the *Behinot* of *Nukva* there, and this is not the place to elaborate on them. I have already explained the doubts in my commentary on the Tree of Life "Panim Meirot and Panim Masbirot", and study it there.

There is a very important rudiment to know here: The *Nekeva* of the above new MA, which is its *Malchut*, remains concealed in *Rosh de Atik*. However, she does not appear at all in all the *Partzufim* below *Atik*.

Know also, that the *Hey Tata'a*, concealed in the above *Rosh de Atik*, manifests in the two bottom thirds of *Netzah* and *Hod de Atik*, though because of that they went out of *Atzilut* as *Dadei Behema*. However, it does not appear in the entire *Atzilut*, but only from her *Behinat He'arah*, and nothing of her *Behinat Atzmut*.

The primary difference between *Kelim de MA* and *Kelim de BON* is during the *Katnut*, meaning in the *Ibur*. On the part of the *Kelim de BON*, there should be a complete *Behinat ZA* even in *Behinat Ibur*, meaning three *Kavim HGT* and three *Kavim NHY*. This is because the *Katnut de BON* is *Hey Tata'a* in the *Eynaim*, leaving two *Kelim* in the *Behinat Atzilut* of all the degrees, which are *Keter* and *Hochma*, and ejects *Bina* and *ZON* to *Behinat BYA*.

Hence, each *Partzuf* has two *Orot Ruach Nefesh*, clothing two *Kelim Keter* and *Hochma*. However, on the part of the *Kelim de MA*, where the *Hey Tata'a* rose in *Keter*, only one *Sefira* remained in the *Atzilut* of all the degrees, namely *Sefirat Keter*. The lower nine of all the degrees went outside the degree.

For that reason there is only *Behinat ZA de Hitlabshut* in the *Zivug* of the *Katnut*, which is *Behinat HGT*, but it has no *Kelim*, while *Komat Malchut de Aviut* does have *Kelim*. Thus, HGT must clothe inside NHY, meaning in *Kelim de Komat Malchut*.

From this explanation you will understand the difference between GAR *de Atzilut* and ZON *de Atzilut*. In GAR *de Atzilut* there are only two *Zivugim*: *Zivug de Katnut*, called *Ibur*, and *Zivug de Gadlut*, though in ZA there are three *Zivugim*: *Ibur, Yenika, Mochin*.

The reason is that there is a great difference between the *Nukvin* (pl. for *Nukva*) of the two *Partzufim Atik* and AA, and the *Nukvin de AVI* and ZON. The *Nukvin de Atik* and AA are from *Behinat Keter de Nekudim* where the breaking did not strike at all. For that reason they were left with all the *Ohr* from the *Eser Sefirot* that extended to them from the *Nikvey Eynaim de SAG*, meaning the entire measure that came out during the *Katnut de Nekudim*.

It thus follows, that during the *Zivug de Atik* and *Nukva* to generate *Behinat Katnut de AA*, called *Ibur*, it is born out of there complete, in *Komat ZA*, which are *Orot de Ruach Nefesh* in *Kelim de HGT NHY*. The *Zachar de Atik* is *Behinat MA*, and there are no *Kelim* in his *HGT* since he is considered ZA of *Hitlabshut*. Yet, through its stay in *Behinat Me'i* (intestine) *de Nukva de Atik*, where her *Katnut* is also from the *Hey Tata'a* in the *Nikvey Eynaim*, he acquires the *Kelim de HGT* operating in the *Nikvey Eynaim*.

Thus, even the first *Zivug* of *Katnut de Atik* and *Nukva* brought out *Partzuf de AA*, complete in *Komat ZA* in *Kelim de HGT* and *Kelim de NHY*. Similarly, when AA and *Nukva* mated for the *Katnut de AVI*, called *Ibur*, they too were born in *Komat ZA*, complete.

This is so because *Nukva de ZA* too does not need her *Zachar* in the *Behinat Zivug de Katnut*, since she is *Behinat Keter de Nekudim*. Hence she gave AVI the *Kelim de HGT* from the *Behinat Hey Tata'a* in the *Eynaim*, and AVI came out in complete *Kelim de HGT* and NHY.

However, they lack GAR, for which they rose a second time for MAN, for *Zivug de Gadlut*, where *Atik* and *Nukva* emanated the GAR at one time for AA. Also, AA and *Nukva* mated and emanated GAR to AVI. It turns out that they were completed in two *Zivugim*.

It is not so with ZA because the *Nukva* is not complete in AVI, even from the *Behinat Katnut de BON*. Hence, even the *Behinat Katnut de BON* needs to receive from her *Zachar* from the *Behinat MA*.

It turns out that the *Zivug de AVI de Katnut* for the *Ibur de ZON* was in *Ibur* by the force of MA. Since MA is only *Komat ZA* of *Behinat Hitlabshut*, and in *Behinat Aviut* it has only *Komat Malchut*, it therefore has only *Kelim de NHY*. As a result, *Komat HGT* must clothe inside NHY.

Because of that ZA is born only on *Komat* NHY, where the *Behinot* HGT is clothed in it, and it has only *Kelim de* MA, which are *Komat Malchut*, where it is divided into NHY by *Tikun Kavim*.

Hence, it needs *Zivug de Yenika* in order to be completed with *Kelim* for HGT. It is so because through *Yenika* from its mother's milk it acquires the *Behinat Kelim* from the *Hey Tata'a* in the *Eynaim*, as it is written, "His eyes are washed with milk, and fitly set."

It acquires *Kelim de* HGT through this *Zivug*, and then *Komat* ZA is fully completed in *Behinat Nefesh Ruach* in it. *Ruach* clothes the *Kelim de* NHY, and in order to acquire GAR too, it needs to rise to MAN for a second *Ibur de Mochin*. Then AVI mate in *Behinat Gadlut*, and give him *Mochin de* GAR, and he is then fully completed.

Thus, ZA is not completed before it undergoes three *Zivugim*: *Ibur Aleph* for *Gimel* within *Gimel*, meaning HGT inside NHY, because it only has *Kelim* from the side of MA at that time. Then *Zivug de Yenika*, by which it acquires *Kelim* from the part of BON, from the *Hey Tata'a* in the *Eynaim*, at which time it acquires *Kelim de* HGT, and HGT expand from within the NHY as they already have *Kelim*. After that, *Ibur Bet de Mochin*, when it acquires its GAR.

However, GAR *de Atzilut*, which are AA and AVI, do not need a *Zivug de Yenika*, since they acquire *Kelim de* BON from the *Zivug de Ibur Aleph* too. This is because *Nukva de Elyon* has complete *Orot de* BON from the *Behinat Hey Tata'a* in the *Eynaim*, and does not need the *Behinat Zachar de* MA for that.

Consequently, as soon as they are born, they have complete *Kelim* for HGT and NHY. However, they need *Ibur Bet de Mochin*. Thus, they do not need more than two *Zivugim*, which are *Ibur Aleph de Katnut* and *Ibur Bet* for *Mochin*.

Now we come to the essence of the Rav's words here. He says: **"in the beginning, it started to sort out the purest among them through the *Ibur Elyon*. From that *Nukva de Atik* was made."** It means the first raising of MAN where all the *Behinot* of *Achoraim de* AVI and YESHSUT and the seven *Orot* of the seven *Melachim* rose, being that they were all contained in the *Masach de Nekudim* that purified and rose to *Behinat Masach de Rosh* SAG (*Ohr Pnimi* item 2).

Then, *Behinat Katnut* of *Atik* and its *Nukva* came out there because *Behinot* BON too, contained in the *Masach* that rose, joined with this new *Zivug*, but with the better parts in them, which is *Behinat Keter de* BON. After that *Atik* and *Nukva* rose to MAN to *Behinat Zivug Bet de Gadlut*, to *Rosh de* SAG.

In that state the *Rosh de SAG* mated with *AB*, which are the *Mochin*. The *He'arat AB* lowers the *Hey Tata'a* from the *Eynaim* of *Rosh SAG* to the *Peh*, like the place of the *Zivug* which occurs in *AB* itself. The *Komat Keter* emerges, *Atik* and *Nukva* come down to their place and produce *Eser Sefirot* from below upward in *Komat Keter* for their *Behinat Rosh*.

Then they expand from above downward to their *Behinot Guf* as well. However, we should remember that their *Behinot Katnut*, which came out in the first *Zivug*, still haven't changed in them. This is because any *Eser Sefirot* of this *Rosh* and *Guf* expanded in the first *Kli de Keter* that they had during the *Katnut*. From *Bina de Keter* upward, *Eser Sefirot de Rosh* on *Komat Keter* came out. From *Bina* down, *Eser Sefirot de Guf* came out.

Thus, *Kli de Keter*, which was but a single *Nekuda* before, now expanded into a complete *Partzuf*, *Rosh* and *Guf*, through the *Sium* of the *Atzilut*.

It is written, **"Aferwards, through Zivug de duchra de Atik with its Nukva, they brought up and sorted Nitzotzot that were fallen below, from the suitable part for Nukva de Arich Anpin. They entered the place of the Ibur as MAN, becoming Behinat Partzuf."**

Interpretation: It is known that all the MAN in general that belong to all four *Olamot ABYA* rose together as *Reshimot* incorporated in the *Masach*, up to *Rosh de SAG*. However, each *Partzuf* took only what relates to its own *Behina*, and left the rest for its following *Partzuf*. The second *Partzuf* also took the *Behinat MAN* from that entirety that belongs to its degree, and left the rest for the *Partzuf* that follows it, and so did all the degrees through the end of *Assiya*.

We have already explained the two *Behinot MAN* that *Rosh de SAG* sorted for the two *Zivugim de Katnut* and *Gadlut de Atik* and *Nukva*. He left all that remains in the general MAN to the sorts of *Atik* and its *Nukva*, for AA and its *Nukva*.

First, *Atik* sorted the *Behinat MAN* relating to the *Zivug de Katnut de AA* and *Nukva*, which is for their very creation, because the essence of the *Partzuf* is from the *Zivug de Katnut*. Conversely, the *Zivug de Gadlut* is not the essence in any *Partzuf*; it is considered as mere addition, being in the *Partzuf* intermittently, not permanently.

Hence, the *Partzufim* of *Atzilut* come out in two *Zivugim*, even the GAR among them. The reason for it has already been explained in previous parts, which is by the ascent of the *Hey Tata'a* in the *Eynaim* through the association of *Midat ha Rachamim* with *Din*.

Consequently, in the *Partzufim* of *Nekudim* the *Hey Tata'a* came out permanently. Here in *Atzilut*, however, the *Hey Tata'a* came out at the *Metzach* permanently, but it is permanently associated with the *Behinat Hey Tata'a* in the *Eynaim*.

Know, that this addition that was made here is the cause for this entire correction. Because the breaking that occurred in *Nekudim* due to the *Parsa*'s weakness, when the new *Ohr* of *Gadlut* fissured the *Parsa*, the *Parsa* no longer had the strength to refrain from expanding the *He'arah* to the Separated *Olamot BYA* too. Thus, *Tzimtzum Bet* was revoked entirely.

Now, however, through the ascent of the *Hey Tata'a* to the *Metzach*, the *Parsa* received great strength from the *Keter*, which is the *Shoresh* of every *Partzuf*. Hence, the *Parsa* covered and fortified so that even during the *Zivug de Gadlut*, when a new *Ohr* comes and fissures the force of the *Parsa*, that new *Ohr* still does not shine below *Parsa de BYA*. It follows that now there is subsistence for the *Gadlut*, as it does not revoke the *Katnut*. This will be explained below.

After AA and its *Nukva* came out in *Behinat Katnut*, AA returned and rose to MAN to *Atik* and *Nukva*. Then *Atik* and *Nukva* sorted the MAN from the collective that SAG left them for AA, meaning *Behina Gimel de Aviut* in the general MAN.

At that time there was a *Zivug* in *Atik* and *Nukva*, and *Eser Sefirot* came out in *Komat Hochma*. This *Koma* is considered *Behinat MA*, for the rule is that all the *Komot* that came out anew are considered *HaVaYaH de MA de Alephin*. That *AA de MA* sorted for it the bottom half of *Keter de Nekudim*, which became its *Behinat Nukva* as he gives her his *Komat Hochma*.

Atik gave the remainder of the MAN after *Komat AA* to AA and his *Nukva*. They sorted form them the MAN that relates to *AVI de MA*, meaning to the two *Zivugim de Katnut* and *Gadlut* that first sorted the MAN that relates to the *Katnut de AVI*. Thus, AVI were born in *Komat ZA*.

Afterwards, AVI rose to MAN to AA and *Nukva*, and they sorted the MAN de *Behina Bet* and generated *Eser Sefirot* in *Komat Bina*. *AVI de MA* descended to their place and dressed *HGT de AA*, while sorting *ZAT de Hochma* and *Bina de BON* for their *Behinat Nukva*.

AA left the remains of the MAN after the sorts to AVI, which in turn, sorted out the MAN that relates to ZON. First, they sorted the MAN that belongs to *Katnut*, mated on the MAN and generated *Katnut de ZON*, which is *Komat NHY* and *HGT* within it.

After that they descended for *Zivug de Yenika* and were completed in *Komat HGT* too. They came down and clothed below *Tabur de AA*, and AVI left for ZON the remains left after the sorts of ZON.

They, in turn, sorted them form *Partzuf Atik de Beria* in the same above manner, *Atik* for *AA* and so on likewise as in the five *Partzufim* of *Atzilut*. Also, *ZON de Beria* sorted from the remains of the general *MAN* that *AVI de Beria* left for them for *Atik* of *Olam ha Yetzira*. *Atik* sorted for *AA* etc. until *ZON de Yetzira*. *ZON de Yetzira* sorted for *Atik de Assiya*; *Atik de Assiya* for *AA de Assiya* etc. until *ZON de Assiya* were sorted in *AVI de Assiya*.

The rest of the sorts of *ZON de Assiya* are already considered complete *Sigim*, unfit to join *Kedusha*. For that reason they fell to the *Klipot*, from which *ABYA de Klipot* were constructed.

However, many *Nitzotzin* of *Kedusha* remained in them, even of the more important among them. They are sorted by the souls of the righteous in each generation until the end of correction.

When all the sorts are through, the construction of *ABYA de Klipot* will fall down, for their entire sustenance will have been sucked out, being the *Nitzotzin* suitable for *Kedusha*. Then it will be said, "He will swallow up death for ever."

21. Similarly, **Arich** sorted for **Nukva de AVI**, and **AVI** for **ZON**, the entire **Behinat Malchut** in them. This is why they are called **Melachim**, because all the **Malchuiot** (pl. for **Malchut**) were made of them.

    Similarly, in every *Eser Sefirot* themselves in each and every *Partzuf*, they were sorted in the above-mentioned order. What could not be sorted and rise in *Olam ha Atzilut*, even for the bottom *Nukva de ZA*, remained in *Beria*.

    Afterwards, all the parts of *Beria* were made of them, with its entire order of degrees. The *Nitzotzot* of *Beria* cannot be sorted by *AVI de Atzilut* since they cannot ascend above *ZON*, though they are sorted out in the *Beten* of *Nukva de ZA* through he *Zivug* with *ZA*.

22. There too it sorts only *Behinat Atik de Beria*. *Atik de Beria* is sorted there. *AVI de Beria* are sorted in *Arich*, and likewise always because it is impossible for any part to be sorted above the place of its degree, neither in place and nor in time. Instead, they follow one another, both in the order of degrees, and in the order of their time of correction. This is explained sufficiently.

23. *Only the *Behina* of the apparent *Malchut* is not in *AA*, but in its *Ateret Yesod*. It is so because all that is *Dechura*, but there is no actual *Nukva*. In *Atik Yomin* too there is no *Nukva* in itself, only the *Ateret Yesod de Atik* is *Nukva*, as in *AA*. However, afterwards, *Malchut* appears from that Upper

most *Reisha de Lo Etyada*, called *Atik Yomin*, who is above all these nine *Sefirot de AA*.

Ohr Pnimi

23. Only the *Behina* of the apparent *Malchut* is not in *AA* etc. …In *Atik Yomin* too.

As we have explained above (*Ohr Pnimi* item 20), the *Hey Tata'a de MA* was concealed in *Rosh de Atik*, and her *Atzmut* does not appear in the entire *Atzilut*.

Malchut appears from that Upper most *Reisha de Lo Etyada*.

It is called *Rosh de Atik Yomin*, which is the first *Rosh* of *Atzilut*, and where the *Hey Tata'a* was concealed. Her *He'arah* appears in *Malchut* of *Olam ha Atzilut*, meaning in *Malchut* that became a complete *Partzuf* for *Nukva de ZA*.

24. This is the meaning of "A virtuous woman is a crown to her husband." In the end of days, she will be greater than the sun, and this is the meaning of "became the chief corner-stone."

When *Malchut* appears below, she appears from that *Reisha de Lo Etyada*. This matter will clarify for you how every *Behinat Malchut* of the Upper *Olam* herself becomes the *Behinat Atik* of the *Olam* below it. It turns out, that the nine *Sefirot* are of *AA*, and the Upper *Reisha de Lo Etyada* above all, is the *Behinat Atik*.

Ohr Pnimi

24. This is the meaning of "A virtuous woman is a crown to her husband." In the end of days, she will be greater than the sun, and this is the meaning of "became the chief corner-stone."

This relates to the concealed *Malchut* in *Rosh de Atik Yomin*. She does not appear in her *Atzmut*, but only when all the *Makifim de Atzilut* enter into *Behinot* inner *Orot* in her lower nine, being the lower nine of *Rosh* and *Guf de AA* with his four *Malbushim*, which are *AVI* and *ZON*.

Afterwards, the hidden *Malchut* in *Rosh de Atik* appears, as it says, "she became the chief corner-stone," being *Rosh ha Aleph*, and all the *Olamot de ABYA* are her upshots.

It is written, "the nine *Sefirot* are of *AA*, and the Upper *Reisha de Lo Etyada* above all, is the *Behinat Atik*." This means that *AA* and all its four dresses, *AVI* and *ZON*, are considered *Hitpashtut* of her nine lower *Sefirot*, while she is *Keter* to them.

Malchut of the Upper *Olam* herself becomes the *Behinat Atik* of the *Olam* below it.

All the *Sefirot de Tachton* are influenced by the *Elyon* through a *Masach*. They are greatly lessened by the *Masach* they travel through, except *Malchut* of the *Elyon*, which does not travel through the *Masach* but fissures the *Masach* and passes to the *Tachton* (see Part 3, Chap 7, item 1).

25. *Regard *AA* and *Atik*. The *Zachar* took the entire *MA*, and the *Nukva* took the entire *BON*, since she is corrected and does not need him. However, from *AVI* onward the males had to first take the *BON* of the *Nekeva*, even the *Katnut* in her, in order to correct it. Afterwards they were given to her entirely and its *Shoresh* from the *Katnut* remained in them.

In *Gadlut*, he takes both his and hers and the *BON* is given to her *Partzuf* alone, while the *MA*, only its *He'arah*, which is *He'arat Hassadim*, but not the gist, since the gist remains in him.

It is the opposite in *BON*, because his gist is in her, with only *He'arah*. Yet, since he took it first, he has a large *Shoresh* from it, and thus his *Daat* is complete. However, the *Nekeva* takes only the *He'arah* from *MA*, and her gist is from *BON*, hence her *Daat* is small, even in *Gadlut*.

Ohr Pnimi

25. Regard *AA* and *Atik*. The *Zachar* took the entire *MA*, and the *Nukva* took the entire *BON*.

The *Zachar de Atik* is *Komat Keter* that came out on the *Hey Tata'a* that descended from the *Metzach* to the *Peh*. This is the new *MA* because all the *Orot* that came out by *Zivugim* in *Olam Atzilut* are called *HaVaYaH de MA*. Also, all the *Orot* and the *Kelim*, whose *Zivug* was made in *Olam ha Nekudim* are called *HaVaYaH de BON*.

Hence, *Nekudat Keter* of *Olam ha Nekudim*, whose Upper half was taken by *Atik* into his *Behinat Nukva* is considered *HaVaYaH de BON*. Thus, the *Zachar* is only *MA* and the *Nekeva* is only *BON*.

Similarly, the *Zachar de AA* is *Komat Hochma* that came out on the *Behina Gimel* in *Olam Atzilut*, hence it is *MA*. His *Nekeva* is the bottom half *de Nekudat Keter* of *Olam ha Nekudim*, hence it is all *BON*.

Since she is corrected and does not need him.

This means that the episode of the breaking of the vessels did not concern *Sefirat Keter de Nekudim* at all; she has all the *Ohr* that came out with her when she was first created. For that reason she is corrected in herself and does not need MA to correct her.

With regard to the *Zivug de Katnut*, she does not even need to receive *Ohr* from the new MA, since her *Ohr* is more important than the MA, as she is from *Behinat Hey Tata'a* in the *Eynaim* (*Ohr Pnimi* item 20). However, she receives her GAR from MA in terms of her *Gadlut*.

From AVI onward the males had to first take the BON of the Nekeva, even the Katnut in her, in order to correct it.

Since there was an annulment in their *Achoraim* due to the breaking of the vessels, hence, even when they are in a state of *Zivug de Katnut*, the BON needs the correction of the new *Ohr de Katnut* of MA. Thus, before it comes to the *Partzuf Nekeva*, the BON had to connect with the *Zachar* inside its *Kelim de MA*, to correct and complete it. Afterwards the *Zachar* gives the BON to the *Kelim* of the *Nekeva*, and the *Zachar* is regarded as the *Behinat Elyon* of the *Nekeva*, even during the *Katnut*.

Thus, the *Shoresh* of BON is regarded as remaining in the *Zachar*, while only a branch of it departs to the *Nekeva*. It is known in every *Elyon* and *Tachton* that although the *Ohr* relates entirely to the *Tachton*, since it passes through the *Elyon*, the gist of the *Ohr* remains in the *Elyon*, and only a branch of it is poured on to the *Tachton*.

Its Shoresh from the Katnut remained in them.

This means that a *Shoresh* of BON remains in the males since they first received it during the *Katnut*. Hence, though they later gave it to their *Nukva*, the gist of the *Ohr* remains in the males, as we have said above.

The MA, only its He'arah etc. but not the gist, since the gist remains in him.

This means that there is *Hitkalelut* of the *Nekeva* in the *Zachar* here. Because BON first comes to the *Zachar*, it is mingled with the MA in the *Zachar*. Thus, BON receives the *He'arah* of MA. Afterwards, when poured on to the *Kelim de Nekeva*, there is also *Behinat Orot de MA* to the *Kelim de Nekeva*, though the gist in her is the name BON.

In the *Zachar*, however, it is the opposite. This is because the gist in him are the *Orot de MA*, and BON that he took due to the *Hitkalelut* of the *Nekeva* in him is only considered *He'arah* in him, not the gist.

His Daat is complete etc. However, the Nekeva etc. her Daat is small, even in Gadlut.

The *Zachar* has complete *Hassadim* and *Gevurot* since *Hassadim* are from MA and the *Gevurot* are from BON. Since the *Shoresh* of BON remains in the

Zachar too, the *HG* in his *Daat* are also complete. However, the *Nekeva* does not have from the *Atzmut* of MA, being the *Hassadim* in *Daat*, but only a *He'arah*, hence her *Daat* is small.

26. This entire **MA and BON *de Gadlut*** is called "the departing addition". None of it remains but the **BON *de Katnut*** in both. This is in ZON. However, the MA and BON always remain in AVI, since they already had complete BON there at the time of the *Melachim*, in all ten *Sefirot*.

   Nonetheless, they too needed the MA and BON in the above way as in ZON, where the gist of the MA is in the *Zachar*, and its *He'arah* is in the *Nukva*. It is the opposite in BON because HB are only from *Bina de MA*, and their *Shoresh* is *Dinim* and not *Rachamim*, though they are MA.

Ohr Pnimi

26. **MA and BON *de Gadlut* is called "the departing addition".**

   Only what came out in the beginning of *Atzilut* is considered the *Etzem* of the *Partzuf*, meaning the *Behinat Katnut* in it. However, what it attains afterwards by new *Zivugim* is regarded as additions to its basic structure, and can depart from it.

   None of it remains but the BON *de Katnut* in both. This is in ZON.

   It seems that we should say "MA and BON in *Katnut*" since the *Katnut* is primarily the MA, and even the BON is rooted in MA and needs it. We must insist and sustain the version, and interpret that he calls MA *de Katnut* by the name "BON". This is because the *Yenika* that manifests the *Kelim de HGT* comes from *Behinat BON*, from *Behinat Hey Tata'a* in the *Eynaim* (see *Ohr Pnimi* item 20). Because this *Behinat BON* is higher than MA, he names the entire VAK "BON".

   Thus, the *Behinot Ibur* and *Yenika de ZA* are considered the very creation of ZON, namely the *Orot* of *Nefesh*, clothed in *Kelim de Ibur*, and the *Orot de Ruach*, clothed in *Kelim de Yenika*. However, *Zivug de Gadlut de MA* and BON, which are *Behinot GAR*, even if they are GAR *de Neshama*, they are considered additions, and depart when there is cause for *Histalkut*.

   In AVI, since they already had complete BON there at the time of the *Melachim*, in all ten *Sefirot*.

   Meaning MA and BON *de Gadlut* because MA and BON *de Katnut* remain even in ZON. This is because they already had complete BON in the time of the *Melachim* from *Behinat GAR* too. It means that the matter of the annulment of the *Achoraim* in them was not because of themselves, but because of the sons, being ZAT.

Hence, after the *BON* was erected once more in *Behinat GAR*, it is considered the *Etzem* of their creation. The rule is that anything that comes out complete in *Olam ha Nekudim* is considered the *Etzem* (essence) of the *Partzuf* here in *Olam Atzilut*. Since it was erected once, it never again departs.

The *Achoraim* of *AVI de Nekudim* were cancelled and they returned to being *Achor be Achor* there. Yet, as it was not because of them, they are considered whole. Hence, once they were corrected in *Atzilut* in *Behinat Panim be Panim*, they never return to *Achor be Achor*, as the Rav said in several places.

Nonetheless, they too needed the MA and BON in the above way as in ZON.

During the *Melachim* there was complete *BON* of *Eser Sefirot* in them, which helped them that MA and BON *de Gadlut* would not depart from them. However, since there was the cancellation of the *Achoraim* in them before they were corrected, they needed sweetening and correction from the MA. Before it clothes in the *Kelim* of the *Nekeva*, it must first connect with the MA, as it is in ZON. For that reason there is MA and BON in the *Zachar*, and MA and BON in the *Nekeva*.

Their *Shoresh* is *Dinim* and not *Rachamim*, though they are MA.

It means that the *Shoresh* of the *Dinim* is there, since "*Dinim* fall from *Bina*" in the form of *Butzina de Kardinuta*, concealed in the *Me'i de Bina*.

27. *This clarifies the connection of the name MA, the new *Ohr*, with the name SAG. Now it is called BON, being the sorts of the seven *Melachim* with the *Achoraim de AVI* too. This became *Zachar* and that became *Nukva*.

Ohr Pnimi

27. **BON, being the sorts of the seven *Melachim* with the *Achoraim de AVI*.**

Meaning from AA downward, as well as in the lower seven *de Atik*. However, GAR *de Atik* do not have any *Achoraim de Keter* in them, much less of ZAT *de Nekudim*.

28. We shall explain the division of the name MA. It is known that the *Yod Sefirot de Atzilut* are divided into five *Partzufim*. However, *Partzuf de Arich* is divided into another two, namely *Atik* and *Arich*.

It is known that the *Taamim* are in *Keter*, the *Nekudot*, in *Hochma*, the *Tagin* in *Bina*, and the *Otiot* in the bottom seven, as it is mentioned in the *Tikkunim*. So they are precisely in the division of the *Eser Sefirot*, whether in AB, SAG, MA or BON.

However, the *Yod Sefirot de Atzilut* made of these connections of MA and BON do not take them in this order.

Ohr Pnimi

28. **The *Yod Sefirot de Atzilut* are divided into five *Partzufim*.**

    This is according to the five known *Behinot*: *Komat Keter* comes out on *Masach de Behina Dalet*, *Komat Hochma* on *Masach de Behina Gimel*, *Komat Bina* on *Masach de Behina Bet*, *Komat ZA* on *Masach de Behina Aleph*, and *Komat Malchut* on *Masach de Behinat Keter*. You already know that *Komat ZA* that comes out on *Behina Aleph* consists of six *Sefirot HGT NHY*, hence the above five *Komot* are regarded as *Eser Sefirot*.

    The *Yod Sefirot de Atzilut* made of these connections of MA and BON do not take them in this order.

    It is so because of the difference between MA and BON. These five *Komot* that came out in *Atzilut* are called the new MA, since any *Hidush Ohr* that came out in *Atzilut* in addition to the *Orot BON* that were already in the *Kelim* during the seven *Melachim*, are called "the new MA. Also, the old *Orot* that were during the *Melachim* are named BON.

    However, you must understand that all the *Orot* of the above five *Komot* that came out on the five *Behinot* in the *Masach* in *Atzilut* itself, are regarded according to the new MA. However, each and every *Koma de MA* takes for itself a single *Sefira* from BON to be her *Behinat Nekeva*. There are changes in them since *Keter de BON* is divided into two; its Upper half connects to *Komat Keter de MA*, and its bottom half connects to *Komat Hochma de MA*, and some more changes.

    Hence, the *Partzufim* of *Atzilut* are found to be not very accurate in their order of *Komot* since the *Behinot* BON in the *Partzuf* must also be taken into consideration.

29. Indeed, *Atik* and *Arich*, called *Keter de Atzilut*, take the two *Behinot* of the name MA between them, which are *Taamim* – *Keter*, and *Nekudot* – *Hochma*. This is because each *Dechura* side of *Atik* is made of *Keter*, being *Taamim de MA*, and each *Dechura* side of *Arich* is made of *Hochma*, being *Nekudot de MA*. Thus, only *Keter de Atzilut*, which is *Behinat Atik* and *Arich*, takes the *Keter* and *Hochma* of MA to the *Dechura* side of them, and only the both of them are called *Keter de Atzilut*.

Ohr Pnimi

29. **Atik and Arich, called *Keter de Atzilut*, take the two *Behinot* of the name MA between them.**

MA is primarily in order to correct the BON. Hence, we name the *Partzufim* according to their relation to the MA, since it is their *Behinat Zachar*. It means that all the *Ohr*, poured in the *Partzufim*, is the *Behinat* MA, and thus it naturally controls their order.

In light of that, since *Atik* and *Arich* are both *Behinat Keter* of the *Nekudim*, they are also considered as *Keter de Atzilut*. Their state is necessarily according to how they relate to MA. *Keter de* MA is the *Behinat Zachar de Atik*, and *Hochma de* MA is the *Behinat Zachar* of AA.

It has already been explained that because of the ascent of the *Hey Tata'a* to the *Keter*, *Hochma* too departed from the *Behinat Rosh de Keter*. Hence, *Partzuf* AA relates to *Partzuf Atik* like a *Guf*, as it is *Hochma de* MA, clothing the *Guf de Atik*, though with regard to BON, they are both *Keter*. This is for the above reason that the situations are controlled by MA, as it is the owner of the *Ohr* in the *Partzufim*.

Keter and Hochma of MA to the Dechura side of them.

We must thoroughly understand that great change that was made here: The *Zachar* and the *Nekeva* of a single *Partzuf*, which are necessarily on the same degree, are compelled to be from two *Sefirot*. Moreover, the *Zachar* is to be from *Sefirat Hochma* and the *Nekeva* from *Sefirat Keter*. There is also, the matter of the division of the *Sefirat Keter* between the two *Partzufim* and why *Atik* did not take the bottom half of *Sefirat Keter de* BON too.

First, we shall explain why all three *Roshim* of *Nekudim* in *Zivug de Gadlut* in AVI *de Nekudim*, connected to AVI to be as *Eser Sefirot de Rosh* in *Komat Keter*, while here in the new MA it was not so. Moreover, in its *Zivug de Gadlut*, the *Hey Tata'a* came out from the *Metzach* and returned to her place in the *Peh* by *He'arat* AB, and the *Eser Sefirot* came out in *Komat Keter*. However, it only helped *Sefirat Keter*, and all other bottom nine *Sefirot* did not return to the *Rosh*. Furthermore, they did not receive anything from the *Zivug*.

The Rav writes that when *Atik* was corrected, it was not corrected from what is below *Atik* at all. Also, when AA was corrected, it was not corrected from what is below it whatsoever, and likewise with AVI and likewise ZON.

You already know the *Shoresh* of the new MA. It is the *Masach de Guf de Nekudim* that raised the *Reshimot* of the seven *Melachim* and the four *Achoraim de* AVI and YESHSUT and the *Achoraim* of NHY *de Keter*. It brought them to *Rosh de* SAG, to the *Behinat Metzach*, which is *Behinat Bina de Galgalta de* SAG. *Komat* ZA *de Hitlabshut* came out on it, and *Komat Malchut de Aviut* from *Bina de Keter* and above (*Ohr Pnimi* item 20).

Since the place of the *Zivug* is *Bina de Keter*, they received *Behinat Achoraim de Bina* there and were corrected *Achor be Achor* in the form of *Tikun Kavim*, called *Gimel Go* (within) *Gimel*. This is so because there is only *Komat Malchut de Aviut* here, and thus there is only *Komat NHY* here. *Komat HGT* that departed is but *Behinat Hitlabshut* and has no *Kelim*, and this is called *Gimel Go Gimel*, or *Behinat Ibur*.

Only the *Ketarim* were made of this *Komat Ibur* in all the *Reshimot* that rose to MAN there, and not all the *Eser Sefirot* in *Keter*, but only from *Bina* upward. This is because the *He'arat Achoraim de Bina* in them did not let them expand to ZON since the force of the *Achoraim de Bina* is only before it expands to *He'arat ZON*.

However, when she expands to *He'arat ZON* she is compelled to arrest her *Achoraim* and mate in *Hochma*, receive *He'arat Hochma* from him for the ZON (Part 7, *Ohr Pnimi* item 24). Thus, ZON is in the same situation here as ZAT de Nekudim, where the *He'arat Rosh* did not reach them because of the *He'arat Achoraim de AVI*.

You find, that besides *Hochma* leaving the *Behinat Rosh* into *Behinat Guf*, ZON *de Keter* itself also departed from *Behinat Rosh* into *Behinat Guf*, since the *Hey Tata'a* stands in *Bina de Keter*. Even the *He'arah* of *Gimel Go Gimel* did not reach them.

There is yet another matter here in the new MA. Since *Hey Tata'a* rose to *Keter*, *Parsa* was greatly strengthened, since as long as *Parsa* was in *Behinat Hey Tata'a* in the *Eynaim* she did not have the strength to exist during the *Zivug de Gadlut de AB SAG* too. This is so because the new *Ohr de Zivug AB SAG* descended and lowered the *Hey Tata'a* from the *Eynaim* to the *Peh*, fissured the *Parsa*, and illuminated in *Nekudim*. Consequently, the *Parsa* did not have the strength to detain the *Ohr* from expanding to BYA, and this is the reason for the breaking.

Now that the force of *Parsa* has been doubled by the *Hey Tata'a* that rose to *Keter*, she was greatly strengthened. Thus, even the *Zivug de Gadlut*, which lowers the *Hey Tata'a* from the *Metzach* to the *Peh* does not cancel the *Gevul de Katnut* of *Parsa* in any way. On the contrary, the *Kelim* only grow.

Thus, the new *Ohr* that descended from the *Zivug de AB SAG* and lowered the *Hey Tata'a* from the *Metzach* to the *Peh*, and the *Eser Sefirot de Rosh de Atik* that came out in *Komat Keter*, were also not cancelled by that ancient *Gevul de Katnut*.

ZON de Keter did not return to the *Rosh*, but by receiving the *Koma* of the *Rosh* from above downward, the *Kelim* grew in a way that *HGT de Guf* became

KHB, NHY into HGT, and new NHY emerged for them. However, they remained in *Behinat Guf*, and the form of *Rosh* did not return on them, as in AVI de Nekudim.

Hence, even though *Atik* was corrected in a complete *Koma de Eser Sefirot* through *Keter*, still, none of it reached *Partzuf* AA. This is because even its own *Guf* did not return to *Behinat Rosh*, much less the rest of the bottom nine *Sefirot*.

Therefore, this entire *Koma de Keter* came out and expanded only on the single *Sefira* of *Keter*, and the rest of the *Sefirot* did not receive anything from it. It was likewise in *Sefirat Hochma*, which expanded in itself by the two *Zivugim* Katnut and Gadlut, into RTS, and none of it reached *Bina* at all, etc. similarly.

Now you will understand that these *Eser Sefirot* in *Komat Keter* that came out in the *Koma de Histaklut Eynaim* of AVI contain within them all the other *Komot* that came out in *Nekudim*. They come here in the new MA one-by-one in five special *Zivugim*, meaning a special *Sefira* in each *Koma*, as has been explained above.

It is also not on an equal *Koma* as it was in *Histaklut Eynaim de AVI*, but one below the other: *Komat Keter* came out only in *Atik*, *Komat Hochma* came out in AA, *Komat Bina* in AVI, and *Komat ZA* in ZON. This is so because each *Tachton* comes out from the *Behinat Guf de Elyon* since the *Hey Tata'a* is above it.

It turns out that *Komat AA* is considered *Behinat Guf* with regard to *Keter*, and is not considered as *Rosh*, but only with regard to *Sefirat Hochma*. Thus, AA lacks the *Behinot GAR de Yechida* because it is considered *Guf* with regard to the *Ohr de Yechida*.

Also, AVI are considered *Guf* with regard to AA, which is *Hochma*. They are only considered *Rosh* with regard to the new *Zivug* made on the *Masach de Behina Bet*, which is *Bina*.

Nevertheless, all three *Partzufim* Atik, AA and AVI, are considered complete *Partzufim* in *Rosh* and *Guf*. AA still has *Rosh* and GAR from the new *Zivug de Behina Gimel*; AVI have *Rosh* and GAR from the new *Zivug de Behina Bet*. It is like the *Partzufim* GASMB de AK where each *Tachton* is a *Guf* to the *Elyon*, though it has complete *Rosh* in itself.

However, since ZON came out only on *Komat ZA*, which is *Nefesh Ruach*, hence they lack the GAR entirely, and came out as *Behinat Guf* without a *Rosh*. Examine the great lessening that occurred because of the ascent of the *Hey Tata'a* to the *Metzach*: Not only did it divide the *Sefirot* and each and every

Sefira came out in its own *Koma*, they also came out one below the other, until it caused ZA to come out without a *Rosh*.

However, through the new *Ohr* that descended from the *Zivug de AB SAG* in *Nekudim*, *Eser Sefirot KHB ZON* came out in *AVI*, and all their *Komot* were equal up to *Keter*, even the *Malchut* in them.

In addition, we must remember that there is a great difference between the *Kelim de GAR* of the *Nekudim* and the *Kelim de ZAT de Nekudim*. The *Kelim de GAR* are from *Behinat* First *Hey*, and have none of the *Behinat Hey Tata'a*.

Those *Kelim* came out by *He'arat NHY de AK* through the *Tabur*, by which the *Hey Tata'a* in the *Eynaim* came down to *Peh* of the *Nekudim* and *AVI* returned to *Behinat Rosh*. However, because *Ima* wants *Hassadim*, she still does not return her *Panim* to *Abba* to receive *Hochma*, except by MAN. These GAR are from the *Behinat Kelim de AVI*, which have no *Behinat Hey Tata'a* (Part 6, *Histaklut Pnimit* item 9).

However, the *Kelim de ZAT* came out by the MAN *de Vav* and *Nekuda* from the *Yesod de AK*. These MAN returned to *AVI Panim be Panim*, mated on the MAN, and generated *Komat Eser Sefirot* from below upward in *Komat Keter*, called *Histaklut Eynaim de AVI*.

From there downward it ejected the seven *Melachim*: First, *Melech ha Daat*; after the *Hizdakchut* to *Behina Gimel* they ejected *Melech ha Hesed* etc. Hence, only the *Koma* from below upward that emerged by the MAN *de Yesod de AK* is considered as *Behinat Rosh de ZON*, but not the *Komot* that emerged before the MAN, in the form of *Panim be Achor*. It is so since they have connection with ZON as they do not have any part in the *Behinat Hey Tata'a*.

It turns that those *Eser Sefirot* that departed to *AVI de Nekudim* in *Komat Keter* should be divided between the GAR in them, which have no connection with ZON, and the ZON in them, considered *Rosh* of *ZAT de Nekudim*. Now you see that these first three *Partzufim Atik*, *AA* and *AVI* that came out in *Nekudim*, are not connected with ZON *de Atzilut* any longer since they are from the *Behinat GAR* in the *Roshim* of *AVI de Nekudim*.

You can therefore understand that there are three *Behinot* in the *Eser Sefirot de Nekudim*, and there is a great difference in the way the are corrected:

- The first *Behina* is the *Behinat Katnut* that emerged in *Nekudim* by the ascent of *Hey Tata'a* in the *Eynaim*, meaning what emerged in their basic creation, being only *Behinat Achor be Achor*.
- The second is *Behinat Panim be Achor* that came out in *Nekudim* by the *He'arat Tabur de AK* that lowered the *Hey Tata'a* from the *Eynaim de Keter*

de Nekudim to the *Peh de Nekudim*. It returned the AVI to the *Rosh*, where *Ima* still remains in the *Achoraim* to *Abba* though she is turned completely into *Behinat Rosh*, "because He delighteth in mercy."

The difference between the first *Behina* and the second *Behina* is that in the first *Behina* where the *Hey Tata'a* was above AVI, AVI had only *Komat ZON*. However, now they have *Komat Keter* since the *Hey Tata'a* is in its place in the *Peh*.

Yet, although *Ima* can receive the *Ohr Hochma*, there is still an imprinted yearning in her by the nature of her creation in *Ohr Yashar* to want only *Ohr Hassadim*. Indeed, there is benefit from that to ZAT *de Nekudim*, that they can now receive *Behinat* complete *Ohr Hassadim* from *Ima*, being the *Behinot Eser Sefirot* in *Komat ZA* that expand to them from *Ima* that returned to the *Rosh*.

- The third *Behina* is the two *Roshim* that came out in GAR *de Nekudim* in *Behinat Panim be Panim*, on the MAN *de Vav* and *Nekuda* that they received from the *Yesod de AK* and their *Behinat* from above downward, called ZAT *de Nekudim*.

The best among them is the first *Behina*, meaning *Achor be Achor* that remained in *AVI de Nekudim*, which did not suffer from the breaking at all. After them it is the second *Behina*, meaning GAR *de AVI* that came out in *Behinat Panim be Achor*, since they are clean from *Hey Tata'a*, and the *He'arat Ruach Nefesh* that expanded in them to ZA is of the same merit.

Hence, there is a great difference between the two above *Behinot*: After they were corrected in *Atzilut*, their correction remained permanent and the blemish of the *Tachtonim* does not cause them any *Histalkut*.

However, this is not the case in the third *Behina*, as it comes by the MAN *de Yesod AK*, which is the *Behinot Vav* and *Nekuda*, meaning there is *Behinat Hey Tata'a* there. For that reason, its correction is not permanent, but all the *Tikkunim* that come in this *Behina* are in the form of ascending and descending, according to the actions of the *Tachtonim*. Remember all the above as it is an introduction to understand the Rav's words before us.

30. **AVI, called Hochma and Bina de Atzilut, take only the Bina of MA between them, which is the Behinat Tagin de MA. ZA de Atzilut and Nukva, which are the seven bottom Sefirot de Atzilut, take the Behinat Otiot of the name MA, which are also the seven bottom Sefirot of the name MA; ZA takes six and Nukva takes the seventh.**

Thus, the division of the *Eser Sefirot de MA* in the *Eser Sefirot de Atzilut* has been thoroughly clarified. You find, that they are not aimed together.

31. Each side of the *Nukva* in *Atzilut* is made of the name BON, since *Atik* takes the *Taamim de BON* to make its *Nukva*, and they are the first five *Sefirot* in *Keter de BON* since every *Sefira* consists of ten. Also, it takes GAR from *Sefirat Hochma* and the first four from *Bina de BON*, and all this is for *Nukva*. Also, it takes seven *Ketarim* for the above-mentioned *Nukva*, from the bottom seven *de BON*.

Arich takes the last five *de Keter de BON* for *Nukva* and *Abba* takes the bottom seven *de Hochma de BON*. *Ima* takes the bottom six *de Bina de BON* and ZON take all the bottom seven *de BON*, except for the *Ketarim* in them, which *Atik* took.

Ohr Pnimi

31. **Atik takes the *Taamim de BON* to make its *Nukva*, and they are the first five *Sefirot* in *Keter de BON*.**

It has already been explained in the previous item that the *Eser Sefirot de Nekudim* that came out all at once there cannot be corrected in the new MA there, but only one by one. Hence, when *Atik*, which is *Sefirat Keter*, was corrected, it could not sort any *Behinat Hochma*.

For that reason the bottom half of *Keter de Nekudim* did not connect with *Behinat Atik de MA*, since it is the *Behinot NHY de Keter* that clothed the *Mochin* in AVI. Hence, they descended from the degree of *Keter* to the degree of *Hochma* and are no longer fit to connect in *Rosh ha Aleph* in *Keter de Atzilut*.

by saying that they are the first five *Sefirot* he means that they are half the degree. Since the time of the ascent of the *Hey Tata'a* in the *Eynaim*, all the degrees have been divided into two halves GE and AHP. Only the Upper half remains in the degree, being GE, but the bottom half went out of the degree and is considered lower than it.

In the Tree of Life (Gate No. 40, Study No. 8) the Rav writes: "This is a great rule by which you will understand everything. The second *Partzuf* is always the Upper half."

This is the most important key in the wisdom that must always be kept before one's eyes, because most of the connections in the wisdom are explained by it. In fact, the Upper part contains only two *Sefirot*, which are the ones that came out when it was first created, called GE, while the bottom part that went out of the degree contains three *Sefirot Bina*, ZA and *Nukva*. However, since they are the two Upper *Sefirot*, they are considered as half.

Also, it takes GAR from *Sefirat Hochma* and the first four from *Bina de BON*.

The reason for it is that the place of the position of the *Rosh de Atik de MA* is from the place of the *Peh de Nekudim* and upward through *Tabur de AK* (*Ohr Pnimi* item 18), meaning the place where GAR *de Nekudim* stand. Hence, everything that remains in GAR *de Nekudim* after the breaking of vessels is taken by the *Zachar de Atik* that clothes them there. It is indeed what came out there when they were first created, which is the actual *Behinat Katnut de* GAR and *Behinat Achor be Achor*.

However, since they are *Behinat Galgalta ve Eynaim* of the degree, he therefore calls them GAR. This is because the whole matter of *Gadlut* is only the return of *Bina* and ZON to the degree because by lowering the *Hey Tata'a* to the *Peh*, *Bina* and ZON return to the degree, and then acquire GAR *de Gadlut*.

Thus, the gist of what emerged in *Katnut* is GAR, meaning *Galgalta ve Eynaim*, and the gist of the addition that comes during the *Gadlut* are *Bina* and ZON. Hence, he names *Katnut* "Panim" or "GAR", and the *Gadlut* he names "Achoraim" or "ZAT".

It turns out that since *Atik Dechura* clothes in the place of GAR *de Nekudim*, it takes everything that remains there of these GAR into his *Behinat Nukva*. However, from *Bina*, being *Ima de Nekudim*, he takes the first four *Sefirot*, meaning *Hesed* of *Bina* too. This is because *Ohr Hesed* is always in *Bina* when she is in *Achoraim* to *Abba*.

He only leaves there when *Ima* turns her *Panim* to *Abba*, as the Rav wrote above (Part 5, *Ohr Pnimi* item 40). The seven *Ketarim* of ZAT *de BON* that *Atik Dechura* took, it took only for its *Behinat Guf*.

Arich takes the last five *de Keter de BON* for *Nukva* and *Abba* takes the bottom seven *de Hochma de BON*. *Ima* takes the bottom six *de Bina de BON* and ZON take all the bottom seven *de BON*.

In order to understand these connections of MA and BON and the necessity in the rations that the Rav ascribed to them, it is necessary to write at some length. Thus a truly comprehensive concept of the *Eser Sefirot de Atzilut* may be given, how they result from one another, both the MA part in each of them, the BON part in each and every one of them, and the necessitated connection in each and every *Sefira*.

Let us briefly repeat the words that have already been explained. It all begins in the ascent of MAN to GAR *de Nekudim* in general, and from there to *Rosh de SAG*, until the *Hey Tata'a* rose to the *Metzach de SAG*. The *Masach* only gained the *Aviut* found in the *Keter*. Such a fine *Aviut* generates only *Komat Malchut*, called NHY because of the *Tikun Kavim* in her.

However, there is also *Behinat Hitlabshut* of the last *Behina* there, which is *Komat ZA de Hitlabshut*. Hence, it is considered that HGT are also clothed in *Kelim de NHY*. This is called "*Gimel Go Gimel*" or "*Ibur de Atik*" (examine closely in *Ohr Pnimi* item 17).

This *Ibur de Atik* is actually *Behinat Ibur* that corrects the general MAN that rose there since it was in the form of twelve months. Hence, it immediately raised all the *Kelim* of the seven *Melachim* from BYA to NHY *de Atzilut* by way of a general *Ibur* to the *Kelim* as the Rav says above (item 3). However, a particular *Ibur* is still necessary, where every *Tachton* is corrected in it by its *Elyon* (see item 20).

It is also called *Zivug de Katnut*, and after that there was a *Zivug de Gadlut*. Know, that there are two *Behinot* here in the *Zivug de Gadlut*: *Panim be Achor* and *Panim be Panim*, because the *Tachton* is only born from the *Zivug Panim be Panim de Elyon*.

Hence there are three *Zivugim* to discern here: 1 - *Zivug de Katnut*, which is *Achor be Achor* and *Ibur*; 2 - *Zivug de Gadlut*, which is the lowering of *Hey Tata'a* from the place of the *Metzach*, which is *Behinat Panim be Achor*, since there is no *Behinat Panim be Panim* but through MAN; 3 - The *Zivug* on the MAN that rose to the *Nukva*, which is *Panim be Panim*.

You also know that all these *Komot* that come out by *Zivugim de Katnut* and *Gadlut* in *Atzilut* are called "the new MA". Moreover, even the *Behinot Masach* and *Aviut* of the *Reshimot*, which are only from the *Sefirot* of the *Eser Sefirot de Nekudim*, being certainly BON, are still considered *Kelim de MA*.

This is so because the *Zivug* from the *Ohr Elyon* came out on them, and they are the measurements of the *Komot* in *Atzilut*. Hence, they necessarily became the *Kelim* to MA, since the *Masach* in *Malchut* of the *Rosh* expands to *Eser Sefirot* from her and within her, making *Kelim* for the *Eser Sefirot de Toch* and *Sof*, called *Guf*.

However, only the *Orot*, meaning the *Reshimot*, the *Nitzotzin* and the old *Kelim* that have already been used for *Halbasha* of *Orot* during the *Melachim* in the GAR and the ZAT, are named BON, and remember that.

Thus, the construction of the *Katnut de Atik* was made of the *Hitkalelut Masach* in the *Hey Tata'a*, from her *Atzmut*, which is the better part of the MAN and the *Reshimot*. It is known that from the perspective of the *Zivug*, the more *Av* is better. However, because of the weakness in the *Masach*, having only

Behinat Keter of its *Aviut*, it therefore raised the *Hey Tata'a* to *Keter*, to *Metzach*, which is *Bina de Keter*, and from here stemmed the *Komat Ibur de Atik*.

The cause for the *Zivug de Gadlut de Atik* is the remains of MAN that was left there in *Rosh de SAG* without any *Tikun*. This is because only *Komat NHY* came out of the *Behinat MA*, connecting with the Upper half of *Keter de BON* in *Tikun Kavim Achor be Achor*.

The rest of the MAN, being all four *Achoraim de AVI* and *YESHSUT*, and the seven *Orot de ZAT*, remained without any *He'arah*. These MAN induced the *Zivug AB SAG* where the *He'arat AB* lowered the *Hey Tata'a* from *Metzach* to *Peh*. Since the *Hey Tata'a* descended in her place, the *Aviut de Behina Dalet* reawakened in the *Masach*, and the *Ohr Elyon* that mated with the *Masach* generated *Komat Keter*.

After the *Aviut de Nekudim* in the *Masach* was recognized, the *Masach* returned to *Peh de Nekudim* and generated *Eser Sefirot de Rosh* in *Komat Keter* from below upward, from *Peh de Nekudim* to *Tabur de AK*. It is the same place of GAR *de Nekudim* (*Ohr Pnimi* item 18).

It has already been explained that this *Behinat Gadlut* is *Behinat Panim be Achor* because HB in these *Eser Sefirot* are not *Panim be Panim* without MAN. Hence, *Komat Keter de Rosh* has not yet expanded into *Behinat Guf*, since *Bina de Rosh* stands *Achor be Achor* with *Hochma*. Thus, only *Behinat Ruach Nefesh* descended to *Guf*, which is *Komat ZA* without *He'arat Hochma*.

Know, that here came the *He'arat Ibur* to half the lower *Keter*. This is because you know that the two halves of *Keter* became a single degree in *Gadlut GAR de Nekudim*. However, because of the breaking of the *Melachim*, where the *Hey Tata'a* returned to the *Eynaim*, the two halves of *Keter* were divided into two degrees once more, *Elyon* and *Tachton*. GE remained in the degree and the AHP departed from there to the lower *Behina*.

Thus, now by the new *Zivug de AB SAG*, the *Hey Tata'a* descended to the place of *Peh* once more, and thus the two halves of *Keter* became a single degree once more.

Yet, the lower half of *Keter* did not return to *Rosh de Atik*. This is because of the double strength that was now made in *Parsa* (*Ohr Pnimi* item 29). However, she received *He'arah* below in her place, and this *He'arah* is the *He'arat Ibur de AA* in *NHY de Atik*, which is from *Rosh de Atik* in the form of *Panim be Achor*.

This is so because the Upper half of *Keter* returned to *Behinat Rosh* completely, by the force of the *Komat Keter* in the *Zachar de Atik*, which gave her

Behinat new *AHP*. Hence, the old *AHP* from *Behinat BON* too, still received a great *Tikun*.

Yet, because *Bina de Atik* is still in the *Achoraim* to *Abba*, these *AHP* can only receive *He'arat Ibur*, and understand that thoroughly. Thus, we have explained the *Rosh* and *Guf de Atik* and *Behinat Ibur de AA*.

After *AA*, which is the bottom half of *Keter*, was completed in all the *Behinot de Ibur* and was born in *Behinat Ruach Nefesh*, it rose to MAN to *Rosh de Atik*, meaning to the Upper half of *Keter*, which is *Nukva de Atik*. Thus, it caused *Behinat Bina de Atik* to return her *Panim* to *Hochma de Atik*. Consequently, the *Zivug* was *Panim be Panim* in *HB de Rosh Atik*.

Behinat GAR reached *Guf de Atik* too, and when the *Aviut de AHP de Keter* was acknowledged from the *Behinat Nekudim* as they were *Behinat Mochin* to *HB de Nekudim*, it descended from there to *Behinat Guf de Atik*. It generated *Eser Sefirot* from below upward in *Komat Hochma*, and from *Behinat Panim be Achor* as well, as *Rosh de Atik* before the raising of the MAN.

The reason it did not come out in *Komat Keter* is because the more important *Behinat Aviut*, which is *Behina Dalet*, was already sucked by *Partzuf Atik* for itself. Hence, only *Aviut de Behina Gimel* remained in the general MAN.

Thus, the *Koma* that came out on *Aviut de Behina Gimel* is called the new MA, and the *Kelim de AHP de Keter* that already served as *Mochin* in *HB de Nekudim* during the *Melachim*, are called BON, and are *Nukva de AA*. However, only *Ruach Nefesh* expanded into their *Behinat Guf* because *Bina de Rosh de AA* is in *Achoraim* to *Hochma*, as mentioned in *Atik*.

Since *AHP de Keter de BON* were corrected in *Behinot GAR* to *Nukva de AA*, *He'arat Ibur* came from her to *ZAT de Hochma* and *Bina de Nekudim*, which are *Behinat AHP de HB* that *Atik* took. This is because *Atik* took *Behinat GE de HB de Nekudim*, which are the *Behinot Katnut* that remained after the breaking of the vessels and the *AHP*, which are the *Achoraim de HB* that were cancelled, which are considered ZAT.

Now they received *He'arat Ibur* from *Nukva de AA* because there is a direct link for *Nukva de AA*, being *AHP de Keter*, with *AHP de HB*, from the time of the *Melachim*. At that time they were clothed in each other and *AHP de Keter* were their *Mochin*. Hence, now too it was fitting that *AHP de HB* would rise to *Rosh de AA* and clothe the *AHP de Keter* there. Thus, they would both be corrected in a single *Tikun*.

However, they cannot ascend because of the strength of the *Parsa*, and for that they receive the *He'arat Nukva de AA* in their place below, and this

He'arah is considered *He'arat Ibur*. It is so because *Bina de Rosh de AA* is still in *Behinat Achoraim* on *Hochma*, and so they receive only the *He'arat Ubar*. Thus, we have explained the *Gadlut de Rosh* and *Guf de AA* in *Behinat Panim be Achor*, and the *Behinat Ibur de Hochma* and *Bina de Atzilut*, called AVI.

AVI *de Atzilut*, being *ZAT de HB de BON*, were completed in all the *Behinot de Ibur* and were born in *Behinat Ruach Nefesh* because of the *He'arat Rosh de AA* in *Behinat Panim be Achor*. Afterwards, AVI rose to MAN to *Nukva de Rosh de AA*, which is *AHP de Keter BON*.

Thus, they caused *Bina de Rosh de AA* to return her *Panim* to *Hochma de Rosh AA Panim be Panim*, and *He'arat GAR* reached *Guf de AA* too. After the *Aviut* in *ZAT de HB* that rose to MAN was recognized, they returned to their place in *Guf de AA*, and generated *Komat Bina* from below upward from the *Behinat Aviut*.

There is also *Komat Hochma* from the *Behinat Hitlabshut*, and they too were in *Behinat Panim be Achor*, as in *Atik* and AA. The reason they did not come out in *Komat Hochma* is because the *Aviut de Behina Gimel* had already sucked AA from the general MAN, and they were only left with *Aviut de Behina Bet*. *Komat Bina* that came out on *Behina Bet* is called the new MA, and the *Behinat Kelim de ZAT de Hochma* and *Bina* is called BON.

After the *Rosh de AVI* was completed in *Behinat GAR de Bina* in *Behinat Panim be Achor*, *He'arat Ruach Nefesh* came to *Guf de AVI*, and *He'arat Ibur* came to *ZAT de Nekudim*. This is so because they are related as *Rosh* and *Guf* of a single *Partzuf* from the time of the *Melachim*. After the ZAT were completed in all the *Behinot de Ibur*, they were born and came outside in *Behinat Ruach Nefesh*.

Thus we have explained *Rosh* and *Guf de AVI* in the *Behinat Katnut de ZON*. MA *de ZON* is the *He'arat Ibur* that received from *Rosh de AVI*, considered *ZAT de MA*, and *BON de ZON* is *ZAT de Nekudim*.

32. *We have clarified that the *Dechura* in *Atik Yomin* was made entirely from *Keter* of the new MA, which are the *Taamim de MA*. The *Nukva* in it is made of the First *Hey de Keter de BON*, which are the *Taamim de BON*, *GAR de Hochma de BON*, the First four of *Bina de BON* and the seven *Ketarim de ZAT de BON*.

Now we shall explain the matter of AA. The *Eser Sefirot* of the *Dechura* in it was made entirely of the *Hochma* of the new MA, which is *Nekudot de MA*, and the *Nukva* in it is made only of the bottom five of *Keter de BON*, which expanded and became complete *Eser Sefirot* in *Nukva*.

33. The *Behinat Dechura de AA* is explained, hence we shall now explain the *Behinat Nukva*, since she is made of the sorts of the *Melachim de BON*. We must clarify the appearance of this sort, and the entire *AA* will be clarified along with it.

This is because the entire *Atzilut* was only sorted and corrected by *Iburim* (pl. for *Ibur*), and every *Partzuf* was corrected and sorted by the *Partzuf Elyon* above it. By mating with the *Nukva*, it sorted the parts that this *Tachton* needs, they were there in the *Nukva* in *Behinat Ibur* of twelve months, and it was corrected.

Ohr Pnimi

33. **Every *Partzuf* was corrected and sorted by the *Partzuf Elyon* above it.**

It is written in the previous item that both the *Ibur* and the *Zivug de Gadlut* of every *Tachton* was made in its *Elyon*. This is because the two *Zivugim de Atik* were made in the *Rosh de Atik*, and the two *Zivugim de AVI* were in *Rosh de AA*. Also, *Zivug ZON* was made in *Rosh de AVI*, as is written and explained above.

By mating with the *Nukva*, it sorted the parts that this *Tachton* needs.

It is written above, in the previous item, that all the sorts from the *Reshimot* and the *Kelim de BON* were made by the *Zivug Zachar* and *Nukva de Partzuf Elyon*. The *Nukva de Elyon* raised the sorts that relate to it, which were on the same degree as her during the *Melachim*, and the *Zachar de Elyon* corrected them with its luminescence.

34. It turns out that the two *Behinot* in *Atik Yomin*, *Dechura* and *Nukva*, mated together, and raised the five parts of the lower *Keter de BON*, as *MAN*. They sorted the *Orot* from the *Behinat Kelim* and were there in *Behinat Ibur* of twelve months, and *AA* was corrected there.

35. We shall first explain the matter of *Partzuf AA*, and how the *Eser Sefirot* in it are divided. Nine *Sefirot* are *Behinat AA*, since the *Nukva* in it does not manifest, and the entire *Behinat AA* is called *Keter* of the general *Atzilut*. This *Keter* is divided into nine *Sefirot*, and this collective is called *AA*.

We have already explained the matter of the *Hitlabshut* of all the *Partzufim* of *Atzilut* one within the other. It turns out that only the *Rosh* of each *Partzuf* appears, and all these *Roshim* are then one below the other, all depicted as a single *Partzuf*, containing the entire *Atzilut* in general.

Since only the *Levush Keter* appeared from the entire *AA*, since even the *Hochma* in it is concealed inside that *Keter*, hence the entire *AA* is only called *Keter*. The two uncovered *Roshim de AVI* come immediately after that and become *Behinat HB* of the general *Atzilut*.

Reisha de ZA comes in their place through its *Tabur* and becomes a *Guf* to the *Atzilut* in general. Then *Nukva de ZA* appears, called *Malchut* of the general *Atzilut*. However, there is not a single *Partzuf* that does not have ten general *Sefirot*, clothing within another *Partzuf* as its separate *Guf*. So are the second in the third, and so are all of them.

Ohr Pnimi

35. **The entire *Behinat AA* is called *Keter* of the general *Atzilut*.**

You must know, that there are three general discernments in all the *Partzufim* of *Atzilut*: The first is the *Behinot Shorashim* to the *Mochin*; the second is the *Behinot Mochin* themselves; the third is *Behinat ZON* that receive the *Mochin*. This matter is necessitated here by the *Partzuf Elyon*, which is *SAG de AK*, as it is known that all the forces in the *Elyon* must necessarily be in its *Tachton* too.

You find there, in the beginning of the rooting of the attribute of *Midat ha Rachamim* with *Din*, meaning the ascent of the *Hey Tata'a* in the *Eynaim de SAG*, that it ejected the *AHP* from all the degrees outwardly. *Rosh SAG de AK* itself acquired that association to the *Eser Sefirot* of its *Rosh*, and the beginning of that *Zivug* of the *Hey Tata'a* in the *Eynaim* came out in it.

Although its degree in itself, did not diminish at all because of this ascent, it became the *Shoresh* to this *Behinat* association, where the *Behinat* breaking of the degree appeared in it as *Se'arot Dikna*.

Hence, two *Behinot Shorashim* emerged opposite it in *Atzilut*, called *Atik* and *AA*. The *Shoresh* for all the *Mochin* that come in the association of *Midat ha Rachamim* with *Din* is *Atik*, similar to *Rosh SAG de AK*, where the *Zivug* of the *Hey Tata'a* in the *Eynaim* was made.

As the departure of the *AHP* could not manifest in the *Rosh SAG* itself, so this matter too did not appear in *Atik*, but only in *AA*, which is of similar value to *Dikna de SAG de AK*. Everything that is done by the *Zivug* in the *Rosh SAG* appears only in its *Dikna*, and so it is in *AA* and *Atik* too, where all the *Zivugim* made in *Atik* for *Mochin de Atzilut* do not appear in *Atik* itself, only in *AA* (see Part 6, Ohr Pnimi item 2).

Thus we have explained the two *Partzufim* of *Atik* and *AA*, considered roots of *Mochin* to *Atzilut*, like *SAG de AK* and its *Dikna*, which are the roots of the association of the *Hey Tata'a* in the *Eynaim*.

After the *Reshimot* in *SAG de AK* were recognized as *Behinat Guf*, they descended to their place in the *Guf*, the place of *Tabur de AK*, where the *Mochin* of the *Hey Tata'a* in the *Eynaim* appeared in *Behinat Rosh*. It is much the same here in *Atzilut*, where after the *Zivug* was made in *AA* and *Atik* on the *MAN* that rose for the *Mochin*, they descend to their place in the *Guf*, to *Chazeh de AA*, to manifest the *Mochin* in its suitable place. They are called AVI *de Atzilut*, meaning the *Mochin*.

Now you can understand the division of AVI *de Atzilut* to the four *Behinot* of AVI. You must only keep in mind all that has been explained regarding the ascent of the *Masach* that was purified from the *Guf de SAG* into *Behinat* renewal of the *Zivug* in *Rosh de SAG*, until it came to ZAT *de Nekudim*, as brought in the two previous parts.

Let us mention the things briefly: The *Masach* that rose from *Guf de SAG* consisted of three *Behinot Reshimot*: *Reshimot de Taamim de SAG* (see Part 6, *Histaklut Pnimit* item 24). MA Elyon *de SAG* came out on their *Zivug* and after the *Zivug* its place was apparent from the *Peh de SAG* through above *Tabur de SAG*. Since the *Taamim* never descended below *Tabur* and did not mix with the inner NHY *de AK* at all, it thus has nothing of *Behinat Hey Tata'a* and is considered as Upper AVI, as the Rav says above (Part 6 item 6).

The second *Behina de Reshimot*, are the *Reshimot* of *Nekudot de SAG*. These are the lower nine *de SAG* that expanded from *Tabur* down to the *Sium Raglin de AK*, where they mixed with the Inner NHY *de AK* and mingled with the *Hey Tata'a*.

The *Eser Sefirot de Nekudim* came out on their *Zivug* in the form of *Hey Tata'a* in the *Eynaim*, which ejected the AHP from all the degrees. After their *Zivug* in *Rosh SAG*, their place in *Tabur de AK* became apparent, and *Rosh ha Aleph* came out from *Tabur* upward to the *Chazeh de SAG*, which is the *Peh de MA Elyon*. GAR *de Nekudim* have two *Roshim*, *Keter* and AVI, whose place is from the *Sium Tifferet* to *Tabur de AK*.

Know, that these three *Roshim* that came out by the *Zivug* on the *Reshimot de Nekudot de SAG* are all called YESHSUT, and they are three *Behinot* YESHSUT. They are called that for the reason the Rav has written above, that the *Behinot* SAG, mixed with the Inner MA and BON *de AK*, are always called YESHSUT. The ones that are clean from this mixture are called Upper AVI.

Since these came out on the *Reshimot de Behinot Nekudot de SAG*, they are necessarily mixed with the *Hey Tata'a* of MA and BON *de AK*. However, they contain three degrees: the first YESHSUT stands from *Tabur de AK* upward. It is the best of them, because the *Hey Tata'a* operates in it from below upward, and it is known that the *Aviut* cannot operate anything above its origin of creation.

Hence, this YESHSUT is considered clean from *Hey Tata'a*; it is not even regarded as *Nekudim*, but is completely similar to *Behinat Taamim* of SAG, meaning the Upper AVI. Yet, it is certainly lower than them for it still has the *Orot* that come from the *Zivug* of *Hey Tata'a*.

Nevertheless, it is considered the *Shoresh* of the *Nekudim*. However, the above-mentioned MA *Elyon*, which is *Behinat* Upper AVI, is not even considered the *Shoresh* for *Nekudim*, since it does not have anything of these *Orot*, related to *Hey Tata'a* in the *Eynaim*.

The second degree is *Rosh ha Bet de Nekudim*, called *Keter*. Since it is *Behinot* AHP of the first YESHSUT. Hence, the force of the *Hey Tata'a* already controls it, and it is thus considered *Behinat Nekudim*. However, in itself, it is divided into *Galgalta ve Eynaim* and AHP in its *Eser Sefirot*, which are two *Roshim*.

For that reason, it is considered that in *Keter* too the *Hey Tata'a* operates from below upward in its *Behinot Nikvey Eynaim*. For this reason, the dominion of the *Hey Tata'a* in the *Eynaim* appears primarily in the third *Rosh*, called AVI *de Nekudim*.

It is considered the *Shoresh* to the *Mochin*, which are AVI, where the *Hey Tata'a* controls, but for itself, it is considered that the *Hey Tata'a* is below it. The third YESHSUT, being AVI *de Nekudim*, are considered the actual *Behinat Nekudim*, meaning *Behinat Hey Tata'a* in the *Eynaim*, where it appears in all its control.

Now we have explained the two *Behinot* of *Atzilut*, which are the roots of *Mochin de Atzilut*, called *Atik* and AA, relating to *Rosh de SAG de AK* and its *Dikna*. The *Zivug* was made on the *Masach* there only in the form of *Hitkalelut* for the *Tachton*, and after the *Aviut* in the *Masach* had been recognized, it had to descend to its place.

This occurred in a similar manner in the *Zivug* in *Atik* and AA, meaning only in the form of *Hitkalelut*, which is merely called *Shoresh* for the *Mochin*. The second *Behina* was also clarified, being AVI *de Atzilut*, which are the complete *Mochin* of *Atzilut*. However, they are not Upper AVI, but only the fourth YESHSUT, relating to the fourth YESHSUT *de SAG de AK*, being AVI *de Nekudim*.

Similarly, the four *Behinot* AVI emerge here too, and the fourth are the *Mochin de Atzilut*, meaning they clothe in ZON *de Atzilut*, considered the receivers of the *Mochin*. The entire matter of this association revolves around them for the management of the world comes only from ZON.

However, although we have clarified four *Behinot* in AVI, they are still considered as only two primary *Behinot*. Upper AVI are one *Behina*, and all three degrees of YESHSUT are considered as one *Behina* too.

ZON *de Atzilut*, which are the receivers of the *Mochin*, relate to ZAT *de Nekudim*, born from the MAN *de Yesod de AK*, called *Shuruk*. They are divided into two *Behinot* in *Atzilut*: the "Big ZON", and the "Little ZON". This is before two *Behinot* came out in ZAT *de Nekudim*, which are the four *Melachim* DHGT from AVI and the four *Melachim* TNHYM from YESHSUT. In *Atzilut* they came out in the same manner: the Big ZON related to DHGT, and the Little ZON related to TNHYM.

It is written, "all these **Roshim** are then one below the other, all depicted as a single **Partzuf**, containing the entire **Atzilut** in general." It means that all the *Partzufim* of *Atzilut* primarily manifest only in ZON. This is the *Hidush Mochin* that was made in *Atzilut*, in the form of the association of *Midat ha Rachamim* with *Din*, which should uncover the matter of the conduct of reward and punishment in this world.

This relates only to ZON, for only in them this conduct applies, that when the *Tachtonim* are worthy, they raise MAN and the *Mochin* appear in ZON, and when they are not worthy, the *Mochin* exit. However, the actions of the *Tachtonim* do not blemish above ZON whatsoever.

Thus, the *Mochin* is primarily for the reception of ZON. However, in order to give them to ZON, they must come down through the previous eight *Partzufim*, *Atik* and *Nukva*, AA and *Nukva*, for *Behinot Shorashim* for the *Mochin*, and AVI and YESHSUT for the *Mochin* itself. ZA cannot receive them but from the fourth YESHSUT, as we've said, and thus they are all one *Partzuf* with one function.

36. Let us explain the order of these nine *Sefirot* divided in it, in AA. AA is different from all the rest because all the other *Partzufim*, whether *Atik*, or AVI or ZON, their *Rosh* is one *Galgalta*, which is the *Behinat Keter* in the *Partzuf*.

    Keter comes from the word **Koteret** (heading), as it is written, "the wicked doth beset the righteous," meaning surrounds him. The *Gulgolet* (Heb. for *Galgalta*) is like one heading, surrounding the entire *Behinat Rosh*.

    There are two **Mochin** within that **Galgalta**, called the HB of that *Partzuf*, *Hochma* on the right and *Bina* on the left. These two are the majority of the *Mochin*. However, the third *Moach* below them is made of those two in general, determining between them, in the middle. It is called the *Daat* of the *Partzuf*. We shall explain what is not included in the *Eser Sefirot* of the *Partzuf*, and all these three *Mochin HaVaYot* will be built inside that *Galgalta*, called *Keter*. After that the seven lower *Sefirot HGT NHYM* will expand in the *Guf* one atop the other in the form of *Kavim*.

37. However, there is only one separated *Mocha* inside that *Galgalta*, called *Hochma de AA*. Since this *Hochma* and that *Mocha* too, contain *Behinat* three *Mochin*, as we will explain later, yet all three are but *Behinat Hochma* itself.

    Thus, it turns out that in that *Reisha de AA* there was only one *Galgalta*, which is *Keter de AA*, and inside it, one *Mocha* which is *Hochma de AA*. However, *Bina de AA* could not stand there in *Behinat Reisha*.

38. We have learned that the reason for it is that *Behinat Nukva de Atik* was made of the First five *de Keter de BON*, where there was never any cancellation or even a blemish. However, the sorting of the *Melachim* began in *Nukva* of *AA* as she was made of the last five *de Keter de BON*, that were a little blemished.

    From there on the flaws add in the rest of the *Partzufim*, as mentioned there. Hence in *Reisha de Atik*, where there was no blemish whatsoever, his *Bina* was able to receive the *Ohr Elyon de AK* that extends within *Reisha de Atik*, when she is up there. For that reason she too stood at *Reisha de Atik*, and then the *Daat*, made of the connection of *HB*, stands there too.

Ohr Pnimi

38. ***Behinat Nukva de Atik* was made of the First five *de Keter de BON*... ...the sorting of the *Melachim* began in *Nukva* of *AA*.**

    It has already been explained above, in the previous item, that *Atik* and *AA* are related in the same manner as *Rosh de SAG* and its *Dikna*. For that reason, *Atik* did not sort from the *BON* for its *Nukva*, but only those *Behinot* that were not controlled by any flaw due to the breaking. This is because the matter of the *Hey Tata'a* in the *Eynaim* that we discern in the descent of the degrees of *SAG de AK* is of similar value to the *Behinat Reshimot de BON*. Its degrees descend according to the blemish they were blemished by the breaking of the vessels.

    That mixture is not at all apparent in *Rosh SAG*, though there is *Hitkalelut Zivug de Hey Tata'a* in the *Eynaim* in it. Similarly, *Atik*, which relates to it, cannot take any *Behina* from the somewhat blemished *BON* by the breaking of the vessels for its construction.

Hence, it did not take from *BON*, but from its *Behinat Katnut*, meaning everything that emerged in it from its very creation, meaning only the Upper half of *Keter BON*, meaning only its *Behinat Galgalta ve Eynaim*. These did not receive anything within them, even from the *He'arat NHY de AK* that emerged through the *Tabur* in the form of *Holam* above the *Otiot*.

For that reason it has nothing of the *Behinot ZAT de Nekudim*, since the *He'arat Holam* through the *Tabur* is the *Shoresh* to the *ZAT de Nekudim*. This is because this *Ohr* descended from *Zivug de AB SAG* made on *MAN de NHY de AK* that rose to them. Also, *NHY de AK* are considered the *Shoresh* of *ZON de Nekudim* since *AVI* generated *ZAT de Nekudim* on their *MAN*.

This *He'arah* that came out through the *Tabur* to *Keter de Nekudim* lowered the *Hey Tata'a* from the *Eynaim de Keter* to *Peh de Nekudim* and returned *AVI* to *Behinat Rosh*. In that state *Keter* itself gained its *GAR* too, since it now has complete *Eser Sefirot* as it acquired its *AHP* from the return of *AVI* to its *Rosh*.

However, before *AVI* returned to the *Rosh*, *Keter* had only *Galgalta ve Eynaim*, which are *Behinot Orot de Ruach Nefesh*. This is because *Orot de HGT* are clothed in *Galgalta* and *Orot de NHY* are clothed in the *Eynaim*.

Hence, although it is not completed by the *He'arat Tabur de AK* but only in the three lower *Kelim Bina* and *ZON*, they still returned *KHB de Orot* to it from the aspect of the *Orot*. This *Bina* and these *ZON* that *Keter* gained by the *He'arat NHY de AK* are considered *Sigim* with respect to *Atik* because the cancellation during the *Melachim* happened in them, and they fell back to *Behinat VAK*. This is called the annulment of *NHY de Keter*.

For that reason *Atik* gave these *Bina* and *ZON de Keter* to *AA*, since it relates to the *Behinat Dikna de SAG*, the place of the manifestation of the *Katnut*, which is at *Rosh de SAG*. Hence, *AA* received *Behinot Bina*, and *ZON de Keter* of the blemished *BON* into its *Behinat Nukva*.

It is written, **"Behinat Nukva de Atik was made of the First five de Keter de BON, where there was never any cancellation or even a blemish."** As it is written, that it was made from the *Behinat Katnut de Keter* that came out in it from its very creation. It remained complete, and not a thing of it was cancelled even a bit.

However, the sorting of the *Melachim* began in *Nukva* of *AA* since she was made of the last five of *Keter de BON* which were a little flawed. This means, as we have explained, that *AA* was made of *Bina* and *ZON de Keter*, which

Keter gained the new *Ohr* of NHY de AK that illuminated on it through the *Tabur*. This *Ohr* was cancelled once more and *Bina* and ZON de *Keter* descended from *Rosh* to VAK once more, hence, they are flawed.

From there on the flaws add in the rest of the *Partzufim*.

This is because *Bina* and ZON that *Hochma* gained by *Ohr* de NHY de AK that came out through the *Tabur* was blemished more than *Bina* and ZON de *Keter*. This is because *Hochma* participated in the MAN de *Shuruk*, which are the *Behinat Hey Tata'a* itself.

Bina and ZON de *Bina* de BON were blemished even more than *Hochma*. This is because *Bina* de *Nekudim* did not extend her *Bina* and ZON by *He'arat Holam*, as *Abba*, but only through the MAN de *Shuruk* that she received from *Yesod* de AK, which is the *Behinat Atzmut* de *Hey Tata'a*, from which ZON were born. The *Behinot* seven *Orot* of ZAT are blemished most since they broke in *Panim* and *Achor* and descended to BYA.

39. The sorting from the *Melachim* that had some flaw n them was in *Reisha de AA*. Hence, his *Bina* is more *Dinim* than *Hochma*, as *Dinim* always awaken from her, since she is *Nukva*. Thus, she could not receive the *Ohr Atik* that clothes inside *Reisha de AA* in a high place in *Reisha*.

This is because there is great *Ohr* there, close to *Atik*, and thus she came down in the *Behinat Garon de AA*. Since she was further there, she had the ability of receiving the *Ohr* of *Atik*.

Ohr Pnimi

39. **In *Reisha de AA* etc. his *Bina* etc. she came down in the *Behinat Garon*.**

It means that these AHP that *Nukva de AA* were made of, consist of *Eser Sefirot* GE and AHP, also considered as *Panim* and *Achoraim*. This is because there are two *Behinot* in them: One – they joined to complement AHP de *Keter*. This is considered *Behinat Galgalta ve Eynaim* in these AHP; Two – they expanded to being *Mochin* to AVI de *Nekudim*.

This is considered as *Behinat* AHP in these AHP. Hence, when *Nukva de Atik* sorted these AHP for the *Nukva de AA* she only sorted *Behinat* GE, which are *Behinot Keter* and *Hochma* de AHP that belong to *Behinat Keter de Nekudim*, which is *Nukva de Atik*.

However, *Bina* and ZON of AHP, which are NHY de *Keter* that turned into *Mochin* in *Hochma* and *Bina* de *Nekudim* are considered as the degrees of AVI de *Nekudim*, and not as the degree of *Keter*. Hence, *Bina* departed from the *Rosh* de AA.

There is yet another important reason that *Bina* could not stand at *Rosh de AA*. The rule is that everything that is not flawed by the breaking received its correction from the new MA, completely and permanently, and never leaves there. However, the *Mochin* do not remain permanently in the flawed *Kelim* by the breaking, but are rather in a state of "coming and going".

Hence, *Behinat AHP de AHP*, namely their *Bina* and ZON, are considered flawed with regard to *Rosh de AA* that received *Komat Hochma* from *Atik*. Hence she cannot receive this great *Ohr* permanently in *Rosh de AA*, and thus descended outside the *Rosh*.

It is written, "**thus she came down in the Behinat Garon de AA. Since she was further there, she had the ability of receiving the Ohr of Atik.**" This is so because with her descent to the *Garon* she receives her *Mochin* temporarily; sometimes she connects with the *Rosh* to a single *Partzuf* and has *Mochin de GAR* from AA, and sometimes she is not connected and then has no *Mochin*. In this manner she is worthy of receiving.

There is a third reason, as the Rav wrote, "**Bina is more Dinim than Hochma, as Dinim always awaken from her.**" Interpretation: you already know that the flaws add and accumulate in the *Partzufim* (item 18 here and *Ohr Pnimi* item 29). This is so because there are three *Behinot* in them: First, what came out in the beginning of *Atzilut*, which were not flawed at all, which *Atik* took. Second, what came out in *Nekudim* by the *He'arat Holam* through *Tabur de AK* from which GAR came *Panim be Achor*. The third is the *He'arat Shuruk* from *Yesod de AK* where GAR came from in *Behinat Panim be Panim*.

These three *Behinot* apply only in *GAR de Nekudim*. After that there is *Behinot ZAT de Nekudim* that broke *Panim* and *Achor*. The best from *Behinat Achoraim de AVI* is what comes from the *He'arat Holam* by the *He'arat Tabur*.

This *He'arah* of *Holam* did not reach the *AHP* from the *Behinat Bina* even in *AHP de Keter*. It is so because *Bina* did not return her *Panim* to *Abba* to receive *He'arat Hochma* from him and complete her *AHP* before the MAN *de Shuruk* that she received from *Yesod de AK* reached her. Thus, all the *Behinot AHP de Bina* are from *He'arat Hey Tata'a*, contained in *Shuruk*. This is the meaning of the *Dinim* awakening from *Bina*.

40. **However, the Bina of the rest of the Partzufim below AA had the ability to stand at the Rosh of the Partzuf. The reason is that Ohr Atik is a greater Ohr than all of Atzilut, since Ohr Ein Sof clothes inside it. Since Atik had already been clothed inside AA, the Ohr was greatly lessened. When AVI return a second time, to clothe AA too, Ohr Atik is found to be very distant from them.**

Thus, their *Bina* has the ability to receive the *Ohr Atik,* after she is distant, while sitting at the *Rosh* of the *Partzuf,* and all the more so in ZON, which drew even farther.

41. *After we have clarified the matter of AA, we shall now clarify the order of its ten *Sefirot,* and how they clothe *Atik Yomin.* We have already explained above that this is the reason it is called *Atik Yomin,* as its seven days clothe AA separately. This is their order: *Keter de AA* clothes *Hesed de Atik,* and *Hochma* to *Gevura,* and *Bina* to *Tifferet.*

42. The reason is that since they are the Upper three of AA, which are *Behinat Reisha* and require more *Ohr* than in the *Guf,* hence a complete *Sefira* of *Atik* is clothed in each of them. However, the lower seven of *Guf de AA* do not require as much *Ohr* as the *Rosh,* hence the last three *de Atik* will suffice to shine in them.

This is their order: *Atzmut NHY de Atik* in *HGT de AA,* as mentioned, and that too is because *HGT de AA* later became *Mochin* in the First Three *de Abba* and *Ima.* Hence, their *He'arah* is primarily in *HGT de AA* to shine for *Mochei* (pl. for *Mochin*) AVI. Afterwards *Ohr* came out alone from *Yesod de Atik* and expanded in *NHY de AA.*

Ohr Pnimi

42. They are the Upper three of AA, which are *Behinat Reisha* and require more *Ohr* than in the *Guf.*

Because *HGT de AA* became *Mochin* to AVI. These words are profound indeed, and require length.

First, we must know that the matter of *Hitlabshut NHY de Elyon* in the *Behinot Mochin* in the *Tachton,* and the matter of the *Halbasha* of the *Tachton* to *Guf de Elyon* are separate matters. Note, that *NHY de Atik* clothe *Mochin* in *Rosh de AA,* and yet, *Rosh de AA* clothes *HGT de Atik,* not *NHY de Atik.*

Also, in AVI, *NHY de AA* clothe in the *Mochin* in *Rosh de AVI,* and yet, the *Roshim de AVI* clothe only *HGT de AA* and not *NHY de AA* at all. The reason is simple: These *NHY de Elyon* that clothe the *Mochin* in the *Tachton* are *Behinat NHY de Eser Sefirot de Rosh de Elyon* and have no dealings with the *Halbasha* of the *Tachton* to the *Guf de Elyon.*

Know, that there are three *Behinot NHY de Elyon:* the first – *NHY de Eser Sefirot de Rosh* of the *Elyon* from its very creation. The second – the *NHY* that appear in it by the ascent of MAN of the *Tachton.* The third – the new *NHY* that appeared in it by the ascent of the MAN of the progeny of the *Tachton.*

We shall understand the matters according to the order of the creation of the three *Partzufim Atik*, *AA*, and *AVI*. You know, that by *Zivug AB SAG* that the *Hey Tata'a* generated from the *Metzach* and lowered to her place in the *Peh*, *Eser Sefirot* came out on *Komat Keter*.

This was done first by *Hitkalelut* of the MAN of *Nekudim* in *Rosh de SAG*, and afterwards, when the *Aviut* of the *Reshimot* was acknowledged, they descended to their place, to *Peh de Nekudim*. There they once more generated *Eser Sefirot de Rosh* from *Peh de Nekudim* to *Tabur de AK* on *Komat Keter*, called *Rosh de Atik* (*Ohr Pnimi* item 20).

This sufficed for *Behinat Rosh de Atik* and to its *Behinat Guf* because *Bina* of this *Rosh* stands as she always does in *Behinat Achoraim* to *Abba*. Hence, she only imparts the *Guf* with *Ruach Nefesh*, and the *Guf* lacks GAR. Thus we have explained the creation of *Rosh* and *Guf de Atik*, and now we shall explain *Partzuf AA*.

Partzuf AA is sorted by *Nukva de Atik*. Since she is the Upper half *de Keter de Nekudim*, meaning the *Behinot ve Eynaim de Keter* that came out when it was first created, through her connection with MA, she now acquired GAR *de Keter*. She extends her AHP from the time of the *Nekudim* once more, meaning the NHY *de Keter* that were then cancelled by the concealment of GAR *de Keter*.

Now that she acquires the GAR by the new MA once more, she returns and draws them to her, to complete her old *Eser Sefirot*. Since these AHP are also from *Behinot* NHY *de AK*, hence, they became MAN there, and caused *Bina de Atik* to return to being *Panim be Panim* with *Hochma*.

It is known that the coming of ZON in the place of *Bina* always awakens *Bina* to return her *Panim* to *Abba*. This is in order to draw *He'arat Hochma* for ZON, who is connected to them to provide them with *He'arat Hochma* from the perspective of *Bina* and ZON *de Eser Sefirot de Ohr Yashar*. It is known that only *Behina Gimel de Aviut* remained in them. This is because *Behina Dalet*, which was in the general MAN, was taken by *Atik*. Hence, only *Komat Hochma* emerged on them.

It turns out that *Nukva de Atik* acquired her *Behinat* AHP from the time of the *Nekudim* by that new *Zivug* that emerged in her. It means that she was once more completed with *Eser* complete *Sefirot* GE and AHP, though not in the *Koma* she has from MA, which is *Komat Keter*, but only in *Komat Hochma*.

Now it is considered to have two *Behinot* of NHY in *Keter de Nukva*. The first is NHY *de Keter* that she has from *Kelim de MA*, and the second, NHY *de Komat Hochma* that she now acquired by the new MAN *de AHP*.

Two *Komot* extend below from this *Zivug*: the first is to the *Guf de Atik* itself, because after *Bina de Rosh* returned *Panim be Panim*, its *He'arah* reaches the *Guf* too. Now the *Guf* gains *Behinot GAR*, but only GAR *de Komat Hochma*, and not *Komat Keter*, as it is in the *Rosh*.

This is so because the *Zivug Panim be Panim*, made in the *Rosh*, was only on the new *Behinot MAN*, which do not have more than *Aviut de Behina Gimel*. The second *Koma* extends to *Behinat Rosh de AA*, to the place of *Chazeh de Atik*, which clothes it from the *Chazeh* to the *Peh*.

Now you can understand the matter of *Hitlabshut NHY de Elyon* to *Mochin* in the *Tachton*. Indeed, they are a part of the *Tachton* and are not fitting to remain in the *Elyon*. This is so because they are the same *AHP* that completed *Nukva de Atik* during the *Zivug* of MAN *de AA*.

Even though they joined her during the *Zivug*, they are still unworthy of remaining in her, since they are from *Behinat Komat Hochma*. After their own *Aviut* had been recognized, their flaw from the time of *Nekudim* becomes known too, that they do not merit being in the place of *Atik*. Hence, they descend to the place of *Guf de Atik* along with *Komat Rosh de AA*.

Here you should know what the Rav writes below, that when they are born, all the *Partzufim* fall to *Beria* and suck there from the two bottom thirds *de Netzah* and *Hod de Atik* there. The reason is that this *Masach*, which contains all the *Reshimot* in the *Achoraim de NHY de Keter* and the four *Achoraim de AVI* and ZAT, this *Masach* is from *Behinat Guf de Nekudim* that rose to *Behinat Rosh de SAG* after its *Hizdakchut*.

From there it descended from degree to degree until it generated all the *Partzufim de ABYA*. Hence, since the *Guf de Nekudim* illuminated in the entire BYA, thus, before the *Aviut* was recognized in its *Guf*, meaning while it was still contained in *Aviut de Rosh*, it could be in *Behinat Atzilut*.

However, after its *Aviut de Guf* is recognized, it is time for the *Koma* to depart from the *Hitkalelut* in the *Rosh* and descend to her own place, to the place it was prior to its *Hizdakchut*. This is called the birth of the *Partzuf*.

Then the *Behinot Guf de Nekudim* become apparent, which were in the *Masach* prior to its *Hizdakchut*, when it was in *Behinot BYA*. Hence, each and every *Koma* that came out on this *Masach* was compelled to come to *Beria* at the moment of its birth, meaning when its *Aviut* is recognized.

However, by *Yenika* from the two bottom thirds of *Netzah* and *Hod de Atik*, which are in *Beria*, they acquire the *Behinat Atzilut* in them once more, until they rise and clothe the *Guf de Elyon*. The same also happened to AA, and after the *Aviut de Guf* in the *Masach* that was in it from *Behinot BYA* too was recognized, it was compelled to leave *Behinat Rosh de Atik* and come to the place of *Beria*, under *Parsa de Atzilut*. This is called the birth of the *Partzuf*.

It turns out that the *Behinot NHY de Mochin* that it received from the *Elyon* remain in the *Guf de Atik*. After AA sucked from the two bottom thirds of *Atik*, returned to *Atzilut* and clothed *HGT NHY de Atik*, it then returned and received the *NHY de Rosh de Elyon*, which clothed in it as *Mochin*.

Thus we see that the beginning of the reception of AA to *NHY de Atik* was while it was still contained in the *Zivug de Rosh de Atik*. However, since during its birth, it was compelled to come down to *Beria*, it must therefore return and receive them from *HGT de Atik* once again.

It was similar in the creation of *AVI* by *Nukva de AA*. This is because *AVI* were made of *Behinat ZAT de HB de BON*, meaning *AHP* that were cancelled from *AVI* after they've lost their *GAR*. During the *Nekudim*, ZAT of these *AVI* were on the same degree as *NHY de Keter de Nekudim*, and also clothed them in *Behinot Mochin*.

Hence, after *Nukva de AA*, which is *Behinat NHY de Keter Nekudim* received *Behinot GAR* by the *Zivug de Atik*, she extended *Behinot AHP de AVI* to *Behinat MAN* too. AA and *Nukva* mated on these MAN *Panim be Panim* and generated *Eser Sefirot* in *Komat Bina*, since only *Aviut de Behina Bet* remained in the *Reshimot*, as AA took *Behina Gimel* for himself.

Two *Komot* came out by this *Zivug*, as with *Atik*, one for *Guf de AA* itself, which was only in *Behinat Nefesh Ruach* before, and could not receive from its *Rosh*, since *Bina* stands in *Achoraim* to *Abba*. Now, through the MAN from *AVI* that returned *Panim be Panim*, *Guf de AA* too received the GAR. However, they are GAR *de Behina Bet*, not from *Behina Gimel*, as it has in the *Rosh*, and a second *Koma* came out to *Rosh de AVI*, whose MAN are theirs.

Here too it is considered that *NHY de AA* clothed in *Rosh de AVI*, meaning *Behinot AHP* that *Nukva de AA* took from the MAN to complete the *Eser Sefirot* during the *Zivug* as with *Atik* for AA. When *AVI* were born, meaning when their *Masach* was recognized, they descended to *Beria* too for the same reason mentioned in AA. The *Behinot NHY* and the *Mochin* remained in *Guf de AA* until they returned to *Atzilut* through the *Yenika* and clothed *HGT de AA*, and then *Behinot NHY* returned and received their *Mochin*.

You should know that AA cannot mate on the MAN *de AVI* but only when it connects and becomes one *Partzuf* with *Atik*. This is because *Nukva de AA* is only half of the bottom *Keter de Nekudim*, which is only *Behinat NHY*. In order to sort out the MAN *de AVI* and mate on them, *Keter* must be as complete as it was during the *Nekudim*, when it clothed for *Mochin* in *AVI de Nekudim*.

Moreover, the *Zivug* is primarily named after the *Nukva de Atik* because the bottom of *Keter* is cancelled and incorporates in one complete degree with the *Elyon* when connecting with its Upper half. The *Tachton*, on the other hand, does not even bear a name, as the Rav says (Part 6 item 6).

Accordingly, you will find that *Atik* gives two kinds of *Mochin* for AA: the first is for *Rosh de AA*, which are *Eser Sefirot* on *Komat Hochma*, clothed in NHY *de Atik* that appeared because of this *Zivug* in *Rosh de Atik*. These NHY descend to AA together with the *Mochin*, since they are unworthy of *Atik*.

Atik gives the second *Mochin* for the *Guf de AA*. This is because the *Guf de AA* cannot receive *Behinat* GAR from its own *Rosh*, as they are *Behinat Panim be Achor*. Only through raising the MAN *de AVI* do *Atik* and *Arich* return to become one *Partzuf*. HB *de Rosh* also return *Panim be Panim* and then descend are impart GAR to *Guf de AA*.

Since that *Zivug* is also named after *Atik*, even the *Mochin de Guf* are imparted from the *Zivug Atik*, though from a low *Koma*, since it is from MAN *de AVI*, which is but *Behina Bet*. Yet, you must understand that the *Mochin de Behina Bet* in *Guf de AA* is also clothed in NHY *de Atik*, meaning the AHP by which *Nukva de Atik* was completed during the *Zivug* of this *Koma de Behina Bet*.

Now we have explained the two *Zivugim de Atik* for AA, and the two *Behinot* NHY *de Atik* that clothe AA. NHY *de Atik* from *Komat Hochma* clothe *Rosh de AA*, and NHY *de Atik* from *Komat Bina* clothe the *Guf de AA*.

Now you can also see that after the *Yenika* of AVI from the two bottom thirds *de Netzah* and *Hod de Atik*, while still in *Beria*, they thus acquire the strength to rise to *Atzilut* and clothe HGT *de AA*. Then they receive the NHY with their *Mochin* from the *Behinat* NHY *de Atik*, clothed in HGT *de AA*.

There are three *Behinot* NHY *de Eser Sefirot de Rosh de Atik* that you find here: 1 – NHY *de Eser Sefirot de Rosh Atik*, from its very creation, from *Komat Keter*. 2 – NHY *de Eser Sefirot de Rosh Atik* that emerged in it out of the *Hitkalelut* of the MAN *de AA*. These are NHY *de Komat Hochma*, clothing the *Mochin de Rosh de AA*. 3 – NHY *de Eser Sefirot de Rosh Atik* that emerged in it out of the *Hitkalelut* of MAN *de AVI*. These are NHY *de Komat Bina*, clothing *Guf de AA* in its HGT. AVI from the *Levushim* of the HGT *de AA* receive *Mochin de* GAR by these NHY *de Atik*, clothed in HGT *de AA*.

It is written, "**since they are the Upper three of AA, which are Behinat Reisha and require more Ohr than in the Guf, hence a complete Sefira** of *Atik*." In other words, *HGT NHY* that give the *Mochin de Rosh* in *Komat Hochma* by its return to *Atzilut* and clothing the *HGT de Atik*. Hence, it needs all three *Sefirot de Atik*, made into the *KHB* in it, while its primary *He'arah de AA* comes from them.

"However, the lower seven of *Guf de AA* do not require as much *Ohr* as the *Rosh*, hence the last three *de Atik* will suffice to shine in them." This means, as we have said, that *NHY de Atik* that shine in *Guf de AA* are low *He'arah* from *Komat Hochma de AA*, and are only from *Komat Bina*. They too stand there primarily to shine *He'arat GAR* in *AVI*.

It is written, "that too is because *HGT de AA* later became *Mochin* in the First Three *de Abba* and *Ima*. Hence, their *He'arah* is primarily in *HGT de AA* to shine for *Mochei* (pl. for *Mochin*) *AVI*." It means that *NHY de Atik*, which clothe *Guf de AA*, give the *Mochin de GAR* to *AVI*.

43. Now you know the reason to what has become known and clarified, that all the *Behinot NHY* of any *Partzuf* from the *Partzufim*, always come as supplements, not as the core. This is why they are considered outside the *Guf*.

The reason is that in the *Rosh* of the *Partzufim* of *Atzilut*, which is *AA*, where all the other *Partzufim* of *Atzilut* clothe and hold, its *NHY* have nothing to rely on in it, in *Atik Yomin*. This is because only the *ZAT de Atik* clothed the First seven *de AA*, and there is only *He'arah* in *NHY de AA*, which stems from *Yesod de Atik* and expands in them. For that reason this whole issue continues in every *NHY* of all the other *Partzufim*.

Ohr Pnimi

43. **Its *NHY* have nothing to rely on in it, in *Atik Yomin*. This is because only the *ZAT de Atik* clothed the First seven *de AA*.**

This means the true *NHY de Rosh Atik*, from its creation, which are at *Komat Keter*. These *NHY* do not clothe *AA* at all, but only from its *Behinat Guf*, which are from *Komat Hochma*, found in *HGT de Atik*, which are *Behinat ZAT de Atik*.

Since it is so, *AA* itself, being *Behinat Keter de Nekudim*, lacks *NHY de Kelim* and *GAR de Orot*. This is so because its *GAR* are from a lower degree, and since *AA* is considered the general *Keter de Atzilut*, and it lacks its *GAR*, hence, all the degrees descending after it are found to be lacking *NHY de Kelim* and *GAR de Orot*. This is so because the *GAR* of each of them is *GAR* of its inferior degree, and its own *GAR* are missing from it, as we have explained regarding *AA*.

It is written, "all the **Behinot NHY** of any **Partzuf** from the **Partzufim**, always come as supplements, not as the core." This is because the *Partzuf* does not acquire its own *NHY* unless by joining and *Hitkalelut* with the *Elyon* to a single *Partzuf*, as we have explained regarding AA becoming one *Partzuf* with *Atik* by the *MAN de AVI* that it received. This *He'arah* is considered an addition, not as the core of the *Partzuf*, but rising and falling, as we will write below.

44. However, on another occasion, my teacher explained them to me more clearly, in the following manner: It is known, that every *Shok* consists of three *Prakin*, as mentioned in the Zohar (VaYechi). However, *Yesod* consists of but two *Prakin*, being the *Yesod* and the *Atara* in it.

    Thus, the two Upper *Prakin de NH de Atik* clothed the *HG de AA*, *Netzah* on the right, and *Hod* in *Gevura* on the left *Kav*; *Yesod* in *Tifferet de AA* and the two middle *Prakin de NH de Atik* in *NH de AA*. Also, *Ateret Yesod de Atik* in *Yesod de AA*, and *Malchut de Atik* in *Malchut de AA*, because a complete *Partzuf* of *Nukva* must be made of it.

    For that reason she took one complete measure. You find, that the two bottom *Prakin de NH de Atik* remained below the entire *NH de AA*, and remained uncovered.

Ohr Pnimi

44. Every *Shok* consists of three *Point in the heart...* ...You find, that the two bottom *Prakin de NH de Atik* remained.

    The difference between *Hitlabshut NHY de Elyon* to *Mochin* in the *Tachton* has already been explained. *Hitlabshut NHY de Elyon* to *Mochin* in the *Tachton*, or in the progeny of the *Tachton*, means *NHY de Eser Sefirot de Rosh*. These are the same *NHY* that completed the *Rosh de Elyon* in *Eser Sefirot* during their *Hitkalelut* in the *Zivug de Rosh de Elyon*. However, the *Halbasha* of the *Tachton* to the *Elyon*, meaning to *HGT NHY de Guf Elyon*, is because the *Tachton* is always on the same degree with the *Guf de Elyon*.

    Now you can see that the rumors brought here in the name of the Rav do not contradict each other whatsoever. He says above that *NHY de Atik* only clothe in *HGT de AA* and not at all in *NHY*, but only *He'arah* emerges from *Yesod de Atik* and expands in *NHY*. This refers to the *Behinat Hitlabshut NHY de Atik* to *Mochin* in *HGT de AA* for the *Rosh de AVI* that clothe those *HGT*.

    He also says here that *NHY de Atik* clothe also *NHY de AA*, as in *HGT de AA*, where the Upper thirds clothe in *HGT de AA* and the middle thirds clothe in *NHY de AA*. This relates to the *Behinat Halbasha* of the *Tachton* to the *Elyon*, which certainly clothes up to the *Sium* of the *Elyon*, meaning through the end of *Atzilut*, since all the *Partzufim* of *Atzilut* end equally. It turns out that even the *NHY de Tachton* necessarily clothe some of the *NHY de Elyon*.

However, we have said above that it speaks of *Behinat Hitlabshut NHY de Elyon* as *Mochin*. It is certain that *NHY de Atik* are clothed only in *HGT*, for the *He'arat Mochin de AVI*, which they clothe there.

Yet, *NHY de Atik* are not at all related to *NHY de AA*, where *ZON* clothe, to clothe in them for *He'arat Mochin*. This is because the *Mochin de ZON* come only by connecting *AA* and *AVI*, and have only *He'arah* from *Behinat Atik*.

This is the precision that the Rav makes above, "**Atzmut NHY de Atik in HGT de AA**, as mentioned, and that too is because *HGT de AA* later became *Mochin* in the First Three *de Abba* and *Ima*. Hence, their *He'arah* is primarily in *HGT de AA* to shine for *Mochei* (pl. for *Mochin*) *AVI*. Afterwards *Ohr* came out alone from *Yesod de Atik* and expanded in *NHY de AA*."

As we have explained in the previous item, this means that only *AVI* rise to *MAN* in *Rosh de Atik* along with *AA*, and thus take the *Atzmut de NHY de Atik* with them, uncovered by their *Hitkalelut* in that *Zivug*. The *Zivug de ZON*, however, is not done there, but only in *AA* along with *AVI*, as we shall explain below.

45. It is known that the *Raglaim* of *AA* end at the *Sof* of *Olam Atzilut*. Thus, these two bottom *Prakin de NH de Atik* in *Olam Beria* are uncovered, without *Levush*. They joined together and clothed in *Malchut de AA*, and there became two *Dadim* to her, on either side of her.

This is the meaning of *Dadei Behema*, which are below the *Raglaim*, from which the *Melachim* that descended in *Beria* sucked before their place was corrected in *AA*, *AVI*, and *ZON*. Even after they were born, each and every *Partzuf* first descended there and sucked from them, and then rose to their place.

Ohr Pnimi

45. Thus, these three bottom *Prakin de NH de Atik* in *Olam Beria*.

These words are seemingly perplexing. What caused the matter of the division of *NHY de Atik* into three thirds in this manner, until *Olam Atzilut* was not enough for them, and the two bottom thirds had to depart to *Olam Beria*? Also, why were all three thirds not clothed in *HGT NHY de AA*, and how are the Upper thirds of *HGT de AA* and the middle thirds of *NHY de AA* related?

These things are indeed deeper than the sea, and we shall explain them here. Know, that the origin of the division of the thirds in this manner extends from NHY de AK. It has been explained above (Part 6, *Histaklut Pnimit* items 14, 26) that because of *Tzimtzum Bet de AK*, where the two *Heyin*, the First and the second, joined together, the point of *Tzimtzum* in the place of *Olam ha Zeh* in *Behinat Malchut de Eser Sefirot de NHY de AK*, rose to the place of *Sefirat Bina de Eser Sefirot de NHY de AK*.

Thus, the three *Sefirot Bina* and *ZON de Eser Sefirot de NHY de AK* remained below the *Sium* of the *Kav de Ein Sof*, meaning below the point of *Tzimtzum*. They became a place for the three *Olamot: Beria, Yetzira, Assiya*, in the above-mentioned two places.

Even afterwards, when the *Ohr* that fissured the *Parsa* descended and clothed NHY de AK, the new *Gevul* did not change because of that. It is so, although ZAT de Nekudim that departed from *He'arat NHY de AK* along with AVI de Nekudim, crossed the new *Gevul* and wanted to expand their dominion below the *Gevul*, meaning in the three *Olamot* BYA. Hence, they broke and remained in BYA, meaning the place of their dominion.

NHY de AK, whose ZON departed and became BYA, and their *Keter* and *Hochma* remained in *Atzilut*. These *Bina* and ZON are merely regarded as the two bottom thirds of these *Eser Sefirot de NHY*, as this is how the AHP that came out of all the degrees is considered.

You will find that the Rav referred to the *AHP de Keter* that came out of *Keter* as Five Bottom *Sefirot de Keter BON*, which are only TNHYM. Also, the principal part of *Sefirat Tifferet*, meaning its Upper third, is considered the Upper half *de Keter*, and only the two bottom thirds of *Tifferet* belong to the AHP.

Thus, six *Sefirot* of the degree, KHB HGT, belong to the Upper half *de Keter*, which is only *Galgalta ve Eynaim*, and four *Sefirot* of the degree, NHYM, belong to the bottom half of the degree. The reason for it has already been explained in Part 7, and there is nothing more to add here.

Hence, it is considered that the six Upper *Sefirot* of the *Eser Sefirot de NHY de AK* remained in *Atzilut*, and only four *Sefirot*, NHYM of these *Eser Sefirot* came out and were made into BYA, meaning from their *Chazeh* downward. Similarly, *Eser Sefirot de NHY de AK* are divided into three thirds, KHB, HGT, NHYM. The two Upper thirds, KHB HGT, remained in *Atzilut*, and only the bottom thirds, which are NHYM, became BYA.

It is known that there is no absence in the spiritual, and the matter of the second *Tzimtzum* that was made in NHY de AK are regarded as merely additions to them. Thus, no change was made in the first NHY de AK, who now end at the *Nekuda de Olam ha Zeh* too, as it is written, "And His feet shall stand upon the mount of Olives."

It is known that *Partzuf Atik de Atzilut* is between AK and the *Partzufim* of *Atzilut*, where *Atzmut Malchut de AK* operates, which is *Behinat Hey Tata'a* before the *Tzimtzum*, meaning *Malchut* concealed in *RADLA*. Her *Atzmut* does not manifest in all the *Partzufim* of *Atzilut* at all, since she is *Midat ha Din*, without the association of *Midat ha Rachamim*, which is the First *Hey*. Hence, it too ends at the *Nekudat Olam ha Zeh*, as the first NHY *de AK* prior to *Tzimtzum Bet*, which is the association of *Midat ha Rachamim* with *Din*.

It turns out that NHY *de Atik* are divided into three thirds, as we have explained above regarding the *Eser Sefirot de NHY de AK*. The two Upper thirds *de NHY*, KHB HGT, stand in *Atzilut* and end equally with all the *Partzufim* of *Atzilut*, meaning on the new *Gevul de Tzimtzum Bet*. The bottom thirds, which are NHYM, are already below the *Sium* of *Atzilut*, expanding in BYA down to the *Nekuda de Olam ha Zeh*, as the first NHY *de AK*.

These two Upper thirds of NHY, which are *Behinot* KHB HGT that remained in *Atzilut*, are so only with regard to the *Kelim*. However, with regard to the *Ohr* in them, they are but HGT NHY, as it is known that HGT NHY *de Orot* clothe KHB HGT *de Kelim*.

It is written, "**the two Upper Prakin de NH de Atik clothed the HG de AA, Netzah on the right, and Hod in Gevura on the left Kav; Yesod in Tifferet de AA.**" It means that the Upper thirds of NHY *de Atik* are KHB *de Kelim* and HGT *de Orot*, hence their place is also in HGT *de AA*.

"**...and the two middle Prakin de NH de Atik in NH de AA. Also, Ateret Yesod de Atik in Yesod de AA, and Malchut de Atik in Malchut de AA.**" This means that the middle *Prakin de NHY de Atik* are HGT *de Kelim* and NHY *de Orot*, hence they clothe NHYM *de AA*. When he says that *Malchut de Atik* clothes *Malchut de AA*, it is not the actual *Malchut de Atik*, but only *Behinat He'arah* from its *Malchut*, since *Malchut de Atik* is concealed in *RADLA* and does not manifest (item 23).

It is written, "**These two bottom Prakin de NH de Atik in Olam Beria are uncovered, without Levush.**" This means that the bottom thirds *de NHY de Atik* expand equally with the *Raglaim* of AK in BYA. However, they are regarded as lacking *Yesod* and *Malchut*.

This is so because there is only *Tikun Kavim* in the form of the association of *Midat ha Rachamim* with *Din*, extending from *Tzimtzum Bet*. Since this *Hitpashtut* is from *Behinat Tzimtzum Aleph*, hence, there is no *Tikun* of the middle *Kav* there, and thus it is only considered as being in two *Kavim*, right and left, without sweetening. Thus, there is only the *Behinat* two bottom thirds *de Netzah* and *Hod* there, without *Yesod* and *Malchut*, but *Malchut* is contained in *Hod*.

Dadei Behema, which are below the Raglaim, from which the Melachim that descended in Beria.

It has already been explained (*Ohr Pnimi* item 42) how the birth of a *Partzuf* makes it fall to the Separated *BYA*. This is because the *Masach* upon which the *Zivug Elyon* for the *Koma* of the *Partzuf* comes from the *Behinat Guf* of the *Nekudim* that illuminated in *BYA*. Hence, this force that the *Reshimot* that the *Masach* consists of remains to shine in *BYA*.

However, when the *Masach* is purified from all the *Aviut de Guf* that was in it, this mixture of *He'arat BYA* was not apparent in it either, meaning as long as it was contained in the *Zivug de Rosh*.

Yet, after the *Aviut* of the *Guf* in the *Masach* was recognized, the force of *He'arat BYA* that was in it immediately appeared, and it was separated from the *Rosh* and descended to its place in *BYA*. Thus, its birth, meaning the recognition of the *Aviut de Guf* in the *Masach*, separates it from the *Behinat Elyon* and brings it to its place, making it fall to *BYA*.

This is the conduct in all the *Partzufim de Atzilut*, since they all came out of the *Masach de Guf Nekudim* that illuminated in *BYA*, except *Partzuf Atik*, which was truly corrected to be able to expand to *BYA*, as it clothes the *Atzmut Malchut de AK* prior to *Tzimtzum Bet*.

The principal *Tikun*, sufficient to raise them to *Atzilut* once more, is the separation of the force of *He'arat BYA* from them, and the attainment of the strong force of *Sium* of *Tzimtzum Bet*, being *Behinat Malchut de AA* that contains all the force of *Sium* of *Atzilut*. This is the meaning of *Dadei Behema*, which are the *Behinat* two bottom thirds *de Netzah Hod de Atik* found in *BYA*.

They joined and connected and were corrected in a single association with *Malchut de AA*. By joining both of them, they became corrected *Dadei Behema* to bestow the strong force of *Tzimtzum Bet* in *Malchut de AA*.

It is written, "**These two bottom Prakin de NH de Atik in Olam Beria are uncovered, without Levush. They joined together and clothed in Malchut de AA.**" This is so because then they can suck the *Shefa de Atzilut* although they stand in *BYA*, as they receive *He'arat Malchut de AA* through the two bottom thirds *de NH de Atik* that are in the same *Olam* as theirs. Finally, they receive the *Behinat Sium de Atzilut* and rise to their place in *Atzilut*.

They are called *Dadei Behema* because *Malchut* is called this when she is without the sweetening from *Midat ha Rachamim*. Their opposite is *Dadei Adam*, indicating that *Malchut* is sweetened in *Midat ha Rachamim*. This is the meaning of standing in *Komat Bina*, which is the *Shoresh* of *Rachamim*. For that reason they are connected in the place of the heart, which is *Bina*, and not below in the *Raglaim*, where there is gripping for the *Klipot*, as it is written, "Her feet go down to death." Hence, it is the place of *Erva*, meaning there is gripping to the exteriors. This is also the meaning of *Behema* being BON in *Gimatria*.

46. Thus we have explained how **ZA** receives his **Mochin,** which is the **Ohr** of his true inner **Atzmut.** When he is in *Gadlut,* they come to him clothed inside the *Achoraim de NHY de Ima* and *NHY de Abba.* All the *Partzufim* are like that too, because the **NHY** of the *Elyon,* their *Hitzoniut,* becomes a *Levush* to the *Mochin* of the *Partzuf* below it and everything enters and expands in *Rosh* and *Guf* to that lower *Partzuf.*

Ohr Pnimi

46. **All the *Partzufim* are like that too, because the *NHY* of the Elyon, their *Hitzoniut,* becomes a *Levush* to the *Mochin* of the *Parzuf* below it, and everything enters and expands in *Rosh* and *Guf* to that lower *Parzuf*:** It is has already been thoroughly explained (*Ohr Pnimi* item 42) that the matter of *NHY de Elyon* which clothe in the *Tachton,* they are *NHY de Eser Sefirot de Rosh,* that come out in *Rosh de Elyon* in the power of the *Tachton's Hitkalelut* in *Zivug de Rosh de Elyon,* that those additional *NHY* are not at all *NHY de Eser Sefirot de Elyon* for they are below its *Koma.* For example, the *NHY de Rosh de Atik,* they are *NHY de Komat Keter,* but the *NHY* that were added to *Atik* due to *Hitkalelut AA* in *Behinat MAN* there, those are *NHY de Komat Hochma.* This is why Rav precisely writes: "their *Hitzoniut,* becomes a *Levush* of the *Mochin* of the *Partzuf* below it", because the *Koma de Behina Gimel* is called *Hitzoniut* to the *Koma de Behina Dalet,* and *AA* took only the *NHY de Behina Gimel,* thus he had taken only the *Hitzoniut de NHY de Atik.* Similarly, all the *Partzufim,* are not actually taking *NHY de Elyon,* but *NHY de Komat* the *Tachton* while it is included in the *Elyon,* which is always one degree lower than *de Elyon* and thus is called *Hitzoniut de Elyon,* or *Achoraim de NHY de Elyon,* And Remember this.

Here are those *NHY de Elyon* becomes *Levush* to the *Mochin de Tachton* and go down with it as it goes out from *Rosh de Elyon* to its place. Because the essence of *Koma's light* clothe those *NHY, and NHY are* clothed with the *Mochin* in

Kelim of the *Tachton* in such a way that those *NHY* they are a means between the *Orot de Tachton* and the *Kelim de Tachton*.

Also know that those *NHY* contains complete *Eser Sefirot Rosh* and *Guf* like there are to the *Mochin* which receive inside them, Because *Netzah* and *Hod* are the *Kelim de GAR* and in them Clothe *HBD* of the *Mochin*. And *Yesod* is the *Kli* to all the *ZAT* of the *Mochin* which are *HGT NHYM*, like it is written in front of us.

47. There is no *Mochin* that is less than three *Behinot HB* and *Daat*. *Hochma* is the *Hesed* line, *Bina* is the *Gevura* line and *Daat* is divided into two: half *Hesed* and half *Gevura*. This is in order to determine between them, as it is written, "for the Lord is a God of knowledge," two *Daats* (pl. for *Daat*). Also, *Hesed* is considered five *Hassadim* and *Gevura*, five *Gevurot*, as mentioned in *Idrat Nasso* (in the Zohar).

Ohr Pnimi

47. **There is no *Mochin* that is less than three *Behinot HB* and *Daat*. *Hochma* is the *Hesed* line, *Bina* is the *Gevura* line and *Daat* is divided into two: half *Hesed* and half *Gevura*:** Since those things are the keys for all the *Mochin de Atzilut*, it is fitting that we Shall speak at length about them. It has already been explained above that all the heads that came out in the beginning, in *Atzilut's Tikun*, even in their *Zivug de Gadlut*, were as *Panim be Achor*. Since *Bina de Rosh* doesn't change her nature because of the *Gadlut* and always stands in *Achoraim* to *Abba* (*Ohr Pnimi* item 31), it follows that *Bina de Rosh* is stopping *ZON de Rosh* from spreading from within her to the outside. Because *ZON* only reveals outside of *Bina* in *He'arat Hochma* as in *ZON de Ohr Yashar*, which have already become known, and since *Bina* is in *Achoraim* to *Abba* and doesn't contain anything but *Ohr de Hassadim*, *ZON* are included within her and does not reveal outside. Now you can understand why the Heads *de Atzilut* are known as *GAR*, because they have nothing but *KHB*, and *ZON* are missing within them due to *Bina* standing in *Achoraim* to *Abba* and does not return her *Panim* back to *Abba*, apart from raising *MAN*.

Now you can understand the origin of *Moach HaDaat*, because by the raising of *MAN*, *Bina* is awakened and comes back *Panim be Panim* with *Abba* and they bring out *Komat Eser Sefirot* on the Man. And then *ZON* are born and reveal in *Rosh de Elyon* itself, where they were missing until now because of *Achoraim de Bina*. And now that *Bina* came back *Panim be Panim*, now *ZON de Rosh* reveal out of them in *He'arat Hochma* as they are worthy. And this new

ZON that revealed in *Rosh* are called *Daat*, since they are really only Rosh's ZAT, which were now added by the raising of the MAN.

And even though they are only ZON, still they have complete *Eser Sefirot* GAR *and* ZAT, because they have *He'arat Hochma* within them. Therefore, it is then distinct, that HGT becomes HBD and NH within them became ZON. Although in their origin they have nothing but *Hey Hassadim* for ZA within *Daat*, which are HGT NH *de Hassadim* and *Hey Gevurot* for *Nukva* within *Daat*, which are HGT NH *de Gevurot*. But the *Bet Hassadim de Hesed* and *Gevura* and the upper third within *Tifferet* returns to be *HBD* by the power of *He'arat Hochma* within them. And so does the *Bet* and third *Gevurot*, which are *Hesed* and *Gevura* and the upper third within *Tifferet*, from the *Nukva*, also became HBD by the power of *He'arat Hochma*. But now they are connected together and are considered one.

It has already been explained above, in the previous item, that NHY *de Elyon*, which are the clothing of the *Mochin*, are also divided to *Eser Sefirot*, That is, they are divided to there thirds, on the three *Kavim*: *Netzah, Hod, Yesod*. That the right *Kav* which is *Netzah* is divided to three thirds: *Hochma Hesed, Netzah*. So does the left *Kav* which is *Hod* is divided to three thirds: *Bina, Gevura, Hod*. And so does the middle *Kav* which is *Yesod* is divided into three thirds: *Daat, Tifferet, Yesod* and *Malchut*.

It is written: "*Hochma* is the *Hesed* line, *Bina* is the *Gevura* line and *Daat* is divided into two: half *Hesed* and half *Gevura*".

It has already been explained above in the previous item, that *Netzah* and *Hod* are *Kelim de* GAR of the *Daat* and *Yesod* is the *Kli de* ZAT of the *Daat*, and accordingly, the same two and a half upper *Hassadim* with the two and a half upper *Gevurot*, which are HGT down to the Chazeh, returned to become HBD. Now *Hochma* has clothed in the right line which are the three thirds within *Netzah*, and has divided there into *Hochma, Hesed, Netzah*; and they are all as *Hochma*. And *Bina* has clothed in the left line, which are three thirds within *Hod*, and has divided there into *Bina, Gevura, Hod*, and they are all as *Bina*. *Daat de Elyon* within GAR *de Daat*, which is called the hidden *Daat*, has clothed in upper third *de Tifferet*. Now it is clear that GAR *de Daat* are HGT, which returned to become HBD. And ZON in *Daat*, which are the two and two thirds of *Hassadim*, and two and two thirds of *Gevurot*, which are two lower thirds of *Tifferet*, and NH, which were left in the *Hassadim* and *Gevurot*, double themselves and becomes complete *Hey Hassadim* and complete *Hey Gevurot*. *Hey Hassadim* are ZA in *Daat de* ZAT and *Hey Gevurot* are Nukva in that *Daat*, and both of them are clothed in the three thirds within the middle line of *Kli de Yesod* which are *Daat, Tifferet, Yesod*, and they are all only as *Daat*.

48. There is no *Mochin* that is less than three *Behinot HB* and *Daat*. *Hochma* is the *Hesed* line, *Bina* is the *Gevura* line and *Daat* is divided into two: half *Hesed* and half *Gevura*. This is in order to determine between them, as it is written, "for the Lord is a God of knowledge," two *Daats* (pl. for *Daat*). Also, *Hesed* is considered five *Hassadim* and *Gevura*, five *Gevurot*, as mentioned in *Idrat Nasso* (in the Zohar).

Ohr Pnimi

46. AK contains.

    Orot stem from it, which are its branches.

49. There were two *Daats* in *Zeir Anpin*, one from *Mochin* that were extended to him from *Abba* and one from *Mochin* that were extended to him from *NHY de Ima*. Each of them consists of five *Hassadim* and five *Gevurot*.

50. The reason for it is that after all he also receives *Mochin de AA* by *Hitlabshut NHY de Atik* in itself. *Atik* does not have two separate *Partzufim, Dechura* and *Nukva*. Rather, they are both one *Partzuf*.

    Hence, there were two *Partzufim* there in ZA de AVI. Two *Behinot Mochin* entered: one in *NHY de Abba* and one in *NHY de Ima*. However, in this *Atik Dechura* and his *Nukva*, they all form one *Partzuf*.

    For that reason there are only three separate *Mochin* in AA. This is also why he has only one *Daat* with five *Hassadim* from the *Dechura* side, the MA in him, and five *Gevurot* from the *Nukva* side, the name BON in him, since all is one *Behinat HaVaYaH*.

51. Remember and do not forget that rule that always, in all the *Partzufim* of *Atzilut*, all the *Hassadim* extend from the name New MA that comes to correct the *Atzilut*, and all the *Gevurot* from the name BON of the sorts of the *Melachim*. This is also the meaning of the *Zivug* to sweeten the *Nukva Gevurot* named BON that are now being sorted anew in every single *Zivug* as MAN by the *Hassadim* from which the new MA extends.

52. Also, it has already been explained there that what *Atik* sorted in the first time was to correct the *Atzmut* of *Partzuf* AA in the beginning of its correction and placed them in AA as *Mochin*.

    Partzuf AA *Zachar* and *Nukva* was made of these HG that *Atik* placed in AA in the first time. They remain there permanently and when AA also returns to sort for AVI, to correct them for the first time, the *Zivug* of *Atik*

Zachar and *Nukva* must precede it. After that they return to extend new *Mochin* to *AA* and *Nukva* so that they can sort the parts of *AVI*.

Afterwards the new *HG* come to them, the *Hassadim* from the name *MA* and the *Gevurot* from the name *BON*. Then the parts of *AVI* are erected there inside the *AA*, as mentioned there.

Thus, there are two kinds of *Hassadim* and *Gevurot*: one, this is the first, to correct the *Partzuf*; two, the new ones, which extend in every single *Zivug* and every single time. These do not stay there permanently; they are only erected and the form of the fetus is made of them, and it is born there.

Ohr Pnimi

51. The *Se'arot* of its *Rosh* are opposite the braches of *AB*, and the *Se'arot Orot* stem from it, which are its branches.

53. *I have notified you before that there is *Behinat Atik* and *Nukva*, *AA* and *Nukva*, and *AVI* and *ZON*. However, there is a difference regarding the above-mentioned *Nekevot*. The *Nekeva* is *Dinim*, and is from the sorts of the *Melachim*. How then can the name *Nekeva* be right there in *Atik* and *AA*, which are totally *Rachamim*, as we've mentioned in the two Idrot (Zohar)?

Moreover, the existence of *Zachar* and *Nekeva* indicates diminution and separation. There is no greater unity as when the *Zachar* is alone.

We have found in many place places in the Zohar and in Idra Raba (a Parasha in the Zohar): "In that image of *Adam* there exists a rule of *Dechura* and *Nukva*, which is not so in *Atik*. We also find in many places that *Behinot Zachar* and *Nekeva* did not begin but from *AVI* downward.

It is thus mentioned in the Idra Zuta (a parasha in the Zohar): "That *Hochma* expanded, and you find *Dechura* and *Nukva*." *Hochma* is the father, *Bina*, the mother, and because of it there is *Zachar* and *Nukva*.

Thus, why do we say that there is *Behinat Nukva* even in *Atik* and *AA*? We find the opposite of that in many places, especially in Parashat Bereshit (in the Zohar): "The reason of all reasons said that called, 'See now that I, even I, am He, and there is no god with Me'.

There is one that merges, such as *Dechura* and *Nukva*, and he said about him: 'I called him one, but he is one, not counted and not merged. Because of that he said 'there is no god with Me,' which is *Behinat Nukva*, called Elohim, which is *Din*."

Ohr Pnimi

52. **AK contains.**

    Orot stem from it, which are its branches.

54. In order to reconcile these texts, you should know that in all the *Eser Sefirot* there are certainly *Zachar* and *Nukva*, but there is a dispute in how they are present. The explanation of the matter is that most of the death is in ZON since the seven *Melachim* that died were in them.

    Hence there is *Zachar* and *Nukva* in separate *Partzufim* from one another. The reason you sometimes find them joined is only when they are *Achor be Achor*. This is because at that time their *Achoraim* are attached together, one wall serves both, and a separation of the *Achor* is required to separate them.

Ohr Pnimi

53. The *Se'arot* of its *Rosh* are opposite the braches of AB, and the *Se'arot Orot* stem from it, which are its branches.

55. However, in AVI there was annulment and not actual death as it was in ZON. Hence there were separate *Behinot Zachar* and *Nekeva* in them too, meaning regarded as two *Partzufim*, as in ZON.

    Yet, there is a great cohesion added there, which is that they are always attached together *Panim be Panim* in one wall that serves both. There is no separation between them whatsoever as in ZON, which connect when they are *Achor be Achor* and separate when they are *Panim be Panim*.

Ohr Pnimi

54. The *Se'arot* of its *Rosh* are opposite the braches of AB, and the *Se'arot Orot* stem from it, which are its branches.

56. This is the reason that they said in many places in the Zohar that AVI never stops the joint connection, they emerge as one and remain as one; one is not separated from the other. Hence their *Zivug* is perpetual and unending.

57. However, in AA, which is considered the *Keter* of the *Nekudot*, even the cancellation did not occur although it is from the last five of *Keter de BON*.

    It is known that there was some annulment in the NHY of *Keter de Nekudim* when they descended to become *Mochin* for AVI. Hence there was also *Behinot ZON* in it, but a correction and additional connection was added to them, being that both were one *Partzuf*, the *Zachar* and *Nekeva* in it. Thus, the *Behinat* name MA in it is placed in each right side and the *Behinat* name BON in it was on the left side in it, and both were cleaved together as one *Partzuf*.

Ohr Pnimi

56. The *Se'arot* of its *Rosh* are opposite the braches of *AB*, and the *Se'arot*

    Orot stem from it, which are its branches.

58. This is the meaning of what is written in the Zohar that *Keter* is a single *Zachar* without a *Nukva*, meaning without a separate *Nukva*. When we say that there are *Zachar* and *Nukva* it is because these two *Behinot* MA and BON are in it, on its right and on its left. They are *Behinot Zachar* and *Nekeva* in every place, but not that it has separate *ZON* in two *Partzufim*; examine that deeply.

    Now you can see how *AVI* clothe *AA* on its right and on its left. It is so because this is how it is in *AA* itself; the right side in it is MA *Dechura* and the left side is BON *Nukva*.

59. In *Atik Yomin*, which is considered the First *Hey* of the *Keter* of *Nekudim*, there was never any cancellation. Hence, *Behinot Zachar* and *Nekeva* in it, namely MA and BON, become completely mixed and they are entirely mingled in one another on the right, in itself, and on its left, and they are not like *AA*.

    This is the meaning of what is written in the Zohar (Idra Raba), "there is no left in that blocked *Atik*, it is all right." The thing is that in *AA* the *Zachar* is on the right and the *Nekeva* on the left. Yet, in *Atik Yomin*, its right side consists of MA and BON, and also on the left side.

    Hence they are equal and there is no difference between its right and its left. However, the *Behinot Nekeva* and *Zachar* in it are in a different form, meaning they are two *Behinot* right and left. It means that there is also *Behinat* MA from the *Panim* side and *Behinat* BON from the *Achor* side between its right side and its left side. In that it is a great and wonderful connection.

Ohr Pnimi

58. *AK* contains.

    Orot stem from it, which are its branches.

60. *Know, that Upper AVI were made thus: *Abba* from the *Nekeva*, Upper half of *Bina de MA* and *Ima* from the *Zachar*, completely *Hochma de BON*. Yet, it is called *Hochma de BON Ima* since it is *Behinat BON*. *Bina de MA* is called *Hochma* since it is *de MA*, and examine that. It turns out that in fact they are both called only *Hochma* and they are *Behinat* First *Yod* in the Name.

Ohr Pnimi

59. The *Se'arot* of its *Rosh* are opposite the braches of *AB*, and the *Se'arot Orot* stem from it, which are its branches.

61. *Ima* is many times greater than *Abba* in three aspects: One, because this is half *Bina de MA* and this is complete *Hochma de BON*. Two, because one is *Hochma* and the other is *Bina*. Three, because one is *MA* and the other is *BON*, whose merit is greater than *MA* since it is *Behinat SAG*. This is because it is known that the *Melachim* that died are all *SAG*.

Hence, you find that *Ima* now came out concealed and clothed inside *Abba*, and because of all these reasons both are called *Abba*, or only *Hochma*, as she is not at all apparent. For that reason they are both the *Yod* in the Name, since *VAD* (*Vav* and *Dalet*) in the filling of *Yod* is shaped as *Hey*.

This is so because *Ima* is concealed inside the *Yod* and is not mentioned, but only a simple *Yod* which is *Abba*. This is the meaning of "crown to her husband."

Ohr Pnimi

60. *AK* contains.

Orot stem from it, which are its branches.

62. *Israel Saba* was made of the lower half of *Bina de MA* and *Tvuna* from complete *Bina de BON* and then both are considered *Bina de MA* and *BON*. Hence, they are both regarded as only *Bina*, and this is the First *Hey* in the Name.

In that state *Abba* is hidden and concealed since he is the *Yod* of the filling *Hey Yod*. This is because now she has no merit over him, as now they are both from *Behinat Bina*. Since he is *Behinat Zachar* he overpowers her. However, in *AVI* the *Ima* has a great advantage over *Abba*.

Ohr Pnimi

61. The *Se'arot* of its *Rosh* are opposite the braches of *AB*, and the *Se'arot*

Orot stem from it, which are its branches.

63. It turns out that in fact *Abba* is the general Upper AVI, the *Yod* in the Name and *Ima* is the general *Israel Saba ve Tvuna*, the First *Hey* in the Name. However, sometimes we call *Abba* and *Israel Saba* – *Abba*, since they are both *Bina de MA*, and *Bina* and *Tvuna* – *Ima*, since they are both only *BON*, which is *Nekeva*.

    Now you can see what is written in a different place about "and I will not come in fury" that *Zivug Israel Saba ve Tvuna* is *Zivug de Lo Pasik* called *Zivug Bina* and *Bina*. But, "and I will not come in fury" is *Hochma* with *Bina*, which is Upper AVI, whose *Zivug* stops.

    It is told in another interpretation that "*Ima* came out from between the arms of *Abba*". This is the meaning of YESHSUT, called "*Ima* came out from under the two arms of the Upper AVI", called that they both come alone.

Ohr Pnimi

62. The *Se'arot* of its *Rosh* are opposite the braches of AB, and the *Se'arot Orot* stem from it, which are its branches.

64. *

65.

Ohr Pnimi

64. The *Se'arot* of its *Rosh* are opposite the braches of AB, and the *Se'arot Orot* stem from it, which are its branches.

66.

Ohr Pnimi

65. The *Se'arot* of its *Rosh* are opposite the braches of AB, and the *Se'arot Orot* stem from it, which are its branches.

67.

Ohr Pnimi

66. AK contains.

    Orot stem from it, which are its branches.

68.

Ohr Pnimi

67. **AK** contains.
    Orot stem from it, which are its branches.
69.
70.
71.
72. *

Ohr Pnimi

71. **AK** contains.
    Orot stem from it, which are its branches.
73.

Ohr Pnimi

72. **AK** contains.
    Orot stem from it, which are its branches.
74.

Ohr Pnimi

73. **AK** contains.
    Orot stem from it, which are its branches.
75.

*Ohr Pnimi

74. **AK** contains.
    Orot stem from it, which are its branches.
76.
77. *

Ohr Pnimi

76. **AK** contains.
    Orot stem from it, which are its branches.
78.

Ohr Pnimi

77. **AK** contains.

Orot stem from it, which are its branches.

79.

80.

Ohr Pnimi

79. **AK** contains.

Orot stem from it, which are its branches.

81.

82.

Ohr Pnimi

81. **AK** contains.

Orot stem from it, which are its branches.

83.

Ohr Pnimi

82. **AK** contains.

Orot stem from it, which are its branches.

84.

85.

Ohr Pnimi

84. **AK** contains.

Orot stem from it, which are its branches.

86.

87.

Ohr Pnimi

86. **AK** contains.

Orot stem from it, which are its branches.

88.

Ohr Pnimi

87. AK contains.

    Orot stem from it, which are its branches.

89. *

Ohr Pnimi

88. AK contains.

    Orot stem from it, which are its branches.

90.

Ohr Pnimi

89. The Se'arot of its Rosh are opposite the braches of AB, and the Se'arot Orot stem from it, which are its branches.

91.

Ohr Pnimi

90. AK contains.

    Orot stem from it, which are its branches.

92.

Ohr Pnimi

91. The Se'arot of its Rosh are opposite the braches of AB, and the Se'arot Orot stem from it, which are its branches.

93.

Ohr Pnimi

92. AK contains.

    Orot stem from it, which are its branches.

94.

PART SIXTEEN

The Three *Olamot Beria Yetzira Assiya*

42. * It is written in the Zohar (Kedoshim) about the secretes of the Torah: "*Adam ha Rishon* did not have anything of *Olam ha Zeh*. One righteous made use of his *Nukva*, and one *Guf* was made of that usage, whose *Ohr* is more than all those angels above etc."

    First, I will explain a certain matter that I had briefly heard from my teacher and then I will elaborate more as much as I heard later on.

43. *Adam ha Rishon* had no part of *Olam ha Zeh*, which is *Olam Assiya*. His *Guf* was from *Olam Yetzira*, his *Nefesh* from *Olam Beria*, his *Ruach* from *Nukva de ZA de Atzilut*, and his *Neshama* from *ZA de Atzilut*. Also, He had *Neshama* to *Neshama* from *Abba ve Ima de Atzilut*.

Ohr Pnimi

43. His *Guf* was from *Olam Yetzira*, his *Nefesh* from *Olam Beria*, his *Ruach* from *Nukva de ZA de Atzilut*, and his *Neshama* from *ZA de Atzilut*. Also, He had *Neshama* to *Neshama* from *Abba ve Ima de Atzilut*.

    We need a close examination here to compare this short text with the elaborate text presented later and with the rest of the articles regarding that matter. We must know that before the sin of *Etz ha Daat* Adam had two *Behinot NRN*; he had *NRN* from *BYA* and also *NRN* from *Atzilut*.

    He also had a *Malbush Hitzon* on them like the current corporeal *Guf* about which it is said, "Then the Lord God formed man off the dust of the ground etc." It is presented below that all the *Olamot* were on a higher level than they are now because from the current *Chazeh de Yetzira* downward was *Mador ha Klipot*, *ZA de Atzilut* was in the place of *Abba* and *Nukva* in the place of *Ima*.

    Beria in the place of *ZA de Atzilut* and *GAR de Yetzira* in the place of *Nukva de Atzilut*. The bottom six of *Yetzira* in the place of the top six of the current *Beria*, *GAR de Assiya* in the place of the bottom four of the current *Beria*, and the bottom six of *Assiya* in the place of the top six of the current *Yetzira*. This is because the *Sium Raglin* was in the place of the current *Chazeh de Yetzira* (see item 55).

    The *Malbush Hitzon* of *Adam ha Rishon* was made of *Malchut de Assiya* called "dust off the earth" and indeed the place of *Beit ha Mikdash* was built from this *Beria de Malchut*. However, *Assiya* was then completely above the current *Chazeh de Yetzira*.

Afterwards he had NRN from BYA, he had *Nefesh Ruach* from *Assiya* and *Yetzira*, which are also called "*Behinat Guf*" of *Adam ha Rishon*, because the VAK are called *Guf*. Finally, he had *Neshama* from *Beria*.

After that he had NRN from *Atzilut*, *Nefesh* from *Nukva de Atzilut* that was clothed in *Olam Yetzira*, and for the clothing of *Nukva* in *Olam Yetzira*, which is *Behinat ZA*. For this reason this *Nefesh* is named *Ruach*.

He had *Ruach* from ZA *de Atzilut* which is clothed in *Olam Beria* and for the dressing of ZA in *Beria*, which is *Behinat Neshama* and YESHSUT. Hence, this *Ruach* is named *Neshama*. In addition, he had *Neshama* to *Neshama* from ZON *de Atzilut*, which are then in the place of *Abba ve Ima*.

It is written, "**His Guf was from Olam Yetzira**," meaning his *Behinot Ruach Nefesh*, called VAK or *Guf*, were both from *Olam Yetzira*. This is because the past *Assiya* stood above *Chazeh de Yetzira* and was thus considered that her *Nefesh*, which also received from *Assiya*, is also *Behinat Yetzira* compared to now.

It is written, "**his Nefesh from Olam Beria**." It means that he had *Behinat Neshama* from *Olam Beria*, meaning his *Behinat Neshama* was from *Olam Beria* and it is called *Nefesh* relating to *Nefesh de Atzilut*. This is the meaning of "**his Ruach from Nukva de ZA de Atzilut**," meaning from the part of *Nukva* clothed in the past GAR *de Yetzira*. It is called *Ruach* because of the *Hitlabshut* in *Olam Yetzira* which is *Behinat ZA* and *Ruach*.

This is the meaning of "**and his Neshama from ZA de Atzilut**." In other words it is from the part of ZA clothed in *Olam Beria*. It is called *Neshama* even though everything that comes from ZA is only *Ruach*. This is because of his *Hitlabshut* in *Beria*, which is *Behinat Neshama* and *Behinat* YESHSUT.

It is written, "**Also, He had Neshama to Neshama from Abba ve Ima**," meaning from ZON that rose and clothed AVI. This is because ZA rose to the place of *Abba* and *Nukva* to the place of *Ima*.

44. The reason why he had no part in *Olam Assiya* is what we will explain about the order of the world and its division. Its place of ruin is opposite the *Klipa*, and the settled world is divided into many divisions: *Hutz la Eretz* is opposite *Assiya* and the whole of *Eretz Israel* is opposite *Yetzira*.

It is written in the Zohar, "The firmaments of *Assiya* exist on *Eretz Israel* to defend it etc." The place of **Beit ha Mikdash** is opposite **Beria** and the **Kodesh Kodashim** is opposite the Upper **Heichal Kodesh Kodashim** of **Beria**.

45. It turns out that since *Adam ha Rishon* was created from the place of his repentance, the *Olam* was always in the form of *Beria*. After he had sinned, he was created in the weekdays. We have already explained in Parashat Pekudei that *Adam ha Rishon* was created by *Zivug ZA* and its *Nukva*, who rose up to the *Heichal* of *Abba ve Ima* where they mated *Panim be Panim* and procreated *Adam* and *Hava*.

46. For that reason ZA was then in the form of *Neshama*, which is *Bina*, and his *Nukva* was in the form of *Ruach*, which is ZA. It is said in that regard in the Zohar, "a man's soul is the candle of God" that *Neshama* is *Dechura* from the Upper Great Tree, and *Ruach* is from the Small Tree.

Ohr Pnimi

46. **ZA was then in the form of *Neshama*, which is *Bina*, and his *Nukva* was in the form of *Ruach*, which is ZA etc. called *Neshama* after ZA being up in the place of *Bina* etc. called *Ruach* after his *Nukva* having been at that time in the place of her husband ZA.**

   It is seemingly perplexing that he contradicts his own words. He says above that ZON rose up to *Heichal Abba ve Ima*, and below in the part (item 57) he says that ZA rose to the place of *Bina* and *Nukva* to the place of ZA.

   The thing is that this speaks of ZA and *Nukva* that remained below clothed in *Olam Yetzira* and *Beria*. When ZA is clothed in *Olam Beria* it must give her from *Bina de Atzilut* because *Beria* receives only from *Bina*, as she is *Behinat Bina de Guf* and a *Behina* receives only from its corresponding *Behina* in the *Elyon*.

   This is the meaning of the text **"called *Neshama* after ZA being up in the place of *Bina*,"** meaning he gives to *Beria* by receiving the *Ohr* above the *Ohr* from the place of *Bina*, which is the corresponding *Behina* of *Beria*.

   It is written, **"called *Ruach* after his *Nukva* having been at that time in the place of her husband Yodin."** This is because the *Nukva* that clothed in *Olam Yetzira* cannot give to *Yetzira* but only from the *Ohr* of ZA which is ascribed to *Behinat Yetzira*.

   In order to give to *Yetzira*, she must be for her in the place of ZA, hence the *Ohr* is named after ZA, which is *Ruach*. Nonetheless, ZON themselves are on a higher degree because *Nukva* is in the place of *Ima*, which is YESHSUT, and ZA is in the place of *Abba*, which is the Upper AVI.

47. **The thing is that ZA, which is *Dechura* Great Upper Tree, where the *Neshama* of *Adam ha Rishon* came from, called *Neshama* after ZA being**

up in the place of *Bina*. The *Ruach* of *Adam* is from *Nukva de ZA* Small Tree, *Nukva*, called *Ruach* after his *Nukva* having been at that time in the place of her husband *ZA*, as explained there in the Zohar.

48. After *Adam ha Rishon* sinned in *Etz ha Daat*, which is *Olam Assiya* that he was commanded not to eat from since he had no part in *Assiya* but only from *Yetzira* upward. Since he broke it and ate from *Etz ha Daat*, which is *Assiya*, he flawed all the *Olamot*. Hence, they all descended from their degree because *Yetzira* clothed in *Assiya*.

Ohr Pnimi

48. In *Etz ha Daat*, which is *Olam Assiya* that he was commanded not to eat from since he had no part in *Assiya* but only from *Yetzira* upward.

The meaning of the *Mitzva* that he was told not to eat from *Etz ha Daat* stems from the *Sium Raglin* of the three *Olamot BYA* that was on the current *Chazeh de Yetzira*. This was the end of the zone of the *Kedusha* and from there down was *Mador ha Klipot*.

It is so because only the first nine of the eight broken *Melachim* were sorted, which are the 248 *Nitzotzin*. However, their *Malchuiot* fell from the *Chazeh* down to the general place of *BYA*, which are the eight *Malchuiot*. Each of them consists of four *Behinot*, which are 32 in *Gimatria*, and they became the *Klipot* that are not good for anything, called *Lev ha Even* (The Stony Heart).

This is so because they are not sorted at all before the end of correction when *Malchut de Tzimtzum Aleph* that was concealed in *RADLA* will appear. Then, even SAM will be a holy angel, as then "He will swallow up death for ever."

It is written, "**he was commanded not to eat from since he had no part in *Assiya* but only from *Yetzira* upward**," meaning the current *Assiya* that is clothed in *Mador ha Klipot* and has contact with the above *Lev ha Even*. This is because the past *Assiya* ended entirely above the *Chazeh* of the general place of *BYA* which is above the current *Chazeh de Yetzira*.

Because of this *Sium* he was given the commandment of prohibition on eating the *Etz ha Daat* so that he would have no contact with the *Klipot* that cling to *Assiya*, meaning the *Achoraim* of *Assiya* that remained *Achor be Achor*. He was forbidden to eat the *Etz ha Daat*, meaning to extend *He'arah* to the *Achoraim* since the *Shefa* would reach the *Kelim* in the above-mentioned *Lev ha Even*, and he would die as in the case of the breaking of the vessels.

Since he broke it and ate from *Etz ha Daat*, which is *Assiya*, he flawed all the *Olamot*. Hence, they all descended from their degree because *Yetzira* clothed in *Assiya*.

It means in the past *Olam Assiya* too, when he stood at the first six of the current *Olam Yetzira*. It was therefore considered *Olam Yetzira* since the *Tachton* that stands in the place of the *Elyon* becomes like him (see item 60). Hence, now after the sin of *Etz ha Daat* he fell to the *Behinat* current *Assiya* that stands clothed in *Mador ha Klipot*. Also, the reason why the eating of *Etz ha Daat* caused the *Hitlabshut* of *Assiya* in the *Klipot* will be explained below (item 52).

49. It follows, that *Eretz Israel* that was opposite *Yetzira* does not receive from it but through *Assiya* because *Yetzira* is clothed in it. Also, *Beria* is clothed in *Yetzira*, *Nukva de Atzilut* clothed in *Beria* and ZA clothed in its *Nukva*. Similarly, all the *Elyonim* of it descended from their degree.

Ohr Pnimi

49. **Eretz Israel that was opposite Yetzira does not receive from it but through Assiya.**

Prior to the sin, *Yetzira* was in the place of *Beria*, the Upper four of *Nukva de* ZA in the place of *Nukva de* ZA and the lower six in the place of the Upper six of *Beria*. Then, *Eretz Israel*, which is opposite the *Yetzira* received from the current *Beria*.

After the sin, the Upper six of *Yetzira* fell inside the past *Assiya*, and the bottom four of *Yetzira* fell to the place of the *Klipot*. This is so because from *Chazeh de Yetzira* downward they fell to *Mador ha Klipot* which is from the *Chazeh* down of the place of BYA.

Thus, *Eretz Israel* cannot receive from its corresponding *Behina*, which is *Yetzira*, except through *Assiya* from before the sin, meaning according to the state that was in the first *Behina* when *Adam ha Rishon* was born.

Beria is clothed in Yetzira, Nukva de Atzilut clothed in Beria and ZA clothed in its Nukva.

Beria that stood at the place of ZA *de Atzilut* descended below *Parsa* because of the sin to the place of the bottom six of *Yetzira* from before the sin, meaning the state at the time of the birth of *Adam ha Rishon*. ZA, which stood in the place of Upper *Abba*, descended to the place of the *Nukva*, to its *Behinat* from the *Chazeh* down, belonging to its *Nukva* and became *Behinat* VAK without a *Rosh*.

Thus, the principle state is the state of the *Olamot* prior to the sin, meaning in the first *Behina* at the time of the birth of the *Neshama* of *Adam ha Rishon*. ZA was in the place of *Abba*, its *Nukva* in the place of *Ima* and *Beria* in the place of ZA. GAR *de Yetzira* in the place of *Nukva de ZA* and her VAK in the place of the top six *de Yetzira* through the *Chazeh*.

After the sin ZA fell from its *Chazeh* downward and became VAK without a *Rosh*, and *Nukva* a *Nekuda*. *Beria* fell below *Parsa* in the place of the bottom six of *Yetzira* and the top four of the past *Assiya*. *Yetzira* fell to the place of the bottom six *de Assiya* and the top four of *Mador ha Klipot* and *Assiya* fell all the way down to the *Eser Sefirot* of *Mador ha Klipot*.

Know, that these bottom four of *Yetzira* from her *Chazeh* down when she fell to *Mador ha Klipot* are sometimes called *Malchut de Yetzira* because anything from the *Chazeh* down of any degree is considered *Malchut*.

His *Guf* is from *Olam ha Zeh*, his *Nefesh* from *Assiya* and his *Ruach* from *Yetzira*, the place where his *Guf* first was.

This is because the *Guf* of *Adam* is always from *Malchut de Assiya*, called "dust" and the *Malbush Hitzon* of its NRN is made of it (*Ohr Pnimi* item 43). The place of the sin when *Olam Assiya* was in the place of the first six *de Yetzira* up to the *Chazeh*, his *Behinat Guf* was also made of the *Behinat* current *Yetzira* because the *Tachton* that rises to the place of the *Elyon* becomes like him.

After he sinned in *Etz ha Daat* and all *Eser Sefirot de Assiya* fell to the place of the *Klipot* his *Guf* was made of *Olam ha Zeh*, which is *Behinat Malchut* of the current *Olam Assiya*. His *Nefesh* was made of the Upper nine *de Assiya* and his *Ruach* was made of the current *Olam Yetzira* in the place of the bottom six of the past *Assiya*.

Also, his *Neshama* was made of the current *Beria* in the place of the bottom six of the former *Yetzira* and he completely lost the NRN *de Atzilut* that he had prior to the sin. You should also know that these NRN *de Beria* that the Rav mentions do not mean that they remained in him after the sin. This is because after the sin nothing was left in him but *Nefesh de Nefesh*, as the Rav wrote in *Shaar HaPsukim*. Rather, it means that after he had repented, he acquired NRN from BYA once again.

50. Now the *Nefesh* of *Adam* was from *Nukva de ZA* that descended in the place of *Nefesh* in *Beria*, and his *Ruach* was from ZA that descended in the place of his *Nukva*. In that, the text that states that *Nefesh* and *Ruach* are *Malchut* and *Tifferet* is correct and does not dispute with the article of *Sabba*, which speaks of after the sin of *Adam*.

Ohr Pnimi

50. Now the **Nefesh** of **Adam** was from **Nukva de ZA** that descended in the place of **Nefesh** in **Beria**, and his **Ruach** was from **ZA** that descended in the place of his **Nukva** etc. does not dispute with the article of Sabba, which speaks of after the sin.

    Explanation: After the sin ZA came down to *Behinat VAK* and he is his *Behinat* from the *Chazeh* down, which belongs to *Nukva*. Thus, ZA descended to the degree of *Nukva* from before, and *Nukva* herself descended to a single *Nekuda* under the *Yesod*. Her bottom nine descended to *Olam Beria*, and you find that the *Nukva* descended to *Beria*.

    This is the meaning of the words of the Rav that when he says that *Nefesh* is from *Nukva* and *Ruach* from *ZA*, he speaks of after the sin of *Adam ha Rishon*, when ZA became VAK and the *Nukva* a *Nekuda* under *Yesod*.

    It is written, "**In that, the text that states that Nefesh and Ruach are Malchut and Tifferet is correct and does not dispute with the article of Sabba, which speaks of after the sin.**" It means that it will not disagree with the text of the Sabba because the Sabba speaks of after the sin, and the words that speak after the sin relate to his words that NR are *Tifferet* and *Malchut*.

51. Now you see how many degrees **Adam ha Rishon** fell. In the beginning his **Guf** was from **Yetzira** and now his **Guf** is from **Olam ha Zeh**, his **Nefesh** from **Assiya** and his **Ruach** from **Yetzira**, the place where his **Guf** first was.

52. Do not be surprised if you will find several places in the Zohar where **Etz ha Daat** is good, **Matatron**, and bad, **Sam'el**. This is because **Etz ha Daat** is not only in **Assiya** where there are **Klipot** mixed with **Kedusha**. However, after **Yetzira** came down and clothed in **Assiya**, **Yetzira** is called "**Etz ha Daat** of good and bad", the name of **Assiya**. Thus we have thoroughly explained what was **Etz ha Daat**.

Ohr Pnimi

52. **Etz ha Daat** is good, **Matatron**, and bad, **Sam'el** etc. However, after **Yetzira** came down and clothed in **Assiya**, **Yetzira** is called "**Etz ha Daat** of good and bad", the name of **Assiya**.

    Interpretation: After the sin the Upper six of *Yetzira* fell to the place of the lower six of *Assiya* and her lower half from the *Chazeh* down fell to the place of the *Klipot*. Hence, she is now half good, meaning her *KHB HGT* through the *Chazeh*, where she stands above *Mador ha Klipot*. She is also half bad, meaning her *TNHYM* from the *Chazeh* down, clothed in *Mador ha Klipot* where the *Tachtonim* cannot receive the *He'arat Yetzira* except when it passes through the *Klipot*.

This is the meaning of "good, *Matatron*", meaning the *Behinat* from the *Chazeh* upward in her, and "bad, *Sam'el*", meaning the *Behinat* from the *Chazeh* down in her, clothed in *Mador ha Klipot*, whose *Rosh* is called "*Sam'el*". This is the meaning of *Etz ha Daat* of good and bad: good from the perspective of *Matatron* and bad from the perspective of *Sam'el*. All this occurred because of the sin of *Etz ha Daat*, though before the sin *Etz ha Daat* was only in *Assiya*.

We must understand that, since before the sin *Olam Assiya* too had no contact with *Mador ha Klipot*. Thus, why was *Olam Assiya* in a state of *Etz ha Daat* of good and bad? Moreover, according to what the Rav writes below (item 87), that on the eve of Shabbat in the twilight, before the sin of *Adam ha Rishon*, all of *BYA* rose to *Atzilut*, and *Yetzira* and *Assiya* rose to the place of *ZON de Atzilut* and were *Panim be Panim*?

After all, *Olam Assiya* was already in the place of *Nukva de Atzilut* with all her *Eser Sefirot*, and how does he say here that she was in a state of *Etz ha Daat* of good and bad? It must not be said that the sin was before that, since after the sin the *Olamot* had already fallen.

They also say in Masechet Sanhedrin that he sinned on the tenth hour, was sentenced on the eleventh, and was expelled from *Gan Eden* on the twelfth. Thus, the sin was after the twilight, and how are there good and bad in *Assiya* that rose to *Atzilut*, since it is written about *Atzilut* that "evil shall not sojourn with Thee"?

When you study the book Shaar HaPsukim, you will find that the Rav himself addressed it and explained it thus: We shall explain for you one rule and that will explain and settle all the mentioned articles. Know, that every *Behinat* middle line from the *Chazeh* down where the *Orot* are uncovered, whether in ZA, in *Nukva de Atzilut*, in *Beria*, or *Yetzira*, or *Assiya*, it is called *Etz ha Daat*.

Thus, when the Rav says here that *Etz ha Daat* is only in *Assiya* it refers to the *Assiya* of every *Partzuf* and every degree of the degrees and the *Olamot*. This is because from the *Chazeh* of every *Olam* and every *Partzuf* downward, it is considered as *Assiya* or *Malchut* of that *Partzuf*, even though they have five *Sefirot TNHYM* there.

However, not all the *Assiya* of the *Partzuf* is called *Etz ha Daat*, only the *Behinat* middle line in it, which is *Yesod*. This is because the three *Kavim de Assiya* are NHY and the middle line is *Yesod*. The Rav describes more accurately in the

Tree of Life that only *Behinat Ateret Yesod* is called *Etz ha Daat*. This is why the Rav writes here that there is only *Etz ha Daat* of good and bad in *Assiya*.

However, the Rav says (Tree of Life) that the sin of *Adam ha Rishon* was in the lower *Gan Eden*, which is *Bina de Malchut de Assiya*. The *Karka* of that *Gan Eden* does not touch this *Eretz* of ours, meaning the *Nekuda de Olam ha Zeh*.

Thus, according to the Rav's words here, *Olam Assiya*, which was already entirely in the place of *Nukva de Atzilut*, was also the *Karka* of the *Gan Eden Tachton* in *Malchut* of *Olam Assiya* that rose in the very place of *Karka de Atzilut* itself. Hence, why does the Rav say there that the *Karka* of the lower *Gan Eden* touched and did not touch our *Eretz* when our *Eretz* was below in the *Hitzoniut* of the *Olamot* that did not rise at all in all the ascents on the eve of Shabbat before the sin (item 88)?

Moreover, only the *Pnimiut* of the three *Olamot BYA* rose before the sin of *Etz ha Daat*, not all the *Hitzoniut* which is *Behinat* from *Chazeh de TNHY de AK* downward that became the place of *BYA* (see item 3). It turns out that the *Karka* of the *Gan Eden Tachton* stood at the *Karka* of *Olam Atzilut* and our *Eretz* is below the *Raglaim* of *AK* with respect to *Behinat Malchut de Tzimtzum Aleph*. The entire *Hitzoniut de BYA* severs them and the distance between them is great, so how does he say that *Karka Gan Eden* touched and did not touch our *Eretz*?

There is indeed great depth here and this is a very important matter. First we must know that even before the sin of *Adam ha Rishon* the *Klipot* came opposite *Olam Atzilut*, but they did not have *Behinat Panim be Panim*, but were merely as *Vav* and *Nekuda*.

In general there are three *Klipot*: *Ruach Se'arah*, *Anan Gadol*, and *Esh Mitlakahat*, which cling to *Noga*. This *Noga* is half good and half bad because when *Noga* is attached to the *Gevul* of *Parsa de Atzilut* she is good, and when the three above *Klipot* cleave to her, she becomes as evil as they.

This is the meaning of the serpent being turned into a rod and the rod turning into a serpent. The three above *Klipot* are the serpent. When *Noga* clings to the *Gevul* of the *Kedusha* she is called "a rod" and she is good, and when the *Klipot* cling to her the rod turns into a serpent and it is bad.

Explanation: the *Klipot* are built from the deficits in *Kedusha*, as it is written, "I shall be filled with her that is laid waste" since *Tzor* is only built out of the ruin of Jerusalem. Thus the *Shoresh* became the *Klipot* immediately with the deficit that was made at the outset of *Tzimtzum Aleph*. This is because of the *Tzimtzum* that was made on *Behina Dalet* to not receive the *Ohr Elyon* into her.

This is considered *Malchut de Klipa* and only *Behinat Nekuda*, meaning merely *Behinat Shoresh*. However, after *Tzimtzum Bet* the *Hey Tata'a* rose to *Nikvey Eynaim* when *Malchut ha Mesayemet* under the place of *Sium Raglin de AK* rose to the place of *Bina de Guf*, which is *Chazeh de Tifferet*.

Then the two bottom thirds of *Tifferet* and *NHYM*, which are *Bina ZA* and *Malchut de Guf* became *Behinat* vacant and empty *Halal* without *Ohr* (Part 16 item 3). Then these three above *Klipot* were made one opposite the other, meaning opposite the three *Kelim Bina ZA* and *Malchut de Guf*, which now remained as vacant *Halal*.

Ruach Se'arah is opposite *Assiya*, which is *Malchut*, *Anan Gadol* is opposite *Yetzira*, which is ZA, and *Esh* Mitlakahat is opposite *Beria*, which is *Bina*. Because this place of *Halal* in *BYA* caused a lessening in *Atzilut*, which is the meaning of the amputee going out with his stilt, there is the *Behinat* three above *Klipot* opposite from *Olam Atzilut* too. However, prior to the sin of *Adam ha Rishon* the *Klipot* were not built, and they were also separated from the *Kedusha*.

This matter of separation of the *Klipot* was made by the force of two great *Tikkunim* that were corrected in *Olam Atzilut*: 1 - The Inner *AVI* were concealed, which are *GAR de Haya*; 2 - *Behina Dalet* was concealed in *RADLA* that the *Mochin de Yechida* come out on.

Explanation: The breaking of the vessels *de ZAT de Nekudim* happened because of the *He'arat AB* that they received during the *Mochin de Haya* that lowered the *Hey Tata'a* to the *Peh* as in *Tzimtzum Aleph*. Then the strength of the *Parsa* was cancelled and the *ZAT de Nekudim* expanded to the restricted place of *BYA*, and hence broke, died and fell to the *Klipot*.

The two above *Tikkunim* were made in *Olam Atzilut* in order to correct that, meaning in order to be able to receive *Mochin de Gadlut* by *He'arat AB* that lowers the *Hey Tata'a* from the *Eynaim* to the *Peh*. However, it is without expanding below *Parsa* to the restricted place of BYA. 1 - The *Hey Tata'a* was concealed in *RADLA*, thus even when *He'arat AB* lowers *Hey Tata'a* to the *Peh* there is no actual *Behinat Malchut* there, only *Yesod de Malchut*; 2 - The Inner *AVI* were concealed, which are the *Behinat GAR de He'arat AB*, and all that remains is *Behinat He'arat VAK de He'arat AB*. This does not expand from above downward at all, only illuminates from below upward, meaning only from the *Parsa* upward.

Thus, you find that the force of *Parsa* is always kept so that it is not cancelled as during the breaking of the vessels and no *He'arah de Atzilut* will expand to the restricted place of *BYA*. Therefore, the *Klipot* were separated from the *Kedusha* altogether because *Kedusha* no longer expands below the *Parsa* and the *Klipot* can no longer rob the *Kedusha* as during the breaking of the vessels.

Now you can understand what the Rav wrote above in item 56. In the first *Behina*, meaning at the time of the birth of the *Neshama* of *Adam ha Rishon*, although ZA rose to the Upper *AVI* and *Mochin de Haya* illuminated, it did not help to make them able to raise all *Eser Sefirot de Olam Yetzira*, only GAR *de Yetzira*, while the *VAK* remained below *Parsa*.

This is so because there is no *Behinat* from above downward in *Mochin de Haya* as the Inner *AVI* were concealed. For that reason it suffices to raise only GAR *de Yetzira*, which are *Behinat* from below upward and can rise to *Atzilut*. The *VAK de Yetzira*, however, did not receive any *Tikun* from these *Mochin* since there is no *Behinat* from above downward in that which expands to the VAK as well.

Now you can also understand what the Rav wrote in the ascents in the second *Behina* on the eve of Shabbat after midnight, when ZA rose to AA and acquired the *Mochin de Yechida*. Still, it only helped GAR *de Olam Assiya* to be able to rise to *Atzilut* but ZAT *de Assiya* remained below the *Parsa* and did not receive any *Tikun* (see below item 80).

This is so because of the concealment of the *Hey Tata'a* in RADLA, and thus even in *Mochin de Yechida* that emerge by the lowering of the *Hey Tata'a* to the *Peh* there is no actual *Zivug* on *Behina Dalet*, only on *Behinat Yesod de Malchut*.

For that reason the *Nukva de ZA* cannot rise there and be mingled in that *Zivug* since there is nothing of her *Behina* there. This is because *Yesod* and *Atara* are *Behinat Nukva* of the *Guf de ZA*, which is good for *Behinat Zivug de ZA* and Leah, being *Behinat* from *Chazeh de ZA* upward and there is no *Hitpashtut* there from above downward to *Behinat* Rachel.

It follows that only *Behinat* from the *Chazeh* upward of ZA rose to AA and received *Ohr Yechida*, and from its *Chazeh* down which is Rachel, *Nukva de ZA*, remained below in *AVI*. They did not receive anything from the *Mochin de Yechida*. Hence in *Assiya* too, only her GAR that could receive from the great *Nukva*, Leah, rose to *Atzilut*. However, ZAT *de Assiya* did not receive anything from these *Mochin* and could not ascend to *Atzilut*.

Moreover, even in the third *Behina* of the eve of Shabbat, at twilight, when the bottom six of *Assiya* rose above *Parsa* to *Atzilut*, it was not a complete ascent by *Zivug* on *Behina Dalet*, as this is utterly impossible. After all, she is concealed in RADLA.

Rather the ascent was as "additions of Shabbat", which is the great dominion of *Kedusha*, as it is written that all the *Dinim* are impregnated in her. Hence, this *He'arah* helped only for the day of Shabbat and not before the *Kodesh* of the Shabbat.

The Rav wrote in the Tree of Life: "*Adam ha Rishon* could correct only the *Olamot Elyonim*, but he did not correct *Olam Assiya* which is all *Klipot* and this *Olam* remained in *Behinat Achor be Achor* etc. The exterior have a hold there among those *Achoraim* between the cleaved, and this is the meaning of 'other gods', meaning other gods that cleave to the *Achoraim*."

Explanation: It is explained that although ZA rose in AA by the *He'arat AB* that lowers the *Hey Tata'a* to the *Peh*, there is still no actual *Hey Tata'a* there. This is because she was concealed. Rather, she is *Malchut de Ima*, contained in *Yesod de Malchut*.

This is enough for it only with *Mochin de Ima* of the *Ohr Yechida*, since there is NRNHY in the *Ohr Yechida* and then ZA received only the *Neshama* of *Yechida*. For that reason only ZA and Leah rise to AA and Rachel remains below.

It is known that *Mochin de Neshama* suffice only to being GAR to the *Behinat* from the *Chazeh* up, but from the *Chazeh* down he remains *Achor be Achor* with Rachel, as it is written, "their hinder parts were inward and their faces outward." It means that there is only *He'arah* for *Kelim de Panim* there, called HBD HGT, but the *Kelim de Achoraim* which are NHY are hidden there inside the HGT.

This is so because they need to hide from the exterior that seize them because all that the exterior want is to annul the ending force of *Parsa* as during the breaking of the vessels. Thus they could receive *He'arat Atzilut* once more as during the breaking of the vessels.

For that reason their hold is on these NHY of *Assiya* that need the *He'arah* from above downward, whose *Tikun* is only by the annulment of the *Parsa*. At that time *He'arat Atzilut* will expand once more to the place of the *Klipot* as during the breaking of the vessels.

It turns out that as long as NHY de *Assiya* are concealed in the form of "their hinder parts were inward" and do not awaken to receive their *Shefa*, the *Klipot* are separated from the *Kedusha*. This is because they cannot suck from the *Kelim de Panim de Assiya* since they only receive from below upward and the *Gevul* of the *Parsa* is well kept to not expand there to the restricted place of BYA where the *Klipot* receive it.

However, when the *Kelim de Achoraim* awaken to suck from the *He'arat GAR* it cancels the *Gevul* in the *Parsa*. This is so because they can only receive from the *Behinat GAR* that comes from above downward and cancels the *Parsa* as in the case of the breaking of the vessels.

This is why the *Klipot* are called "other gods". The Rav explained that it is because they cleave to the *Achoraim*. In other words, if the *Achoraim de Assiya*, which are the above *NHY*, would extend *Shefa GAR* from above downward the *Shefa* will instantly reach the *Klipot* since they are their actual *Behina*, meaning *Behinat Lev ha Even*.

The Rav writes that *Olam Assiya* is all *Klipot* (item 144) because in fact they hold to the *Achoraim de Yetzira* too. Even *Olam Yetzira* which is corrected in *Mochin de Haya* cannot receive them but only in its *GAR*, meaning from below upward because of the above reason that the Inner *AVI* were concealed. For that reason they have a hold also from *Chazeh de Yetzira* downward.

However, this is only half of *Yetzira*, not all of it. Conversely, in *Olam Assiya* where the entire *Behina Dalet* was concealed in *RADLA*, which is the gist of *Olam Assiya*, all of it is considered *Klipot*. This is because all that she extends from her share downward comes in the *Klipot*, which are the remains of the *Melachim* in the form of *Lev ha Even*.

This was the sin of *Adam ha Rishon*. He extended *GAR de Haya* that shine inside the *Achoraim de Assiya* and *Yetzira*, meaning that pass the *Gevul* of the *Parsa* as in the case of the breaking of the vessels. By so doing he too caused the breaking of the vessels because all his organs fell inside the *Klipot*. He also caused the *Olamot* to descend, and the bottom four of *Yetzira* and all *Eser Sefirot de Assiya* were greatly blemished since they were clothed in *Mador ha Klipot* (see item 94).

It is written, "*Adam ha Rishon* could correct only the *Olamot Elyonim*. However, he did not correct *Olam Assiya* which is purely *Klipot*, and this *Olam* remained in *Behinat Achor be Achor*. There, in those *Achoraim*, since there are many *Klipot* there the waste is more than the food and there is hold for the exterior among these *Achoraim* among the cleaved. This is the meaning of 'other gods'."

This means that *Kelim de Achoraim de Olam Assiya* are only corrected by manifestation of *GAR de Haya* and the manifestation of *Malchut de Behina Dalet* concealed in *RADLA*. She extends the *Mochin* from above downward and cancels the *Gevul* of the *Parsa de Tzimtzum Bet*.

Since this manifestation does not happen in the six thousand years before the end of correction, it follows that there is no correction and sorting to those *Achoraim de Assiya*. This is because they are *Behinat Lev ha Even*, whose only desire is for that *Shefa*, since this is their share. Their entire sustenance and vitalizing force is out of that desire.

The bottom six of *Assiya* rose to *Atzilut* in the third *Behina* of the eve of Shabbat at twilight and the *Yetzira* and *Assiya* became *Panim be Panim* (item 87). However, this was only because of the addition of Shabbat, which is the authority of *Kedusha* of the day of Shabbat itself, as it is said "All the judgments are impregnated in her."

However, it was not because of the raising of MAN and the sorts since there is no sorting for them throughout the six thousand years. Hence, although the *Achoraim de Assiya* appeared there and became *Panim be Panim*, with regard to the weekdays they are still considered *Achor be Achor*.

The addition of Shabbat dominates only on the day of the Shabbat, meaning after the Shabbat is sanctified. This is the meaning of the words of the sages, that if he had waited with his *Zivug* to the day of Shabbat, there would have been no hold to the exteriors. His whole sin was that he rushed in his *Zivug* while it was still weekday.

It is written in the Tree of Life that "the *Karka* of the Garden touches and does not touch our *Eretz*." Because of the ascent that was made in the addition of Shabbat when the *Karka* of the Garden rose to *Atzilut*, it certainly had no contact with our *Eretz*.

Indeed, before he sanctified the Shabbat she was still connected with other gods that cleave there to the *Achoraim*, as with regard to weekdays there weren't any sorts. It follows that she touches our *Eretz*, which is the restricted *Behina Dalet* who is forbidden to receive any *He'arat Atzilut*.

In this manner she touches from the perspective of the weekdays and does not touch from the perspective of the addition of Shabbat. The sin of *Adam ha Rishon* in eating *Etz ha Daat* means that he extended *Mochin* in the *Zivug* of *Yetzira* and *Assiya Panim be Panim* on a weekday.

These *Mochin* cancel the *Gevul* of the *Parsa* and come in the *Klipot*. This gives strength to the serpent, which consists of all three *Klipot*, to enter the lower *Gan Eden* and touch the *Ateret Yesod*, called *Etz ha Daat*.

This is the meaning of the tree shouting and saying, "Do not touch me!" The Rav wrote in the Tree of Life that by this touching, all the Upper *Mochin* that *Adam* acquired in these three *Behinot* of the eve of Shabbat, called *Zihara Ela'a* (Upper Radiance), fell and clothed in a *Guf* of *Olam ha Zeh* of the *Klipot*.

In Beit Shaar HaKavanot (*Ohr Pashut* item 19) it is explained in implication. Thus we have thoroughly explained the matter of *Etz ha Daat* which is only in *Assiya* and that it is all *Klipot*. From here you will also understand that the matter of *Etz ha Daat* and the matter of the breaking of the vessels are indeed the same matter, except this was in the *Olamot* and that was in the *Neshamot*.

53. **In this explanation we settle both verses. One says "And God created man" and the other says, "Then the Lord God formed man." The *Guf* of *Adam* was made of *Yetzira*, hence the word "created" and after *Beria* descended and clothed in *Yetzira* it is as though he was created from *Beria*, hence the word "formed."**

Ohr Pnimi

53. **The *Guf* of *Adam* was made of *Yetzira*, hence the word "created" etc. after *Beria* descended and clothed in *Yetzira* it is as though he was created from *Beria*.**

As ZA is *Behinat Yetzira de Atzilut*, so *Adam ha Rishon* is discerned as the bottom *Yetzira de BYA*, meaning from the aspect of *Ohr de Tolada*. In this aspect he has no part in *Bina* which is *Beria* and is not fitting for *Behinat Neshama* and *Mochin*.

Instead, because of the ascent of the *Hey Tata'a* to *Nikvey Eynaim*, *Bina* herself expanded to *Behinat ZON*, called *Yetzira* and *Assiya*, or *ZAT de Bina*, in the form of *VAK* without a *Rosh*. In consequence, *ZON* were rooted in *Bina*.

Hence, although in principle *ZA* is *VAK* without a *Rosh*, when it rises to MAN to *Bina* and returns the *AVI Panim be Panim*, in consequence YESHSUT acquire their GAR, thus *ZA* also acquires *Behinat Rosh*. The rule is that everything that the *Tachton* induces in the *Elyon* returns to the *Tachton* in the same measure.

Consequently, *Adam ha Tachton* too can receive the *Behinat Rosh* from the *ZON* because after the *ZON* rise to *AVI* they become like them. Thus, although in the beginning of its creation, *Adam* is not worthy of *Behinat Rosh* because he has no part in *Beria*, yet through his ascent to MAN to *ZON* he causes them *Behinat GAR* from their *Chazeh* down too.

Since except the ascent of *Adam* to MAN ZON did not have *Behinat GAR* but only from the *Chazeh* up, he also acquires by himself that measure that *Adam* caused to extend in *Chazeh de ZON* down and attains *Behinat GAR* as they do. The discernment is that *Adam*, which is *Yetzira*, rose to *Beria* because he received GAR from *Behinat Beria* and equalized with her. You should also remember that *BYA*, *Bina*, *ZON* and *NRN de Adam ha Rishon* are one matter both in *Atzilut* and in the lower *BYA*.

During the birth of *Adam ha Rishon* the *Olamot* were already in the form of *Beria*, as the Rav wrote that *Yetzira* and *Assiya de Atzilut* were already in the place of *Beria de Atzilut*. This means that ZON *de Atzilut* have already ascended to *AVI de Atzilut* hence the lower *BYA* and *NRN de Adam ha Rishon*, which are their *Tolada*, were thus born in *Behinat Beria*.

The *Guf* of *Adam ha Rishon*, which is *Yetzira*, came out in the place of the top six *de Beria*, by which they had *Rosh* in *Atzilut* in the place of ZON. The *Rosh* itself, called *Bina* or *Beria*, was in the place of *ZA de Atzilut*, and the *Garon*, which is GAR *de VAK* or GAR *de Yetzira*, was in the place of *Nukva de Atzilut*.

This is the meaning of, "Then the Lord God formed man etc." This is because there was a complete *Yetzira* in a complete *Rosh* from *Atzilut* since *HaVaYaH Elokim* implies perfection since *Yetzira* acquired the very same virtue of *Beria*.

However, after the sin when *Beria* descended once more to being *Yetzira*, which means that the *Mochin de* GAR that ZA caused YESHSUT departed, YESHSUT descended to VAK without a *Rosh* which is *Yetzira*. Also, the *Mochin* from ZA departed and he returned to *Behinat VAK* without a *Rosh*.

Hence, all this is considered that *Beria* descended to being *Yetzira*. This is the meaning of "And God created man etc." It is so because *Elokim* designates *Behinat Mochin de Katnut* due to the *Behinat Beria* that became VAK without a *Rosh*.

That settles a difficult question: *Beria* is more important than *Yetzira*. Hence, why does it write in "formed" a full *HaVaYaH Elokim*, and in "created" only the name *Elokim*? According to the words of the Rav we can thoroughly understand that "formed" relates to the complete *Yetzira* after she had been turned into actual *Beria* and acquired *Rosh* from *Atzilut*. This is why the full name is used. "Created", however, relates to his *Behina* after the sin on *Behinat VAK* without a *Rosh*, meaning on *Beria* that fell to being like *Yetzira*. This is why it only writes the name *Elokim*, indicating *Katnut*.

Therefore we should not ask why it is written, "created" when it should have written "formed". The answer is that he did not return to actual *Behinat Yetzira*, as then it would never have been suitable for GAR.

Instead, he returned to BYA and is therefore still worthy of reforming his actions so as to raise MAN anew to ZON and extend *Mochin de Gadlut* in the same amount that he causes in the *Elyonim*. This is the precision of "created", designating that he still holds to *Beria*, though to *Katnut* of *Beria*.

54. **Now we will explain a matter which is discussed elaborately and then we will explain the superficiality of the above-mentioned text. First we will explain the matter of the order of the degrees of the *Olamot* and how they stood in the beginning, before *Adam* was created, and also how they**

descended from their degree after he had sinned. Know, that the number of the *Olamot* itself did not change and they are always four, *Atzilut, Beria, Yetzira Assiya*.

55. However, their order of degrees was thus since the entire place of *Eser Sefirot* of the current *Olam Assiya* as well as the place of the four bottom *Sefirot* of the current *Yetzira* were empty and vacant. There in that place was *Mador ha Klipot*.

56. The bottom six of *Assiya* were in the place where now the first six of *Yetzira* are and the first four of *Assiya* were in the place where the last four of *Beria* are now. The last six of *Yetzira* where in the place where the first six of *Beria* are now and the first four of *Yetzira* were in the place where *Nukva de ZA de Atzilut* now is.

You already know that she only takes the place of the last four of *ZA*, namely *Netzah Hod Yesod Malchut* in him. She stands opposite them from behind, hence the name *Dalet*, since her place is only in the four mentioned *Sefirot*.

Ohr Pnimi

56. **The bottom six of *Assiya* were in the place where now the first six of *Yetzira*.**

Here we must remember what the Rav wrote above (item 20) that only *ZON* are sorted in the *Beten* of *Ima* and nothing more, and *Rosh de Beria* is sorted in *Beten Nukva de ZA de Atzilut*.

The rule is that every *Partzuf* is emanated in its adjacent Upper degree. You can see that according to the current state of the *Olamot*, *ZA* is in *Behinat VAK* and *Nukva* in *Behinat Nekuda* from the perspective of the permanent state. From that state it is impossible that the *Rosh* of *Beria* will come out from the *Beten* of *Nukva de Atzilut*.

This is so because when even for herself she is not a *Partzuf*, how can she emanate a second *Partzuf* below her? The rule is that the *Partzuf* cannot emanate a *Partzuf Tachton* below it before it grows to *Behinat Neshama* in itself (see item 60).

The Rav elaborated here to explain the order of the emergence of *BYA* from its beginning so as to teach us that the *Olamot* were not in the same situation as *ZA* is now, in a state of *VAK* and *Nukva* in *Behinat Nekuda*. Rather, *ZA* was then in *Komat Abba* which is *Behinat Mochin de Haya* and *Nukva* was in *Komat Ima* which is *Mochin de Neshama*. Then *Beria* could be sorted in the

Beten of *Nukva* until she was completed and could sort the *Olam Yetzira*, and also *Yetzira* sort *Olam Assiya*.

With the above we can also understand the order of the state of the three *Olamot BYA* that the Rav wrote here. It is known that when the *Tachton* rises to its *Elyon* it becomes exactly like the degree of the *Elyon*, as the Rav will write in item 60.

It follows, that *Nukva* that rose to *Komat Ima* becomes completely like *Ima* and everything that is emanated from *Ima* is considered as the degree of ZA. This is because only *Behinot* ZA are sorted in *Ima's Beten* (item 20). Thus, the *Eser Sefirot de Beria* must have been in the place of ZA because when *Nukva* is in *Behinat Ima* then *Beria*, which is emanated from it, is in the degree of ZA.

Also, since *Olam Beria* was then in the degree of ZA, the first four *Sefirot* of *Olam Yetzira* that emanates from it are considered to be in the degree of *Nukva de* ZA which clothes ZA from his *Chazeh* downward. Since *Beria* is in the degree of ZA the *Ne'etzal* from ZA is always his *Behinat Nukva*.

However, there are two degrees in the *Nukva*: *Achor be Achor* with the ZA from the *Chazeh* down, and *Panim be Panim* with the ZA on an equal *Koma*. The general state of the *Olamot* was still in *Behinat Achor be Achor* before *Adam ha Rishon* was created, as it is known that ZON themselves, when they rose to *AVI*. Consequently, they were still in a state of *Achor be Achor*.

This is so because ZA rose to *Abba*, called Upper *AVI* and *Nukva* rose only to *Ima*, called YESHSUT. It follows that *Nukva* clothes there only from the *Chazeh de* ZA downward in the same manner as the *Halbasha* of YESHSUT to the Upper *AVI*.

Thus, the Upper ZON are also only in *Behinat* from the *Chazeh* down *Achor be Achor*. Thus, although *Olam Yetzira* received the *Behinat Nukva de* ZA because of its exit from *Beria* which was *Behinat* ZA, she only received the first degree of *Nukva*, meaning *Behinat Chazeh de* ZA *Achor be Achor* downward.

For that reason only the first four of *Yetzira* became the degree of *Nukva de* ZA, but the bottom six of *Yetzira* descended to the current *Behinat Beria*, meaning below *Parsa de Atzilut*. This is because the *Behinat Nukva de* ZA takes only four *Sefirot* while being *Achor be Achor* from the *Chazeh* down and the rest of her *Sefirot* are in *Beria*.

Also, since *Olam Yetzira* became the degree of *Nukva de* ZA, it is considered that *Olam Assiya* that comes out of it, the first four *Sefirot de Assiya* became the degree of *Olam Beria*. This is because in *Beten de Nukva de* ZA only *Olam Beria* is sorted.

However, *Nukva* herself had only the first four *Sefirot* in *Atzilut* and the six lower *Sefirot* were in the degree of the first six of *Olam Beria*. Hence only the first four *Sefirot* of *Olam Assiya*, which is sorted by her, were in *Olam Beria* since they extend from the first four *Sefirot de Nukva*.

Yet, her six bottom are considered to have been emanated from the bottom six of *Nukva* that were on the degree of *Beria*, and everything that comes from the degree of *Beria* is considered as the degree of *Yetzira*. For this reason the bottom six of *Olam Assiya* descended to the first six of *Olam Yetzira*.

Thus we have thoroughly explained the necessity of the state in the *Olamot* and their degree, that they must be as in the order that the Rav explains here. This is because no sorting is possible in the *Beten* of *Nukva* before she acquires *Partzuf Neshama*.

It follows that she must clothe *Ima* and since the *Nukva* already stood in the degree of *Ima*, then all the states that the Rav has already written must be so. You will also learn here that all the *Olamot BYA* came out of *Nukva de Atzilut*.

This is because not only did *Olam Beria* come out of *Nukva* that is in the place of *Ima*, when *Olam Assiya* emerged from *Yetzira*, the *Yetzira* was literally in the degree of *Nukva de Atzilut*. It follows that *Olam Assiya* too came out of *Nukva de Atzilut*, but from the *Behinat Achor be Achor de Nukva*.

57. All *Eser Sefirot* of *Beria* were in the place which is now **ZA de Atzilut** in all its *Eser Sefirot* and his **Nukva de Atzilut** was then in the current place of **Abba ve Ima de Atzilut**. The *Olamot* continue similarly from **Abba ve Ima de Atzilut** upward to the highest degree, to **Ein Sof**, higher than their current degree and we need not elaborate here.

58. Indeed there is a question here. We have already learned that the lowest degree in the entire *Atzilut* is higher than every thing below it through the end of *Assiya* etc. similarly in all the degrees. This is so because even the bottom degree in *Beria* is greater than every thing below it, which are *Yetzira* and *Assiya*.

    Thus, how did we say above that *Olam Yetzira* had only its Upper four above where *Nukva de Atzilut* now stands and the rest of the bottom six *Sefirot de Yetzira* remained below in the place that it is now *Beria*? After all, all the *Olamot* could stand at the lowest degree *de Nukva de Atzilut*, which is beneath it.

59. The answer to that is that when it is written in a different place that the lowest degree in the higher *Olam* is greater than everything below it, it does not relate to quantity and a measurement of limited space. Rather, it is discerned

in the quality of the *Ohr* itself being better than everything below it. In that aspect of quality and merit it contains everything that is below it.

In comparison, we see that the last drop in a human being's brain contains everything that exists below it in the entire human body. It is so although we see that it is not so with respect to the size of the place. Moreover, a single organ of the body such as the thigh of the leg is bigger than the size of the entire head.

Ohr Pnimi

59. Quantity and a measurement of limited space. Rather, it is discerned in the quality of the *Ohr* itself.

    This must not be confused with an imaginary place. Rather, quality means the number of disparities in form in the degree without differentiations of merit and importance in it. This is how he explains that it is true that the smaller degree in the *Elyon* is greater than everything below it.

    Yet, this is still a qualitative difference, not a quantitative difference. For example, *Malchut* in the *Elyon* is greater than all the *Olamot* and *Sefirot* below it. Hence, it is impossible for the two *Sefirot* below her to be in *Malchut de Elyon*. According to the quantity there is only one form in *Malchut de Elyon*, which is why it is considered as merely one *Sefira*.

    For that reason she cannot accept within her two *Sefirot* that have two different forms from one another, which necessarily require two separate places. The reason is that the *Sefira* is the *Behinat Ohr*, and the place is the *Behinat Kli* related to it.

    Thus, the four *Sefirot* of *Yetzira* cannot be in the place of one *Sefira* of *Malchut de Atzilut*, but it requires four *Sefirot* of *Malchut de Atzilut*. This is because every *Sefira* requires its own unique place, as every disparity of form in the *Ohr* necessitates a disparity of form in the place, which is the *Kli*.

60. I also believe I had heard from my teacher a different answer regarding this. It is that this is only meant to be when every single degree is in its proper place because then the measure of the lowest degree in the higher *Olam* is greater than everything below it.

    However, when *Olam Beria* rises to *Olam Atzilut Beria* returns to being in the degree of *Atzilut* itself and requires the same amount of space as if it is *Atzilut* in itself, etc. similarly.

    Hence, when *Yetzira* rises to *Nukva de Atzilut*'s place she returns to being in her merit. Then the first four *Sefirot* of *Yetzira* require the same measure of space as the *Nekeva* of *Atzilut,* whose measure is also four *Sefirot de Atzilut.*

Ohr Pnimi

60. When *Olam Beria* rises to *Olam Atzilut Beria* returns to being in the degree of *Atzilut.*

    This is very simple. There is no issue of imaginary places here, but of quality of merit. When you say that the *Tachton* rises to the place of the *Elyon* it means that its *Tzura* has been equalized with the *Elyon*. Hence, it is necessary that when *Beria* rises to the place of *Atzilut* it becomes exactly like *Atzilut*, and remember that in all the places.

61. Let us return to the first matter. Before *Adam* was created the *Sium* of *Assiya* was at the end of the sixth *Sefira* of the current *Olam Yetzira* and the bottom four *de Yetzira* were all vacant, and all the *Eser Sefirot* of the current *Assiya* too. Together they are fourteen *Sefirot* and there was the section of all the *Klipot*.

62. That place of the fourteen *Sefirot* was then the zone of the *Olamot*, such as we place in every town a Shabbat Zone around it. This is the meaning of the words of our sages why He is called *El Shadai*, since He said to His world *Dai* (Heb: enough).

    Interpretation: As these four *Olamot* ABYA expanded when they reached the place of *Sium* of the sixth *Sefira* of the current *Yetzira*, He said to them "*Dai*, do not expand and do not enter the zone of the above-mentioned fourteen." Instead, they would remain a *Halal* for the *Klipot* as was mentioned.

Ohr Pnimi

62. That place of the fourteen *Sefirot* was then the zone of the *Olamot*, etc. Shabbat Zone around it.

    This implies to the Shabbat Zone of two thousand *Amah* that is given and added to the territory of the town where it is permitted to go out of town.

    The thing is that Shabbat means the dominion of *Atzilut* in all the *Olamot* because the three *Olamot* BYA rise to *Atzilut* there as the Rav writes below. This is the meaning of the verse, "let no man go out of his place on the seventh day."

    The city one dwells in on Shabbat implies the place of *Olam Atzilut* where the *Olamot* rose. Hence he is forbidden to go out of his city on the day of the Shabbat, as the *Olamot* do not go out of *Atzilut* on the day of the Shabbat.

Yet, our sages added another two thousand *Amah* around the city where it is permitted to go out of the city without breaking "let no man go out of his place on the seventh day." This requires explanation why it is not considered an exit outside his place.

We must understand these words, since on Shabbat all the *Olamot* rise to *Atzilut* and the same sixteen *Sefirot* through the current *Chazeh de Yetzira* also remain empty of the *Ohr* of *Kedusha*. Thus, the Shabbat Zone was made above in the place of *Parsa* between *Atzilut* and *Beria*, meaning the place where *Atzilut* ended. Why then is it permitted in exit and is not considered exit outside the zone until the place of *Chazeh de Yetzira*?

To understand that we must remember everything that the Rav wrote above in this Part in items One through Eight and in *Ohr Pnimi* there, meaning the explanation of the place of *BYA*. All of these thirty *Sefirot de BYA*, the sixteen and the fourteen that the Rav deals with here relate primarily to the thirty *Sefirot* of the place of *BYA*. They are called the *Hitzoniut* of the three *Olamot BYA* which do not rise even on the day of Shabbat, as the Rav writes below.

He says about them that at the end of the sixteenth *Sefira* it is the Shabbat Zone and is prohibited to enter in the zone of the fourteen *Sefirot* below. It explains there that this place *BYA* was made of half of *Partzuf Tifferet* and *NHY de AK* that remained under the *Parsa de Atzilut* during *Tzimtzum Bet*.

This was because of the ascent of *Malchut ha Mizdaveget* to *Nikvey Eynaim* and *Malchut ha Mesayemet* rose to the place of the half of *Tifferet*, which is *Bina de Guf*. There the place of *Sium Kav Ein Sof* was made which is *Parsa de Atzilut*, and from there down there remained an empty and vacant space without *Ohr*.

Hence, half *Tifferet* and *NHY de AK* remained empty without *Ohr* and are called the place of the three *Olamot BYA*, meaning where the three *Olamot BYA* are destined to expand.

See in *Ohr Pnimi*, the rest of the text, that the place for *Olam Beria* was made of the bottom half of *Tifferet*, the place for *Olam Yetzira* was made of *NHY* and the place for *Olam Assiya* was made of *Malchut*.

We know what the Rav writes for us that you have not a tiny *Nitzotz* in all four *Olamot ABYA* that has not four *Behinot ABYA* in itself. Thus, even within those *TNHY de Partzuf Nekudot de SAG de AK* that remained under the *Parsa de Atzilut* to the place of *BYA*, they are also considered as four *Behinot ABYA* in themselves.

This is so because those *TNHYM* expand to *Eser Sefirot HBD HGT NHYM* where *HBD* is the *Rosh*, *HGT* is the *Behinat Atzilut* in it until the *Chazeh*, and from *Chazeh* to *Sium de Tifferet* it is *Beria* in it. *NHY* are *Yetzira* and *Malchut* is the *Assiya* in it.

Thus the principal dominion force of *BYA* in it appears only from the *Chazeh* down, meaning from the *Sium* of the sixth *Sefira* of *Yetzira* downward. However, from the *Chazeh* up it is still *Behinat Atzilut* compared to the *Kelim*, even though it is empty of *Ohr Elyon* because of the *Parsa de Atzilut* above it that has already ended the *Kav Ein Sof* there.

Now we have thoroughly explained the great difference between the sixteen *Sefirot* from the *Chazeh* up in *BYA*'s place and the fourteen *Sefirot* from the *Chazeh* down in it, even when it is completely empty of *Ohr*, meaning immediately after *Tzimtzum Bet*. Even then it is considered that *Behinat BYA* is not apparent in the *Kelim* until the *Chazeh* since they are *Behinat Rosh* and *Atzilut* in the *Kelim*. The force of *BYA* is only apparent in them from the *Chazeh* down.

Now we can thoroughly understand the matter the Shabbat Zone of the two thousand *Amah*, permitted in exit although they are outside the city. The Rav says that they are opposite these sixteen *Sefirot* from *Chazeh de BYA* upward. From the *Behinat Ohr* in them they are already *BYA* since they are below *Parsa de Atzilut*. Therefore they are considered to be outside the city.

Yet, since from the *Behina* of the *Kelim* they are still *Atzilut* until the sixth *Sefira* of *Yetzira*, it is therefore still permitted to go there since it is not considered an exit outside *Atzilut*.

The reason is that they are still considered *Atzilut* from the perspective of the *Kelim*, hence the prohibition of "let no man go out of his place" does not apply to them. It is so because from the perspective of the *Kelim* they are still *Atzilut*.

The matter of the number of two thousand years implies the two *Sefirot Keter* and *Hochma* in them because *HBD* is *Rosh* and *Keter* and *HGT* are *Atzilut* and *Hochma* since the five *Sefirot KHB ZON* are called *Rosh* and *ABYA*. We find that until *Chazeh de Yetzira* they are only two *Sefirot Keter* and *Hochma* and from the *Chazeh* down they are *Bina* and *ZON*.

This is why the Rav writes that they are called Shabbat Zone, since Shabbat is *Behinat Atzilut* and at the *Sium* of the sixth *Sefira de Yetzira* it is the zone of *Atzilut*. From there down begins the *BYA* in them, being the fourteen bottom *Sefirot*.

You will not be perplexed by what the Rav wrote above that *Rosh* is *Beria* and *HGT* through *Chazeh* is *Yetzira* and from the *Chazeh* down it is *Assiya*. The value of the *Orot* is on one side and the value of the *Kelim* is on another.

What the Rav wrote to us in several places, that there is not a tiny *Nitzotz* in the entire *ABYA* that does not have *Behinat ABYA* within it, these are the values of the *Kelim*. Even the corporeal *Guf* is considered to have *Keter* and *ABYA*. Its *Rosh* is *Behinat Keter*, from *Peh* to *Chazeh* it is *Atzilut*, from *Chazeh* to *Tabur* it is *Beria*, and from *Tabur* down it is *Yetzira* and *Assiya*.

Although compared to the *Orot* there isn't even *Ohr Malchut* in it before it acquires the *Eser Sefirot de Assiya* called Cycles, yet, even a fetus in its mother's womb already has these *Eser Sefirot*. No *Kli* will be added to it when it grows, but it is merely that the *Kelim* are not fitting for their task before they acquire the *Orot* ascribed to them.

Because of that, we mostly name the *Kelim* after the *Orot* dressed in them. The Rav writes above regarding the *Guf* of *Adam ha Rishon* that his *Rosh* is *Beria*, meaning *Neshama* and *HBD*, his *Guf* which is *HGT* is *Yetzira*, meaning *Ruach*, and from the *Chazeh* down he is *Assiya*, meaning *Ohr Nefesh*.

This discernment is according to the values of the *Orot* clothed in him. In addition, in that regard it is considered that the *Rosh* and the *HGT* through the *Chazeh* are considered the First nine *Sefirot* in the *Guf*, which are *Keter* and *ABY* and from the *Chazeh* down it is only for *Sefirat Malchut* in him, called *Assiya*.

This is so from the *Behinat Hitlabshut Orot* in the *Kelim* since every emergence of an act in the *Kelim* is only according to the *Orot* clothed in them.

When we are concerned with discerning only the values of the *Kelim*, such as here concerning the Shabbat Zone where the prohibition applies chiefly to the places that are the *Kelim*, we have to discern ten complete *Sefirot* in them *KHB ZON*. These are called *Rosh* and *ABYA* each emerging from its opposite *Behina* in the *Shorashim Elyonim* until "one higher than the high" by way of branch and root. Hence this also applies to a corporeal *Guf*.

It is written, "**When they reached the place of Sium of the sixth Sefira of the current Yetzira, He said to them "Dai, do not expand and do not enter the zone of the above-mentioned fourteen." Instead, they would remain a Halal for the Klipot.**"

It has been explained (*Ohr Pnimi* item 56) at the end of the item, that all these three *Olamot BYA* were emanated from *Nukva de Atzilut* and even *Olam Assiya* emerged from *Nukva de Atzilut*. This is because her *Elyon* which is *Olam Yetzira* was then in *Behinat* actual *Nukva de Atzilut*.

Thus, even *Olam Assiya* can only expand through the *Sium* of the current *Chazeh de Yetzira*, meaning only in the measure of the sixteen *Sefirot* which are *Behinat Atzilut de BYA*. However, they could not expand from the *Chazeh* down, where they are already *Behinat BYA* from the perspective of the *Kelim* too. This is because the force of *Sium de Kav Ein Sof* made in the *Parsa* below *Atzilut* begins to show its authority there in *Chazeh de Yetzira* meaning after the *Sium* of the *Rosh* and *Atzilut de BYA*.

For that reason no upshots of *Nukva de Atzilut* can expand there since the dominance of the *Sium de Kav Ein Sof* made in *Tzimtzum Bet* leave these fourteen *Sefirot* as vacant *Halal*. It is written, "they would remain a *Halal* for the *Klipot*."

As *Olam ha Zeh* was made in *Behinat* vacant *Halal* in *Tzimtzum Aleph*, so from *Chazeh de Yetzira* down it became a vacant *Halal* in *Tzimtzum Bet* because the force of *Sium de Parsa* below the *Atzilut* begins to manifest there.

You can relate the matter to what is written in *AA de Atzilut* that this *Masach* in *Peh de AA* that generates *Bina de AA* outside the *Rosh* does not appear at all in its exit place at the *Peh*, but only in the place of its *Chazeh*. Hence, *AVI* that stand from the *Peh* to the *Chazeh* still have *Rosh* and GAR. Only YESHSUT, which stand from his *Chazeh* down remain in *Behinat* VAK without a *Rosh* because of this *Masach*.

We have elaborated in different places, but here too the power of *Sium* in the *Parsa* below *Atzilut* is *Behinat Peh de Rosh* with regard to *BYA*, hence beginning only at *Chazeh de BYA*. From there down the vacant *Halal* is made for the *Klipot*.

63. Now we shall explain the matter of *Adam ha Rishon,* how he expanded in these *Olamot*. I have already notified you in the article Studied in the House of Eliyahu, section The World Exists Six Thousand Years, in Parashat Bereshit, regarding the sin of *Adam ha Rishon,* that *Adam ha Rishon* contained three *Olamot*, which are *Beria Yetzira* and *Assiya*.

64. This is the order of his *Hitpashtut* in them: The *Rosh* of *Adam ha Rishon* was in *Olam Beria*, which is now the place of *ZA de Atzilut* and his *Garon* was in the first four of *Yetzira*, which is now the place of *Nukva de Atzilut*. You already know that *Nukva de Atzilut* is called *Gan Eden,* thus only his *Garon* was placed in *Gan Eden*.

65. From there downward his entire *Guf* was outside *Gan Eden* in a manner that his whole *Guf* was place in the last six of *Yetzira* and in the first four of *Assiya*. These are now the measure of place of the entire *Olam Beria*.

66. However, the *Guf* of Adam was divided into two divisions, because *Yesod de Bina* expands until the *Chazeh* and the *Orot* inside it are covered. From

the *Chazeh* down the *Orot* are uncovered, as we explain regarding the *Hassadim* that expand in *Tifferet de ZA*.

For that reason his *Guf* was divided into two *Olamot,* the covered Upper half was placed in the last six of *Yetzira* and the revealed lower half was placed in the first four *de Assiya*.

67. It turns out that his *Guf* was primarily above in *Yetzira*, as it is known that the *Guf* implies the *Vav* of *HaVaYaH* and *Yetzira* is also implied in the *Ot Vav* itself. The *Raglaim* of *Adam ha Rishon* were placed at the bottom four of the past *Assiya* which are now the first six of *Yetzira*. Thus we have explained the *Hitpashtut* of *Adam ha Rishon* in three *Olamot Beria Yetzira Assiya* when he was created.

68. Now we will explain the matter of *Adam ha Rishon* when he was created, as our sages wrote in the Midrash and the Talmud, how we connect it to what we have explained. Our sages said that the *Guf* of *Adam ha Rishon* was created from *Eretz Israel*, his *Agavot* (buttocks) from *Bavel* and from Akra DeAgma (a city in Babylon).

To explain that we must also explain what they said in the *Tikkunim* that *Yetzira* controlled *Eretz Israel* and *Assiya* controlled *Hutz la Eretz, Ever ha Yarden, Suria* etc. What all these discernments mean. We have explained that before *Adam* was created the *Olamot* were higher in degree.

Ohr Pnimi

68. *Hitpashtut* of *Adam ha Rishon* in three *Olamot Beria Yetzira Assiya* when he was created.

This entire article was explained above in Part 8 and study it there.

69. We have also explained that his *Guf* was from *Eretz Israel*. You already know that only *Yetzira* controls *Eretz Israel*, not *Assiya*. Yet, at that time the last six of *Yetzira* were in the place where the first six of *Beria* are now.

70. The *Guf* of *Adam* was of the last six of the past *Yetzira*, because the *Guf* means the *Ot Vav*, and *Yetzira* is also *Ot Vav*. Thus, *Yetzira* controls *Eretz Israel* and you find that the *Guf* of *Adam* was from *Eretz Israel* which is from *Yetzira*, which is between two *Olamot Beria* and *Assiya*. Also, the *Guf* of *Adam* is the middle of the whole of *Adam*.

71. However, the last *Sefira* of the six *Sefirot* of *Yetzira* is called *Malchut de Yetzira, Nukva de ZA de Yetzira* which is now the sixth *Sefira* of *Olam Beria*. This is the meaning of *Ever ha Yarden*, the place of the children of Gad and the children of Reuben. It is considered *Malchut* of the past

Yetzira with all first three of the past Assiya, which are now the four bottom Sefirot de Beria.

72. All these four bottom Sefirot of the current Beria are the meaning of Ever ha Yarden, and they are Tifferet and Netzah and Hod and Yesod of the current Beria. However, Malchut of the current Beria that was then the fourth Sefira de Assiya is called Suria and her degree is worse than Ever ha Yarden.

73. It turns out that the past Malchut de Yetzira was the past Ever ha Yarden and the current Malchut de Beria was Behinat Suria. The last six of the past Assiya, which are the first six of the current Yetzira, were Hutz la Eretz since these were then Behinat Assiya. It is known that Assiya hangs in Hutz la Eretz and controls there, and we have already explained that the Raglaim of Adam ha Rishon were from Hutz la Eretz.

74. It is known that each Regel (leg) is divided into three Prakin. The two upper Prakin in both Raglaim, called his Agavot, were from Bavel and from Akra DeAgma, as mentioned in the Gmarah.

75. Do not be surprised by that because they are very close to Eretz Israel, as it is written in the Midrash and the Yerushalmi about that man who was plowing with his cow. It ran away from him and he chased it until they reached Bavel before night.

Thus, the Guf from Eretz Israel is not far from his Agavot from Bavel, since these are the two upper Prakin proximate to the Guf. The other lower four Prakin in both his Raglaim were from the other lands in Hutz la Eretz.

Ohr Pnimi

75. The Guf from Eretz Israel is not far from his Agavot from Bavel, since these are the two upper Prakin proximate to the Guf.

Eretz Israel is Behinat Olam Yetzira. Prior to the sin her First four were in Nukva de Atzilut and her lower six were in the First six of Beria, meaning HBD HGT through Chazeh de Beria.

Our sages do not speak of the Rosh and Garon of Adam ha Rishon, but only from his Guf which is Behinat lower six de Yetzira that were then in the First six of Beria. Also, Malchut de Yetzira that stands in the place of Chazeh de Beria is Behinat Ever ha Yarden, containing the First four of Assiya too, which then clothed the lower four TNHY de Beria. The Behinat Guf de Adam ha Rishon was made of them, from the Chazeh down to the end of his Tifferet.

Malchut of the First four of *Assiya* that was in the place of the current *Beria* is *Behinat Suria*, close to *Bavel*. The *Raglaim* of *Adam ha Rishon* are *Behinat* bottom six of *Assiya* that clothe the First six of *Yetzira* until the *Chazeh*. This place is *Behinat Hutz la Eretz*, hence you find that his *Raglaim* are from *Behinat Hutz la Eretz*.

However, the *Raglaim* are divided into three thirds. His two Upper thirds, called his *Agavot*, are from *Behinat* two Upper thirds *de VAK de Assiya*, which are *Behinat Bavel*, proximate to *Suria*, which is *Malchut* of the First four of *Assiya*.

The part of his *Guf* from the *Chazeh* down to *Sium Tifferet* is made of those. The two Upper thirds of *VAK de Yetzira*, namely *Bavel*, are found to be close to *Behinat Eretz Israel*, meaning *Malchut de Yetzira* that was in *Chazeh de Beria* like his *Agavot*, close to his *Guf*.

76. Now we have explained how *Adam ha Rishon* took from the entire *Olam ha Zeh* and his *Guf* was stretched over three *Olamot Beria Yetzira Assiya* too, and all is one. Thus we have explained the first *Behina*, how the *Olamot* were when *Adam ha Rishon* was created. We also explained how his *Rosh* and *Garon* were inside *GE* and his *Guf* in the rest of the *Olam*.

Ohr Pnimi

76. The first *Behina,* how the *Olamot* were when *Adam ha Rishon* was created.

We must know that this first *Behina* is considered the "constant" of *Mochin de BYA*, but they descended from their place because of the sin of *Etz ha Daat*.

77. Now we will explain the second *Behina* after *Adam ha Rishon* was created and the Creator placed him in *Gan Eden*. It was then half of the sixth day and onward, at which time *Kedusha* is necessarily added in all the *Olamot*, as we explain regarding the eve of Shabbat.

The *Olamot* begin to rise above their place from the fifth hour of the eve of Shabbat and *Kedusha* is added to them. It is as we mention regarding the excess *Hey* mentioned in verse, "And there was evening and there was morning, the sixth day." It implies the fifth hour.

Ohr Pnimi

77. The *Olamot* begin to rise above their place from the fifth hour of the eve of Shabbat etc. It is as we mention regarding the excess *Hey*.

Explanation: The six days of *Bereshit* are *HGT NHY*. Thus, the sixth day is *Yesod*, in which all five days were sweetened and corrected, which are *HGT*

NH. This is the meaning of the Sixth Day "And the heaven and the earth were finished etc." For this reason *Yesod* is called *Kol* (Heb: all), because it contains five *Sefirot* HGT NH.

The sixth day itself is divided into twelve hours. The first six are five *Hassadim* in *Yesod*, which are the sweetening of the five days HGT NH from the aspect of the *Hassadim*. You find that the sixth hour is its own *Behina* from the aspect of *Hassadim*.

The last six hours are the sweetening of the five days HGT NH from the aspect of the *Gevurot* in them, and the sixth hour and the twilight is its own *Behina* from the aspect of the *Gevurot*, sweetening the five *Gevurot* HGT NH.

The sweetening falls mainly on the fifth day, which is *Hod*, namely *Malchut* that is close to the *Klipot*. This is the reason for the excess *Hey* of the sixth day, implying the fifth hour, which is the *Hesed* that is ascribed to *Sefirat Hod*.

Thus, when the fifth hour on the eve of Shabbat comes, the *Olamot* begin to rise up from their place and *Kedusha* is added to them. This is so because then all five days HGT NH have been sweetened from the aspect of the five *Hassadim* in the *Yesod*, and hence there is an ascent to all the *Olamot* above their place.

78. Thus we shall now explain what was renewed that eve of Shabbat after midnight when *Adam* was created and entered *Gan Eden* with all his *Guf*. When he was created only his *Rosh* and *Garon* were in *Gan Eden*, and the rest of his *Guf* was in *Olam ha Zeh*. Now, however, he entered *Gan Eden* entirely.

79. The *Olamot* rose in the following manner: ZA rose to the place that is now the place of AA. *Nukva* rose to the place that is now the place of *Abba*, and *Beria* rose to the place that is now the place of *Ima*. Also, *Yetzira* in the place of ZA and *Assiya* in the place of *Malchut Nukva de ZA*.

Ohr Pnimi

79. **The *Olamot* rose in the following manner: ZA rose to the place that is now the place of AA.**

ZA *de Atzilut* first came out only in *Behinat* VAK without GAR, considered its "permanence", and the GAR that he later acquired is considered "inconsistent additions". Similarly, BYA came out in the first *Behina* in the *Behinat* VAK in them, because *Beria* came out in the place of ZA *de Atzilut*, which is *Behinat* VAK.

Also, *Yetzira* came out in the place of *Nukva de* ZA, clothing from the *Chazeh* down, when the *Nukva* has only *Behinat* VAK without GAR. This is considered the "permanent" of BYA, had it not been for the sin that lowered them below Parsa.

Now at the fifth hour on the eve of Shabbat Kedusha was added to them (see Ohr Pnimi item 77). BYA acquired Mochin of Behinat addition, meaning the GAR in them, because ZA rose to the place of AA and Nukva to the place of Abba, meaning Upper AVI, where Nukva procreated the Mochin for Olam Beria.

Mochin de Beria were emanated from the Upper AVI since Nukva rose there, and everything that emanated from the Upper AVI is considered YESHSUT. Hence, Olam Beria was then made in the degree of YESHSUT de Atzilut and acquired her GAR.

Similarly, Beria emanated Mochin for Olam Yetzira and through these Mochin the Yetzira became the degree of ZA de Atzilut. This is because everything that emerges and emanates from the degree of YESHSUT is considered the degree of ZA. Then Yetzira too acquired her Mochin de GAR.

Similarly, Yetzira emanated Mochin to Olam Assiya. Because Yetzira is now in the degree of ZA, the Mochin de Assiya were made in the degree of Nukva de Atzilut clothing ZA from his Chazeh downward, Achor be Achor, since she is the next degree after ZA.

You find that now the Assiya is in the state of Olam Yetzira in the first Behina, where GAR de Assiya clothe the Nukva de Atzilut and her bottom six remain under the Parsa clothing the First six of the current Olam Beria.

This is so because Nukva de Atzilut herself in the place she rose, also clothes ZA only from the Chazeh down since ZA rose to the place of AA and Nukva did not rise there with him. Instead, she remained in AVI, clothing ZA from the Chazeh down as has been explained above in the first Behina in the bottom six of Yetzira.

80. The first four of Assiya rose because this is the measure of **Nukva de ZA**, only four Sefirot. The other six Sefirot de Assiya are in the place of the first six of the current Beria. Yet, AVI de Atzilut and everything above them also rose above their degree in this order, and we should not elaborate in them.

81. Know, that the principal place of the Olamot and their genuine degree is in this order, and this is their rightful place for all times. The reason is that ZA should grow to be like Arich Anpin and should therefore rise up to there. Also, the place of Arich Anpin should be the place of ZA because by that it becomes Arich.

81. The principal place of the *Olamot* and their genuine degree is in this order, and this is their rightful place for all times etc. ZA should grow to be like **Arich Anpin**.

It means that the whole matter of *Olam ha Tikun* is about reviving the seven *Melachim* that died during the breaking of the vessels in *Olam Nekudim*. This will mean the revival of the dead and *Gmar ha Tikun*.

However in the beginning of *Olam ha Tikun*, when the new MA came out and revived the *Melachim*, not all were corrected, but some were corrected and some were not corrected. Consequently, all the degrees descended from their place.

GAR *de Atik* clothed on the place of GAR *de Nekudim* and HGT NHYM *de Atik* on the place of HGT NHYM *de Nekudim*. GAR *de AA* clothed on HGT *de Atik*, meaning on the place of HGT *de Nekudim*, and AVI and ZON on ZAT *de AA* in the place of TNHYM *de Nekudim*.

It turns out that AA descended to the place of ZA *de Nekudim*, because his GAR clothe HGT *de Atik* that stand in the place of HGT *de Nekudim*, which are ZA. ZA himself descended to *Behinat* VAK *de* NHY *de Nekudim* since AVI clothe HGT *de AA*, which in turn clothe NHY *de Atik* that stand in the place of TNHYM *de Nekudim*.

ZA clothes VAK *de* VAK *de AA* and is therefore located in the place of VAK *de* VAK *de* NHY *de Nekudim*. It follows that the degrees descended significantly since AA descended to the degree of ZA *de Nekudim* and ZA descended to VAK *de* VAK *de* NHY *de Nekudim*.

It is written, "**ZA should grow to be like Arich Anpin** etc. the place of **Arich Anpin should be the place of ZA because by that it becomes Arich.**" It means that AA stands in the place of ZA of *Olam ha Nekudim*, meaning the place of HGT *de Atik* that took the place of HGT *de Nekudim*, which are ZA.

Before ZA rises and clothes his HGT in *Olam ha Nekudim*, all the degrees are still in a state of descent. It is written, "**Know, that the principal place of the Olamot and their genuine degree is in this order,**" meaning that ZA will rise and take the place of GAR *de AA*, which is the true place of ZA.

Also, *Nukva's* place was in *Nekudim* in the place of NHY *de Nekudim*, meaning from the *Chazeh* of ZA *de Nekudim* downward. Now during the descent of the degrees the GAR of the Upper AVI stand there clothing HGT *de AA* which clothe NHY *de Atik*, which are the place of NHY *de Nekudim*.

Similarly, the real place of the three *Olamot BYA* is in the place of *YESHSUT* and *ZON de Olam Atzilut*. This is because these three *Olamot BYA* are discerned as the new *NHY* that came out to *ZA* during the emergence of *Gadlut de ZAT de Nekudim* with the *Mochin de AB SAG* that came out. This is because the *Mochin de AB* lowered the *Hey Tata'a* from the *Eynaim* and raised the *AHP* that fell to the *Guf* back to the *Eser Sefirot de Rosh*.

Also, as a result, the *TNHY* that fell below *Parsa* to the place of *BYA* returned, joined the *ZAT de Nekudim* and became *Behinat Atzilut*. However, they broke because the *Parsa* was not yet in its fullest power. In consequence, the *Ohr* expanded to these new *NHY de BYA* from above downward, meaning to the place of *BYA*. As a result, they broke and died since they breached the *Gevul* of the *Parsa*.

However, if the *Orot* of the new *NHY* had not expanded into *BYA* but would rather have raised the new *NHY* from *BYA* above *Parsa*, as in the case of *Olam ha Tikun*, then they would not have been broken. They would have remained with all the *Orot de Atzilut* forever.

Now you can see that the whole issue of the sorting of *BYA* is these new *NHY* that joined the *ZAT de Nekudim* when they were already in *Gadlut*. They broke because they wanted to receive the *Orot de Atzilut* in their place in *BYA*, and must now sort them and raise them from the place of *BYA* to be once more *Behinat* new *NHYM* to *Olam Atzilut*.

This will be the *Tikun* and the revival of the dead. You find that the true place of *BYA* is in the place of *YESHSUT* and *ZON de Atzilut* because after *ZA* and *Nukva* return to their place in *Nekudim*, these *BYA* must be their *Behinat* new *NHY*, clothing *Nukva* from the *Chazeh* down.

Since *Nukva* is the place of *AVI* then her new *NHY*, which are *BYA* are from the *Chazeh* down of the *Nukva* in the place of *YESHSUT* and *ZON*. This is because *YESHSUT* and *ZON* are clothed from the *Chazeh* down of *AVI*, and thus the real place of the three *Olamot BYA* at the time of *Gmar Tikun* is in the place of *YESHSUT* and *ZON de Atzilut*.

This thoroughly explains the words of the Rav how this order that was on the second *Behina* on the eve of Shabbat is the true state of *ZON* and *BYA*.

82. **Nukva of ZA in the place of Abba**, as it is written, "by wisdom founded the earth," as "Father founded his daughter." It is also the meaning of "Ye shall keep the sabbath therefore, for it is holy." "Keep," which is the **Nukva** becomes "holy," which is **Abba**.

This is the meaning of the text "it is holy," because the *Nekeva* returns to being holy, and *Beria* rose in *Ima*, as you know that *Ima* nests in her abdomen." Also, *Yetzira* in the place of ZA because ZA nests in the angel and *Assiya* in *Nukva de ZA* because *Malchut* nests in the *Ofan*, which is *Assiya*.

83. You find that this is the worthy place for the order of the degrees of the *Olamot*, and you now find that all the lower *Olamot* of *Beria Yetzira* and *Assiya* were in the place of *Atzilut* except the last six of *Yetzira*. Those were then at the First six of the current *Beria*.

84. This was the meaning of the *Ibur* of the *Ir* (town) mentioned in the Talmud. It is because these bottom six protrude and exit *Olam Atzilut* like a pregnant woman whose *Ubar* protrudes outside her body.

Ohr Pnimi

84. Protrude and exit *Olam Atzilut* like a pregnant woman whose *Ubar* protrudes outside her body.

This is the meaning of the *Ibur* of the *Ir* presented in Masechet Iruvin. When you come to measure the zones you do not measure from the wall of the city but go seventy *Amah* and some margins and begin to measure from there. These seventy *Amah* are called the *Ibur* of the *Ir*, considered as though they are still within the wall of the city.

The Rav says that these lower six of *Assiya* that remained below *Parsa de Atzilut* in the place of the first six of the current *Beria* are considered to have remained as one *Guf* with *Olam Atzilut*. It is like a pregnant woman whose *Ubar* and *Beten* protrude outside her *Guf*. This is the meaning of the *Ibur* of the *Ir*, which is considered like the *Ir* itself although already outside the wall.

We must understand these words. How can you say that the last six *de Assiya* are one *Guf* with the *Atzilut* when *Parsa* interrupts between them? How are these first six of *Beria* different than the rest of the *Sefirot de BYA*, and also, what is the resemblance to the *Ibur* of an *Ir*?

The thing is that *Parsa* is the *Behinat Sium* on *Ohr Atzilut* that is made at half the *Tifferet*, which is *Bina de Guf* by the power of the ascent of the *Hey Tata'a* in the *Nikvey Eynaim*, which occurred during the emergence of the *Nekudim*. As a result, *Malchut ha Mizdaveget*, meaning the *Peh* of the *Rosh* rose to *Nikvey Eynaim*, which is *Bina de Rosh*. Then the *Eser Sefirot de Rosh* came out from *Bina* upward, and the *Eser Sefirot* from above downward into *Behinat Guf* expanded from *Nikvey Eynaim* downward.

The *AHP* of the *Rosh* went outside the *Rosh* and were contained in *Behinat Guf* and *Malchut ha Mesayemet* that prior to that stood in the *Etzbaot Raglaim*, rose from there to the place of *Bina de Guf*, called *Tifferet*, meaning to the *Chazeh*. There at the *Chazeh* she ended the *Partzuf* and the two thirds *Tifferet* and *ZON* remained below the *Sium* of the *Partzuf*, meaning below *Atzilut* (see above *Ohr Pnimi* items 2 and 3).

This is indeed difficult since the *Hey Tata'a* rose to *Bina*, only the *Hotem Peh* should have gone outside the *Sium* of *Atzilut* since the *Zivug* was made in *Bina*. Why did the *Hey Tata'a* rise in the middle of *Bina*, meaning under *GAR de Bina*, by which the *ZAT de Bina* herself went outside the *Rosh* and outside *Atzilut*?

Indeed this is the meaning of "*Abba* took *Ima* out for her son and *Abba* himself was corrected with *Dechura* and *Nukva*." This is because *GAR de Bina* are called YESHSUT. *Malchut* rose in *GAR de Bina* and *Abba* himself was corrected there in *Dechura* and *Nukva*, which is the meaning of *Eynaim* and *Nikvey Eynaim*. Hence, the *Awzen*, which is *ZAT de Bina*, called YESHSUT, went outside the *Rosh* into *Behinat Guf*.

Also, the two thirds of *Tifferet*, which are *Behinat ZAT de Bina de Guf*, called YESHSUT went out of *Atzilut* because of that. This correction was in order to provide *Mochin* for ZA which is the son of YESHSUT. Had YESHSUT not gone outside, there would have been no presence of *Mochin* for ZA (see item 33).

Thus you find that from the aspect of the ascent of the *Hey Tata'a* in the *Eynaim* only, *ZAT de Bina* did not have to go outside *Parsa de Atzilut*. This is the meaning of the two lower thirds of *Tifferet* that were made into *Olam Beria*.

However, this was a special *Tikun* by Upper AVI who took the *Hey Tata'a* within them in order to eject *ZAT de Bina* outside the *Rosh* and outside *Atzilut* so as to provide *Mochin* for ZA. Hence, YESHSUT are considered the *Beten* of AVI, protruding outside the *Guf de AVI*.

Yet, they are still considered as the *Guf de AVI* itself because this is the protrusion and the exit outside the *Guf de AVI*. It is not because of a flaw in them, but only for her *Ubar*, being ZA who did not have *Mochin* anyhow.

Thus, the place of *Olam Beria* was made of two thirds of *Tifferet*, which are *ZAT de Bina de Guf* that remained below the *Parsa* and expanded to *Eser Sefirot de Beria*. The First seven are *Behinat ZAT de Bina* and from the *Chazeh* downward they are *Behinat ZON*.

Hence, these First seven of *Beria*, which are KHBD HGT through the *Chazeh*, are already under the *Parsa de Atzilut*. Yet, since they do not exit *Atzilut* because of their own flaw but in order to give *Mochin* to ZON, they are regarded as being from the *Parsa* upward, inside *Atzilut*.

It is rather like a pregnant woman where the *Ubar* protrudes outwardly, meaning as the *Beten* protrudes outside the *Guf* in a pregnant woman, which is not because of her, but because of the *Ubar* in her. Similarly, the exit of these First seven of *Beria* outside *Atzilut* is because of the *Ubar* in her, which is ZON to whom she wants to give *Mochin*. It turns out, that in herself she is still *Guf de Atzilut*, although she protrudes and exits below *Parsa de Atzilut*, as this is not because of a flaw.

Now you can also see the meaning of the *Ibur* of the *Ir*, which is not included in the two thousand *Amah* of the Shabbat Zone. The *Ir* means *Olam Atzilut*, as written in *Ohr Pnimi* item 62. On the day of the Shabbat all the *Olamot* are in the form of *Atzilut* and the zone of the two thousand *Amah* are opposite the two *Sefirot* ZON *de Hitzoniut* of the place of BYA which cannot rise to *Atzilut*. They remain below *Parsa*, empty without *Ohr*.

They are in the place of *Rosh* and *Atzilut de Kelim* since there is an opposite value between the *Kelim* and the *Orot*. Although *Rosh* and *Atzilut* of the place of BYA are *Keter* and *Hochma* from the aspect of the *Kelim*, they are ZA and *Nukva* from the aspect of the *Orot*.

Hence, these two thousand *Amah* are not measured from near the city wall, which is *Parsa de Atzilut*, but we leave and add seventy *Amah* and some margins, opposite these seven *Sefirot de Beria* KHBD HGT and the *Chazeh*. Each *Sefira* contains ten and the *Behinat Chazeh* is the "margins".

These seven *Sefirot de Beria* are still discerned as *Guf de Atzilut* and the matter of their protrusion outside *Olam Atzilut* resembles a protrusion of a *Beten* outside a woman's *Guf*, which is not because of her, but because of the fetus. For this reason we measure the Shabbat Zone only from *Chazeh de Beria* downward until the general *Chazeh* of the place of BYA.

It is written, "**these bottom six protrude and exit Olam Atzilut like a pregnant woman etc.**" He wishes to say that even the bottom six of *Assiya* that remained then below *Parsa* inside the place of the First six of the current *Beria*, are also considered to have been in *Atzilut*. This is because the place of these First seven *de Beria* is discerned as the actual *Ibur* of the *Ir*, meaning like a pregnant woman.

85. **Now you find that the bottom four *de Beria* and the entire *Olam Yetzira* and *Assiya* which are the place of twenty-four *Sefirot* were then all vacant,**

empty and *Halal*. It was in the form of Shabbat Zone, which is two thousand *Amah* except for the last fourteen *Sefirot,* which became a permanent section for the *Klipot*. The other ten Upper *Sefirot* were in the form of Shabbat Zone.

Ohr Pnimi

85. **Permanent section for the *Klipot*.**

This is so because she has only temporary residence in all three *Olamot BYA*, as it is written in the Zohar: "*Ima* nests in *Kursaya*, ZA nests in *Yetzira* and *Malchut* nests in the *Ofan*." Nesting means temporary residence. The reason is that on Shabbats and Good Days they return to their place in *Atzilut*, and *BYA* remains completely empty of *Kedusha*.

Yet, the *Klipot* that have acquired permanent residence from the *Chazeh de BYA* downward never leave there throughout the six thousand years. They do not leave there even on Shabbats and Good Days.

However, regarding the first sixteen *Sefirot de BYA* from the *Chazeh* upward, after the sin the *Klipot* built a great construction. It is written, "God hath made even the one as well as the other," and they occupy their share in the first sixteen *Sefirot* too throughout *Komat BYA*. However, they do not have permanent residence there since on Shabbats they must leave the first sixteen *Sefirot* from the *Chazeh* up.

This is so because during the ascent of the *Olamot* on Shabbat these sixteen *Sefirot* become completely empty, having neither *Kedusha* nor *Klipot*. Yet, they do not leave from *Chazeh de BYA* downward even on Shabbat. This is the meaning of the words of the Rav, "**except for the last fourteen *Sefirot*, which became a permanent section for the *Klipot*.**" This means that they never leave there until the end of correction.

We must understand the reason why the first sixteen are so different from the last fourteen, and also what is the matter of the permanent residence and temporary residence which is said both about *Kedusha* and about the *Klipot*.

First we must remember that the place of *BYA* is one matter and the *Olamot BYA* with everything inside them, *Kedusha* and *Klipot*, are a separate matter. The difference between them is very big because the place of *BYA* was made of the *Kelim* of *NHY de Partzuf Nekudot de SAG de AK*. They remained below *Parsa* by the renewal that occurred there in *Tzimtzum Bet*, where the *Atzilut* ended on the *Chazeh* of this *Partzuf*.

You find that the *Kelim* themselves are from *Tzimtzum Aleph* but the renewal of the ascent of the *Hey Tata'a* in the *Nikvey Eynaim* lowered them below *Atzilut* and they were emptied of their *Orot*. Thus, the *Kelim* of the place of BYA are from *Behinat Tzimtzum Aleph*, but the three *Olamot* BYA and the *Partzufim* in them, both *Kedusha* and *Klipa*, came primarily from *Tzimtzum Bet*.

It is so because they came out during the *Gadlut de Eser Sefirot de Olam ha Nekudim* with the *Hitpashtut* of the new *Ohr de AB de AK* that lowered the *Hey Tata'a* back to its place in the *Peh de Rosh* and returned the AHP to the *Rosh*.

Afterwards, when the *Mochin* expanded from *Rosh* to ZAT they lowered the *Nekudat Sium* too from the place of the *Chazeh de Partzuf Nekudot de SAG* to the place of *Sium Raglin* as before. Then ZAT *de Nekudim* expanded through the *Nekuda de Olam ha Zeh*, equal to the *Raglaim* of AK. Since they breached the *Gevul* of the *Parsa* that was made during the *Katnut de Nekudim*, they broke because of that and died.

It is known that all four *Olamot* ABYA of *Olam ha Tikun* were made of these ZAT that died as well as ABYA *de Klipot* because some were corrected and some were not corrected. ABYA *de Kedusha* were made of those that were corrected where the *Kelim de Panim* became *Olam Atzilut*, and the three *Olamot* BYA were made of the *Kelim de Achoraim*.

What remained after ABYA *de Kedusha* and could not be corrected was made into ABYA *de Klipot*, thus both BYA *de Kedusha* and BYA *de Klipot* emerged and were made after *Tzimtzum Bet*. However, BYA's place came out entirely during *Tzimtzum Aleph* like all the *Partzufim* of AK, and *Tzimtzum Bet* only diminished it to lower it outside *Atzilut*.

The reason that some were corrected and some were not corrected is that the breaking of the vessels was because *Malchut de Tzimtzum Aleph* that became a vacant *Halal*, became *Av* again in *Kelim de ZAT*, as they crossed the *Gevul* of the *Parsa*. Hence, only the First nine *Sefirot* of each *Melech* of the ZAT could be sorted, but *Malchut* of every *Melech* could not be sorted since she was in *Behinat* vacant *Halal* from *Tzimtzum Aleph*.

However, because of their breaking, all the *Behinot* were mixed with one another and each *Behina* that is sorted and rises from BYA has 320 *Nitzotzin*, which are all seven *Melachim*. This is so because with *Melech ha Daat* they are eight *Melachim*. Each *Melech* contains *Eser Sefirot*, and in each *Sefira* there are four *Behinot HB TM*, thus 320.

Since *Malchut* in each *Eser Sefirot* was not sorted you find that there are eight *Malchuiot* here where in each *Malchut* there are four *Behinot HB TM*, which are thirty-two *Nitzotzin*. This is the meaning of *Lev ha Even*, since these thirty-two *Nitzotzin* of the *Malchuiot* are considered the vacant *Halal* of *Tzimtzum Aleph*. They are unfit for any correction and must be separated from the *Kelim*. Without it, it is impossible to revive them.

It turns out that they are 320 *Nitzotzin* in general, but only the first nine of them can be sorted and revived, which are the 248 *Nitzotzin*. The *Malchuiot* among them are the thirty-two *Nitzotzin* and have no *Tikun* at all and must be separated from the *Kelim*, as it is written, "and I will remove the stony heart out of their flesh."

Hence, the place of *BYA*, which is *TNHY de Nekudot SAG de AK* was divided into two *Behinot* in the same manner, its First nine and the *Malchut* in it. In itself it expanded into *Eser Sefirot HBD HGT NHYM*. All first nine in it *HBD HGT* through the *Chazeh* stand where *Orot* clothe the *Kelim*, and only its *Malchut* stands from the *Chazeh* downward (*Ohr Pnimi* item 3). It turns out that everything that fell to its *Behinat Malchut* which is from its *Chazeh* down is not suitable for sorting because they are *Behinat Lev ha Even*.

It is written, "**the last fourteen Sefirot, which became a permanent section for the Klipot.**" It means that the *Klipot* do not leave there even on Shabbat because there is *Behinat Malchut* of the place of *BYA* where *Lev ha Even* fell, which cannot be corrected throughout the six thousand years.

It turns out that the *Klipot* do not move from there and acquire permanent residence there though the sixteen Upper *Sefirot* from the *Chazeh* upward in the place of the 248 *Nitzotzin* rise on Shabbat. At that time they become *Atzilut* once more and the *Klipot* that are opposite the 248 *Nitzotzin* all cancel on the day of Shabbat. Hence, that place became completely empty then and has neither *Kedusha* nor *Klipa*.

We divide the place of *BYA* and say that from the *Behinat Kelim*, *HBD HGT* through the *Chazeh* is considered the *Behinat Keter Hochma* in it, meaning *Rosh* and *Atzilut*. Also, from the *Behinat Hitlabshut* of the *Orot* in the *Kelim*, all nine *Sefirot* in it are considered to be in *HBD HGT* through the *Chazeh*, and only *Malchut* is from the *Chazeh* down.

Similarly, all the *Olamot* are divided in the same manner because the nine *Sefirot* of the first *Olamot* in general are in *AK* and *Atzilut* through the *Parsa*, where *Nukva de ZA* is. From *Parsa* down there is nothing of the nine original *Sefirot*, only the *Hitpashtut* of *Nukva de ZA*, meaning *Malchut* alone.

All these *Partzufim de BYA* are *Behinat Ohr* of *Tolada*. Yet, from the *Behinat Hitpashtut Orot* in the *Kelim* from *Parsa* downward it is considered to be the three *Olamot BYA*, which are the three *Komot Bina* and *ZON* while *AK* and *Atzilut* are considered as merely *Keter* and *Hochma*. In other words, it is just as we have said in the two discernments of the place of *BYA* and also in every single item, because everything that exists in the general always abides in the particular too, even in the very last item.

You find that there are two *Behinot* of *Eser Sefirot*: the original *Eser Sefirot* and *Eser Sefirot* of *Ohr* of *Tolada*. The *Sium* of the original nine *Sefirot* is in *Malchut de Atzilut* and the *Sium* of the nine *Sefirot* or the *Ohr* of *Tolada* is in the place of *Chazeh* of the place of *BYA* that ends there, and remember that.

This is only according to the state of *BYA* in the first *Behina* that the Rav wrote here, which is the permanent state of *BYA*. What they acquired in the second *Behina* and in the third *Behina* is an addition in them.

Also, the descent that the *Olamot* descended afterwards because of the sin of *Adam ha Rishon* and the last four of *Yetzira* and the *Eser Sefirot* of *Assiya* that descended from the *Chazeh* of the place of *BYA* downward is the matter of the great lessening and descent from their permanent state. It is considered as *Hitlabshut* of *Kedusha* in *Klipot* because from the *Chazeh* of the place of *BYA* downward it is the place of the *Klipot*.

Printed in Dunstable, United Kingdom